THE ACTS OF THE APOSTLES

Sacra Pagina Series

Volume 5

The Acts of the Apostles

Luke Timothy Johnson

Daniel J. Harrington, S.J.
Editor

A Michael Glazier Book
THE LITURGICAL PRESS
Collegeville, Minnesota

Cover design by Don Bruno.

A Michael Glazier Book published by Liturgical Press.

ISBN 13: 978-0-8146-5807-9
ISBN 10: 0-8146-5807-5

Library of Congress Cataloging-in-Publication Data

Johnson, Luke Timothy.
    The Acts of the Apostles / Luke Timothy Johnson ; Daniel J. Harrington, editor.
        p.   cm. — (Sacra pagina series ; v. 5)
    "A Michael Glazier book."
    Includes bibliographical references and indexes.
    ISBN 0-8146-5807-5
    1. Bible. N.T. Acts—Commentaries. I. Harrington, Daniel J.
II. Bible. N.T. Acts. English. Johnson. 1992. III. Title.
IV. Series: Sacra pagina series ; 5.
BS2625.3.J64   1992
226.6'077—dc20   92-36900
                                                                    CIP

CONTENTS

II. The Expansion of God's People

III. The Apostle to the Gentiles

IV. THE IMPRISONED APOSTLE

Indexes

EDITOR'S PREFACE

Sacra Pagina is a multi-volume commentary on the books of the New Testament. The expression *Sacra Pagina* ("Sacred Page") originally referred to the text of Scripture. In the Middle Ages it also described the study of Scripture to which the interpreter brought the tools of grammar, rhetoric, dialectic, and philosophy. Thus *Sacra Pagina* encompasses both the text to be studied and the activity of interpretation.

This series presents fresh translations and modern expositions of all the books of the New Testament. Written by an international team of Catholic biblical scholars, it is intended for biblical professionals, graduate students, theologians, clergy, and religious educators. The volumes present basic introductory information and close exposition. They self-consciously adopt specific methodological perspectives, but maintain a focus on the issues raised by the New Testament compositions themselves. The goal of *Sacra Pagina* is to provide sound critical analysis without any loss of sensitivity to religious meaning. This series is therefore catholic in two senses of the word: inclusive in its methods and perspectives, and shaped by the context of the Catholic tradition.

The Second Vatican Council described the study of "the sacred page" as the "very soul of sacred theology" (*Dei Verbum* 24). The volumes in this series illustrate how Catholic scholars contribute to the council's call to provide access to Sacred Scripture for all the Christian faithful. Rather than pretending to say the final word on any text, these volumes seek to open up the riches of the New Testament and to invite as many people as possible to study seriously the "sacred page."

DANIEL J. HARRINGTON, S.J.

PREFACE

This commentary on Acts is written as the companion to the *Commentary on Luke* in the *Sacra Pagina* series, and continues the interpretation begun there. For each section of the text it provides a fresh translation from the Greek, a set of detailed notes, an interpretation, and a short bibliography. All this is preceded by an introduction setting out the principles governing the interpretation, and a general bibliography.

In the translation of Acts, I aim at clarity and readability. This has sometimes demanded difficult decisions between alternative readings. The issues involved in such choices are discussed in the notes. I have been willing, not without an awareness of loss, to sacrifice Luke's biblicisms and complex sentences in favor of shorter sentences and idiomatic equivalents. The challenge of providing a gender-inclusive translation within the constraints of Greek syntax and biblical symbolism has proven more daunting in the case of Acts than in the Gospel. True, there are no treasured *logia* of the Lord to be tortured into more inclusive shape. But the text as a whole is pervasively androcentric, as shown by Luke's frequent greeting in the speeches, "Men Brethren" (*andres adelphoi*), which I could do no better with than "Brothers."

Every commentary stands within a long tradition of scholarship and depends on that tradition. Every commentary also inevitably engages in a bit of selective cannibalism. Perhaps the best thing a commentary can hope for, indeed, is to provide some nourishment to its readers and some usable pieces for the commentator of the next generation. As I worked my way through Luke's narrative, several earlier commentaries provided useful information and alternative perspectives. For specific comments on textual, lexical and historical matters, the commentaries of Cadbury/ Lake and F. F. Bruce were valuable. From the side of German scholarship, the commentaries of Conzelmann and Haenchen were regularly checked. A different but no less valuable sort of help was given by Metzger's textual commentary, which has made everything so much easier for his successors. And as many before me, I was given help on difficult grammatical and syntactical points by Moule and Zerwick.

Among the things each commentator takes from predecessors are guides to the extensive literature of the Hellenistic world pertinent to interpreting Luke-Acts. The Book of Acts touches in one way or another virtually every aspect of life in the first century Mediterranean world. Few of us have complete command of that world. The process of polite borrowing is therefore widespread. Ultimately, all of us are in debt to J. J. Wettstein! I have certainly profited from following up leads provided by my predecessors, and by the always impressive entries in the lexica of Liddell-Scott-Jones-McKenzie and Bauer-Arndt-Gingrich-Danker. No citation or reference has been included here, however, that has not personally been checked and verified, and many more have been added than have been handed on. Indeed, on checking out the references given by earlier commentaries, I found some to be inaccurate or inappropriate, and have eliminated them.

A commentary should not, however, simply provide a catalogue of cross-references and arcane information about the text. It ought to *interpret the text.* In that task, the present work situates itself between the approaches of the major commentaries listed above. Cadbury/Lake and Bruce treat Acts primarily as a historical source, and are therefore strong on factual data but weak on meaning. Haenchen, in contrast, is the great pioneer in seeking a creative author at work in Acts, so his interpretation of specific incidents is often lively and insightful. Unfortunately Haenchen suffers from the typical German embarrassment at the theology of Luke-Acts, and tends to equate historical with factual, so that any inconsistency in the story is taken to legitimate the conclusion that Luke was simply writing "pious fiction." Most of all, Haenchen is unable to break out of an atomistic approach to each segment, and see the meaning Luke was creating with his story as a whole.

I have tried to respect the character of Acts as an apologetic history, which means that while taking the factual level of the story seriously, I do not stop at that level. I recognize that what we would call "fictional shaping" is a feature not only of ancient but also of modern historiography whenever it attempts a narrative account of events, and that it is in such shaping that we discover the literary and religious purposes of the author.

Most of all, I have tried to deal with the literary self-presentation of Luke-Acts as a whole, which means that Acts is read as the continuation of the Gospel of Luke. The reader will discover in the notes and interpretations a constant cross-referencing between volumes, as I seek in my discussion of each part to encourage a vision of the whole. I am convinced that it is in the whole of Luke-Acts, in its narrative argument, that the author's most deliberately intended meaning is to be discovered.

In the preface to the Commentary on Luke, I paid tribute to Adrian Hastings for opening my eyes to the distinctiveness of Luke's Gospel. In an even more obvious fashion, all contemporary scholars working in Luke-Acts owe an immeasurable debt to the magnificent labors of Jacques Dupont, who in matters great and small has brought learning, insight, and integrity to the study of Christianity's first historian. I take special note as well of the recent two-volume interpretation of Luke-Acts by Robert Tannehill, which in very many ways is congenial to the approach of this commentary.

This paragraph concludes two years spent in the pages of Luke-Acts. I thank God for the great privilege of having this chance to learn, and I thank those human mediators through whom the opportunity presented itself: Michael Glazier, who first sponsored this series and allowed me to write on both volumes; Daniel Harrington, who has been the gentlest of editors; and the editors of The Liturgical Press, for saving the series and giving it (and me) their full support. My wife Joy and my daughter Tiffany have had to deal with fatigue and irritability for a long period of time; they have done so graciously, and my gratitude to them cannot adequately be stated. I hope that the product in some fashion is compensation for the pain of the process.

May 4, 1991

ABBREVIATIONS

Biblical Books and Apocrypha

Gen	Nah	1-2-3-4 Kgdms	John
Exod	Hab	Add Esth	Acts
Lev	Zeph	Bar	Rom
Num	Hag	Bel	1-2 Cor
Deut	Zech	1-2 Esdr	Gal
Josh	Mal	4 Ezra	Eph
Judg	Ps (*pl.*: Pss)	Jdt	Phil
1-2 Sam	Job	Ep Jer	Col
1-2 Kgs	Prov	1-2-3-4 Macc	1-2 Thess
Isa	Ruth	Pr Azar	1-2 Tim
Jer	Cant	Pr Man	Titus
Ezek	Eccl (*or* Qoh)	Sir	Phlm
Hos	Lam	Sus	Heb
Joel	Esth	Tob	Jas
Amos	Dan	Wis	1-2 Pet
Obad	Ezra	Matt	1-2-3 John
Jonah	Neh	Mark	Jude
Mic	1-2 Chr	Luke	Rev

Periodicals, Reference Works, and Serials

AnBib	Analecta biblica
AnGreg	Analecta Gregoriana
ANRW	Aufstieg und Niedergang der römischen Welt
AusBR	Australian Biblical Review
BAG	W. Bauer, W. F. Arndt, F. W. Gingrich, and F. W. Danker, *Greek-English Lexicon of the NT*
BDF	F. Blass, A. Debrunner, and R. W. Funk, *A Greek Grammar of the NT*

BETL	Bibliotheca ephemeridum theologicarum lovananiensium
Bib	Biblica
BibKir	Bibel und Kirche
BJRL	Bulletin of the John Rylands University Library of Manchester
BSac	Bibliotheca Sacra
BZNW	Beihefte zur ZNW
CBQ	Catholic Biblical Quarterly
CNT	Commentaire du Nouveau Testament
CurTM	Currents in Theology and Mission
EstBib	Estudios biblicos
ETR	Études théologiques et religieuses
EvQ	Evangelical Quarterly
ExpTim	Expository Times
HeyJ	Heythrop Journal
HR	History of Religions
HTKNT	Herders theologischer Kommentar zum Neuen Testament
HTR	Harvard Theological Review
ICC	International Critical Commentary
Int	Interpretation
ITQ	Irish Theological Quarterly
JAAR	Journal of the American Academy of Religion
JB	Jerusalem Bible
JBL	Journal of Biblical Literature
JETS	Journal of the Evangelical Theological Society
JSNT	Journal for the Study of the New Testament
JSNTSup	Journal for the Study of the New Testament — Supplement Series
KJV	King James Version
LD	Lectio Divina
LS	Louvain Studies
LumVie	Lumière et vie
LXX	Septuagint
MT	Masoretic Text
NAB	New American Bible
NCB	New Century Bible
NEB	New English Bible
NICNT	New International Commentary on the New Testament
NIGTC	New International Greek Testament Commentary
NIV	New International Version
NJB	New Jerusalem Bible
NJBC	New Jerome Biblical Commentary
NovT	Novum Testamentum
NovTSup	Novum Testamentum, Supplements
NRSV	New Revised Standard Version
NT	New Testament
NTM	New Testament Message
NTS	New Testament Studies

OT	Old Testament
RB	Revue biblique
REB	Revised English Version
RSR	Recherches de science religieuse
RSV	Revised Standard Version
SBLDS	SBL Dissertation Series
SE	Studia Evangelica
SEA°	Svensk exegetisk arsbok
SJT	Scottish Journal of Theology
SNTSMS	Society for New Testament Studies Monograph Series
Str-B	H. Strack and P. Billerbeck, Kommentarzum Neuen Testament
TDNT	G. Kittel and G. Friedrich (eds). *Theological Dictionary of the New Testament*
THKNT	Theologischer Handkommentar zum Neuen Testament
TrinJour	Trinity Journal
TToday	Theology Today
USQR	Union Seminary Quarterly Review
WBC	Word Biblical Commentary
WTJ	Westminster Theological Journal
ZAW	Zeitschrift für die alttestamentliche Wissenschaft
ZNW	Zeitschrift für die neutestamentliche Wissenschaft
WMANT	Wissenschaftliche Monographien zum Alten und Neuen Testament

INTRODUCTION

The *Acts of the Apostles* is the second part of the two-volume composition that scholars call *Luke-Acts*. It is written by the author of *The Gospel of Luke*—possibly but not certainly the Luke who was a companion of Paul (Col 4:14)—and shares the same outlook as well as many of the same themes. Like the Gospel, Acts has a short prologue which connects this composition to "the first word (*logos*)" addressed by Luke to his reader-patron Theophilus (Acts 1:1; see Luke 1:1-4). The prologue briefly recapitulates the first volume as concerning "what Jesus said and did" before being taken up into heaven in the sight of his followers. Acts then continues the story of Jesus into the story of the early church, from its birth at Pentecost to its success among the Gentiles all the way to Rome.

Here is Luke's original and decisive contribution to Christian literature and theology. Others before him had written gospels (Luke 1:1). But he was the first to create a sustained narration of Christian beginnings. The story need not have been told at all. Or it could have been organized in any number of ways. It is Luke's genius to have convinced readers from his day to the present that things not only happened the way he said, but had to have happened that way.

What is most impressive in this is not the story's historical verisimilitude, but the way Luke used it to give literary shape to a theological vision. Like Paul, Luke saw the work of the Holy Spirit as the replication in the lives of believers of the messianic pattern enacted first by Jesus (see 1 Cor 2:16; Phil 2:5; Gal 6:2). Luke communicates his conviction through a narrative, and with such success that Christians subsequently took it as self-evident that the working of God's Spirit in human freedom did not cease with Jesus but continued in the lives of the disciples. Luke's account of Pentecost (Acts 2:1-42) is therefore not only an artistic success, but also the creation of a narrative connection between the work of God in Jesus and in believers.

The present commentary on Acts is itself a second volume, following my commentary in this series on *The Gospel of Luke*. Like Acts, this present volume also needs a less extensive prologue than that in the previ-

1

ous commentary. In that earlier introduction, the framework for reading both volumes as a single story was established. Everything said there about the identity of the author, the circumstances of composition, the genre and purpose of the work, and the literary methods used by the author, need not be repeated in detail. Instead, some of the issues that are of particular relevance for this volume will briefly be considered.

A. *The Text of Acts*

Luke-Acts is best understood when read as a carefully constructed narrative whose story-line is itself the vehicle of meaning. But *which* version of the narrative should be read? Acts presents a particularly acute form of a problem found everywhere in the New Testament, namely establishing the Greek text that is the basis for any interpretation.

As with all NT writings, the critical text of Acts is derived from the evidence supplied by many ancient manuscripts, in the case of Acts including some fragmentary papyri from the third century. Such manuscripts normally display a considerable range of minor variations within a framework of substantial agreement. It is therefore usually possible to construct a critical text by an eclectic method of adjudication between different readings, using the standard rules of textual-criticism: generally the reading is to be preferred that derives from the most ancient and reliable manuscripts, that is shorter (scribes tend to expand more than contract texts), and that is "harder" (i.e., least likely to represent "improvement" by a well-meaning scribe).

In the case of Acts, however, a small body of manuscripts called the "Western Text Tradition" (represented most fully by *Codex Bezae Cantabrigiensis,* called "Codex D" throughout this commentary), present a rather consistent *alternative* version of Acts. This group of manuscripts obviously has its own internal points of inconsistency due to scribal tendencies. But as a group it contains a version of Luke's story up to ten percent longer than that found in the majority textual tradition (usually called the "Alexandrian Tradition").

Because it tends to aim at a smoother Greek style, to amplify stories (especially by the addition of details), and to reveal certain tendencies (such as an emphasis on the rejection of the Jews and on the Holy Spirit), it appears certain to most contemporary scholars—although vigorous protestations to the contrary continue to be made—that the Western Tradition taken as a whole does not contain the original text of Acts. Neither is it probable that this text comes from an authorially revised edition. In all likelihood what we have is an unusually sustained scribal redaction. The translator of Acts cannot, on that account, automatically dismiss the

Western readings when considering specific passages; each of its readings must be considered on its own merits.

In this commentary, however, the Western textual variants will be considered in the notes only when they show a genuinely different version of a passage. Otherwise, so complex are the issues and arguments, detailed discussion of all the variants would needlessly distend the commentary, as well as deflect it from its main goal, which is a comprehensive reading of Luke's story.

B. *Acts as History*

The prologue to Luke's Gospel (1:1-4) identifies his entire narrative as a form of historical writing. But Acts more obviously moves beyond the framework of a Hellenistic biography into that of a properly historical account. Because it is unprecedented and unparalleled in its attempt to provide a sequential account of the nascent Christian movement, Acts must also respond to questions posed by critical historiography.

1. *Sources*

The question of which sources Luke might have used is different and more difficult for Acts than for the Gospel. We have no clearly identifiable "Mark" or hypothetical "Q" to help us discern what comes from tradition and what is owed to Luke's redaction. Luke apparently had no overall guide for his extended narrative. He says he had "examined everything carefully from the start" (Luke 1:3), which means he had done his own research into "the matters that have been brought to fulfillment among us" (Luke 1:1). This suggests that not only the ordering but also much of the gathering of the data was part of his pioneering task. But did he have any partial written sources available to him?

Attempts at isolating such sources have been frequent. Some have thought to disentangle a "Jerusalem" source from an "Antioch" source for the first chapters of Acts. The "We Passages" found in the latter part of the story (Acts 16:10-17; 20:5-15; 21:8-18; 27:1–28:16) offer another plausible candidate. Source theorists fail to agree, however, on the existence, provenance, or even extent of such hypothetical sources. The reason is simple. As we have seen in the case of the Gospel, Luke rewrites his sources thoroughly. If we did not have an extant version of Mark, we would never be able to detect with certainty where Luke was using him as a source. Since in the case of Acts we have no standard of comparison, the detection of specific sources is even more hopeless.

To question the possibility of identifying sources, however, is not to deny that Luke *used* sources, only that we can locate or verify their presence. Nor is it to deny that Luke had available to him information from earlier tradents. He could have gathered information from a variety of locations, either in person or from those whom he calls "eyewitnesses and ministers of the word" (Luke 1:2). But such information was most likely available to him in anecdotal rather than in an ordered form.

As for the fullness and value of such information, it should be obvious that Luke had more and better facts for the later parts of his story than for the earlier. When we analyze the first chapters of Acts (virtually everything having to do with Jerusalem), we are struck by how very little real "stuff" Luke had available to him: the ascension story and Pentecost, a healing account, some trials, a punishment, and the stoning of Stephen. The rest of these marvelously busy scenes are filled out by Luke himself with summaries, speeches, and vivid descriptions.

Even passages rooted in earlier tradition undoubtedly owe their present literary form to Luke's artistry. It may be a "fact" for example, that the apostles suffered at the hands of the Sanhedrin in the community's early days (compare 1 Thess 2:14-15), but there is no reason to think that Luke had available transcripts of their hearings (Acts 4–5); the scenes as we read them are his dramatic creations. The same must be said of Peter's discourses to the crowds or the prayers of the community. For this first part of Acts, the historian can see that Luke's creative scope was most ample, simply because he was unconstrained either by narrative precedent or wealth of information. Whatever historical basis there is to his account must be found at the level of substance and pattern rather than at the level of detail or specific incident.

For the second part of Acts, in contrast, especially when the story picks up the travels and travails of Paul in Chapter 13, the information available to Luke seems to have been both more substantial and reliable. Some of it may have come directly from Paul or his associates. Luke may even have been the eyewitness responsible for the "We Passages." The historian is also better able to make judgments on this part of the story because of the other kinds of evidence available: topographical, archaeological, and literary.

Above all, a check is provided by a number of Paul's extant letters. There is a considerably detailed overlap between the narrative of Acts 16–20, and the incidental facts we can elicit from 1 and 2 Corinthians, 1 and 2 Thessalonians, Galatians, and Romans. Although arguments continue to be made that the reason for such overlap is that Acts used Paul's letters in constructing his story, the evidence does not really support that position. Not only does Luke not tell us a great deal that he could have told us if he were using Paul's letters—about the Galatian mission, for example, or the Corinthian controversies—but in the places of overlap there are so many points of discrepancy that the hypothesis of independent information rather than of literary dependence seems more likely. The relative independence of the accounts makes their testimony all the more valuable, as much when they disagree as when they agree.

2. *Reliability*

How accurate is Luke's account when measured against our other information? In general, he is impressively precise in matters of local color and detail. Places are where he says they are; things seemed to have worked pretty much the way he describes them; he accurately records the titles, functions, and time of tenure of various local officials. He captures the peculiarities of different regions. All of these suggest an author close to the scene. When Paul's movements in Acts are compared to those reported in his letters, furthermore, it appears that despite his selection and shaping of materials, Luke provides a reliable if partial framework for reconstructing that portion of Paul's career. Indeed, Acts is indispensable for any attempt at such reconstruction. Where we can check him on details, Luke's factual accuracy in the latter part of Acts is impressive.

Such factual fastidiousness, however, needs careful evaluation. A perfect rendering of local detail and color, after all, is also a characteristic of good fiction! We are more confident that Luke got his "world" right than that he got exactly right the sequence or meaning or character of events that form the substance of his narrative. We are aware, first of all, that he is highly selective in what he tells us. The exclusive concentration on Paul rather than on all of the apostles in the latter part of Acts is itself a deliberate interpretive choice. And even if the framework is essentially factual, it is nevertheless evident that its adornment with individual scenes is due to Luke's literary powers. As in the Gospel, he creatively shapes his vignettes in imitation of biblical models or motifs, and in conscious appropriation of Hellenistic literary and social tropes.

In Luke's treatment of Paul, for example, we see his hero placed in settings and scenes evocative of Hellenistic models. At Lystra, Paul and Barnabas are taken for Zeus and Hermes (Acts 14:8-18); the scene recalls Ovid's tale of Baucis and Philemon (*Metamorphoses* 8:613-738). His speech at Athens before Epicurean and Stoic philosophers (17:16-34) reminds us of the vivid scenes of philosophic debates in that city sketched by Lucian of Samosata (*The Eunuch*). His reception by the natives of Malta after his shipwreck (28:1-6) evokes the similar scene in Dio Chrysostom's *Oration* 7 ("The Euboean Discourse").

The use of biblical imagery for the characterization of Paul is even more obvious. Luke fits Paul into his overall literary presentation of Jesus' followers as his prophetic successors. Paul is a man filled with the Holy Spirit, speaking God's word with boldness, working signs and wonders, and creating division among the people. It is true that within this literary stereotyping Luke manages to capture as well some of the Pauline characteristics we know from his letters: his consciousness of a mission to the Gentiles, his working as part of a team, his use of urban centers to spread the gospel, even a hint of Paul's distinctive self-consciousness (20:25-35) and view of Torah (13:39). The Paul who is most familiar to us, however, is not even hinted at by Acts. There is no suggestion that Paul ever wrote a letter! In a word, Luke exercises considerable literary license in his shaping of Paul's portrait, just as he does in his presentation of Jesus and the other apostles.

There are also some major discrepancies between the evidence in Paul's letters and in Acts. The first concerns Paul's relations with the Jerusalem community. In Gal 2:1-10, Paul reports on a critical meeting between himself and the "Pillars" of the Jerusalem church concerning the validity and future of his Gentile mission. Acts 15 also reports on a meeting of the leadership in Jerusalem concerning the same issue. The sources disagree, however, concerning the occasion, the precise participants, the process, and the conclusions of the meeting, as well as the sequence of events leading up to and following it. This disagreement in detail may also, of course, be taken as confirmation of the essential historical fact that sometime in the first generation Paul and other leaders met in Jerusalem to discuss the Gentile initiative.

A similar and possibly even more puzzling problem concerns Paul's great collection of money among his Gentile communities for the church in Jerusalem. His letters repeatedly return to this task in its practical and symbolic dimensions (Gal 2:10; 1 Cor 16:1-4; 2 Cor 8-9; Rom 15:25-28). It is therefore strange that although Luke reports a gathering of Paul's delegates prior to his final Jerusalem journey (20:4-6), and that Paul carried with him a sum of money sufficiently large for Felix to have hopes for a bribe (24:26), he has Paul refer to it only obliquely in a defense speech, "I came to bring my nation alms and offerings" (24:17). And when Paul meets James in the city, neither leader mentions Paul's great gift. Instead, James suggests another gesture of reconciliation involving the use of money (21:23-24)!

Luke certainly knows more than he is telling us. Why is he so circumspect? Is it because Paul's fears (Rom 15:31) were realized and his gift was not accepted? We cannot be sure. Even more oddly, Luke does involve Paul in a collection for the poor in Jerusalem, not as a gesture of reconciliation between Gentile and Jewish churches at the end of his career, but as an act of almsgiving from the Antioch community before Paul began his Gentile mission (see Acts 11:29-30; 12:25). Once more, the historian can state rather confidently that Paul at some point took part in a major relief effort for the Jerusalem church. Concerning the details of timing and significance, however, the account in Acts appears to be impossible to reconcile entirely with the version in Paul's letters.

Concerning Luke's use of sources and his historical reliability, therefore, extreme positions should be avoided. It is true that we cannot, because of Luke's artistry, determine the extent or even the existence of written sources. But this does not imply that Luke did not make use of tradition, or that he made up events solely from his imagination. Likewise, because Luke selected and shaped his story does not mean that it is simply fiction. These are false alternatives. All historical writing, after all, demands a selection and creative shaping of materials, and all great histories have a large component of imagination. It is unrealistic to hold Luke to a standard of "perfect factual accuracy," failing which he is dismissed as a novelist. Narrative can be significantly shaped by an author's imagination and still report substantial historical information. No responsible historian dismisses Josephus' *Antiquities of the Jews* or Suetonius' *Lives of the Caesars* because they are embroidered with gossip and exaggeration. Recognizing the *ways* in which Luke literarily shapes his narrative, in fact, is an important step toward recognizing the *kind* of history he was attempting to write.

C. *Acts as Apology*

Luke had no intention of writing a scientific, disinterested history—if in fact there is such a thing. He tells us that he is writing for the purpose of giving "full confidence" (*asphaleia*) to his readers by the way he tells the story "in sequence" (*kathexēs*, see Luke 1:4). As a whole, Luke-Acts should be read as an Apology in the form of a historical narrative. The burden of Luke's defense is not demonstrating the philanthropic character of the Christian movement (to influence the Roman Empire), or proving the benevolence of the Empire (to influence believers). Nor did Luke write simply to provide a defense for Paul as he faced his trial before imperial authorities, or to shape a defense for Paul as a teacher of Israel before a jury of theologically influential Jewish Christians.

Luke's Apology is rather in the broadest sense a theodicy. His purpose is to defend God's activity in the world. Luke-Acts ostensibly addresses a wider audience in the clothing of Greek literature; but its main interest is to construct a continuation of the biblical story for Gentile believers in order to help them come to grips with the profound puzzle generated by their own recent experience.

At the most obvious level, Luke-Acts celebrates the success of the Gentile mission. Paul's final words in Acts, "this word of salvation has been sent to the Gentiles, and they will listen" (28:28), is meant to be understood as a prophecy that is—like all prophecies in Luke-Acts—brought to fulfillment. Theophilus and the readers he represents are among the fruits of this mission. Much of the narrative of Acts is devoted to showing how God willed and directed this surprising choice of "taking from among the Gentiles a people for His name" (Acts 15:14), and how the human agents of this expansion had to struggle to keep up with God's initiative and understand it (see especially Acts 10–15). Luke's Gospel had intimated from the start that "all flesh will see the salvation that comes from God" (Luke 3:6). In Acts, we see God's will enacted, as Paul (in particular) is shown to be the "light of revelation to the Gentiles" prophesied by the old man Simeon (Luke 2:32; see Acts 13:47).

The success of this mission has, however, created a serious problem of confidence in the very God who accomplished it. The Gentiles have been converted only, it seems, because the Jews have rejected the Gospel. Luke shows Paul repeatedly failing to convert his countrymen, and twice during his active ministry he has him solemnly declare a turn to the Gentiles (Acts 13:46-47; Acts 18:6). This pattern of rejection reaches its climax in the final encounter between Paul and the Jewish leaders in Rome, when despite the fact that some of his listeners were convinced by his demonstration, he directed against those who disbelieved the blindness passage from Isaiah 6:9-10 before announcing his prophecy concerning the Gentile mission (28:25-27).

It appears therefore that the Jews have missed out on the promises that God had made specifically to "Abraham and his descendants" that they would be the recipients of God's blessings (Luke 1:55, 73; Acts 3:13; 7:16; 13:26). If the Jews of Luke's own day have not converted to the Messiah, and if demographically Christianity is becoming predominantly Gentile, then believers are faced with an unpleasant choice: either the present Jews are correct and Jesus is not Messiah and therefore the Gentile believers are not authentically God's people; or, God has not been faithful to his promises to the Jews and has abandoned them as his people.

Luke's readers need "assurance" (*asphaleia*), because either option seems to convict God of deception and disloyalty. The question posed both by the inclusion of the Gentiles and the exclusion of the Jews is: does God keep his promises? If God is *not* faithful, then the Gentiles who now enjoy God's favor are really no better off than the Jews, for if God abandoned the people of the promise, the Gentiles could be rejected even more easily. Can the Gentiles be "secure" in their own possession of the blessings?

Luke intends to give this assurance by the "orderly" character of his narrative. He will show *by the sequence of events in the story* how God in fact did offer the blessings to Israel in the first proclamation of the good news in Jerusalem, and that great numbers of Jews actually accepted the message and received the blessings of Abraham (which, as we shall see, Luke defines as the gift of the Holy Spirit, Acts 3:25). The part of his story dealing with the first community in Jerusalem (Acts 1-8) is of particular importance, since it provides the hinge between the first rejection of Jesus (in the Gospel) and the account of the Gentile mission. By showing that in this first community there was a "restoration of Israel," Luke can subsequently describe the Gentile mission not as a replacement of Israel but as its legitimate continuation.

A number of frequently noticed tendencies in Acts make sense within Luke's overall apologetic concern: his emphasis on the large number of Jewish *conversions* in the Jerusalem narrative; his stress on the *continuity* of the missionary effort leading from Jerusalem to the Diaspora, and his concern to show the fundamental *cooperation* among all the Christian missionaries; and most of all, his *portrayal of Paul* as one who not only "opened a door of faith to the Gentiles" (14:27), but continues to offer the word of salvation as well to his fellow Jews (Acts 14:1; 16:13, 16; 17:1, 10; 18:4, 19:8; 28:23), and can express the essence of his message simply as "the hope of Israel" (28:20).

D. *Literary Dimensions of Acts*

The introduction to the commentary on Luke's Gospel provides a fairly full discussion of literary elements found in both volumes. Here we need note only how some of Luke's literary techniques apply in particular to the second volume. What was said in the earlier volume about Luke's Greek style, for example, and especially about his habit of imitating the Greek of the Septuagint, should be assumed throughout the reading of Acts. Only the briefest recapitulation concerning narrative devices is needed for the reader of the present volume.

1. *Narrative Devices*

Already in the Gospel, Luke had taken over from Mark the use of narrative *summaries*. In Acts, they are even more important, enabling him to provide a sense of fullness to a narrative otherwise low in specific factual content. The first chapters of Acts have three "major summaries" (2:42-47; 4:32-35; 5:12-16), to which we owe much of our impression of the first community's inner life. Similar if smaller summaries are used throughout Acts to provide narrative transitions (see 5:42; 6:7; 9:31; 12:24; 19:20).

Like other Hellenistic historians, Luke uses *speeches* as narrative filler, especially in the first section of Acts, where there are nine speeches of lesser or greater length (1:4-8, 16-22; 2:14-40; 3:12-26; 4:8-12, 24-30; 5:35-39; 7:2-53), constituting fully half the narrative to that point. The speeches obviously represent Luke's sense of what should have been said on the occasion, as well as his authorial commentary on the events he is relating.

Another typical device of Hellenistic narratives is the *journey*. In the Gospel, Luke took the tradition of Jesus' journey to Jerusalem and shaped it into a major literary construction (Luke 9–19). Acts shows us Paul making a series of journeys (13:4–14:28; 15:36–18:1; 18:18–19:1; 20:1–21:16). The most dramatically depicted is his final sea-voyage from Caesarea to Italy (27:1–28:16), an account which puzzles interpreters as much for its length and detail as for its apparent irrelevance to the development of Luke's story. Like the summaries and speeches, however, the journeys give an author the chance to organize otherwise disparate incidents, to develop aspects of character otherwise left implicit, and above all to give the reader a sense of spaciousness and elapsed time.

As the similarity between the journeys of Jesus and Paul suggest, Luke is also fond of the literary device of *parallelism.* He has Peter and Paul work similar wonders (compare Acts 3:1-10 with 14:8-11, and 10:36-40 with 20:7-12) which in turn resemble those worked by Jesus (Luke 5:17-26; 8:40-56). Peter and Paul face similar threats (compare Acts 8:9-13 with 19:13-19) and enjoy similar miraculous escapes (compare Acts 12:6-17 with 16:25-34). Parallelism enables Luke to draw connections between his characters and to create a dynamic tension between discrete parts of his story.

2. *Literary Structure*

Two of Luke's literary devices are of particular importance for shaping the narrative of Luke-Acts as a whole: his use of Geography, and his use of Prophecy.

a. *Geography*

In the Gospel, Luke moves the narrative toward Jerusalem. In Acts, the geographical movement is, in the most obvious sense, away from Jerusalem. The pronouncement by Jesus in 1:8, "You shall be my witnesses in Jerusalem and in all Judea and Samaria and to the end of the earth," is fulfilled in the subsequent narrative: the account of the first church in Jerusalem (Acts 1-7) is followed by stories concerning the evangelization of Judea and Samaria (8–12), and by the much longer treatment of the gospel spreading to Asia Minor and Europe, ending with Paul's arrival in Rome (13–28).

Several specific aspects of this geographical movement in the Acts account are worth noting. First, the sense of spatial expansion is closely connected to the portrayal of the Gentile mission. Readers take this so much for granted partly because of Luke's literary achievement: he has wonderfully joined a spatial progression to a demographic phenomenon (conversion of Gentiles more than Jews), and has joined this to a cultural transformation (an ever-increasing sense of the "Greek World" as the story progresses).

A second aspect of the geographical movement is the way Luke punctuates the triumph of the mission in each new territory with a symbolic conquering of evil powers. In Jerusalem, Peter strikes dead Ananias and *cf. the plague contests in Exod.* Sapphira who had taken Satan into their hearts (5:1-11). In Samaria, Peter rejects the overtures of the magician Simon, rebukes him, and wins his recognition (8:9-24). In Cyprus, Paul overcomes the magical powers of the "false Jewish prophet" Bar-Jesus (13:4-12) and in Philippi, the forces of divination and soothsaying (16:16-18). In Asia Minor, the "seven sons of a Jewish high priest named Scaeva" who tried to work exorcisms in the name of Jesus are routed (19:11-20). In Malta, Paul is thought to be a criminal because he is bitten by a deadly viper (see Luke 10:19), but when he survives he is regarded as a god (28:1-6).

In these "turf-wars" between Christian missionaries and other spiritual powers, Luke shows how "the word of the Lord grew and prevailed mightily." The powers of exorcism that were at work in the prophet Jesus (Luke 4:33, 41; 6:18; 8:2, 26-39; 9:37-43; 11:14) are at work as well in his prophetic successors (see Luke 9:1) and signify the same reality: where the powers of evil are overcome, the power of God is present, "If it is by the finger of God that I cast out demons, then the kingdom of God has come upon you" (Luke 11:20).

The third aspect of the geographical movement in Acts is that it is not simply outward. Each movement of the Gospel away from Jerusalem also circles back to it (see 8:14; 11:1-18, 29-30; 12:25; 15:2; 18:22; 19:21; 20:16; 21:13; 25:1). Luke is concerned to show that the expansion of Christianity into the wider world and among the Gentiles took place in continuity and communication with the original community in Jerusalem.

The geographical structure of Luke-Acts therefore makes Jerusalem the *center* of Luke's narrative. The reason is that Jerusalem is the place where the story of "the prophet and the people" reaches its climax.

b. *Prophecy*

Luke's most comprehensive way of structuring his entire two-volume work is by means of literary prophecy. The reader of this commentary can refer to the lengthy argument on this point made by the introduction to the commentary on the Gospel. The points made here are meant to serve as a reminder that Luke's use of "prophecy and fulfillment" goes far beyond that found in any other NT writing. For Luke, it does not refer only to the way in which events in Jesus' life (and for him, the life of the Church) fulfill prophecies first enunicated in Torah ("Moses, the Prophets and the Psalms," Luke 24:44), but also—and of equal importance—to the fulfillment of prophecies uttered by characters within Luke's own narrative.

Of particular importance are Luke's "Programmatic Prophecies," statements uttered at critical junctures in the story which provide an authorial commentary on the events which follow. The most obvious example of such a programmatic prophecy is Jesus' announcement in Acts 1:8 that his followers would be his witnesses in Jerusalem, Judea and Samaria, and the end of the earth; the rest of Acts, as we have seen, functions as the narrative fulfillment of that prophecy (see also 3:22; 11:27; 13:46-47; 19:21; 20:25; 21:11; 23:11; 27:22; 28:28). Such fulfillment of prophecy not only serves to strengthen Luke's presentation of the missionaries as prophetic figures moved by the Spirit, but also helps Luke's reader to perceive how "the matters that have been brought to fulfillment among us" are events directed by God. Sometimes Luke employs the pattern within so tight a compass that the events *immediately* following a prophetic statement serve to fulfill that statement, often ironically (see, for example, 7:51-60 and 13:40, 48-49).

E. *The Prophetic Structure of Luke-Acts*

Luke's literary use of prophecy extends to the portrayal of his characters and to the overall structuring of his two-volume work. The pervasive use of prophetic imagery and pattern is a key to understanding how Luke managed so convincingly to make his story of Jesus and of Christian beginnings a prolongation of biblical history. The first section of Acts is of particular importance for detecting Luke's literary and religious intentions, precisely because in this part of his story the author was least constrained by the demands of tradition. The reader of this commentary might want to consult the much fuller argument displayed in the introduction to the commentary on the Gospel of Luke. The main points of the argument are these:

1. Luke portrays the apostles as prophets: in Acts, all believers are given the Spirit, but Luke uses stereotypical imagery to describe his protagonists, an imagery which in the biblical parlance is unmistakably prophetic.

2. Jesus is portrayed as the prophet like Moses: the prophetic spirit at work in the apostles comes from the risen Jesus, who is identified as the prophet "like Moses" promised by Deut 18:15-18. He is now the "raised prophet" who speaks authoritatively through the wonders and speech of the apostles.

3. Moses reveals the basic prophetic pattern: In the section of Stephen's speech (Acts 7) devoted to Moses, Luke structures the account to make it correspond precisely with the story of Jesus as Luke himself tells it: the prophet is sent a first time to save Israel, but out of ignorance the people reject him. He is forced to go away, but while in exile is empowered by God and sent a second time to offer salvation, this time with powerful signs and wonders. If the people reject him again, they will be sent into exile rather than he. It is in this way that Luke understands the story of Jesus to have been found in "Moses and all the prophets" (Luke 24:27).

4. The prophetic pattern structures Luke-Acts: the first chapters of Acts, and in particular Stephen's speech, provide the key to reading all of Luke-Acts as the story of "the Prophet and the People." Luke uses the prophetic pattern established by his reading of the Moses story to structure his entire two-volume work. The Gospel is the time of the first sending of the prophet. Acts continues the story of the prophet's second and more powerful sending to the people, with the offer of a second chance at accepting "God's visitation," and thereby their salvation.

5. Acts should be read in the light of the Gospel: just as Luke's first volume can best be understood in the light of these literary patterns established in the first section of Acts, so that elements in his presentation of Jesus and the disciples and their opponents that might otherwise remain at best implicit are revealed in clearer and more explicit form, the narrative in Acts must also be read as the continuation and confirmation of the Gospel story. The Gospel has shown us Jesus as the prophet sent by God to "visit the people," and who carries out his mission of "good news to the poor" by his works of mercy and his teaching—what the prologue of Acts calls "everything that Jesus began to do and teach" (Acts 1:1). His invitation to the poor and the outcast to join the restored people of God is heard by them gladly, but he is rejected by the leadership of the people and put to death. After his resurrection, he appears to those who had followed him in his ministry, and instructs them to wait in the city until they receive the "power from on high" (Luke 24:49), which will enable them to "preach in his name to all nations beginning in Jerusalem" (24:47).

The geographical centering of Luke's story in Jerusalem and the literary pattern of the acceptance or rejection of God's Prophet converge in the account of the founding of the Christian community in Acts 1–7. Here the story of the prophet and the people comes to its *climax:* will God send the Prophet again to the people with a second offer of salvation? Will they reject the Prophet still a second time? Will they then be definitively rejected from the people? Or, will the offer of the blessings be received within Judaism? The critical questions are posed and answered in these chapters. However lengthy, detailed, or fascinating the remainder of the Acts narrative might be, in dramatic terms it must be considered strictly *denouement.* The crisis concerning God's fidelity to his people is resolved in the narrative of Acts 1–7; the rest of the story simply extends that resolution to its pleasing conclusion.

F. Religious Themes

In the Introduction to the Commentary on the Gospel of Luke, a number of religious emphases that applied to Luke-Acts as a whole were listed and discussed: world-affirmation, the great reversal, salvation, the word of God, conversion, the response of faith. A number of additional religious emphases emerge more explicitly in Acts. An awareness of them can make the reading of Luke's dramatic story a richer experience by suggesting certain consistent religious preoccupations that might not be obvious on the surface of his story-telling.

1. The Holy Spirit

Acts can appropriately be called the "Book of the Holy Spirit." Luke not only includes five separate accounts of the Spirit's dramatic "outpouring" on believers (2:1-4; 4:28-31; 8:15-17; 10:44; 19:6)—demarcating, it will be noted, the geographical and demographical progress of the "Word of God"—but also shows the Spirit actively intervening in the story, impelling and guiding it (see Acts 8:29, 39; 10:19; 11:15; 13:2; 15:28; 16:6; 20:22; 21:4, 11). Because Luke understands this Spirit to be the "spirit of prophecy" (Acts 2:17-21) that derives from the resurrected Lord (2:33), he is able to link Jesus and his followers in a prophetic succession like that of Moses and Joshua (Deut 34:9) or Elijah and Elisha (2 Kgs 9–14).

Something more than a literary device is at work here, however, for Luke has grasped the Pauline principle that the Spirit's essential work is not extrinsic but intrinsic, the transformation of human identity. The work of the Holy Spirit is not revealed only in the spectacular manifestations of "speaking in tongues and prophesying," although Acts has plenty of those activities (2:4; 10:44-46; 13:2; 19:5-6; 21:7-11); it is not found only in the ability of missionaries to proclaim and work wonders "in the name of Jesus"; it is found above all in their ability also to imitate the suffering of the Messiah (5:41; 7:59; 9:16; 12:4; 14:22; 16:23; 20:19, 22-24, 35; 21:11-14). By establishing a narrative role for the Holy Spirit, Luke has taken a significant step towards the eventual theological recognition of the Holy Spirit as a "person."

2. *The Life of the Church*

Luke obviously considers the Holy Spirit itself to be the "life-principle" of the Church, and in his narrative he provides an impressively full portrait of the messianic people of God. Like Paul, Luke is a witness first of all to the conviction that God's concern in history is the shaping of "a people for his name" (15:14). Luke thinks in terms of the social reality of "the church" (*ekklēsia*; 5:11; 8:1, 3; 9:31; 11:22; 12:1, 5; 13:1; 14:23, 27; 15:3, 22; 16:5; 18:22; 20:17, 28). In the "major summaries" of Acts 2:42-47 and 4:32-37, he sketches the inner life of this community in idealistic terms: its practicing baptism with an accompanying reception of the Holy Spirit, listening to the teaching of the apostles, being of one mind and heart, sharing all possessions, breaking bread in households, joining in prayer.

That these descriptions are not entirely idealized, however, is shown narratively by the recurrence of these activities in Luke's short vignettes of community life punctuating the mission exploits of the apostles. Thus he multiplies the instances of community prayer (1:24; 4:24-30; 6:4, 6; 12:5, 12; 13:2; 16:25; 20:36; 21:5, 14) and worship, including the breaking of bread (20:7). He shows communities sharing their possessions (6:1-7; 11:27-30), and "listening to the teaching of the apostles" (6:1-7; 11:1-18; 15:30-35; 20:7-12, 17-35). The apostles, in turn, are not simply traveling evangelists, but are leaders of communities who are concerned for their identity and stability, including the establishment of local leaders (6:1-7; 8:14-24; 11:22-26; 14:21-23; 15:22-27, 31-32, 36; 19:21-22; 20:2, 17, 28).

cf. p. 279

3. *The Discernment of God's Activity*

Luke brings together the themes of the Church and the Holy Spirit in the attention he pays to the process of human decision-making. The mission, as we have seen, is willed, initiated, impelled, and guided by God through the Holy Spirit. God moves ahead of the other characters. But at the human level, Luke shows how difficult and intricate is the effort of the Church to keep up with God's action, follow God's initiatives, understand the precedents being established. Luke carefully describes several major decisions taken by the Church in its earliest days: the election of Matthias (1:15-26); the decision to continue preaching despite persecution (4:23-31); the choosing of the seven (6:1-6); the acceptance of Paul as an apostle by the Jerusalem community (9:26-30).

Most elaborately, the entire narrative of Acts 10–15 is devoted to the stages of a church decision concerning the admission and status of Gentiles. With literary artistry and genuine theological sensitivity, Luke shows through the narrative itself how the diverse experiences of God's action by individuals are slowly raised to the level of a communal narrative, which in turn must be tested by the entire community in a difficult and delicate process of disagreement, debate, and the discernment of the Scripture. By means of carefully constructed narrative, Luke communicates a vision of the Church as a community of moral discourse and of discernment of the Spirit.

4. Universality

The work of the Holy Spirit in history is not confined by the precedents established by human perception, institution, or Scripture. The essential drama of Luke's narrative is found in the breathtaking sweep of the Spirit's work. The wind that swept over the Twelve and their company at Pentecost is not understood by Luke to be a power meant for them alone, but a power for the restoration (first) of Israel, and then for the salvation of all humans. There could scarcely be a better way to signal that the same Spirit that was at work in the Messiah who proclaimed good news to the poor and the outcast among the people and called them to a place in God's banquet was also at work in his followers, than to show Jesus' prophetic successors proclaiming the same universal offer of salvation, not only to those who are by heritage part of "God's people," but to "everyone whom the Lord our God calls to him" (Acts 2:39).

The clearest expression of the theme of universality is the Gentile mission, which dominates Luke's narrative after chapter nine. The beginning for Luke was Peter's epochal preaching to the household of Cornelius (10:34-48), quickly followed by the mission to the Greeks in Antioch (11:19-25) and the extended campaigns of Paul with his fellow workers Barnabas, John-Mark, Silas, Timothy, Aquila, Priscilla, Apollos, Erastus, Sopater, Aristarchus, Secundus, Gaius, Tychichus, and Trophimus the Ephesian (see chs. 13–21). But even before that, Luke shows us the proclamation of good news to the despised Samaritans (8:4-13), to the Ethiopian eunuch (8:27-39), and to the simple folk in the cities of Lydda and Joppa (9:32-43). These early forays represent a continuation of Jesus' outreach to the despised and marginal members of the people.

The conversion of Gentiles is the clearest exemplification of Luke's conviction that all people "will be saved through the grace of the Lord Jesus" (15:11), but not the only one. The theme of universality is found in the way the Christian mission is made available to all kinds of people, whether powerful or weak, wealthy or poor, male or female: the message is constantly enunciated through proclamation or through merciful action, to poor widows (9:39) and provincials (14:15-18) and merchants (16:14), and jailers (16:30-32), and sailors (27:25) as well as powerful military officers (10:34-48), proconsuls (13:7), governors (24:10), kings (26:2), and philosophers (17:18).

If such is the case, we would also expect that the same salvation remains extended to the Jews, for they are preeminently the people whom God has visited. Luke struggles with the historical reality that the majority of Jews in the first generation did not accept the offer of salvation represented by the prophet Jesus, and that in his own generation, the mission to the Jews appears either vestigial or futile. As we have seen, the shaping of his account responds to the crisis of faith this historical development presents to Gentile believers. Despite all that, Luke never completely lets go of the "hope of Israel" (28:20).

As in the Gospel, he resists portraying the rejection of the Jews as total or uniform. In the Jerusalem narrative, it is the leadership that opposes the apostles just as it had Jesus (4:1-2, 5-21; 5:17-42; 6:12-15; 9:1-2). The ordinary people are shown not only to look favorably on the church (2:47) but also to convert in great numbers in response to the apostles' proclamation; Luke notes the progressive growth of the community (made up of Jews) in 2:41, 47; 4:4; 5:14; 6:1, 7, and makes clear that the increments are in the thousands (2:41; 4:4). A significant portion of historical Judaism, in other words, became part of the restored people of God in Jerusalem.

We have seen that the restoration in Jerusalem was a critical element in Luke's apologetic argument, demonstrating that God was faithful to his historical people. This opens the way for the secure spread of the good news to the Gentiles. But Luke does not leave Israel behind. Even at Pentecost, the number of those who converted included Jewish pilgrims from the Diaspora (2:5-11). And when Paul begins his mission, it is consistently to his fellow Jews in the Synagogue that he first preaches (13:5; 14:1; 16:13, 16; 17:1-2, 10; 18:4; 19:8). And even though Paul's message is rejected there, and he explicitly says he is turning to the Gentiles (13:46-47; 18:6), he never stops trying to convince his fellow Jews. Indeed, the final scene in Acts has Paul trying to preach Jesus to the Jewish leaders in Rome "from the law of Moses and the Prophets" (28:23).

He had, furthermore, some success, even in the Diaspora. In each place, Luke shows among the Jews not a total but a partial rejection of the gospel. Many Jews and God-fearers do join the Church (13:43, 49; 14:1; 17:4, 11; 19:9). The opposition and rejection come not from all but from "some" (19:9), even if that "some" occasionally appears as a clear majority (17:5; 18:6). The point is that Luke need not have included any of this success. His repeated emphasis on it is deliberate. Acts does not even end with a total abandonment of the Jews, despite Paul's use of the Isaiah blindness passage and his programmatic turn to the Gentiles, "they will listen" (28:28), for even in that place some of the Jewish leaders "were convinced by what he said" (28:24). The story of Luke-Acts as a whole shows that however difficult it is to discern in the complexities of historical events, God's will remains constant to "seek a people for his name," which means both the visitation of the Gentiles and also the rebuilding of "the dwelling of David which has fallen" (Amos 9:11; Acts 15:14-16).

BIBLIOGRAPHY

This selection out of a vast body of scholarship includes only works in English, and which will be useful for the reading of Acts as a whole. There is some overlap with the bibliography given in the Introduction to the commentary on the Gospel of Luke, but the present list focuses particularly on Acts. More technical references to scholarship on specific points (including non-English works) are provided throughout the commentary at the end of each unit; even these fuller references provide only a small sample of an ever burgeoning bibliography. An impressively full collection of bibliography up to 1984 is provided by R. Pesch, *Die Apostelgeschichte* 2 vols. (EKK 5; Zurich: Benziger Verlag, 1986).

Barrett, C. K. *Luke the Historian in Recent Study*. London: Epworth, 1961.
_____. "Is There a Theological Tendency in Codex Bezae?" *Text and Interpretation*. Ed. E. Best and R. McL. Wilson. Cambridge: Cambridge University Press, 1979, 15-27.
Bovon, F. *Luke the Theologian: Thirty-three years of Research (1950–1983)*. Trans. K. McKinney. Princeton Theological Monograph Series 12. Allison Park, Penn.: Pickwick Publications, 1987.
Brawley, R. L. *Luke-Acts and the Jews: Conflict, Apology, and Conciliation*. SBLMS 33. Atlanta: Scholars Press, 1987.
Brown, S. *Apostasy and Perseverence in the Theology of Luke*. Analecta Biblica 36. Rome: Pontifical Biblical Institute, 1969.
Cadbury, H. J. *The Book of Acts in History*. New York: Harper and Brothers, 1955.
_____. *The Making of Luke-Acts*. New York: MacMillan Co., 1927.
Carroll, J. T. *Response to the End of History: Eschatology and Situation in Luke-Acts*. SBLDS 92. Atlanta: Scholars Press, 1988.
Cassidy, R. J. *Society and Politics in the Acts of the Apostles*. Maryknoll, N.Y.: Orbis Books, 1987.
Conzelmann, H. *The Theology of St. Luke*. Trans. G. Buswell. New York: Harper and Row, 1961.

Introduction

19

Dahl, N. A. "'A People for His Name' (Acts XV.14)." *New Testament Studies* 4 (1957–1958) 319–327.

_____. "The Story of Abraham in Luke-Acts." *Studies in Luke-Acts.* Eds. L. E. Keck and J. L. Martyn. Nashville: Abingdon Press, 1966, 139–158.

Dibelius, M. *Studies in the Acts of the Apostles.* Trans. Mary Ling. London: SCM Press, 1956.

Donelson, L. R. "Cult Histories and the Sources of Acts." *Biblica* 68 (1967) 1–21.

Dupont, J. *The Sources of the Acts: The Present Position.* Trans. Kathleen Pond. New York: Herder and Herder, 1964.

_____. *The Salvation of the Gentiles: Studies in the Acts of the Apostles.* Trans. John Keating. New York: Paulist Press, 1979.

Ellis, E. E. "The Role of the Christian Prophet in Acts." *Apostolic History and the Gospel.* Eds. W. Gasque and R. Martin. Exeter: Paternoster Press, 1970, 55–67.

Enslin, M. "Once More, Luke and Paul." *ZNW* 61 (1970) 253–271.

Epp, E. J. *The Theological Tendency of Codex Bezae Cantabrigiensis in Acts.* SNTSMS 3. Cambridge: University Press, 1966.

Esler, P. F. *Community and Gospel in Luke-Acts: The Social and Political Motivations of Lukan Theology.* SNTSMS 57. Cambridge: University Press, 1987.

Filson, F. "The Journey Motif in Luke-Acts." *Apostolic History and the Gospel.* Eds. W. Gasque and R. Martin. Exeter: Paternoster Press, 1970, 68–77.

Foakes-Jackson, F. J. and K. Lake, eds. *The Beginnings of Christianity. Part I: The Acts of the Apostles.* 5 volumes. London: MacMillan and Co., 1920–1933.

Garrett, S. R. *The Demise of the Devil: Magic and the Demonic in Luke's Writings.* Minneapolis: Fortress Press, 1989.

Gasque, W. W. "A Fruitful Field: Recent Study of the Acts of the Apostles." *Interpretation* 42 (1988) 117–131.

_____. *A History of the Interpretation of the Acts of the Apostles.* (Peabody, Mass.: Hendrickson Publishers, 1989.

Gaventa, B. "Towards a Theology of Acts: Reading and Rereading." *Interpretation* 42 (1988) 146–157.

Goulder, M. D. *Type and History in Acts.* London: SPCK, 1964.

Haenchen, E. "The Book of Acts as Source-Material for the History of Early Christianity." *Studies in Luke-Acts.* Eds. L. E. Keck and J. L. Martyn. Nashville: Abingdon Press, 1966, 258–278.

Harnack, A. *New Testament Studies III: The Acts of the Apostles.* Trans. J. R. Wilkinson. Crown Theological Library 27. London: Williams and Newgate, 1909.

Hemer, C. J. *The Book of Acts in the Setting of Hellenistic History.* WUNT 49. Tübingen: J. C. B. Mohr (Paul Siebeck), 1989.

Hengel, M. *Acts and the History of Earliest Christianity.* Trans. J. Bowden. Philadelphia: Fortress Press, 1980.

Jervell, J. *Luke and the People of God.* Minneapolis: Augsburg Press, 1972.

_____. *The Unknown Paul: Essays on Luke-Acts and Early Christian History.* Minneapolis: Augsburg Press, 1984.

Johnson, L. T. *A Commentary on the Gospel of Luke.* Minneapolis: The Liturgical Press (Michael Glazier Books), 1991.

_____. "On Finding the Lukan Community: A Cautious Cautionary Essay." *SBL 1979 Seminar Papers.* Ed. P. J. Achtemeier. Missoula: Scholars Press, 1979, 87–100.

_____. *The Literary Function of Possessions in Luke-Acts.* SBLDS 39. Missoula: Scholars Press, 1977.

_____. *Decision-Making in the Church: A Biblical Model.* Philadelphia: Fortress Press, 1983.

Karris, R. J. "Missionary Communities: A New Paradigm for the Study of Luke-Acts." *Catholic Biblical Quarterly* 44 (1979) 80–97.

Keck, L. E. and Martyn, J. L. eds. *Studies in Luke-Acts.* Nashville: Abingdon Press, 1966.

Kurz, W. S. "Luke-Acts and Historiography in the Greek Bible." *Society of Biblical Literature 1980 Seminar Papers.* Ed. P. J. Achtemeier. Chico: Scholars Press, 1980, 283–300.

_____. "Narrative Approaches to Luke-Acts." *Biblica* 68 (1987) 195–220.

_____. "Narrative Models for Imitation in Luke-Acts." *Greeks, Romans, and Christians: Essays in Honor of A. J. Malherbe.* Ed. D. L. Balch et al. Minneapolis: Fortress Press, 1990, 171–189.

Lampe, G. W. H. "The Holy Spirit in the Writings of St. Luke." *Studies in the Gospels.* Ed. D. E. Nineham. Oxford: Basil Blackwell, 1955, 159–200.

Lindars, B. *New Testament Apologetic: The Doctrinal Significance of the Old Testament Quotations.* Philadelphia: Westminster Press, 1961.

Lüdemann, G. *Early Christianity according to the Traditions in Acts: A Commentary.* Minneapolis: Fortress, 1989.

Maddox, R. *The Purpose of Luke-Acts.* Edinburgh: T & T Clark, 1982.

Mattill, A. J. "The Date and Purpose of Acts: Rackham Reconsidered." *CBQ* 40 (1978) 335–350.

Menoud, Ph.-H. "Jesus and His Witnesses: Observations on the Unity of Luke's Work." *Jesus Christ and the Faith.* Trans. E. M. Paul. Pittsburgh: Pickwick Press, 1978, 149–166.

Moessner, D. " 'The Christ Must Suffer': New Light on the Jesus-Peter, Stephen, Paul Parallels in Luke-Acts." *Novum Testamentum* 28 (1986) 220–256.

Moule, C. F. D. "The Christology of Acts." *Studies in Luke-Acts.* Ed. L. E. Keck and J. L. Martyn. Nashville: Abingdon Press, 1966, 159–185.

O'Neill, J. C. *The Theology of Acts in its Historical Setting.* London: SPCK, 1961.

Pervo, R. I. *Profit with Delight: The Literary Genre of the Acts of the Apostles.* Philadelphia: Fortress Press, 1987.

Praeder, S. M. "Luke-Acts and the Ancient Novel." *SBL 1981 Seminar Papers.* Ed. K. H. Richards. Chico: Scholars Press, 1981, 269–292.

Ramsay, W. *St. Paul the Traveller and Roman Citizen.* New York: Putnam, 1904.

Schwartz, D. R. "The End of the Line: Paul in the Canonical Book of Acts." *Paul and the Legacies of Paul.* Ed. W. S. Babcock. Dallas: SMU Press, 1990, 3–24.

Sterling, G. E. "Luke-Acts and Apologetic Historiography," *SBL 1989 Seminar Papers.* Ed. D. Lull. Atlanta: Scholars Press, 1989, 326–342.

Talbert, C. H., ed. *Perspectives on Luke-Acts.* Danville, Va.: Association of Baptist Professors of Religion, 1978.

_____. *Luke-Acts: New Perspectives from the SBL Seminar.* New York: Cross-road, 1984.

Tannehill, R. C. *The Narrative Unity of Luke-Acts: A Literary Interpretation.* Vol. I: *The Gospel according to Luke.* Philadelphia: Fortress Press, 1986; Vol. II: *The Acts of the Apostles.* Minneapolis: Fortress Press, 1990.

_____. "Israel in Luke-Acts: A Tragic Story." *Journal of Biblical Literature* 104 (1985) 69–85.

Taylor, J. "The Making of Acts: A New Account." *RB* 97 (1990) 504–524.

Tiede, D. *Prophecy and History in Luke-Acts.* Philadelphia: Fortress Press, 1980.

Trites, A. A. "Some Aspects of Prayer in Luke-Acts." *SBL 1977 Seminar Papers.* Ed. P. J. Achtemeier. Missoula: Scholars Press, 1977, 59–77.

van Unnik, W. C. "The 'Book of Acts,' the Confirmation of the Gospel." *Novum Testamentum* 4 (1960) 26–59.

_____. "Luke's Second Book and the Rules of Hellenistic Historiography." *Les Actes des Apôtres: traditions, rédaction, théologie.* Ed. J. Kremer. Gembloux: J. Duculot, 1979, 37–60.

Walasky, P. W. *"And so We Came to Rome": The Political Perspective of St. Luke.* SNTMS 49. Cambridge: University Press, 1973.

Walker, W. O. "Acts and the Pauline Corpus Reconsidered." *JSNT* 24 (1985) 3–23.

Wilcox, M. *The Semitisms of Acts.* Oxford: Clarendon Press, 1965.

Wilson, S. G. *The Gentiles and the Gentile Mission in Luke-Acts.* SNTMS 23. Cambridge: University Press, 1973.

_____. *Luke and the Law.* SNTMS 50, Cambridge: University Press, 1983.

Commentaries on the Acts of the Apostles

Bruce, F. F. *The Acts of the Apostles.* London: Tyndale Press, 1951.

Conzelmann, H. *Acts of the Apostles.* Trans. J. Limburg, A. T. Kraabel, D. H. Juel. Hermeneia; Philadelphia: Fortress Press, 1987.

Haenchen, E. *The Acts of the Apostles.* Trans. B. Noble, et al. Philadelphia: Westminster Press, 1971.

Juel, D. *Luke-Acts: The Promise of History.* Atlanta: John Knox Press, 1983.

Lake, K. and Cadbury, H. J. *English Translation and Commentary.* Vol. IV of *The Beginnings of Christianity.* Ed. F. J. Foakes-Jackson and K. Lake. London: MacMillan and Co., 1933.

Metzger, B. M. *A Textual Commentary on the Greek New Testament.* New York: United Bible Societies, 1975.

Munck, J. *The Acts of the Apostles.* Anchor Bible 31. Garden City: Doubleday, 1967.

Neill, W. *The Acts of the Apostles.* New Century Bible Commentary. Grand Rapids: Eerdmans, 1973.

TRANSLATION, NOTES, INTERPRETATION

I. THE RAISED PROPHET AND THE RESTORED PEOPLE

1. *Prophecy and Enthronement* (1:1-11)

1. Theophilus, the first book I composed was about everything Jesus began to do and to teach 2. up to the day he was lifted up. Through the Holy Spirit, he commissioned the apostles whom he had selected. 3. To them also after his suffering he showed himself to be alive by means of many convincing signs. He appeared to them for forty days and spoke of things concerning the kingdom of God. 4. And as he ate with them, he ordered them, "Do not withdraw from Jerusalem, but await the promise of the father which you heard from me, 5. because John baptized with water, but after a few days you will be baptized with the Holy Spirit." 6. Those who had gathered together therefore asked him, "Lord, are you restoring the kingdom to Israel at this time?" 7. He said to them, "The times and the seasons that the father has reserved to his own authority are not yours to know. 8. Instead, you will receive a power from the Holy Spirit coming upon you. And you will be my witnesses in Jerusalem and in all of Judea and Samaria and to the end of the earth." 9. After he said these things, while they were watching, he was lifted up. A cloud took him up away from their sight. 10. And as they were gazing into heaven at his departure, two men in white clothing stood near them 11. and said, "Men of Galilee! Why do you stand looking into heaven? This Jesus who was lifted up from you into heaven, will come in the same way that you saw him going into heaven."

Notes

1. *Theophilus:* Although the vocative appears later in the Greek sentence (compare Philo, *Every Good Man is Free* 1; Josephus, *Against Apion* 1:1), this translation shifts the address, "O Theophilus," to a position that enables a more natural sentence in English. Theophilus is Luke's "intended reader," possibly a patron who is already instructed in "the matters brought to fulfillment among us," but whom Luke thinks needs "assurance." Luke seeks to provide it by the ordered way he writes his narrative (see Luke 1:1-4).

   the first book I composed: The term *logos* literally means "word," but is applied to speeches, discourses, or as here, to literary compositions (see, e.g., Plato, *Parmenides* 127D). Luke uses the adjective "first" (*prōtos*) rather than the expected "earlier/former" (*proteros;* see Philo, *Every Good Man is Free* 1; Josephus, *Against Apion* 2:1), but in Hellenistic Greek the differences between such constructions were not rigorously maintained.

   began to do and to teach: Luke sometimes uses the verb *archō* ("begin") as a sort of helping verb (e.g., Luke 3:8; 4:21), but can also use it more deliberately to demarcate the start of Jesus' active ministry, as in Luke 3:23, Acts 1:22, and here. Jesus' practice of teaching is highlighted throughout the Gospel (Luke 2:46; 4:15, 31; 5:3, 17; 6:6; 13:10, 22; 19:47; 20:1, 21; 21:37; 23:5), as that of the apostles will be throughout Acts (4:2, 18; 5:21, 25, 28, 42; 11:26; 15:35; 18:11; 20:20; 21:28; 28:31).

2. *the day he was lifted up:* The translation simplifies a complex Greek sentence. Jesus' ascension (*analēmpsis*) was adumbrated already in Luke 9:51 at the beginning of his journey to Jerusalem, and in 9:31 was described as the *exodos* that he had to fulfill. Its importance is signalled by its double recital in Luke 24:51 and Acts 1:9-11; the ascension forms the hinge between the two volumes. In Acts 1:22, it distinguishes the ministry of Jesus and that carried out by his witnesses. The use of the verb *analambanō* echoes the account of the ascension of Elijah in LXX 2 Kgs 2:9-11.

   through the Holy Spirit: The Greek phrase is placed awkwardly between "commissioned the apostles" and "whom he selected," so that it modifies neither clearly. The translation therefore moves it to the beginning of a new English sentence, so that it modifies both, which is probably what the author intended it to do. The Gospel account does not explicitly involve the Holy Spirit in either the selecting of the apostles or their commissioning, but Luke sees all of Jesus' activities as directed by the Spirit (Luke 4:1, 14, 18, 36; 10:21).

   commissioned the apostles: The translation gives maximum formality to *entellomai,* which could also be translated as "commanded" (compare Luke 4:10; Acts 13:47). As mentioned above, the Greek syntax is difficult; the translation makes an independent sentence out of a circumstantial participle (*enteilamenos*), whose tense indicates an action prior to Jesus' being taken up. The "selection" (or "election/choice," *eklegomai*) of the Twelve is still earlier, before the Sermon on the Plain (Luke 6:13). In context, this "commissioning" refers to Jesus' prophecy concerning his witnesses in Luke 24:46-49, which is restated below in Acts 1:8. The "Western Text" (see Introduction for a discussion of this textual tradition represented mainly by Codex D) explicates the commission, "and commanded them to preach the gospel."

3. *many convincing signs:* The term *tekmērion* is otherwise unattested in the NT, but is found in discussions of Greek rhetoric as a form of proof. Aristotle (*Rhetoric* 1357B) refers to a popular understanding of *tekmērion* as "proven and concluded"; see the use in Wis 5:11; 19:13; 3 Macc 3:24. Luke's concern for "evidence" accords with his overall intention of providing "assurance" to his reader (Luke 1:4). Note his emphasis on physical evidence in Luke 3:22 (the baptism) and 24:38-40 (the resurrection). Such "evidences," we imagine, would figure in the rhetorical disputations carried out by the apostles (Acts 9:29; 17:1-3; 18:4, 19; 19:8; 28:23).

appeared to them for forty days: More literally, "through forty days." The Greek participle *optamenos* is once more made an independent verb, in order to provide a clearer English sentence. The forty-day period during which appearances took place is a distinctive Lukan contribution to the resurrection traditions. Some apocryphal gospels expand this time of special revelation to the apostles even further; see, for example, the *Epistula Apostolorum*, *The Apocryphon of James* (550 days), and especially *Pistis Sophia* 1, ". . . after Jesus was raised from the dead, he spent eleven years discoursing with his disciples . . . ." For Luke, the number 40 would naturally seem to be associated with the figures of Moses and Elijah (Exod 34:28; Deut 8:2; Ps 90:10 [LXX]; 1 Kgs 19:8).

concerning the kingdom of God: Throughout the Gospel, Jesus proclaimed the kingdom of God (Luke 4:43; 6:20; 7:28; 9:2, 11, 60, 62; 10:9, 11; 11:2, 20; 12:31-32; 13:18, 20, 28-29; 14:15; 16:16; 17:20-21; 18:16-17, 24-25, 29; 19:11; 21:31; 22:16, 18, 29-30; 23:42). The apostles will continue this proclamation (Acts 8:12; 14:22; 19:8; 20:25; 28:23, 31).

4. *as he ate with them:* The precise translation of *synalizomai* is difficult, though the general sense is clear enough. This translation takes "sharing salt (*alas*) together" in its extended sense of "sharing a meal," which the cross-references to Luke 24:36-48 and Acts 10:41 seem to support.

do not withdraw from Jerusalem: The Greek indirect discourse, "he ordered them not to withdraw," is changed to direct discourse at this point rather than in the next clause, to avoid both an awkward transition, and the need to add a clarifying phrase such as "he said" (see RSV). The content of the instruction echoes the "remain in the city" of Luke 24:49, and is an instance of the way Luke centers his story geographically in Jerusalem.

which you heard from me: So awkwardly does the Greek shift to direct discourse in this clause that Codex D adds an additional phrase, "through my mouth," to ease the transition. The "promise of my father" exactly repeats Luke 24:49 and refers to the Holy Spirit, which Luke understands as the fulfillment of the promise God made to Abraham (Acts 3:25-26).

5. *you will be baptized with the Holy Spirit:* This carefully balanced statement picks up the contrast which is found in the gospels as a prophecy of John the Bap-

tist. Both Luke 3:16 and Matt 3:11 add ''and in fire'' to John's statement in Mark 1:8, ''he will baptize you with the Holy Spirit.'' Luke will immediately combine these symbols in his Pentecost account (2:1-4). He also has Peter cite this saying as a ''word of the Lord'' in Acts 11:16.

6. *restoring the kingdom to Israel:* Luke uses a general designation for the questioners, ''those who had gathered together,'' perhaps because he has a larger group than the apostles in mind (see Acts 1:13-14). The verb ''restore'' (*apokathistanō*) is used by Luke with this meaning only here (compare Luke 6:10). The question seems to be related to the tradition concerning the ''restoration of all things'' expected of the figure Elijah, and fits the Lukan portrayal of Jesus in the pattern of the prophet like Moses. Thus, the LXX of Mal 3:23 uses this verb when it says that Elijah will ''restore (*apokatastēsei*) the heart of a father toward his son and the heart of a man toward his neighbor,'' a passage alluded to in Luke 1:17. The LXX of Sirach 48:10, in turn, speaks of Elijah turning a heart of a father toward his son and ''restoring (*katastēsai*) the tribes of Jacob.'' See the evidence of this tradition in Mark 9:12; Matt 17:11.

7. *the father has reserved to his own authority:* The relationship between the Greek verb *tithēmi* (literally, ''place''), and the phrase in the dative case, ''his own authority (*exousia*)'' could be translated as in the RSV, ''which the father fixed by his own authority.'' The meaning in either case is much the same, with the emphasis placed on the inaccessibility of God's plans to their knowledge. Like Paul in Rom 11:25-36, Luke sees the fate of Israel as a ''mystery'' that escapes easy human analysis.

8. *power from the Holy Spirit:* In Luke 24:48, the prophecy was stated as ''you will be clothed with power from on high.'' The spatial image of the Spirit ''coming down on'' corresponds to that of Jesus ''going up into heaven,'' and recalls the gospel accounts of the annunciation to Mary (Luke 1:35) and the baptism of Jesus (3:22).

you will be my witnesses: The prophecy explicitly picks up Luke 24:48, ''you are witnesses of these things.'' The category of ''witness'' is one of Luke's most inclusive for the followers of Jesus (Acts 1:22; 2:32; 3:15; 5:32; 7:58; 10:39, 41; 13:31; 22:15, 22; 26:16). For the carrying out of the prophecy, see 6:3; 13:22; 14:3; 23:11.

to the end of the earth: As noted in the Introduction, the geographical sequence provides a rough outline of the book: it begins with the ministry in Jerusalem (compare ''beginning from Jerusalem'' in Luke 24:47) in chs. 1–7, followed by the spread of the good news to Judea and Samaria in chs. 8–12, and then the mission all the way to Rome, chs. 13–28. The precise meaning of *eschatou tēs gēs* (''end of the earth'') relies on the context. In Herodotus, *Persian Wars* 3:25, for example, the ''ends of the earth'' is applied as a geographical designation to Cambyses' campaign against the Ethiopians; in Strabo, *Geography* 1, 1, 6, again, it is Ethiopia which is called the end of the earth. In Dio Chrysostom, *Oration* 13:9, in contrast, the philosopher is given instruction by the oracle to continue his preaching ''to the uttermost parts of the earth'' (*heōs an . . . epi to hystaton apelthēs tēs gēs*), which in context seems to mean simply, "everywhere." In the LXX, the term "end of the earth" occurs frequently, and has less the sense of a specific geographical locality, than of universal extent (see e.g., Deut 28:49; Ps 134:6-7; Isa 8:9; 14:21-22; 48:20; 49:6; 62:11; Jer 10:12; 16:19; 1 Macc 3:9). The determination therefore that the expression means something like Rome here, rather than, for example, "end of the land (of Israel)," depends on the way one understands the overall ground-plan of the narrative, although in *Psalms of Solomon* 8:15 the Roman enemy is called "someone from the end of the earth."

9. *he was lifted up:* Rather than the verb *analambanō*, Luke here uses *epairō* in the aorist passive. The fact that this is the only time he uses the verb in this sense (compare Luke 6:20; 11:27; Acts 2:14; 22:20) only reminds us how flexible is Luke's diction: in Luke 24:50 he uses *dihistēmi* and *anapherō* to describe the ascension. Here he also uses *analambanō* (Acts 1:2, 11) and *poreuomai* (1:10, 11). The constant is the phrase "into heaven" (*eis ton ouranon*) in Luke 24:51; Acts 1:10, 11.

cloud took him up: The verb *hypolambanō* is translated literally as "take up," so that the cloud is the vehicle of ascent, as it is for the "two witnesses" (who are meant to be understood as Moses and Elijah) in Rev 11:12. A cloud is involved in the ascent of Enoch in 2 *Enoch* 3:1 (it is a whirlwind in 1 *Enoch* 39:3), in the death of Moses as described by Josephus, *Antiquities of the Jews* 4:326, and very elaborately in the description of Jesus' ascension in the *Epistula Apostolorum* 51. An alternative translation of *hypolambanō* would have the cloud "receive him" out of their sight (Haenchen).

10. *two men in white clothing:* The description recalls the "two men in shining garments" seen by the women at the tomb (24:4), who in turn echoed the description of Moses and Elijah at the transfiguration, discussing with Jesus the *exodos* he was to fulfill in Jerusalem (Luke 9:30). The allusion seems more likely since both Moses and Elijah are figures to whom tradition accredited an "ascension into heaven" (see Deut 34:6; Philo, *Life of Moses* 2:291; 2 Kgs 2:11-12).

11. *men of Galilee:* The translation retains "men" since the Greek has *andres*, as it does also in 1:10. In fact, the vocative of *anēr* is used frequently in Acts for public discourses (1:16; 2:14, 22, 29, 37; 3:12; 5:35; 7:2; 13:15-16, etc.). The Galilean origin of the first believers has been stressed repeatedly in the last portion of the Gospel (Luke 22:59; 23:5, 49, 55). The declaration made by the two men functions very much like that given the women at the empty tomb (see the Interpretation).

this Jesus: By no means does Jesus disappear from the pages of Acts. Compared to some 86 uses of his personal name in the Gospel are some 68 occurrences in the Acts narrative. The expression "this Jesus" (*houtos ho Iēsous*) recurs in 2:32, 36, and matches the designation "this Moses" in 7:35.

will come in the same way: The Greek reads literally, "will come thus, in the manner you saw him going." The point of similarity would seem to be the cloud, which in the NT appropriation of Daniel's vision (Dan 7:13) becomes the vehicle for the expectation of Jesus' future return as the Son of Man (Matt

24:30; 26:64; Mark 13:26; 14:62; Rev 14:14; Luke 21:27). Luke repeats the phrase "into heaven" (*eis ton ouranon*) four times in verses 10-11. Codex D omits the third occurrence, but it probably should be included as part of Luke's original emphasis (compare Acts 7:55-56).

INTERPRETATION

Consistent with the advice of Lucian of Samosata's treatise, *How to Write History* 55, Luke's prologue to his second volume is not only shorter than that to the Gospel, but it briefly summarizes the contents of the first narrative before moving on. We can observe the same sort of practice in Josephus, *Against Apion* 1:1 and 2:1. The *recapitulative* character of Acts 1:1-11 is important to bear in mind if the reader is not to be distracted unnecessarily by questions concerning multiple and conflicting accounts of the ascension. Lucian advises the historian: "the first and second topics must not merely be neighbors but have common matter and overlap."

The best way to make sense of this opening section of Acts, therefore, is to grasp that not only the first five but the first eleven verses in their entirety function as a transition to a new stage in the story, a transition wherein the author does not provide new material but rather reworks and elaborates a part of the story already told. The reader, I think, is meant to imagine the gestures and words in Acts 1:1-11 as an elaborate variant of those in Luke 24:36-53.

The constraints imposed by the prologue form make for a somewhat scrambled syntax, but Luke manages to provide this fairly impressive review of the Gospel contents: 1) the teaching and actions of Jesus in his ministry; 2) the selection of the apostles; 3) Jesus' suffering; 4) his resurrection appearances; 5) his eating with the disciples; 6) his commission of them as witnesses from Jerusalem to the nations; 7) the promise of the Spirit; 8) his ascent into heaven. What matter if the details are various or the order is not entirely the same? This part of the story is scarcely the stuff of scientific history no matter how it is told: the subject, after all, is that of spiritual transformation and empowerment.

Recognizing the literary function of this opening, we can observe more closely those elements that Luke considers important enough for his subsequent narrative to elaborate and emphasize. We notice that he does not consider it necessary to do more than touch on the ministry, suffering, and resurrection. In contrast, he does place special emphasis on the question put to Jesus by his followers, on Jesus' prophecy concerning their mission of witness, and on the message delivered to his disciples at the ascension. Consideration of these elements will enable us to appreciate the special perspective Luke gives to this second part of his story of the Prophet and the People.

The question of the disciples concerning the restoration of the kingdom to Israel (1:6) follows naturally on Jesus' discourse concerning "the kingdom of God" (1:3). We are equally curious: what is the relationship between these kingdoms, and how do they connect to the kingship of Jesus that Luke has been so concerned to establish in the latter portion of his Gospel (see Luke 11:2, 20; 12:22; 13:18-21; 17:20-21; 19:11-27, 38; 22:29; 23:2, 37, 38, 42)? At issue in this question is the legitimacy of Jesus' claim to be Messiah, as well as the Gentiles' assurance of being part of God's people. Jesus' response is nuanced and therefore not fully satisfying. He deflects speculation about "times and seasons," without denying that God has such dispositions within his authority (1:7).

More significantly, Jesus shifts the focus from "knowledge" to mission. We see in this not only a dramatic contrast to the preoccupation of later apocryphal gospels with the revelatory activity of the risen Lord (e.g., *Epistula Apostolorum, Pistis Sophia, The Sophia of Jesus Christ*), but also the real answer to the question concerning the "restoration" of the kingdom to Israel. Jesus' answer contains a redefinition of "kingdom" and therefore of the Christian understanding of Jesus as Messiah. The kingdom of God is not a territory or political realm. It is the rule of God over human hearts. It is initiated in the prophetic work of Jesus, not only in exorcisms and healings, but above all in the "healing of the people": the call of the outcast into fellowship. Now, because Jesus is enthroned as King-Messiah, he can pour out the Spirit on his apostolic successors through whom his rule will be exercised over the people (Acts 2:33-36).

The "kingdom for Israel" will mean for Luke, therefore, the restoration of Israel *as a people of God.* For him, this means its reception of the Holy Spirit, its recognition of the apostles as leaders of the people, and its enjoyment of the messianic blessings of spiritual friendship and harmony (Acts 2:41-47; 4:32-37). This restoration will take place through the witnessing activity of the apostles after they receive "a power from the Holy Spirit" (1:8).

By no means, then, does Luke reject the idea of a restoration of the rule of God for Israel, or simply replace it with a more universal notion of "God's kingdom." Instead, he redefines God's rule as the rule over an obedient people, and he relates the restoration of this people within Israel dialectically to the universal mission "to the ends of the earth": one precedes the other, the second builds on the first. Luke invites the reader to discover the mystery of "times and seasons" by the reading of his own narrative.

By having Jesus respond to the most pressing question of both disciples and readers at the very beginning of his second volume, Luke further elaborates his literary presentation of Jesus as Prophet. Jesus commissions his followers, but also in the most obvious sense predicts their future (1:8). The reader will learn from the subsequent story-line how this "programmatic prophecy" of Jesus is fulfilled, since the geographical arrangement of the narrative precisely matches his prediction.

Three times already, the Holy Spirit has been mentioned: as working through Jesus' selection and commission of his apostles (1:2), as the baptism that will bring on them "the promise of the father" (1:4-5), and as a "power coming down on them," enabling them to be witnesses (1:8). The repetition builds an anticipation for the immediate fulfillment of the prophecy. But Luke has also suggested that the instruments through which the Spirit will work as it did in Jesus will be his apostles. As he is a prophet, so will they be prophetic figures. We are therefore primed to recognize in Jesus' ascension the condition for a transmission of prophetic power like that found in the stories of Moses (Deut 34:9) and Elijah (2 Kgs 2:9-22). This succession is suggested as well in the phrase "my witnesses" (*martyres mou*), for the ambiguity of the Greek genitive allows us to understand it in a two-fold sense: the apostles will witness *to* Jesus, and they will also be *his* witnesses, that is, his prophetic representatives to the people.

Luke's account(s) of Jesus' ascension are unique in the NT but not within Hellenistic literature. The Roman Poet Ovid describes the ascension of Romulus into heaven in his *Metamorphoses* 14:805-851: the founder of the city continues to legislate even as he rises to join the gods (see also Ovid, *Fasti* 2:481-509). In the Jewish tradition, the ascension of Elijah in a fiery chariot and whirlwind (2 Kgs 2:11) was most impressive, and set the precedent for descriptions of other such ascents: thus, Enoch is described as ascending in a whirlwind (*1 Enoch* 39:3). In his *Antiquities of the Jews* 4:326, Josephus seems concerned to describe Moses' disappearance "in a cloud" in naturalistic terms, to avoid the suggestion of a return to the divinity. But Philo describes Moses' ascension in a manner similar to Ovid's depiction of Romulus: Moses continues to prophesy even as he ascends (*Life of Moses* 2:291). Building on Luke's version (and these other traditions), the ascension of Jesus becomes even more elaborately described in such Christian apocryphal writings as *The Apocryphon of James* 14–16, the *Epistula Apostolorum* 51, and *The Martyrdom and Ascension of Isaiah* 11:22-33.

The specific Lukan understanding of the ascension can rapidly be sketched. First, Luke clearly understands it to be Jesus' enthronement as King, and therefore as Messiah. By means of this ascent, Luke enables us to envisage the resurrected Jesus not as a resuscitated corpse or wraith, but as one living in power, "at the right hand of God" (LXX Ps 109:1; Acts 2:34-36; 7:55). Second, Jesus' physical removal is for Luke the condition for the gift of the Holy Spirit. Moses has to leave in order for Joshua to work with his prophetic spirit (Deut 34:9); Elijah had to depart in order for Elisha to gain a double portion of his prophetic spirit (2 Kgs 2:9). So long as Jesus was physically present, he was available only to those he directly encountered; by the Spirit he became powerfully present to many through his prophetic successors.

These observations can help us appreciate two further aspects of Luke's remarkably restrained depiction of the actual ascent. The symbolism of the cloud is connected in the biblical tradition not only to the Son of Man (discussed in the notes) but even more so to the prophetic figures Moses (Exod 19:16) and Elijah (1 Kgs 18:44). This linkage moves us to assess more carefully the action of the disciples and the message of the two men to the disciples. They are undoubtedly to be grasped together. The resemblance between these two men in white garments to those who appeared with Jesus at the transfiguration (Luke 9:30) as well as to the two men who spoke to the women at the tomb (Luke 24:4-5) is obvious. There is good reason to think that they imaginatively represent Jesus' prophetic predecessors who ascended, Moses and Elijah (see esp. Luke 9:31, and the note on Luke 24:4).

The form of the men's question to the disciples, furthermore, formally resembles the challenge put by the two men to the women who came to the tomb. There it was, "why are you seeking the one who lives among the dead?," followed by the correction, "he is not here but has been raised!" (Luke 24:5-6). Here it is, "why do you stand looking into heaven?," again followed by a correction: "he will come in the same way you saw him going into heaven" (Acts 1:11). It is obvious what was wrong with the women seeking the living one among the tombs. But what is wrong about the apostles gazing into heaven?

Perhaps a clue is provided once more by the literary prototype of Elijah. Before Elijah departed, he was asked by Elisha for a double portion of his prophetic spirit. Elijah told him this was a hard request, but that if Elisha *saw him departing*, then he would receive the gift; if he did not, then he would not receive it (2 Kgs 2:10). Elisha did see him go up in the fiery chariot and whirlwind, and did receive a double portion of the Spirit. Luke's emphasis on the disciples "seeing him" as he ascends (Acts 1:9) picks up this literary motif; we know that they will also receive the promised Spirit. But to do so, they must obey the command to return to the city and await that empowerment.

The message from the two men (perhaps Elijah and Moses) therefore has the same double function as their message to the women at the tomb. By seeking Jesus in the tomb, the women certify that he is not there, he is raised. But they are then told to "remember" how this was a fulfillment of Jesus' own prophecy (Luke 24:6-8). The empty-tomb account looks backward to the ministry of Jesus. The ascension account, in turn, looks forward to the ministry of his successors. The two men therefore now confirm that Jesus has ascended and that the disciples have witnessed it. But they are not to stand there, gazing, for the presence of Jesus will be with them precisely in the spiritual outpouring they are about to experience. It is for them to return to the city to be empowered for their prophetic witness.

For Reference and Further Study

Dupont, J. "*ANELĒMPHTHĒ* (Actes 1, 2)." *Etudes sur les Actes des Apôtres.* Lectio Divina 45. Paris: Editions du Cerf, 1967, 477–480.

Lohfink, G. *Die Himmelfahrt Jesu: Untersuchungen zu den Himmelsfahrts-und Erhohungstexten bei Lukas.* Studien zum Alten und Neuen Testament 26. Munich: Kösel-Verlag, 1971.

Menoud, Ph.-H. "The Plan of the Acts of the Apostles." *Jesus Christ and the Faith.* Trans. E. M. Paul. Pittsburgh: Pickwick Press, 1978, 121–132.

Palmer, D. W. "The Literary Background of Acts 1:1-4." *NTS* 33 (1987) 427–438.

Parsons, M. *The Departure of Jesus in Luke-Acts: The Ascension Narratives in Context.* JSNTSS 21. Sheffield: JSOT Press, 1987.

Rétif, A. "Témoignage et Prédication Missionaire dans les Actes des Apôtres." *NRT* 73 (1951) 152–165.

Schwartz, D. R. "The End of the Gē (Acts 1:8): Beginning or End of the Christian Vision?" *JBL* 105 (1986) 669–676.

Tiede, D. L. "The Exaltation of Jesus and the Restoration of Israel in Acts 1." *HTR* 75 (1986) 278–286.

van der Horst, P. W. "Hellenistic Parallels to the Acts of the Apostles: 1, 1-26." *ZNW* 74 (1983) 17–26.

van Unnik, W. C. "Der Ausdruck '*heōs eschatou tēs gēs*' (Apostelgeschichte 1:8) und sein alttestamentliche Hintergrund." *Sparsa Collecta.* Leiden: E. J. Brill, 1973, 1:386-401.

Wainwright, A. W. "Luke and the Restoration of the Kingdom to Israel." *ExpT* 89 (1977–78) 76–79.

Wilson, S. G. "The Ascension: A Critique and an Interpretation." *ZNW* 59 (1968) 269–281.

2. *Preparing the People* (1:12-26)

12. They then turned back to Jerusalem from the mountain called Olivet. It is close to Jerusalem, about a Sabbath Day's journey. 13. When they had entered they went up to the upper room where they were staying. Peter and John and James and Andrew, Philip and Thomas, Bartholomew and Matthew, James son of Alphaeus and Simon the Zealot, and Judas the son of James: 14. these were all united as they continued in prayer with the women, and Mary the mother of Jesus, and his brothers. 15. In these days, Peter stood in the midst of the brothers, a crowd of about 120 people gathered in one place. He said, 16. "Brothers, the scripture which the Holy Spirit spoke beforehand through the mouth of David had to be fulfilled. It concerned Judas, the one who became guide for those arresting Jesus. 17. For he was numbered among us. He was apportioned a share of this service. 18. (This man thereupon bought a field from the payment for his wicked deed. But he fell headlong. He burst open in the middle and all his bowels spilled out. 19. This became known to all those living in Jerusalem. As a result, that field came to be called in their own language 'Hakeldama,' that is, 'field of blood.'). 20. For it is written in the Book of Psalms, 'Let his dwelling-place become deserted and let there be no one dwelling in it,' and also, 'Let another take his office.' 21. It is necessary therefore that one of these men who accompanied us during all the time the Lord Jesus went in and out among us, 22. beginning from the baptism of John up to the day he was taken up from us, become a witness to his resurrection with us." 23. They presented two, Joseph the one called Barsabbas, who was given the name Justus, and Matthias. 24. They said in prayer, "O Lord, knower of the hearts of all! Show which one of these two you have chosen 25. to take the place in this service and apostleship, which Judas left by going to his own place." 26. They cast lots for them. And the lot fell on Matthias. And he was counted in with the eleven apostles.

NOTES

12. *mountain called Olivet:* This is the site mentioned by Luke alone in his version of Jesus' entry into the city (Luke 19:29), and as his resting place during the ministry of teaching in the temple (21:37). Bethany is named as the place of ascension in Luke 24:50, which Luke 19:29 locates at Olivet. He therefore treats them as identical, although the distances given by Josephus (*Antiquities of the Jews* 20:169) for Olivet and by John 11:18 for Bethany diverge considerably. *Sabbath Day's journey:* See the command in Exod 16:29, and the rabbinic discussion in *M.Erub.* 4:1-11. Luke uses the language not only to remind his readers of the proximity to Jerusalem (in fulfillment of Jesus' command in Luke 24:49), but also to portray Jesus' followers as faithful Jews (compare Luke 23:54-56).

13. *the upper room:* Although he uses a different word here (*hyperōon*), Luke may have in mind the same "upper-room" (*anagaion*) as that used for the last supper in Luke 22:12. For the upper-room as a place for assembling, see Acts 9:37, 39; 20:8.

    Peter and John and James: This is Luke's second apostolic list (see also Mark 3:13-19; Matt 10:1-4). The names are the same as in Luke 6:13-16, with variations in order only. John, who plays a role in Acts as Peter's companion (3:1, 3, 4, 11: 4:13, 19; 8:14), is now listed with James (whose death is mentioned in Acts 12:2) ahead of Andrew, who has no narrative role. Less significantly, Thomas is shifted to the position following Philip. The most noteworthy change is the omission of Judas Iscariot, which motivates the account that follows.

14. *united as they continued in prayer:* The adverb translated as "united" (*homothumadon*) is peculiar to Luke in the NT, and one of his favorite expressions either for the spiritual unity of the believers (2:46; 4:24; 5:12; 8:6; 15:25) or their opponents (7:57; 12:20; 18:12; 19:29). The theme of prayer spans both volumes (Luke 3:21; 5:16; 6:12; 9:28-29; 11:1-4; 18:1; 22:41-44, 46; Acts 1:24-25; 4:24-30; 6:6; 8:15; 9:11, 40; 10:9, 30; 12:12; 13:3; 14:23; 16:25; 20:36; 21:5; 28:8).

    with the women: Luke means the women who had followed Jesus from Galilee (8:1-3) who witnessed his death (23:49), his burial (23:54-56), and his resurrection (24:1-10, 22). They are now to share the gift of the Spirit (Acts 2:17). Codex D misses the special role these women play in Luke's narrative, and adds the words "and children," which demands the translation "with their wives and children," a domestic touch Luke probably did not intend!

    Mary the mother of Jesus: The inclusion of Mary cannot be accidental. This is Luke's first mention of her by name since the infancy narrative, for he omits the negative implications concerning the family of Jesus found in Mark 3:31-35 and 6:3. As Mary has the Spirit overshadow her to give birth to the prophet-messiah (Luke 1:35), so is she present at the gift of the Spirit that gives birth to the Church, one of those "daughters of Israel" who have the spirit of prophecy (Acts 2:17).

15. *Peter stood in the midst of the brothers:* The temporal reference "in these days," makes a clear connection between this story and the foregoing listing of disciples. Codex D changes "brothers" (*adelphoi*) into "disciples" (*mathētai*), possibly to avoid confusion with the "brothers of Jesus" listed there.

    a crowd of about 120 persons: This is the only time Luke uses the word "name" (*onoma*) to mean "person," perhaps in dependance on LXX Num 1:18, 20, 22, etc. The number 120 has significance because of the twelve apostles and through them, the "twelve tribes" of the restored Israel (see esp. Luke 22:29). *M. Sanh.* 1:6 gives 120 as one opinion concerning the minimum size a city would need to be in order to have a legitimate synagogue. Like *homothumadon*, the phrase *epi to auto* ("in one place"/"together") is a favorite of Luke's (Acts 2:1, 22, 47; 4:26; 14:1). It derives from the LXX translation of *yaḥad* ("at one"/"together"), as in Pss 2:2; 132:1. At Qumran, *hayaḥad* is almost a technical term for the community (see e.g., 1QS 1:1; 3:7).

16. *brothers:* An insoluble obstacle to any translation hoping to be gender inclusive is Luke's persistent habit of using "men" (*andres*) so frequently in the Acts narrative, as here: "men brothers" (see also 2:14, 22, 29, 37; 3:2; 5:35; 7:2, 26; 13:15, 16, 26, 38; 14:15; 15:7, 13; 17:22; 19:35; 21:28; 22:1; 23:1, 6). This translation will simply eliminate the "men" part of such phrases, since nothing is really added to the English by retaining it.

Holy Spirit . . . through the mouth of David: For the form of the introduction, compare 4:25. David is also called author of the psalms in Luke 20:41-42 and Acts 2:25. Because the psalms are, like all of Scripture, regarded as prophetic (Luke 24:44; Acts 1:20; 13:33), they can be ascribed to the Holy Spirit (compare Acts 28:25). A similar conviction is reflected in Rom 1:2.

had to be fulfilled: A classic expression of early Christian conviction concerning prophecy and fulfillment. Luke characteristically uses the impersonal verb *dei* ("it must") in such statements about the inexorability of the divine will (see Luke 9:22; 17:25; 24:7, 26, 44; Acts 3:21; 9:16; 14:22), and especially in connection with the fulfillment of scriptural passages (Luke 22:37; 24:26, 44; Acts 1:21; 17:3). The term "scripture" (*graphē*) is in the singular, referring to the first citation from Ps 68:26 (LXX) in v. 20: it "had" to be fulfilled and already has been; the second text remains to be fulfilled by the election of Judas' replacement.

the one who became guide: The translation breaks up a longer Greek sentence. As in Luke 6:16, the verb *ginomai* is here taken in its strong sense of "become," rather than the weaker sense of "was." It is striking that Peter begins his description of Judas with the specific recollection of Luke 22:47. The use of *syllambanō* ("arrest") directly recalls the scene described in Luke 22:54.

17. *numbered among us:* The attention to "numbering" throughout this passage cannot be missed. The use of *katarithmeō* ("number") is a chilling reminder of Luke's account of Satan's entering Judas in Luke 22:3, where he adds, "he was from the number (*arithmos*) of the twelve."

apportioned a share of this service: Luke uses a complex symbolism of possessions throughout the passage. The verb *lanchanō* can mean "to obtain by lot," and by extension, "to obtain a portion" of something. The term translated "share," in turn, derives precisely from the context of casting lots; a *klēros* is, in the first instance, a "lot." In the biblical tradition, the notion of "inheritance" (*klēronomia*) associated with the land is inextricably tied to the idea that the various tribes received their portions "by lot" from God (see Num 16:14; 26:55; 33:53). The connection to "ministry" or "service" (*diakonia*) is established in this tradition by the "lot" (*klēros*) apportioned to the Levites (Num 18:21-26). They received no land, but their portion was the Lord— they were supported by tithes from all the other tribes. In the present case (as 1:25 makes even more explicit), the "service" refers to the apostolic role. Luke is preparing a language for the "casting of lots" later in the passage (1:26) and for the transmission of the ministry in 6:4.

18. *this man thereupon:* In the translation, parentheses are used to bracket this section of the speech, which functions rhetorically as an aside that brings the

reader up to date. The Greek demonstrative *houtos* is given full strength, and the connective *oun* is treated as a narrative transition rather than as inferential. Luke's account of Judas' actions and fate is notably different from that found in Matt 27:3-10.

bought a field: The specific etymology given by 1:19 ("field of blood") demands this translation of *chōrion*. But the imagery of "falling headlong" and of a "dwelling-place" suggests something more of a farm or country estate with buildings on it, rather than simply a bare "field."

payment for his wicked deed: The Greek phrasing recalls the characterization of "wicked mammon" in Luke 16:9, and the genitive could allow the translation, "wicked reward," but the translation given better fits the actual context. It is not the money that is wicked, but Judas' way of getting and spending it.

fell headlong: We are to think of him falling from a height, perhaps from a building; certainly we should not try to harmonize this with the version of Judas' suicide by hanging in Matt 27:5. A similar sequence is found in *bT Ḥullin* 56b: "A gentile once saw a man fall from the roof to the ground so that his belly burst open and his entrails protruded." A pitching headlong of the wicked is found in Wis 4:19, and a splitting of the bowels in the killing of Amasa in 2 Sam 20:10. Compare as well the miserable end of Herod in Acts 12:23. For death by falling off a ladder on a farm, see Chariton of Aphrodisias, *Chaereas and Callirhoe* 1, 3, 1.

19. *Hakeldama, that is, 'field of blood':* This is the one detail shared with Matt 27:9. Luke adds the Aramaic original, and emphasizes the spread of the news to the Jerusalemites, whereas Matt says that the name endures "to this day." Both expressions indicate that this is an aetiological story. For a similar aetiological account, see Plutarch, *On the Malice of Herodotus* 15 (*Mor.* 858B).

20. *let his dwelling-place become deserted:* The citation is from Ps 68:26 [LXX] with some slight modifications, such as changing the pronouns to the singular so that they fit Judas. The term *epaulis* ("dwelling-place") makes us think of Judas' purchase as a farm rather than a field. Psalm 68 is rather frequently used in NT apologetic (see for example Mark 15:23, 36 and parallels; John 2:17; Rom 11:9-10; 15:3). What is odd in this application to Judas is that he is the evildoer but it is the property that is cursed!

let another take his office: Only the conjunction *kai* (translated here as "and also") joins this citation from LXX Ps 108:8 to that from Ps 68:26. This is the only direct citation from Ps 108 in the NT, and it is interesting that the application works best because of the LXX translation. The Hebrew *pĕhudātô yiqqah 'aḥer* is best understood in its context to mean, "may another seize his goods." The LXX's rendering of *pĕhudâ* by *episkopē* ("office/magistracy") works very well for Luke's purposes. It is used in 1 Tim 3:11 for the "office of overseer (*episkopos*)," a position that Luke recognizes in Acts 20:28.

21. *it is necessary therefore:* This use of *dei* ("it is necessary") echoes that in 1:16, and with the two scriptural passages structures the passage. The first "must" dealt with the defection and death of Judas; the second with the fulfilling of the second passage, "let another take his office."

22. *beginning from the baptism of John:* In several other places, Luke uses the baptism of John to demarcate the beginning of Jesus' ministry (Luke 3:23; 16:16; Acts 1:5; 10:37; 11:16; 13:24-25; 18:25; 19:3-4). For "witness to the resurrection" as defining the apostolic role, see especially Acts 4:33.

23. *they presented two:* A small but fascinating variant in Codex D makes "presented" singular, which would make Peter the nominator rather than the community. This would clash with the procedure suggested by Acts 6:5-6, but would delight later ecclesiastics eager to find Petrine primacy in the NT texts.

    Joseph, the one called Barsabbas: Despite this belated inclusion in the apostolic circle, Matthias is never again mentioned in the NT. Neither does Joseph Barsabbas reappear, although Acts 15:22 has a "Judas, the one called Barsabbas," who is sent with Paul and Barnabas to the church at Antioch. Is there a confusion or repetition of names? In the light of Acts 4:36, where another Joseph is "called Barnabas by the apostles" (using the same verb, *epikaleō,* in the same aorist passive tense), it may be possible to see the addition of "Justus" here not simply as a Latin surname, but as a symbolic renaming by the apostolic circle ("just"/"upright"/"righteous").

24. *knower of the hearts of all:* The epithet *kardiognōstēs* is used of God again in 15:8. That God knows human hearts is axiomatic in the biblical tradition (see Deut 8:2; LXX Ps 7:9; 43:21; 64:6; 139:23; 1 Cor 4:5; 14:25; Heb 4:12; 1 John 3:20; Rev 2:23).

25. *by going to his own place:* Some mss read *klēros* ("lot"), but the external textual evidence and the literary play on the word *topos* ("place") argue convincingly that it is the best reading. The term *topos* can be used to refer to one's place of final destiny, as in Tob 3:6 or 1 Clement 5:4, or (with the same phrase, "his own place"), Ignatius of Antioch, *Magnesians* 5:1. And there may be a reference to the death or fate of Judas here. But there is also a play on "his own place" (*ton topon ton idion*) meaning the abandonment of the apostolic circle symbolized by his purchasing of his property, in contrast to the apostles who had "left their own things" (*ta idia;* Luke 18:28). The infinitival phrase "going to his own place" does not describe activity subsequent to his apostasy, but is the symbolic expression of his apostasy.

26. *they cast lots for them:* The scribal correction of *autois* to *autōn* makes the sentence read more easily, "they cast *their* lots," instead of "they cast lots *for them,*" but is probably not original. The practice of casting lots as a mechanism for determining God's choice was traditional in Judaism (see Lev 16:8; Num 26:55; 33:54; Josh 19:1-40; Mic 2:5; Jonah 1:7-8) and is attested as a practice contemporary to earliest Christianity at Qumran (see *1QS* 5:3; 6:16).

    counted in with the eleven apostles: Luke uses a rare Greek verb (*synkatapsēphizomai*) which joins the notions of "voted in" and "reckoned" (see Acts 19:19). The translation seeks the same combination. Despite the correction of Codex D to "twelve," the number eleven should be retained as the harder reading. The sense is, "with the *other* eleven apostles."

INTERPRETATION

It is Luke's stated intention to provide his reader "assurance" by the sequence of events in his story (Luke 1:1-4). But seldom does the sequence reveal his religious concerns so clearly as in this passage, where the main point is made by its surprising placement. Why does Luke have the ascension of Jesus followed by a list of apostles in which the absence of Judas is glaring (Acts 1:13-14)? And why does Luke highlight the failure of Judas by so elaborately describing the election of his replacement (Acts 1:15-26)?

this is
no excep-
tion: he
needs a
narrative
delay of
10 days
btw 1:3
and 2:1
The sequence at first appears even more puzzling because Luke ordinarily has his literary prophecies fulfilled by the narrative as rapidly as possible. In this case, he has several times repeated the promise of the Holy Spirit both at the end of the Gospel (24:49) and at the beginning of Acts (1:5, 8). He has shown the disciples obediently returning to the city, to await the "power from on high" (24:49; Acts 1:12). We naturally expect to see an account of that fulfillment at once.

If Luke interrupts this natural flow, it is because he must deal with a problem left over from the Gospel. The seriousness with which he takes the problem and the narrative attention he devotes to its solution are both instructive. As the unfinished list of the apostles shows, the circle of the twelve has been broken. One of those chosen to be among the twelve by Jesus (Luke 6:12-16) and given the authority to preach and to heal (Luke 9:1), as well as to exercise rule over the twelve tribes of Israel (Luke 22:29-30), turned into a traitor with a heart possessed by Satan (Luke 22:3) and led Jesus' enemies to arrest him (Luke 22:47). Luke has made clear from the feeding of the five thousand (9:17) as well as from his prophecy at the last supper (22:30) that the significance of the number twelve was in relation to the restored people of Israel. As Jesus gathered the nucleus of this people around himself, he was preparing a new leadership over the people to replace those leaders who rejected the visitation of the prophet.

The betrayal of Judas was therefore more than simply the failure of an individual. It splintered the numerical and symbolic integrity of that group which constituted the beginning and essential authority of the restored people of God. Peter after all had also denied Jesus. But Peter's failure was one of weakness, and both his fall and restoration were foretold by Jesus. Jesus said that he would turn to strengthen his brothers (Luke 22:32), and it is in just such a role that we find him in this passage, standing in the midst of them to interpret the Scripture authoritatively in the light of the divine will, just as Jesus himself had done (1:15-22).

Judas' sin, however, was an apostasy from his apostolic office, and therefore a threat to the fulfillment of Jesus' promise and the whole plan of God. The defection of Judas posed a unique problem and demanded a unique solution. When others of the Twelve died, there would be no need to replace them. Why? Because once the Twelve had definitively been constituted at the heart of the people *and the Spirit bestowed,* the faithful Israel would have come into existence, and the promise of God would have reached fulfillment. This is why Judas had to be replaced before Pentecost, because the integrity of the apostolic circle of Twelve symbolized the restoration of God's people.

Luke's literary art is evident not only in the placement of the story but also in its composition. Peter's speech surely derives from Luke's sense of what should have been said on the occasion, and reflects in particular his convictions concerning the "necessity" of scriptural texts reaching fulfillment. We note how the double use of "it is necessary" (1:16, 21) in connection with the two verses from the psalms (1:20) gives a rhetorical symmetry to the passage. The historical Peter would not, we think, have had to identify Judas to his listeners in an extended aside, or refer to the place name Hakeldama as being "in their own dialect," or make use of texts from the psalms that would serve his rhetorical purpose only in the Greek translation of the Septuagint (LXX) not in the Hebrew.

As so often, however, Luke gives the entire scene the appropriate "color" for the time and place, recalling indeed the sort of language and practice of another Jewish sect of the first century that saw itself as the remnant people of God. The Dead Sea Scrolls from Qumran offer a number of parallels to the concerns reflected in this passage: the symbolism of Israel reflected in a leadership of twelve (*1QS* 8:1), the interpretation of the psalms with reference to the community's own experience (*4QpPs37* 2:6-25), the sharing of community possessions (*1QS* 5:1-3; *CD* 10:18-20), the casting of lots for decisions (*1QS* 5:3; 6:16). Such verisimilitude suggests some sort of tradition behind the story, but the shaping of it is certainly Luke's.

We can detect Luke's hand above all in his account of Judas' end, because we can compare it to the version in Matt 27:3-10. The only thing the accounts really have in common is the violent death and the name of the field. Otherwise, the versions differ in every respect. In Matthew, Judas repents his action and tries to return the money to the priests, confessing that he had sinned (Matt 27:3-4). He then goes out to hang him- cf. 2 Sam self. His repentance is late and ineffectual, but it is real, and is expressed 17:23 by his return of the money. It is the priests who use it to purchase a burial field for foreigners (Matt 27:7), and the name derives from the fact that "blood-money" was used for its purchase (27:8). Finally, Matthew concludes with a free composite scriptural citation (using Zech 11:11-12 and Jer 32:8-9) applied to the price of the field, not the fate of Judas (Matt 27:9).

In Luke's version everything, including the scriptural citations, centers on the defection of Judas as one of the Twelve. And as he does so often,

Luke uses the disposition of possessions as symbolic. Judas does not return the money as a sign of repentance, but goes to buy a farm with the payment for his wicked deed (1:18). This action stands in direct contrast to his "having a share in this ministry" (1:17). Rather than be one of those who "left their own things" and will "sell their farms" and "call nothing their own," Judas separates from the group by his purchase of property for himself. We notice that like Ananias and Sapphira, who will later be described as doing the same thing, Judas is said to have been possessed by Satan (Luke 22:3; Acts 5:3), and to have "entered into a conspiracy" to get the money (Luke 22:4-6; Acts 5:9). Spiritual disaffection is symbolized by physical acquisitiveness.

In similar fashion, Judas' fate and that of his property is intertwined. He dies on the farm and his dwelling place is to be deserted (1:20). And, as his *property* is vacant, so is his place in the apostolic circle; therefore, "let another take his office" (1:20). Each stage of the story is symbolized by the disposition of possessions: Judas' apostasy from the Twelve is expressed by the buying of a farm, his perdition is expressed by the desertion of the property, that empty property expresses the vacancy in the apostolic circle. That Luke intends just such an interpenetration of the notion of authority and the symbolism of property is shown by the final statement concerning Judas, that he left his "place" (*topos*) in the ministry precisely by his "going to his own place" (*ton topon ton idion*, 1:25).

The story is not "about" the use of possessions, but Luke uses the evocative power of possessions-language to tell the story of Judas' defection and the restoration of the apostolic circle. By so doing, he has not only solved the problem posed by Judas' betrayal by reintegrating a leadership of the Twelve for this people that awaits the promised gift of the Holy Spirit, but he has also prepared his readers to see in the restored people a community that calls nothing its own and shares all its possessions as a sign of its spiritual unanimity (Acts 2:41-47; 4:32-37).

FOR REFERENCE AND FURTHER STUDY

Benoit, P. "La Mort de Judas." *Synoptische Studien.* Ed. J. Schmid and A. Vögtle. Munich: Karl Zink Verlag, 1953, 1-19.

Brown, S. *Apostasy and Perseverance in the Theology of Luke.* Analecta Biblica 36. Rome: Pontifical Biblical Institute, 1969, 53-97.

Dupont, J. "La destinée de Judas prophetisée par David (Actes 1, 16-20)." *Etudes sur les Actes de Apôtres.* Lectio Divina 45. Paris: Editions du Cerf, 1967, 309-320.

_____. "Le douxième apôtre (Actes 1:15-26): à propos d'une explication récente." *The New Testament Age.* Ed. W. C. Weinrich. Macon, Ga: Mercer University Press, 1984, 1:139-145.

Fuller, R. H. "The Choice of Matthias." *Studia Evangelica.* Ed. E. A. Livingstone. Berlin: Akademie Verlag, 1973, 6:140-146.

Haenchen, E. "Judentum und Christentum in der Apostelgeschichte." *ZNW* 54 (1963) 155-187.

Jervell, J. *Luke and the People of God.* Minneapolis: Augsburg Publishers, 1972, 75-112.

Lohfink, G. "Der Lorsvorgang in Apg. 1, 26." *BZ* n.s. 19 (1975) 247-249.

Masson, C. "La Reconstitution du Collège des Douze." *RTP* series 3, 5 (1955) 193-201.

Menoud, Ph.-H. "Additions to the Group of the Twelve Apostles according to the Book of Acts." *Jesus Christ and the Faith.* Trans. E. M. Paul. Pittsburgh: Pickwick Press, 1978, 133-148.

Wilcox, M. "The Judas Tradition in Acts 1:15-26." *NTS* 19 (1972-3) 438-52.

3. *Pentecost: The Gift of the Spirit* (2:1-13)

1. When the day of Pentecost arrived, all of them were together in one place. 2. Suddenly there was a sound from heaven like that of a strong wind blowing. It filled the whole house where they were sitting. 3. Individual tongues as of fire appeared to them and sat upon each one of them. 4. All were filled with the Holy Spirit. They began to speak in other languages just as the Spirit gave them to declaim. 5. There were pious Jews from every nation under heaven dwelling in Jerusalem. 6. When this sound occurred, a crowd gathered. They were confused because each was hearing them speak in his own language. 7. They were astonished and amazed. They said, "Look, are not all of these people who are speaking Galileans? 8. So how can each of us hear in our own native language? 9. Parthians and Medes and Elamites, as well as dwellers of Mesopotamia, Judea and Cappadocia, Pontus and Asia, 10. Phrygia and Pamphylia, Egypt and the parts of Libya around Cyrene; also those of us visiting from Rome, 11. both Jews and proselytes, Cretans and Arabs: in our own languages we are hearing them speaking of the great deeds of God." 12. They were astonished and confused, asking each other what this meant. 13. But others mockingly declared that they were filled with new wine.

Notes

1. *day of Pentecost:* The Greek construction is paraphrastic and solemn, like that in Luke 9:51. The term *pentekostē* (+ *hēmera* = "fiftieth day") occurs as a translation of the "Feast of Weeks" only twice in the LXX (Tobit 2:1; 2 Macc 12:32).

Ordinarily the LXX translates literally *heortē hebdomadōn* (see Exod 34:22). The legislation for the feast in Exod 23:16; 34:12; Lev 23:15-21; Deut 16:9-12 shows its agricultural and nomadic roots in the offering of first fruits and lambs. It is one of the three great pilgrimage feasts of ancient Israel; see Paul's eagerness to be in Jerusalem for this feast in Acts 20:16.

2. *a sound from heaven:* The loud sound recalls the noise of the Sinai theophany (Exod 19:16-19), and a strong wind is associated with the theophany to Elijah (1 Kgs 19:11-12) as well as with Elijah's ascension (2 Kgs 2:11). In this case, the sound is *compared* to that of a blowing wind; it is the sound that fills the house, not a wind.

3. *individual tongues as of fire:* Literally, "divided" (*diamerizō;* see Luke 11:17-18; 12:52-53; 22:17; 23:34). The translation "individual" is used because the tongues are separated from each other rather than divided within (or "forked"); the RSV translates nicely, "distributed." Once more, the particle *hōsei* marks a *comparison* to fire. For fire (*pyr*) as a regular feature of biblical theophanies, see Gen 15:17; Exod 3:2; 13:21-22; 14:24; 19:18; 24:17; Deut 4:12, 24, 33, 36; 5:4; 10:4; 1 Kgs 19:12; 2 Kgs 2:11; LXX Ps 17:9. Note in particular the combination of "sound" and "fire" in LXX Ps 28:7, "the voice of the Lord flashes forth in flames of fire." The most obvious connection, of course, is to the "Holy Spirit and fire" that is their promised baptism (Luke 3:16).

4. *filled with the Holy Spirit:* Luke uses the aorist passive of *pimplēmi* ("to fill"), as he does with reference to the Holy Spirit in the Gospel infancy section (Luke 1:15, 41, 67) and also in Acts (4:8; 9:17; 13:9). Here is the fulfillment of the promise made by Jesus (Luke 24:49; Acts 1:4-5, 8).

   in other languages: In context, this is the appropriate translation of *heterais glōssais,* for Luke stresses the communicative rather than the ecstatic dimensions of their speech. Such speech accompanies the gift of the Spirit as well in Acts 10:45 and 19:6; otherwise we find it in the NT only in Mark 16:17 ("new tongues"), and in Paul's extensive discussion (1 Cor 12-14). Assessing the NT evidence against the backdrop of Hellenistic religious phenomena leads to the conclusion that such *glōssolalia* originally referred to a form of ecstatic (speech-like) babbling that was widely associated with mantic prophecy (see Cicero, *On Divination* 1, 32, 70-71; Plutarch, *On the Obsolescence of Oracles* 14 [*Mor.* 417C]; 40 [*Mor.* 432C-F]; and Apuleius, *The Golden Ass* 8:27). This form of prophecy was highly esteemed, for it was thought to derive from direct possession by the deity (*enthusiasmos;* see Plato, *Phaedrus* 244A-B; *Timaeus* 71E-72B; Plutarch, *The E at Delphi* 6-24 [*Mor.* 387B-406F]). An example of it can be found as well in the *Testament of Job* 48-52, when Job's daughters speak with "angelic" languages.

   gave them to declaim: Luke emphasizes that the Spirit itself directed (*edidou* = "was giving") each one's speech. The translation "declaim" aims at the sententious character of the proclamation suggested by *apophthengomai* (compare 2:14 and 26:25).

5. *pious Jews:* The term *eulabēs* (translated "pious") is used by Luke elsewhere in its specifically religious connotation (Luke 2:35; Acts 8:2; 22:12). Some *mss*

had trouble with the apparently unnecessary inclusion of the word "Jews"—who else, they thought, would be in Jerusalem?—but the specific description here as in v.11 helps Luke make his literary and religious point.

dwelling in Jerusalem: Although Josephus tells us of the large crowds in Jerusalem for this feast (*Antiquities of the Jews* 14:337; 17:254; *Jewish War* 1:253; 2:42-43), Luke does not refer to such temporary pilgrims. His use of *katoikountes* (compare 1:19; 4:16; 7:2, 4; 9:22, etc.), indicates Jews who had come from all over the world to settle in the city. Such a mixed population in the city is supported not only by Acts 6:9, but also by scattered references in Josephus (for example, *Jewish War* 1:397, 437, 672).

6. *a crowd gathered:* Is literally "the" crowd (*plēthos*). Luke uses the term both for loose assemblages and for formal bodies (Luke 1:10; 2:13; 5:6; 6:17; 8:37; 19:37; 23:1, 27; Acts 4:32; 5:14, 16; 6:2, 5; 14:1, 4; 15:12, 30; 17:4; 19:9; 21:22, 36; 23:7; 25:24; 28:3). In this case the role of the crowd is similar to that awaiting Zechariah's emergence from the temple in Luke 1:10.

7. *astonished and amazed:* Luke uses the crowd to provide dramatic perspective on the event; the reader appreciates the dimensions of the occurrence from its effect on these observers. Luke uses a full range of strong mental reactions. They have been called "confused" (*synched*, 2:6), and now "astonished" (*existēmi*, see Luke 2:47; 8:56; 24:22; Acts 2:12; 8:9, 11, 13; 9:21; 10:45), and "amazed" (*thaumazō*, see Luke 1:21, 63; 2:18, 33; 4:22; 7:9; 8:25; 9:43; 11:14, 38; 20:26; 24:12, 41; Acts 3:12; 4:13; 7:31; 13:41).

8. *our own native language:* The Greek is literally, "each in his own language in which we were born." The contrast again focuses attention on this remnant community as made up of "Galileans" (2:7; see 1:11, 14).

9. *Parthians and Medes and Elamites:* Such lists of "nations" are found already in Gen 10:2-31, and are elaborated in Jewish apocryphal works such as *The Sibylline Oracles* 3:160-172, 205-209, and Pseudo-Philo's *Biblical Antiquities* 4:3-17. Lists which stress the presence of Jews in various lands are found in Philo, *Embassy to Gaius* 281-282, and *Against Flaccus* 45-46. Luke's list presents a number of problems. Some of them are textual: should "Judea" be included at all (its presence is odd in a list of "foreigners"), or is it a later scribal interpolation? Are the "Cretans and Arabs" at the end of the list likewise a later addition that spoils the climax of "both Jews and proselytes"? Other questions are interpretive: what is the principle of selection, and what the perspective on the world given by this map? Do names appear because they have dense Jewish populations, or because they are important for the Christian mission? Hypotheses abound, but none can be proven. Among these first three names, Parthia is the contemporary empire that threatens Rome from the East. But the Medes (2 Kgs 17:6; Dan 5:31) and the Elamites (Isa 11:11; 22:6) are ancient kingdoms no longer politically active in the time of Luke's writing. "Parthians and Medes" do appear together as enemies of Israel in 1 *Enoch* 56:5.

9.-10. *Cappadocia . . . Pamphylia:* These are all districts in Asia Minor which as a whole had a strong Jewish population (see Philo, *Embassy to Gaius* 245).

Pontus was Aquila and Priscilla's place of origin (Acts 18:2). The geographical sequence makes the placement of "Judea" even more problematic.

Egypt . . . Cyrene: These are the North African coastal territories nearest to Palestine: Alexandria in Egypt is the homeland of Apollos (Acts 18:24). Cyrene is the home of the Simon who helped Jesus carry his cross (Luke 23:26), of some missionaries who preached to the Greeks in Antioch (Acts 11:20), and of an Antiochean leader named Lucius (Acts 13:1).

visiting from Rome: The special designation of those "visiting" (*epidēmountes*) strengthens the point made in v. 5 about those "dwelling" (*katoikountes*). The term means to dwell in a place as an alien (see Acts 17:21; 18:27).

11. *both Jews and proselytes:* This is a summary rather than a separate ethnic entry. Building on the idea of the "sojourner" (*ger;* see Exod 23:4; Lev 16:29; Num 9:14; Deut 1:16), which was translated in the LXX by *proselytos* ("one who has approached"), the term "proselyte" came to mean one who converted from paganism to Judaism. Considerable reflection was devoted within Judaism to figures like Ruth who were taken to be the models for such conversion, and to the topic of proselytism generally (see for example, *Leviticus Rabbah*, Wayikra 1,2; *bT Sanh.* 99b; *Aboth de Rabbi Nathan* 1, 15). The great abundance of such passages in the rabbinic literature, together with NT evidence such as Matt 23:15; Acts 6:5; 13:43; 15:21, not to mention the production of writings such as *Joseph and Aseneth*, testify to the historical fact that Judaism was an active missionary religion in the first century (see also Josephus, *Antiquities of the Jews* 20:38-48).

Cretans and Arabs: These names are anticlimactic, and may come from an interpolation, although no *ms* evidence supports that suggestion. Crete figures in Paul's journey to Rome (Acts 27:7-21) and as Titus' place of ministry (Titus 1:5). Paul also mentions Arabia as a place for his early missionary work (Gal 1:17).

the great deeds of God: The term *megaleia* is used only here by Luke, but it echoes a fairly frequent biblical refrain (Deut 11:2; LXX Ps 70:19; 105:21; Sir 17:8; 18:4; 42:21; 43:15; 2 Macc 3:34; 7:17).

12. *astonished and confused:* Luke used *existēmi* ("astonished") in v. 7, and adds *diaporeō*, which he had used in Luke 9:7 for the confusion of Herod over Jesus' identity (see also Acts 5:24; 10:17). The verb *thelō* ordinarily means "desire," but is here used idiomatically, as it is also in Acts 17:18, 20.

13. *mockingly declared:* The participle *diachleuazontes* is an intensive of *chleuazō* ("jeer"/"mock"), found also as the response to Paul's proclamation of the resurrection in Acts 17:32, and is here treated as an adverb.

filled with new wine: As the term *gleukos* suggests, "new wine" is also "sweet wine" and therefore a quick stimulus to drunkenness. States of ecstasy accompanied by drunkenness were not unknown in Mysteries like that of Dionysius (Bacchus); see Ovid, *Metamorphoses* 3:528-545; 4:25-30. Philo is able to play on this combination with his oxymoron "sober intoxication" to describe the mystic state (*On the Creation* 69-71), and Lucian of Samosata refers to being "drunk on the discourse" of the philosopher Nigrinus (*Nigrinus* 5).

For an example of crowd confusion over the meaning of an oracular pronouncement, see Heliodorus, *The Ethiopians* 2, 36, 1.

INTERPRETATION

The narrative suspense built by Luke is about to reach a first resolution. In fulfillment of the repeated promise and prophecy of Jesus, the apostles and their company are about to receive the "power from on high" that is the Holy Spirit (2:1-13). Already in this event, there is the restoration of the remnant people. But then, the gift will be interpreted and offered to the Jewish population of Jerusalem (2:14-36), and it will be received by thousands of those dwelling in the city (2:37-47). By the end of this sequence, Luke will have answered the question of God's fidelity to his promises.

The gift of the Holy Spirit at Pentecost (Acts 2:1-13) has exercised such powerful influence over the Christian imagination that it is somewhat startling to realize just how slender and spare an account it is. The description of the event itself takes only four verses (2:1-4), and is extraordinarily circumspect; the major part of the passage concerns the response of observers (2:5-13). In terms of empirical phenomena, there is just the noise that fills the house, and the speaking of the community in diverse tongues. The sound is *compared* to a strong wind blowing, and the tongues that "appear to them" (the disciples, not the crowd) are again *compared* to fire.

Luke's point is not the pyrotechnics of theophany, but spiritual transformation. The real "event" of Pentecost is the empowerment of the disciples by the Holy Spirit. If we compare this narrative to other NT passages (such as John 20:22-23 and 1 Cor 15:45) we can even say that Luke's Pentecost story is a rendering of the primordial Christian experience of the resurrection. Here the emphasis is not on what happened to Jesus, but what happened to them: the "fact" of Jesus' new life is verified by the "fact" of their new experience of power, manifested by their bold proclamation of "the great deeds of God." But even this speech phenomenon is ambiguous. The response of the crowd is mixed, and Peter must interpret the ecstasy in terms not of drunkenness but of the bestowal of an eschatological prophetic spirit deriving from the crucified and raised Messiah (2:14-36).

Still, it is tempting to be distracted by the allusive symbolism used to express the event. What connection is there between Luke's description and the symbolism associated with the Jewish Feast of Weeks (Pentecost)? In other accounts dealing with the outpouring of the Spirit, after all, Luke mentions speaking in tongues (10:46; 19:6), but nowhere else does he have sound or wind or fire. The real difficulty here is determining what symbolism was available to him when he wrote. After the destruction of the temple in C.E. 70, it is clear that Pentecost was universally understood by Jews to be the celebration of the giving of Torah on Mt. Sinai: "It is the day on which the Torah was given" (*bT Pes.* 68b). But was this the understanding during Luke's time? The main piece of evidence is *The Book of Jubilees* 6:17-21 (ca. 150 B.C.E.), which speaks of the Feast of Weeks as a covenant-renewal feast.

Whether or not other Jews connected the giving of Torah to their celebration of Pentecost, Luke certainly could have made the connection, if not to the feast itself, at least to the event of giving Torah. There are several reasons for thinking that he did so. First is the widespread use in Judaism of fire as a symbol for Torah (see *bT Ta'anith* 7a; *bT Bab. Bath.* 78b; *Sifre on Deuteronomy* Ber. 343). Torah is also compared to other things in the Talmud, to be sure, and fire is used for all sorts of theophanies (see Notes). But nowhere is the same cluster of symbols found all together except in the LXX description of Sinai (Exod 19:16), with its repeated emphasis on the *sound*, and the "descending of God upon it in fire" (*dia to katabebekēnai ep' autǫ ton theon en puri*, Exod 19:18).

Second is the striking development of this symbolism by Philo Judaeus, (*On the Decalogue* 33), who explicitly attaches the giving of the Law by God to the communication of speech by flame: "Then from the midst of the fire that streamed from heaven there sounded forth to their utter amazement a voice, for the flame became articulate speech in the language familiar to the audience, and so clearly and distinctly were the words formed by it that they seemed to see rather than hear them" (*On the Decalogue* 46).

Third is Luke's consistent use of the Moses typology for the story of Jesus. So thoroughly does Luke use the Moses story elsewhere (see Introduction), that it would be surprising if the use of sound and fire and languages here did not allude to the Sinai event. In fact, as we shall see, Luke has the short reference to the giving of the law through Moses in the Stephen speech (Acts 7:38) exactly match the description given by Peter of the bestowal of the Holy Spirit (Acts 2:33). Moses "received living words to give to us"; Jesus "received the Holy Spirit, poured out this thing you see and hear."

The full understanding of the event must come to the reader, of course, through the interpretation given by Peter's speech. Now we must pay some attention—as Luke clearly desires—to the audience gathered by the sound and the ecstatic utterance.

Rather than an amorphous crowd such as so often listened to Jesus, Luke carefully delineates this first audience for the proclamation of Jesus as Messiah and Lord. It is striking first of all that he uses the literary device of the list of nations. As the notes suggest, a variety of questions can be put to the list concerning the criteria for inclusion, the view of the world it reveals, the possible numerical symbolism that may have been disrupted by interpolations. These matters of detail should not distract the reader, however, from Luke's basic point, which he makes with great clarity: the giving of the Holy Spirit at Pentecost took place in the presence of Jews from all over the world. And through Peter's speech, the invitation to share in this gift will be made (2:38). Already in this first fulfillment of the promise, therefore, Jews from the Diaspora are included. Just as the Twelve represent the nucleus of the people that is being restored, so does this audience represent all the lands to which the Jews had been dispersed.

It is in this light that we can understand the clear literary parallelism that Luke has established to the genealogy of Jesus in Luke 3:23-38. Immediately after the gift of the Spirit in Jesus' baptism (Luke 3:21-22), the generations of Jews are traced all the way back to Abraham, and even further, to Adam. Now, after this "baptism in the Spirit" of the apostles and their company, Luke lists all the lands from which Jews have gathered. The parallelism fits the pattern of Luke's story: Jesus is the prophet who sums up all the promises and hopes of the people before him; in his apostolic successors, that promise and hope (now sealed by the Spirit) will be carried to all the nations of the earth.

For Reference and Further Study

Bovon, F. "Le Dieu de Luc." *RScR* 69 (1981) 279-300.

Brinkman, J. A. "The Literary Background of the 'Catalogue of Nations' (Acts 2, 9-11)," *CBQ* 25 (1963) 418-427.

Cerfaux, L. "Le symbolisme attache au miracles des langues." *Recueil Lucien Cerfaux* Vol. 2 Biblioteca Ephemeridum Theologicarum Lovaniensium VI-VII; Gembloux: J. Duculot, 1954, 183-187.

Kremer, J. *Pfingtsbericht und Pfingstgeschehen: Eine exegetische Untersuchung zu Apg. 2, 1-13.* Stuttgarter Bibelstudien 63/64. Stuttgart: Verlag Katholisches Bibelwerk, 1973.

Lake, K. "The Gift of the Spirit on the Day of Pentecost." *Beginnings* V:111-121.

Lohse, E. "Die Bedeutung des Pfingtsberichten im Rahmen des lukanischen Geschichtswerkes." *Die Einheit des Neuen Testaments.* Göttingen: Vandenhoeck & Ruprecht, 1973, 178-192.

van der Horst, P. W. "Hellenistic Parallels to the Acts of the Apostles (2:1-47)." *JSNT* 25 (1985) 49-60.

Wilder, A. "Variant Traditions of the Resurrection in Acts." *JBL* 62 (1943) 307-318.

4. *Peter's Pentecost Sermon* (2:14-36)

14. Peter stood with the eleven. He lifted his voice and declaimed to them, "Judeans and all those dwelling in Jerusalem! Let this become known to you! Pay attention to my words! 15. It is not as you think, that these people are drunk, for it is only the third hour of the day. 16. Instead this thing is what was spoken of by the prophet Joel: 17. 'It will happen in the last days, says God: I will pour out from my spirit upon all flesh, and your sons and your daughters will prophesy. Your young men will see visions. Your old men will dream dreams. 18. Indeed, I will pour out from my spirit in those days upon my men servants and women servants, and they will prophesy. 19. I will provide wonders in heaven above and signs on earth below, blood and fire and a cloud of smoke. 20. The sun will be changed into darkness and the moon into blood before the great and manifest day of the Lord arrives, 21. and everyone who calls on the name of the Lord will be saved.' 22. Israelites, listen to these words! Jesus the Nazorean was a man accredited to you by God, as shown by the powerful deeds, the wonders and the signs that God did through him among you, as you yourselves know. 23. This man, who was delivered up by the set plan and foreknowledge of God, you killed by crucifixion through the hands of lawless people. 24. Him God has raised! He has loosed the pangs of death because he could not be held by it. 25. For David said about him: 'I have seen the Lord before me always, because he is at my right hand, so that I not be shaken. 26. My heart has been glad because of this, my tongue has rejoiced. More than that, my flesh will dwell in hope 27. because you will not abandon my life to Hades, nor will you let your holy one see corruption. 28. You have made known to me the paths of life. You will fill me with gladness in your presence.' 29. Brothers, I can tell you with confidence concerning the patriarch David that he died and was buried. And his tomb is among us to this day. 30. Therefore since he was a prophet and knew that God had sworn to him by an oath that he would seat one of his descendants upon his throne, 31. he looked ahead and spoke concerning the resurrection of the Messiah, that neither was he left in Hades nor did his flesh see corruption. 32. This Jesus, whose witnesses we all are, God has raised up. 33. Lifted up to the right hand of God, therefore, and receiving the promise that is the Holy Spirit, he has poured out this which you are seeing and hearing. 34. For David did not ascend into the heavens, yet he says, 'The Lord said to my Lord, sit at my right hand 35. until I put your enemies as a footstool for your feet.' 36. Therefore let the whole House of Israel know for certain that God has made him both Lord and Messiah, this Jesus whom you crucified!"

NOTES

14. *all those dwelling in Jerusalem:* Peter's greeting ties his speech to the audience described in 2:5-13. The term *Ioudaioi* can mean simply "Jews," but since that

is assumed for all the listeners here, the meaning "Judeans" is probably better (as in Luke 23:51; Acts 10:39).

pay attention to my words: Is literally, "let it be put in your ears" (*enōtizomai*), used only here in the NT, but frequent in the LXX (e.g., Gen 4:23; Exod 15:26; Job 32:11; LXX Ps 5:1; Joel 1:2). Compare "place in your ear" (Luke 9:44).

15. *only the third hour of the day:* The adverb "only" is supplied by the translation to make the point clear; nine in the morning is too early to be drinking, much less be drunk. The experience of glossolalia is, however, sufficiently ambiguous to require interpretation.

17. *in the last days, says God:* Although the citation from Joel 3:1-5 agrees substantially with the LXX, there are several changes that in all likelihood represent alterations made by Luke to fit the text to the context. Two of them are in the first line: 1) The LXX reads *meta tauta* ("after these things"), which Luke changes to *en eschatais hēmerais* ("in the last days"), thereby making Pentecost part of an eschatological scenario. 2) Less significantly, except that it reveals the premise of all prophetic texts, Luke adds "says God (*theos*)" to the LXX.

upon all flesh: The term "flesh" (*sarx*) here means "humanity," as it does also in Luke's citation from Isaiah 40:5, "all flesh will see the salvation that comes from God," (Luke 3:4-6). Both texts bear an implicit universalism. For the moment, however, the gift of the Spirit is for the "sons and daughters" of Israel. Note the physicalism of "pouring out" and "filling up," as though the Spirit were a fluid. Such concrete imagery is frequent in religious texts that speak of divine power and gifting.

see visions . . . dream dreams: these are not utopian fantasies, but specifically prophetic modes. For the vision (*horasis*) as the vehicle of prophecy, see LXX Num 24:4, 16; 1 Sam 3:1; 2 Sam 7:17; Ps 89:19; Hos 12:10; Mic 3:6; Obad 1:1; Nah 1:1; Hab 2:2-3; Zech 10:2; Isa 1:1; 13:1; 19:1; Jer 14:14; Lam 2:9; Ezek 1:1; 8:3; 40:2; Dan 4:20; 8:1. And for the "dream" (*enupnion*) as a regular if ambiguous mode of prophecy, see Gen 37:5; 41:8; Deut 13:1-5; 1 Sam 28:15; Zech 10:2; Jer 28:25-32, 36; Dan 1:17; 2:1; 4:2. Whether or not he uses the term *horama* ("vision"), Luke has visions play an important role for his prophetic characters in the narrative (Acts 7:31, 55-56; 9:3-10, 12; 10:3, 17, 19; 11:5; 16:9-10; 18:9; 27:23).

18. *my men servants and my women servants:* By adding the word "my" (*mou*) to the LXX, Luke makes the recipients servants of God. Note the gender inclusiveness in "sons and daughters," and now *douloi kai doulai*.

they will prophesy: The best mss contain the addition, *kai prophēteusousin* ("and they will prophesy"), to the LXX text of Joel. It certainly fits Luke's perception of the event, and strengthens the identification of the gift as a specifically prophetic spirit, made already by v. 17.

19. *signs on earth below:* Luke has altered the LXX text by adding "above" (*anō*) to the "wonders (*terata*) in heaven," as well as the words "signs" (*sēmeia*) and "below" (*katō*). As a result, he has made the text foretell the working of "wonders and signs" (*terata kai sēmeia*), which he uses to identify the prophetic figures in his story (see 2:43; 4:16, 22, 30; 5:12; 6:8; 8:6, 13; 14:3; 15:12).

In the LXX, the phrase is associated above all with Moses and the exodus story (Exod 4:8, 9, 17, 28, 30; 7:3, 9; 10:1, 2; 11:9-10; Num 14:11-12; Deut 4:34; 6:22; 7:19; 11:3; 26:8; 29:3; LXX Ps 77:43; 104:27; 134:9). Of special importance is the connection of the phrase to the portrayal of Moses as a *prophet,* as in Deut 34:10-12: "The Lord has not raised up a prophet in Israel like Moses whom the Lord knew face to face, in all his signs and wonders which the Lord sent him to do in Egypt . . . before all of Israel." That Luke exploits this tradition is clear from his application of it to Moses in 7:36, and immediately to Jesus in 2:22.

20. *great and manifest day of the Lord:* Some *mss* omit *epiphanē,* which here has the meaning "manifest/evident" rather than "glorious/notable," for Luke exploits the text primarily to show that the gift of the Spirit is eschatological in that it inaugurates the new age, but is not yet the climax or the end; the adverb *prin* ("before") should be taken seriously. As in Jesus' eschatological discourse in Luke 21:5-36, there is a distinction between the time of witnessing with signs and wonders, and the cosmic events that will precede the coming of the Lord. For the "day of the Lord/Son of Man" and "day of judgment" and "that day," see Luke 10:12; 12:46; 17:22, 24, 26, 30; 21:6, 23, 34; Acts 17:31.

21. *calls on the name of the Lord:* This part of Joel's text is cited also by Paul (Rom 10:13; see 1 Cor 1:2; 2 Tim 2:22; Heb 11:16). The expression echoes through Acts (7:59; 9:14, 21; 22:16). "Salvation" is thematic in Luke-Acts (see e.g., Luke 1:69; 2:11; 7:50; 8:36, 50; 15:1-32; 19:9-10; Acts 7:25; 15:11; 28:28).

22. *accredited to you by God:* The verb *apodeiknymi* has a range of meanings from "display" to "appoint." Luke seems to combine several senses. Jesus was "assigned/appointed" by God to this people as prophet; but he was also "displayed/demonstrated" to them as such by his wonders. The translation tries to capture something of both ideas. The Greek sentence as a whole is complex, with several dependent clauses clustered about two main verbs: "you killed," and "God raised."

powerful deeds, the wonders and the signs: With "powerful deeds" (*dynameis*), Luke connects this proclamation of Jesus to his presentation in the Gospel (Luke 4:14, 36; 5:17; 6:19; 8:46; 9:1; 10:13, 19) and the presentation of the apostles in Acts (3:12; 4:7, 33; 6:8; 8:13; 19:11). They have received the *dynamis* from on high (Luke 24:49; Acts 1:8) that enables them to do what Jesus had done (Acts 10:38). For "wonders and signs," see the note on v. 19. It is striking that Luke immediately picks up this aspect of the Joel citation: the prophetic spirit being poured out comes from the prophet Jesus!

God did . . . among you: The image of Jesus as prophet is strengthened by having God do the wonders *through* him (compare Acts 10:38). The phrase "among you" echoes that concerning Moses in Deut 34:10, ". . . before all Israel." The prophet's work is among the people.

23. *set plan and foreknowledge:* The term translated "set" is *hōrismenos,* from *hōrizō,* "to set aside" or "determine" (see Rom 1:4). Luke uses it similarly in the Gospel (22:22) and in Acts 10:42; 17:31. For the "plan of God" (*boulē tou theou*) in history, see Luke 7:30; 23:51; Acts 4:28 (again with *prohōrizō*); 5:38; 13:36;

20:27. Apart from Rom 9:19; Eph 1:11 and Heb 6:17, Luke is the only NT writer to use the term this way. For God's "foreknowledge" (*prognōsis*), compare Rom 8:29 (with *prohōrizō*); 11:2; 1 Pet 1:2, 20; 2 Pet 3:17.

you killed by crucifixion: The same verb for "kill" (*anairō*) is used here as in Luke 22:2; 23:32; Acts 5:33, 36; 7:21, 28, etc. The term for "crucify" (*prospēgnymi*) means literally to "affix" and is found only here in the NT; the participle is translated by a noun. In contrast to most of his other statements concerning Jesus' death (with the exception of Acts 10:39), Luke does not mitigate the blame of the people by invoking their "ignorance" (3:17) or putting the primary blame on the leaders (Luke 24:20; Acts 13:27), unless here the "lawless men" be taken to mean the "wicked" leaders rather than the "law-less" Gentiles. The bald charge at the end of the speech, "whom you crucified" (*estaurōsate*) is equally straightforward.

24. *loosed the pangs of death:* A wonderful example of the LXX shaping Luke's language. The term "pangs" is odd, here, especially with "loose." It translates the Greek *ōdinai* which refers in particular to "birth-pangs" or "throes of birth." But in LXX 2 Sam 22:6 (and Ps 17:5, 6), in a song of David, it appears as "pangs of death" (and "pangs of hades," as in the *ms* variant here), because the LXX translators read the Hebrew *ḥebel* ("pang") rather than *ḥebel* ("cord"). We find here therefore a clear if unconscious echo of the Septuagint.

25. *I have seen the Lord before me always:* The citation from LXX Ps 15:8-11 is exact. It is a psalm attributed by its title to David, and therefore is taken as reflecting his personal experience, a point Peter will use in his messianic application to Jesus. The citation is full of phrases that, seen from the perspective of Jesus' resurrection, appear to anticipate it: thus, the Messiah never loses sight of the Lord, and (in v. 9) this is the basis for his flesh dwelling in hope.

27. *abandon my life to Hades:* As elsewhere in Luke-Acts, *hades* is equivalent to the Hebrew *sheol*, the place of the dead (Luke 10:15; 16:23; compare Gen 37:35; Num 16:30; Ps 6:5). In addition to the hope of not seeing physical corruption (compare LXX Job 33:31 [A]; Ps 106:20), the motifs of the "paths of life" and "gladness in your presence" also suggest resurrection. The term translated "holy one" (*hosios*) has the specific sense of one dedicated to God. In the LXX, it translates the *ḥasid*, or "saint" (see especially Pss 4:2; 11:1; 17:25; 29:4, etc.). Luke will use this same citation in combination with another from Isa 55:3 in a later speech by Paul (Acts 13:34-35).

29. *can tell you with confidence:* The Greek construction *exon eipein meta parrēsias* suggests a *captatio:* "It is allowed to speak plainly," or, "don't be offended if I point out;" (compare Aelius Aristides, *Oration* 6:2). The term "patriarch" is actually used rarely in the LXX (only in 1 and 2 Chr, five times, as well as 4 Macc 7:19), and apart from Acts 7:8-9 and Heb 7:4, this is the only use in the NT. For the tradition about David's tomb in Jerusalem, see Josephus, *Jewish War* 1:61.

30. *since he was a prophet:* That the author of the psalms was a prophet is axiomatic for Luke (see Luke 20:41-42; 24:44; Acts 1:16, 20; 4:25; 13:33-36). In the

present case, David "looked ahead" (*proidōn*) and was able to speak in the psalm about the resurrection of his descendant, the Messiah.

sworn to him by an oath: The wording here is very close to that in LXX Ps 131:11. Note that this verse in the psalm is preceded by "for the sake of David your servant do not turn away the face of your anointed one (*christos = messiah*)," which clearly legitimates the messianic application of the next verse (see also LXX Ps 88:4). These passages allude to the dramatic promise of a perpetual Davidic dynasty by the prophet Nathan in 2 Sam 7:12-16. The Dead Sea Scrolls from Qumran show that the messianic interpretation of this passage was present in contemporary Judaism; see *4QFlor* 1:7-13. Luke also refers to this promise in Luke 1:32-33.

32. *witnesses we all are:* Luke thus has Peter fulfill Jesus' prophecy in Luke 24:48 and Acts 1:8, and his own criterion of apostleship, that one should be a witness to the resurrection (Acts 1:22).

33. *right hand of God:* The phrase anticipates the use of LXX Ps 109:1 in v. 34 below. It is linked to the previous citation by the verse that Peter does *not* quote. After "gladness in your presence," the LXX of Ps 15:11 continues, "delights are in your right hand (*dexia*) forever." The symbolism derives from the secular custom of sitting a king's favorite at his right hand (2 Kgs 2:19; 1 Chr 6:39; 1 Esdr 4:29; 9:43; Neh 8:4), and the image of God's "right hand" as the source of power, life, and salvation (Exod 15:6; LXX Pss 17:35; 25:10; 43:3; 47:10; 59:5; 97:1; 117:16; 137:7).

the promise that is the Holy Spirit: The Greek genitive is epexegetical: the Holy Spirit is the content of the promise (see Luke 24:49; Acts 1:4). For Luke, this means the promises made to the patriarchs (Luke 1:55, 73; Acts 3:13, 25; 7:17); the gift of the Holy Spirit realizes the blessings promised to Abraham (Acts 2:39; 7:17; 13:23, 32; 26:6). For the sequence "receive . . . pour out," compare what is said of Moses and the Law in 7:38, "received . . . to give." The use of *encheō* ("pour out") connects to the prophecy of Joel in 2:17.

34. *sit at my right hand:* A direct citation from LXX Ps 109:1, perhaps the most extensively employed text in early Christian apologetic (see Mark 12:36; 14:62; 16:19; Matt 22:44; 26:64; 1 Cor 15:25; Eph 1:20; Col 3:1; Heb 1:3, 13; 8:1; 10:12; Rom 8:34). The text is used in the controversy over David's son in Luke 20:42-44.

36. *whole House of Israel:* The somewhat archaic expression (LXX Pss 97:3; 113:20; 117:2; 134:19) characterizes this Jewish population as the people of God (Israel) that is being challenged by Peter's address (compare Acts 7:10, 42, 46, and the use of "House of Jacob" in Luke 1:33). The phrase "know for certain" uses the adverbial form of the term *asphaleia*, which is critical to his entire composition (compare Acts 16:23; 21:34; 22:30; 25:26).

Lord and Messiah: By this statement, Peter makes clear that the "Lord" they can call on to be saved (2:20) is Jesus. The title *kyrios* is particularly associated with the resurrection (see 4:33), and the confession "Jesus is Lord" seems to have been one of the earliest in Christianity (1 Cor 12:3; Rom 10:9). Luke uses the titles of Jesus both before and after the resurrection accounts: for

"Messiah," see Luke 2:11, 26; 4:41; 9:20; 20:41; for "Lord," see Luke 2:11; 10:1; 11:39; 12:42; 22:61.

INTERPRETATION

Ancient historians used the speeches of their characters to communicate to the reader the wider implications and the deeper meaning of the events being described. Lucian of Samosata advised the historian to observe the principle of *prosōpopoiia*: "let his [i.e., the person introduced to make a speech] language suit his person and his subject." At the same time, however, the author was allowed considerable leeway for his own artistry: "you can play the orator and show your eloquence" (*How to Write History* 58).

Luke observes these canons in the many speeches he strews through his story. He may have structured some of these discourses on the foundation of traditional preaching patterns, but the specific rhetorical turns in each speech come from him rather than some source. The speeches sound authentic because of his artistry: he does practice *prosōpopoiia*, and makes each discourse appropriate to the speaker and the occasion. The speeches in the first part of Acts, for example, have many semitisms that give them a distinctly "biblical" and even archaic feel. At the same time, Luke uses his speeches in service to his larger narrative: not only do the words interpret the present event, they provide a "programmatic prophecy" for events yet to follow within the narrative. The speeches in Acts provide authorial commentary on the narrative.

We can observe these features in Peter's first great "missionary discourse" in Acts (2:14-36). Luke has shown the Spirit falling on the followers of Jesus so that they speak ecstatically. He has gathered a crowd of Jews from all over the Diaspora. Drawn by the noise, they hear Galileans speaking the powerful deeds of God each in his own language. They are confused and wonder what the event might mean, though some dismiss it as a case of drunken excess. Interpretation is needed.

As Peter stands to address the crowd, we can appreciate, if only for a fleeting moment, how Luke has developed the scene in a manner true to the religious sensibilities of the Gentile world. In the oracle shrines such as that of Delphi, the revelations of the god often took place in a kind of ecstatic utterance that looked like the glossolalia of Pentecost. The oracles were rendered intelligible by the shrine official called the *prophētēs* ("prophet"), who "translated" the language of the god (see Plato, *Timaeus* 72B; Herodotus, *Persian Wars* 8:135). Within this religious typology, Peter is presented as the cult "prophet" who will make the utterances of the God intelligible. But that is not what Peter does. Luke puts a twist on religious phenomenology. First, he makes the speech of the glossolalists already intelligible to the listeners; it does not require "translation." Second, he has the prophet Peter interpret the *event* rather than the speech.

By no means is the speech a casual collection of assertions. It is a rhetorically sophisticated argument, involving the refutation of common opinion (that the disciples could be drunk [2:15] or that David was speaking of himself in the psalms [2:29-30]); an appeal to the audience's own experience, both past (they knew of Jesus' powerful deeds [2:22], they killed Jesus [2:23, 36]) and present (the things they see and hear [2:33]); an appeal to eyewitness testimony (of the apostles [2:32]); and an appeal to scriptural prophecy concerning this event (2:17-21) and its cause (2:25-35).

Luke first has Peter define the *nature* of this event, which involves as well a preliminary statement of its *cause:* The speech of the disciples does not derive from drunkenness, but from the gift of God's Spirit. But Luke alters the citation from LXX Joel 3:1-5 in several important ways, making the Spirit's outpouring an eschatological, and above all a prophetic event (see the detailed observations in the Notes). By so doing, he also makes the Joel prophecy a programmatic statement for the rest of the narrative: the reader will recognize those who are "filled with the Holy Spirit" and who "work signs and wonders among the people" as prophets in the line of Moses, just as the description of Jesus immediately after the citation as one who worked "powerful deeds, wonders and signs" during his ministry mark *him* as a prophet.

Luke's more difficult task is to have Peter demonstrate that the immediate *cause* of this eschatological event is the resurrection of Jesus. Once more there is a contrast between natural perception and religious claim, just as there was between the options of "drunkenness from new wine" and "the gift of the Spirit." Now, however, it is expressed as a contrast between the perception of Jesus as one who was simply crucified and killed, and one who is resurrected Lord and the bestower of the Spirit, or, in even bolder terms, as a contrast between their activity ("you killed") and God's activity ("God raised up"). How can Peter support this claim? He can appeal to his audience's perception of this ecstasy, but that is itself, as we have seen, ambiguous. He can appeal to the testimony of Jesus' followers, but that is understandably suspect. His best support is given by an midrashic application of messianic texts from Torah.

Peter's interpretation builds on a number of widely shared presuppositions: a) that the psalms were authored by David; b) that David was God's "anointed"; c) that God had promised an eternal dynasty to David through his descendants; d) that the things spoken of in the psalms would refer therefore either to himself or to his descendant, the Messiah (compare, for example, *Midrash Tehillim* 42/43:5; 60:3; 87:6).

Luke has Peter work with two psalms that can be read messianically. Psalm 15:8-11 [LXX] clearly speaks of one who "sees the Lord always," whose "flesh has not seen corruption," who has been shown the "paths of life." All these point to one who is resurrected and alive in the presence of God. But, asserts Peter, this cannot apply to the historical David. Not only does everyone know he died and was buried, his tomb is still among them (2:29). Therefore, the text must apply to his messianic successor, whom David as a prophet could foresee (2:30). The Messiah is one who experiences resurrection.

This leads to the second text, from Ps 109:1 [LXX]. As we have seen from the earlier controversy between Jesus and the Sadducees concerning this passage (Luke 20:41-44), its proper understanding involves the proper identification of the "Lords" concerning whom the text speaks. Consistent with the practice of the LXX, the title "Lord" should refer not to an earthly king, but to God. Therefore the text speaks not of an earthly, but of a heavenly enthronement at the "right hand of God." Once more, Peter can state that nowhere in the tradition is David believed to have ascended to God's presence (2:34). Therefore, the text must apply to his messianic successor, who has ascended to the right hand of God (2:33). These texts show, therefore, that the Jesus whom they crucified was not dead. By his resurrection he has been enthroned in God's presence as "Lord," and, as these texts of David prove, also "Messiah."

Luke joins the entire discourse together by asserting that the resurrected Messiah, who has been enthroned at God's right hand, is the source of the Holy Spirit at work in them: "having received from the father the promise that is the Holy Spirit, he has poured out this that you are seeing and hearing." Perception, experience, and meaning are all united in the conviction that Jesus is not dead but alive as powerful Lord. The challenge that Peter puts to his hearers, therefore, is to change their perception of Jesus and his followers, to share the meaning given by the conviction that Jesus is Lord, and to partake in the experience of the eschatological, prophetic Spirit being poured out. Not for the last time in Acts, humans are challenged to respond to the activity of God in their midst.

For Reference and Further Study

Dibelius, M. "The Speeches in Acts and Ancient Historiography." *Studies in the Acts of the Apostles.* Trans. M. Ling. London: SCM Press, 1956, 138–185.

Dillon, R. J. "The Prophecy of Christ and His Witnesses according to the Discourses of Acts." *NTS* 32 (1986) 544–556.

Dupont, J. "Apologetic Use of the Old Testament in the Speeches of Acts." *The*

Salvation of the Gentiles. Trans. J. Keating. New York: Paulist Press, 1979, 129–159.

Evans, C. "The Prophetic Setting of the Pentecost Sermon." *ZNW* 74 (1983) 148–150.

Fitzmyer, J. "David, 'being therefore a Prophet . . .' (Acts 2:30)." *CBQ* 34 (1972) 332–339.

Gourgues, M. "Lecture Christologique de Psaume CX et Fête de la Pentecôte." *RB* 83 (1976) 5–24.

Juel, D. "Social Dimensions of Exegesis: The Use of Ps 16 in Acts 2." *CBQ* 43 (1981) 543–556.

Rese, M. *Alttestamentliche Motive in des Christologie des Lukas.* SNT 1. Gütersloh: Gerd Mohn, 1969.

Wilckens, U. *Die Missionsreden der Apostelgeschichte.* WMANT 5. Neukirchen: Neukirchener Verlag, 1961.

Zehnle, R. *Peter's Pentecost Discourse.* SBLMS 15. Nashville: Abingdon Press, 1971).

5. *Portrait of a Restored People* (2:37-47)

37. When they heard this, they were stunned. They said to Peter and to the rest of the apostles, "What shall we do, brothers?" 38. Peter said to them, "Repent! Let each of you be baptized in the name of Jesus Messiah for the forgiveness of your sins, and you will receive the gift of the Holy Spirit. 39. For the promise is for you and for your children, and all those far off, whomever the Lord our God summons." 40. He bore witness with many other words and he exhorted them by saying, "Be saved from this twisted generation!" 41. Those who accepted his message were thereupon baptized. That day about three thousand persons were added. 42. They were constant in their attention to the teaching of the apostles, the fellowship, the breaking of bread, and the prayers. 43. Every person felt awe because of the wonders and signs being done through the apostles. 44. All the believers were together. They held all things in common. 45. They were selling their property and possessions, and were distributing them to everyone according to each one's need. 46. Every day they continued together in the temple. They broke bread in their houses. They shared food with gladness and in simplicity of heart. 47. They praised God and had favor among all the people. Every day the Lord was adding those who were being saved to the community.

NOTES

37. *they were stunned:* The Greek has the verb *katanyssomai* with *tēn kardian* as the accusative of respect. The verb appears only here in the NT, but translates

six different Hebrew terms in the LXX, ranging in meaning from "anger" (Gen 34:7) through "struck silent" (Lev 10:3; Isa 47:5) and "stung" (Sir 12:12) and "humbled" (1 Kgs 20:27-29; Ps 108:16) to "sorrowful/remorseful" (Gen 27:38; Sir 14:1; 20:21; 47:20). Luke wants us to see a deeply emotional response appropriate to conversion; see the RSV's "cut to the heart," and *Joseph and Aseneth* 6:1; 8:8.

what shall we do: The artificiality of "the rest of the apostles" here, when Peter is so clearly the spokesperson, fits Luke's concern for their communal leadership over Israel according to Jesus' prophecy in Luke 22:30; compare "with the eleven" at the start of the speech (2:14). The audience's character ("those who were with them and heard") and response ("show us!") is expanded by Codex D. The question itself echoes that of the people to John the Baptist (Luke 3:10; see also 3:12, 14; and variations of the form in 10:25; 12:17; 16:3-4; 18:18, 41).

38. *repent:* The term *metanoeō* is used in the LXX for God's "repenting" (=changing his mind), as in Amos 7:3, 6; Joel 2:13-14; Jer 4:28. In the NT the verb and noun (*metanoia*) appear frequently for human conversion: in Luke's Gospel, see 3:3, 8; 5:32; 10:13; 11:33; 13:3, 5; 15:7, 10; 16:30; 17:3-4, and above all the prophecy of Jesus that they would proclaim "in his name a repentance for the forgiveness of sins" (Luke 24:47). In Acts, see 3:19; 5:31; 8:22; 11:18; 13:24; 17:30; 19:4; 20:21; 26:20.

baptized in the name of Jesus Messiah: The ritual of repentance associated with John the Baptist (Luke 3:7-16; Acts 1:5; 11:16; 19:4) is taken over as the ritual of initiation by the messianic community, thus "in the name of Jesus Messiah" (see also Acts 8:16; 10:48; 19:5). The phrase "in the name of Jesus" recurs throughout Acts as the power and authorization for apostolic activity (3:6, 16; 4:10, 12, 17-18, 30; 5:28, 40-41; 8:12; 9:16, 21, 27, 28; 15:26; 16:18; 19:13, 17; 21:13; 22:16; 26:9). Other NT texts confirm the picture given by Acts concerning baptism as the primordial Christian ritual (Rom 6:3-4; 1 Cor 1:13-17; 10:2; 12:13; 15:29; Gal 3:27; Eph 4:5; Col 2:12; 1 Pet 3:21).

for the forgiveness of your sins: Here is a point of continuity with the baptism of John (Luke 1:77; 3:3) and also the ministry of Jesus (Luke 5:20-21, 23-24; 7:47, 49; 11:4; 23:34). Jesus commands forgiveness among the disciples in Luke 17:3-4, and tells them to proclaim forgiveness "in his name" (Luke 24:47). Acts shows the messianic community as one of forgiveness (5:31; 10:43; 13:38; 22:16; 26:18).

the gift of the Holy Spirit: Twice more (Acts 10:45; 11:17), Luke will refer to the Holy Spirit as a "gift"; as with the term "promise," we are to understand "Holy Spirit" as epexegetical, that is, as *being* the gift. In Acts the giving of the Spirit is not always coincident with baptism. It comes after baptism with the laying on of hands in 8:15-16 (also 19:5-6), whereas it precedes and motivates baptism in 10:47-48. Luke is not interested in constructing a self-consistent theory of sacraments.

39. *the promise is for you:* For a discussion of the language of promise (*epangelia*) as used by Luke, see the note on Luke 24:49. Here it can be stated briefly

that like Paul (see Gal 3:14-16), Luke identified the Holy Spirit with the "promise to Abraham" of blessings from God. In the strictest sense, this constitutes a "spiritualization" of the blessing, although one that has real and visible
social consequences, as Luke's subsequent description of the community
shows. For the phrase "those far off," see the LXX of Isa 57:19, a text which
could be read as applying to the Gentile mission (compare Eph 2:17).

our God summons: The verb *proskaleomai* has just such a peremptory tone; more
than an invitation, it is an official demand: see Gen 28:1; Exod 3:18; 5:3; Amos
5:8, and Luke's further use in Acts 5:40; 6:2; 13:2, 7; 16:10; 23:17-18, 23. The
phrase here echoes Joel 3:5b, whose importance for understanding the entire passage is discussed in the Interpretation.

40. *be saved from this twisted generation:* The phrase "be saved" is in the passive
(not "save yourselves," as in the RSV). It picks up the "will be saved" of
the Joel citation (2:21). Notice as well the characterization, "those being saved"
in 2:47. To be saved from a larger population obviously means to be part of
a remnant people. For "twisted generation" see Deut 32:5, as well as LXX
Ps 77:8; Luke 9:41; 11:29.

41. *who accepted his message:* Codex D corrects "accepted" to "believed," but compare the use of *apodechomai* in Luke 8:40; 9:11; Acts 18:27; 21:17; 28:30. The
numerical increase in believers is noted again in 2:47; 4:4; 5:14; 6:1, 7.

42. *constant in their attention:* The periphrastic *ēsan proskarterountes* (as in 1:14; 2:46;
6:4; 8:13; 10:7) could be translated "persevered in." In such summaries, Luke
wants to show continuing and consistent patterns of behavior. The four elements listed in this verse are elaborated by vv. 43-47.

teaching of the apostles: For this apostolic activity, see 4:2, 18; 5:21, 25, 28, 42.
The apostles continue the teaching ministry of Jesus (Luke 4:15, 31-32; 5:3,
17; 6:6; 13:10, 22; 19:47; 20:1, 21; 21:37; Acts 1:1).

the fellowship: Although the term *koinōnia* can refer to spiritual communion
(1 Cor 1:9; 10:16; 2 Cor 6:14; 13:13; Gal 2:9; Phil 1:5; 2:1; 3:10; Heb 13:16;
1 John 1:3), here it obviously refers to the sharing of material possessions,
elaborated in v. 45 as well as in 4:32-37 (see also Rom 15:26; 2 Cor 8:4; 9:13).

the breaking of bread: This undoubtedly refers to more than ordinary meals.
The presence of the resurrected Jesus is noted at the "breaking of the bread"
in Luke 24:35. Luke emphasizes the connection between meals and Jesus'
presence (Luke 24:41-42; Acts 1:4; 10:41). The ritual is noted again in 2:46;
20:7, 11; see also 1 Cor 10:16; 11:24.

43. *wonders and signs:* Luke thus certifies that the prophetic Spirit (2:19) that was
at work in Jesus (2:22) is also at work in the apostles. For "fear" (*phobos*) as
religious awe, see Luke 1:12, 65; 7:16; Acts 5:5, 11; 19:17.

44. *held all things in common:* The phrase *epi to auto* is here translated "together,"
but in v. 47 as "the community"; for the linguistic problem, see the note on
Acts 2:1. The Greek phrase *panta koina* ("all things in common") is an unmistakable allusion to the Hellenistic *topos* concerning friendship, that "friends

hold all things in common" (*tois philois panta koina*). The proverb itself is widely distributed (see, e.g., Plato, *Republic* 449C; Aristotle, *Nichomachean Ethics* 1168B; *Politics* 1263A; Plutarch, *The Dialogue on Love* 21 [*Mor.* 767E]; Philo, *On Abraham*, 235), and was a feature of utopian visions of society. The community of possessions was not an ideal within Rabbinic Judaism (see e.g., *Pirke Aboth* 5:10), but at Qumran there was a very strict community of possessions (*1QS* 5:1-3, 14-16, 20; 6:17-22, 24-25; 7:24-25; 8:22-23; 9:3-11; *CD* 9:10-15; 10:18-20; 12:6-7; 13:14-15; 14:20; 20:7), based however not in an ideal of friendship but on the demands placed by a strict ritual purity (see *1QS* 9:3-11).

45. *selling their property and possessions:* The verbs are in the imperfect to denote customary behavior, and serve to generalize what may have been exceptional acts of generosity. Note that Codex B reduces the impression of universality, "as many as had property . . . ." The term translated "property" (*ktēmata*) can mean possessions in general but often means real property such as land (compare Acts 5:1, 3, 8; also, Sir 28:24; 36:25; 51:21; Hos 2:15; Joel 1:11). The term translated "possessions" derives from a word for existence or being and is used extensively in the LXX (2 Chr 35:7; Ps 77:48; Prov 8:21; 13:11; 18:11; 19:14).

according to each one's need: Neither the process of collection nor distribution is described; at this point, Luke wants to show the sharing of possessions as a spontaneous outgrowth of the Spirit, rather than as an institution. The disciples are fulfilling the commands of their teacher (Luke 6:30-36). The term "need" (*chreia*) recurs in 4:35 and 6:3.

46. *together in the temple:* Luke again uses *homothumadon* to express unanimity of spirit, as in 1:14; 4:24; 5:12. By using *hieron* rather than *naos,* he means that they assembled in the temple precincts (identified in 5:12 as Solomon's Portico). As the climax of Jesus' ministry in Jerusalem was carried out in the environs of the temple (Luke 20:1, 21:5, 37, 38; 22:52-53), so is it the place where his followers congregate for prayer (Luke 24:53; Acts 2:46; 3:1) and for teaching (5:20, 25, 42).

broke bread . . . shared food: This statement expands the "breaking of bread" in v. 42. The household is the place for these meals, and will increasingly be mentioned as the locus for cult activities (5:42; 8:3; 11:14; 16:15, 31-32; 18:8; 20:20). The term "gladness" (*agalliasis*) is one that suggests eschatological joy in the presence of the Lord (see Luke 1:14, 44, 47; 10:21, and compare LXX Pss 9:2; 12:5; 19:5; 20:1; 30:7; 39:16; 44:7; 80:1; 83:1; 99:2; 117:15). The term *aphelotēs* ("simplicity of heart"), on the other hand, is found only here in the NT and does not occur in the LXX. It appears related to *haplotēs,* which has the sense of simplicity and generosity, as opposed to double-mindedness and grudging envy (see Luke 11:34; Rom 12:8; 2 Cor 8:2; 9:11, 13; 11:3; Eph 6:5; Col 3:22, and Jas 1:5).

47. *favor among all the people:* The contruction with *charis* ("favor") is somewhat unusual (compare 4:33). This is Luke's first use of *laos* ("people") in the Acts narrative. As in the Gospel, he uses it especially in the religious sense of "people of God" (see Luke 1:10, 17, 68, 77; 2:10, 31-32; 7:16, 29; 18:43; 20:1,

6, 9, 19, 26, 45; 21:38; 22:2; 23:35; 24:19; Acts 3:12, 23; 4:2, 10, 21; 5:12-13, 20, 25, 26; 6:8, 12).

those who were being saved: The present participle asks to be translated as progressive; the characterization picks up Peter's plea, "be saved" in 2:40, and Joel's prophecy, "will be saved" in 2:21.

to the community: The phrase *epi to auto* is placed so awkwardly that some *mss* omit it, even though external attestation and the difficulty it creates argue in favor of its inclusion, as in the 26th edition of Nestle-Aland on which the present translation is based. If we remember that in the LXX, the phrase frequently translates the Hebrew *yahad* (e.g., Pss 2:2; 4:9; 33:4; 36:38), and that at Qumran, *hayahad* is practically a technical term for "community" (see *1QS* 1:1, 12; 8:2; 9:2), the translation "community" here seems appropriate.

INTERPRETATION

The conclusion of Peter's Pentecost speech is one of the most dramatic moments in Luke-Acts. In fulfillment of Jesus' prophecy, his followers have been filled with his prophetic spirit. Peter challenges them to accept what God has done in making "this Jesus whom you crucified" both Messiah and Lord. Will the people respond positively or will they refuse "God's visitation" once more? On their decision rests Luke's entire argument concerning God's fidelity to Israel: despite their rejection of Jesus as Messiah, they are given a second chance through the apostles' message; but will God's fidelity be met with human faith?

Luke suggests which way their decision will go by having them "stunned" by Peter's declamation, and asking the question put to John the Baptist by the populace, "What shall we do?" At the death of Jesus, Luke showed the reader a people ready for repentance; when they observed the death of Jesus, they had turned back to the city beating their breasts in a gesture of remorse (Luke 23:48). Now, hearing Peter's message, they are ready to do what is required by God's action. Their question also allows Peter (and the author) the chance to unfold the meaning of the event. This is all in fulfillment of the prophecy of Jesus that after being empowered, his apostles would proclaim repentance for the forgiveness of sins in his name (Luke 24:47-49).

Even more clearly, Peter interprets this outpouring of the Spirit and its extension to them in terms of the promises of God to Abraham. Yes, it will be extended (and we shall see it extended through the narrative of Acts) to those "far off," but first in sequence comes this offer to the Jews in Jerusalem. They can "be saved" as a remnant (2:40) and become part of God's restored people (2:39).

Peter's words, "whomever the Lord our God summons," (2:39) echoes a part of the prophecy of Joel that is not cited in his speech, but may repay closer attention. After the first part of Joel 3:5, "all who call on the name of the Lord will be saved," there is another line. In the Hebrew, it reads, "for in Mount Zion and in Jerusalem, there shall be those who escape, as the Lord has said, and among the survivors shall be those whom the Lord calls" (RSV). This is impressive enough, and as many readers have observed, the phrase, "whom the Lord calls" connects the Joel citation to Peter's challenge.

But when we consult the LXX translation, which Luke was unquestionably using for the composition of his work, we find another rendering of Joel 3:5b: "For it will be in Mount Zion and in Jerusalem *that there will be a remnant (estai anasōzomenos), just as the Lord said, and they will be preached the good news (euangelizomenoi), those whom the Lord summons.*" As so often in midrash, a verse that is not cited is the most influential. In this case, the *reason* why the prophecy of Joel is so perfect for the interpretation of Pentecost is because it contains both an outpouring of the Spirit *and* the proclamation of the good news to a restored remnant of the people Israel, all this taking place in Jerusalem!

Luke resolves the narrative suspense by showing mass conversions in response to Peter's challenge. Three thousand Jews in the city are baptized and enter the messianic community (2:41). Although Luke will be careful to note further such increments, this one is fundamental, for in it we find the realization of the restored people of God within historic Judaism. Those who repent receive the Holy Spirit, have their sins forgiven, and enjoy the blessings God promised to Abraham, which derive precisely (in Luke's understanding) from the gift of the Spirit itself.

That such is Luke's perception of these first conversions is shown by the first of his "summaries" (2:42-47), showing the inner life of the community. It has long been recognized that these summaries are Luke's own creation. He had fragments of tradition (meaning in this case also continuing practice) on which to build, but he elaborates such fragments into an idyllic picture of the first Christian community. In the present case, the very brief summary in 2:42, with its four elements (teaching of the apostles, fellowship, breaking of bread, prayers) is elaborated in vv. 43-47: as in the Gospel accounts about Jesus, "teaching" is expressed in terms of "wonders and signs" that create awe; fellowship is elaborated in terms of the sharing of possessions; the breaking of bread in terms of meals shared in homes; and "the prayers" in terms of attendance at the temple and praising God.

Luke's portrait of this first community is obviously idealized. Not that the first believers could not have been intense in their unity and joy; they probably were, even though Luke himself will shortly show us some aspects of controversy and failure that occurred very quickly (5:1-11; 6:1-6; 11:29). But the description is idealized in the literary sense, especially in his use of the language associated in Hellenistic philosophy with the *topos* on friendship, when he characterizes the community as having *koinōnia*, and holding all their possessions in common (*panta koina*).

A Hellenistic reader would recognize in Luke's description the sort of "foundation story" that was rather widespread in Hellenistic literature. An early example is Plato's *Critias*, which pictures the early days of Athens as a time when "none of its members possessed any private property, but they regarded all they had as the common property of all" (110 C-D). Another example is Ovid's description of the "Golden Age" of humanity (*Metamorphoses* 1:88-111). Political thinkers like Plato saw such sharing of possessions as a feature of the ideal state (see *Republic* 420C-422B; 462B-464A; *Laws* 679B-C; 684C-D; 744B-746C; 757A), although Aristotle with equal vigor rejected the ideal of community possessions (*Politics* 1261A-1267B).

Some philosophical schools saw the sharing of possessions as the perfect fulfillment of the ideal of friendship, and the late *Life of Pythagoras* by Jamblichus describes the founding of the Pythagorean community at Croton in terms remarkably similar to those used by Luke (6:29-30; see also Porphyry's *Life of Pythagoras* 20). Even the descriptions of the Essenes by Hellenistic Jewish writers bear many of the same features; see Josephus, *Jewish War* 2:122-127, and even more so Philo's *Every Good Man is Free* 77, 79, 84-85.

By using this *topos*, Luke communicated to his readers in vivid fashion that the gift of the Spirit brought about a community which realized the highest aspirations of human longing: unity, peace, joy, and the praise of God. I do not mean to suggest that the ideal of *koinōnia* was simply a literary theme in earliest Christianity; evidence for the intense sharing of possessions (although probably not in an institutionalized "community of possessions"), is found in Paul (Gal 2:10; 1 Cor 16:1-4; 2 Cor 8-9; Rom 15:25-31; Phil 4:15-20), and in other early Christian literature (such as the *Didache* 4:5-8 and the *Letter of Barnabas* 19:8), and is even given grudging recognition from an outsider (Lucian of Samosata, *Passing of Peregrinus* 13). But Luke's appropriation of this ideal in his description of the Jerusalem church has had an unparalleled impact on later Christians who looked back to the Apostolic Age as the time when the Church was most perfectly realized. For fifth-century monks like Cassian (*Institutes* 2:5; 18:5) and for liberation theologians of the twentieth century, Luke's description has provided a utopian vision of what the Church might be in its finest realization.

For his immediate first-century reader, Luke has answered the most pressing question concerning the fate of Israel. Yes, he has shown, God has proven faithful to his promises to Abraham. Despite the first rejection of the prophet Jesus, God raised him up and empowered his followers with his Spirit so they could offer salvation "in his name" yet another time. And it was accepted: in the city of Jerusalem there was realized a "restoration of the people" who enjoyed the blessings given by the Spirit. In one sense, Luke could have ended his story right at this point. Or, he could have moved immediately to the Gentile mission. Why he continues the Jerusalem account the way he does will become evident as we observe his shift in attention to the new leaders over the restored Israel, the apostles.

For Reference and Further Study

Cadbury, H. J. "The Summaries of Acts." *Beginnings* 5:392-402.

Cerfaux, L. "La Composition de la première partie du livre des Actes." *Recueil Lucien Cerfaux*. Biblioteca Ephemeridum Theologicarum Lovaniensium VII-VIII. Gembloux: J. Duculot, 1954, 63–103.

Dupont, J. "Community of Goods in the Early Church." *Salvation of the Gentiles*. Trans. J. Keating. New York: Paulist Press, 1979, 85–102.

Mealand, D. L. "Community of Goods and Utopian Allusions in Acts II-IV." *JTS* n.s. 28 (1977) 96–99.

Menoud, Ph.-H. "The Acts of the Apostles and the Eucharist." *Jesus Christ and the Faith*. Trans. E. M. Paul. Pittsburgh: Pickwick Press, 1978, 84–106.

Mussner, F. "Die *Una Sancta* nach Apg 2, 42." *Praesentia Salutis*. Düsseldorf: Patmos-Verlag, 1967, 212–222.

Zimmermann, H. "Die Sammelberichte der Apostelgeschichte." *BZ* n.f. 5 (1961) 71–82.

6. *The Working of the Raised Prophet* (3:1-26)

1. Now Peter and John were going up into the temple at the ninth hour, the hour of prayer. 2. A certain man who was lame from birth used to be carried and placed every day next to the gate of the temple called Beautiful, so he could beg for alms from those entering the temple. 3. When he saw Peter and John going into the temple he began to ask for alms. 4. Peter (with John) looked at him intently. He said, "Look at us." 5. And he paid attention to them since he was expecting to receive something from them. 6. But Peter said, "I do not have silver and gold. But what I have, this I give you: in the name of Jesus Messiah the Nazorean, rise and walk!" 7. And seizing him by the right hand, he raised him up. His feet and ankles were immediately strengthened. 8. He jumped up, stood, and began to walk. He went with them into the temple. He was walking and leaping and praising God. 9. The whole people saw

him as he walked and praised God. 10. They knew that he was the very
one who used to sit by the Beautiful Gate of the temple. They were filled
with astonishment and amazement at what had happened. 11. As he
held on to Peter and John, the whole people in astonishment surged
toward them at the Portico called Solomon's. 12. Seeing this, Peter
responded to the people: "Israelites, why are you astonished at this?
Why are you staring at us, as though by our own power or piety we had
enabled him to walk? 13. The God of Abraham, of Isaac and of Jacob, the
God of our fathers, has glorified his child Jesus, whom you handed over
and rejected in the presence of Pilate when he had decided to release
him. 14. You rejected the holy and righteous one, and requested that
a murderer be released to you. 15. The author of life whom you murdered, him God has raised from the dead. Of this we are witnesses! 16.
And his name — by faith in his name — has strengthened this man whom
you see and recognize. And the faith that comes through him has given
him this wholeness in front of you all. 17. Now brothers, I know that
you acted in ignorance, just as your leaders did also. 18. But God has
thus brought to fulfillment the things he had foretold through the mouths
of the prophets about the suffering of his Messiah. 19. Repent, therefore, and turn back for the removal of your sins 20. so that seasons of
refreshment might come from the Lord and he might send the Messiah
designated for you, Jesus. 21. It is necessary for heaven to receive him
until the times of restoration of all things, of which God spoke through
the mouths of his holy prophets from of old. 22. Moses said, 'The Lord
your God will raise up for you a prophet like me from among your
brothers. You will obey him in whatever he tells you. 23. But every person who does not obey that prophet will be destroyed from the people.'
24. Indeed, all the prophets who spoke from Samuel onwards also announced these days. 25. You are the children of the prophets and of the
covenant that God made with your ancestors when he said to Abraham,
'In your descendants all the families of the earth will be blessed.' 26.
Having raised up his child, God sent him first to you, in order to bless
you by turning each one of you away from your evil deeds."

Notes

1. *into the temple . . . hour of prayer:* The translation renders the narrative *de* as
   "now." With this slight transition, Luke connects the healing narrative—a
   "wonder" done through the apostles (2:43)—with the previous summary:
   they are "frequenting the temple" and "praising God" (2:46-47). The evening temple service goes back to the instructions of Exod 29:38-42; Num 28:1-8;
   see Josephus, *Antiquities of the Jews* 14:66. That it was also a traditional time
   for prayer is suggested by Dan 6:10; 9:21, and *m.Tamid* 5:1; 6:4.

2. *lame from birth:* The *chōloi* ("lame") are listed among those receiving messianic
   healing by Jesus in Luke 7:22, and parabolically as among the "outcasts" in-

vited to the eschatological banquet (Luke 14:13, 21); see also Acts 8:7; 14:8. According to Lev 21:16-18, a lame man could not "approach to offer the bread of his God"; that is, he was excluded from priesthood, just as a lame lamb could not be offered because of its "blemish" (Deut 15:21; Mal 1:8, 13). The same sort of exclusion from full participation is envisaged in the Qumran writing 1QSa 2:5-6. The circumstances of the lame man's placement at the gate recall those of the beggar in the parable of Luke 16:20.

gate . . . called Beautiful: We cannot be sure of this gate's identity. Josephus mentions a "Bronze Gate" on the east side of the temple in *Jewish War* 2:411, and specifically stresses its value as being greater than those "plated with silver and gold," since it was made of Corinthian bronze (*Jewish War* 5:201), but he never mentions a gate called "Beautiful." Neither does the extensive description of the temple gates in *m.Midd.* 1:3-5, although the identification of the "Nicanor Gate" on the east side again involves its being made out of bronze rather than the overlaid gold of the other gates (*m.Midd.* 2:3). The Mishnah retains a tradition concerning a "miracle" connected to this gate, though not the one related by Luke (see *Tosephta Sotah* 2:4). No more than with the location of Solomon's Portico (3:11) can we be certain of Luke's knowledge or literary intention: does he intend his readers to catch a play on the "silver and gold" associated with the temple gates?

beg for alms: The sharing of possessions through almsgiving (*eleēmosynē*) was an important expression of "doing justice (*ṣedekâ = dikaiosynē*)" in Judaism. See, for example, Tob 1:3, 16; 2:14; 4:7-11; 12:8-9 and the representative statements from the Rabbinic tradition in *m.Peah* 1:1; *Pirke Aboth* 1:2; *Aboth de Rabbi Nathan* 4; *bT Ber.* 5b; 8a; *bT Shab.* 156b; *bT Rosh ha Shanah* 16b; *bT Git.* 7a-b. One reason why the rabbis resisted an institutional sharing of possessions was that it would make the practice of this commandment impossible; see especially *Exodus Rabbah*, Mishp. 31:3-5. Luke also esteems almsgiving (see Luke 11:41; 12:33; Acts 9:36; 10:2, 4, 31; 24:17).

4. *looked at him intently:* Codex D has an elaborate paraphrase in which the lame man does the "intent looking." The translation places "with John" within parentheses to show the awkwardness of its placement in the Greek sentence. As elsewhere (2:14, 37), Luke struggles to make the apostolic action communal.

5. *since he was expecting:* The circumstantial participle *prosdokōn* is treated as explanatory. Luke creates a moment of suspense by this passing reference to the beggar's expectation. The reader then hears with him first disappointing words, then those of unexpected blessing.

6. *silver and gold:* For the possible allusion to the decoration of the temple gates, see the note on v. 2. There is certainly narrative sense to Peter's assertion, since Luke has thus far only shown a community of possessions (2:44) and not the apostles as the administrators of it, a narrative development (4:32–5:11) that has its own logic. The contrast between "silver and gold" and some inward quality of virtue (as in Luke 16:10-13) is commonplace in Hellenistic moral teaching (e.g., Plutarch, *On Love of Wealth* 1 [*Mor.* 523D]; Epictetus, *Discourses* 3, 3, 5-13; 3, 7, 19-28; 3, 9, 15-22; 3, 26, 34-36). For the incommensurability of the divine power and human currency, compare Acts 8:18-24.

name of Jesus Messiah the Nazorean: For the apostolic activity carried out "in the name of" Jesus, see the note on 2:38. The emphasis in the speech that follows on the "name" (*onoma*) as source of power and identity is striking if a bit confusing (3:16; see also 4:7, 10, 12, 17, 18). This translation has deliberately maintained the more archaic-sounding "Messiah" rather than "Christ," and "Nazorean" rather than "of Nazareth." Luke's use of *Nazōraios* seems to reflect a religious as well as a geographical background; see the note on Luke 18:37, and compare Luke 1:26; 2:4, 39, 51; 4:16; Acts 10:28, with Acts 2:22; 4:10; 6:14; 22:8; 26:9. Luke's reference to the "sect of the Nazoreans" in 24:5 seems to demand recognition of this titular use of the term.

rise and walk: Although some *mss* omit "rise" (*egeire*) here, it is surely part of the original text, not despite but because it echoes Luke 5:23 (Jesus' healing of the paralytic). The allusion to Jesus' resurrection in this and the next verse is unmistakable: the power that comes from the prophet whom God "raised up" is "raising up" this man.

8. *began to walk:* As at other places in Luke-Acts (e.g., Luke 4:39; 5:6), the imperfect has an inchoative sense. The use of the adverb *parachrēma* ("immediately") is typical for Lukan wonders (Luke 1:64; 4:39; 8:44, 47, 55; 13:13; 18:43; Acts 5:10; 12:23; 13:11). Again, its use in the Gospel healing of the paralytic (Luke 5:25) is especially noteworthy.

leaping and praising God: Luke devotes extraordinary attention to the signs of healing: after the strengthening of feet and ankles, he lists seven verbs: the man leaps up, stands, walks, enters, walks, leaps, and praises. The use of the cognate terms *exallomenos/allomenos* for "leaping" may recall the LXX use of *allesthai;* in Judg 14:6, 19; 15:14; 1 Sam 10:10, the verb describes the Spirit's "leaping" on a charismatic leader of the people. Note also the phrase, "the lame man shall leap like the hart and the tongue of the dumb sing for joy" in LXX Isa 35:6, in fulfillment of the promise that God would "strengthen the weak hands and make firm the feeble knees" (Isa 35:3) in the context of the restoration of the people in Mt. Zion (Isa 35:1-10). Luke will again use the verb in Paul's healing of a cripple (Acts 14:10). The response of "praising God" is typically Lukan (Luke 2:20; 5:25-26; 7:16; 13:13; 17:15; 18:43). The use of "praise" (*aineō*) here echoes the description of the community in 2:47: the goal of healing is restoration to a people that praises God.

10. *astonishment and amazement:* A response by onlookers is standard for NT healing stories (see Luke 4:36; 5:26; 7:16; 8:37, 56; 11:14; 13:17; 18:43). This one is unusually elaborate, matching the unusual attention to the signs of healing. The heightened emotions are reminiscent of Hellenistic novels like Chariton of Aphrodisias, *Chaereas and Callirhoe* 3, 5, 3, or Heliodorus, *The Ethiopians* 4, 9, 1). The emphasis on *recognition* of the lame man by those who knew him previously reminds us of John 9:8-12, 20. "Astonishment" (*thambos*) is used in Luke 4:36; 5:9, and is picked up in the next verse as well by *ekthambos.* "Amazement" (*ekstasis/exhistēmi*) is found in Luke 2:47; 5:26; 8:56; 24:22; Acts 8:9, 11, 13; 9:21; 10:45; 12:16.

11. *whole people . . . surged toward them:* Is literally "ran together toward them." The entire verse is reworked by Codex D, and complicates the problems already present concerning Luke's knowledge of the temple and the location of Solomon's Portico (mentioned in Josephus' *Jewish War* 5:184-185). Such mass responses by a city populace is another staple of Greek Romances like Heliodorus, *The Ethiopians* 4, 21, 1-3.

12. *by our own power or piety:* The manifestation of *dynamis* ("power") has been obvious. The issue is its source: are Peter and John to be regarded as the sort of "divine men" whose miracles showed them to be partakers of the divine *dynamis* because of their great wisdom or virtue (here *eusebeia*, "piety")? For the classic portrayal of such a figure, see Philostratus, *Life of Apollonius of Tyana* 3:18; 8:5; 8:7. A deflection similar to that carried out by Peter is attributed to Paul in Acts 14:15.

13. *glorified his child Jesus:* The one whose power is at work is identified in the first place as the "God of our fathers," in a characterization that recalls the theophany to Moses in Exod 3:6, 15. The term *pais* can be translated as "child" or "servant." In the latter sense, it is used in the LXX particularly of "Moses my servant" (Joshua 1:7, 13; 9:24; 11:12, 15; 12:6; 14:7; 18:7; 1 Chr 6:49; 2 Chr 24:9). It is used also of the mysterious figure of the Isaianic "servant songs." The glorification of "his child/servant Jesus" recalls specifically Isa 52:13, "my child (servant) will be glorified exceedingly." Matt 12:18 uses the term with reference to Jesus in a citation from Isa 42:1. Luke applies it to "Israel your child" in Luke 1:54, and "David your child" in Luke 1:69. After the present occurrence, it reappears in the titular sense in Acts 3:26; 4:25, 27, 30, and occurs in other early Christian writings outside the NT, such as the *Didache* 9:2; 10:2; *1 Clement* 59:2-4; *Letter of Barnabas* 6:1; 9:2; *Martyrdom of Polycarp* 14:1; 20:2. As so much else in this speech, the title has an archaic feel.

    whom you handed over and rejected: The sentence structure is similar to that in Acts 2:23-24 and 10:39-40: "*whom* you killed, *this one* God raised." The same "kerygmatic formula" is used of Moses in 7:35. The recollection of Jesus' death is here more detailed than in Peter's first speech, with the "handing over" (*paradidōmi*) recalling both the passion prophecies (Luke 9:44; 18:32) and the passion narrative (20:20; 22:4, 6, 22, 48). The verb translated "reject" is *arneomai* (literally "deny"), which recurs in the next verse.

    decided to release him: Peter recalls the hearing before Pilate in Luke 23:1-23, where Pilate three times tries to release Jesus (23:4, 16, 22) only to give in to the people's demand (23:24). Barabbas is identified as a man thrown into prison for rioting and as a murderer (Luke 23:18-19, 25).

14. *holy and righteous one:* The title "Holy One" is properly God's (see Lev 11:44-45; LXX Ps 77:41; 98:5; 102:1). It is applied to Jesus in Luke 1:35 and by scriptural allusion in 2:23. The demons address him as "holy one of God" (Luke 4:34). In Acts 4:27-30, the community prayer designates Jesus the "holy child/servant (*pais*)." The designation "righteous" (*dikaios*) recalls especially the acclamation of the centurion at the cross of Jesus (Luke 23:47), and is used

of Jesus again in Acts 22:14. The title is related to the understanding of Jesus as the "righteous one [who] will live by faith" in Hab 2:4 (see Rom 1:17; Gal 3:11; Heb 10:38) and the "righteous servant" of Isa 53:11 (see 1 John 1:9; 2:1, 29).

15. *author of life:* The epithet *archēgos tēs zōēs* is difficult to render exactly, since its range of possible meanings runs from "originator/founder" (e.g., Josephus, *Against Apion* 1:130) through "cause" (e.g., Josephus, *Antiquities of the Jews* 7:207) to "pioneer/hero" (e.g., Heb 12:2). Luke uses it again in combination with "savior" (*sōtēr*) in Acts 5:31, which is similar to Heb 2:10, "author of salvation"; the combination is picked up by the early Christian writing 2 *Clement* 20:5. The intended contrast here is obviously between the one who gives life, and the murderer who takes it away.

16. *by faith in his name:* Not only does this statement as a whole interrupt Peter's "kerygmatic statement," (thereby linking the healing even more directly to the event of Jesus' resurrection), but it is garbled in Greek. The translation places this phrase within dashes in order to indicate its parenthetic character: it serves to qualify the bald statement, "his name has strengthened." The next statement about faith, however, is almost as confusing, "the faith that comes through him." The author is struggling, it appears, to join the objective power of "the name" working through the apostles, with the subjective necessity of "faith" to make that power operative. For the relationship of faith to salvation in Luke-Acts, see Luke 5:20; 7:9, 50; 8:12, 25, 48, 50; 17:19; 18:42; Acts 14:9; 15:11.

    this wholeness: The choice of *holoklēria* here rather than a word such as *hygiēs* ("healthy") might be deliberately evocative. As the "lame" (*chōlos*) was ritually "blemished" and therefore excluded from the people's worship, so did the LXX use the term *holoklēros* to designate unblemished animals acceptable to the Lord (e.g., Isa 1:6; Zech 11:16).

17. *acted in ignorance:* The qualification is important for the structuring of Luke's story: the fact that there were mitigating circumstances for the first rejection of the prophet legitimates the second offering of salvation through his prophetic emissaries. The statement here picks up the prayer of Jesus on the cross (Luke 23:34) and is an essential component of the Moses story in Acts 7:25. In contrast to other such statements, Luke includes the leaders in this exculpation.

18. *has thus brought to fulfillment:* Peter strikes one of the central themes of Luke-Acts, that the events in the story of the prophet and the people fulfill the prophecies of Torah (Luke 1:1), most specifically the necessity of the Messiah's suffering before entering his glory (Luke 24:26-27, 44-46; Acts 17:2-3).

19. *repent . . . and turn back:* For "repent" (*metanoeō*) see the note on 2:38. The LXX uses *epistrephō* ("turn back") more frequently to translate the Hebrew *šub/tešubah* for human repentance and conversion (e.g., Hos 3:5; 5:4; Amos 4:6, 9; Joel 2:13; Zech 1:3; Mal 3:7; Isa 9:13; 19:22; 55:7; Jer 3:10; Ezek 18:32). The term appears in the "blindness" prophecy of Isaiah 6:9, cited by Mark 4:12; Matt 13:15 and Acts 28:27. Luke also alludes to the use in Mal 3:4 in

Luke 1:17. In the sense of "repent," Luke uses *epistrephō* in Luke 17:4; 22:32; Acts 9:35, 40; 11:21; 14:15; 15:19; 26:18, 20.

removal of your sins: The word choice is unusual, since *exaleiphō* is used in the LXX almost entirely in the negative sense of "blotting out" a person or people (see Gen 7:23; Exod 32:32-33; Lev 14:22; Deut 9:14; 25:6; 2 Kgs 14:27; Ps 9:5; 68:28). Only in Isa 43:25 do we find a usage that anticipates Luke's: "I will blot out your sins."

20. *seasons of refreshment:* The expression as such occurs only here, and its specific meaning is not clear. In the literal sense, the terms *anapsychō/anapsyxis* refer to the sort of respite or refreshment that comes from a good drink of water (e.g., Judg 15:19; 2 Sam 16:14; 2 Macc 4:46). The verb is used for the sabbath rest of slaves and animals in Exod 23:12, for the soothing of Saul's spirit by David's music in 1 Sam 16:23, for the cessation of suffering in Ps 38:14, for the revival of the people in 2 Macc 13:11. The noun occurs only once, but most intriguingly: in Exod 8:15 it refers to the respite in punishment from plagues that comes when Pharaoh obeys Moses! Although the relation between these "seasons" (*kairoi*) and the "times (*chronoi*) of restoration" or the sending of the Messiah is not entirely clear, Luke *does* immediately connect the people's conversion to their refreshment by means of a purpose construction (*hopōs*, "so that"). The translation "from the Lord" simplifies the septuagintalism "from the face of the Lord" (compare LXX Pss 9:3, 26; 16:2, 9; 17:8).

Messiah designated for you: The prefix *pro-* in the verb *procheirizomai* does not demand its being taken in a temporal sense of "predestined." The perfect passive participle here bears the sense: "one who stands chosen by God." The verb is used in the LXX for the selection of twelve men to carry the ark (Josh 3:10), but even more striking is Exod 4:13: Moses begs God not to send him to Pharaoh, "I pray that another capable one be chosen, whom you will send." Note the resemblance to the present passage in these elements: a) one chosen; b) who will be sent; c) other than Moses; d) and empowered. In the light of v. 22 below, this is indeed suggestive.

21. *necessary for heaven to receive him:* Luke uses his characteristic construction with *dei* ("it is necessary") for events in the divine plan (compare Luke 24:7, 26, 44; Acts 1:16, 21). The "receiving" of Jesus into heaven obviously refers to the ascension (1:9-11), which promises his return "in the same manner."

restoration for all things: The term *apokatastasis* picks up the question concerning Israel in 1:6; for a discussion of the term's antecedents, see the note and interpretation on that verse. Here, the problematic term is *pantōn* ("all things") and its relationship to the relative clause (*hōn*) following. Should the sentence be read "the times of restoration of everything that God spoke of," which places the emphasis on the fulfillment of prophecy and treats "restoration" in the weaker sense of "establish" (see the RSV)? Or—as in the present translation—should the stress be put on "restoration of all things" in the strong sense of "rebuild" or "reconstitute" (see Acts 15:16), with the relative clause playing only a secondary role?

22. *raise up for you a prophet like me:* Luke merges a citation from LXX Deut 18:15-19, in which Moses predicts the "raising up" of a prophet like himself, with two phrases ("every person" and "will be destroyed from the people") from the LXX of Lev 23:29. In effect, Luke replaces the threat already present in Deut 18:19 ("I will take vengeance") with a formulation that stresses exclusion *from the people.* The passage from Deut 18:15-19, together with that from Deut 34:9-12, generated in Judaism an expectation for a "prophet like Moses" that is fairly widely attested (see e.g., the Samaritan *Memar Marqah* 4:3, and John 1:21; 6:14; 7:40). The use of precisely this text from Deut 18 by the Qumran sectarians is especially fascinating (see *4QTest* 5-8). Note that this is also the text that is attributed to Moses himself in Stephen's speech (Acts 7:37).

    obey him in whatever he tells you: Luke alters the LXX text slightly to fit the citation to the context. The translation of *akousesthe* as "you will obey" rather than "you will listen" better captures the precise *kind* of listening Luke has in mind (compare LXX Exod 19:5; 24:3). The formula "destroyed from the people" in 3:23 uses a verb that ordinarily means simply to be done away with physically (as in Deut 1:27; 2:34), but appears in this combination to mean "cut off from the people" for a variety of offenses, in LXX Gen 12:14; Exod 12:15, 19; 22:20; 30:33; 31:14; Ps 36:28; 72:27; 100:8.

24. *indeed all the prophets:* This is a notoriously difficult sentence both in structure and sense. The rendering "indeed" aims to capture the unusual *kai pantes de.* The translation also tidies the cluttered syntax by shifting *hosoi elalēsan* ("whosoever spoke") back to "the prophets." Other cosmetic improvements have been attempted to make the sentence yield an acceptable if not altogether clear sense. Left unclear are questions such as: why "from Samuel onwards," and why "whosoever spoke"? No translation is adequate to such a confused text, but the essential point comes through, that the prophets spoke about the present days.

25. *children of the prophets:* The expression has a general meaning rather than the specific one found in 1 Kgs 21:35; 2 Kgs 2:3, 5, 7, 15 for prophetic bands called "sons of the prophets." For "children of the covenant," compare Ezek 30:5; the phrase is not so widely used as one might expect (see *1QM* 17:8). A similar way of stating the special status of the Jews is found in Rom 9:4-5.

    all the families of the earth will be blessed: There are four such promises to Abraham in Genesis (12:3; 18:18; 22:18; 26:4). The citation resembles most LXX Gen 22:18, with two exceptions: Luke uses the passive "will be blessed" rather than the reflexive "will bless themselves" captured by the LXX *eneulogeomai;* he also replaces "nations" (*ethnē*) with "families" *patriai*, (compare *phylai*, "tribes," in Gen 12:3). This translation treats *sperma* ("seed") as plural "descendants," since Luke is not making the same messianic midrashic use of the singular that Paul does in Gal 3:16. Luke emphasizes the promise to Abraham in Luke 1:55, 73; Acts 7:5-6, 16-17.

26. *having raised up his child:* As elsewhere in this speech, the word-order in Greek is difficult. For the meaning of *pais* ("child/servant"), see note on v. 13. The mention of "raising" Jesus here is not accidental; it connects him to the

"prophet like me whom God will raise up" (v. 22). The Mosaic imagery is obvious.

sent him first to you: The adverb *prōton* is here taken to define the order for the offer of salvation: first to the Jews, and then to the Gentiles (compare Rom 1:16). This reading conforms to the overall plan of Luke's work with its special emphasis on sequence. The participle *eulogounta* ("blessing") is treated as a purpose clause. It establishes a direct connection to the foregoing citation: in the gift of the Spirit that comes from the resurrection of Jesus, they are sharing in the Abrahamic blessings!

INTERPRETATION

The healing of the lame man at the beautiful gate of the temple (3:1-10) sets up and gains its depth of meaning from Peter's speech to the crowd that is brought together by the wonder (3:11-26). And together, they perform a valuable narrative function for the author, who wants to shift his readers' attention to a new stage in the story. Luke has shown how the blessings of God are being enjoyed by the restored people who responded to the Pentecost proclamation. Now he must show how in fact the apostles carry on the prophetic power of Jesus in their deeds and words, and how they are to be the leaders over this restored people, "judging the twelve tribes of Israel" (Luke 22:30).

The healing story follows the usual pattern of such accounts in the Gospel tradition but is unusually well developed in each of its parts. Such descriptive intricacy invites speculation on the possible deeper resonances of meaning the story may contain. It is certainly clear at once that Luke uses this story to exemplify the elements of his summary in 2:42-47: We see the apostles frequenting the temple in order to pray; they have no money to give a beggar; they work "signs and wonders" in this healing; they stimulate a positive response among the people. But by having all these community qualities enacted by Peter and John, Luke shifts our attention to them rather than to the community as a whole.

The choice of healing a lame man is scarcely arbitrary. It serves several literary roles. As the notes indicate, many of the linguistic details of the story resemble those in Luke 5:17-26; for the reader of his story as a whole, the parallel between the accounts would not be missed: the apostles have the same power to heal as was at work in Jesus. The resemblance is more striking in that both accounts explicitly raise the issue of "what authority" is at work in the performance of the wonder (Luke 5:21-24; Acts 4:7). By means of this literary parallelism Luke communicates the simple point that the apostles are prophetic successors of Jesus.

The healings of Jesus, we saw throughout our reading of the Gospel, served a broad symbolic function within Luke's story of the Prophet and the People. Jesus did not only heal bodily ailments; his cures worked to "heal the people of God." His healing of the outcast and marginal in the population enacted his mission to "proclaim good news to the poor" (see especially Luke 7:18-23). The end-point of Jesus' healings was the restoration of the sick person to full participation in the life of the people. The same point is surely being made in this healing of a lame man by the apostles, and the point is carried by the symbolism associated with the temple cult.

A number of separate contrasts are being played out simultaneously in the story. The lame man (as the notes have shown) is marked by Torah as "blemished," a condition that excludes an animal from being used for sacrifice, and a human being from becoming a priest. But when he is commanded by Peter to rise and walk, the man is able to leap through the temple precincts, "praising God." The healing worked by the apostles makes the temple truly "a house of prayer" (Luke 19:46) even for one considered an outcast but now made "whole."

There is also the odd comment of Peter about not having silver or gold. We cannot be sure that Luke intends his reader to catch an allusion to the rich adornment of the temple gates (see notes). But we can be sure that Peter is invoking a power transcending the wealth and power of human establishments. As his speech and later confrontation with the authorities will make even clearer, the power at work to heal comes from one who was himself rejected and scorned. If, then, "his name" can cause a lame man to "rise" and skip through the porticos of the temple in ecstatic praise of God, then Jesus surely must be the "prophet whom God raised up."

By attaching Peter's speech immediately to the healing (with the healed man still clinging to his arm!), Luke has dramatically established another connection between the apostles and Jesus. Like him, they are now "teaching in the temple," and like him as well, their teaching is intimately connected to the powerful deeds they perform. But by making these points so well, Luke has also made Peter's next great speech (3:11-26) very difficult reading.

Anyone who has tried to work through the speech in Greek comes away with a sense of frustration at two sorts of problems that may be related to each other. First is the tangled state of syntax throughout the speech. Second is the uncertain connection in ideas. Underlying both problems is an unusually high proportion of "primitive" language whose precise import is not obvious. So daunting is this cluster of difficulties that some readers suggest that we have here a badly translated Aramaic original that takes us back to Peter himself and the earliest of all Christian proclamations. Certainly, such hypotheses have some general plausibility, and in this case, some of the "back translations" into Aramaic work rather well.

As our notes to this section demonstrate, however, the "biblical" language Luke uses here derives from the Septuagint, and it is less likely that he was using a primitive source than that he was, as elsewhere, deliberately "archaizing" Peter's discourse. As for the disjunctions in syntax, they are best understood as the result of trying to compress complex connections within too small a space. Although we customarily speak of a "speech" or "discourse," after all, it is good to remember that Peter's address consists of only eighteen (English) sentences!

Three aspects of Peter's speech should be noted. The first is the connection it draws between the healing of the lame man and the resurrection of Jesus (3:16). The difficulty of doing this when using periphrases such as "in the name of" creates some of Luke's syntactical difficulties. But by placing this assertion right in the middle of his kerygmatic statement about the death and resurrection of Jesus (3:13-18) Luke has made his central affirmation powerfully: the power at work in Peter and John is not their own but comes from the "child whom God glorified," Jesus. The healing enacts what had been announced by Peter's Pentecost sermon: the prophetic Spirit poured out on the apostles is one that works "wonders and signs" just as Jesus had worked "powerful deeds, wonders, and signs" (Acts 2:19, 22, 32).

The second noteworthy aspect of the speech is the elaborate attention it pays to the rejection portion of the kerygmatic statement. In contrast to Peter's Pentecost speech, which focused primarily on the reality of the resurrection and the gift of the Spirit, here we find a stress placed on the people's rejection of Jesus at the time of his first visitation: they preferred a murderer to the author of life, and demanded Jesus' death even when Pilate wanted to release him (3:13-15). The charge is devastating, all the more so when the people as a whole are implicated as much as their leaders. At the same time, Luke has Peter offer two mitigating circumstances to their first rejection of the prophet. One was that both they and their leaders had acted in ignorance (3:17). The other was that although they did not know it, God was fulfilling his predictions about a suffering Messiah (3:18). These qualifications open up the possibility for repentance, both for people and for leaders. Their first rejection was not final. They are not excluded from the offer of salvation. In fact, "in the name of Jesus" it is being offered to them now. But the stakes are obviously higher. Now they know. They can no longer appeal to ignorance. The fact of God's raising up Jesus is manifest in the deeds he works through the apostles. This second offer of salvation is not veiled.

This brings us to the third aspect of Peter's speech, its call to conversion. Even more than in the Pentecost speech, the emphasis is put on the fact that it is "the God of our fathers" who raised Jesus from the dead, and that these deeds of power represent an offer of hope to "Israelites" as the "people of God" (3:9, 11, 12, 13). This Messiah, Peter says, was designated "for them" (3:20). The blessing of Abraham that is now being proclaimed in the resurrection Spirit is sent "first to you" (3:26). At the same time, the call to conversion has a double edge, containing both promise and threat.

The promise is that their conversion will mean the "wiping out" of their sins (3:19) and a turning of each person from one's wicked deeds (3:26). This will lead to their enjoyment of the "seasons of refreshment" (3:20). The connection of this immediate result with the "sending of the Messiah" and the "restoration of all things" is deeply problematic and perhaps irresolvable. Two things can be stated with fair certainty: first, Luke does see the realization of a people of God in Jerusalem as some sort of "restoration of the people" enjoying the messianic blessings; he has already established that in 2:42-47, and the "seasons of refreshment" offered in 3:20 seem most logically to be an extension of that blessing (see 3:26) to the rest of the people in the city: they too can share in these blessings if they have "faith in this name" and accept the blessing that comes from the Spirit. But, second, Luke does not see this as yet a "restoration of *all things*," which will involve the return of the Messiah as Son of Man. Consistent with his eschatological scenario sketched in Luke 21:5-36, Luke separates the time of witness from the end-time.

Peter's speech also contains a threat, enunciated by the mixed citation from Deut 18:15-19 and Lev 23:29 (Acts 3:22-23). This citation serves the double function of establishing with absolute clarity the connection between the resurrected Jesus and the "prophet like Moses" whom God promised to "raise up," and of serving as a programmatic prophecy for the next section of the narrative: depending on their response to this "raised prophet" who challenges them through the deeds and words of the apostles will the fate of the people be decided. Will they "obey this prophet" who now speaks to them unmistakably in "signs and wonders," and thereby enjoy the Abrahamic blessings and be counted among the restored people? Or will they reject the prophet a second time, now in full knowledge and deliberation? If they do, Peter makes clear, they will definitively be "destroyed from the people" that God is forming.

For Reference and Further Study

Dupont, J. "Les discours de Pierre dans les Actes et le chapitre xxiv de L'évangile de Luc." *l'Evangile de Luc.* Ed. F. Neirynck. Biblioteca Ephemeridum Theologicarum Lovaniensium XXXII. Gembloux: J. Duculot, 1973.
Hamm, D. "Acts 3:1-10: The Healing of the Temple Beggar as Lukan Theology." *Bib* 67 (1986) 305-319.

Kurz, W. "Acts 3:19-26 as a Test of the Role of Eschatology in Lukan Christology." *SBL 1977 Seminar Papers.* Ed. P. J. Achtemeier. Missoula: Scholars Press, 1977, 309–323.

Matera, F. J. "The Responsibility for the Death of Jesus according to the Acts of the Apostles." *JSNT* 39 (1990) 77–93.

Mussner, F. "Die Idee der Apokatastasis in der Apostelgeschichte." *Praesentia Salutis.* Düsseldorf: Patmos-Verlag, 1967, 223–234.

Robinson, J. A. T. "The Most Primitive Christology of All?" *JTS* n.s. 7 (1956) 177–189.

Schmitt, J. "L'église de Jérusalem, ou la 'restoration' d'Israel." *RevScRel* 27 (1953) 209–218.

Ziesler, J. A. "The Name of Jesus in the Acts of the Apostles." *JSNT* 4 (1979) 28–41.

7. *The Response by People and Leaders* (4:1-22)

1. As they were speaking to the people, the priests and officer of the temple and Sadducees confronted them, 2. upset because they were teaching the people and proclaiming in Jesus the resurrection of the dead. 3. They seized them and put them in custody until the following day, for it was already evening. 4. But many of those who had heard the word believed. And the number of the men was about five thousand. 5. The next day their leaders and elders and scribes gathered together in Jerusalem, 6. as did Annas the chief priest and Caiaphas, and John and Alexander, and whoever belonged to the chief-priest's family. 7. Having stationed them in the middle, they began questioning them: "By what sort of power or by what sort of name did you do this thing?" 8. Then Peter was filled with the Holy Spirit. He said to them, "Leaders of the people and elders! 9. If we are being examined today concerning a kindness for a sick man, by which this man has been saved, 10. let it be known to all of you and to the entire people of Israel that it is through the name of Jesus Messiah the Nazorean—whom you crucified but whom God raised from the dead—it is through him that this man stands before you healthy. 11. This is the stone that was scorned by you the builders. He has become the cornerstone! 12. And salvation is in no other, for neither is there another name under heaven given to humans by which we must be saved." 13. When they saw the boldness of Peter and John, and grasped that they were unschooled and common, they were astonished—and they recognized that they had been with Jesus. 14. And since they could see the person who had been healed standing there with them, they could say nothing in opposition. 15. They ordered them to leave the council-chamber, and began to consult with each other. 16. They said, "What shall we do with these fellows? The fact that they per-

formed a sign is known to all the inhabitants of Jerusalem. It is obvious. We cannot deny it. 17. But to keep it from spreading even further among the people, let us warn them not to speak any more to anyone in this name." 18. After summoning them, they ordered them to put a complete halt to proclaiming or teaching in the name of Jesus. 19. But Peter and John answered them by saying, "You judge whether it is righteous before God to obey you rather than to obey God. 20. For we are unable to stop speaking of the things we have seen and heard." 21. So having given warning, they released them, since they had found no way of punishing them because of the people: they were all giving glory to God because of what had happened. 22. For the man who experienced this sign of healing was more than forty years old.

NOTES

1. *priests and officer of the temple:* Some *mss* have "chief-priests" (*archiereis*) to bring this list of opponents into line with Luke's passion account (Luke 19:47; 20:1, 19; 22:2, 4, 50, 66; 23:4, 10, 13), but since "priests" is the harder reading, it is to be preferred. Luke is not in any case overly precise in such designations. Note, for example, that the *stratēgos tou hierou* ("officer of the temple") appears in the *plural* in Luke 22:4, 52. Josephus has temple "guards" (*phylakoi*) reporting to a *stratēgos*; we are to picture a temple security force (Josephus, *Jewish War* 6:294). Luke's essential point is that these are the *leaders* as distinct from the ordinary folk.

   confronted them: Luke uses *ephistēmi* for sudden appearances (Luke 2:9, 38; 4:39; 21:34; Acts 6:12; 10:17; 11:11; 12:7; 22:13). The translation tries to capture the sense demanded by the context (compare Luke 20:1).

2. *upset:* The verb *diaponeuomai* has the literal sense of "being worn down," but as it is used in Mark 14:4 and Acts 16:18, it connotes irritation and exasperation. Compare the reaction of the head of the synagogue in Luke 13:14.

   preaching in Jesus the resurrection of the dead: A wonderfully concise characterization of the kerygma. Codex D seems to have misunderstood Luke's intention by putting "announcing Jesus in the resurrection of the dead." Compare Luke's language in Acts 4:33. It is fitting that the Sadducees appear as the opponents at this point, for they are introduced in the Gospel as "those who deny the resurrection" (Luke 20:27). Indeed, they are pictured as fighting with the Pharisees over the point in Acts 23:8. On this school within Judaism, see the notes on Luke 20:27, and Josephus, *Antiquities of the Jews* 13:297-298; 18:16-17, and *Jewish War* 2:164-165.

4. *the number . . . five thousand:* The contrast to the response of the leaders is deliberate and part of Luke's larger literary pattern. Large numbers of the ordinary people believe and join the community. For the use of "men" (*andres*) in counting, compare Luke 9:14, where in fact five thousand is also the number involved. The point here is not the actual number, but the evidence of substantial growth among the populace.

5. *their leaders and elders and scribes:* Although the use of "their" makes for awkward English, Luke is making a point: at issue in the next sequence of stories concerns who the leadership over the restored people really is to be. For these titles, see the note on Luke 19:47. "Leaders" (*archontes*) is a more general designation, whereas "elders" (*presbyteroi*) and "scribes" (*grammateis*) are categories of membership in the Jewish Council (the Sanhedrin, see 4:15, below), that deliberated under the close scrutiny of the Roman occupation; see Josephus, *Antiquities of the Jews* 12:142; *m.Sanh.* 1:6; 4:3; Acts 5:21, 27, 34, 41; 6:12, 15; 22:30; 23:1, 6, 15, 20, 28).

6. *Annas . . . Caiaphas:* As in Luke 3:2, the names are joined, although Annas held office from 6 to 15 C.E. and Caiaphas, his son-in-law, from 18 to 36 C.E. (Josephus, *Antiquities of the Jews* 18:26-35).

   John . . . Alexander: These names are otherwise unknown, unless Codex D's replacement of "John" with "Jonathan" is original, in which case the reference could be to the Jonathan whom Josephus names as a son of Annas and successor to Caiaphas as chief-priest (*Antiquities of the Jews* 18:95).

7. *what sort of power . . . name:* The adjective *poios* is generalizing (compare Luke 6:32, 33, 34; 9:55; Acts 7:49). Because of the distinction between "power" (*dynamis*) and "name" (*onoma*), the question addresses the source and authority for the healing. Compare the question put to Jesus by the leaders in Luke 20:2, *en poia exousia tauta poieis,* ("by what sort of authority are you doing these things?").

8. *filled with the Holy Spirit:* This phrase is part of Luke's stereotypical characterization of his main characters as prophets, both in the Gospel (1:15, 41, 67; 4:1) and in Acts (2:4; 4:31; 6:3, 5; 7:55; 9:17; 11:24; 13:9).

9. *kindness for a sick man:* The term translated "kindness" (*euergesia*) can also have a much more official sense of "benefaction" such as would be performed as a public service by a wealthy benefactor for a Greek city-state (see Plato, *Laws* 850B; Aristotle, *Politics* 1286B). Note the use particularly in Wis 16:11; 2 Macc 6:13; 9:26. The term *asthenēs* ("weak/sick") is used here much as it is in Luke 10:9 and Acts 5:15-16.

   has been saved: The perfect passive tense points to the present condition of being healed (compare *tetherapeumenon* in v. 13). The use of *sōzō* ("save") here is deliberate, picking up the theme of "those calling on the name of the Lord being saved" established by 2:21 and carried by 2:47. The theme will be stated explicitly in v. 12.

10. *known to you all:* As in 2:14 and 2:36, Peter's answer to the leaders becomes a proclamation to "all of Israel." For the form and content of this statement, compare 3:13-16. For "Jesus Messiah the Nazorean," see the note on 3:6.

11. *stone that was scorned:* This is Luke's second application of LXX Ps 117:22 to the leaders. The first time was at the end of Jesus' parable of the vineyard (Luke 20:17), which the leaders recognized as addressed specifically to them (20:19). Two aspects of the present citation are noteworthy: a) Luke replaces the verb *apodokimaō* ("reject") of the LXX with the verb *exoutheneō* ("scorn"),

a verb he uses elsewhere to characterize the attitude of leaders (Luke 18:9; 23:11); b) he explicitly adds the words "by you" (*hyph' hymōn*) before "the builders," a creative emendation of the LXX text that makes it fit his narrative purposes.

the cornerstone: The phrase *kephalē gōnias* (literally "head of a corner") is used in Matt 21:42; Mark 12:10; Luke 20:17, and 1 Pet 2:7. It is related to *akrogōniaios* (Isa 28:16; Eph 2:20; 1 Pet 2:6), which more properly refers to the "capstone" joining the sides of an arch at the top. Either term points to this stone as the essential one for construction: the prophet they have rejected is the basis for the restored people God is calling together.

12. *salvation is in no other:* The Greek sentence is awkward and somewhat tautologous; the second clause, however, does make clear that the "no other" means "no other name given to humans" (or: "among humans"), and that "salvation" means "by which we must be saved." The theme of salvation in the name of Jesus is announced explicitly, and involves, as we have seen, physical, spiritual, and social dimensions.

13. *the boldness of Peter and John:* The quality of *parrēsia* ("boldness/frankness/free speech") was particularly associated with philosophers of the Cynic strain (see Dio Chrysostom, *Oration* 32:11; 77/8:37, 45; Lucian of Samosata, *Demonax* 3, 11). Lucian of Samosata, in fact, personified "Frankness" (*Parrēsiadēs*) and made it a spokesperson for Philosophy in his dialogue, *The Dead Come Back to Life*. The LXX, in contrast, has only a few uses of the term (Esth 8:13; Job 27:10; Prov 1:20; 10:10; 13:5; Wis 5:1; Sir 25:25; 1 Macc 4:18; 3 Macc 4:1; 7:12). Luke uses both noun and verb forms to identify his prophetic characters, a nice example of his blending of prophetic and philosophical images (Acts 2:29; 4:29, 31; 9:27-28; 13:46; 14:3; 18:26; 19:8; 26:26; 28:6, 31).

unschooled and common: The term *agrammatos* literally means to be illiterate (=without letters), but is extended to mean lack of education generally (Plato, *Timaeus* 23A; Epictetus, *Discourses* 2, 9, 10). This is the only use in the NT. The term *idiotēs* derives from *idios* and has the first sense of being a "private person," and by extension, one who is uncouth and ignorant (see Lucian, *Alexander the False Prophet* 30). It can also be used, as here, to mean someone lacking in a professional lore: Aristotle contrasts an *idiotēs* to a philosopher (*Politics* 1266A). Paul uses the term in the broader sense in 1 Cor 14:16, 23 and in the narrower sense in 2 Cor 11:6. In the present case, the epithet may bear some of the implications of the Pharisaic distinction between the Associate and the *'am-ha'ares* (see *m.Demai* 2:2-3; 3:3).

14. *could say nothing in opposition:* The use of *anteipein* deliberately picks up Jesus' prophecy concerning his witnesses (Luke 21:15): "I will give you speech and wisdom such that all those opposing you will not be able to resist or contradict (*anteipein*)."

16. *do with these fellows:* The deliberative question in this case has the same form but a much different spirit from that in 2:37. The translation of *anthrōpois toutois* as "these fellows" aims at the contempt implicit in all the council's first encounter with the apostles.

that they performed a sign is known: The placement of *gnōstos* ("known") before *sēmeion* ("sign") leads some translations to take it as modifying that noun (RSV: "notable sign"). But although the word order is unusual, the meaning here is closer to Luke's other uses of the term (see 1:19; 2:14; 4:10; 9:42; 13:38; 15:18; 19:17; 28:22, 28). For rhetorical reasons, this translation makes "it is obvious" a separate statement from those on either side. Luke strikes once more the theme of the *public* character of the prophetic ministry.

19. *to obey you rather than to obey God:* As in 3:23, the verb *akouō* is translated as "obey" to make clear the kind of hearing meant. Peter's response here (and even more clearly in 5:29) recalls Socrates' defense before the Athenian judges: "I shall obey God rather than you, and while I have life and strength I shall never cease from the practice and teaching of philosophy" (Plato, *Apology* 29D). Socrates provided the prototype for brave opposition to tyranny in the name of God, as in the case of the Maccabees (see 2 Macc 7:2; 4 Macc 5:16-24; Josephus, *Antiquities of the Jews* 17:158-159).

21. *found no way to punish them:* The participle *heuriskontes* is read as explanatory. For the pressure put on the leaders by the people, compare Luke 19:48; 20:6, 19, 26; 21:38; 22:2). In the first part of Acts, Luke continues the theme of the division between leaders and people.

22. *sign of healing:* This phrase crystallizes two aspects of the narrative sequence: a) the healing was a "sign" worked by the apostles that showed the prophetic power of Jesus was indeed operative through them; b) the healing (salvation) of a lame person symbolized the restoration of the people, particularly the outcast. Literarily, this apparent aside actually frames the entire section of 3:1-4:22.

more than forty years old: There is an obvious temptation to see a symbolic resonance here, except that Luke uses the specific number forty (well-hallowed by the biblical tradition) so frequently: for Jesus' stay in the desert (Luke 4:2), and with the disciples after the resurrection (Acts 1:3); for Moses' age when he first approached his fellow-Israelites (Acts 7:23), and his years in exile (7:30) and the years spent leading the people through the wilderness (7:36, 42; 13:18); for the period of Saul's reign (13:21) and of the number of conspirators against Paul (23:13, 21)! In any case, noting the duration of a sickness is common in healing narratives (Mark 5:25; 9:21; John 5:5; 9:1; Luke 8:43; 13:11; Acts 9:33); compare Philostratus, *Life of Apollonius of Tyana* 3:38.

INTERPRETATION

The best way to appreciate Luke's shaping of his story at this point is to step back and observe the sequence of events as a whole. We see that after showing us the community of believers who represent the restored Israel (2:42-47), Luke shifted our attention to the apostles: Peter and John heal the lame beggar at the gate of the temple (3:1-10), and Peter addresses the crowd that gathers with another speech calling for conversion, this one concluding with a threat as well as a promise (3:11-26). Now, in rapid sequence, Luke shows us the apostles brought to a hearing and dismissed (4:1-22), praying for and receiving power (4:23-31), working powerfully within the people (4:32–5:16), then brought to a second trial (5:17-42).

Luke forces our attention on the apostles in order to resolve the next issue in his story: the people have been restored within Jerusalem, but what is the legitimate leadership over Israel? Is it the leadership of the Sanhedrin that first rejected the prophet, or is it the leadership of the Twelve who are Jesus' prophetic successors? Will Jesus' prophecy that they were to "rule over the twelve tribes of Israel" (Luke 22:30) be fulfilled within the narrative? Luke will show us in this sequence how the apostles become the true leaders of the faithful Israel.

To do this, he employs the same literary pattern that I have so emphasized throughout this commentary, the pattern established by the prophet Moses. As we shall see in Stephen's speech, Moses was sent a first time to the people, and was rejected; he went away, was empowered by God, and returned to the people working signs and wonders; he was rejected a second time (Acts 7:17-44). We will also observe that Luke uses a similar pattern in his narration concerning the patriarch Joseph (Acts 7:9-16). And, throughout Luke's story of Jesus, we have seen the same pattern structuring Luke-Acts as a whole: the first sending of Jesus the prophet and his rejection; his empowerment in the resurrection and second sending through the apostles who work signs and wonders; their second offer of salvation with the mixed response of acceptance and rejection (see Introduction).

Now Luke uses a miniature version of the same pattern for the interaction of the apostles and the Jewish leaders. There is the first trial and rejection; the empowerment and works of wonder; then the second trial and a final closure. Within the overall story, then, we have this compressed drama, which will demonstrate two points: that the erstwhile leaders are being cut out of the people God is restoring, because they will not listen to "the prophet God has raised up" (in fulfillment of the programmatic prophecy of 3:23); and that the Twelve have in reality become the effective leaders of *ho laos*, the populace considered as "the people of God."

Once we grasp this pattern, we can better appreciate the details of the passage. We see, for example, the function of 4:1-4: Luke opposes the reaction of the common people to that of the leaders, continuing his theme of a division within the people. Many of the ordinary people who hear Peter's words believe, and the community grows to five thousand. It is only the leaders who are "upset" at the apostles and arrest them.

The stage is now set for the next sequence. We know that the people favor the apostles. But the leaders still have ostensible power.

In the confrontation itself, Luke draws the sharpest possible contrast between the apostles and the sanhedrin. The apostles fulfill Jesus' prediction concerning them that they will bear witness for him, and that their opponents will not be able to contradict them (Luke 21:13-15). What is particularly striking is the emphasis on the apostles' boldness (*parrēsia*). This is a characteristic of the philosopher that Luke joins to the image of the prophet. Peter and John speak and act with an openness and boldness at least equal to that of Jesus; indeed, they defend themselves in a way that Jesus (shockingly, for ancient critics) did not.

The prophetic Spirit, in other words, is *even more powerfully* at work in them because of the resurrection of Jesus. And the issue of rejection or acceptance of the prophet is stated even more sharply. Whereas Jesus had applied the "stone which the builders rejected" passage from Ps 117:22 to the leaders parabolically and obliquely in Luke 20:17-19, Peter casts it at these leaders directly: Jesus is the stone scorned *"by you the builders."* In contrast to his other kerygmatic statements, Peter does not end this one with a call to conversion. What use? The leaders responded to his last speech with his arrest! No, the leaders are cutting themselves out of the people by their refusal to heed the prophetic challenge; the string needs only to be played out.

In contrast to the burning simplicity of the apostles' prophetic/philosophical witness is the double-mindedness (we should say "bad faith") of the leaders. Luke's use of irony here is subtle. The leaders are upset because the apostles are proclaiming "in Jesus the resurrection of the dead" (4:2). Yet they cannot deny the evidence that resurrection power is at work through the apostles. The man has been cured: they see him standing there, they acknowledge that the whole city knows about it. And yet when they ask "what power or name" made him whole, and Peter answers that it is the power of the resurrected Jesus, they refuse to acknowledge it, even though Luke has them pay ironic tribute to the power of Jesus at work in the apostles: they can see the apostles do not have learning, yet they speak with boldness, so "they recognized they had been with Jesus"!

The end of the passage marks the contrast emphatically. Peter and John align themselves with the Socratic tradition of integrity: they must obey God rather than humans. They cannot stop speaking of "what they have seen and heard." But the leaders deny "what they have seen," the healed man in front of them; and they deny "what they have heard," the prophet's voice. They take refuge in political maneuvering; they cannot deny the reality of the healing, but they can engage in "damage control." They will not obey the prophet, but they can try to keep the word from spreading even further. They forbid the apostles to speak to anyone in Jesus' name. Will their power overcome that of the prophet? We must read on to see.

For Reference and Further Study

Jervell, J. "The Twelve on Israel's Thrones." *Luke and the People of God*. Minneapolis: Augsburg, 1972, 75–112.
Johnson, L. T. *The Literary Function of Possessions in Luke-Acts*. SBLDS 39. Missoula: Scholars Press, 1977, 46–47, 68–69, 192–193.
Marrow, S. B. "*Parrhēsia* and the New Testament." *CBQ* 44 (1982) 431–446.
Schenke, L. "Die Kontrastformel Apg 4, 10b." *BZ* n.s. 26 (1982) 1–20.
Schlier, H. "*Parrēsia*," *TDNT* 5 (1967) 871–886.
Tannehill, R. "The Composition of Acts 3–5: Narrative Development and Echo Effect." *SBL 1984 Seminar Papers*. Ed. K. H. Richards. Chico: Scholars Press, 1984, 217–240.

8. *The Power of the Apostles* (4:23–5:11)

23. When they had been released they went to their associates and told them everything the chief-priests and elders had said. 24. Those who heard it lifted a common voice to God. They said, "Master! You are the creator of the heaven and the earth and the sea and of all things that are in them. 25. You are the one who said—through the mouth of David your servant, our father, through the Holy Spirit—'Why were the nations arrogant and the peoples making silly schemes? 26. The kings of the earth drew up their lines and the rulers gathered together against the Lord and against his anointed one.' 27. For in this city they did truly gather together against your holy child Jesus whom you anointed: Herod, and Pontius Pilate, with the Gentiles and the peoples of Israel, 28. in order to accomplish everything your hand and your will had determined should happen. 29. And now, Lord, look at their threats! Enable your servants to speak your word with complete boldness 30. by stretching out your hand for healing and signs and wonders to be done through the name of your child Jesus." 31. And as they were praying, the place where they were gathered was shaken. They were all filled with the Holy Spirit and were speaking the word of God with boldness. 32. Now the assembly of believers had one heart and soul, nor did any one of them having something call it one's own. Instead, they had everything in common. 33. The apostles were bearing witness to the resurrection of the Lord Jesus with great power. And great favor was on all of them. 34.

Neither was anyone among them needy, for whoever owned fields or possessed houses sold them, and carrying the proceeds from the things sold, 35. laid them at the feet of the apostles. Then distribution was made to each one according to anyone's need. 36. Joseph, who was called Barnabas by the apostles (translated, the name means "son of consolation"), was a Levite, a Cypriot by birth. 37. He sold a field that he owned, brought the yield and laid it at the feet of the apostles. 5:1. But a certain man named Ananias, together with his wife Sapphira, sold some property 2. and with the collusion of his wife held something back from the profit. Bringing a certain portion he laid it at the feet of the apostles. 3. But Peter said, "Ananias, why has Satan filled your heart to falsify the Holy Spirit and hold back some of the price of the field? 4. Was it not yours before you sold it, and after you sold it, wasn't it in your control? Why then did you make this plan in your heart? You have not lied to humans but to God." 5. When Ananias heard these words he fell down dead. And everyone who heard of it felt great fear. 6. The younger men got up, wrapped him in a cloth, carried him out, and buried him. 7. After an interval of about three hours, his wife also came in, without knowing what had happened. 8. Peter responded to her, "Tell me whether you sold the field for such an amount." "Yes," she said, "for such an amount." 9. Peter said to her, "Why did you enter into agreement to test the Spirit of the Lord? Look, the feet of those who buried your husband are at the door, and they will carry you out." 10. At once she fell at his feet and died. When the young men came in they found her dead. They carried her out and buried her next to her husband. 11. Great fear came over the whole Church and over all who heard about these things.

Notes

23. *went to their associates:* The translation of *pros tous idious* (literally, "to their own") is both difficult and critical to the interpretation of the passage. Who is meant by those the RSV translates as "friends"? The community as a whole, or the other apostles? I translate "associates" because the literary logic of the passage in context demands seeing them as the apostles rather than the community as a whole.

24. *those who heard:* Codex D adds the pious phrase, "and recognizing the working of God," but the external attestation supports the shorter reading. Similarly, at the beginning of the prayer, Codex D adds *ho theos* ("God"), so that it reads, "Master you are the God who created."
    creator of the heaven and the earth: For the title "master" (*despotēs*), see the prayer in Luke 2:29. The designation of God as the creator of all is a biblical *topos* (e.g., Gen 14:19; Exod 20:11; Isa 37:16; LXX Ps 145:6), and is repeated almost verbatim in Acts 14:15 and 17:24.

25. *you are the one who said:* The text for this verse is very confusing, with a combination of excess phrases and unusual word order. In order to give a straight-

forward rendering in English, this translation shifts the attributive participle ("you are the one who said") to the beginning of the sentence, and places the doubled qualifying phrases between dashes ("through the mouth/through the Holy Spirit" and "your servant-child [*pais*]/our father"). The idea that God spoke through the psalms of David has already been well established (Luke 24:44; Acts 1:16; 2:25, 30-31).

why were the nations arrogant: This is a direct citation from LXX Ps 2:1-2, with no authorial emendations. Luke will have Paul quote directly from Psalm 2:7 in Acts 13:33 (see also Heb 1:5; 5:5). The verb *phruassō* is normally used in the middle voice for the noise made by whinnying horses and by extension to human wild, wanton, or arrogant behavior (see LXX 2 Macc 7:34; 3 Macc 2:2, and the use of the noun *phruagma* in LXX Hos 4:11; Zech 11:3; Jer 12:5; Ezek 7:24; 24:21). The translation of *ethnē* as "nations" rather than as "Gentiles" is appropriate to the psalm, although Luke's pesher adaptation will require an alteration.

making silly schemes: Or: "pursue empty things." The verb *meletaō* means to "take care for" or "pursue" (compare Josh 1:8; Job 27:4; LXX Ps 1:2; 34:28; Isa 59:3; 1 Tim 4:15). This first line of the psalm is explicated by the second.

26. *and against his anointed one:* One could also translate, "and against his messiah" (*kata tou christou autou*) which is precisely the way Luke is reading the psalm. As in Peter's Pentecost speech (2:25-35), a psalm of David is opened to a messianic reading. The late rabbinic *Midrash Tehillim* on Psalm 2 applies the words "against his anointed" to the revolt against Aaron in the past (3) or against the "lord Messiah in the time-to-come" (3), perhaps in battle against Gog and Magog (4).

27. *did truly gather together:* Luke applies the words of the psalm point by point to the passion of Jesus and the circumstances of the community. This style of interpretation most resembles the pesher-midrash carried out at the Qumran community (see especially 1QpHab, 4QpNah, and 4QpPs37). The plausibility of the application is heightened by Luke's use of the same verb in his narrative for the "gathering together" (*synagō*, Luke 22:66; Acts 4:5) as is used in the psalm.

against your holy child: Here *pais* appears again as a title for Jesus, whereas in 4:25, it was used of David. On the meaning of the term, see the note on 3:13 and 3:16. As in 3:14, Jesus is also here called "holy" (*hagios*).

whom you anointed: The use of *chriō* is striking, reminding us of the virtually etymological sense in which Luke understands Jesus to be "messiah = anointed" (compare Luke 4:18 and Acts 10:38, as well as Luke 9:20).

Herod and Pontius Pilate: Herod fills the role of "the kings" in the pesher interpretation. Only in Luke's Gospel does Herod play a role in the passion account (Luke 23:7, 8, 11, 12, 15). Pilate, of course, fills the role of "the rulers" as he does also in the passion narrative (Luke 23:1-6, 11-13, 24, 52).

Gentiles: The same Greek word (*ethnē*) is used here as was translated "nations" in the psalm citation. The reason for the shift is that Luke in his application is clearly thinking of "representatives" of the nations as individual figures playing a role in Jesus' death (see Luke 23:47; Acts 2:23), rather than "the nations" as entities.

peoples of Israel: A similar judgment must be made about the odd plural "peoples." Some *mss* have the singular, but the plural is better attested, and as the obviously harder reading, to be preferred. It is a harder reading because, as we have seen, Luke in his passion account tries to eliminate "the people" from participation in the passion of Jesus (see only Luke 23:13). Acts, it is true, is more straightforward in its charge against the people as a whole (2:23, 36; 3:13-14). Why then the plural? The most obvious reason is to retain the words in the form of the citation (important for pesher-style interpretation). But the plural also enables Luke to involve *individual* Jews in the death of Jesus (such as the rulers), as he does individual Gentiles, without jeopardizing the special place of "the people" as a religious designation for Israel.

29. *look at their threats:* The term apeilē picks up the "threat" (*apeileō*) levelled against the apostles by the Sanhedrin in 4:17, and makes the transition from the suffering of Jesus at the hands of rulers, to the present suffering of the community in the person of the apostles: the rulers are "gathering" against them as well (4:5); the succession of prophets is marked by rejection and suffering as much as by wonderworking.

enable your servants: Literally, "give to your servants to." In this case "servant" is *doulos* (see Luke 12:37, 43-47; 17:7-10; Acts 2:18; 16:17) rather than *pais*. For "boldness" (*parrēsia*) as a prophetic/philosophical quality, see the note on 4:13.

30. *stretching out your hand:* Luke uses a common biblical idiom for the use of power (see LXX Ps 54:20; 137:7; Sir 7:32) as he does also in v. 28, above. Of particular interest is the association of this expression with Moses and the "signs and wonders" he performed in the Exodus (see Exod 3:20; 4:4; 6:8; 7:5, etc.).

healing and signs and wonders: The "healing" (*iasis*) picks up the event that started this sequence, the healing of the lame beggar at the gate of the temple (3:1-10). "Signs and wonders," on the other hand, is Luke's signature phrase for identifying the work of the prophetic Spirit (2:19, 22, 43; 4:16, 22). Following the phrase "stretching out your hand" with its Mosaic connections, the prophetic imagery is obvious.

31. *place . . . was shaken:* As at Pentecost, there is both a physical and linguistic sign of the Spirit's coming in power. It is obvious that for one to "speak the word of God" when filled with the Holy Spirit is essentially to play the role of prophet (see Deut 18:19; Amos 1:1; 3:1; 4:1; 7:16; Mic 1:1; Joel 1:1; Jonah 1:1; Zech 1:1; Isa 1:10; 28:14). The qualification that they spoke this word "with boldness" indicates that the power they prayed for was granted (see v. 29).

32. *assembly of believers:* The connective *de* is here translated as "now," to suggest the sort of narrative transition Luke seems to intend, from the empowerment of the apostles to the demonstration of that power within the community of believers (*hoi pisteusantes* = those who had come to believe). As at several

other places in Luke-Acts, the term *plēthos* invites translation in the more technical sense of "assembly" rather than "multitude" (compare Luke 8:37; 23:1; Acts 6:2; 14:4).

one heart and soul: The presence of the Hellenistic *topos* on friendship is obvious (see notes on 2:42-47). The idea that "friends are one soul (*mia psychē*)" is attested as early as Euripides, *Orestes* 1046, and is quoted as proverbial by Aristotle, *Nichomachean Ethics* 1168B. See also Plutarch, *On Having Many Friends* 8 [*Mor.* 96F], and generally for the theme of "likeness" in friendship, see Plato, *Lysis* 214B; Cicero, *On Friendship* 14, 50; 19, 69; 21, 80. This distinctive way of envisaging friendship, with its implications for sharing possessions, is for the most part absent from the Old Testament. The phrase *mia psychē* does appear as the translation of the Hebrew *leb yaḥad* in 1 Chr 12:38, and the phrase, "heart and soul" is frequent enough (see Deut 6:5; 10:12; 11:13, etc.), but the connection of "one soul" with "holding all things in common" is so frequent in the Hellenistic literature, that there can be no doubt Luke is appropriating that tradition; indeed, the addition of "heart" in this case may serve to provide a more biblical feel.

had everything in common: The phrase is identical to that used in 2:44; for the location of the proverb "friends hold all things in common," see the note on that verse. Here the specification that "none called anything he had his own" especially echoes passages like Plato, *Critias* 110C-D. The phrase also introduces an element of complexity: ownership was not utterly renounced (see 5:4), but all grasping onto individual possessiveness was.

33. *bearing witness to the resurrection:* The verse is not misplaced, as we might at first think, for Luke intends to place the apostles into the middle of the community's life, so that "authority" and "possessions" will again reinforce each other. The "great power" of their proclamation is matched by their place in the collection and distribution of the community goods. The translation here reflects the most likely text, although the word order of the Greek is unusual, leading to several textual variants (compare 4:2).

great favor was on all of them: In contrast to 2:47, where the community was said to enjoy *charis* "with the whole people," the construction with *epi* here, and the context, suggests another meaning, that they enjoyed the favor of God, as in LXX Exod 3:21: "I will show favor to this people" (see also 11:3; 12:36, and especially 33:12-13 and Ps 83:11). The two notions are complementary, but the emphasis here, as the next note suggests, is on God's blessing rather than human approval.

34. *anyone among them needy:* The use of *endeēs* ("needy") makes this an allusion to Deut 15:4: "When the Lord God blesses you in your land, there will be no needy person (*endeēs*) among you." Deut 15:5 states the condition for this blessing: "When you obey the voice of the Lord your God to keep all these commandments that I have commanded you this day." The commandments in question had to do with the sharing of possessions (Deut 15:1-18). The messianic community has "heard the voice of the prophet" and has shared its possessions, and thereby is enjoying the blessings promised by God. The

idealized character of this is suggested by the distribution "according as any had need" (4:35; see 2:45), and from the evidence offered by 6:1 and 11:27-30. The Rabbinic midrash on Deut 15, in fact, found the same tension between this promise of no need (15:5), and the continuing presence of the poor person in Israel (15:7); see *Sifre on Deuteronomy.*

35. *at the feet of the apostles:* The phrase is repeated three times (see 4:36; 5:2), and represents a significant departure from the summary in 2:42-47. In the biblical idiom, "being at the feet" of another means to be in a state of submission or obedience (see Josh 10:24; 1 Sam 25:24, 41; 2 Sam 22:39; Pss 8:7; 17:10; 46:4; 98:5; 131:7; 109:1). Luke uses the language the same way (Luke 7:38, 44-46; 8:35, 41; 10:39; 17:16; Acts 10:25; 22:3). To lay something at the feet of another is therefore the body language of self-disposition spelled out by possessions, specifically a statement acknowledging the power and authority of another over the self and what one has. The apostles are now placed at the center of the community collection (and, by implication) dispersal of goods.

36. *called Barnabas by the apostles:* Compare the story of Matthias' election in 1:23. The "translation" is linguistically faulty (the name actually means "son of Nebo"), but is thematically apposite: Barnabas is indeed a character who will be a "consoler/advocate" as he works as a mediator between Paul and the Jerusalem community (9:27; 11:22, 30; 12:25). His introduction at precisely this point in the narrative is not accidental. We know that in the biblical idiom, the giving of a name to others signifies having authority over them (see e.g., Gen 2:19; 17:5; 19:39; 25:26, 36; also *Joseph and Aseneth* 15:7). Barnabas is therefore shown to be doubly submissive to the apostles: he receives a new name from them and lays his possessions at their feet.

    levite, a Cypriot by birth: The tribe of Levi was dedicated to the Lord, and since "their portion is the Lord" (Deut 12:12; 14:29; Josh 14:3, 4; 18:7), the tradition was that they held no land, even though Josh 21:1-41 catalogues the cities and properties supposedly given to them from the lands of other tribes. By NT times, Jews who traced their descent to Levi certainly held property (Josephus, *Life* 68-83). The fact that Barnabas was from Cyprus connects him to the missionaries from there (Acts 11:19-20; 21:16) and fitted him to be Paul's companion for the first missionary trip there (Acts 13:4). It is also the place to which he returned after his dispute with Paul (15:39). For the flourishing Jewish population in Cyprus, see Josephus, *Antiquities of the Jews* 13:285-288.

37. *brought the yield:* Luke uses the term *chrēma* here ("money/yield"), which is roughly equivalent to *tima* ("worth/price"), used in 4:34 and 5:2. Barnabas' action is the sort of specific action which appears to form the basis for Luke's summaries.

5:1 *with his wife Sapphira:* The couple is associated throughout the story, for the essence of their action is conspiracy. Thus, she "colluded" in the fraud (5:2) and perpetuated it (5:8). In dramatic terms, the presence of Sapphira enables Luke to suggest a shadow counter-community of avarice, over against the spirit-community that shares its possessions.

sold some property: The term *ktēma* is used equivalently with *chōrion* ("field") in 5:8. Their action of selling and donating mimics that of Barnabas and the other believers (4:35, 37).

2. *held back something from the profit:* The verb *nosphizomai* is at home in contexts of financial fraud (see 2 Macc 4:32). The LXX usage that draws the reader's attention is Josh 7:1, the story of Achan. After Israel conquered Jericho, its inhabitants and goods were placed under the "ban" (*ḥerem*). But "they kept something back" (*enosphisanto*) from those possessions dedicated to the Lord. Structurally, Luke's story bears a strong resemblance to that in Joshua 7:1-26.

3. *Satan filled your heart:* In the case of Judas also, betrayal was attributed to Satan's entering his heart (Luke 22:3), and his apostasy was expressed through the purchase of property of his own (Acts 1:18, 25). Jesus had warned Peter that "Satan will seek you out" (22:31) and in such "testing of the Spirit" (5:9) we find Peter "strengthening his brethren" (22:32). Satan is no match for the Spirit-filled Peter. As in the Gospel, the ability to see into the hearts of others is the mark of a prophet (Luke 5:22; 7:39; 9:47; 24:38; *Joseph and Aseneth* 23:8).

to falsify the Holy Spirit: The Greek can be rendered "lie to (against) the Holy Spirit," but the use of *pseudomai* with the accusative can mean "falsify," and that seems the sense intended here; by their behavior, they counterfeit the actions generated by the Spirit, thus they "falsify" the Spirit's work. In the next verse, by contrast, the verb governs the dative case, and "lie" is a better translation.

4. *in your control:* The sentence is difficult mainly because of its pregnant construction, literally, "remaining it remained to you; sold, it was in your authority." The sharing of goods, we see, was voluntary. Ananias neither had to sell nor to share. Not ownership of property is the fault, but conspiracy which shatters the unity of the church and threatens the prophetic authority of the Twelve.

make this plan: A double level of intentionality runs through the story. At one level the battle is between the cosmic forces of the Holy Spirit (leading to sharing) and Satan (leading to fraud); people are "filled" with one or the other. At the other level, human freedom is invoked: Ananias could have kept his property, yet he "made this plan" with his wife. Such is the tension in religious narratives, made explicit in Peter's statement, "You have not lied to humans but to God."

5. *fell down dead:* Literally, "having fallen down, he expired." Luke uses *ekpsychō* here and for the death of Sapphira in 5:10. It is used by the LXX for the death of Sisera in Judg 4:21. Peter does not strike him dead. Nor does he pronounce a judgment of death. But on hearing his prophetic declaration, Ananias dies.

6. *the younger men:* We have no information as to who these might be or what their role was. Luke probably does not intend a technical designation, since *neōteroi* is used here and *neaniskoi* is used in 5:10. Perhaps they are simply

the youthful men who can do the heavy work of lifting, carrying, and burying. There may be, however, a further echo of the Achan story in the Book of Joshua. When Joshua decrees the ban, those who take out the family of Rahab and "set them outside the camp of Israel" are called the *neaniskoi* (Josh 6:23; see the antecedents for the removal from the camp in Lev 10:4).

7. *without knowing:* The contrast with v. 2 ("with the collusion of his wife") is deliberate. The conspiracy is broken by the prophetic judgment of Peter. Sapphira is in ignorance of what happened to her co-conspirator.

9. *enter into agreement:* Literally, "why was it agreed upon among you?" The term *symphōneō* is ironic. Their "harmony" in collusion was a mockery of the "one soul" that led the community to share its possessions in common.

    test the Spirit of the Lord: The theme of "testing the Lord" is connected with the wilderness part of the Exodus story (Exod 17:2, 7; 20:20; Num 14:22; Deut 33:8; LXX Pss 77:41, 56; 94:9; 105:14), and therefore to the imagery of the prophet like Moses (see Luke 4:2; 11:16; Acts 15:10). Note that it is not Peter the person, but the prophetic *Spirit* that comes from "the Lord" who is being tested.

10. *fell at his feet:* The irony of Sapphira's unintended obeisance to the apostle is surely deliberate. They falsified the gesture of genuine submission when they laid only a portion of their possessions "at the feet of the apostles," and now the conspirators fall "at the feet" of the apostles whose authority they had challenged.

11. *fear came over the whole Church:* The response of fear/awe is frequent in Luke-Acts (see Luke 1:12, 65; 2:9; 7:16; 8:37; Acts 19:17, and especially the earlier summary, 2:43). In the present story, this is the second time the response of fear is noted (see 5:5), and adds "the whole Church" to the sentence "fear fell on all who heard." This is the first use of the term *ekklēsia* in Luke-Acts (in contrast to Matt 16:18; 18:17). It corresponds well to the *plēthos tōn pisteusantōn* ("assembly of believers") in 4:32, with which it brackets the section. Luke's use of the term throughout the rest of Acts maintains the sense of the "assembly of God" found also in Paul (see 1 Thess 1:1; 1 Cor 1:2; 2 Cor 1:1). It is the realization of the *qahal Yahweh,* the assembly of the people of God (see LXX Deut 4:10; 9:10; 18:16; 23:1; Josh 9:2; Judg 20:2; Pss 21:22, 25; 25:12; 34:18; 39:9; 67:26); as the LXX of Deut 31:12 combines the terms: *ekklēsiasas ton laon,* "having churched the people!"

INTERPRETATION

Luke has shown how God fulfilled his promise to Abraham by establishing within Jerusalem a Jewish people enjoying the blessings of the Spirit. But the question next requiring answer concerns the leadership over this restored Israel. Will it be those "leaders of the people"—above all the chief priests and members of the Sanhedrin—who put the prophet to death in his first visitation? They certainly seem to be in charge. Or will it be the apostles whom Jesus said would "rule over the twelve tribes of Israel" (Luke 22:30)? Luke has focused his reader's attention on this issue, by following the apostles from their healing of the lame beggar (3:1-10) to their first hearing before the Sanhedrin (4:4-22). They were sent away by the leaders with the stern warning to cease preaching. But Peter declared they would obey God rather than humans. The battle between leaders is joined; who will emerge as the effective rulers of the restored Israel?

In the sequence we now examine, Luke provides the answer to that question. If we are to grasp his literary intention, we must first answer correctly the puzzle presented immediately by 4:23. When Luke says that Peter and John left the Sanhedrin and returned *pros tous idious* ("to their own"), whom does he mean? We must understand this to refer to the other apostles, rather than the community as a whole. The subsequent events therefore concern the apostolic circle.

As Moses was rejected a first time, then withdrew to be empowered by God, before being sent back in a second visitation with even greater power (Acts 7:17-44), and as Jesus was rejected a first time, then withdrew in order to be enthroned at God's right hand, so that he could empower his followers with the Spirit in a second visitation of the people, so we see the apostles repulsed in the first hearing, then withdrawing. Now, like Moses and Jesus, they are empowered (4:23-31).

In the prayer of the apostles, we can observe once more how Luke's midrash of the Septuagint contemporizes the texts of the psalms, first with reference to the suffering of Jesus, and then with reference to the threats being made against them (4:24-28). What they ask for in prayer is *power*, expressed by the imagery of God's outstretched hand, and to be manifested in healing, signs and wonders—the signs of the Spirit's presence in prophets (4:29-30). The apostles then receive an additional outpouring of the Spirit that enables them to proclaim the word with the quality that had they had requested, prophetic boldness (*parrēsia*, 4:31). Shortly, we will see this power demonstrated in public among the people (5:12-16), and observe the climactic confrontation between the Twelve and the erstwhile leaders (5:17-42). That confrontation will provide his complete answer as to who are the leaders over Israel.

But before that, Luke shows his readers how powerfully the leadership of the Twelve is being exercised within the nucleus of the restored Israel, the messianic community (4:32–5:11). We notice that this section is bracketed by the terms "assembly of believers" (4:32) and "Church" (5:11). As with the summary of 2:42-47, Luke opens a window on the inner life of the first community. But in contrast to that first summary, the entire point of this one is to show the authority of the apostles. After having read this much of Luke-Acts, we are no longer surprised to find him using his favorite symbolism for relationships and power, the use of possessions.

There are some small touches concerning the community as a whole. Luke continues to exploit the Hellenistic *topos* of friendship by saying that all the believers were "one mind and heart" (4:32), for one of the classic definitions of friends was that they were "one mind" (see Notes). He also continues to portray the first community in terms suggesting the ideal realization of the people of God: thus, they have "great favor" shown to them by God (4:33), and the sign of this is that there is "no needy person" among them (4:34; see Deut 15:4 and Notes). The primitive community in Jerusalem, Luke tells us, realizes for a moment the best ideals both of Hellenism and Judaism concerning life together.

But now we see the apostles situated at the very center of this community sharing. The statement that they were witnessing with great power (4:33) is a deliberate intercalation into the description of sharing, joining the spiritual authority of the apostles to this community activity. Then, in 4:35, the believers who have sold property are shown "laying at the feet of the apostles" the proceeds, which are then dispersed according to need. No more graphic image can be imagined for the community's recognition of the apostles' authority.

The generalized picture given by the summary is given sharp and specific definition by the actions (positive and negative) of Barnabas (4:36-37), and of Ananias and Sapphira (5:1-11). In opposite ways, these vignettes use the language of possessions to converge at the same point concerning the prophetic authority of the apostles.

Barnabas will play a key role later in Acts as the person who mediates between Paul and the Jerusalem Church, and therefore between the restored people within Judaism and "the people for his name" God will choose from among the Gentiles (Acts 15:14). Since his narrative role is to provide continuity, Luke appropriately and typically assures the reader first of Barnabas' utter submission to the Twelve. He does this in twofold fashion, by having the symbolic name "son of consolation" given to him by the apostles, and by having him "lay at the feet of the apostles" the profit from the property he sold (4:36-37). When Barnabas next appears in the story it is as an advocate for the dangerous Paul (9:27). In the light of what Luke has told us here, neither the Twelve nor the reader can doubt Barnabas' trustworthiness in that task.

The story of Ananias and Sapphira makes the same point about the apostles' authority through negative example. Several elements in Luke's account (see Notes) remind us of the story of Achan in the Book of Joshua, when in defiance of the command to place all the inhabitants and goods of Jericho under the ban, Achan held something back for himself (7:1). Israel therefore suffered at the hands of its enemies (7:13). God tells Joshua that the one who committed the offense must himself be placed under the ban, that is, be destroyed. After a ritual process of elimination, Achan is identified, and Joshua demands from him the truth. Achan confesses (7:19) and is then stoned to death by the entire community (7:25).

These elements are common to both stories: a deceitful holding back of goods, a confrontation with God's spokesperson, and the cutting of the miscreants from the people by death. But there are also these important differences: a) the property of the Christian community is not itself called sacred, or under the ban; b) in confrontation with Peter not the truth but a lie is told; c) the community is not said to suffer any hardship because of the fraudulent action; d) there is no stoning by the community as a whole but merely the prophetic word of the apostle. The detailed allusions and structural similarities do suggest, however, that Luke used the story of Achan as a rough model for his own. Certainly he was giving a similar message: the misappropriation of possessions was an offense against the community and against God and required punishment of the most radical sort. But in Luke's story, Peter's role is much greater than was Joshua's, and the offense is understood much more specifically as a "testing of the spirit" at work in the apostles, that is, as a direct challenge to their authority.

The community was constituted as "one mind and heart" by the Spirit of God. It was the Spirit that led them to call nothing their own and share all their possessions. But this couple "falsified the Spirit" in the first place by their breaking the unanimity of intention; they "colluded" in their action. They were hoping that by counterfeiting the gesture, they could both partake of the community life and "hold back something of their own." Once more, Luke uses the language of possessions to express self-disposition. Like Judas, this couple had Satan enter their hearts; like Judas, they broke fellowship by seeking something of their own.

The couple's biggest mistake, however, was in thinking that they were dealing simply with another human gathering. They did not recognize that they were "lying to God, not to humans." And as an essential element in this error, they failed to recognize that the apostles were not simply human administrators who could be fooled by the gesture of "laying possessions at their feet." They did not recognize that God is the "knower of hearts" and that by testing these apostles they were challenging *prophets*; Peter meets the challenge easily. He shows himself to be a prophet by cutting through their conspiracy: he can read their hearts and knows before they can even speak a lie that they have "falsified the Spirit" by their fraud. The power of his prophetic presence is so palpable that when he states the truth to each of the conspirators, they die.

Luke has shown us within the messianic community the fulfillment of his programmatic prophecy in Acts 3:19-23. Those who "listen to the voice of the prophet" whom God raised up by obeying the apostles are sharing in the promised blessings. But those who do "not listen to that prophet" are being "destroyed from the people." All who hear it are afraid. The Church is in fear. But will the authority of the prophets over the people still be stifled by the physical might of the erstwhile leaders in the Sanhedrin? In the next sequence, Luke returns the reader to the impact made by the apostles among the larger population as they return from their empowerment with further "signs and wonders" (5:12-16), and to their final confrontation with the leaders (5:17-42).

FOR REFERENCE AND FURTHER STUDY

Brock, S. "Barnabas, *huios paraklēseōs.*" *JTS* 25 (1974) 93–98.

Capper, B. "The Interpretation of Acts 5:4." *JSNT* 19 (1983) 117–131.

Degenhardt, H.-J. *Lukas Evangelist der Armen.* Stuttgart: Katholisches Bibelwerk, 1965, 165–171.

Derrett, J. M. D. "Ananias, Sapphira, and the Right of Property." *Downside Review* 89 (1971) 225–232.

Dupont, J. "Community of Goods in the Early Church." *Salvation of the Gentiles.* Ed. J. Keating. New York: Paulist Press, 1979, 85–102.

_____. "L'Union entre les premières chrétiennes dans les Actes des Apôtres." *NRT* 91 (1969) 898–915.

_____. "La prière des apôtres persecutés (Actes 4, 23-31)." *Etudes sur les Actes des Apôtres.* Lectio Divina 45. Paris: Editions du Cerf, 1967, 521–522.

Gerhardsson, B. "Einige Bemerkungen zu Apg. 4:32." *ST* 24 (1970) 142–149.

Horn, F. W. *Glaube und Handeln in der Theologie des Lukas.* Göttinger Theologische Arbeiten 26. Göttingen: Vandenhoeck & Ruprecht, 1983, 35–49.

Menoud, Ph.-H. "La Mort d'Ananias et de Sapphira (Actes 5:1-11)." *Aux Sources de la Tradition Chrétienne.* Biblioteque Théologique. Neuchatel: Delachaux et Nièstle, 1950, 146–154.

9. *The Second Trial* (5:12-42)

12. Many signs and wonders were done among the people through the hands of the apostles. They all were together at Solomon's Portico, 13. and none of the rest dared to approach them. But the people exalted them. 14. And so great grew the number of those believing in the Lord, multitudes of both men and women, 15. that they even carried out the sick into the streets and put them on cots and pallets, so that when Peter

passed by even his shadow might fall on them. 16. Indeed, gatherings from towns around Jerusalem came together, carrying sick people and those afflicted with unclean spirits. All of them were healed. 17. But the chief priest rose up and with him all those of the Sadducean school. They were filled with envy. 18. They arrested the apostles and put them in the public jail. 19. But during the night an angel of the Lord opened the doors of the jail. As he led them out he said to them: 20. "Go! Stand in the temple! Speak to the people all the words about this life!" 21. They listened and they went about dawn into the temple and began teaching. Now when the chief priest and his associates arrived, they called together the Sanhedrin and the whole council of the children of Israel. They sent to the jail for them to be brought. 22. But when the attendants got there, they did not find them in the jail. They went back and announced, 23. "We found the jail securely locked and the guards standing by the doors. But when we opened up we found no one inside." 24. When they heard these words, the officer of the temple and the chief priest were perplexed by them: what might happen next? 25. But someone arrived to tell them, "Look, the men you put in prison are standing in the temple and teaching the people." 26. Then the officer went off with his assistants. They led them back, but not with force, for they feared that the people might stone them. 27. They brought them in and stood them before the Sanhedrin. The chief priest questioned them: 28. "We strictly ordered you to stop teaching in this name. And look! You have filled Jerusalem with your teaching. And you are set on bringing down on us this man's blood!" 29. Peter and the apostles answered, "It is necessary to obey God rather than humans. 30. The God of our fathers raised up Jesus whom you killed by hanging him on the tree. 31. Him God has exalted to his right hand as leader and savior, to give repentance and forgiveness of sins to Israel. 32. And we are witnesses of these things, as well as the Holy Spirit whom God has given to those who obey him." 33. Those who heard were enraged and wanted to kill them. 34. But a certain Pharisee stood up in the Sanhedrin. His name was Gamaliel. He was a teacher of the law respected by all the people. He ordered the men to be put outside for a short time. 35. Then he said to them, "Israelites, watch carefully what you are about to do with these fellows. 36. For before these days Theudas rose up saying about himself that he was somebody. About four hundred men joined him. He was killed and all those who obeyed him were dispersed and came to nothing. 37. After him, Judas the Galilean rose up in the days of the census and led a people in revolt. Then he perished and all those who obeyed him were scattered. 38. Now concerning these present matters, I tell you: withdraw from these people and let them be. Because if this plan or this work is from humans it will be destroyed. 39. But if it is from God, you will not be able to destroy them, and will find yourselves fighting God!" They heeded him. 40. They summoned the apostles. They beat them, commanded them not to speak in the name of Jesus, and released them. 41. They left the Sanhedrin rejoicing because they had been considered worthy of being despised in behalf of the name. 42. Through every day in the temple and in houses they did not cease teaching and preaching the good news that the Messiah was Jesus.

NOTES

12. *signs and wonders:* For the literary significance of the phrase, see the note on Acts 1:19. The apostles now demonstrate even more spectacularly the fulfillment of the prayer in 4:30.

    they were all together: The implied subject of the sentence is "the apostles." Luke's focus remains on them as it has since 3:1, rather than on the community as such. The mention of Solomon's Portico establishes a connection to 3:11, and sets up the later statement in 5:25.

13. *none of the rest dared to approach them:* This text is ordinarily regarded as so difficult that it has generated emendations and "back translations" into Aramaic. The difficulty, however, is a false one caused by two errors: a) reading "they were all" in 5:12 as though it applied to the entire community rather than the apostles; b) reading the verb *kollasthai* as though it were a technical term for "joining the community." Based on these misjudgments, a conflict is perceived: v. 13 seems to say no one joined, yet v. 14 says the community grew. In fact, there is no contradiction. The LXX uses *kollaomai* for a variety of "adherences," according to context, from "allegiance to the Lord" (Deut 6:13; 10:20; 2 Kgs 18:6) to a neutral "physical proximity" (Deut 28:16; 29:20; Ruth 2:8, 21; 2 Kgs 5:27; Sir 19:2). Luke also uses the term flexibly and by no means as a technical expression for conversion (even in Acts 17:4); see Luke 10:11; 15:15; Acts 8:29; 9:16; 10:28. If, in fact, we read "they were all" as meaning the apostles, and "the rest" as referring to everyone else who was afraid to approach the apostles physically—not surprisingly in light of the Ananias story—the text makes perfect sense. The apostles appear as numinous figures, and like the *mysterium tremendum et fascinosum*, they both repel and attract.

14. *so great grew the number:* This verse also provides options for translation, depending on whether the phrase *tō̧ kyriō̧* ("in the Lord") is taken with "added to" or "believing in." The RSV, for example, translates, "More than ever, believers were added to the Lord." The present translation tries to take seriously the *mallon . . . hōste* construction of the sentence.

15. *sick into the streets:* The scene is reminiscent of those concerning the healing ministry of Jesus in Luke 4:40; 5:19; 6:18-19, but even heightened. "Cots" is *klinaria*, a diminutive of *klinē* which Luke had preferred in the story of the healed paralytic in Luke 5:18. "Pallet" is *krabbaton* which was used by Mark 2:4-12 and John 5:8-11 in their versions of the paralytic's healing (see also Acts 9:33).

    even his shadow might fall on one of them: Literally, "his shadow might overshadow." For the resonances of *episkiazein* in the LXX, see the note on Luke

1:35. The image of healing by sheer presence here is striking and perhaps even shocking. Nothing in the Gospel tradition is close to it, except perhaps the healing of the woman by touching Jesus' garment (Luke 8:43), or the healing of the centurion's slave at long distance (Luke 7:1-10). The divine *dynamis* is so powerfully present in Peter that it radiates automatically. The closest image in Hellenistic literature may be in the inscriptions and accounts connected to healing shrines such as Epidaurus, where the presence of the suppliant in the healing space is itself sometimes efficacious (see, e.g., Aelius Aristides, *The Sacred Tales* 2:71; 3:22). Certainly within Luke's own work, however, the divine *skia* is powerful in its effect, as we see from the annunciation (Luke 1:35) and the transfiguration (9:34). Codex D amplifies the verse in anticipation of v. 16: "they were being set free from every illness that each one of them had."

16. *gatherings from towns:* The connective "Indeed" in the translation tries to capture the sense of the literal: "But even the multitude (*to plēthos*) from the cities (*poleis*) around Jerusalem came together." No English translation can be both precise and idiomatic. For "unclean spirits" as the work of Satan in humans, and Jesus' ministry as one of liberating humans from them, see Luke 4:33, 36; 6:18; 8:29; 9:42; 11:24.

17. *rose up:* This is a biblicism (see Gen 22:3), which functions as a sort of transition; Luke uses it from time to time (Luke 1:39; 15:18, 20; 23:1; Acts 9:18; 14:20; 22:10). The sentence could as easily be translated, "The chief priest and those with him . . . were filled with envy."

Sadducean school: The term *hairesis* has its original sense of a "choice" of school or party within a larger tradition. In Greek philosophy, it was used for one's allegiance to a particular set of teachings and traditions (see, e.g., Diogenes Laertius, *Lives of Eminent Philosophers* 1:18, 20). Josephus uses the term for his description of the "sects" within Judaism (*Jewish War* 2:118-119). Luke will use it also for the Pharisees (Acts 15:5; 26:5) and for the Christian movement itself, thereby capturing precisely the place of this messianic movement within first-century Judaism (Acts 24:5, 14; 28:22). For the connections of the Sadducees to the wealthy and aristocratic class, see Josephus, *Antiquities* 13:298; 18:17.

filled with envy: Luke uses the term *zēlos* which could be distinguished theoretically from *phthonos*, (as in Aristotle, *Rhetoric* 1388A-B), but often was used synonymously (Plato, *Symposium* 213D; Plutarch, *On Brotherly Love* 14 [*Mor.*485D-E]). Luke's attribution of this vice to the leaders taps into a Hellenistic *topos* on envy, which consistently connects envy with the urge to kill (Plato, *Laws* 869E-870A; Plutarch, *On Brotherly Love* 17 [*Mor.*487F]). This commonplace is taken over in Hellenistic Jewish literature (Wis 2:24; Philo, *On Joseph* 12; *Testament of Simeon* 2:7, 11). Luke will later apply it as well to the brothers of Joseph (Acts 7:9) and to the Jews who oppose Paul (Acts 17:5).

18. *in the public jail:* Three terms are used more or less equivalently in the passage: *dēmosia, phylakē* (v. 19), and *desmōtērion* (v. 21). If we had to distinguish them, the first would be roughly equivalent to "city hall," the second to "the

guard house," and the third, to "the lock-up." As in contemporary usage, the distinctions are irrelevant. Codex D adds the colorful but irrelevant detail concerning members of the Sanhedrin "and each one of them went to his own place (*ta idia*)."

19. *angel of the Lord:* These messengers from God play an important role through substantial portions of Luke-Acts (Luke 1:11, 26; 2:9, 13; 22:43; 24:23; Acts 8:26; 10:3, 7, 22; 11:13; 12:7-15, 23; 27:23). Luke will narrate more elaborate escapes from prison for Peter in 12:6-11 and for Paul in 16:26-31. The present account has perhaps its strongest parallel in Euripides' *Bacchae*, which portrays the followers of the cult of Bacchus persecuted by a leader. He seeks to stop the movement by imprisoning its followers (346-357), and one of its leaders (510-519). But the cult-followers are freed from prison by Bacchus himself (615-640).

20. *words about this life:* Literally, "words of this life." The phrase is unusual, but can be compared to Paul's statement in 13:26, "word of this salvation." Jesus is called "author of life" in 3:14.

21. *Sanhedrin and the whole council:* The terms *synedrion* (which is used in Luke 22:66; Acts 4:15; 6:12, 15; 22:30; 23:1, 6, 15, 20, 28; 24:20) and *gerousia* (which Luke uses only here, although he uses the synonym *presbyterion* in Luke 22:66; Acts 22:5) are more or less equivalent. Luke uses them in combination for the sake of solemnity: he wants to emphasize the formality of the leaders' rejection, and also their humiliation.

24. *were perplexed:* The verb is *diaporeō*, as in Luke 9:7 and Acts 2:12. The "officer of the temple" (*stratēgos tou hierou*) is appropriately reintroduced at this point (see 4:1), since it is his "assistants" (*hypēretai*, translated elsewhere as attendants or ministers), who must go to the temple to coax back the apostles.

26. *feared that the people might stone them:* Literally, "feared lest (*mē*) they be stoned"; for stoning as a punishment for blasphemy, see the note on Luke 13:34. The theme of the leadership's fear of "the people" (*ho laos*) goes back to the Jerusalem section of the Gospel (Luke 20:19; 22:2). Nothing could better indicate: a) the division between the leadership and the people; b) the prestige of the apostles in the peoples' eyes (it is blasphemy to oppose them); c) the fact that effective power over the populace has passed to the apostles.

28. *we strictly ordered you to stop teaching:* The ancient mss are divided between reading this as an interrogative: ("Did we not order you?"), and as a statement. The harder reading is the declarative, since the verb *epērataō* ("question") introduces it, and scribes would understandably correct for consistency. The adverb "strictly" tries to capture the force of the cognate accusative (another of Luke's biblicisms), which would read literally, "we commanded you a command." The reference is to the order issued at the first hearing (4:18).

you are set: Literally, "you intend," or "you will" (*boulesthe*), a term used for a fixed intention. This will be turned ironically by their intention to kill the apostles in v. 33, below. The phrase "bringing blood on" someone means to assign blame for a death (see Gen 4:10-11; 2 Sam 1:16; Hos 12:14; Ezek

18:13; 33:2-4). Remarkably, there is a faint echo here of Matt 27:25, but even more emphatically, of Luke 11:50-51. The chief priest is not wrong, for Peter in Acts 4:10-11 has certainly placed the blame for Jesus' death squarely on the leaders.

29. *it is necessary to obey God:* For the background to this statement in the defense of Socrates, see the note on 4:19. Just such patterns of repetition with variation led earlier generations of scholars to find diverse sources in Acts. It is more likely that Luke uses repetition in the literary fashion we have suggested. Note here, for example, these distinctive elements: a) rather than ask the leaders to judge (4:19), Peter here states the principle flatly; b) and he uses it to launch just such a kerygmatic statement (implicating the leaders) that the chief priest has forbidden, very much as a challenge.

30. *by hanging him on the tree:* The pattern of this statement is familiar from 2:22-24; 3:13-15; 4:10-11, but the diction is distinctive. The verb *diacheirizomai* ("kill") is a more severe form of "lay hands on," and is used in the NT only here and Acts 26:21. The term *xylon,* on the other hand, has a richer set of associations. It literally means "wood" or "tree." In the first sense it can be used for the "clubs" carried by those arresting Jesus (Luke 22:52) or of the "stocks" into which Paul is placed (Acts 16:24). But its more interesting use in the NT is for the cross (Acts 10:39; 13:29; Gal 3:13; 1 Pet 2:24), which derives from the LXX usage for "hanging" (Josh 8:29; 10:24), and above all from the curse passage of Deut 21:23: "cursed be everyone who hangs upon a tree," a text that continued to be disputed between messianist and non-messianist Jews long after the time of the NT (see Justin Martyr, *Dialogue with Trypho* 73, 86-91).

31. *leader and savior:* The word "leader" (*archēgos*) is translated as "author" in 3:15; see the note on that verse for discussion. The title *sōtēr* ("savior") is applied to Jesus in Luke 2:11 and Acts 13:23; for the theme of salvation in Luke-Acts, see the Introduction to the *Commentary on the Gospel of Luke,* and the note on Luke 1:47.

    forgiveness of sins to Israel: Throughout the Jerusalem section of Acts, Luke maintains a steady focus on the offer of salvation made to Israel (1:6; 2:36; 4:10, 27; 5:21); note the recurrent use of "Israelites" in 2:22; 3:12; 5:35. For the theme of forgiveness of sins and its connection to repentance, see the note on Acts 2:38.

32. *God has given to those who obey him:* Peter's statement is provocative: this is said, after all, by one already identified as "full of the Holy Spirit" (4:8). A similar sort of statement, using the quality of "wisdom" is attributed to Apollonius of Tyana (*Life* 4:44).

33. *enraged . . . wanted to kill:* Luke uses a particularly vivid verb to express their reaction: they were "torn apart" (*diapriō*); compare the Sanhedrin's response to Stephen's speech in 7:54. In the note to v. 17, the connection between envy and murder in the Hellenistic *topos* on envy was observed; see also *Testament of Gad* 4:5-6; *Testament of Joseph* 1:3; *Testament of Benjamin* 7:1-2.

34. *certain Pharisee:* Since Gamaliel's interjection is often read in positive terms, it is taken as evidence for Luke's supposed positive attitude toward the Pharisees in contrast to other Jewish leaders. Throughout the commentary on the Gospel, it has been noted how this perception is false. In Acts, Luke will show that the Christians share the Pharisees' convictions concerning the resurrection of the dead, but that does not indicate that the Pharisees as individuals are more benignly viewed; on the contrary, they fail to follow up their own convictions by not acknowledging the resurrection of Jesus. As the Interpretation will also show, Gamaliel's is far from a positive portrayal. On the Pharisaic "school" within Judaism, see note on Luke 5:17 and Josephus, *Jewish War* 2:166; *Antiquities of the Jews* 13:293-298.

Gamaliel: In Acts 22:3, Paul claims to have had Gamaliel as his teacher; since Paul was at that time also a persecutor of the Church, one would hesitate to presume that in our author's eyes Gamaliel is positively inclined toward the Messianists! There were several great rabbinic teachers with this name. The one meant here is the first, Rabban Gamaliel I (the Elder). He was in the first generation of Tannaim, possibly a descendant of Hillel. He should be distinguished from R. Simeon ben Gamaliel I (his son) who was contemporaneous with the war against Rome (see Josephus, *Life* 189–198), and R. Gamaliel II, according to tradition the successor of Johanan ben Zakkai at Yabneh (ca. 90-110 C.E.), and our Gamaliel's grandson. For the slender body of teaching associated with Gamaliel I, see *m.Peah* 2:6; *m.Orlah* 2:12; *m.R.H.* 2:5; *m.Shek.* 6:1; *m.Yeb.* 16:7; *m.Git.* 4:2; *m.Sotah* 9:15, and possibly *Pirke Aboth* 1:16. For the expression "teacher of the law" (*nomodidaskalos*), compare Luke 5:17.

36. *Theudas rose up:* Luke uses the same verb here and in the next verse as he uses for the "raising up" of the prophet Jesus (*anhistēmi*; 2:24, 32; 3:22, 26). In the description of Theudas and Judas the Galilean, we meet a classic problem for assessing Luke's historical accuracy, because of the discrepancy between him and our other major source, Josephus, *Antiquities of the Jews* 20:97-99. They agree that Theudas was a popular leader and came to a violent end, but disagree on the dating. Josephus puts Theudas during the prefecture of Fadus, therefore about 45-46 C.E., at a time not only *after* the revolt of Judas the Galilean (in contrast to Luke) but also *after* the time when Gamaliel could have made this speech (around 37 C.E.?). Since we have no independent controls, it is impossible either to harmonize or utterly dismiss either version.

saying . . . that he was somebody: In fact, according to Josephus, *Antiquities* 20:97, he claimed to be a *prophētēs*, a prophet! Josephus himself has the same reaction as Gamaliel, dismissing Theudas as a *goēs*, or charlatan. Of particular interest, however, is that Theudas placed himself in the tradition of "prophets like Moses," since he promised his followers that he would command the Jordan to be parted and his followers could go through dry-shod (*Antiquities* 20:98). Some have suggested that Luke used Josephus' account, but it seems incredible that he should have omitted this aspect if he had seen it in Josephus, since it fits his own themes so precisely. His reticence and allusiveness in this case suggest the use of an independent tradition. Codex D adds the word *megan*, to make, "saying he was somebody great." This could represent a textual infiltration from the story of Simon Magus (Acts 8:9), or the perception of both Simon and Theudas as *goētai*.

37. *Judas the Galilean:* Josephus once more gives us considerable information on Judas, who fomented a revolt against the Roman census around 6 c.e. The revolt itself was not successful, but Judas was at the least a model to which the zealot movement looked (see Josephus, *Antiquities of the Jews* 17:271-272; 18:1-10; *Jewish War* 2:117-118; 7:252-258). Luke deviates from Josephus on two counts: a) he agrees that the revolt took place in the time of the census, but dates it differently from Josephus (see the note on Luke 1:5; 2:2); b) he places Judas *after* Theudas (*meta touton* = "after this one"), whereas Josephus puts Judas first in sequence (although even he must work to clarify things in *Antiquities* 20:102). For Gamaliel's historical lesson, of course, questions of dating are irrelevant.

    led a people in revolt: The verb *aphistēmi* means literally to "stand away from," but can mean (ordinarily in the passive rather than the active as here) "revolt" (as in Herodotus, *Persian Wars* 1:95). The noun *laos* is here anarthous, and should be understood as "a group of people." Some *mss* heighten the effect by adding quantitative adjectives.

    who obeyed him were scattered: The term "obey" (*peithomai*) is used twice in verses 36 and 37; it picks up the related verb "obey a leader" (*peitharchein*) in verses 29 and 32. There is a definite literary play involving the obedience of God rather than humans, running through this passage; see the Interpretation. The verb "scatter" (*diaskorpizein*) is used in the LXX for the total devastation of enemies (Num 10:35; Ps 52:5; 58:11; 67:10, 30; 88:10; 105:27).

38. *let them be:* The expression *aphete autous* could mean either to release them or to allow them. Here, the net result is much the same. Codex D and other ancient *mss* greatly expand verses 38-39. In the present verse, the most interesting expansion is "without defiling your hands," which is an appropriate note for a Pharisee!

    from humans it will be destroyed: There are two conditional sentences in these verses. Luke uses a future conditional in the first, suggesting a remoter possibility, and a simple conditional in the second, suggesting a more likely possibility; his syntax reveals his (not Gamaliel's) perception. A principle roughly equivalent to Gamaliel's is attributed to R. Johanan the Sandalmaker in *Pirke Aboth* 4:11: "Any assembling together that is for the sake of heaven shall in the end be established, but any that is not for the sake of heaven shall not in the end be established."

39. *not be able to destroy them:* The verb *kataluō* ("destroy") is used in both sentences; some *mss* have *auto* ("it") in this clause, rather than *autous* ("them"), probably because it would better match the singular suggested by the disjunctive *boulē* or *ergon* in the previous verse. Codex D expands the statement to include "neither you nor kings nor tyrants."

    fighting God: Literally, "you are found to be fighters against God (*theomachoi*)."

The term is found in 2 Macc 7:19; Epictetus, *Discourses* 3, 24, 24; Lucian of Samosata, *Zeus Rants* 45; Philostratus, *Life of Apollonius of Tyana* 4:44.

they heeded him: In light of Peter's challenge in 5:29-32, the irony here is intense. The Sanhedrin heeds Gamaliel, which means that they "obey humans rather than God." Gamaliel's superficially benign statement is in effect a self-condemnation. When they do not obey the prophet they *are* "fighting God."

41. *worthy of being despised:* This is an oxymoron that is typically and uniquely Christian in its transvaluation of terms. They are despised "in behalf of the name" (see the note on 2:38), so that in their suffering as in their proclamation, the apostles follow the pattern of the prophet (see the sayings of Jesus in Luke 6:22-23).

42. *they did not cease:* This concluding statement serves to demonstrate that the apostles do not obey humans but God, and they are able to do so with impunity. Luke even excludes the Twelve from the great persecution that will scatter the other leaders after Stephen's martyrdom (8:3). The phrase "in houses" (*kat'oikon*), picks up the expression of the summary in 2:46.

the Messiah was Jesus: The Greek phrase *euangelizomenoi ton christon Iēsoun* can be read several ways: the translation here tries to respect the word-order and the central point of the early proclamation.

INTERPRETATION

After showing the authority of the apostles within the community, not only over teaching and possessions but even over life and death, Luke places them once more in public, at Solomon's Portico in the temple, and striding through the streets (5:12-16). His point is clearly to demonstrate that Peter and the other apostles are truly "rulers of the twelve tribes of Israel." Even though he depicts them in terms of almost frightening numinosity—the people are afraid to approach them at the temple, they do not seek to touch Peter but only hope for his shadow to fall on them — the apostles also exercise the compellingly attractive force of the Holy. They draw ever more converts to the community. People drag their sick into the streets and even from the neighboring villages to be healed by them.

Everything in this description is heightened and extreme, but can be understood simply in terms of the opening line: "great signs and wonders were being performed through the apostles among the people." This line tells us that it is the prophetic spirit of Jesus working through his followers, more powerful even than when he was alive, because now he has been exalted to the right hand of God (5:31). The power let loose in Israel—in the world—is not to be controlled by human manipulation.

Such is the setting for the second trial of the apostles before the Sanhedrin (5:17-42). Although there are superficial similarities to the first hearing in 4:5-22 (Peter's statement about obeying God rather than humans, his kerygmatic statement, the warning and dismissal from the assembly), the placement in the overall narrative together with the distinctive elements in this hearing make it tell quite a different tale.

For the reader, the outcome is no longer in doubt. The question whether the apostles would be—could be—subdued by the political power of the Sanhedrin has been answered by God in their empowerment with the Spirit and their spectacular display of prophetic activity. This second trial, therefore, is, for the reader, not truly as dramatic as the first. To compensate, the reader is allowed to enjoy the rich irony and even humor with which Luke has laced this vignette. Thus, Luke invokes extra pomp in describing the gathering of the council (5:21), only to show its impotence: God has arranged the prisoners' escape by night, and the jailers sent to lead the apostles to the council for their hearing must report back to the waiting assembly that the cell is empty despite locked doors and standing guard; and while the leaders are still standing in embarrassed perplexity at this news, the report comes that the escapees are freely teaching the people in their customary place. How great is the divide between these leaders and the people? They must go and escort the apostles back, but show no force, for they are afraid the people will stone *them!* All their warnings and even their beatings, we understand, are empty: God is at work in the apostles, and they will not be stopped.

Less humorous is Luke's depiction of the Sanhedrin as filled with envy (5:17) and rage that led to the desire to murder (5:33). So a deeper and darker level of irony is also present in the text. The chief priest charges Peter with bringing the responsibility for Jesus' death on their heads (5:28) and in his response Peter unapologetically does exactly that once more, "you killed him by hanging him on a tree" (5:30). Even more strikingly, the Sanhedrin's response of murderous rage is directed to Peter's statement that God had given the Spirit to all who obeyed him. They respond to the offer of "repentance to Israel" with the intent to kill its proclaimers (5:31-33).

But the irony is found most clearly in the advice given by Gamaliel to the Sanhedrin (5:34-39). Remarkably, Gamaliel's little speech is often interpreted as entirely benign, and even as evidence for Luke's positive appreciation of the Pharisees. So to understand it is to miss entirely the signals the author himself has given us.

This was not Gamaliel's first encounter with the apostles, or even (we should think) with Jesus. Luke specifically identifies him as a Pharisaic member of the Sanhedrin (5:34), and the authority carried by his speech as well as his prestige among the people suggest he is one of its leaders. He had, therefore, been part of the condemnation of Jesus (Luke 22:66-73). Furthermore, he had confronted the apostles Peter and John and had seen the man healed by them standing before him; he saw their *parrēsia* and knew it had to come from Jesus (4:13-14). He had just now heard Peter declare again that the Jesus they had killed was powerfully alive at God's right hand (5:31). What does he do? He sends the apostles from the room, and with his colleagues formulates a *plan of action* based on historical prudence! Fundamentally, he advises a "wait and see" attitude.

His argument from historical analogies reveals his thinking. We notice that the use of the term "rose up" with reference to Theudas and Judas echoes the language used of "the prophet like Moses" and particularly of Jesus, whom God "raised up." Gamaliel's use is unconsciously ironic, for his entire point is to reduce Jesus to the status of those "would-be" prophets and kings. His argument runs like this: they "rose up," but then they were killed, and their followers were scattered. His implication is that the same thing will probably happen here. But he has missed the message concerning Jesus. Jesus rose up as a prophet and was killed, yes. But the reality to which the apostles are witnessing is that he has been "raised up" in a new and powerful way, and his followers are not being scattered, but are just now being gathered in ever growing numbers: *this* is the difference between the precedents and Jesus!

There is, therefore, no comparison between Jesus and these others who died and whose followers were scattered. The signs and wonders being done by the apostles show that Jesus has been raised and is gathering a people *now*, and calls for a response. Gamaliel's prudent advice about this "plan or work" (*boulē ē ergon*) is therefore really an example of bad faith. He is (in the sense Luke uses the term of the Pharisees and teachers of the law), a "hypocrite," for he wants to appear to be righteous, and he has all the right convictions, but he will not respond to the prophetic call before him. Like the Pharisees and teachers of the Law described in Luke 7:29, he "rejects God's plan (*boulē*)." There is even greater irony in the fact that the council "listens to" Gamaliel. They do not respond in faith; they listen to humans rather than to God; they do not obey the voice of the prophet; the result, as we know from Acts 3:23, is that they are being cut out of the people.

When Luke shows the apostles triumphantly preaching Jesus as Messiah in the temple (5:42), undaunted by the council's beatings or threats, shown to be empowered and guided by God's Spirit, he has answered for his readers the question concerning the leadership over Israel. Not the faithless members of the Sanhedrin but the Twelve are truly "ruling over the twelve tribes of Israel." But before Luke can close this critical section of his story, and show how the good news reached beyond Jerusalem and how the people of God would come to encompass even Gentiles, he must show how that leadership is passed in continuity from the Twelve to those who will carry it "to the ends of the earth."

FOR REFERENCE AND FURTHER STUDY

Horsley, R. A., and Hanson, J. S. *Bandits, Prophets, and Messiahs: Popular Movements at the Time of Jesus.* Cambridge: Harper and Row, 1985.
Nauck, W. "Freude im Leiden: zum Problem einen Urchristlichen Verfolgungstradition." *ZNW* 46 (1955) 68–80.
Schwartz, D. R. "Non-Joining Sympathizers (Acts 5, 13-14)." *Bib* 64 (1983) 550–553.
van der Horst, P. W. "Peter's Shadow: The Religio-Historical Background of Acts 5:15." *NTS* 23 (1976–1977) 204–212.

10. *The Succession of Prophetic Authority* (6:1-15)

1. During this time, as the number of disciples was increasing, there was a complaint made by the Hellenists against the Hebrews, that their widows were being slighted in the daily distribution. 2. The Twelve therefore summoned the assembly of disciples. They said, "For us to abandon the word of God in order to serve at tables is not acceptable. 3. Brothers, select from among you seven approved men who are full of the Spirit and of wisdom, whom we can put in charge of this responsibility. 4. And we will continue in prayer and in the service of the word." 5. The speech pleased the entire assembly. They chose Stephen, a man full of faith and of the Holy Spirit, and Philip and Prochorus and Nicanor and Timon and Parmenas and Nicolaus, an Antiochean proselyte. 6. These they stood before the apostles, and when they had prayed, they laid their hands on them. 7. The word of God grew, and the number of disciples in Jerusalem multiplied considerably, with even a large crowd of priests becoming obedient to the faith. 8. Now Stephen, full of grace and of power, was performing great wonders and signs among the people. 9. But some people from the synagogue called "The Freedmens', Cyrenians', and Alexandrians'," and some of those from Cilicia and Asia, were getting up and disputing with Stephen. 10. They were not able to stand against the wisdom and the spirit by which he was speaking. 11. Then they prompted men to say "we have heard him speaking blasphemous words against Moses and God." 12. They agitated the people and the elders and the scribes. They confronted him, seized him, and led him to the Sanhedrin. 13. They set up false witnesses to say, "This person never stops speaking against this holy place and the law. 14. For we have heard him saying that this Jesus the Nazorean will destroy this place and will change the customs that Moses handed down to us." 15. As all those sitting in the Sanhedrin gazed at him attentively, they saw his face like the face of an angel.

NOTES

1. *a complaint:* Literally, "there was a grumbling (*gongusmos*)": the term is used by the LXX for the grumbling of the Israelites against the Lord in the wilderness (Exod 16:7-12; Num 11:1; 17:5). Luke shows considerable narrative skill in placing the dispute at this point. The conflict is seen to result from the natural stress created by rapid community growth, with needs outstripping administration. This is the first time that *mathetes* ("disciple") appears in Acts, but it will recur frequently hereafter (6:7; 9:1, 10, 19, 25; 11:26, 29; 13:52, etc.).

Hellenists . . . Hebrews: A classic problem for the interpretation of Acts: to whom does Luke refer by these designations? Because Luke is the first author we know of to use the term *hellēnistēs* (and its use by later Christian writers to contrast pagans and Christians was unavailable to him), our judgment must be based on Luke's own usage. Even that determination is made more difficult by a textual variation in a key passage (11:20). Nevertheless, some clarity is possible. Is Luke making a linguistic or ethnic distinction? His practice elsewhere is illuminating. He uses the term "Hebrew" (*hebraios*) only here, but when he uses the adjective *hebrais* it is always to refer to the "Hebrew dialect," (Aramaic), in other words, as a linguistic category. In the present case, therefore, the "Hebrews" would naturally mean Jews who speak exclusively or mainly Aramaic. When Luke wants to make an *ethnic* contrast between Jew and Greek, he does not use the term *hellēnistēs*, but the term *hellēn*. Four out of Luke's seven uses of this term make the ethnic distinction explicit (14:1; 16:1; 19:17; 21:18—see also *hellēnis* in 17:12), two contain it implicitly (17:4; 19:10), and the last (11:20) is a textually disputed passage. As for the term *hellēnistēs*, the only definite uses are here and in a very similar passage (9:29). Given this evidence, the suggestion that Luke meant by *hellēnistēs* "Greek Gentiles" in the present passage has little to recommend it, particularly since Luke takes such pains to show the gradual development of the Gentile mission *after* the close of the Jerusalem narrative. Luke is therefore here making a linguistic distinction: *hellēnistēs* refers to a Jew who predominantly speaks Greek. Some of them were probably from the Diaspora (see Acts 2:7-12; 4:36; 6:9), although Greek was widely spoken in Palestine as well.

widows were being slighted: The verb *paratheōreō* can mean "overlook," but in this context, the note of discrimination suggested by "slighted" is appropriate. In any land-based, patriarchal economy, some categories of people are chronically needy: the orphans, the transients ("sojourners") and the widows. The laws of Torah gave special attention to their care (Deut 10:18; 14:29; 16:11, 14; 24:17, 19-21; 26:12-13). Failure to care for such poor folk bore a curse: "cursed be he who prevents justice due to the sojourner or the fatherless and the widow" (Deut 27:19). Among the prophets, "doing justice for widows" was shorthand for covenantal loyalty (Mal 3:5; Isa 1:17, 23; 10:2; Jer 5:28 [LXX]; 7:6; 23:3; Ezek 22:7; Ps 93:6). A classic expression is given to this conviction by Jas 1:27: to "neglect widows" is a fundamental betrayal of covenantal loyalty. In the Rabbinic tradition, "doing justice" (*ṣedekâ*) was spelled out in terms of organized community almsgiving; see the next note, and with repect to widows in particular, see *m.Ket.* 4:12; 11:1-6; 12:3-4; *m.Git.* 5:3. Every welfare system has difficulties balancing need and resources, as well as fairness in distribution; compare Paul's discussion in 1 Tim 5:3-16.

in the daily distribution: Literally, "the daily service" (*diakonia*); The same term will be used in the phrase "service of tables" (6:2) and "service of the word" (6:4). Luke consistently joins the exercise of authority to service at table and the disposition of possessions (Luke 9:1-17; 12:35-48; 16:1-13; 19:12-27; 22:24-30; Acts 1:15-26; 2:42-47). The allusion to the "daily distribution" corresponds with what we know of organized Jewish charity in local communities. Each community would offer a daily "soup kitchen" for transients and the destitute, and a "chest" for meeting long-term needs; see e.g., *m.Peah* 5:4; 8:7; *m.Demai* 3:1; *Pirke Aboth* 5:9; *bT Meg.* 27a; *bT Bab.Bat.* 8a-9a; *bT R.H.* 4a-5b.

2. *summoned the assembly of disciples:* The sense of *plēthos* here is that of a deliberative body rather than a loose assemblage. Luke may even be thinking of a representative group rather than the entire (by his reckoning now quite large) community of believers. For all the prophetic authority of the Twelve, it is striking that on such critical decisions the discernment of the community is invited.

   to abandon . . . is not acceptable: The verb *kataleipō* is strong: to "leave behind," or "forsake." The pressures of community growth and the needs of the poor outstrip the administrative capability of the Twelve; a distribution of roles is required. The issue is not a moral one but rather of what is "fitting" or "appropriate" (*arestos;* compare LXX Deut 6:18; 12:8, 25; Tob 3:6; Prov 21:3).

3. *select . . . approved men:* Although Luke ordinarily uses the verb *episkeptein* in the sense of "visit" (Luke 1:68, 78; 7:16; Acts 7:23; 15:14, 36), here it means to "select by examination or review." The term "approved" (*martyroumenos*) means having one's actions or character witnessed to by others (Luke 4:22; Acts 10:22; 16:2; 22:12; also 1 Tim 5:10; 3 John 12).

   full of the Spirit and of wisdom: Some *mss* have "the Holy Spirit," which we would expect with the indeclinable adjective *plērēs* (see Luke 4:1; Acts 6:3; 7:55), but just such expectations of consistency were what led scribes to alter texts; in this case the shorter version is also the best attested.

   put in charge of this responsibility: The verb *kathistēmi* echoes the parable of Jesus in Luke 12:42, "Who then is the faithful household manager, the sensible one, whom the master will set over (*kathistēmi*) his household slaves to give them their rations at the appointed times?" The term *chreia* is literally "need" (as in 2:45 and 4:35), but is used in a generalized sense of "duty."

4. *in prayer and in the service of the word:* Luke can use "word of God" for the entire mission (4:31; 6:2, 7; 8:14; 11:1; 12:24; 19:20), so the "service" here probably means more than simply preaching. For the apostles in prayer, see 4:23-30, and now, before their laying on of hands (6:6). The combination makes for a striking definition of ministry.

5. *they chose Stephen:* Like Barnabas, introduced quietly in 4:36, Stephen is a pivotal figure in the narrative, helping to link the Jerusalem ministry with

that in the Diaspora. His death (7:59) closes the Jerusalem section of the story, and provides the impetus for the geographical spread of the gospel (8:2). Even later in the story, he is looked back on as a turning point (Acts 11:19; 22:20). The verb *eklegomai* ("choose") is the same used for the selection of the Twelve by Jesus (Luke 6:13), and has rich resonances in the biblical tradition (Num 16:7; Deut 4:37; 7:7; 10:15; 12:5; Ps 32:12; 77:68).

Philip: The only one of the seven to play a narrative role besides Stephen, Philip brings the gospel to Samaria (8:5), and proclaims the good news to the Ethiopian (8:29), and along the coast from Azotus to Caesarea (8:40). Paul visits him there on his last trip to Jerusalem (21:8). Philip also has the character of a prophet, since he proclaims "the word" (8:1), does signs and wonders (8:6, 13), is led by the Spirit (8:29, 39), and even has daughters who prophesy (21:9).

Prochorus . . . Nicolaus: Of the remaining five, we know nothing beyond the fact that their names are Greek, and even this would not be exceptional for Diaspora Jews. Nicolaus is identified as a "proselyte from Antioch," and we saw some proselytes from the Diaspora at Pentecost (2:10). Antioch, of course, will play a major role later in the story, beginning in 11:19. There is no particular reason to credit the ancient tradition that connects him to "the Nicolaitans" opposed by Revelation 2:6, 15.

6. *laid their hands on them:* The gesture symbolizes the transfer of power. It appears in sacrificial rites (Exod 29:10, 19; Lev 1:4, 11; 4:15; 16:21), and in Num 8:10 as part of the ordination of priests: "When you present the Levites before the Lord, the people of Israel shall lay their hands upon the Levites." Even more impressive is the formal transfer of authority from Moses to Joshua ("a man in whom is the Spirit") through this gesture (Num 27:18-23; see also Deut 34:9). These passages make clear that the gesture signified that the people should now obey Joshua just as they had Moses (Num 27:20; Deut 34:9). In Luke, the laying on of hands appears as a part of Jesus' healings (which Luke clearly understands as a communication of power) in Luke 4:40; 13:13. In Acts, the gesture accompanies the bestowal of the Spirit in baptism (8:17, 19; 19:6), healings (9:12, 17; 28:8), and commissioning for ministry (13:3).

7. *word of God grew:* This is one of Luke's regular notices of community growth within Jerusalem (2:41, 47; 4:4; 5:14). It is quite possible that the background for the motif lies in Isa 2:3, "For the law shall go out of Zion, and the word of the Lord (*logos tou theou*) out of Jerusalem." The translation "with even a large crowd of priests" takes seriously the consequential implication of the Greek particle *te*. The conversion of "many priests" may not represent an inconsistency within Luke's theme of the division within the people (despite the textually uncertain 4:1), because the priestly class in Jerusalem was a vast and in many ways marginalized population. Estimates of numbers are always difficult, but by comparing ancient testimonies concerning numbers involved in the regular temple services (e.g., 1 Chr 12:26-28; *Letter of Aristeas* 95; Josephus, *Against Apion* 2:108; 2:119; *m. Yom.* 2:1-7) we can estimate many thousands of persons in this category. There is also evidence that the priests were disaffected from the ruling hierarchy, at least during the period of the

war with Rome (see Josephus, *Antiquities of the Jews* 20:181; *Jewish War* 2:409-410).

obedient to the faith: Luke uses the term "the faith" here in an absolute sense, as roughly equivalent to "the community of faith." Compare 13:8; 14:22. For the dative as the object of *hypakouō*, see Luke 8:25; 17:6.

8. *great wonders and signs among the people:* Stephen is described as a prophet: he is filled with the Holy Spirit and wisdom (6:5, 10; 7:55), he works "wonders and signs" with great "power" (*dynamis*); these are the marks of the prophet (see Acts 2:19, 22, 43; 4:16, 22, 30; 5:12). Equally important is the note that he did his wonders "among the people" (see 2:12, 47; 3:12; 4:1, 10; 5:12). Some *mss* try to correct the present description of "full of grace and power" by supplying either "faith" or "spirit," to correspond with 6:5. The Western Text also felt compelled to add after "the people" this phrase: "through the name of the Lord Jesus Christ," probably under the influence of 4:30.

9. *the synagogue called the "Freedmans', Cyrenians', and Alexandrians' ":* Luke's overall point here is clearer than the specifics. He wants to show that Stephen is attacked without provocation by Diaspora Jews who frequent (one or more) synagogues within the city. That there were such synagogues in the city is certainly true; according to a (late) tradition in *jT Meg.* 73d, there were 480 synagogues in the city; compare Acts 24:12. That synagogues had such titles is also clear, both from inscriptions (such as the door inscription found at Corinth of "synagogue of the Hebrews"), and from references such as *jT Meg.* 73d and *bT Meg.* 26a. The best archaeological evidence is provided by the "Theodotus inscription" found in Jerusalem. What is unclear is how to read the series of genitives in this sentence: does Luke intend them to be distributive, so that there could be as many as five synagogues represented, or does he intend (as this translation takes it) one synagogue, with perhaps two other groups (Cilicians and Asians) also pitching in? Still other combinations are possible. A further puzzle is the designation "Freedmen's" (*libertinōn*), since it is the only social rather than regional designation. Some *mss* correct it to "Libyans." Some scholars try to connect it to the freedmen descendants of the Jews taken captive to Rome by Pompey (Philo, *Embassy to Gaius* 155-157).

10. *stand against the wisdom and the spirit:* Jesus had told his disciples that the Holy Spirit would instruct them when they came to trial (Luke 12:12), and also that he would give them "a wisdom that none could oppose" (Luke 21:15). The Western Text expands this verse considerably, making the opponents' inability to defeat Stephen in public the reason for their conspiracy against him; this would make the sequence resemble even more fully the passion narrative of Jesus (Luke 20:19).

11. *they prompted men to say:* The subject of the sentence remains the *tines* ("some people") from the synagogues. They are the main authors of this trouble. The verb *hypoballō* has the sense of "putting someone up to something" or of subornation (see *Testament of Simeon* 3:3, and the sending of "spies" against Jesus in Luke 20:20).

blasphemous words: For the meaning of "blasphemy," see the note on Luke 5:21. Luke shifts the charge of blasphemy from the trial of Jesus (compare Mark 14:64; Matt 26:65) to the trial of Stephen. The content of the alleged blasphemy "against Moses and God" (a strange sequence!) is made more explicit in verses 13-14. Elsewhere, Luke can use "Moses" when referring to Torah (Luke 5:14; 16:19, 31; 20:28; 24:27; Acts 3:22; 15:1, 21; 21:21; 26:22).

12. *they agitated the people:* The subject is still the people from the synagogues, rather than the false witnesses who are their agents. Their activity echoes the charge made against Jesus that he "stirs up the people" (*anaseiei ton laon,* Luke 23:5).

    led him to the Sanhedrin: Luke is careful to make this shift from popular arrest to formal hearing; it is the leadership that will hear and formally reject Stephen. The sequence again resembles that of Jesus' passion: the confrontation (Luke 22:47-53), the arrest (22:51), and the taking to the council (*apēgagon auton eis to synedrion autōn,* 22:66).

13. *false witnesses:* As with the accusation of blasphemy (6:11), Luke transfers the "false witnesses" from the trial of Jesus (Mark 14:56-57; Matt 26:59-60) to here. "Making false witness" is condemned by the decalogue (Exod 20:16), and the problem of false accusations against a neighbor is dealt with in Deut 19:16-18. Legislation did not make the vice go away (see Exod 23:1; LXX Pss 26:12; 34:11; Prov 6:19; 12:17; 14:5; 19:5; 24:43). For the Sanhedrin rules for testing witnesses, see *m.Sanh.* 3:6; 5:1-5.

    this holy place and the law: For "holy place" as a sanctuary, see Lev 10:13-18; 14:13; 16:24; 24:9, and specifically for the temple, LXX Pss 23:3 and 67:5. The phrase "this place" more often refers to the land (Deut 1:31; 9:7; Jer 7:3-20; 14:3), but it can also be used with reference to the temple (2 Chr 6:20-21). The charge against Stephen is very close to that later placed against Paul (Acts 21:28). For "the law," see Luke 2:22, 23, 24, 27, 39; 10:26; 16:16-17; 24:44; nowhere does Jesus speak against the law as such. Nor does Stephen, who calls it "living oracles" (7:38) and says that it was delivered by angels (7:53).

14. *will destroy this place:* Once more Luke has taken a charge that the other Synoptic Gospels make an essential part of Jesus' trial, and placed it here (see Mark 14:58; 15:29; Matt 26:61; 27:40; see also John 2:19-21). The precise role to be played by the temple in God's plan for the people had always been hotly debated in Judaism, and certainly was in the first century. There was not only the dispute over the sanctuaries of Samaria and Jerusalem and the challenge to the Jerusalem cult as unworthy (and the replacement of it by the community of the pure) by the Qumran community (e.g., 1QS 8:4-10). Hellenistic Jews like Philo, despite their devotion to the temple in Jerusalem and willingness to pay taxes to it (Philo, *Embassy to Gaius* 216; 313), were also able to "spiritualize" its meaning in terms of individual piety (see Philo, *On Dreams* 1:149, 256). Neither in apocalyptic literature was there a standard view concerning the heavenly or eschatological temple, much less the Messiah's relationship to it (see e.g., *Book of Jubilees* 1:23-29; 4:26; *1 Enoch* 25:1-7; 53:6; 71:1-17; 90:28-36; *2 Baruch* 4:2-7; *Testament of Benjamin* 9:2-3).

change the customs: The wording of this charge is particularly interesting. Luke uses *ethē* rather than "commandments" or "laws." He considers the ritual obligations specific to Jews as part of their ancestral heritage, but not necessarily to be taken over by Gentile believers; thus the Jews have their "customs" (see Luke 1:9; 2:42; Acts 15:1; 21:21; 28:17), just as the Gentiles have their "customs" (Acts 16:21; 25:16). We can observe a similar usage in the apologetic writing of Philo (see *Embassy to Gaius* 315, and the equivalent use of *nomima* and *ethē* in *Embassy* 360, 362). It is used in the LXX only in writings originating in Greek, for customs of pagans (Wis 14:16; 1 Macc 10:89; 2 Macc 13:4), or for Jewish practices as perceived by pagans (2 Macc 11:25; 4 Macc 18:5).

15. *like the face of an angel:* The comparison can be found in the LXX of Esth 15:13, and in the LXX of Dan 3:92 for the young men in the furnace, *"homoiōma angelou theou."* In the *Palestinian Targum* on Gen 33:10, the phrase "face of God" is piously replaced with: "I have seen thy face as though I had seen the face of an angel." See also the *Acts of Paul and Thecla* 3 (probably based on Gal 4:14), and the face of St. Polycarp "filled with grace" before his death in *The Martyrdom of Polycarp* 12:1. As at the transfiguration of Jesus (9:29), the change of countenance indicates that Stephen is an authoritative spokesperson for God.

Interpretation

Luke has successfully portrayed a restored people and the authority of the Twelve over it. Now, he prepares for the second stage of Jesus' programmatic prophecy in Acts 1:8, that the Gospel would move out from Jerusalem to Judea and Samaria and to the ends of the world. He does this, typically, by establishing a continuity of ministry, which for Luke means a succession of prophetic authority.

The basic lines of the account appear at first to be simple, but as repeated attempts to get at the historical reality in back of the story have shown, the appearance is deceptive. There is a gap between what the story seems to be saying, and what it is actually doing within the narrative. We can begin to bridge that gap by first carefully assessing its distance.

The apostles appear to resolve a problem created by a dispute over the daily distribution by appointing seven administrators (6:1-6). But it is not at all clear how the apostles' abandonment of their administrative tasks would solve the purported problem: why would seven administrators be more effective than twelve? Or, if we are to conclude from the Greek names of the seven that they were to take over the care of the "Hellenist" widows, who would look after the "Hebrew" widows once the apostles left their station? The reason the apostles give for their action is also puzzling. They claim that they need to leave administration because it makes them "abandon the word of God" (6:2). But the entire narrative from 4:1 to 5:42 has demonstrated how impressively the apostles have served the word, and the power of their prayer (4:23-31).

Even more bewildering is the outcome of their decision. Yet this final puzzlement also provides the clue for the proper understanding of the passage. The seven were selected precisely to be "in charge of this responsibility" of the daily distribution (6:3). But although the entire narrative from this point until the end of chapter 8 is devoted to two of the seven (Stephen and Philip), neither of them has the slightest connection to the "service of the tables." Instead, they are portrayed as *prophets* who continue the work of the twelve: they are filled with the power of the Holy Spirit, they preach God's word, they work signs and wonders among the people. The sole difference is the sphere of their activity: Stephen disputes the Hellenistic Jews in the city, Philip begins the preaching to Samaria and Judea.

The problem of this passage is therefore this: there is no obvious connection between the purported role of the seven and their actual function. They were supposed to be in charge of community possessions but they turn out to be prophetic preachers. There seems to be, in fact, only the most tenuous connection between the account of their placement over community possessions and the description of their actual ministry.

The discrepancy disappears when we remember Luke's consistent habit of using authority over material possessions as a symbol for spiritual authority. The twelve were shown to be ruling Israel not only by the proclamation of the word, but by their administration of the tables. Now Luke wants to show how spiritual authority was bestowed on those who would carry the gospel to the Diaspora. He needs to show that these Hellenistic missionaries were fully prophetic figures, like the Twelve; but he also wants to show that their authority is derived from that of the Twelve and in continuity with it. He accomplishes both tasks by having the seven placed over the distribution of goods. The transfer of spiritual power (through the laying on of hands) is symbolized by the taking on of "table service" (as it was for Jesus and the Twelve).

The very disjointedness of the account is therefore the best evidence that Luke's main preoccupation was in establishing this transition of leadership. The symbolism is not entirely successful—it has certainly eluded many readers who obsessively search for the historical underpinnings of the account. And once Luke has established the image, he abandons it; no more is said about the seven's role in the community goods. But the symbolism has done its basic work: the reader, even if at a subliminal level, recognizes the appropriateness of the seven's appointment to table service, and without hesitation accepts them as the worthy prophetic successors of the Twelve.

The transitional character of the passage is demonstrated also by the way in which Luke then describes Stephen. He is described in precisely the terms used of Jesus and the Twelve, that is, as a prophet: he is filled with the spirit and power, he "works signs and wonders among the people," and like the prophets before him, he generates a divided response. This time, however, those who oppose the prophet are, fittingly, themselves Hellenistic Jews from the Diaspora. Like the rejection of Jesus at Nazareth (Luke 4:16-30), the rejection of Stephen the Hellenist anticipates the conflict that will meet all those who preach the good news in the synagogues of the Diaspora.

But Stephen is not himself a preacher in the Diaspora. His proclamation and rejection take place in Jerusalem. In this respect as well, Stephen is a pivotal figure: he anticipates the future success and conflict of the mission among the nations, but his death also puts a close to the Jerusalem narrative. Luke joins these functions by having Stephen hounded by Hellenistic Jewish opponents, who challenge, confront, agitate and cause his arrest, but then by having his formal hearing and rejection take place before the official Jewish court, the Sanhedrin. The same "leaders of the people" who arrested, tried, and arranged for Jesus' death (Luke 20-23), and who also resisted the preaching of the apostles by arrest, trial, and beating (Acts 4-5), now sit to hear the proclamation of one whose "face like an angel" shows even them that he is a messenger from God (6:15).

That Luke intends the reader to perceive Stephen as a prophet like Jesus is obvious not only from the stereotypical prophetic characteristics in his ministry, but above all from the description of his end. When we examine the account of Stephen's death, we will see the connections drawn explicitly (7:55-8:2). But even in this opening scene, Luke has done three things to show the continuity between Jesus and Stephen. First, by making Stephen's wisdom impossible to refute, he shows that he is one of the witnesses prophesied by Jesus, to whom Jesus has given a "mouth and wisdom" that could not be countered (6:10; see Luke 21:15). Second, the succession of events leading to Stephen's speech imitates the sequence of Jesus' passion: the open confrontation, the suborning of spies, the agitation of the populace, the arrest, and the delivery to the council (6:10-12). Third, Luke has shifted to Stephen's "passion" elements that the other Synoptists made part of Jesus' passion: not Jesus but Stephen has "false witnesses" stand against him and accuse him; not Jesus but Stephen has the charge of "blasphemy" laid against him; not Jesus but Stephen is accused of speaking against the temple. The effect of this overlapping is to insure the reader's perception of Stephen as an authentic witness in continuity with the prophet Jesus; it does not matter that he was appointed by the Twelve; the same prophetic spirit is at work in him. The pattern of the prophet is enacted in his words and in his deeds, in the division he creates in the people, and in his rejection and suffering.

Finally, as in the hearing before Pilate the charge against Jesus was stated three times with variations (Luke 23:2, 5, 14), so is the charge against Stephen: the false witnesses first accuse him of blasphemous words against "Moses and God" (6:11); then before the council they say that Stephen "speaks against this holy place and the law" (6:13), and finally, this is explicated in 6:14 as "Jesus the Nazorean will destroy this place and change the customs that Moses handed down to us."

Before these charges are made, Luke has given the reader no opportunity to hear Stephen. He has thus created an even more dramatic context for Stephen's speech. Will Stephen confirm these charges? We already know that he will not speak "against Moses and God." But will he speak against the holy place and the Law? The answer to this may depend somewhat on what the accusers mean by those terms, which makes the fullest statement of the charge in 6:14 the most important. We notice that "blasphemy against God and Moses" comes down to a very narrow and self-involved definition of Jewish identity: the stability of the temple, and the immutability of the "customs handed down to us."

So self-protective and external an understanding of "God and Moses"—of the nature of God's people in its covenantal relationship with God—is obviously subject to a sharp prophetic challenge. Stephen's response will not be a narrow response to this narrow vision, but a sweeping condemnation of the religious attitudes that legitimate such rigidity and defensiveness, and with it, a closure to God's activity in the Spirit.

For Reference and Further Study

Boismard, M. E. "Le Martyre d'Etienne (Acts 6, 8-8, 2)." *RScR* 69 (1981) 181–194.

Cadbury, H. J. "The Hellenists." *Beginnings* 5:59–74.

Daube, D. "A Reform in Acts and its Models." *Jews, Greeks, and Christians*. Ed. R. Hammerton-Kelly and R. Scroggs. Leiden: Brill, 1976, 151–163.

Grundmann, W. "Das Problem des hellenistischen Christentums innerhalb der Jerusalemer Urgemeinde." *ZNW* 38 (1939) 45–73.

Kodell, J. "The Word of God Grew: The Ecclesial Tendency of *Logos* in Acts 6, 7; 12:24; 19:20." *Biblica* 55 (1974) 505–519.

Lienhard, J. "Acts 6:1-6: A Redactional View." *CBQ* 37 (1975) 228–236.

Moule, C. F. D. "Once More, Who were the Hellenists?" *ExpT* 70 (1958–59) 100–102.

Simon, M. *St. Stephen and the Hellenists in the Primitive Church*. London: Longmans, Green and Co., 1958.

11. *Stephen's Speech: Promises to the Patriarchs* (7:1-16)

1. The chief priest said, "Are these things so?" 2. He said, "Brothers and fathers, listen! The God of glory appeared to our father Abraham while he was in Mesopotamia before he settled in Haran. 3. He said to him, 'Go from your land and from your family, and come to the land that I will show you.' 4. Then he left the land of the Chaldeans. He settled in Haran. And from there, after the death of his father, God moved him into this land in which you are now dwelling. 5. But he did not give him an inheritance in it, not even a foothold. But he promised to give it as a possession to him and to his descendants after him, even though he had no child. 6. And this is the way God spoke, that his 'descendants will sojourn in a foreign land and it will enslave them and treat them badly for four hundred years.' 7. 'Furthermore,' (God said), 'I will judge the nation that they will serve. And after that they will leave and will worship me in this place.' 8. And he gave him a covenant of circumcision. Thus he became the father of Isaac and circumcised him on the eighth day. And Isaac became the father of Jacob, and Jacob of the twelve patriarchs. 9. The patriarchs were envious of Joseph. They sold him into Egypt. But God was with him 10. and rescued him from all his afflictions, and gave him favor and wisdom in the presence of Pharaoh, the king of Egypt. He appointed him governor over Egypt and over all his household. 11. But a famine and great affliction came over all of Egypt and Canaan. Our fathers could not find food. 12. But Jacob heard that there was grain in Egypt. He sent our fathers a first time. 13. And in the second visit, Joseph made himself known to his brothers and the family of Joseph was made known to Pharaoh. 14. Joseph sent for and summoned Jacob his father and his whole family of seventy-five people. 15. Jacob went down into Egypt. He himself and our fathers died. 16. They were transferred to Shechem and were placed in the tomb that Abraham had purchased for a sum of silver from the sons of Hamor in Shechem."

NOTES

2. *the God of Glory appeared:* The expression *theos tēs doxēs* is unusual, appearing otherwise only in LXX Ps 28:3. Since the term *doxa* ("glory") has the sense of "presence/radiance," it more often appears as "glory of the Lord" (Exod 24:16; Lev 9:6) or, more rarely, as "glory of God" (Ezek 10:19). For this first call of Abraham neither the biblical account nor the Jewish narratives based on Genesis refer to a vision, but only an "oracle" (Philo, *On Abraham* 62). In LXX Gen 12:7, however, the expression "the Lord appeared (*ōphthē*) to Abraham" does appear. It is possible that the "vision of glory" here anticipates 7:55, where Stephen also "sees the glory of God."

our father Abraham: The figure of Abraham and the promises God made to him are of central importance for Luke's story; see Luke 1:55, 73; 3:8, 34;

13:16, 28; 16:22-30; 19:9; 20:37; Acts 3:13, 25; 13:26. For Abraham as "father" of the Jews, see Luke 3:8; 16:24, 30; Rom 4:12, 16. In his speech, Stephen consistently aligns himself with the ancestors ("our fathers," 7:11, 12, 19, 38, 44, 45), until the end, when he attacks the audience and "your fathers" (7:51-52).

before he settled in Haran: Luke's sequence of events does not agree with the LXX of Gen 11:3–12:5, nor with the version of *The Book of Jubilees* 12:12-15, or Pseudo-Philo's *Biblical Antiquities* 8:1-3, or Josephus' *Antiquities of the Jews* 1:154. But the wording in Philo's *On Abraham* 67 could suggest that Abraham rather than his father Terah was the agent of the move from Ur of the Chaldees to Haran (see Gen 11:38).

3. *go from your land:* This is a citation from the LXX of Gen 12:1, with only small alterations: a) Luke omits "and from your father's house," and b) adds the adverb *deuro,* here translated as "come." Compare *The Book of Jubilees* 12:22-23, Heb 11:8, *1 Clement* 10:3.

4. *God moved him:* This builds on the LXX of Gen 12:5, "they came into the land of Canaan." The translation supplies "God" in the Greek phrase "he moved him," for the sake of clarity. According to Gen 11:33, Abraham's father Terah died in Haran before Abraham's departure for Canaan, but compare *Book of Jubilees* 12:28-31.

5. *an inheritance:* According to Gen 15:7, God told Abraham that he would "give you this land as an inheritance" (see also Gen 22:17; 28:4). Compare Heb 11:8-10, 13-16, which expands on the significance for faith of this time of sojourning in the land of promise. The translation "foothold" is literally "foot's length" (*bema podos,* see Deut 2:5). Luke is emphasizing that the promise was not yet realized.

promised to give it as a possession to him: The language of "inheritance" (*klēronomia*) and of "promise" (*epangelia*) is found together in 2 Macc 2:17-18, but otherwise is surprisingly absent from the LXX, particularly in light of the NT's predilection for the notion of "promise" (Luke 24:49; Acts 1:4; 2:33, 39; 13:23, 32; 26:6; Rom 4:13-20; 9:4, 8-9; 15:8; 2 Cor 1:20; Gal 3:14-22, 29; 4:23, 28; Eph 2:12; 3:6; 6:2; Heb 4:1; 6:12-13, 15, 17; 8:6; 9:15; 10:36; 11:9, 13, 17, 33, 39). After the word "promised," here, the rest of the verse paraphrases the LXX of Genesis, most clearly 48:4 (because of the term "possession," *kataschesis*), but also Gen 13:15 and 17:8.

he had no child: The genitive absolute construction *ouk ontos autǭ teknou* is read as concessive. See also Gen 15:2; 16:1, and compare Josephus, *Antiquities of the Jews* 1:183; *The Book of Jubilees* 14:2.

6. *descendants will sojourn in a foreign land:* Although the Greek sentence is in indirect discourse, the translation (with some awkwardness) places that part of it dependent on Gen 15:13-14 in direct quotation. Luke makes some changes from the LXX, such as the substitution of *gē allotria* (which is used in Exod 2:22 and 18:3) for *gē ouk idia* ("a land not their own"). The collective noun *sperma* ("seed") is here translated in the plural, as in Luke 1:55 and Acts 3:25.

The term *paroikos* means a resident alien (see Exod 2:22; 18:3; Lev 25:23; Deut 14:21; 23:7).

enslave them and treat them badly: The citation from Gen 15:13 continues. The Greek has *auto*, whose neuter singular is meant to refer back to *sperma*, even though the LXX has *autous* ("them"); consequently some *mss* correct the text to make it harmonize with the LXX. Luke also omits the LXX phrase *kai tapeinosousin* ("and humble them").

7. *I will judge the nation:* Apart from the exchange of a *kai* for the LXX's *de*, the citation continues from Gen 15:14. The phrase put in parentheses ("God said") is added by Luke; compare the Joel citation in Acts 2:17. The verb *krinō* in Gen 15:14 translates the Hebrew *din*, which has the sense of "passing in judgment" (see LXX Pss 7:8; 53:1; 71:2; 134:14). In context, of course, the judgment consisted in the plagues and exodus.

worship me in this place: In LXX Gen 15:14 and in *The Book of Jubilees* 14:14, we find "they will come out with many possessions." Luke replaces this with a paraphrase of Exod 3:12, "when you lead my people from Egypt, you will worship God on this mountain." Note that Luke uses *topos houtos* ("this place") in the sense of "this land" rather than as in the accusation of 6:13-14. Pseudo-Philo's *Biblical Antiquities* 8:3 has the promise but omits any mention of future suffering. Josephus, *Antiquities of the Jews* 1:185 keeps all the elements of the Genesis citation but rewrites and expands them.

8. *covenant of circumcision:* The expression itself is unusual, but it captures the gist of Gen 15:18; 17:1-4, 10-14, 19-22. Circumcision was actually the "sign" of the covenant God made with Abraham (Gen 17:11). According to Gen 17:23-27, Abraham proceeded to circumcise everything male in his vicinity, including himself and his son Ishmael, even before the birth of Isaac. Josephus (*Antiquities* 1:192) supplies this motivation for circumcision: "that his posterity should be kept from mixing with others." At this point in its version, *The Book of Jubilees* 15:25-34 expatiates on the eternal character of the covenant of circumcision and how some have forsaken it. In contrast, Pseudo-Philo's *Biblical Antiquities* 8:3-4 completely ignores the ritual, as does Philo's *On Abraham* 111-166.

Isaac . . . the twelve patriarchs: Luke moves with great rapidity through the next part of the story, since his interest is really in Joseph: the circumcision of Isaac on the eighth day (Gen 21:4); the birth (and implied circumcision) of Jacob (Gen 25:19-26), and of Jacob's twelve sons (Gen 29:31–30:24; 35:16-18), who are here called "patriarchs"; for the rarity of this expression, see the note on 2:29. Pseudo-Philo's *Biblical Antiquities* is almost as brief, adding only the interesting information that Job married Dinah, Jacob's daughter (8:8; see also *Testament of Job* 1:6). In contrast, *The Book of Jubilees* 29-38 pays considerable attention to these characters, revealing at points a close resemblance to the traditions found in the *Testaments of the Twelve Patriarchs*.

9. *the patriarchs were envious of Joseph:* In the LXX of Genesis, the brothers of Joseph are said to hate him (37:4) and be jealous of him (37:11), which led to their

seeking to kill him (37:28). *The Book of Jubilees* 39:1-2 omits this aspect of the story entirely. Pseudo-Philo's *Biblical Antiquities* 8:9 retains only the "hatred" from the LXX. In fragment two of Artapanus' *On the Jews*, there is only the mention that Joseph was "plotted against" by his brothers. Josephus, in sharp contrast, exploits the elements that he recognizes as part of the Hellenistic *topos* "On Envy," and develops them in *Antiquities of the Jews:* the brothers have "envy and hatred" *(phthonos kai misos,* 2:10-13), which makes them seek to kill (2:18). Philo, in turn, elevates "envy" into the theme of this section of *On Joseph:* the brothers are filled with envy *(phthonos,* 5, 17), hatred (5), disturbance and upheaval (10), grief and anger (10-11), and rage leading to murder (12). Not surprisingly, this aspect of the story is emphasized throughout the *Testaments of the Twelve Patriarchs,* as in *Testament of Gad* 3:3; 4:5-6; 5:1; *The Testament of Joseph* 1:3-4; and especially the *Testament of Simeon* 2:6-7, 11, 14; 3:2-3; 4:4-9. The *topos* continues to be developed in Christian writings such as Jas 3:13–4:10; *1 Clement* 4:9; 5:2, and Basil the Great, *Homily* 11:4. We have seen already how Luke attributes the arrest of the apostles in 5:17 to envy.

God was with him: This echoes the recurrent phrase, "the Lord *(kyrios)* was with Joseph" in Gen 39:2, 21, 23; see *Book of Jubilees* 39:4. Philo summarizes, "everything he said or did was under God's directing care" *(On Joseph* 37). Note what is said about Jesus by Peter in Acts 10:38, "because God was with him."

10. *rescued him from all his afflictions:* After Joseph's initial favor with his master, the attempt to seduce him by Potiphar's wife (Gen 39:6-18) led to his imprisonment (39:20) and neglect for over two years (41:1), before he was restored (41:39). For a poetic rendering, see LXX Ps 104:15-20. The sequence is retold with novelistic color by Josephus, *Antiquities of the Jews* 2:41-86, and with predictable moral reflections by Philo, *On Joseph* 40-104.

favor and wisdom: This phrase picks up the LXX Gen 39:4: Joseph found *charin enantion tou kyriou autou,* and Gen 41:33, 38-39, where Joseph is said to have the spirit of God in him, and to be more prudent and understanding than others. See *The Book of Jubilees* 40:5; Philo, *On Joseph* 106; Josephus, *Antiquities of the Jews* 2:87. Note that the same qualities are attributed to the young Moses (Acts 7:22) and the young Jesus (Luke 2:52).

appointed him governor over Egypt: The LXX of Gen 41:40 has "you will be over my house," and 41:41, "Behold, I am setting you over all the land of Egypt." Genesis elaborates Joseph's honors and services (41:42-57), including his marriage to an Egyptian named Aseneth (41:50). Understandably from the standpoint of Jewish national pride, this part of the story is enthusiastically emphasized by Josephus, *Antiquities of the Jews* 2:87-94 and Philo, *On Joseph* 119-162. *The Book of Jubilees* 40:10 pays Joseph's reign its highest compliment, "there was no Satan and there was no evil." In fragment two of Artapanus, *On the Jews,* Joseph is credited with the organization of Egyptian agriculture. The Joseph legend is expanded even further in the novel, *Joseph and Aseneth,* which portrays his wife as a prototype for proselytes.

11. *famine and great affliction:* The wording derives from Gen 41:54, 56, 57, and 42:5; see also LXX Ps 104:16. The words "and great affliction" appear to be a Lukan addition, since it is found neither in the LXX nor in the parallel accounts. We have learned that God released Joseph from all *his* afflictions (7:10); now Joseph will rescue his family from theirs. For the expression "could not find food," compare LXX Ps 36:19; the term *chortasma* originally meant fodder for animals, but see *chortazō* in Luke 6:21; 9:17; 15:16; 16:21.

12. *there was grain in Egypt:* The LXX of Gen 42:2 has Jacob tell his sons, "Look, I have heard that there is grain (*sitos*) in Egypt." Gen 41:57 made it clear that people were coming from other lands to purchase Egyptian grain.

    sent our fathers a first time: Here is the sort of small detail that reveals a great deal about an author's perceptions. This distinction between a "first" and "second" visit is unique to Luke and important for the structuring of his story, since it corresponds both to the two-fold visitation of Moses, and of Jesus (in his ministry and through his prophetic successors). According to Gen 42:8, at the first visit (42:6-25), "Joseph knew his brothers but they did not recognize him (*ouk epegnōsan auton*)." Luke will make the motif of recognition explicit in the next verse. Thus the theme of "ignorance" in the time of the first visitation applies equally to Joseph, Moses, and Jesus. Since it is in the text of Genesis, the Jewish commentators can scarcely ignore it, but it is not exploited in any significant fashion by Josephus, *Antiquities of the Jews* 2:97, or Philo, *On Joseph* 165-167. In contrast, Pseudo-Philo's *Biblical Antiquities* 8:10 is striking because this is one of the few details included in its spare reworking, but nothing more is done with it.

13. *Joseph made himself known to his brothers:* The verb *anagnorizō* can mean either "recognize" or "make oneself known," and although in the end they come to the same thing, the echo of LXX Gen 45:1 demands the translation given here. The "recognition scene" is a staple of Hellenistic Romances (e.g., Longus, *Daphnis and Chloe* 4:20-36). We note that it is after the "recognition" that the family of Joseph is "saved" through being made known to Pharaoh and being brought down to Egypt; see Josephus, *Antiquities of the Jews* 2:160-165.

14. *summoned Jacob his father:* This comes from LXX Gen 45:9. Luke passes rapidly through the final stages of the patriarchal narrative: Jacob coming down to Egypt (46:8) with his family (48:26). Luke follows the LXX of Gen 46:27 in giving the number of the family as seventy-five, rather than the seventy of the Hebrew text, which is found also in Josephus, *Antiquities of the Jews* 2:176; *The Book of Jubilees* 44:33; the calculations in Pseudo-Philo's *Biblical Antiquities* 8:11-14 are very confused.

15. *he himself and our fathers died:* The death of Jacob is recounted in Gen 49:33, that of Joseph in Gen 50:26. In Exod 1:6 it is noted, "Joseph died and his brothers, and all that generation."

16. *transferred to Shechem:* This simple conclusion has a number of difficulties based on the confusing doublets in Genesis concerning the purchase of burial-sites by the patriarchs, and the diverse traditions of where people actually were buried: a) Both Abraham and Jacob purchased burial places in Canaan; b)

Abraham bought his from Ephron the Hittite in Hebron (Gen 23:10-19); c) Jacob bought his from the sons of Hamor the father of Shechem (a person) in Shechem (a place) in Gen 33:18-20. d) But according to Gen 50:13, in accordance with his own request (Gen 49:31), *Jacob* was taken by his sons to *Abraham's* burial site at Hebron—where Abraham and Sarah and Isaac and Rebecca and Leah were already interred. This obviously confuses things, but it agrees with Josephus, *Antiquities of the Jews* 2:199-200 and *The Book of Jubilees* 45:15; 46:9-10. e) A final element of confusion is introduced by Josh 24:32, which says that the bones of *Joseph* were taken to the cave bought by *Jacob* from the sons of Hamor. f) Luke has therefore either confused these traditions, or telescoped them into one.

INTERPRETATION

Stephen's speech in response to the chief priest's question is the longest single discourse in Acts, so long that some sort of division into sections is necessary. The speech is so structured, however, that the damage done by such dismemberment is not severe. The present discussion will take up some general considerations and then look more closely at the part of the speech dealing with Abraham and Joseph. An evaluation of the speech in its literary context will be deferred until the next section, after the text as a whole has been examined.

From the beginning, of course, we must listen to the speech as the creation of Luke and as serving his literary goals. It is futile and even fatuous to seek to find in these words the special theological outlook of the historical "Hellenists" represented by Stephen. Not only in style and diction, but above all in its religious perceptions, this discourse represents the special vision of Luke himself. Indeed, it is in Stephen's speech that we find most clearly articulated not only our author's interpretation of the biblical story, but also his understanding of how that story is continued in Jesus and the apostles. Stephen's speech is, as a whole, the key Luke provides his readers for the interpretation of his entire two-volume narrative.

We do not examine the speech, therefore, with a narrow preoccupation concerning its historicity, or its manner of responding to the charges placed against Stephen. Does Stephen answer the question concerning the Law and the Temple? In one obvious sense, no, for he does not even take up the charges in the form they were made. But in a more important sense, he responds to the real issue underlying those attacks: are the Messianists renegade Jews, or do they have a legitimate reason to claim that they are the authentic realization of the people of God? The way Luke has Stephen make this argument is, consistently enough for an author who believes in the convincing character of narrative, through a retelling of that people's history.

Those readers who object that the greater part of Stephen's speech is beside the point simply show that they have not grasped what the point is. Luke is working very much like a Hellenistic historian when he has Stephen deliver a history lesson at this critical moment. Herodotus shows us two sides in a fierce battle giving speeches which defend their claims by means of ancestral traditions (*Persian Wars* 9:26-27). Thucydides also has lengthy speeches filled with historical reminiscence that are uttered at moments of crisis (*Peloponnesian War* 1, 3, 68-70; 2, 6, 35-47). Josephus recounts how, while being derided and under fire from missiles, he addressed the defenders of the city of Jerusalem and tried to persuade them to surrender to the Romans. How did he do this? By a lengthy speech in which he recounted all the precedents for their predicament from the people's story in the Bible (*Jewish War* 5:376-419)!

What all such recitals have in common is the way in which they select and shape a tradition in order to justify or support a specific understanding of it. Perhaps the most useful way to understand Stephen's speech, in fact, is as an example of such "biblical retellings" within Judaism. The sectarians at Qumran used *The Book of Jubilees* as well as their own *Genesis Apocryphon* and *Damascus Rule* to provide a basis for their own claim to being God's particular people by retelling the ancient story in a way that pointed to them. In a less markedly sectarian fashion, Jewish apologists like Philo in his *On Abraham, On Joseph,* and *Life of Moses,* and Artapanus in his *On the Jews,* and Pseudo-Philo in his *Biblical Antiquities,* and Josephus in his *Antiquities of the Jews,* interpreted the narratives about the patriarchs and Moses for their Hellenistic readers by retelling them in terms those readers could appreciate.

The notes have indicated the many points at which Stephen's speech resembles or differs from such Jewish narrative interpretations. But the most important insight to be gained from reading Luke's version within this comparative context is that the precise understanding of Israel's past that Luke wants to communicate becomes clearer. Luke was up to a similar task as his fellow apologists, but the claims he was defending were distinctive, and had to do with faith in the prophet Jesus. Luke therefore is part of the development of specifically Christian apologetic. Like Paul in Galatians and Romans, like the author of Hebrews and James, like Clement and Barnabas and Justin, Luke seeks to legitimate the messianic appropriation of Torah by showing how Torah itself demanded such an appropriation. This central conviction provides the principle of selection for his Bible story, and the basis for its shaping.

Certain literary impressions are immediate, once Stephen's speech is placed within this comparative framework. The first is its author's remarkable power of compression; although long by the measure of other speeches in Acts, this discourse is truly extensive only in the amount of material it manages to cover. The second is the way Luke not only uses biblical diction but the actual text of the LXX. This is, of course, most obvious in the direct citations (e.g., 7:3, 5, 6). But Luke also uses actual snippets of biblical texts to construct the discourse (see notes for examples). The closest parallel to the way he works the biblical text into his own may be in Pseudo-Philo's *Biblical Antiquities*. The third impression that emerges from comparison to other such recitals is our author's tight focus on certain characters and patterns. The characters are Abraham, Joseph, and Moses. The patterns require a closer analysis.

Luke has Stephen begin with Abraham, which is natural enough when the discourse concerns the story of the people. Beginning with Abraham, all the way to the final accusation, Stephen associates himself with his listeners: Abraham is not "your father," but "our father." The debate, therefore, is within the family as to what constitutes authentic family membership. The first clues to Luke's understanding are given by the details in the Abraham story he includes or emphasizes.

The most important feature of the Abraham story for Luke is that it is one in which God is the main actor. God is the first subject mentioned (7:2) and his are all the main actions: God appears (7:3), speaks (7:3, 6), moves (7:4), gives an inheritance (7:5), promises (7:5), judges (7:7), gives a covenant (7:8). Luke does not emphasize Abraham's faith, indeed does not even mention it. Abraham merely goes and dwells (7:4), begets and circumcises (7:8). The focus is on God's promise and the way it will reach fulfillment in a time beyond Abraham. God appears where and when he wishes, directs and moves peoples, and issues promises that are open-ended, to be fulfilled in often surprising ways. Luke will show such paradoxical realizations of the promise in the saving figures of Joseph and Moses. But in fact, for Luke the story of Abraham reaches its true fulfillment only now in the messianic realization of the promise.

In the section of the story dealing with Joseph (7:9-16) we can see even more clearly how Luke exploits aspects of the biblical account to make it point forward to the present. First is the way in which Joseph himself is a type of Jesus. The imaging here is less dramatic than in the case of Moses, but is nevertheless visible. In verses 9-10, we see how Joseph is rejected by his brothers (because of their envy) and sold into Egypt, but that this fate is reversed by God: God is with him and frees him from all his afflictions, he finds favor with the king, he is installed as ruler over Egypt. The one rejected by his own people, in other words, is empowered through God's intervention, and is now in a position to save the ones who rejected him.

The second feature of the Joseph story is the way Luke exploits the double visit of the family to the presence of Joseph. The first visit is one in which they do not recognize Joseph, although he knows them. The second visit is one in which Joseph makes himself known, they recognize him, and therefore they can be saved from their affliction caused by famine (verses 11-13). Already in the Joseph story, therefore, Luke shows the pattern that will be developed even more fully in his description of Moses, and which will structure his portrayal of Jesus as the prophet like Moses: the rejected and rescued savior, the double visitation with the possibility of further acceptance or rejection.

For Reference and Further Study

Barrett, C. K. "Old Testament History according to Stephen and Paul." *Studien zum Text und zur Ethik des Neuen Testaments*. Ed. W. Schrage. BZNW 47. Berlin: Walter de Gruyter, 1986, 57–69.

Bihler, J. *Die Stephanusgeschichte*. Münchener Theologische Studien 1, Historische Abteilung 30. München: Max Huebner, 1963.

Dahl, N. "The Abraham Story in Luke-Acts." *Studies in Luke-Acts*. Eds. L. E. Keck and J. L. Martyn. Nashville: Abingdon Press, 1966, 139–158.

Dupont, J. "La structure oratoire du discours d'Etienne (Actes 7)." *Bib* 66 (1985) 153–167.

Kilgallen, J. *The Stephen Speech: A Literary and Redactional Study of Acts 7, 2-53*. Analecta Biblica 67. Rome: Pontifical Biblical Institute, 1976.

Mundle, W. "Die Stephanusrede Apg. 7: Eine Martyrerapologie." *ZNW* 20 (1921) 133ff.

Richard, E. *Acts 6:1–8:4: The Author's Method of Composition*. SBLDS 41. Missoula: Scholars Press, 1978.

_____. "The Polemical Character of the Joseph Episode in Acts 7." *JBL* 98 (1979) 255–267.

12. Stephen's Speech: The Prophet Moses (7:17-53)

17. "As the time approached for the promise which God declared to Abraham, the people increased and grew larger in Egypt 18. until another king ascended in Egypt who had not known Joseph. 19. He tricked our people. He treated our fathers harshly, making them expose their infants so they would not survive. 20. At that time, Moses was born, and he was beautiful in God's eyes. He was nurtured for three months in his father's house, 21. but when he had been exposed, Pharaoh's daughter took him and raised him as her own son. 22. Moses was educated in all Egyptian wisdom. And he was powerful in his words and

deeds. 23. When he was forty years old, he decided to visit his brothers, the children of Israel. 24. He saw someone being treated unjustly. He defended him and vindicated the oppressed man by striking down the Egyptian. 25. He thought that his brothers would understand that God was giving them salvation through his hands. But they did not understand. 26. The next day he came upon them as they were fighting. He urged them to make peace. He said, 'Men, you are brothers. Why are you doing injustice to each other?' 27. But the one who was abusing his neighbor repulsed him. He said, 'Who appointed you ruler and judge over us? 28. Are you seeking to kill me the way you killed the Egyptian yesterday?' 29. At this remark, Moses fled. He became a sojourner in the land of Midian. There he had two sons. 30. After forty years, an angel appeared to him in the desert of Mount Sinai, in the flame of a burning bush. 31. When Moses saw it, he was astonished at the vision. As he approached to observe it, there was a voice from the Lord: 32. 'I am the God of your fathers, the God of Abraham, Isaac and Jacob.' Moses began trembling. He did not dare to look. 33. The Lord said to him, 'Take the sandals off your feet, for the place where you stand is holy ground. 34. I have indeed seen the oppression of my people in Egypt, and I have heard their groaning, and I have come down to rescue them. Now come, I will send you on a commission to Egypt.' 35. This Moses whom they rejected when they said, 'Who made you ruler and judge,' this one God sent out as both ruler and redeemer with the hand of the angel who had appeared to him in the bush! 36. This one led them out! He worked wonders and signs in the land of Egypt, and in the Red Sea, and in the wilderness for forty years. 37. This is the Moses who said to the children of Israel, 'God will raise up a prophet like me from among your brothers.' 38. This is the one who was in the assembly in the desert, with the angel who spoke to him on Mount Sinai, and with our fathers. He received living words to give to us! 39. Our fathers did not want to obey him. Instead they rejected him. And they turned back in their hearts to Egypt. 40. They said to Aaron, 'Make gods for us who will go before us, for this Moses who led us out of the land of Egypt, we do not know what has happened to him.' 41. And during that period they made a calf. They brought a sacrifice to the idol. They rejoiced in the works of their hands. 42. But God turned, and handed them over to worship the hosts of heaven, just as it is said in the Book of the Prophets, 'Did you offer me victims and sacrifices for forty years in the desert, house of Israel? 43. Rather you raised a tent to Moloch and the star of your god Raiphan, and the images you made to worship them. So I will exile you beyond Babylon.' 44. The tent of witness was in the desert for our fathers, just as the one who spoke to Moses commanded it to be made according to the model which he had seen. 45. It was brought in by our fathers who had received it in their turn when with Joshua they took possession of the nations that God drove out before our fathers, until the days of David. 46. He found favor with God and asked to find a dwelling for the God of Jacob. 47. And Solomon built a house for him. 48. But the Most High does not dwell in the works of hands. As the Prophet says, 49. 'Heaven is my throne. Earth is the footstool for my feet. What sort of house will you build for me, says the Lord, or what resting place for me? 50. Has not my hand made all things?' 51. You are stiff-necked people, and are uncircumcised both in your hearts and your ears! You are always resisting the Holy Spirit! As your fathers did, so do you. 52. Which of the prophets did your fathers not persecute? And they killed the ones who foretold the coming of the righteous one. Now you have become his betrayers and murderers! 53. You are the ones who received the law as commandments from angels, yet you did not keep it."

NOTES

17. *as the time approached:* Together with v. 20, "at that time," Luke locates the Moses story with reference to the fulfillment of the promises to Abraham. Notice the concern for dating in vv. 20, 23, 26, 30, 36, 42, 45.

promise which God declared to Abraham: This is obviously a Lukan shaping of the narrative, a look backward to 7:5 which establishes the pattern of "prophecy/fulfillment." Compare Luke 1:53, "Remembering his mercy as he spoke to our fathers, to Abraham and his descendants forever," and 1:73, "to show mercy to our fathers and remembering his holy covenant that he swore by oath to Abraham our father." Such attention to the fulfillment of the promises is found also in Pseudo-Philo's *Biblical Antiquities* 9:3; 10:2.

people increased: This is taken from LXX Exod 1:7. Rather than use "the children of Israel" of the LXX, Luke uses the term "the people" (*ho laos*). Josephus puts this in terms of the Hebrews' aptitude for labor, wealth and prosperity, which generated envy among the Egyptians, "a voluptuous people, slack to labor" (*Antiquities of the Jews* 2:201).

18. *another king ascended:* The line comes from LXX Exod 1:8, with the biblicism "rose up" translated as "ascended." He takes the verb "trick" (*katasophizomai*) from Exod 1:10 and "treat harshly" (*kakoō*) from Exod 1:11. The phrase *to genos* ("family/race") is here translated as "people." Luke moves over the specifically economic oppression directly to the decree concerning children.

19. *expose their infants:* Luke abbreviates the account. Pharaoh at first tried to kill the children through midwives, but failing at that, ordered the drowning of sons in the Nile (Exod 1:15-22). Only the verb *zōogoneō* (here translated as "survive") is lifted from Exod 1:17, 22. Josephus attributes Pharaoh's action to a prophecy concerning Moses' future greatness and the threat he would pose to the kingdom, and adds that parents who did not obey the decree were themselves to be put to death (*Antiquities of the Jews* 2:205-208).

20. *Moses was born:* For the temporal connection to the promises, see the note on 7:17. The role of Moses' family is considerably elaborated, including the fact that the attempt to save Moses was owed to revelations in dreams, by

Josephus, *Antiquities of the Jews* 2:210-217, and Pseudo-Philo, *Biblical Antiquities* 9:3-10.

beautiful in God's eyes: The term *asteios* derives from the LXX of Exod 2:2, and has a range of meanings from "urbane/witty" to "comely/pretty" (see Num 22:32; Judg 3:17; Jdt 11:23). Luke adds the pious dative of respect, *tō theō* (with reference to God = "in God's eyes"). Philo, *Life of Moses* 1:9, says that Moses had "an appearance of more than ordinary beauty (*asteioteran*)." Josephus revels in the unusual ease of Moses' delivery (*Antiquities of the Jews* 2:218), but defers mention of his physical beauty to the impression made on Pharaoh's daughter by the first sight of him (2:224).

nurtured for three months: Exodus 2:3-4 speaks rather of "hiding" the child, which is followed closely by *The Book of Jubilees* 47:3, and Josephus, *Antiquities of the Jews* 2:218. Philo has Moses secretly "nursed at his mother's breast" for three months (*Life of Moses* 1:9). The oddest version is Pseudo-Philo's *Biblical Antiquities* 9:12, which has Jochabed hide him for three months in her womb!

21. *Pharaoh's daughter took him:* The verb *anaireō* comes from LXX Exod 2:5; when used in the middle, it means to "take up" something, and can be used in the specific sense of "taking up/owning" a child (e.g., Plutarch, *Life of Antony* 36:3). The Western Text adds "in/by the river" after the word "exposed," to make clearer Moses' location when found.

raised him as her own son: Exod 2:10 has "he became to her as a son." Josephus supplies the name Thermuthis to the daughter (*Antiquities of the Jews* 2:224), whereas *The Book of Jubilees* 47:5 calls her Tharmuth, and Artapanus, *On the Jews,* calls her Meris, and adds that she was barren (Frag. 3). This last aspect, in turn, is psychologically developed by Philo, *Life of Moses* 1:12-15.

22. *educated in all Egyptian wisdom:* In vv. 20-22, Luke uses the classic biographical triad of "birth, nurture, education" (*gennēsis, trophē, paideia*), as he will also of Paul in Acts 22:3; see examples in Plato, *Crito* 50E, 51C; Philo, *Life of Moses* 2:1; *Against Flaccus* 158. There is nothing about Moses' youth in the Exodus account, but the lives of great figures require legendary elaboration where the historical record fails, as we see in Pseudo-Callisthenes, *Life of Alexander of Macedon* 1:13-19, and *The Infancy Gospel of Thomas.* The same is true for Moses. Josephus has a sketch of a childhood challenge of Pharaoh (*Antiquities of the Jews* 2:233-235) and says that he was "educated with the utmost care" (2:236). Philo pays particular attention to the education, stressing his training by Greek teachers, but also Assyrian, Chaldean and Egyptian instructors (*Life of Moses* 1:21-24), but Philo typically expatiates on Moses' growth in moral virtue (1:25-31). A countervailing tendency is found in *The Book of Jubilees* 47:9, which insists that "Amran, your father, taught you writing," and says nothing further of Moses' education at court. Likewise Pseudo-Philo's *Biblical Antiquities* 9:16 says that his mother maintained his Hebrew name of Melchiel. Cultural competition reaches its apex in Artapanus, *On the Jews,* frag. three, which makes Moses the teacher of Orpheus and the source of everything worthwhile in Egyptian culture. Josephus also has an

extensive recital of Moses' adult activities before his encounter with his countrymen (*Antiquities of the Jews* 2:238-253). In its brevity and essential components, Luke's treatment of Moses' childhood resembles his summary concerning Jesus in Luke 2:52: "Jesus made progress in wisdom and stature and in favor both with God and people."

powerful in his words and deeds: This does not derive from Exod but is Luke's authorial addition. The very wording, *dynatos en logois kai ergois autou* echoes the description of Jesus in Luke 24:19, *prophētēs dynatos en ergō kai logō* ("a prophet powerful in deed and word"; see also Acts 2:22). This characterization, in fact, contrasts with his own protestation in Exod 4:10-17, but does fit his depiction as an orator by Josephus, *Antiquities of the Jews* 3:13-23.

23. *forty years old:* According to Deut 34:7, Moses was a hundred and twenty years old when he died. Luke divides this into three equal sections: a) the period up to his first visit of the people (7:23); b) the period of exile and empowerment (7:30); c) the period of exodus and wandering in wilderness (7:36). At this point, LXX Exod has only, "when he became great (*megas*)," and according to *The Book of Jubilees* 47:10, Moses was then about "three weeks of years."

decided to visit: The phrase, "his brothers the children of Israel" comes directly from LXX Exod 2:11, but the rest is Luke's. The phrase translated "decided" is a biblicism, "rose in his heart to" (see Luke 24:38, and see Jer 3:16; 39:35; 51:21; Ezek 38:10; Isa 65:16). The term *episkeptein* here has something of its sense of "observe/examine," but Luke uses it in the special meaning of "God's visitation" (see e.g., Gen 21:1; 50:24-25; Exod 3:16; 4:31; 13:19; 32:34; Luke 1:68; 7:16; 19:44 and Acts 15:14).

24. *striking down the Egyptian:* Luke basically follows the LXX of Exod 2:11-12, retaining the phrase *pataxas ton Aigyption*, but omitting Moses' "looking this way and that" before acting, and his burying him in the sand afterward, although the Western Text adds this phrase to Acts.

25. *understand . . . did not understand:* This is lacking entirely from Exod and from any of the parallel Jewish retellings of the Moses story. It represents a distinctive Lukan contribution and is an obvious connection to his story of Jesus, whose first rejection by his people is also attributed to "ignorance" (Acts 3:17). We have observed the theme of recognition also in the Joseph story (Acts 7:13). For the theme of "salvation" in Luke-Acts, see e.g., Luke 1:47, 69, 71, 77; 2:11, 30; 3:6; 19:19; Acts 5:31, and especially Luke 24:21, "we had hoped that he was the very one who was going to liberate Israel."

26. *came upon them as they were fighting:* The notice concerning the next day comes from Exod 2:13 ("the second day"). The translation "came upon" is literally in the Greek "appeared (*ōphthē*) to them." Codex D adds "and he saw them doing injustice" after the word "fighting" (from Exod 2:14); this would create a verbal link to v. 24.

urged them to make peace: The imperfect of the verb *synallasō* ("to enter into communication/reconcile") is conative: he was attempting to reconcile them. The phrase *eis eirēnēn* is not only redundant but is striking for several other reasons: a) Exod 2:14 has one of the Hebrews "doing injustice" to another, and Moses takes the part of the one being injured, only to be rebuked by the other (see likewise *The Book of Jubilees* 47:11). But Luke makes Moses a neutral mediator, with both "doing injustice" (see 7:26). b) By so doing, he embellishes the image of Moses as a sage, one of whose works is to make peace (see Dio, *Oration* 22; 38; 77/78; Lucian of Samosata, *Demonax* 9; Philostratus, *Apollonius of Tyana* 1:15). c) The theme of peace is associated with the ministry of Jesus, so that Luke has established another connection between Moses and Jesus (Luke 1:79; 2:14, 29; Acts 10:36).

doing injustice to each other: The LXX of Exod 2:11 has Moses ask, "Why are you beating your neighbor?" The strain Luke has placed on the text by his re-reading is shown by the next verse, in which "the one who was abusing his neighbor" responds to Moses, even though Luke had them both "doing injustice." The question has a deeper edge within Luke-Acts as a whole: like the brothers of Joseph who out of envy sought to kill him, and like these contentious Israelites, so do the hearers of Stephen reject Jesus and the apostles and the one speaking to them, "doing injustice."

27. *repulsed him:* The verb *apōtheō* is literally "to thrust away"; the rejection is both verbal and physical. The verb is used frequently by the LXX for *God's* "rejection" (Judg 6:13; 1 Sam 12:22; LXX Ps 42:2; 43:9, 23; 59:1; Hos 4:6; 9:17; Jer 2:37; Ezek 5:11). The words of the rejection are taken verbatim from LXX Exod 2:14, and will be repeated in v. 35.

29. *at this remark, Moses fled:* Literally "at this word." Exod 2:15 has Moses fearful that Pharaoh would "hear this word (*rhēma*)," and when Pharaoh "heard this word (*rhēma*)" he seeks to seize Moses, so Moses flees. The Jewish apologists had various ways of dealing with this embarrassing incident. *The Book of Jubilees* 47:12 is very close to Acts, giving as the motivation for the flight, "because of these words." In sharp contrast, Pseudo-Philo's *Biblical Antiquities* 9:16–10:1 omits the entire sequence, moving directly from Moses' childhood to the plagues. Artapanus' *On the Jews* gives a novelistic account of a rivalry between Moses and the Egyptian king; it was the assassin sent by the king to kill Moses that Moses himself killed, forcing him to flee (frag. three). Josephus also attributes Moses' flight to an envious plot against him, but does not have Moses' killing anyone (*Antiquities of the Jews* 2:254-256). Philo combines these elements, retaining the killing of the Egyptian as in Exodus, but also including a royal plot against Moses (*Life of Moses* 1:43-46).

sojourner in the land of Midian: Acts uses a more dramatic term, "fled" (*ephugen*) for Moses' departure than does the LXX of Exod 2:15, which has "withdrew" (*anechōrēsen*). The LXX term gives Philo the chance to treat Moses' exile as a kind of philosophical retreat, during which he prayed for the oppressors, but also went through spiritual training exercises, both "theoretical and practical," reading and reflecting (*Life of Moses* 1:47-48). In effect, Philo has Moses appear as the prototype for the Therapeutae (see *The Contemplative Life* 18–32). Moses' sons Gershom and Eliezer are mentioned in Exod 2:22 and 18:3-4.

30. *an angel appeared to him:* This comes from LXX Exod 3:2, except that Luke lacks "of the Lord" after angel, a lack supplied by the Western Text tradition. On

the basis of this verse, Luke continues to refer to the "angel" throughout the rest of the speech, even when the LXX itself does not have it (7:35, 38, 53). The LXX's own use of the expression (originally probably a euphemism to avoid mention of the divine name, derived from the Hebrew *malak Yahweh* is sporadic enough to justify Luke's practice (compare Exod 14:19 and Luke 7:35, Deut 33:2 and Luke 7:53). The event here recounted is critical to Luke's recital, but is slighted in the Jewish parallels. *The Book of Jubilees* 48:1-2 passes over it entirely. The omission in Pseudo-Philo's *Biblical Antiquities* 10:1-6 is even more dramatic. Artapanus, *On the Jews*, gives only a naturalistic account of the bush, separating it from "a divine voice" that instructed Moses (frag. three). Josephus also seem to want to distinguish between the "amazing prodigy" of the bush, and "the divine oracles that issued from the fire" (*Antiquities of the Jews* 2:266-269). Philo devotes the most attention to the event, including quite a lovely symbolic interpretation of the burning bush as the people who are oppressed but never consumed (*Life of Moses* 1:65-66, 69). The angel, in turn, is a "symbol of God's providence which all silently brings relief to the greatest dangers, exceeding every hope" (1:67).

31. *astonished at the vision:* The "vision" (*to orama*) comes from LXX Exod 3:3, but the psychological reactions here and in 7:32 ("began trembling") are owed to Luke. The verb *katanoeō* means to "observe closely/examine/study." Compare Luke 6:41; 12:24, 47; 20:23; Acts 11:6; 27:39.

32. *God of your fathers:* Luke drops the verb *eimi* from what is actually a mixed citation, mainly from LXX Exod 3:6. The phrase "God of your (pl) fathers" comes from Exod 3:15 in place of the singular in Exod 3:6. The Acts textual tradition is uncertain how many times "God" (*ho theos*) should appear in the statement.

33. *the sandals off your feet:* In the LXX of Exod 3:5, this command precedes the identifying statement of 3:6. It may be important for Luke's overall argument in the speech that "this ground" is identified as "holy" (from Exod 3:5), since that would relativize the claims about "this holy place" that formed part of the charge against Stephen (Acts 6:13). "Holy," he suggests, is where the presence of God is. The Messianists argue that this presence is among them in the Spirit.

34. *I have indeed seen:* The emphatic translation seeks to capture the semitism, "seeing I have seen" (*idōn eidon*). Once more, Luke has deftly combined fragments from several verses in LXX Exod to create a condensed version made up of the actual words of Scripture. Here he combines pieces from Exod 3:7, 8, and 10, with only these alterations: a) rather than *kraugēs autōn* he has *stenagmou autōn*, and b) he has God send Moses "to Egypt" rather than "to Pharaoh king of Egypt." The verb *apostellō* is here translated with its full force ("send with a commission"), to communicate the importance of the term for Luke's theme of prophets sent out by God (see Luke 1:19; 4:18; 7:27; 9:2; 10:1; 11:49; Acts 3:20, 26).

35. *this Moses:* The speech takes a dramatic rhetorical turn from narrative to a series of declarative statements (running from v. 35 to v. 39). The sentences

are hinged by the five-fold repetition of the demonstrative pronoun ("this/this one") and three relative pronouns, all pointing to *Moses*. The form of this first declaration is particularly interesting, for it matches precisely the "kerygmatic" statement of *Jesus'* rejection and vindication in Acts 3:13-15, and has precisely the same import: the one rejected by humans is accepted and established in power by God, to be sent back once more, this time with greater power (see also Acts 2:23, 36; 10:39). This rhetorical shaping is entirely Luke's and has no parallel in the Jewish versions of the Moses story.

whom they rejected: The link to Jesus is even more obvious since Luke uses the verb *arneomai* (to deny) for this rejection rather than the *apōtheō* of 7:27; *arneomai* is the verb used for the denial of Jesus in the kerygmatic statement of 3:13-15. And as the statement about Jesus contained a recital of the passion events, so does this one about Moses point back to the words of rejection spoken in 7:27. The parallelism is exact and undoubtedly deliberate.

sent out as both ruler and redeemer: For the significance of *apostellō*, see the note on 7:34. The term "ruler" (*archōn*) derives from 7:27, but "redeemer" (*lutrōtēs*) is not used in the Exodus account; it is applied to God in LXX Ps 18:4; 77:5, and the use of *lutrōsis* in LXX Ps 110:9, "he sent redemption to his people," may echo the exodus story (see LXX Ps 110:4-5). On the other hand, *archōn* is very close to *archēgos* ("author/leader") which is used for *Jesus* in Acts 3:15; 5:31. As for "redemption," it too is a Lukan theme (Luke 1:68; 2:38), which appears in the expectation concerning Jesus expressed in Luke 24:21. The Jewish parallels have various alternative designations: Artapanus, *On the Jews*, says the voice "bade him campaign against Egypt," and understands Moses to be a general leading an army (frag. three). Josephus likewise has him sent as "commander and leader" (*stratēgos kai hēgemōn*) in *Antiquities of the Jews* 2:268. Philo also designates him as "leader" (*hēgemōn*) in *Life of Moses* 1:71.

the hand of the angel: For the use of the "angel of the Lord," throughout the speech, see the note on 7:30. The stretching out of the hand as a gesture of power is discussed in the note on Acts 4:30. The image is used heavily in Exod 4:2, 4, 7, etc. The complete expression "right hand of the one who appeared in the bush" is found in LXX Deut 33:16.

36. *wonders and signs in the land of Egypt:* For this language in connection to the Moses story, see the note on Acts 2:19. The statement here most resembles that in Deut 34:11. The stereotypical character of the language can be seen from its appearance in *The Book of Jubilees* 48:4, 12; Philo, *Life of Moses* 1:77, 90, 91. The threefold division into a) the land of Egypt, b) the Red Sea, and c) the wilderness, shows that the prophetic power was active throughout Moses' ministry among the people.

37. *this is the Moses who said:* Coming immediately after the "kerygmatic" statement of Moses rejection/vindication, and the statement of his wonders and signs, this citation from Deut 18:15 points unmistakably to the figure of Jesus, to whom the same passage was applied in Acts 3:22. Luke's typological intentions at this juncture can scarcely be denied. They are made even clearer by some *mss* that add "to him you shall listen." The focus on Moses as prophet

in Luke's rendition is all the more impressive for its relative absence in the
parallel Jewish retellings of the exodus story. Philo clearly considers Moses
as a prophet "of the highest quality," but develops this theme almost entirely
in terms of Moses' delivery of oracles (*Life of Moses* 1:156, 2:188-291). In *Antiquities of the Jews* 4:329, Josephus shows dependence on Deut 34:10 by declaring
that there was none to equal Moses as a prophet, but he seems to under-
stand the "prophet to be raised up" as Joshua, whom Moses appointed to
succeed him "both in his prophetic functions and as commander in chief"
(4:165).

38. *assembly in the desert:* The term *ekklēsia* is translated elsewhere in Acts as
"church," and derives from the LXX translation of the Hebrew's *qahal Yahweh* in passages such as Deut 4:10; 23:1-2. This picture of Moses as go-between
for God and people is wonderfully sketched by Philo, *Life of Moses* 2:166, who
terms Moses mediator and reconciler and protector and intercessor. This role
for Moses is developed also in the Rabbinic tradition in such passages as *Sifre
on Deuteronomy* 33:1 and *Exodus Rabbah*, Ki Thissa 47:9. For the presence of
the angels, see note on 7:30.

    received living words to give to us: As pointed out in the note on Acts 2:33, the
pattern "who received/to give" is the same as that attributed to Jesus with
regard to the Holy Spirit: "having received/he poured out." As Moses for
the Law, we understand, so Jesus with the Spirit. The phrase "living words"
(or "oracles" = *logia*) does not occur in the LXX, but the connection between
the Law and life is constantly drawn (e.g., Deut 4:1, 33; 5:26; 16:20; 30:15;
32:45; also LXX Ps 118:25, 50, 154).

39. *our fathers did not want to obey him:* Here and in the previous verse, many *mss*
have second person pronouns "you/your" rather than "us/our." The problem is obvious and difficult to resolve: at what point, if any, does Luke want
to show Stephen distancing the Messianists from the past tradition? Oddly
enough, the *ms* evidence for "you" in the previous verse is impressive, but
the context argues against it. In the present verse, by contrast, the reading
"your" would seem demanded by the negative tone, but the *ms* evidence
is actually weaker for "your" than it is for "our" in this verse. This interpretive interjection makes the desert generation the forerunner of the present
generation, which also does not want to "listen to the prophet (Deut
18:15-19)." The discourse takes on an entirely dark coloration from this point
on, matched only by the recountal in Qumran's *Damascus Rule* (*CD* 3:7-11).

    they rejected him: This is again Luke's interpretation, making the disobedience
of the people a rejection of the prophet. Luke's literary intention is clear from
the fact that he uses again the same verb (*apōtheō*) as for the first "repulsion"
(7:27). This is now the second rejection, made despite the "signs and
wonders" done in their midst. The phrase "hearts turned back to Egypt"
is based on LXX Num 14:3, "It is therefore now best for us to turn back to
Egypt."

40. *make gods for us:* The direct statement is found in LXX Exod 32:1 and repeated
in Aaron's report to Moses in Exod 32:23; Luke only eliminates the slighting

"this man Moses" from the LXX and changes *ginomai* from the perfect to the aorist tense.

41. *they made a calf:* The verb form *moschopoieō* ("to make a calf") is based on but not found in LXX Exod 32:4. It corresponds to the "things made by hand" (*cheiropoiētoi*) in Acts 7:48. In fact, Philo has Aaron report to Moses, "They have fashioned a god, the work of their own hands (*cheiropoiētōn*) in the form of a bull" (*Life of Moses* 2:165). Like the scene of Moses killing the Egyptian, Josephus omits this embarrassing incident (*Antiquities of the Jews* 3:98). In contrast, Pseudo-Philo develops the scene at considerable length (*Biblical Antiquities* 12:1-10). Like Luke's, his recital is as much about the people's infidelity as it is about God's fidelity.

    brought a sacrifice to the idol: This is based on LXX Exod 32:6, although that text does not use the term "idol" (*eidōlon*), the making of which is forbidden by the decalogue (Exod 20:4; Deut 5:8); the term is generally associated with Gentile worship (Gen 31:19; 1 Kgs 11:2; 2 Chr 11:15; LXX Ps 113:12; Wis 14:11).

    rejoiced in the works of their hands: See above on "the works of hands" and its connection to idolatry in the LXX (e.g., Lev 26:1, 30; Judg 8:8; Wis 18:8; Isa 2:18; 10:11; 16:12; 19:1; 21:9; 31:7; Dan 5:4, 23). Luke's choice of the verb *euphrainō* ("rejoice") is particularly cutting, since it is based on LXX Exod 32:6, "the people sat to eat and drink but rose up to play," but uses the term used consistently by the LXX for the rejoicing that the people were to do at the feasts of Yahweh (Lev 23:40; Deut 12:7, 12, 18). For the golden calf as paradigmatic symbol of idolatry, see also Paul in 1 Cor 10:7-14.

42. *God turned and handed them over:* The verb *strephō* ("turn") can be either intransitive (as in "God turned away") or transitive (as in "God turned them"); that the latter is intended is clear from the use of "handed over" (*paradidōmi*); as in Rom 1:24, 26, 28 (also in a discourse on idolatry), this suggests that God allowed the people to become captive to the consequences of their own evil choices (compare Exod 21:13; Lev 26:25; Num 21:3; Deut 1:27; LXX Ps 9:35; 26:12; 40:2; 62:10).

    Book of the Prophets: Luke elsewhere refers to the "Book of the Psalms" (Luke 20:42; Acts 1:10) and the "Book of the Words of Isaiah the Prophet" (Luke 3:4). Here he refers to the collection of the twelve ("minor") prophets.

    did you offer me victims: The citation is almost exactly from LXX Amos 5:25-27, with only small alterations. The form of the original question (*mē*) demands the negative response, "no." We are expected therefore to place the emphasis in this citation on the pronoun *moi* ("to me"), which the declarative sentence in the next verse (v. 43) explicates: the golden calf shows that the people in the wilderness (even there!) did not worship the true God but worshipped the idols that found later counterparts in Canaan. The wilderness is therefore not portrayed in terms of a honeymoon period, but is already a period of disobedience and idolatry. There is a striking parallel to this passage in the *Damascus Rule* from Qumran. First it uses the passage from Amos 5:26-27 to proof-text the exile that happened because of Israel's disobedience; second, it uses Amos 9:11 to speak of the authentic community at Qumran which replaces the disobedient people, "I will raise up the tent of Jacob," the same text that Luke will use later in Acts 15:16; third, it then speaks of the "Books of the Prophets whose sayings Israel despised" which will be honored in the sect (*CD* 7:14-17).

43. *the images you made:* Note that the use of *typous* ("images") here provides a point of contrast to the next verse (7:44) which has God providing Moses with a *typos* of the true sanctuary.

    beyond Babylon: The translation treats the conjunction *kai* as inferential, "so." The change of LXX Amos 5:27's "Damascus" to "Babylon" is Luke's major textual alteration, reflecting hindsight on the historical experience of the community. The lesson, of course, is that those who reject the prophet are themselves rejected. When Moses was rejected the first time, he went into exile. Now, when they reject Moses a second time, they go into exile.

44. *tent of witness:* This tent, a sanctuary designed by God, stands in contrast to the "tent of Moloch" raised by the people in the previous verse. The first mention of the *skēnē martyriou* is in Exod 27:21. It was the place where the "ark of testimony" is kept (Exod 26:33), and is the sanctuary (*hagiasma*) built according to the pattern (*paradeigma*) shown Moses by God on the mountain (LXX Exod 25:8) or, in the verse quoted by Luke, "according to the image (*typos*) that he saw" on the mountain (LXX Exod 25:40) at the same time the people were building the calf below. Philo the platonist delighted in the occasion given him by the LXX verse to contrast the "immaterial forms of the objects" and the "patterns conceived in the mind" to the actual "sanctuary molded by hand (*hieron cheiropoiēton*)," (*Life of Moses* 2:71-88).

45. *when with Joshua they took possession:* Josh 4:16 says that the ark of testimony was brought into the land, and in Josh 18:1 the tent of witness is set up in Shiloh, where the lots for the distribution of the land were cast (Josh 19:51). Note that the "taking of possession" (*kataschesis*) fulfills the promise made to Abraham (Acts 7:5).

    until the days of David: The tent of witness is still functioning at Shiloh in 1 Sam 2:22, and when David brings the ark into Jerusalem, he puts it in a tent (2 Sam 6:17). David expresses his desire to build a temple in 2 Sam 7:2, because "the ark of God dwells in a tent." The oracle of the prophet Nathan voices God's disapprobation of David's plan: "I have not dwelt in a house since the day I brought up the people of Israel to this day, but I have been moving about in a tent for my dwelling" (2 Sam 7:6). Instead, God promises David to build *him* a house, and that David's offspring would "build a house for my name and I will establish the throne of his kingdom forever" (2 Sam 7:13). Here is the basis both for Solomon's claim to *be* that descendant, and his temple to be "God's house," as well as the lingering messianic expectation that another "descendant of David" would establish an eternal kingdom (see Luke 2:32-33).

46. *a dwelling for the God of Jacob:* The term *skēnōma* can also be translated as "tent," but since it refers specifically to the Temple here, the translation "dwelling" seems preferable. More noteworthy is the difficult textual problem in this

verse. The best reading, because better attested and definitely "harder" is "a dwelling for the house (*oikos*) of Jacob," rather than "God (*theos*) of Jacob." There are three reasons for overturning the rules of textual criticism, here: a) the language clearly forms an allusion to LXX Ps 131:5, "until I find a place (*topos*) for the Lord, a dwelling for the God of Jacob (*skēnōma tō theō Iakob*)"; b) the *autō* in the next verse makes good sense if the reading here is God rather than Jacob ("Solomon built a house for him"); c) This reading makes better sense of the emphatic declaration in v. 48, "*God* does not dwell."

47. *Solomon built a house for him:* The building of the Temple by Solomon is described by 1 Kgs 5:1–7:51. When it is completed, Solomon has the "tent of meeting" with the ark of the covenant brought into the Temple (1 Kgs 8:4). The tent is not mentioned again.

48. *does not dwell in the works of hands:* The claim made for Solomon's Temple was that God "dwelt" (*katoikeō*) there (1 Kgs 8:27, 53; 2 Chr 6:1; LXX Pss 9:11; 67:16; 131:14; 135:21). But as shown in the note on 7:41, the phrase "works of hands" is used in the LXX for idols (e.g., LXX Isa 16:12). It is important to note that Luke has Paul state the same principle in Acts 17:24 to a pagan audience: "This Lord who is ruler of heaven and earth does not dwell in temples made by hand (*cheiropoiētois naois*)." The shock here is to see it turned against the Jewish Temple. But there is a tradition of such criticism in Israel. Like kingship itself, the building of the Temple did not meet unanimous approval (see e.g., 1 Kgs 8:27; 2 Chr 6:8). Even the oracle legitimating its being built was in the form of a conditional clause: "if the commandments are kept" (1 Kgs 6:11-13). The prophets in particular warned against the tendency of people to rely on ritual rather than obedience, and put false confidence in the presence of God in the Temple as surety for their survival (see Jer 7:1-34; Amos 5:25-27; Mic 3:9-12; Isa 1:12-17). For the variety of views in first century Judaism concerning the role of the Temple, see note on 6:14. Luke's inclusion of the Temple among "works made by hands" as opposed to a "house not made by hands" represents the specific messianic convictions concerning Jesus (see also Mark 14:58; Heb 9:11, 24; also 2 Cor 5:1). The same contrast is made concerning circumcision in Col 2:11 and Eph 2:11.

49. *heaven is my throne:* This is a direct citation from LXX Isa 66:1, with only minor modifications: a) he shifts "says the Lord" from the end to the middle; b) he replaces the second *poios* ("what sort") with *tis;* c) he adds *ouchi* in the last line to make a question in place of Isaiah's declarative. The prophetic authority backs the attack on the Temple's claim to be the "dwelling place" or "rest" (*katapausis*) of God (see LXX Ps 131:13-14). This text is alluded to by Matt 5:34, and is cited by the *Letter of Barnabas* 16:2 and Justin Martyr's *Dialogue with Trypho* 22:11.

51. *you are stiff-necked people:* The speech takes another rhetorical turn to direct denunciation, with the accompanying shift to "your fathers." The words of Torah are appropriated concerning the desert generation, that they were "stiff-necked" (*sklērotrachēloi*, Exod 33:3, 5; Deut 9:6, 13, 27).

uncircumcised: Since circumcision is what separates Jew from Gentile ("the

uncircumcised in the flesh," Judg 14:3; 1 Kgs 14:6; 17:6; 2 Chr 28:3; Isa 52:1),
the charge of being "uncircumcised" is tantamount to a charge of not be-
longing to the people. The specification of "heart" (see Lev 26:41; Ezek 44:7,
9) and "ears" (Jer 6:10) means that in terms of internal disposition and obedience they do not keep the covenant; see Jer 6:10: "Look, their ears are uncircumcised and they are not able to hear." Compare Paul in Rom 2:25-29,
and the metaphorical use of "circumcision of the foreskin of the heart" in
conjunction with "stiffness of neck" in the Qumran writings, *1QS* 5:5; *1QpHab*
11:13. In the present speech, the charge takes on force from the "covenant
of circumcision" in 7:8.

resisting the Holy Spirit: This echoes lxx Isa 63:10, which recounts the blessings of God to Israel, then laments, "they have been disobedient and grieved
his Holy Spirit, and he turned them to enmity, and he himself fought against
them." The reader is reminded in particular of Peter's statement about the
Holy Spirit given to those who obey God (Acts 5:32), and how those who
"falsified" or "tested" the Holy Spirit have been "cut off from the people"
(Acts 5:1-11; 3:23), and of Jesus' words concerning the unforgivability of
blasphemy against the Holy Spirit (Luke 12:10).

52. *which of the prophets:* Stephen's question picks up a theme established by the
Gospel: the prophets were badly treated in the past, but the false prophets
were treated well, by "their fathers" (Luke 6:23, 26).

killed the ones who foretold: The theme of killing the prophets is also well established by the Gospel: the Pharisees and Lawyers build tombs to the
prophets their ancestors killed, and thereby collude in the killing (Luke
11:47-48); they are liable for the blood of all the prophets shed since the creation of the world (11:50); they will kill "the prophets and apostles" the wisdom of God sends to them (11:49); Jerusalem is the "killer of the prophets
and stoner of those sent to her" (13:34)! For Jesus as the "righteous one,"
see Luke 23:47; Acts 3:14.

betrayers and murderers: The responsibility for Jesus' death is now placed
squarely on the leadership (compare Luke 24:20; Acts 4:10; 5:30) without any
mitigation by "ignorance."

53. *by commandments from angels:* The use of *eis* with the accusative is odd, but
is probably to be read as equivalent to *en* instrumental; compare Paul in Gal
3:19, *diatageis di'angelōn.* Early evidence for Torah being given by the instrumentality of angels is not extensive. Of the texts cited in support of the
tradition, Gal 3:19 and Heb 2:2 are certain, but Christian; *The Book of Jubilees*
1:29, Philo, *On Dreams* 1:141-143, and Josephus, *Antiquities of the Jews* 15:136,
are all possible but debated; *Testament of Dan* 6:2 is unlikely.

yet you did not keep it: The *kai* is here translated as "yet" to capture the sense
of the intended contrast. The verb *phylassō* is regularly used for the "obser-
vance/keeping" of the commandments (Exod 12:17; 19:5; 20:6; 31:14; Deut
4:2; lxx Ps 118:8-9, 44; Prov 4:4; see also Rom 2:26; Gal 6:13, and compare
Luke 11:28; 18:21; 21:24-25). The charge that people have not lived up to their
own convictions or speech is one of the most common elements in the polemic

of the ancient world; see, e.g., Plutarch, *On Stoic Self-Contradictions* 1-2 (*Mor.* 1033B-D); Seneca, *Moral Epistles* 20:1; Lucian of Samosata, *Hermotimus* 79; *Timon* 54-55; see also Paul in Rom 2:17-24.

INTERPRETATION

The major portion of Stephen's speech centers on Moses (7:17-44), before coming to a rapid conclusion (7:45-53). It is in fact by understanding the role of Moses that we can best determine the overall function of Stephen's speech in the narrative of Acts. Moses himself, of course, appears as one in a series of figures that God had sent to the people for their salvation. From one point of view—that of God's care for his people and fidelity to his promises—the speech is an example of "salvation history": God makes the promises and works in history to accomplish them.

But from another perspective—and now we must recognize that Luke writes his history from the perspective of a commitment to Jesus as the Messiah and the messianic community as the realization of the authentic Israel—the story is a tragic one of rejection and infidelity on the part of the people. In tone, Stephen's speech resembles most the interpretations of Israel's past that we find in the Qumran writings, especially in the *Damascus Rule:* the history of infidelity of Israel in the past helps to legitimate the claims of the present community to be the authentic realization of Israel in the present.

The specific issues of the charges against Stephen concerning "the Law" and "the Temple" are not addressed by the speech in a way that would please Stephen's imagined accusers. Stephen's response is instead an interpretation of Israel's history in terms that are specifically messianic. Luke wants to show that far from "blaspheming God and Moses" (6:11), the Messianists are actually far more faithful than are their opponents to the genuine story of God and his prophets, above all the prophet Moses. He does this, in short, by reading the biblical story in terms not of commandments and shrines, but in terms of promise and fulfillment, of prophetic sendings, and the challenge to obedience.

In a very real sense, we see in Stephen's speech the emerging Christian understanding of the "Jewish religion" as *Christians* understood it to have been, or should have been. This version, naturally, is not one that non-Messianist Jews themselves have ever taken to represent *their* reading of their tradition. Most Jews have not seen a conflict between obedience to the commandments and faith in God, between allegiance to the Temple and the avoidance of idolatry.

But in light of the crucified Messiah Jesus, allegiance to whom means a new understanding of obedience to God (not totally definable by commandments) and in light of the resurrection of Jesus and the power of his Holy Spirit, the acceptance of which means a new understanding of "the holy place" in terms of a community (rather than a physical shrine), the Christians appropriated for themselves that part of Israel's tradition that had always been skeptical of institutions like kingship and Temple, and gave them an even sharper edge. For these Messianist Jews, true obedience to God (and therefore genuine membership in the people) meant that in a choice between the national shrine and the experience of the Holy Spirit, one had to obey the experience of the Spirit. Luke's recital concerning Moses is critical to this reinterpretation of the biblical story.

The notes show in detail how Luke's treatment of Moses differs from that of parallel Jewish retellings of the Exodus story. It is clear that Luke has selected and shaped the materials of the tradition in order to emphasize Moses as a prophet and as the type of Jesus, the "prophet whom God would raise up." Throughout the earlier narrative, the reader has been alerted to the connection between Jesus and Moses. The link was stated most clearly at the end of Peter's speech in 3:22-23, with the citation of Deut 18:15-19 concerning the prophet like Moses, whose voice must be heeded.

As we examine the speech itself closely, the detailed ways in which Luke makes the story of Moses anticipate that of Jesus emerge. Moses is born at the time when the fulfillment of the promises to Abraham was approaching, as was Jesus. Moses grew in wisdom and favor, as did Jesus. Moses visited his brethren seeking to give them salvation, through a message of peace, as did Jesus. He was mighty in word and deed, as was Jesus. But it is in the pattern of prophetic rejection and acceptance, above all, that we see how deliberately Luke has made the story of the two prophets match. Moses "visits" his people a first time, but because of their ignorance, they reject him, and he must depart into exile. But while in exile, he encounters God and is empowered by him to be "sent with a commission" to his people once more. In this "second visitation," Moses works "wonders and signs" in unmistakable fashion as he "led them out." And as Jesus received the Holy Spirit to pour out on his followers, so did Moses "receive living words to give" to the people in the wilderness. Despite this second more powerful offer of salvation, Moses is rejected a second time. The people prefer the golden calf to the sanctuary revealed to Moses on the mountain. They turn to idols. As a result, God turns from them and hands them over to idolatry, with the result that this time *they* end up in exile.

The pattern of "the prophet and the people" could scarcely fit better. And the fact that this is entirely due to Luke's literary skill is made obvious from the comparison to other such recitals in which no such pattern can be found. Even those parallels that share something of Luke's style of narration, like Pseudo-Philo's *Biblical Antiquities,* or something of his prophetic critique, like the Qumran *Damascus Rule,* lack this specific attention on Moses as rejected prophet.

The way in which Luke molds the Moses story provides us with an important clue to the way he handles traditions. In no place does he distort the text of the Septuagint; in fact in most places, he uses the very words of Scripture. But he selects and shapes according to his own preoccupations, creating from thoroughly traditional material a distinctive rendition. As we read his version of the Moses story, we begin to understand just how *Luke* reads Torah, how he understands its overall message. Therefore we are better able to understand what he means when he says that "Moses and all the prophets" contained the message that the Messiah had to suffer before entering his glory (Luke 24:27, 44), for he has now shared with us his reading of "Moses and the Prophets" as a tale of God's visitations that were turned away by a faithless people, a vision very close to that attributed to Jesus himself in the parable of the vineyard (Luke 20:9-18).

We understand from this Moses story as well not only how Luke understands Jesus to be a prophet, but also how he understands the apostles to represent the "second visitation" to the people. As Moses went away in exile and returned in power, so did Jesus, but his second sending was in the power of the Spirit at work in his prophetic successors. They speak for "the raised prophet," and it is obedience or disobedience toward them that will determine who will be included in the restored Israel or definitely "cut off from the people," for now there can be no appeal to ignorance. As the people then rejected Moses a second time and as a result were sent into exile, so now, Stephen's final attack makes plain, these "leaders of the people" are rejecting the voice of his prophetic spokesperson Stephen, and are being cut off from the people God is forming.

Stephen's speech therefore also provides Luke's most explicit interpretation of his entire narrative, and shows us the logic of its two-fold structure. Appearing at the very end of the Jerusalem narrative (indeed, itself ending that narrative) it provides the reader with the key to understanding everything that had happened in the story of Jesus and the apostles up to this point. The Jerusalem narrative has been all about the second offer of salvation, posing the question whether the people would accept the prophet this time or not. Luke has provided the answer: yes, many, even thousands of the people in the city "listened to the prophet" and joined the messianic community.

To whom, then, is this final closure, this tragic tale of rejection told? To the same people Jesus addressed the parable of the vineyard: the leaders, the members of the Sanhedrin. They were the ones mainly responsible for the first rejection (although even they could be excused by ignorance, Acts 3:17). But they then rejected the apostles in full knowledge of the "signs and wonders" done by them (4:1–5:42). Now another prophet ordained by the apostles, full of the Holy Spirit and wisdom, who has worked signs and wonders among the people, stands before the Jewish leadership. He accuses *them* of continuing in the present generation the tradition of hardness of heart, disobedience and resistance to the Holy Spirit, and of killing the prophets. We already suspect what the Sanhedrin's response to such an accusation will be.

FOR REFERENCE AND FURTHER STUDY

Johnson, L. T. *The Literary Function of Possessions in Luke-Acts.* SBLDS 39. Missoula: Scholars Press, 1977, 50–52, 70–76.

Kilgallen, J. J. "The Function of Stephen's Speech (Acts 7, 2-53)." *Bib* 70 (1989) 173–193.

Moessner, D. "The Christ Must Suffer: New Light on the Jesus-Peter, Stephen, Paul Parallels in Luke-Acts." *NovT* 28 (1986) 220–256.

Sylva, D. "The Meaning and Function of Acts 7:46-50." *JBL* 106 (1987) 261–275.

Thornton, T. C. G. "Stephen's Use of Isaiah LXVI, 1." *JTS* 25 (1974) 432–434.

Via, J. E. "An Interpretation of Acts 7:35-37 from the Perspective of Major Themes in Luke-Acts." *SBL 1978 Seminar Papers.* Ed. P. J. Achtemeier. Missoula: Scholars Press, 1978, 209–223.

13. *The Death of a Prophet* (7:54–8:3)

54. When they heard these things, they were enraged and ground their teeth at him. 55. But filled with the Holy Spirit, he gazed into heaven. He saw the glory of God and Jesus standing at the right hand of God. 56. He said, "Look, I see the heavens opened and the Son of Man standing at the right hand of God." 57. Shouting loudly, they held their ears. They rushed at him all together. 58. They threw him out of the city. They stoned him. And the witnesses placed their clothing at the feet of a young man named Saul. 59. They stoned Stephen as he called out and said, "Lord Jesus, receive my spirit." 60. Falling to his knees, he cried out loudly, "Lord, do not hold this sin against them." And when he had said this, he died. 8:1. Now Saul agreed with his being killed. And on that day there began a great persecution against the Church in Jerusalem. Everybody except the apostles was scattered across the regions of Judea and Samaria. 2. Pious men buried Stephen. They mourned him greatly.

3. But Saul continued to inflict outrage against the Church. He went into one house after another. He dragged out both men and women. He handed them over to prison.

NOTES

54. *they were enraged:* The Greek is literally, "they were ripped through their hearts"; Luke uses the same phrase for the Sanhedrin's response to Peter in 5:13. For "grinding the teeth" as a sign of hostility and rage, especially of the wicked against the righteous, see LXX Job 16:9; Pss 34:16; 36:12; 111:10; Lam 2:16. The phrase "grinding of teeth" (*brygmos tōn odontōn*) is used for those excluded from the kingdom in Matt 8:12; 13:42, 50; 22:13; 24:51; 25:30 and Luke 13:28.

55. *filled with the Holy Spirit:* Stephen has already been identified in prophetic terms (6:10), but this designation emphasizes that those who have "always resisted the Holy Spirit" and "killed the prophets" are doing so again in the rejection of Stephen.

    the glory of God: Three separate connections are established by Stephen's vision of the *doxa tou kyriou:* a) he is connected to the story of the people, which began with the appearance of the "God of glory" to Abraham (Acts 7:2); Stephen is therefore a legitimate spokesperson for the people; b) *doxa* is associated with Jesus, especially with his resurrection (Luke 9:31-32; 24:26; Acts 3:13); thus, Stephen is a witness (*martys*) to the resurrection, a status explicitly affirmed by Paul in Acts 22:20; c) *doxa* is also associated with the coming of the Son of Man (Luke 9:26; 21:27), which sets up the content of Stephen's vision. For the experience of visions at the death of a martyr, see *The Martyrdom and Ascension of Isaiah* 5:7; *The Passion of SS. Perpetua and Felicitas* 10-13. In *The Martyrdom of SS. Carpus, Papylus and Agathonica* 39, there is the vision of "the glory of God."

    Jesus standing at the right hand: The Western Text adds "the Lord," after "Jesus." The image of Jesus "at the right hand" obviously derives from LXX Psalm 109:1, which was used as a proof-text for Jesus' resurrection in Luke 20:42; Acts 2:34; 5:31. But why is Jesus standing, rather than sitting (as in the psalm verse)? The posture could be interpreted variously, as cultic (see Lev 14:11; Ps 22:3), prophetic (Ezek 1:21; 2:1-2), or forensic, with Jesus playing the role of advocate (Gen 18:22; Exod 8:20; 9:13; Zech 3:1-8; Jer 18:20), or even of judge (Isa 3:13). "Standing" was also the traditional posture of those attending God in the heavenly court (see LXX Ps 81:1; Zech 3:1-8; Isa 6:2; compare Gabriel in Luke 1:19, "one who stands in the presence of God"). In the light of Stephen's plea to "receive my Spirit," the posture of Jesus could also symbolize accceptance or welcome; "standing up" is the corresponding posture of those who are to welcome the Son of Man (Luke 21:36).

56. *the heavens opened:* Stephen's statement of his vision is required for the listeners to respond. The vision of the heavens opening is similar to Jesus' baptism in Luke 3:21; in fact, some *mss* change the participle here from *diēnoigmenous*

to *anẽogmenous* to be consistent. For the "opening of heaven" as a prelude or condition of visions, see LXX Isa 63:19; 3 Macc 6:18; *2 Baruch* 22:1; *Corpus Hermeticum* 13:17, and especially John 1:51 (for the Son of Man!) and Rev 4:1; 19:11; Luke will have the heavens open again for Peter's vision in Acts 10:11.

Son of Man standing: For a discussion of this title generally, see the note on Luke 5:24. In light of the Gospel narrative (and v. 55, above), the identification of the Son of Man with Jesus is obvious (Luke 5:24; 6:5; 7:34; 9:22, 26, 44, 56, 58; 11:30; 12:8, 10, 40; 17:22, 26, 30; 18:8, 31; 19:10; 21:27, 36; 22:22, 48; 24:7). The Son of Man saying closest to this vision is in Luke 9:26, which speaks of his coming "in his glory and that of the father and of the holy angels." Compare also the declaration of Jesus before the Sanhedrin in Luke 22:69, "from now on the Son of Man will be sitting at the right hand of the power of God." As in the present verse, the images of Dan 7:13 and Ps 109:1 are combined.

57. *held their ears:* The physical gesture is wonderfully expressive of Stephen's charge that they are "uncircumcised in ears" (7:51). They do everything to keep from hearing the prophet's proclamation that Jesus is the one raised to the presence of God. The "all together" (*homothumadon*) may echo ironically the "one mind and heart" of the Christian fellowship (2:46; 4:24; 5:12); in this case the unanimity is one of rejection.

58. *threw him out of the city:* This resembles the attempt of Jesus' townspeople to kill him (Luke 4:29) and also Paul's stoning in Acts 14:29. In fact, *m.Sanh.* 6:1 legislates that the person to be stoned should be taken outside the court, and cites the passage from Lev 24:14 about bringing the cursed person outside the camp. For stoning as the specific punishment for blasphemy, see *m.Sanh.* 7:4.

witnesses placed their clothing: The witnesses are those identified as "false witnesses" in 6:13. *m.Sanh.* 6:3 says that the man (but not the woman) to be stoned has his clothing stripped off, but here it is the witnesses who strip off their *himatia* (outer cloaks). It was the proper procedure for the witnesses themselves to cast the stones (*m.Sanh.* 6:4). This is the first mention of Saul (Paul) in the story, and Luke has him recall the event in 22:2. The phrase "at the feet" is suggestive in light of Luke's use of it in 4:35, 37 and 5:1. If he uses the gesture consistently, it signifies recognition of Paul as a leader of those opposed to Stephen, a position that he will immediately assume in 8:3.

59. *receive my spirit:* Stephen dies in imitation of Jesus, who said at the end, "Father into your hands I entrust my spirit" (Luke 23:46), which was itself a reminiscence of LXX Ps 30:6. For the recommendation of such a prayer on the lips of the dying righteous person, see *bT Ber.* 5a. The difference is that Stephen is literally "calling on the name of the Lord" (*epikaleō*), in fulfillment of the Joel prophecy in Acts 2:21: "everyone who calls on the name of the Lord will be saved." Jesus is now "Lord" (*kyrios*) who stands at God's right hand to receive Stephen.

60. *falling to his knees:* This is the body language of submission and prayer (LXX Isa 45:33; Phil 2:10; Eph 3:14; Rom 11:4; 14:11; Luke 5:8), as we see also in

Acts 9:40; 20:36; 21:5. In this instance, the imitation of the prayer of Jesus seems deliberate (Luke 22:41).

hold this sin against them: According to *m.Sanh.* 6:2, the condemned man can cry out a prayer for his own forgiveness, "May my death be an atonement for my sins." It even adds the rider that if the condemned person knows that false-witnesses have caused his death, he can pray, "Let my death be an atonement for all my sins excepting this sin." Stephen, in contrast, addresses Jesus again as "Lord" who as judge can assign blame or forgive not himself but those who have unjustly brought about his death. The verb *histēmi* is used as in LXX Gen 6:18; 9:11; 17:7; 26:3; Exod 26:9, as "establish/count." Stephen again imitates Jesus who before his death asked God to forgive those who killed him (Luke 23:34).

when he had said this, he died: The phrasing is precisely that used for the death of Jesus in Luke 23:46, except that for Stephen Luke replaces "expired" with "fell asleep" (*koimaomai*), an obvious and widely used euphemism for dying (compare Gen 47:30; 2 Sam 7:12; 1 Kgs 11:21; 14:20; 1 Cor 15:6, 18; 1 Thess 4:13-15; 2 Pet 3:4).

8:1. *Saul agreed with his being killed:* When recounting the event in Acts 22:20, Paul uses the same verb (*syneudokeō*). In Jesus' attack on the Lawyers who "agreed with" (*syneudokeō*) the deeds of their fathers by building tombs for the prophets the ancestors had killed, this translation adopted the stronger term "colluded with." Something of the same strength should be read into Paul's "agreement" here. A reading between the lines, in fact, suggests that Paul may well have been the instigator of the trouble in the first place: a) he was from Cilicia as were some of those who attacked Stephen (6:9), and in fact when he converts, must himself argue with these same Diaspora Jews (9:29); b) there is the symbolism of the clothing placed at his feet, which for Luke is a gesture of recognizing authority; c) there is the fact that Paul is directly described as the leader of the following persecution (8:3).

a great persecution: But one that notably avoids the apostles, whom the narrative has already established as untouchable. Nor does it last long, for Luke notes in 9:31 that the Church throughout "all" of Judea, Samaria, and Galilee was at peace. The "everybody," in fact, seems to mean mainly the Hellenist Christians, for they are the ones whose labors Luke now begins to follow (8:4; 11:19).

across the regions of Judea and Samaria: Whatever the historical basis for the persecution, its literary function as a narrative transition device is obvious. The Jerusalem section is now essentially closed. The story will move on to the next fulfillment of Jesus' prophecy in 1:8: his witnesses will be "in Judea and Samaria and the ends of the earth."

2. *pious men buried Stephen:* This is another echo of the Gospel story, for a "good and righteous" Joseph of Arimathea arranged for the burial of Jesus (Luke 23:50). The mourning (or lamentation, *kopetos*) also recalls that made over Jesus by the women of Jerusalem (23:27, 48). The legislation of *m.Sanh.* 6:6 allows burial of the body only after the flesh had wasted away, and forbids open lamentation.

3. *inflict outrage:* The verb *lymainomai* suggests both physical harm and insult or indignity. Thus the boar "ravages" the forest (LXX Ps 79:13) and King Asa "ravages" the people (2 Chr 16:10). See also Amos 1:11; Isa 65:25; LXX Jer 51:2; 48:18; Ezek 16:25. For its use in the context of a Gentile persecution of Jews, see Philo, *Embassy to Gaius* 134.

dragged out: Everything in the description points to arbitrary and violent anger. Saul is portrayed as one who "breaks and enters," violently dragging people off to prison; for the verb *syrō* in this sense, see 2 Sam 7:13; Isa 28:2; 4 Macc 6:1; Acts 17:6). Paul will himself be subject to such "dragging out" in Acts 14:19.

handed them over to prison: Compare Paul's own summary statements in Acts 22:4 and 26:10. Just as the apostles had, so these now persecuted fulfill the prophecy of Jesus that his followers would be "handed over to synagogues and prisons" (Luke 21:12; see also Acts 12:4; 16:23).

INTERPRETATION

The death of Stephen provides an example of how Luke relates speech to narrative in a pattern of self-fulfilling prophecy (see Introduction). Not only does Stephen's speech recount the history of Israel's rejection of the prophet Moses, but it closes with the direct indictment of the Sanhedrin: "As your fathers did, so do you" (7:51). They therefore are the ones who always resist the Holy Spirit and kill the prophets (7:51-52). Now Luke ensures we do not miss the point by showing us once more that Stephen in fact is just such a prophet: he is "filled with the Holy Spirit" and as he gazes into heaven he sees at the right hand of God "the righteous one" whom they had betrayed and murdered (7:55).

Just as Jesus' evocation of the prophets Elijah and Elisha in Luke 4:25-27 had moved his townspeople from anger to murderous rage, so does Stephen's announcement of the vision of the Son of Man drive the Sanhedrin to murder. They thus fulfill precisely the point of his accusation. They resist the Holy Spirit speaking through the prophetic figure Stephen. They kill him. And by so doing they join the long history of those who rejected and killed the prophets.

In contrast, Stephen is deliberately portrayed by Luke in terms that insistently evoke the passion and death of Jesus. As did Jesus, so does Stephen have grace and power, and works wonders and signs among the people (6:8); he enters into dispute with those who challenge him (6:9; see Luke 20:1-7), including those who are sent as spies (6:11; see Luke 20:20). He is arrested (6:12; see Luke 22:54), and brought to trial before the Sanhedrin (6:12-15; see Luke 22:66-71). Stephen has false witnesses accuse him (6:13), an element left out of Luke's passion narrative, though found in the Synoptic parallels of Mark 14:56 and Matt 26:59.

Stephen is taken out of the city to be executed (7:58) as was Jesus (23:32). At his death, there is the disposition of clothing (7:58), though not of his own as it was for Jesus (Luke 23:34). Stephen prays that his spirit be accepted (7:59) as did Jesus (Luke 23:46). Stephen asks forgiveness for his murderers (7:60) as did Jesus (23:34). Stephen is buried by pious people (8:2) as was Jesus (Luke 23:50-55).

The major contrast between the death of Jesus and of his witness Stephen (apart from the mode of execution) is the fact that Jesus was portrayed as keeping silence in the face of his accusers, whereas Stephen's speech is precisely the sort of response to an accusation a sage would be expected to make (7:1-53). But even this is in fulfillment of Jesus' prophecy: "I will give you speech and wisdom such that all those opposing you will not be able to resist or contradict" (Luke 21:15).

It should not surprise us at this point that Luke has fitted his portrayal of Stephen so close to that of Jesus, for it is his concern not to emphasize the personality of his characters but rather their prophetic power that is effected by the Holy Spirit. Thus the succession of prophets who speak the word of God and work signs and wonders among the people and cause a response of both acceptance and rejection, runs from Moses through Elijah and Elisha, and John the Baptist, to Jesus, and from him to the apostles and now to Stephen. The same power of the Spirit will shortly be shown as operative in Philip and Barnabas and Paul, as the good news moves beyond Jerusalem to the wider world.

The death of Stephen, in fact, provides the first major transition in the Acts narrative. The Jerusalem story is effectively ended except for those necessary contacts with the Church there that the narrative will demand. In the space of these first four chapters, Luke has answered all the questions requiring an answer for his reader Theophilus to have "assurance" (Luke 1:4): the Prophet rejected by the people was empowered and sent again with the offer of salvation; it was accepted by multitudes in the city and rejected only by the leaders; the restored people of God recognized the authority of the Twelve over it, and as the community grew, this authority was passed on peacefully to those who would spread the gospel beyond Jerusalem. All that remains is for Luke to show that the people will grow to include the Gentiles represented by his reader.

At this point, in fact, he introduces the character who will be most responsible (at least in this narrative) for that Gentile mission. In contrast to his future partner Barnabas, Paul (at this point Saul) is introduced in completely negative terms. We are not told, but we are led to suspect, that his role in the death of Stephen was greater than the text itself explicitly tells us. Certainly the fact that the stoners of the prophet lay their clothes at Saul's feet suggests, in Luke's index of symbols, that Paul is the author of the plot against him. Even if that is not Luke's intention, there is no mistaking the role that Saul immediately begins to play. He is ferocious in his persecution. In the scattering of the Hellenist missionaries from Jerusalem, Luke prepares for the narrative sequence in chapter eight. In his sketch of Saul as the fomenter of the persecution, he prepares for the narrative of his conversion in chapter nine.

FOR REFERENCE AND FURTHER STUDY

Barrett, C. K. "Stephen and the Son of Man." *Apophoreta*. Eds. W. Eltester and F. H. Kettler. Berlin: A. Töpelmann, 1964, 32–38.

Doble, P. "The Son of Man Saying in Stephen's Witnessing, Acts 6:8–8:2." *NTS* 31 (1985) 68–84.

Owen, H. P. "Stephen's Vision in Acts VII, 55-56." *NTS* 1 (1954–1955) 224–226.

Sabbe, M. "The Son of Man Saying in Acts 7:56." *Les Actes des Apôtres: traditions, rédaction, théologie*. Ed. J. Kremer. Biblioteca Ephemeridum Theologicarum Lovaniensium 48. Gembloux: J. Duculot, 1979, 241–279.

Talbert, C. H. "Martyrdom in Luke-Acts and the Lukan Social Ethic." *Political Issues in Luke-Acts*. Eds. R. Cassidy and P. Sharper. Maryknoll, N.Y.: Orbis Press, 1983, 99–110.

II. THE EXPANSION OF GOD'S PEOPLE

14. *The Mission in Samaria* (8:4-25)

4. Those who were scattered then went about proclaiming the good news of the word. 5. Philip went down to a city of Samaria. He proclaimed the Messiah to them. 6. The crowds all paid close attention to the things being said by Philip when they heard and saw the signs that he was performing. 7. For many of them had unclean spirits that came out with a great roar. And many who were paralyzed or lame were healed. 8. And there was great joy in that city. 9. Now a certain man named Simon had been in the city earlier. He did magic and amazed the nation of Samaria. He declared himself to be someone great. 10. Everyone from small to great heeded him. They said, "This is the Power of God, the one called Great!" 11. They stayed devoted to him for a long time because he amazed them by his magical deeds. 12. But both men and women were baptized when they believed Philip in his proclamation of the good news of the kingdom of God and of the name of Jesus Messiah. 13. Even Simon himself believed. And once he was baptized, he

stayed constantly attentive to Philip. When he saw the signs and great deeds of power that were happening, he was amazed. 14. When the apostles in Jerusalem heard that Samaria had accepted the word of God, they sent Peter and John to them. 15. They went down and prayed for them that they might receive the Holy Spirit, 16. for it had not yet come down on any of them. They had only been baptized in the name of the Lord Jesus. 17. Then they placed hands on them and they received the Holy Spirit. 18. When Simon saw that the Spirit was given through the laying on of hands, he brought them money. 19. He said, "Give this power to me too, so that whomever I lay hands on will receive the Holy Spirit." 20. But Peter said to him, "May your silver go with you to destruction, because you thought that God's gift could be acquired with money. 21. There is no portion or share for you in this word, for your heart is not right before God. 22. Repent from this wickedness of yours! Pray to the Lord that your heart's intention might be forgiven, 23. for I see that you are in a bitter gall and a web of wickedness." 24. Simon answered, "You pray to the Lord for me so that none of the things you have said happens to me." 25. After they bore witness and spoke the word of God, they turned back to Jerusalem, and continued to preach the good news to many Samaritan villages.

NOTES

4. *good news of the word:* This verse is obviously transitional, and with v. 25 provides a frame around the passage. The translation is awkward, since the verb *euangelizomai* ("preach the good news") is combined with "word" (*logos*) as its (redundant) direct object. Some *mss* of the Western Tradition fill out the phrase by having "word of God," at least partially because of its use later in the story (8:14, 25; see also 4:31; 6:2, 7). The absolute *logos* is better attested, and also appears in 8:21.

   a city of Samaria: For the tensions between Jews and Samaritans in the first century, and for the place of Samaria in Luke's work, see the notes on Luke 9:52; 10:33; 17:6. Luke ordinarily means the whole territory when he refers to Samaria, so even though the *ms* evidence for a definite article before "city" is strong, there is greater probability—especially in light of the indefinite character of v. 8, "in that city,"—that Luke intended it to be anarthrous. It is typical of Luke to locate the mission in urban centers.

   proclaimed the Messiah: Luke uses the absolute *christos* with some frequency (Luke 3:15; 4:41; 20:41; 23:2; 24:26, 46; Acts 3:8; 9:22; 17:3; 26:23). Like Stephen, Philip was ostensibly ordained to oversee the distribution of charity (6:5), but also like him turns out to be a prophetic proclaimer of the kingdom of God.

6. *crowds all paid close attention:* The verb *prosechō* is used three times in the passage. Here it has the sense of mental attentiveness. In verses 10-11, it has more the sense of a commitment of the heart, so that *proskartereō* in 8:13 is

virtually synonymous. The story involves competition for conversion. The preacher with more power wins more adherence. The Greek adverb *homothumadon* is awkwardly placed; the translation by "all" aims at the uniformity or consistency of their response.

heard and saw the signs: Although the notion of "hearing" signs is awkward, the accusative + infinitive construction makes "signs" the natural object of both seeing and hearing. An alternative rendering would be "heard him and saw the signs," but the point of the sentence is how the miracles made the words attractive. The motif of "working signs" is part of Luke's stereotypical presentation of his leading characters as prophets (see note on Acts 2:19).

7. *unclean spirits that came out:* The Greek sentence is anacolouthic, since the verb "came out" refers back to "many" rather than "unclean spirits," as Luke intended. Ancient *mss* offer alternatives and scholars suggest emendations, but Luke's intended meaning is transparent even through the jumbled syntax. More significant is the way in which the portrayal of Philip's wonder-working as exorcisms and healing shows continuity with the ministry of Jesus, in which exorcisms (Luke 4:33, 36; 6:18; 7:21; 8:2, 29; 9:42; 11:24) represent the kingdom of God's battle against the demonic realm (see the notes on Luke 4:5 and the Interpretation of Luke 11:14-26).

with a great roar: Literally, "shouting with a great voice." The verb *boaō* ("cry out") is sometimes used in contexts of prayer or plea (Luke 18:7, 38; see LXX Exod 8:12; 1 Sam 7:8), but often simply means a loud cry. The exact phrase is used for the yell of Potiphar's wife in LXX Gen 39:14. The sign of a successful exorcism is some sort of physical manifestation (see Luke 4:35, 41; 8:33; 9:42; 11:14, and Lucian of Samosata, *Lover of Lies* 16).

paralyzed or lame: As with exorcisms, the healing of physical disorders signals the arrival of the kingdom of God; compare Luke 5:17-26; 7:22; 9:1-2, 6, 11; 13:11-17; 14:13, 21; Acts 3:1-10; 5:15-16.

9. *a certain man named Simon:* Luke here provides a narrative flashback to the period before Philip's arrival; Simon was there before him (*prohypērchen*), and his success preceded that of the gospel. In later Christian writings, the character of Simon is greatly expanded: Justin Martyr, *Apology* 1:26; *Dialogue with Trypho* 120:6; *Acts of Peter* 4-32; Pseudo-Clementine *Homilies* 2, 22-24; Irenaeus, *Against Heresies* 1, 23, all deal with Simon. The accounts do not entirely agree, but it is certain that sources other than Acts contributed to these portrayals. Although much of the material concerning him is clearly legendary, Simon was undoubtedly a historical figure, and associated at least eponymously with some variety of Gnosticism.

he did magic: In v. 11, Luke repeats that he did "magic deeds." That Simon was a magician is stated also by Justin, *Apology* 1:26; *Dialogue with Trypho* 120:6. The Pseudo-Clementine *Homilies* 2, 22, 3 claims that he learned magic in Egypt (see also 2, 24, 1). The *Acts of Peter* gives examples of his feats, especially the ability to "fly" (levitate?) that won him fame in Rome but also led to his death (4, 32). The category of "magic" is difficult. The term derives from the ancient Persian priests, the *magoi* (see Herodotus, *Persian Wars* 1:101,

120; Pliny the Elder, *Natural History* 30, 2, 1-5; and Matt 2:1). In the study of religion, magic has sometimes been distinguished from religion in terms of its attempt to rationally control transcendent powers through precise rituals and recipes with automatic and predictable results. The distinction may have theoretical validity, but is sometimes hard to apply to specific phenomena. Magic was a widely diffused aspect of Hellenistic religion (see e.g., Apuleius, *The Golden Ass* 1:8-11; 2:6, 3:28-30; Heliodorus, *The Ethiopians* 6, 14-15; Pseudo-Callisthenes, *Life of Alexander of Macedon* 1:1-10), and led to the production of magical recipe books such as the *Great Magical Papyrus*. But it was also a term (like and in combination with the term *goēs*) that was used polemically against marginal or disapproved religious practices (see *Letters of Apollonius of Tyana* 1, 2, 5, 8, 16, 17). Thus Jews (Juvenal, *Satires* 6:542-547) and especially Moses (Pliny the Elder, *Natural History* 30, 2, 11; Eusebius, *Preparation for the Gospel* 9, 8, 1-2) had the reputation of being magicians among outsiders. For that matter, so did Jesus (see Origen, *Against Celsus* 1:6, 28, 38). Designating Simon as a magician, therefore, may in part have a historical basis and in part reflect the desire to diminish the religious claims of Simon's devotees. Note that for Luke, magic is consistently associated with demonic powers, and therefore part of the resistance put by "the other kingdom" to the kingdom of God (Acts 8:20; 13:10; 19:13-20).

amazed the nation of Samaria: The term *ethnos* ("nation") has the sense of "people" (compare 10:22, 35; 13:19). The verb "amaze" (*existēmi*) is one of Luke's favorites both in the Gospel (2:47; 8:56; 24:22) and in Acts (2:7, 12; 9:21; 10:45; 12:16), mainly in connection with wondrous deeds. It is no surprise therefore to find it used three times in the present passage (8:9, 11, 13).

10. *Power of God, the one called Great:* The adjective "great" (*megas*) is anticipated by the previous verse, "he declared himself to be someone great." The precise meaning or nature of this title (if it was such) is debated, particularly since our other accounts present variations of it. Justin Martyr says that the Samaritans trusted Simon and that he declared he was "God above all power and authority and might" (*Dialogue with Trypho* 120:6). This agrees basically with what he also tells us in *Apology* 1:26, "he was thought to be a god," and the Samaritans "confess this man as their first God." The claims for Simon are impressive but a bit lower in *Acts of Peter* 4, "he says that he is the great power of God, and that without God he does nothing." Likewise in Pseudo-Clementine *Homilies* 2, 22, 2, Simon calls himself the "Mighty Power of God," as well as another designation, "The Standing One" (2, 22, 3). In Irenaeus, *Against Heresies* 1, 16, 1-3, Simon appears mythologized as an aeon within a Valentinian-type Gnostic framework, become incarnate to save Helena his consort. The convergent point of all the testimonies is that Simon claimed considerable importance in his own right (and was therefore not simply an effective magician).

11. *they stayed devoted:* The structure of the sentence is similar to that in v. 6 concerning Philip: the wonders performed gain attention and devotion. Theurgy is here an essential part of missionary work as a means of attracting attention and winning allegiance.

12. *were being baptized:* Like the first converts in Jerusalem, the ones who come to belief (*pisteuō*) were baptized as the sign of their commitment. The "preaching of the kingdom of God" establishes Philip's ministry as continuous with that of Jesus (Luke 4:43; 6:20; 8:1; 9:2, 11; 16:16; 17:21; Acts 1:3), but the inclusion of the "name of Jesus Messiah" connects him to the form of that proclamation made by the apostles before him (Acts 2:38; 3:6, 16; 4:10, 17, 30; 5:28, 40).

13. *Simon himself believed:* Luke's is the only ancient source that has Simon become a Christian. In the other accounts, his distinctive claims remain independent. In Pseudo-Clementine *Homilies* 3:29-58, for example, Simon is the head of an independent group and debates Peter for three days in Caesarea.

    he was amazed: Luke's apologetic interest is here obvious: the *magos* whose wonders had created amazement and a following among the crowds is now in turn "amazed" at the deeds performed by Philip, and becomes *his* devotee!

14. *the apostles in Jerusalem:* Luke wants us to see the Twelve as a unified group, exercising control over the mission. But the only persons among the Twelve who played a role in the Jerusalem narrative were Peter and John, who appeared as leaders and spokespersons (Acts 3:1, 3, 4, 11; 4:13, 19). Now when Luke wants to have the collective leadership accredit this new missionary endeavor, he has no choice but to place Peter and John in the position of those "sent out" by the apostolic board. This is the last mention of John in the story, apart from the passing reference in 12:2. As in the earlier passages, he remains silently in Peter's shadow.

15. *might receive the Holy Spirit:* The apostles fulfill the other part of their mission, which was to pray (Acts 6:4). For the inconsistent relationship of baptism to the empowerment by the Holy Spirit, see the note on Acts 2:38. The main thing Luke is interested in here is having the new mission certified by the Jerusalem leadership. We will see the same concern in 11:1-18 and 11:22.

17. *placed hands on them:* For the background and significance of this gesture, see the note on Acts 6:6. As in v. 15, Luke makes *pneuma hagion* anarthrous, as he frequently does (Acts 1:2, 5; 2:14; 4:8, 25; 6:5); the translation "the Holy Spirit" is still appropriate.

19. *this power:* Having fulfilled their respective literary functions, both John and Philip disappear from the scene, leaving Peter to face Simon as he had Ananias and Sapphira. The term for power here is literally "authority" (*exousia*) as in Luke 4:6, 32, 36; 5:24; 9:1; 10:19; 19:17. The magician's characteristic interest appears in Simon's desire to connect the possession of the Spirit to a specific ritual without reference to dispositions such as faith: "whomever I lay hands on." His offer of money (from which the Church derived the term "simony" for the purchase of spiritual positions) also reflect the magician's perception of such wonders as a question of skill that can be taught.

20. *go with you into destruction:* For the verb "to be" (*eimi*) with the phrase *eis apōleian* ("into destruction"), see Theodotion's version of LXX Dan 2:5. Luke here uses the optative, which expresses a wish. As for "destruction" (*apōleia*),

it is combined with "hades" in lxx Prov 27:20, and seems to bear the sense of a "final destruction" also in passages such as Sir 51:2 (see 51:6); Isa 33:2; 34:12; Ezek 26:19-21. In the nt, see John 17:12; Rom 9:22; Phil 3:19; 1 Tim 6:9; 2 Pet 2:1, 3; 3:16. The passages which most resemble the present one are Matt 7:13; 2 Pet 3:7; 2 Thess 2:3 and Rev 17:8. Compare also Peter's declarations to Ananias and Sapphira (5:1-11).

God's gift: The term *dōrea* ("gift") points back to Acts 2:38, where the gift is identified as the Holy Spirit (see also 10:45; 11:17). It also provides a nice contrast to the outlook of magic. Magic seeks a craft that can rationally control the divine powers; it has no real place for "gift" as the free disposition of the divine apart from human manipulation. However much Luke portrays his characters as thaumaturges, this critical distinction is never lost. God's freedom always moves ahead of his characters.

21. *portion or share:* The terms *meris* and *klēros* are virtually synonymous, as can be seen in such passages as Deut 12:12; 18:1; Josh 14:4; 18:7; lxx Ps 15:5; 72:26; 118:57; see also 2 Cor 6:15 and especially Col 1:12. The language of "lot" (*klēros*) here is reminiscent of the passage recounting Judas' replacement; see the notes on Acts 1:17, 26.

in this word: As in the case of Judas (Acts 1:15-26), the issue posed by Simon's offer does not concern identity or membership in the people, but participation in the work of ministry; as in 6:4, "the word" stands for the apostolic ministry.

heart is not right before God: That Peter can "see" the heart of Simon is, as we have noted throughout the commentary, a typical way of showing that he is a prophet (see Luke 5:22; 7:39; 9:47; 24:38; Acts 5:2). The adjective "straight" (*euthus*) takes on the transferred sense of "morally/religiously upright" (see Judg 17:6; 21:25; 2 Sam 1:18; 19:6; 1 Kgs 11:33, 38; compare Luke 3:4-5; Acts 13:10).

22. *repent . . . be forgiven:* Peter uses the same terms (*metanoeō/aphiēmi*) as at the conclusion of the Pentecost speech (2:38), but in this case the offer is conditional: *ei ara* introduces an indirect question whose sense is, "if possible" or "if perhaps"; compare Acts 17:27. The translation retains "heart's intention," in order to be consistent with the seeing of the heart that Peter is doing. The term *epinoia* can mean simply "thought" (Wis 6:16) but very often has the sense of a wicked intention, as here (see Wis 9:14; 14:12; 15:4).

23. *bitter gall and a web of wickedness:* The phrase "bitter gall" (*chōlē pikra*) appears in the lxx only in Prov 5:4, in the context of going after loose women, that is breaking covenant. The words gall (*chōlē*) and "bitterness" (*pikra*) do also occur together in Deut 29:17, to describe the consequences of turning to other gods in idolatry. The phrase here seems to reflect that background (see also the allusion to Deut 29:17 in Heb 12:15). The term *syndesmos* (literally "bond") occurs with "wickedness" only in Isa 58:6, where the Lord declares that the only feast desired is to "loose every bond of wickedness."

24. *pray to the Lord for me:* In this version, Simon capitulates quickly. Codex D adds detail to his statement, and concludes by noting that he wept profusely.

Is this variation a play on the Gospel tradition in which his namesake-now competitor Simon Peter also wept (Luke 22:62)? In other ancient accounts of the rivalry, Simon Magus is not so easily overcome. The Pseudo-Clementine *Homilies* 3:29-58, as we have noted, recount a three-day debate between Simon and Peter in Caesarea. Justin claims that Simon came to Rome and was even honored as a God by a statue dedicated to him (*Apology* 1:26). And in the *Acts of Peter*, there is repeated mention of how Peter drove Simon out of Judea (5, 9, 17); but still he is still powerfully active in Rome, and must be bested by Peter all over again (11-15, 23-32).

25. *to many Samaritan villages:* This is a fine example of how Luke builds on a single incident to create the impression of a more general phenomenon. By having the apostles return to Jerusalem, he maintains contact with the center of the mission, but by having them preach to villages on the way, he shows that the apostles not only approved the Samaritan mission but also took an active role in it.

INTERPRETATION

Luke now begins to show his reader how the second part of Jesus' prophecy in Acts 1:8 came to fulfillment in the spread of the messianic community beyond Jerusalem into Samaria and Judea. Already in this first vignette concerning the mission to Samaria we can observe and appreciate Luke's ability to use an apparently artless recital to serve his literary and religious goals.

It is obvious at the literary level, for example, that the persecution in Jerusalem that affects everyone but the apostles (8:1) serves as an ideal narrative transition. The mission to Samaria and beyond does not appear therefore as a result of human calculation, but as the accidental by-product of persecution. At the religious level, however, Luke does not in the least regard this sequence of events as accidental; it is characteristic of him to see the play of human freedom as the space within which God's will can be enacted. In this case, the tragedy of rejection in Jerusalem turns out to be an opportunity for those outcast from the people called the Samaritans. Some readers call this triumphalism and find it repugnant. Fairer readers would call it belief in providence, and wonder why it is offensive. Much of the tension in Luke's narrative from this point on has to do with the dialectic of rejection and acceptance, and with humans trying their best to catch up to God's action in the world.

This first step outside Jerusalem prepares the way for much larger and more dangerous expansions of the people and with it the vision of what God is doing in history (in chapters 10–15). The Samaritans are not Gentiles. Indeed they lay claim—not without some justice—to being an ancient and deeply traditional form of the religion of Israel. In their eyes, it was the Judeans who were the interlopers and innovators. But in the eyes of contemporary Judeans, they were at best among the "lost sheep" of Israel. The evangelization of them by Philip therefore continues the work of Jesus in reaching out to the marginal and outcast among the people and inviting them to a full participation in the restored people of God forming around the Prophet whom God raised up.

Luke is consequently concerned to show the continuity between this first initiative taken by the Hellenist missionaries and the Church in Jerusalem. Demonstrating such continuity is of first importance for the "security" (*asphaleia*) he is trying to provide his Gentile readers (Luke 1:4). Every link between themselves and the Church of origins is important to their own sense of sharing in God's blessings.

Continuity is shown first by the portrayal of Philip. The function of Luke's stereotypical portrayal of his characters as prophets by now should be obvious. Philip proclaims the kingdom of God (8:12) and works signs and powerful deeds among the people (8:6, 13). He is thereby shown to carry on the work of Jesus himself and of the apostles (see notes). Like them, as well, the "signs" he performs are not simply tricks or demonstrations of power. They have to do with the driving out of unclean spirits, and the healing of the sick (8:7). Those illnesses of body and spirit by which Satan exercises rule over humans in his alternative kingdom must be attacked and overcome. In this outward movement of the Gospel, Luke makes the "kingdom of God" take on a geographical connotation: territory is literally being wrested from the power of demons and brought under God's rule.

The second way Luke demonstrates the continuity of this new venture with the Church in Jerusalem is through the validating actions of the Twelve. When they hear of Philip's work, they send Peter and John to confirm it by the laying on of their hands (8:14-17). Thus there is an actual physical link with the Jerusalem community and that in Samaria, as power is communicated through the hands of the apostles. More than that, Luke shows the apostles taking an active role in this geographical expansion, as they preach in many Samaritan villages on their way back to Jerusalem (8:25).

Something else Luke has accomplished by bringing the apostles down from Jerusalem is getting Peter in position to confront the magician Simon. As the notes indicate, the figure of Simon becomes elaborated in later Christian literature, and there are a number of questions that could be discussed concerning the "historical Simon": was he truly a magician or rather the center of a cult? Was he a founder of Gnosticism or only a convenient eponym for heresiologists seeking to find roots for that later noxious growth?

We leave aside such questions not only because answering them is difficult and distracting (if indeed even possible) but for the more principled reason that the "historical Simon" is no more pertinent to the understanding of Luke's story than is the "historical Gamaliel" or the "historical Paul," or even the "historical Jesus." Trying to understand Luke's literary and religious intentions by appeal to extra-textual references is both a sporadic business (we have lots of material for some characters and none for others) and an irrelevant one. It is as a character in the story that we must come to grips with Simon.

Simon is one of a series of characters within the narrative who represent the powers opposed to the kingdom of God, and who by resisting the prophets provide the occasion for a confrontation and decisive demonstration of God's power over Satan and the demonic realm. In the Gospel, Judas provided the paradigm for such characters. His betrayal of Jesus was motivated by Satan entering his heart (Luke 22:3), and his rejection was symbolized by his use of possessions (Acts 1:17-25). In the Jerusalem Church, Ananias and Sapphira also allow Satan to enter their hearts, and their conspiracy against the Holy Spirit is symbolized by their holding back of possessions (Acts 5:2).

Now, in this new territory being claimed for God, the demonic powers in Samaria find their representative in the magician Simon. It is not much of a battle: the wonderworker whose deeds earlier had made crowds gasp and gather around him (8:10) is himself stunned by the thaumaturgic power of Philip. He believes, is baptized, follows Philip around like a devotee (8:13). But when he sees the transmission of the Spirit through the apostles' laying on of hands, he cannot resist the instincts from his theurgic past. Here is a technique worth purchasing, a way of gaining a "share" in the leadership of this movement (8:18-19). Once more the use of possessions symbolizes the disposition of the heart. Although Simon is now a Christian, his "heart is not right" with God; he is in that "bitter gall and web of wickedness" that is the attitude of the demonic realm, manifested in the attempt to control and manipulate cosmic forces (8:23).

In several ways, Peter's confrontation with Simon resembles his encounter with Ananias and Sapphira (5:1-11). He is the prophet who knows the desires and intentions of the heart even when they are not spoken. He identifies the way in which the use of possessions has signaled that disposition. His rebuke teaches the sinning party (and most of all the reader) the proper understanding: in the case of Ananias and Sapphira that the sharing of a portion of property could not counterfeit the genuine spiritual sharing of the community, nor mock the prophetic authority of the apostles; in the case of Simon, that the power operative in the apostles (and the community) was not in anyone's control but was the "gift of God" subject only to God's free disposition (8:20).

The main point of contrast with the cases of Judas or Ananias and Sapphira is that they died. In the case of Simon, Peter levels an appropriately strong anathema: his silver and he can go together to destruction (8:20), but he also holds out hope for repentance and forgiveness (8:22), and from Simon's plea for Peter's prayer (8:24), the reader expects that in fact he does get his heart straight with God.

We will see similar confrontations between Paul and the forces of magic and sorcery (the tools of Satan) as the gospel moves into Gentile territory (13:6-11; 16:16-18; 19:11-20; 28:3-6). Each of these stories has its distinctive elements. But each also serves to show how the rule of God conquered the forces of evil as the gospel moved outward from Jerusalem into the wider world.

For Reference and Further Study

Barrett, C. K. "Light on the Holy Spirit from Simon Magus (Acts 8:4-25)." *Les Actes des Apôtres: traditions, rédaction, théologie*. Ed. J. Kremer. Leuven: University Press, 1979, 281-295.

Bergmeier, R. "Die Gestalt des Simon Magus in Act 8 und in der simonianischen Gnosis—Aporien einer Gesamtdeutung." *ZNW* 77 (1986) 267-275.

Casey, R. P. "Simon Magus." *Beginnings* 5:151-163.

Cerfaux, L. "Simon le magicien à Samarie." *Recueil Lucien Cerfaux*. Biblioteca Ephemeridum Theologicarum Lovaniensium VI-VII. Gembloux: J. Duculot, 1954, 1:259-262.

Derrett, J. M. D. "Simon Magus (Acts 8, 9-24)." *ZNW* 73 (1982) 52-68.

Garrett, S. R. *The Demise of the Devil: Magic and the Demonic in Luke's Writing*. Minneapolis: Fortress Press, 1989, 61-78.

Gourgues, M. "Esprit des commencements et ésprit des prolongements dans les Actes: note sur le 'Pentecôte des Samaritaines,' (Actes viii, 5-25)." *RB* 93 (1986) 376-385.

Meeks, W. A. "Simon Magus in Recent Research." *RSR* 3 (1977) 137-142.

15. *Philip and the Ethiopian* (8:26-40)

26. An angel of the Lord spoke to Philip. He said, "Rise up and go southward along the desert road that goes from Jerusalem to Gaza." 27. He got up and went. And look, there was an Ethiopian who had gone up to worship in Jerusalem. He was a eunuch, an official of Candace, queen of Ethiopia. He was in charge of her entire treasury. 28. Now he was returning, sitting on his chariot and reading the prophet Isaiah. 29. The Spirit said to Philip, "Approach and get close to this chariot." 30. When

Philip had run up, he heard him reading Isaiah the prophet. He said, "Do you understand the things you are reading?" 31. And he replied, "How can I, unless someone guide me?" So he invited Philip to get up and sit with him. 32. Now the passage of Scripture that he was reading was this: "As a sheep led to the slaughter, and as silent as a lamb before its shearer, so he does not open his mouth. 33. In his lowliness his judgment was taken away. Who will recite his generation? For his life is taken away from the earth." 34. The eunuch responded to Philip, "I beg you, about whom does the prophet say this? Is it about himself or about someone else?" 35. Philip started to speak. Beginning from this Scripture, he proclaimed to him the good news about Jesus. 36. As they went down the road, they came to some water. The eunuch said, "Look at the water. What prevents me from being baptized?" 38. He ordered the chariot to stop. Both went down into the water, Philip and the eunuch, and he baptized him. 39. But when they came up out of the water, the Spirit of the Lord carried Philip away. The eunuch saw him no more, for he continued on his way rejoicing. 40. But Philip found himself in Azotus. And traveling through all the towns until he came to Caesarea, he continued to proclaim the good news.

NOTES

26. *angel of the Lord spoke:* For the intermediary role of angels throughout the narrative, see Luke 1:11, 13, 26, 28; 2:9-10, 13; 22:43; Acts 5:19; 10:3, 7, 22; 12:7-15, 23; 27:23. Luke's symbolic world is one in which the possibility of angels speaking to humans is widely accepted (Acts 23:9). The intervention of the angel at this point is particularly striking because of the frequent use of this language in Stephen's speech (7:30, 35, 38, 53). In v. 29, it is the Spirit who speaks to Philip.

southward: The term *mesēmbria* ("middle of the day") is used to designate noon (see Gen 18:1; 43:16) but can also mean "south" (as in Dan 8:4, 9). Here the construction with *kata* and the geographical relationship of the places named (Gaza is far south of Samaria and Jerusalem) suggests the translation "southward." The Greek continues, "the road going down from Jerusalem to Gaza. This was desert." The final sentence is probably an aside to the reader rather than part of the angel's message to Philip, but in this translation, the extra sentence is reduced to the adjective "desert."

27. *an Ethiopian:* Ethiopia is the land bordering Egypt to the south (Ezek 29:10) known in the Bible as the ancient land of Cush (Gen 2:13). Hellenistic fascination with the exotica of such places is reflected in texts such as Pliny the Elder, *Natural History* 6:180-197; Heliodorus, *The Ethiopians*; Pseudo-Callisthenes, *Life of Alexander of Macedon* 3:18-23; Philostratus, *Life of Apollonius of Tyana* 3:20. Ethiopia figures in a text of Isaiah concerning the restoration of the people: "In that day the Lord will extend his hand to provoke to emu-

lation the remnant of the people that is left, that which is left from Assyria and from Ethiopia and from Babylon . . . he will raise a sign (*sēmeion*) for the nations and will gather the outcasts of the people and those scattered from Judah he will gather from the four corners of the earth" (Isa 11:11; see also Zeph 3:10).

a eunuch: It was not uncommon for castrated males to hold positions of importance in oriental courts (see Herodotus, *Persian Wars* 8:105; Philostratus, *Life of Apollonius of Tyana* 1:33-36). Indeed, in LXX Jer 41:19, the Hebrew term for eunuch is translated as *dynastēs*, the term here translated as "official." Because both terms are used in this passage, however, it seems certain that Luke intends us to see this man as sexually mutilated. According to LXX Deut 23:2, such a condition precluded full participation in the assembly. In Isaiah 56:4-5 is the promise that "eunuchs who keep my sabbaths" and hold fast to the covenant would be given a place in God's house. It is probable, however, that the prohibition against those "smitten in the flesh" in the Qumran vision of the messianic community would exclude them (*1QSa* 2:5-6).

Candace, Queen of Ethiopia: According to Pliny the Elder, *Natural History* 6:186, this is a dynastic rather than a personal name; the title occurs again in Pseudo-Callisthenes, *Life of Alexander of Macedon* 3:18. Eusebius declares that Ethiopia was still ruled by a woman in his day (*Ecclesiastical History* 2, 1, 13).

29. *get close to this chariot:* This message is delivered by "the Spirit" rather than an angel, as in v. 26. The point is the same: Philip is being directly guided by God. The verb translated "get close to" is *kollaō*, which is so disputed in the interpretation of Acts 5:13. The use here indicates that it means above all physical proximity.

30. *heard him reading Isaiah the prophet:* It was customary in the ancient world to read aloud, even when alone; in *Confessions* 6:3, Augustine puzzles over bishop Ambrose's habit of silent reading, as though it were something genuinely odd. The reading and study of Torah was also audible (*Pirke Aboth* 6:5). Although the study of Torah was ordinarily communal, even reading it alone was considered praiseworthy (*Aboth de Rabbi Nathan* 8). There are a handful of stories about Rabbis studying and discoursing when on a journey (*bT Hag.* 12a, 14a; *bT Erub.* 54b).

understand the things you are reading: Every text is capable of different levels of apprehension. At the most elementary level, early Rabbis made a distinction between what was "written" (*kitab*) and what was "read" (*qere*) in the text of Torah; more elaborate distinctions between *peshat* ("literal meaning"), *darash* ("applied or extended meaning"), and *sod* ("mystical meaning") were to follow. Christianity would develop similar distinctions between literal, moral, and allegorical readings of its texts. In the present case, Philip's question derives from the conviction that the prophets contained deeper meanings for the future. There is a similar word play on *ginōskō/anaginōskō* in 2 Cor 3:2.

31. *unless someone guide me:* The Greek construction is somewhat odd, but not unprecedented: the protasis has the future indicative and the apodosis *an*

+ the optative. The term "guide" (*hodēgeō*) means literally to lead along a road (see Matt 15:14; Luke 6:39), but gains the transferred sense of "leading" in righteousness or wisdom in passages such as LXX Ps 5:8; 22:3; 26:11; 72:24; 118:35; Qoh 2:3; Wis 9:11; 10:10; John 16:13. For a *hodēgos* as a spiritual guide because of the knowledge of Torah, see Rom 2:19. The ability to provide the proper interpretation (*pesher*) to Scripture was the special claim of Qumran's "Teacher of Righteousness" (see *1QpHab* 2:2).

32. *passage of Scripture:* This is a direct citation from the LXX of Isaiah 53:7-8, with only these alterations: a) the best text of Acts has the aorist *keirantos* rather than the LXX's present participle *keirontos;* b) a harder call is the addition of "his" (*autou*) after "lowliness." Although rarely cited directly, this "suffering servant" song from Isaiah exercised a profound influence on early Christian language about Jesus (see, e.g., John 12:38; 1 Pet 2:21-25; Rom 10:16).

33. *in his lowliness:* Or, "in his humiliation"; the Greek has *tapeinōsis*, which provides a possible allusion both to Luke's theme of "lowering/raising" (Luke 1:52; 3:5; 14:11; 18:14), and to the specifically Christological use of "humiliation" by Paul in describing the *kenōsis* of the Messiah (Phil 2:5-11).

his judgment was taken away: Interpreting the details of the Isaiah citation is difficult at three levels: a) the Hebrew is notoriously obscure; b) the LXX translation seems to have also been a matter of guesswork: for example, the same Greek verb (*airō*) is used to translate two quite different Hebrew verbs (*lqh* and *gzr*) in two successive lines, and the translation of the Hebrew *mishpat* by *krisis* also produces questions; c) it is not clear how *Luke* was reading the LXX. In the present case, the phrase *hē krisis autou ērthē* could mean "his justice was taken away" (meaning "his justice was denied," RSV), or "his judgment was taken away" (meaning his condemnation was lifted/removed). Luke himself uses *krisis* to mean "judgment" in Luke 10:14 and 11:31-32, but in a sense close to the Hebrew *mishpat* ("doing righteousness") in Luke 11:42.

recite his generation: The term "generation" (*genea*) means here as it does frequently the people living at a particular time (Gen 7:1; 50:23; Exod 1:6; LXX Ps 9:27; Luke 1:48, 50; 21:32; Acts 13:26). The term *diēgeomai* would ordinarily mean "to relate/recite," as in a narrative of God's wonderful deeds (LXX Ps 54:17; 104:2). This is also the consistent meaning in Luke-Acts (Luke 8:39; 9:10; Acts 9:27; 12:17). But how would Luke understand this line? As pointing to the inability to recite the story of Jesus' descendants because his life was cut off? This would fit the Hebrew Isaiah, but less easily the LXX. Another possibility is attractive, particularly in light of the use of *airō* in the next line: Isaiah is read as pointing to the surprising *fact* of having generations of faithful to follow him because his "life was taken up from the earth."

his life is taken up from the earth: Here is the most dramatic deviation from the Hebrew in the LXX version. It is the only time in all of Torah that the verb *gzr* ("to cut off"), is translated by *airō* ("to lift"). The Hebrew definitely means the servant dies, his life is "cut off from the earth." But the LXX can be read by the Messianist who confesses a resurrected prophet as "life is lifted from the earth."

34. *about himself or about someone else:* The eunuch's question is the pertinent one for those who were convinced that Scripture was fundamentally prophetic in its significance. At Qumran, *pesher* interpretation made just such specific applications of ancient texts to contemporary persons and events (*1QpPs37* 4:1-25; *1QpHab* 2:1-15).

35. *beginning from this Scripture:* The biblicism "opened his mouth," which is used in the LXX for solemn (Job 11:36; 33:2; 35:6) or prophetic discourse (Exod 4:12, 15; Ezek 3:27; 29:21; 33:22), is here translated simply as "started to speak." Notice the similarity to Jesus in Luke 24:27, "beginning with Moses and all the prophets he interpreted for them the things concerning himself in all the Scriptures."

    the good news about Jesus: The very ambiguity of the Isaiah passage made diverse interpretations of it possible, including the messianic: see *Targum Pseudo-Jonathan* on 52:13; *bT Sanh.* 98b. It is of course the Christians who take the text as referring specifically to a suffering Messiah; see Justin Martyr, *Dialogue with Trypho* 13.

36. *what prevents me:* Compare the use of *kōluō* ("prevent") in Luke 18:16, where Jesus allows the children to approach, and in 11:52, where Jesus accuses the lawyers of preventing others from entering the kingdom. In Acts 10:47 and 11:17, the verb is connected to baptism, as it is here. In the Western Text, another verse follows this one, recounting an act of faith required from the eunuch: "He said to him, 'It is allowed if you believe with all your heart.' He answered, 'I believe Jesus Christ is the son of God.' " This verse is absent in the earliest and best *mss*, but is attested as early as Irenaeus, *Against Heresies* 3, 22, 8.

39. *Spirit of the Lord:* As in vv. 26 and 29, the direct intervention of God could hardly be made more explicit. Some early scribes spotted the inconsistency between having "an angel" speak to him in v. 26 and "the spirit" in v. 29, and used this verse as an opportunity to clarify matters: "The Holy Spirit fell on the eunuch, but the angel carried away Philip." The *ms* evidence suggests that this, like v. 37, is a scribal addition. For the Spirit's moving about prophets in this fashion, compare Ezek 11:24; 1 Kgs 18:12; 2 Kgs 2:16.

    on his way rejoicing: As frequently in Luke-Acts, "joy" is a specific response to God's work in the world (Luke 1:14, 28; 2:10; 6:23; 8:13; 10:17, 20; 13:17; 15:5, 7, 10, 32; 19:6, 37; 24:41, 52). In the Gospel, the only exceptions are the "unholy joy" of Judas (22:5) and Herod (23:8). In Acts, note especially the apostles "going on their way rejoicing" after being persecuted (5:41), and in the previous story, the "great joy in that city."

40. *found himself in Azotus:* The passive "was found" (*heurethē*) is here properly translated as reflexive. Azotus is north of Gaza along the coast. Luke again dramatically illustrates how the mission is impelled and directed by the Holy Spirit. Philip is now pictured as working his way up the coast to Caesarea, where we will see him when Paul visits there in Acts 21:8. Thus another single incident is expanded by means of geographical references and the imperfect tense to a larger missionary enterprise.

INTERPRETATION

The story of Philip and the Ethiopian reveals once more how Luke can use the slenderest of vignettes to serve his larger literary purposes. The tale itself possesses the lively charm of Luke's best anecdotes: the reader's imagination delights in the visual images of the prophet whisked from place to place by the Spirit, of the elegant chamberlain sitting in his roomy chariot muttering over the prophetic scroll while wheeling down the desert road, of Philip running up to and beside the chariot, politely asking and answering questions *while running,* of the two men going down together into the water in that deserted territory.

Readers schooled in the preoccupations of Hellenistic authors recognize Luke's typical fascination with the exotic and with social rank. However fleeting these early Christian brushes with the powerful—even the bureaucratic powerful—they are exciting. The eunuch may be marginal within the Pharisaic definition of the people of God, but he is a mighty person in his own land (over all the queen's treasury!). His chariot is capacious enough for himself and the scrolls and a guest. He speaks elegant Greek. He has a driver. And best of all, he hears and believes the message about Jesus. It is no small part of apologetic literature to emphasize how one's special claims have met with approval from respectable people (see e.g., Josephus, *Against Apion* 1:176-212).

Readers schooled in the symbols of the Bible appreciate the story at another level. Already alert to the way in which Philip has been identified as a prophet by Luke's stereotypical characterization (being filled with the Spirit, working signs and mighty works of power, proclaiming the word of God), this reader would delight in the oblique allusions to the prophet Elijah suggested by Philip's being addressed by an angel (2 Kgs 1:15), carried from place to place by the Spirit (1 Kgs 18:12), and running down the road with the chariot of a powerful person (1 Kgs 18:46).

Still deeper prophetic resonances would be stirred by the vision of an Ethiopian eunuch coming to the Temple to worship, the recollection of texts like that of Isa 11:11, which includes Ethiopians among the remnant people that God is gathering (see text in notes); or Isa 56:3-5, which promises that eunuchs who keep the Sabbaths and the covenant will not be "a dry tree" cut off from the Lord, but will find an honored place in the people; or like Zeph 3:9-10, which envisages a day when Yahweh would change the speech of all peoples to a pure speech "that all of them may call on the name of the Lord and serve him with one accord," and elaborates, "from beyond the rivers of Ethiopia my suppliants, the daughter of my dispersed ones, shall bring my offering." The conversion of the Ethiopian eunuch gives voice to these muted tones of universality in the prophets.

Readers schooled in the preoccupations of contemporary historical inquiry find other fascinating aspects to the story. They ask, for example, whether the Ethiopian was a proselyte or a God-fearing Gentile, and look for clues in the account for evidence in support of either. What difference would it make? If the eunuch were a Gentile, then this story and not the conversion of Cornelius would mark the real start of the Gentile mission. The reader sensitive to the literary contours of Luke-Acts recognizes, of course, that the main issue is whether *Luke* meant the reader to see this as the start of the Gentile mission, and the answer to that is easy. The enormous effort Luke put into the Cornelius sequence (chapters 10–15) would make no sense at all if Cornelius did not represent a fundamentally new step. Whoever the "historical Ethiopian" might have been, therefore, Luke clearly wants his readers to see him as part of the "ingathering of the scattered people" of Israel.

Another sort of historical question pertains to the way this passage was read in early Christianity. There are elements in the story which suggest it has a certain aetiological character. Certainly, Eusebius understood the story to mark the beginning of the Gentile mission, and in particular the beginning of Christianity in Ethiopia, for the eunuch "was also the first to return to his native land and preach the Gospel of the knowledge of the God of the universe . . . so that by him was actually fulfilled the prophecy which says, 'Ethiopia shall stretch out her hand to God' (Ps. 67:32)" (*Ecclesiastical History* 2, 1, 13). The Ethiopian Church could therefore trace its origin to this story.

That the text may have served a still further aetiological function is suggested by scribal additions to the text. Even in its simplest form, the text presents itself as something of a paradigm for baptismal procedures: not only the "preaching of the good news of Jesus" and the interpretation of the Scripture as preparation, but above all the evocative question "what prevents me?," which elsewhere in Luke-Acts appears in connection with acceptance or rejection from the community, and specifically with the admissibility of baptism (see Notes). Finally, there is the solemn entry into the water with its fascinatingly redundant note that "both of them, Philip and the eunuch" went down.

Textual evidence suggests that this passage may in fact have been used with specific reference to the practice of baptism in the early Church. When the eunuch asks what prevents him, the Western Text adds a demand from Philip for belief, and an explicit confession of faith by the eunuch (v. 37, see Notes). And after the baptism, some manuscripts make explicit that the Holy Spirit came upon the Ethiopian (v. 39). It is an odd but intriguing fact, finally, that one of our earliest manuscript of Acts (P50) is a papyrus fragment containing Acts 8:26-32 and Acts 10:26-31, texts that are joined primarily by the fact that both deal with conversion and baptism, and both containing the word *kollaomai* ("to join"). The physical condition of the papyrus suggests that it was written rapidly and with several corrections, then folded over. These characteristics are consistent with the possibility that it was used as an *aide-memoire* in preaching, perhaps even on the occasion of a baptism.

The reader of the present commentary, however, is primarily interested in how this incident advances Luke's overall literary and religious goals. In terms of its place and function within the narrative, we see how the programmatic prophecy of Jesus in Acts 1:8 continues to be fulfilled. Philip had spread the gospel in Samaria; now he works throughout the territory of Judea and up the coast to Caesarea. In terms of Luke's presentation of the Christian missionaries, we see not only how Philip is portrayed in prophetic terms, but even in terms reminiscent of Jesus: as Jesus on the road to Emmaus opened the meaning of the Scripture concerning himself, so does Philip on the road to Gaza open the text of Isaiah to the Ethiopian, showing how it speaks of Jesus.

The dramatic interventions of the angel and the Spirit serve to highlight Luke's fundamentally religious perspective on the story: the mission is not first of all a result of human enterprise but of the Spirit's impulse. The Christian missionaries are constantly trying to keep up with God's action. Finally, with regard to the theme of the expansion of God's people, we see that as with the Samaritans, the conversion of the Ethiopian does not yet represent a formal opening to the Gentiles, but rather to those who were marginalized within the people of God. The eunuch certainly qualifies, at least in terms of his sexual condition, as one who did not enjoy the full privileges of participation in the people. But he is also portrayed as deeply pious: going on pilgrimage, reading the prophet, eager to understand its meaning, responsive to the message about Jesus. He is one of the righteous from among every nation, whom God is calling to the restored people.

For Reference and Further Study

Decock, P. B. "The Understanding of Isaiah 53:7-8 in Acts 8:32-33." *The Relationship between the Old and the New Testament*. Neotestamentica 14. New Testament Society of South Africa, 1981, 111–133.

Dinkler, E. "Philippus und der *ANER AITHIOPS* (Apg. 8, 26–40)." *Jesus und Paulus*. Eds. E. E. Ellis and E. Grässer. Göttingen: Vandenhoeck & Ruprecht, 1975, 85–95.

Gaventa, B. *From Darkness to Light: Aspects of Conversion in the New Testament*. Philadelphia: Fortress, 1986, 98–107.

George, A. "L'Esprit saint dans l'oeuvre de Luc." *RB* 85 (1978) 500–542.

Martin, C. J. "A Chamberlain's Journey and the Challenge of Interpretation for Liberation." *Semeia* 47 (1989) 105–135.

O'Toole, R. F. "Philip and the Ethiopian Eunuch (Acts viii, 25–40)." *JSNT* 17 (1983) 25–34.

Seccombe, D. "Luke and Isaiah." *NTS* 27 (1981) 252–259.

Tannehill, R. *Narrative Unity* 2:107-112.

van Unnik, W. C. "Der Befehl an Philippus." *Sparsa Collecta*. Leiden: Brill, 1973, 1:328-339.

16. *Saul Encounters the Risen Lord* (9:1-19a)

1. Now Saul was still breathing threat and murder against the Lord's disciples. He approached the chief priest. 2. He requested from him letters to be sent to the synagogues in Damascus, so that if he found anyone following the Way, whether man or woman, he would lead them bound back to Jerusalem. 3. As he was on his way he came close to Damascus. Suddenly a light from heaven flashed around him. 4. He fell to the ground. He heard a voice saying to him, "Saul, Saul, why are you persecuting me?" 5. He answered, "Who are you, Lord?" And it said, "I am Jesus, whom you are persecuting. 6. But you get up! Go into the city. You will be told what it is you must do." 7. The men traveling with him stood there speechless. They heard the voice, but they saw nothing. 8. Saul got up from the ground. But when he opened his eyes, he saw nothing. Leading him by the hand, they brought him into Damascus. 9. For three days he could not see, and he neither ate nor drank. 10. There was a certain disciple in Damascus whose name was Ananias. In a vision the Lord said to him, "Ananias!" He answered, "Here I am, Lord!" 11. The Lord said to him, "Get up, go to the street called 'Straight,' and look in Judas' house for a Tarsian named Saul. For look, he is praying, 12. and he has seen in a vision a man named Ananias coming and placing his hands on him so that he could see." 13. Ananias answered, "Lord, I have heard about this man from many people, how many evil things he has done against your holy ones in Jerusalem. 14. And here he has authority from the chief priests to bind all those who are calling on your name." 15. The Lord said to him, "Go, for this man is my chosen vessel to carry my name before nations and kings and children of Israel. 16. For I will show him how much he must suffer for my name." 17. Ananias left and went into the house. He laid his hands on him. He said, "Brother Saul, the Lord Jesus who appeared to you on the road has sent me so that you can recover your sight and be filled with the Holy Spirit." 18. And at once something like scales fell from his eyes. He regained his sight, and getting up, he was baptized. 19a. He took food and gained strength.

NOTES

1. *still breathing threat and murder:* The adverb "still" (*eti*) nicely connects this continuation of the Saul saga with its initial stage in 8:1-3. The phrase "breathing threat" forms an allusion to the story of an earlier persecutor of the Jews, Apollonius, in 4 Macc 4:1-14: "with threats" (*meta apeilōn*) he entered the temple to plunder it, before he was forestalled by "angels on horseback" (see also 2 Macc 3:22-30).

   approached the chief priest: Saul takes the initiative, but Luke three times in this sequence reverts to the authority from the Jewish leaders. In 9:14, Ananias speaks of the "authority" (*exousia*) Paul had from them, which is what he sought by means of these "letters" (*epistolai;* see also 26:10, 12). Luke continues to show the Jewish leadership at the head or intimately involved with the efforts to extirpate the Jesus movement (Luke 20:1, 19; 22:2, 4, 7, 50, 52, 54, 66; 23:4, 10, 13; 24:20; Acts 4:1, 6, 23; 5:17, 21, 24, 27; 7:1). In Acts 22:5, Paul says that "all the council of elders" (*pan to prebyterion*) joined in giving him the letters.

2. *requested from him letters:* In effect, Saul seeks the sort of Letters of Recommendation with which we are familiar from 2 Cor 3:1; 3 John; Rom 16. It is not at all certain, historically, that the chief priest had such powers of extradition. The letter in 1 Macc 15:15-24, if authentic, commands kings to turn over miscreants to Simon the Chief Priest. See also Josephus, *Antiquities of the Jews* 14:190-195, and for the power of extradition given to Herod, *Jewish War* 1:474.

   to the synagogues in Damascus: It is stunning evidence of Luke's selectivity that he tells us nothing about the spread of Christianity to this important urban center, just as he neglects to relate a Galilean mission despite knowing there was one (9:31). Throughout the Diaspora, the synagogue (or "House of Prayer," *proseuchē*), was the institutional focus for Jewish identity (Philo, *Against Flaccus* 48; *Embassy to Gaius* 312). For the large Jewish population in Damascus, see Josephus, *Jewish War* 2:561, and especially 7:368.

   anyone following the Way: Luke's use of the term "Way" (*hodos*) is distinctive. Already in the OT, this word for "road" took on the obvious metaphorical sense of "manner of life" (LXX Ps 1:1, 6; 2:12; 118:29), a sense it retains in the NT (Rom 3:17; 1 Cor 12:31; Jude 11). Luke elsewhere refers to "the way of salvation" (Acts 16:7) and "the way of God" (18:26); and he alone uses the absolute "Way" to designate the messianic movement as such (9:2; 19:9, 23; 22:4; 24:22), and self-consciously in 24:14, "this way they call a sect." The language is reminiscent of the ethical tradition concerning the "two ways" that we find, e.g., in *1 Enoch* 91:18; *2 Enoch* 30:15; *Testament of Asher* 3:1-6:5; *Sibylline Oracles* 8:399; and in Christian literature, *The Didache* 1-6; *Letter of Barnabas* 18-21.

3. *a light from heaven flashed around him:* The adverb *exaiphnes* ("suddenly/unexpectedly") is used for the appearance of the heavenly choir in Luke 2:13 and the seizing of the youth by a spirit in Luke 9:39. The appearance of light (*phōs*) is especially associated with the presence of God (see LXX Ps 4:6; 35:9;

55:13; 77:14; 88:15; 96:11; 103:2; Wis 7:26; Isa 2:5; 60:19; 1 John 1:5-7; 1 Pet 2:9; Jas 1:17). The verb translated "flashed" (as lightning, *periastraptō*) is used only here, and forms another connection to the story in 4 Macc 4:10. The flashing of lightning is a feature of theophanies in Exod 19:16; 2 Sam 22:15; Ps 17:14; 76:18; 96:4; 143:6; Ezek 1:4, 7, 13; Dan 10:6; see also Luke 9:29; 10:18; 17:24; 24:4. In Paul's defense speech (22:6), he calls this a "great light." In 26:13 he calls it brighter than the sun, and has it surround his companions as well as himself.

4. *Saul, Saul, why are you persecuting me:* The voice from the light not only recalls the voice from the bush in Exod 3:3 ("Moses, Moses"), and from Mt. Sinai (Exod 19:16-20), it also shows the reader that the risen Lord remains active—he is indeed a character in the narrative! For the repetition of the name, compare the call of Jacob (Gen 46:2) and especially of Samuel (1 Sam 3:4, 10). For the identification of Jesus with those sent in his name, see especially Luke 10:16.

5. *who are you, Lord:* The title *kyrios* ("Lord") should be taken at full value. Saul does not yet know it is *Jesus* who is Lord, but he recognizes that he is involved in a theophany! Such dialogue within a revelatory experience clearly serves the literary function of making the import of the experience clear to the reader (see Gen 15:1-6; Exod 3:4-15; Judg 6:11-18; 13:8-20).

    Jesus, whom you are persecuting: Some *mss* add the title "The Nazorean" to the name Jesus. The use of the personal name alone is very striking: it is the person Jesus who is alive in a new and more powerful way, and identified with his followers. The personal character of the early Christian belief in the resurrection could not be more clearly stated.

6. *but you get up:* The *alla* ("but") is emphatic; the burden of this revelation is not information about Jesus, but a commission for Saul. The verse has a number of interesting textual variants. Some *mss* (especially in Latin and other versions) add either here or in verse 4 the statement reported in Paul's speech (26:14), "it is hard for you to kick against the goad," and from the speech in 22:10, the question, "what shall I do?" Some also add the description of Paul as "trembling and astonished." All of these embellishments are lacking in the best Greek *mss*.

7. *heard the voice but they saw nothing:* The three accounts of the event differ in detail. In 22:9, the exact opposite of this is stated: the companions saw the light but did not hear the voice! In 26:13, the light seems to fall on all, but Paul adds, "*I* heard the voice." In that version, however, all the travelers fall to the ground, whereas here and in 22:7, only Paul does so. For the theme of seeing but not hearing in theophanies, compare Deut 4:12; Wis 18:1; Dan 10:7.

8. *he saw nothing:* Some Latin *mss* add color to the account by having Paul say to his companions, " 'raise me from the ground,' and when they raised him, he saw nothing." Other *mss* have "no one" (*oudena*) rather than "nothing" (*ouden*). Paul will later bring a similar blindness on his opponent, the magician Elymas, as a punishment (Acts 13:11).

9. *neither ate nor drank:* The precise significance of this detail is difficult to evaluate. At the most obvious level, it shows that Paul is going through a holy period of transition, a stage of liminality, whose end is shown by his resuming the taking of food in 9:19. Fasting can be associated with a period of preparation for receiving a revelation (see Exod 34:28; Deut 9:9; Dan 9:3; 10:2-3; 4 *Ezra* 5:13, 20; 6:31; 2 *Baruch* 9:2; 12:5; 20:5), and also with repentance (Jer 14:12; Neh 1:4; Joel 1:14; Jonah 3:8). The account in Acts 13:1-3 makes the first option more likely: Paul places himself in a position to receive further guidance from the Lord. The early practice of fasting before baptism (*The Didache* 7:4; Justin Martyr, *Apology* 1:61) may have found some of its foundation in this passage. The explicit mention of "three days" is provocative, especially since Luke is concerned to conform Paul to the image of Jesus, and Jesus declares such a fast for himself before his death and resurrection (Luke 22:16, 30), but there is not enough evidence to support an argument for a deliberate allusion.

10. *here I am, Lord:* Ananias is identified as a disciple (*mathētēs*), and in Paul's speech of 22:12 is described as a person "pious according to the Law." The pattern of call and response is similar to that in 1 Sam 3:4, 10. His eager response is a sign of his obedience. Luke has now introduced the important plot-device of the vision (*horama*): see 9:12; 10:3, 17, 19; 11:5; 12:9; 16:9-10; 18:9. For its use in the LXX, see Gen 15:1; 46:2; Dan 1:7; 7:1, etc.

11. *Judas' house:* The vivid details in the message—the name of the street, the owner of the house, the place of Paul's origin—are compatible both with reliable historical traditions, and good story-telling. There is no possibility of verifying which is operative here.

    he is praying: Prayer and fasting is a standard combination (Jer 14:12; Neh 1:4; Esth 4:16; Mark 9:29; Luke 2:37; Acts 13:2-3; 14:23). The reader is shown that although Paul is an oppressor of the Church, he is also open to God's revelation according to the norms of Jewish piety.

12. *he has seen in a vision:* The narrator does not tell us of the vision directly, but only through the means of another vision. Luke uses this device of mutually interpretive visions to great effect in Acts 10; it is a masterful way of merging individual experiences into a shared narrative.

13. *I have heard about this man:* For such dialogue within a vision, see the note on v. 5. In this case, Ananias is allowed not only to voice his (understandable) reluctance to encounter such a dangerous person, but to help the reader deal with the obvious objections; thus, too rapid or repugnant a rehabilitation is avoided. Human hesitancy is legitimate, but can be overturned by the command of the Lord. Ananias' version of the events also puts a slightly different construction on them. For the first time, Luke uses the term "holy ones/saints" with reference to the community (see also 9:41; 26:10), a designation met frequently in Paul (Rom 1:7; 1 Cor 6:1; 2 Cor 1:1; 8:4, etc). Saul is here explicitly said in v. 14 to have "authority" (*exousia*) from the chief priest. And the phrase, "all those calling on your name" echoes the programmatic statement in Acts 2:21, "all those who call on the name of the Lord will be saved."

15. *my chosen vessel:* Literally, "a vessel of election for me." The term *skeuos* can mean any sort of instrument (see 1 Thess 4:4; Heb 9:21), and sometimes is used in contexts of divine instrumentality (see LXX Jer 27:25; Rom 9:21-23; 2 Tim 2:20-21), but because in this case it "carries/bears" the Lord's name, the translation "vessel" is appropriate. The image is remarkably like that used by Paul himself in 2 Cor 4:7, "we have this treasure in earthenware vessels." This designation of Paul as "chosen," in turn, associates him with the description of Jesus as the "elect one" (Luke 9:35; 23:35).

nations and kings and children of Israel: The term *ethnē* here could also naturally be translated as "Gentiles," particularly if the textual variant calling for a definite article were read. Like the prophecy of Jesus in Acts 1:8, this is a programmatic prophecy for Paul's career. He will carry the gospel to the Gentiles (13:46-47), and defends himself before King Agrippa (26:2-23) and expects to do so before Caesar (25:12). What is most striking in the statement, however, is the climactic position of "children of Israel." They are not left behind in Paul's mission; he continues to preach to his fellow Jews until the very end of the story (28:23-28).

16. *must suffer for my name:* The use of "must suffer" (*dei . . . pathein*) places Paul directly and deliberately in the line of suffering prophets like Moses and Jesus (see Luke 9:22; 17:25; 22:37; 24:7, 26). To suffer for "Jesus' name," in turn, means that he does so as Jesus' representative (see Luke 6:22; 21:12, 17; Acts 5:41). In view of the frequently perceived "triumphalism" of Luke's portrayal of Paul, this note of suffering struck from the very beginning is impressive.

17. *laid hands on him:* For the various dimensions of this gesture, see the note on Acts 6:6. In the present case, the laying on of hands both works a healing (compare Luke 5:13; 13:13; Acts 4:30; 5:12), and bestows the Holy Spirit (see Acts 8:17-19; 19:6).

Brother Saul: The use of the name, the title "brother," and the physical gesture of touching, all register as recognitions of Paul's acceptance as a member of the community. Some *mss* omit "Jesus" after the word "Lord," but it is probably to be read. Once more we see how Luke uses visions and dialogue to construct a community narrative. Here, Ananias incorporates Paul's own experience into his statement: the same Jesus had appeared to them both!

filled with the Holy Spirit: The actual bestowal is not described, but see Acts 13:9, where Paul is said to be "filled with the Holy Spirit." All the believers are "filled" with the prophetic spirit of Jesus (Acts 2:4), but we shall see how Luke will portray Paul as one of the "men of the Spirit" who represent this power in a special fashion.

18. *scales fell from his eyes:* The expression is obviously intended as metaphorical (*hōs*) rather than literal. Paul "was blind but now can see"; the Light that blinded him paradoxically relieved him of his spiritual blindness.

he was baptized: It is important for Luke that Paul—so ambiguous and dangerous a figure—be fully incorporated into the life of the community. The baptism completes Paul's ritual passage out of the sacral state he was in since his vision, a return to profane existence signalled by his taking of food.

INTERPRETATION

The character who will dominate the rest of Luke-Acts now emerges from the shadows. At the level of narrative architecture, we can admire the way in which Luke has arranged the sequence of events. He began the account of Saul with the young man holding the garments and agreeing to the stoning of Stephen, then carrying out a systematic campaign of terror in Jerusalem (8:1-3). Next Luke turned to the spread of the mission to Samaria and Judea in 8:4-40. By so doing, he accomplished two things: first, he prepared the reader to imagine Christians existing in other places, so that without ever telling us about a mission to Damascus, we can picture Saul going to find some there; second, he allowed some time to elapse so that it makes sense for Saul to seek new territories for persecution beyond Jerusalem. When we therefore read in 9:1 that Saul was "still breathing threat and murder," we find no difficulty in picking up the story just as Luke intended.

But the portrayal of Saul's transformation from persecutor to apostle is one that requires all of Luke's literary delicacy. How can the narrator make plausible one of history's most stunning and inexplicable turnabouts, when Paul himself, who based his authority as an apostle precisely on this experience (1 Cor 9:1; 15:8) was always required to include as part of his apologetic the embarrassing fact that he had been a "persecutor of the Church" (1 Cor 15:8; Gal 1:11-17; Phil 3:6; 1 Tim 1:13), without ever finding universal acceptance of his claims or credentials?

The difficulty facing Luke is indicated in part by the fact that he provides three versions of the event, here in direct narration (9:1-19a) and twice more in Paul's defense speeches (22:3-21; 26:9-18). The disagreement in detail between the three versions (see notes) is less significant than what the repetition tells us about Luke's perception of the event. The turning of a Pharisaic persecutor into the apostle of the Gentiles is a paradox so profound that it requires multiple retellings, with each version bringing out some further nuance of significance. Saul's conversion, after all, is the paradigmatic expression of the ironic truth spoken by Gamaliel (5:38-39): no one worked harder to extirpate the messianic movement than this agent (as Luke has it) of the chief priest; his failure to stop it and his being transformed into its boldest advocate stands for Luke and his readers as the surest sign that the crucified Messiah was indeed Lord, that their movement "was from God."

No more than Paul himself does Luke engage in any psychological explanation of Paul's murderous rage against the Messianists; he does not appear interested in the conversion as the resolution of intrapsychic conflicts, or for that matter even as a personal spiritual experience. He does not even mention the conscious reasons why Saul might have wanted to eliminate the Christians, such as the desire to defend Torah against the blasphemous claims made for a crucified (and therefore cursed) Messiah. Paul's personality or motivations before or after the event appear to have little significance for Luke's story. However important Paul turns out to be, he is *not* Luke's main character. He is but one of the human characters who enact the larger drama of God's fidelity to his promises. Luke's concern therefore is for the more properly religious dimensions of the event: how this unexpected turnabout was caused by the direct intervention of the risen Jesus in history, and how the "conversion" of Paul was in reality the call of a prophet.

As with the story of Pentecost, Luke has the daunting challenge of putting in narrative terms what is essentially an internal transformation. The empowerment of the first believers by the Spirit was depicted in terms of wind and flame and sound. This case is even more difficult. Between his leaving for Damascus to bind and imprison Messianists, and his first proclaiming of Jesus as "Son of God" in the Damascus synagogues, something fundamentally world-altering happened to Saul. Reduced to basics, what happened involved the (by definition incommunicable) personal experience of the risen Lord, and the ritual acceptance into the community. To give narrative life to that bald statement, Luke employs models and symbols available to him in the tradition.

In the flashing light and commanding voice of the sudden Damascus Road encounter, for example, we can discern the elements of the Old Testament theophanies, in particular those associated with Moses (Exod 3:3; 19:16-20). The scene appears to use other more specific literary prototypes as well. Luke's account has verbal and structural similarities to the story in 4 Maccabees 4:1-14 (itself elaborating the account in 2 Maccabees 3:7-34), concerning the attempt by Apollonius to plunder the treasury of the temple; that oppressor of the people met "'angels on horseback [who] appeared from heaven with flashing armor" and knocked Apollonius to the ground. Deflected from his wicked plan by "divine justice," he ends by being a friend of those he sought to harm. But Saul is more than simply a persecutor made ally, and he encounters more than angels.

An even more impressive array of thematic similarities is found in the account of Aseneth's conversion from paganism to the Jewish faith of her husband-to-be, the Patriarch Joseph, in the Hellenistic Jewish novel, *Joseph and Aseneth*. The beautiful maiden who had scorned Joseph repented her arrogance with seven days of fasting (10:17) followed by extensive prayers (12:1-15). Then the heavens open, and a great light shines about her (14:2). She falls on her face (14:3). A man from heaven appears to her, and calls out her name twice, "Aseneth, Aseneth" (14:4, 7). She asks his identity, "who are you, tell me" (14:5, 8; see also 15:12). The man answers, "I am chief of the house of the Lord and commander of the host of the Most High'' (14:8). She is told to get up, and she will be told what the messenger has to say (14:8). At the end of the vision, she washes her face with living water (14:15), and is given both a prediction and reassurance concerning her future (15:2-6). This is an impressive set of parallels. But something more than conversion to Judaism is happening to Saul, and his encounter is with more than an angelic messenger. Nor was his vision prepared for by prayer and fasting; it happened while he was still rabid for persecution. Saul's prayer and fasting follow his encounter with Jesus and prepare for his entry into the messianic community.

Luke has therefore used elements from familiar traditions about theophanies, conversion, and the overturning of oppressors, but he has put them together in distinctive fashion. Like Paul's own brief allusions to the event (1 Cor 9:1; 15:8; Gal 1:15-16), Luke understands the encounter as an experience of the resurrected one. But unlike the accounts in the Gospel, where Jesus can be mistaken for a stranger on the road, or even the vision of Stephen of the Son of Man standing at the right hand of God, Saul's experience of Jesus is as the overwhelming power of the Holy One. There is something terrible and inexorable about the flashing light and the probing voice. Paul needs to ask who *is* this Lord, but he knows at once that it is ''Lord,'' the commanding, transcendent power of God. It is not immediately clear what will be demanded of him, but his experience from the beginning is of a commanding presence: ''You get up and go.''

Distinctive to Luke's account as well is the identification of the risen Lord with the community. The dramatic effect of the declaration, ''I am Jesus whom you are persecuting'' is immediate. Luke could scarcely have found a more effective way of establishing the living relationship and presence of the raised prophet with those who continued to live and speak and act with his prophetic spirit. And for Saul, if the living and powerful Lord identifies himself with this community, then joining this community is the sign of obedience to his presence. The one who caused suffering for those ''who call on the name'' of the suffering Messiah is now to be shown ''how much he must suffer for the sake of the name.'' Not only the identification between Jesus and the community, but between Saul and Jesus is established in this mystical encounter.

As the story moves into Damascus, we meet another example of what is becoming a familiar Lukan literary trait, the building of a shared experience and of a common story, by means of multiple visions. We first saw him use this technique in Luke 24, where the multiple experiences of the risen Jesus by diverse witnesses became, by means of telling and retelling, a community experience and narrative. We will see him use the same technique even more elaborately in Acts 10–15.

In this case, the vision (including dialogue) with Ananias, which has as one of its components the report of a simultaneous vision being experienced by Saul, serves several narrative functions. Since Ananias as a disciple is perceived as a reliable character—and demonstrates himself to be such by his willing response, "here I am, Lord," to the calling of his name—he can be used as a means of spelling out some of the implications of Paul's experience: he, not Saul, is now told that Saul must suffer for the name, and that he will be a chosen vessel to bear the name to the nations. Ananias can also serve as the community's (and reader's) spokesperson in voicing reluctance and fear at so rapidly accepting into fellowship this murderous fellow, thus providing Luke with the opportunity to have the divine voice override such human resistance to his work.

This first telling of the story is in fact simple and unadorned. Contemporary readers, perhaps schooled in religious phenomenology, can see vividly the classic stages of a *rite de passage:* entry into the mystery, liminality, re-entry into the profane realm. But for the character Saul, there are no props! For him, this is not ritual enactment, but the frightening reality of being swept into a power beyond human control, and we best read this first telling as the raw recountal of a man struck blind by a great light, overwhelmed by a commanding voice, led helplessly by the hand to the city, sitting in darkness, fasting, praying, waiting . . . for what?, and finally being brought by means of greeting as brother, and the laying on of hands, and the pouring of water, into the community of those he had hated.

Later retellings will help elaborate the deeper significance of the themes implicit within this gripping tale of frightening religious experience: the connections between a living voice and the resurrected one, between being blinded by light and becoming a light to the Gentiles. Both Saul and the reader will need to reflect again on this powerful and pivotal story.

For Reference and Further Study

Gaventa, B. *From Darkness to Light: Aspects of Conversion in the New Testament.* Overtures to Biblical Theology 20. Philadelphia: Fortress Press, 1986.

Gill, D. "The Structure of Acts 9." *Bib* 55 (1974) 546-548.

Hedrick, C. W. "Paul's Conversion/Call: A Comparative Analysis of the Three Reports in Acts." *JBL* 100 (1981) 415-432.

Lohfink, G. *The Conversion of St. Paul: Narrative and History in Acts.* Trans. B. Malina. Chicago: Franciscan Herald Press, 1976.

Mullins, T. Y. "New Testament Commission Forms, especially in Luke-Acts." *JBL* 95 (1976) 603-614.

Munck, J. "La Vocation de l'Apôtre Paul." *ST* 1 (1947) 130-145.

Stanley, D. M. "Why Three Accounts?" *CBQ* 15 (1953) 315–318.
Windisch, H. "Die Christusepiphanie vor Damaskus (Acts 9, 22, und 26) und ihre religionsgeschichtliche Parallelen." *ZNW* 31 (1932) 1–23.

17. Paul's Reception in Jerusalem (9:19b-30)

19b. He stayed with the disciples in Damascus for some days, 20. and he immediately began to proclaim in the synagogues concerning Jesus that he was the Son of God. 21. All those who heard were astonished. They were saying, "Is he not the one who in Jerusalem ravaged those calling on this name? And didn't he come here for the very purpose of putting them in bonds to drag them before the chief priests?" 22. But Saul grew ever more powerful. He confuted the Jews dwelling in Damascus by proving that this one was the Messiah. 23. When a considerable period of time had gone by, the Jews made a plan to kill him. 24. But their scheme was made known to Saul. They were even keeping watch at the gates day and night so that they could kill him. 25. But his disciples took him and let him down by night through the wall, by lowering him in a basket. 26. When he arrived in Jerusalem, he tried to join the disciples. But everyone feared him. They did not believe that he was a disciple. 27. But taking hold of him, Barnabas led him to the apostles. He related to them how on the road he had seen the Lord and had spoken to him, and how in Damascus he had spoken boldly in the name of Jesus. 28. So he remained with them, going and coming within Jerusalem, boldly speaking in the name of the Lord. 29. He was even speaking and disputing with the Hellenists. But they determined to kill him. 30. And when the brothers found out, they brought him down to Caesarea, and they sent him on to Tarsus.

NOTES

20. *immediately began to proclaim:* The imperfect tense is here inchoative: "he set about proclaiming." The adverb *eutheōs* ("immediately") signals the precipitousness of Saul's new activity, felt both by his first hearers, and undoubtedly by Luke's reader as well. He takes everyone by surprise. By having Saul begin in the synagogue, Luke establishes the pattern for Paul's preaching throughout the rest of the narrative: he always begins in the synagogues and only when rejected there moves to other venues (13:5, 13-16; 14:1; 16:13, 16; 17:1; 18:4; 19:8). According to Paul's own *narratio* in Gal 1:17, he went to Arabia after his call, and then returned to Damascus.

concerning Jesus . . . Son of God: In the Greek, Jesus is the direct object of the verb: "he proclaimed Jesus," with the *hoti* clause providing the specific aspect of the message concerning Jesus. The reader of Luke-Acts is not surprised by the designation *huios tou theou* (Luke 1:32, 35; 3:22; 4:3, 9, 41; 22:70), but in Acts (apart from the textually suspect 8:37), this is the only explicit use of the title. For its use in Paul's letters, see Rom 1:3; 2 Cor 1:19; Gal 2:20; Eph 4:13.

21. *ravaged those calling on this name:* The verb *portheō* denotes violent oppression and plundering; it is not found in the LXX except for the violence done by Antiochus IV against Jerusalem in 4 Macc 4:23, and as a charge against their murderers by the Jewish martyrs in 4 Macc 14:4. It is, however, the term used by Paul himself for his persecution of the Church (Gal 1:13, 23). Indeed, the reaction here attributed to the Damascenes is put by Paul himself in the mouth of the Jerusalem Christians: "He who persecuted us is now preaching the faith he once tried to destroy" (Gal 1:23).

22. *ever more powerful:* The verb *endunamoō* is used in some *mss* of the LXX in Judg 6:34 for the Spirit's taking possession of Gideon, and in 1 Chr 12:18 for the Spirit coming upon the prophet Amisai. In the NT it is a Pauline term (Rom 4:20; Eph 6:10); of particular interest is Paul's use of it for his own ministry (Phil 4:13; 1 Tim 1:12; 2 Tim 4:17) and for that of his delegate Timothy (2 Tim 2:1). Some *mss* want to make clear that more than physical strength is meant, so they add "in the word," which only indicates that the scribes did not catch the verb's biblical associations.

    confuted . . . proving: Here and in the next verse, Luke for the first time uses the term *Ioudaios* as designating a group separate from the Christians. The usage is frequent throughout the narrative dealing with Paul's ministry. The verb *synchunō* means literally "to confuse," in the sense of "mixing up." The second verb (*symbibazō*) can either mean to demonstrate—as in reaching a logical conclusion (see 16:10)—or simply "to teach" (as in Exod 4:12, 15; Lev 10:11; Deut 4:9; 1 Cor 2:6). The verse could also be translated, therefore, as "he confused them by teaching that Jesus was the Messiah." Some Latin *mss* from the Western Text tradition inexplicably add the words "in whom God was well pleased."

23. *considerable period of time:* Literally, "when sufficient days were filled"; Luke uses *plēroō* for the completion of a span of time, as in Luke 21:24; Acts 7:23, 30 (see also *synplēroō* in Luke 9:51; Acts 2:11).

24. *scheme was made known:* The term *epiboulē* has the specific sense of a plot made against another (Herodotus, *Persian Wars* 1:12), and will be used again in 20:3, 19 and 23:30 for plots made against Paul by his Jewish opponents.

    keeping watch: Luke uses the verb *paratēreō*, which he used in the Gospel for the hostile attention paid Jesus by his opponents (Luke 6:7; 14:1; 20:20). In 2 Cor 11:32, Paul relates the incident in this fashion: "At Damascus, the governor under King Aretas guarded the city of Damascus in order to seize me." Paul does not attribute the attempt to Jewish opponents, although earlier in the passage he mentions having received "five times at the hands of the Jews forty lashes less one" (2 Cor 11:24). Some *mss* conform Luke's version to that in 2 Corinthians.

25. *his disciples took him:* The translation is based on the best Greek text, even though "his disciples" is very strange. Luke does not elsewhere speak of Paul's disciples, but only of the Lord's disciples. But the word order does not seem to support the best alternative for the genitive *autou*, namely the accusative *auton*, although this is supported by the Vulgate.

lowering him in a basket: Luke's version is almost identical to that of Paul in 2 Cor 11:33: "And I was let down in a basket through the wall, and I escaped from his hands." The two verses in the respective sources combine similarity and dissimilarity in such fashion as to suggest independent traditions rather than literary dependence. In 2 Cor 11, it should be noted, Paul lists the event as something that gives evidence of his "weakness."

27. *taking hold of him:* Barnabas begins to live up to his designation as "son of consolation" (4:36). He acts as mediator between Paul and the Jerusalem leaders. The verb *epilambanomai* is a favorite of Luke's (see Luke 9:47; 14:4; 20:20, 26 [with a different sense]; 23:26; Acts 16:19; 17:19; 18:17; 21:30, 33; 23:19).

led him to the apostles: The incident provides a classic case of disagreement with Paul's account in Gal 1:17-19. Paul takes an oath in support of his version that after his call he did not go up to Jerusalem until three years had passed, and then spoke only to Cephas, seeing "none of the other apostles except James the Lord's brother."

how on the road he had seen the Lord: A remarkable example of Luke's technique of building a shared story. Barnabas validates Paul's experience for the Jerusalem leadership (and also for the reader) by reciting it in a straightforward and unequivocal fashion.

28. *going and coming:* Luke uses a similar expression in 1:21 for the "coming and going" of Jesus among his disciples during the time of his ministry. Luke intends us to see Paul as enjoying the full fellowship of the Jerusalem community. It is difficult to reconcile this, however, with Paul's own statement in Gal 1:22, "I was still not known by sight to the churches of Christ in Judea."

boldly speaking in the name of the Lord: Luke uses a periphrastic imperfect to suggest a continuing activity. He uses this note of "boldness" (*parrēsiazomai*) with special reference to Paul's ministry (see 13:46; 14:3; 18:26; 19:8; 26:26; 28:31), although he attributes *parrēsia* to the other apostles as well (2:29; 4:13, 29, 31).

29. *disputing with the Hellenists:* In a narrative reversal, Luke has Saul fighting with the same group he had formerly represented (and perhaps even led) in the battle against Stephen (6:9-14).

determined to kill him: Literally, "put their hands to killing him." Luke uses the same verb as in the Gospel prologue (Luke 1:1) for those who had attempted narratives before him (see also Acts 19:13). The verse has the narrative function of showing that Saul was not the only Jewish persecutor, and

also to show that he was already starting to "suffer for the name," in fulfillment of Ananias' vision (9:16).

30. *sent him on to Tarsus:* The rallying of the brethren around Saul helps show
his acceptance by the Jerusalem community; the practical effect of removing
him from the scene is to bring peace to the community (9:31). The reader
understands that Saul is returning to his hometown in Cilicia (see 9:11). He
will undergo a similar hurried removal to Caesarea in an attempt to save his
life at the end of his career (Acts 23:23-24).

INTERPRETATION

Our main interest in this interpretation of Luke-Acts is discovering
how the literary shaping of the narrative effects the author's stated religious purpose. But since the form of the narrative is historical, the issue
of accuracy arises whenever the story touches on matters in the public
(and potentially verifiable) realm, or when it relates matters found in other
sources as well. Such is the case here, where Luke recounts the events
following Saul's conversion experience, and such will be ever more frequently the case in his recitation of Paul's movements. As we examine
such issues, our concern is not a final adjudication concerning historicity,
but a finer perception of Luke's literary fashioning.

The historian is relieved to find that Paul's solemn but *ad hoc* recollec-
tions in Gal 1:11-24 and 2 Cor 11:32-33 give substantial support to the
basic historicity of Luke's version without in any way suggesting that Luke
used Paul's versions to construct his own. The historian therefore has
the happy task of sorting through the differences in detail between essentially independent witnesses. The substantial areas of agreement are:
a) Paul's resurrection experience took place in the area around Damascus. Luke makes this explicit (9:1-9); Paul implies it by saying that he
"returned to Damascus" (Gal 1:17). b) Paul had an extended ministry
after his call, whether specifically in Damascus (Acts 9:20-25) or in Arabia and then Damascus (Gal 1:17). c) Paul had to escape Damascus under
threat to his life by means of a basket let down through the city wall (2
Cor 11:32-33; Acts 9:25). d) Paul visited the Jerusalem Church in the early
part of his ministry before going to Syria and Cilicia (Acts 9:26; Gal 1:21),
even though he faced suspicion there (Gal 1:23; Acts 9:26). e) Paul met
with at least some of the apostles in Jerusalem (Acts 9:27; Gal 1:19). f)
Barnabas was Paul's companion in at least one meeting in Jerusalem (Acts
9:27; Gal 2:1). g) After his first trip to Jerusalem, Paul worked in the territory of Cilicia (Gal 1:21; Acts 9:30).

There are any number of disagreements in detail: a) Paul makes a point
about the passage of time between his independent ministry in Arabia

and Damascus, and his first trip to Jerusalem, whereas Luke allows us to imagine a passage of time, but gives the impression of only a short one. b) Paul says he was opposed by King Aretas in Damascus, whereas Luke attributes his troubles to a plot by the Jews of that city. c) Paul insists that on his first visit he saw none of the apostles except Cephas and James, whereas Luke has simply that he saw "the apostles." d) Paul does not leave room for a period of ministry within the Church in Jerusalem, whereas Luke explicitly emphasizes it. e) Paul has Barnabas accompany him on the trip only "after fourteen years," and simply as another companion like Titus, whereas Luke has him as the essential mediator between Paul and the apostles.

Because Paul takes an oath that he is not lying (Gal 1:20), scholars sometimes take his version to be the factually accurate one, and dismiss Luke's version either as purely a fabrication or even as representing the sort of position that Paul was trying to oppose in Galatia. But while the critical historian is obliged to recognize that taking an oath on one's sincerity is impressive, it hardly guarantees factual accuracy. It might actually suggest that the facts were sufficiently ambiguous to require such a vehement self-justification. The historian would do better to grant each author his sincerity, recognize that each had an interest in shaping the events a certain way, and rejoice in the realization that such narrative tendencies actually work toward establishing the essential historicity of those points held in agreement.

We can observe briefly, then, the ways in which Luke's divergences from Paul can be seen as part of his consistent literary and religious preoccupations. It should cause us no surprise that Paul emphasizes his independence from Jerusalem in his account, for the authenticity of his experience and apostolate was under active threat. Neither does it surprise us that Luke emphasizes Paul's connection with Jerusalem, not because he has a desire to relativize Paul's significance, but because *all* of the missionaries in Acts are brought into connection with the Jerusalem leadership as quickly as possible. Luke's interest is showing how the gospel moved out into the Gentile world in continuity with the restored people of God in Jerusalem.

Luke therefore establishes narrative links between Paul and the other apostles. In this passage we see two of them: the first is the role played by Barnabas. We saw how in 4:36-37 Luke portrayed him as doubly submissive to the Twelve, receiving a new name from them and recognizing their authority by laying his possessions at their feet. Now he lives out his new identity as "son of consolation" by functioning as mediator between Saul and the Church. We will see him play the same role again in 11:22, when as an agent for the Church in Jerusalem, he recruits Saul for the mission. The second narrative link is the early visit by Saul to this

Church. Paul is probably right about the delay in time and the limited nature of his first visit. But Luke is concerned to show the essential unity between the various missionaries, and therefore emphasizes the acceptance of Paul by the whole Church and his period of activity within it.

By bringing Saul back to Jerusalem, Luke is also able to develop two of his own narrative themes. The first is the deeply paradoxical character of the persecutor turned apostle: Luke returns him as suppliant to the community he had tried to destroy, and then face as opposition those very Hellenists he had formerly supported or even led. And as he had colluded in their attempts to eliminate Stephen, so is he now the object of their murderous intentions.

This leads to the second theme, the fulfillment of the prophecy that Saul would have to suffer for the name of Jesus. In Luke's portrayal, Saul does not return to Jerusalem in triumph and recognition as an apostle. He is feared, suspected; they do not think he is even a sincere disciple. He must rely on Barnabas to intervene in his behalf. This is suffering. Then, even more obviously, there is the second plot against his life by Diaspora Jews, creating danger for himself and sufficient discomfort for the community that it swiftly removes him from the scene. Luke will portray Paul in terms of prophetic power later in the story. But in these first glimpses he is very much "an earthenware vessel," not yet recognized as fully worthy of carrying the Lord's name.

FOR REFERENCE AND FURTHER STUDY

Cambier, J. "Le voyage de S. Paul à Jérusalem en Act. ix, 26ss et le schéma missionnaire théologique de S. Luc." *NTS* 8 (1961–1962) 249–257.

Dupont, J. "Les trois premières voyages de Saint Paul à Jérusalem." *Etudes sur les Actes des Apôtres.* Lectio Divina 45. Paris: Editions du Cerf, 1967, 167–171.

Gaventa, B. "The Overthrown Enemy: Luke's Portrait of Paul." *1985 SBL Seminar Papers.* Ed. K. H. Richards. Atlanta: Scholars Press, 1985, 439–449.

Giles, K. N. "Luke's Use of the Term *ekklēsia* with Special Reference to Acts 20:28 and 9:31." *NTS* 31 (1985) 135–142.

Johnson, L. T. *Decision-Making in the Church: A Biblical Model.* Philadelphia: Fortress Press, 1983, 65–67.

Loning, K. *Die Saulustradition in der Apostelgeschichte.* Münster: Aschendorff, 1973.

Menoud, Ph.-H. "Le sense du verbe *porthein* (Gal 1:13, 23; Acts 9:21)." *Apophoreta.* Ed. W. Eltester. BZNW 30. Berlin: A. Töpelmann, 1964, 178–186.

Slingerland, D. " 'The Jews' in the Pauline Portion of Acts." *JAAR* 54 (1986) 305–321.

Townsend, J. T. "Acts 9:1-29 and Early Church Tradition." *SBL 1988 Seminar Papers.* Ed. D. Lull. Atlanta: Scholars Press, 1988, 119–131.

Wainwright, A. W. "The Historical Value of Acts 9:19b-30." *Studia Evangelica.* Ed. E. A. Livingstone. Berlin: Akademie Verlag, 1973, 6:589–594.

18. *Wonders Worked by Peter (9:31-43)*

31. The Church throughout all of Judea and Galilee and Samaria therefore had peace. It was being built up and was progressing in the fear of the Lord. It was growing in the comfort given by the Holy Spirit. 32. Now as Peter was going through every place, he went down also to the holy ones who were dwelling in Lydda. 33. And there he found a certain man whose name was Aeneas. He was paralyzed, lying for eight years on a cot. 34. So Peter said to him, "Aeneas, Jesus Messiah is healing you. Get up! Make your bed!" And he got up at once. 35. Everyone dwelling in Lydda and in the Sharon saw him, and these turned to the Lord. 36. Now in Joppa there was a certain woman disciple whose name was Tabitha. Translated, this means Dorcas. She was generous in her good works and in her giving of alms. 37. But during that period of time she grew sick and died. They washed her. They placed her in an upper room. 38. Since Lydda was close to Joppa, the disciples heard that Peter was there. They sent two men to him with this request: "Do not delay! Come over to us!" 39. Peter rose and went with them. When he arrived, they led him to the upper room. All the widows came up to him weeping. They showed him the tunics and cloaks that Dorcas made when she was with them. 40. Peter sent all of them outside. Getting to his knees, he prayed. Then, turning to the body, he said, "Tabitha, Arise!" She opened her eyes and saw Peter. She sat back up. 41. He gave her his hand and raised her. He called the holy ones and the widows. He presented her to them alive. 42. This became known all through Joppa, and many believed in the Lord. 43. He stayed in Joppa with a certain Simon, a tanner, for many days.

NOTES

31. *Judea and Galilee and Samaria:* This is a summary like those in 2:41-47; 4:32-37; 5:12-16; 6:7. The ordering of the regions raises the same sort of questions concerning Luke's knowledge of Palestinian geography as Luke 17:11. The mission to Judea and Samaria has been narrated, but Luke never speaks of the evangelization of Galilee, and in fact this is his only formal acknowledgement of the existence of the Church there.

the Church . . . had peace: In this list of positive qualities, that of peace (*eirēnē*) is the most striking, not only because of the implication that it was Saul's removal that made it possible (9:30), but also because the bringing of peace is so associated with the Lukan conception of the good news (Luke 1:79; 2:14, 29; 7:50; 8:48; 10:5-6; 12:51; 19:38, 42; 24:36; Acts 7:26; 10:36). As with his earlier summaries, Luke highlights some aspect of God's blessing enjoyed by the community.

being built up: The present participle of *oikodomeō* refers to a continuing process of identity formation and stabilization, if the term has the same sense that it does in Paul (1 Cor 8:1, 10; 10:23; 14:4, 17; Rom 14:19; 15:2; 2 Cor 10:8; 12:19; 1 Thess 5:11).

progressing in the fear of the Lord: The participle of *poreuomai* ("to go") is here used as in the LXX translation of the Hebrew *halak*, to designate a way of living; see, e.g., LXX Ps 18:9; 33:11; 110:11; Prov 1:7; 8:13; 10:27; 16:4; Sir 1:11; 19:20; see also Luke 1:12, 65; 2:9; 5:26; 7:16; 8:37; Acts 2:43; 5:11; 19:17.

growing in the comfort: The verb *plēthunō* is used by Luke in Acts 6:1, 7; 7:17 and 12:24 to refer to numerical increase. Here it means qualitative growth. The phrase "comfort given by the Holy Spirit" (*paraklēsē tou pneumatos tou hagiou*) is dative, either of reference or perhaps of instrument. They are growing in that quality of comfort, or because of that comfort, they are able to grow.

32. *dwelling in Lydda:* Peter is pictured as making a circuit of the churches (*dia* + genitive), "moving through" them all. Lydda was a town in Judea (1 Macc 11:34) between Jerusalem and Joppa. Pliny the Elder lists the town as one of the ten Toparchies (local government areas) in Judea (*Natural History* 5:70; see Josephus, *Jewish War* 3:55). Josephus says "in size it was not inferior to a city," and names it as a place where the Roman Governor of Syria sat to settle a dispute (*Antiquities of the Jews* 6:130). Once more Luke assumes rather than narrates the founding of the Church in that important place.

33. *he was paralyzed:* Compare the story of the healing of the paralytic by Jesus in Luke 5:17-26, and those healed by the apostles in Samaria (Acts 8:7). For the length of the illness, compare Acts 4:22. The use of personal names throughout this entire section is noteworthy.

34. *make your bed:* The translation of *strōson seautō* (Literally "spread/strew for yourself") is difficult, because the sense of *strōnnumi* in the imperative could be: "make your bed for yourself" or "set the table for yourself." The point of the command, however, is perfectly clear: it is a demonstration of the reality of the cure; compare Jesus' command to the paralytic to take up his bed and walk (Luke 5:24).

35. *these turned to the Lord:* The translation tries to capture the nuance of *hoitines* by using "these." As in Acts 8:6-8, the healing functions as a stimulus to conversion. The residents of "the Sharon" (note the definite article) are those living in the coastal plain between Joppa and Caesarea (see LXX Isa 33:9). For the shift from town to region, see 8:25, 40.

36. *Tabitha . . . Dorcas:* The designation *mathētria* ("woman disciple") is used only here in the NT; it appears as a designation of two students of Plato in Diogenes Laertius, *Lives of the Philosophers* 4, 2. The name Tabitha is Aramaic, related to the Hebrew *zebi* (*zebiah*), meaning a gazelle. *Dorkas*, which in Greek also means a gazelle, is used by the LXX to translate the Hebrew term in Deut 12:15; 2 Sam 2:18; and most notably as a metaphor for the beloved in the Song of Songs 2:9; 8:14.

generous in her good works: The adjective "generous" translates the Greek *plērēs* ("full of"). The doing of "good works" in fact could be taken to include the giving of alms (see, e.g., Tob 3:2 and possibly Titus 3:14). For the importance of almsgiving as an articulation of piety within Judaism, see the notes on Luke 11:41; 12:33 and Acts 3:2. In Acts 10:2, Cornelius will be described in similar terms.

37. *during that period of time:* Literally, "but it happened in those days . . . ." Luke wants the reader to picture her sickness and death occurring during the time when the events in Lydda were happening.

    washed her: This is part of the normal process of preparing a body for burial, although it is striking that anointing is omitted (see *m.Shab.* 23:5). For the "upper room" (*hyperōon*), compare Acts 1:13 and 20:8. There is perhaps a faint verbal echo of the story in 1 Kgs 17:19, in which the widow of Sarepta places the dead body of her son in the *hyperōon*.

38. *do not delay:* The verb *okneō* ("shirk from/hesitate") is used in just such requests in LXX Num 22:16; Judg 18:19; Tobit 12:6, 13; Sir 7:35. The sending of two men may reflect the command of Jesus (Luke 10:1) and community practice in early Christianity (Acts 3:1; 8:14; 13:2; 22:23).

39. *rose and went with them:* Elements in this story prepare the reader for the still more significant narrative about Cornelius that will immediately follow. Here, the reader learns how Peter is willing to respond to requests made of him by messengers (see 10:23).

    all the widows: The designation with the definite article and no further qualification raises the question whether Luke thinks of them as a definite, organized group, either as ministers or as recipients of charity (see note on Acts 6:1, and 1 Tim 5:3-16). Are they Tabitha's cohort, or the recipients of her alms? The determination would not seem to affect the meaning of the story. In dramatic terms, however, their mute weeping and show of garments serves as an impressive replacement for a direct request that Tabitha be restored to them.

40. *Tabitha, arise:* The verb *anistēmi* is used regularly by Luke for the resurrection of Jesus (Luke 9:22; 18:33; 24:7, 46; Acts 2:24, 32; 3:26; 13:32). There is considerable resemblance between this account and the raising of the little girl by Jesus (Luke 8:49-56): the use of messengers, the weeping bystanders, the exclusion of outsiders from the room, the call to rise ("Little girl, rise up," Luke 8:54), the taking by the hand.

41. *presented her to them alive:* The Greek *parestēsen autēn zōsan* is virtually identical to that used for the resurrection appearances of Jesus in Acts 1:3: *autois parestēsen heauton zōnta.*

42. *many believed in the Lord:* As with the healing of Aeneas, the healing functions as a stimulus to conversions. The response of the people is a standard feature of healing narratives. It is noteworthy here that "belief in the Lord (Jesus)" is an implicit recognition that the power at work through Peter is not his own but comes from the raised prophet.

43. *Simon, a tanner:* Such details as name and occupation give a sense of verisimilitude to the account. Peter's new residence at Joppa sets the locale for the next development in the narrative (10:6, 17, 32). Given Peter's professed fastidiousness about clean and unclean (10:4), it is puzzling that he should

reside with one whose trade puts him among the chronically unclean (see *m.Ket.* 7:10). Of course, Peter himself is among those considered by the Pharisees as *hamartōlos* (Luke 5:8). In any case, the detail could actually derive from tradition, and it is doubtful whether Luke could assume so subtle a knowledge of rabbinic casuistry among his readers that this designation could be taken as significant.

INTERPRETATION

A significant aspect of Luke's narrative artistry is the way he interweaves separate strands of tradition into a single coherent story. Luke inserted the conversion and first preaching efforts of Saul (9:1-30) after stories about the evangelization to the outcast of the people by Philip (Acts 8:1-40), and then, by removing Saul from Jerusalem to Tarsus (9:30) was able by means of a simple summary statement concerning the state of the Church in the territories of Judea, Samaria, and Galilee (8:31), to pick up once more with the mission of Peter in Judea.

By this subtle alternation, he has accomplished two important narrative impressions: first, the reader inevitably sees the career of Saul (Paul) as intimately involved and entwined with that of the other missionaries; second, the reader sees the unprecedented and dangerous initiative toward the Gentiles being taken first, not by the suspect former persecutor, but by Peter (Acts 10-11).

These two miracle stories therefore serve as something of a narrative transition. Geographically, they draw Peter from Jerusalem to the coastal city of Joppa, and therefore closer in the reader's imagination to the wider world of the Gentiles, which boundary will be crossed in the story of Cornelius' conversion. Before Peter is led by God to this dangerous decision (one so unprecedented that the entire section of chapters 10-15 struggles with it), these miracle stories serve to refocus the reader's attention on Peter as the one through whom the power of the Lord is truly at work.

Although the two stories share the basic form of healing accounts, they are also unusually detailed. The image of Peter as circuit rider, visiting churches in a regular round is memorable, as is the communication between churches by means of messengers. The reader is told of place names and personal names, and time or length of illness, and occupations or associates. It is almost as if Luke wanted, for historical or literary reasons, to root the unlikely developments to follow in the soil of the everyday and verifiable.

But if Luke is in fact himself constructing the sequence if not the substance of these stories—if, as is likely, he shaped general traditions about Peter as wonderworker into these specific narratives in this specific place—we can ask what particular narrative function they serve in their present form. It is fairly obvious that the healing of a paralytic and the resuscitation of the widow are meant to echo the similar accounts told about Jesus (Luke 5:17-26; 7:11-16), and the still earlier prototypes provided by the prophets Elijah and Elisha (1 Kgs 17:17-24; 2 Kgs 4:32-37). Peter is validated once more as an authentic representative of the line of prophets who "work signs and wonders among the people."

The stories also point the reader forward to the Cornelius episode and its long sequel, not only by placing Peter in Joppa and showing the reader how eager he is to respond to the appeals brought by messengers, but above all by showing that the power at work is that of the resurrected Lord, who himself "raises" to new life. Notice that Peter tells both Aeneas and Tabitha to "rise up" (*anastēthi*), using the word associated so frequently with the resurrection of Jesus. The reader is given an early signal that the conversion of the Gentiles that Luke will now relate is to be understood similarly as coming from the "Holy Spirit," that is the power of the resurrected one, and also as itself an extension of the "resurrection/rebuilding" of Israel (Acts 15:16-17).

FOR REFERENCE AND FURTHER STUDY

Kreyenbuhl, J. "Ursprung und Stammbaum eines biblischen Wunders." *ZNW* 10 (1909) 265–276.
McConnachie, J. "Simon a Tanner (Acts 9:43; 10:6, 32)." *ExpT* 36 (1924–1925) 90.
Neirynck, F. "The Miracle Stories in the Acts of the Apostles." *Les Actes des Apôtres: traditions, rédaction, théologie.* Ed. J. Kremer. Gembloux: J. Duculot, 1979, 169–213.
Tannehill, R. *Narrative Unity.* 2:125-127.

→ pp. 15-16 §3
cf. p. 279

19. *Two Visions* (10:1-23a)

1. There was a certain man in Caesarea named Cornelius. He was a centurion from the Cohort known as The Italian. 2. He was pious, and together with his whole household, feared God. He was generous in giving alms to the people, and he prayed to God constantly. 3. At just about the ninth hour, he saw clearly in a vision an angel of God approaching him and saying to him, "Cornelius!" 4. He stared at him and became very fearful. He said, "What is it, Lord?" He said to him, "Your prayers and your almsgiving have arisen as a memorial offering to God. 5. Now, send men to Joppa. Summon a certain Simon who is called Peter. 6. He is lodging with the Simon who is a tanner. His house is by the sea."

7. When the angel who spoke to him departed, he called two household servants and a pious soldier from his staff. 8. Once he had related everything to them, he sent them to Joppa. 9. The next day, they were still on the road and approaching the city, when Peter went up to pray on the roof around the sixth hour. 10. He grew hungry, and wanted to eat. But while they were preparing a meal, he went into a trance. 11. He saw heaven opened and some thing like a great sheet being let down onto the earth by its four corners. 12. In it were all the four-footed creatures and snakes of the earth, as well as the birds of the sky. 13. A voice said to him, "Get up, Peter, kill and eat." 14. But Peter said, "Not at all, Lord, for I have never eaten anything common or unclean." 15. So yet a second time a voice addressed him, "Things God has cleansed, you stop making common." 16. This happened three times. Then suddenly the thing was taken up into heaven. 17. As Peter was puzzling over what the vision he had seen might mean, there were the men who had been sent by Cornelius to search out Simon's house, standing at the gate. 18. Shouting, they asked whether the Simon called Peter was lodging there. 19. And as Peter was still going over the vision in his mind, the Spirit said to him, "Look, three men are looking for you. 20. Now get up and go down, and without debating about it in any way, go with them, because I have sent them." 21. So Peter went down to the men. He said, "I am the one you are seeking. What is the reason for your being here?" 22. They said, "The centurion Cornelius, a man who is righteous and fears God, attested moreover by the whole nation of the Jews, received a revelation from a holy angel to bring you to his house and hear words from you." 23. He thereupon invited them in and showed them hospitality.

NOTES

= C. Maritima   50 km north of Tel Aviv. from AD 6, seat of R.

1. *in Caesarea:* Built on the site of Straton's Tower (Pliny the Elder, *Natural History* 5:69; Strabo, *Geography* 16, 2, 27), this coastal city was the location for *prefect (JAF,* some of Herod the Great's magnificent building projects, including its splendid *AB 3/:* port (Josephus, *Antiquities of the Jews* 15:331-341). Its population was primarily *H5-16,* Gentile, and it became the headquarters for Vespasian during the Jewish War *448),* (Josephus, *Jewish War* 3:409-413). In the narrative of Acts, Philip had already reached Caesarea with his preaching (8:40), and Saul had stopped there on his way to Tarsus (9:30). It will figure in the story again in 12:19; 18:22; 21:8, 16; 23:23, 33; 25:1, 4, 6, 13.

a centurion from the Cohort known as The Italian: The reader is reminded at once of the earlier centurion (=leader of 100 men) who sent messengers to Jesus with a request for help (Luke 7:1-10). There is archaeological evidence for a Second Italian Cohort (*speira*= app. 600 men) stationed in Syria around 69 C.E., but we have no evidence supporting the presence of the unit named here in Caesarea for the period 41–44 C.E.; see Josephus, *Antiquities* 19:365-366.

2. *pious . . . feared God:* The adjective *eusebēs* here and in 10:7 has much the same force as *eulabēs* (Luke 2:25; Acts 2:5; 8:2; 22:12), denoting specifically religious reverence (see Sir 11:17; 13:17; 27:11; 39:27; 2 Macc 12:47; Acts 17:23; 2 Pet 1:3; 2:19). The designation of Cornelius as one "fearing God" (see note on Acts 9:31) inevitably raises the difficult issue concerning "God-fearers" and their relationship to first-century Judaism. Luke's use of the expressions "those who fear God" (*hoi phoboumenoi ton theon;* 10:1, 22, 35; 13:26) and "those who reverence God" (*hoi sebomenoi [ton theon];* 13:43, 50; 16:14; 17:4, 17; 18:7), together with scattered references elsewhere (e.g., epigraphy, Josephus, *Against Apion* 2:39; 2:282-286; *Antiquities of the Jews* 14:116-117; Juvenal, *Satires* 14:96-108), have led to a variety of scholarly positions concerning the existence or status of a group of Gentiles who were not formally proselytes (full converts, with circumcision and the observance of the laws), but who nevertheless frequented the synagogue and tried to live as much as they could by the code of Torah. The evidence best supports the position that there were in fact such people, and that the early Christian mission found a fertile soil for its message among them, but that they did not have an official status or title. Cornelius, in any case, is the perfect example of the type, for although he is clearly understood to be Gentile (10:22, 35, 45; 11:1, 18), yet he follows the religious practices of Judaism, and associates himself with "the people."

with his whole household: Luke tends to use *oikos* and *oikia* interchangeably to mean either "house" or "household." In 10:24, we are told that Cornelius gathers his "kinsmen and close friends" (*syngeneis kai tous anankaious philous*) who would make up the extended family of the Hellenistic "household," together with the servants (*oiketai,* 10:7). Compare also 16:33-34.

giving alms . . . prayed: The piety (*eusebeia*) of Cornelius is expressed in traditional terms; for the combination of prayer and almsgiving, see Tob 12:8; Matt 6:2-6; *Didache* 15:4; 2 *Clement* 16:4. In Cornelius' case, each activity is given specification: he gives alms "to the people (*tǭ laǭ*)," meaning to the Jews, like the centurion of Luke 7:5. His prayer is characterized as *dia pantos,* a term that in the LXX consistently translates the Hebrew *tamid* ("continually"), which occurs especially in cultic contexts (Exod 25:29; 27:20; Lev 24:2, 8; 2 Sam 9:7, 10; 1 Chr 16:37, 40; 2 Chr 9:1; Ps 15:8; 24:15; 33:1; 33:17; 39:11; 50:3, etc.).

3. *just about the ninth hour:* Luke's use of both *hōsei* and *peri* is redundant, and leads to the colloquial translation, "just about." For the ninth hour (three in the afternoon) as a set time for sacrifice and prayer, see the note on Acts 3:1.

he saw clearly in a vision: As in the story of Saul's calling, Luke uses the literary device of a double vision to advance the action and provide material for interpretation. Such use of visions is not restricted to the biblical tradition (Gen 15:1-6; Exod 3:1-6; Judg 6:11-16; 13:2-7); it is a staple of Hellenistic novels, e.g., Longus, *Daphnis and Chloe* 2:26-27; Chariton of Aphrodisias, *Chareas and Callirhoe* 2, 9, 6; Pseudo-Callisthenes, *Life of Alexander of Macedon* 1:5, 30, 33. There are even examples of the technique of double vision, as in Achilles Tatius, *Clitophon and Leucippe* 4, 1, 4-8; and Apuleius, *The Golden Ass* 11:6, 13; 11:22.

angel of God: In contrast to the visions (or perhaps better, "auditions") of Saul and Ananias, Luke again employs the *angelos* as the deliverer of the message (Luke 1:11, 26; 2:9; Acts 7:30; 8:26).

4. *became very fearful:* Luke extends Cornelius' reaction to the apparition by having him "gaze attentively" (*atenizō;* Luke 4:20; 22:56; Acts 1:10; 3:4, 12; 6:15; 7:55), and experience "terror" (the adjective *emphobos* suggesting a high degree of fear; Sir 19:24; Luke 24:5, 37; Acts 24:25).

   a memorial offering to God: Luke's language combines two notions: in using *mnēmosynon* ("memorial offering") he uses the LXX word used to translate the Hebrew *zikron* and *azekarah,* terms used for the cereal offerings made to God (Lev 2:2, 9, 16; 5:12), and whose odor (in an anthropomorphic image) rises to the presence of the Lord, so that he "remembers" the person making the sacrifice (Lev 6:15; Sir 38:11; 45:16). In LXX Ps 111:6, the term is used in a transferred sense for the righteous person (*dikaios*) who will be "onto an everlasting memorial." See also Sir 35:7, "the sacrifice of a righteous man is acceptable and the memory of it will not be forgotten." The second notion, which develops in Judaism during this period (for rabbinic Judaism primarily after the fall of the Temple), is that prayer and charity or even the study of Torah are in effect "spiritual sacrifices" that are roughly equivalent to those offered in the Temple (see the note on *dia pantos* in v. 3). See e.g., Tob 12:12; *Aboth de Rabbi Nathan* 4; *Tanchuma* Wayera 1; *1QS* 8:1-9; *4QFlor* 1:1-6; in the NT, see Phil 4:18; Rom 12:1; Heb 13:15-16; 1 Pet 2:5.

5. *summon a certain Simon:* Luke uses the verb *metapempomai* ("send for/summon") for the first time; it reappears in 10:22, 29; 11:13; 20:1; 24:24, 26; 25:3. Some *mss* omit the *tina* ("certain") in v. 5, either out of a sense of respect or to avoid the awkward repetition in the next line; this translation avoids it by rendering the second *tina* with a definite article, "the Simon who." Some *mss* also expand v. 6 by adding, "he will speak to you what you must do."

7. *from his staff:* Literally, "of those attending him (*tōn proskarterountōn autǫ*)." For the sense of the participle, see Acts 1:14; 2:42, 46; 6:4; 8:13; the noun "staff" tries to supply the proper military equivalent. The adjective "pious" (*eusebēs*) tells us that this soldier shares Cornelius' values (10:2) and will represent him well.

8. *related everything to them:* The verb *exēgeomai* could also be translated as "narrated." The recital here plays the same role as in Luke 24:35, and in Acts 9:27 (using *diēgeomai*), namely to bring a private experience into the public realm (see also Acts 15:12, 14).

9. *around the sixth hour:* The reading "sixth hour" is preferable to the *mss* reading "ninth hour," not only because it is attested by both Alexandrian and Western traditions, and works well to explain Peter's hunger (at noon), but also because scribes would be tempted to find literary synchronicity between Cornelius' and Peter's visions, such as we find in *Tobit* 4:17.

10. *went into a trance:* Literally "there came (*egeneto*) upon him a trance (*ekstasis*)." Some *mss* seek to improve the banality of *egeneto* and replace it with

epesen, so the trance "fell upon him." Luke will use *ekstasis* for a visionary state again in 11:5 and 22:17, although in Luke 5:26 and Acts 3:10 he used it for the "ecstatic" emotional response of the crowd to healings. The LXX uses *ekstasis* to translate the Hebrew *tardemah* that "falls" on Adam in Gen 2:21 and on Abraham in Gen 15:12.

11. *some thing like a great sheet:* Luke uses the historical present (*theōrei*) for vividness (see also v. 27). The opening of heaven is a standard feature of visions; see the note on Acts 7:56 for references. The Greek literally has a "certain instrument/vessel/thing (*skeuos*) descending," with the next clause functioning as a comparison: "like (*hōs*) a great sheet." The next participle (*kethiemenon*) described the mode of descent: it is being "let down" by/at its four "corners" (*archais*). The image is sufficiently obscure to have generated a number of textual variants, none of which substantially affects the meaning.

12. *all the four-footed creatures:* The list is meant to be inclusive of all creatures (compare Gen 1:24; Rom 1:23) without making any distinctions between them, such as were legislated by Lev 11:1-47, which concludes, "to make a distinction between the clean and the unclean, and between the living creature that may be eaten and the living creature that may not be eaten" (Lev 11:47).

14. *not at all, Lord:* The adverb *mēdamōs* expresses a strongly felt negative, found in the NT only here and in Peter's repetition of the story in 11:8. The LXX uses it for similar sorts of responses (Gen 18:25; Jonah 1:14; Ezek 21:5). The most striking antecedent is Ezek 4:14: the Lord tells the prophet that the people will eat their bread unclean, and the prophet replies, "Not at all, Lord God, I have never defiled myself, from my youth up to now . . . ." The phrase *koinos kai akathartos* is strictly redundant, although Luke may have felt the need for both terms since he had previously used *koinos* only in its meaning of "shared" (Acts 2:44; 4:32), and *akathartos* only with reference to "unclean spirits" (Luke 4:33, 36; 6:18; 8:29; 9:42; 11:24; Acts 5:16; 8:7). In Hellenistic Jewish writings, the term *koinos* is sometimes used for things considered ritually "unclean" (Heb. *ḥol*); see 1 Macc 1:47, 62; Josephus, *Antiquities of the Jews* 3:181; 11:346; 12:320. In the *Letter of Aristeas* 315 the term is used to describe "profane" men. This last reference is particularly instructive, in fact, for it deals with a revelation in a dream to Theopompus, explaining why he had suffered a mental upset for thirty days: "it was due to his meddlesome desire to disclose the things of God to common man."

15. *things God has cleansed:* The verb *katharizō* ("to declare clean") is the one used by the LXX for the pronouncements of the priests on matters of ritual impurity (Lev 13:6, 13, 17; and Luke 11:39); see also the use in Mark 7:19, "he declared all food clean" (*katharizōn panta ta brōmata*), and its application to the healing of lepers in Luke 4:27; 5:12-13; 7:22; 17:14, 17. The implication is that all things God created are declared clean by him, and are not affected by human discriminations; the *mē* with the present imperative has the sense, "*stop* making common." The statement's deeper implications will be developed as the story unfolds.

16. *this happened three times:* The repetition is to show the divine initiative overcoming human resistance, which symbolizes the narrative development to follow: Peter resists God's initiative, then the leaders in Jerusalem (11:1-18), then the members of the Pharisaic party in Antioch (15:1-2).

17. *puzzling over . . . might mean:* Here and in the next verse, Luke invites the reader into the human perplexity of Peter: the meaning of the vision is not obvious. For the meaning of *diaporeō*, see Luke 9:7; Acts 2:12 and 5:24. The phrase "might mean" translates the optative of *eimi*, as in Luke 1:29.

19. *still going over the vision in his mind:* Coming close after v. 17, the present participle in the genitive absolute construction gives the sense of a continuing mental struggle. The verb *dienthumeomai* is found neither in the LXX or in the other NT writings.

    the Spirit said to him: The ambiguity of the vision is followed by the clarity of the divine command. Peter is not only addressed by the Spirit, but is told that God is at work in the disposition of this affair. The reader understands with Peter that it was not only the human Cornelius who sent messengers, but that "I sent them out."

20. *without debating about it:* The participle *diakrinomenos* has a double nuance that is important for the development of the story. *Diakrinō* can mean to "doubt/hesitate" (as in Jas 1:6) with the result that one is "double-minded" (Jas 4:8). It can also mean to "make discrimination/choose between" (as in Jas 2:4). Peter in effect is told not to be filled with doubts about the course of events which will eventually lead him to understand how he is not to discriminate between people (see 11:2, 12; 15:9).

22. *attested moreover:* The particle *te* in this case seems to give a special emphasis which the translation "moreover" seeks to capture. Luke uses *martureō* in the passive participle to mean a person's reputation (as in Acts 6:3; 22:12). Compare the recommendation of the centurion in Luke 7:5.

    received a revelation: The verb *chrēmatizō* is used with some frequency for the receiving of an oracle (*chrēsmos*) from a divinity (see e.g., Plutarch, *The Obsolescence of Oracles* 46 [*Mor.* 435C]; Lucian of Samosata, *The Mistaken Critic* 8; Josephus, *Antiquities of the Jews* 3:212; LXX Jer 32:30; 33:2; 36:23; 37:2). In the NT, see Matt 2:12, 22; Heb 8:5; 11:7, and Luke 2:26. Notice that the messengers not only represent Cornelius' own understanding of the experience, but expand it, "to hear words from you."

    showed them hospitality: The verb *xenizō* is used three more times in the passage; in 10:6, 18, it has the middle form and means "to lodge." Here it is active, and means, "to provide lodging." Given the symbolism of hospitality in the ancient world (see e.g., Heb 13:2; 2 John 10-11; 3 John 10; Matt 25:35-44), Peter's acceptance of them as people signifies as well an openness to their message (see also Acts 17:20; 28:7). Hospitality was one of the virtues of the sage within Rabbinic Judaism as well (see *Pirke Aboth* 1:5; *Aboth de Rabbi Nathan* 7; *bT Shabb* 127a).

INTERPRETATION

The story of the conversion of the centurion Cornelius with his whole household sets in motion the most critical phase of the expansion of God's people. Having secured the promises of God to Israel in his portrait of the restored people in Jerusalem (Acts 1-7), Luke has shown his reader how the good news spread both geographically and demographically, reaching in the evangelization of the detested Samaritans and the sexually mutilated Ethiopian those who would be considered at best marginally Jewish by the strict standards of the Pharisees (Acts 8).

After the interlude devoted to the call of Saul who would be the elect vessel for carrying the name to the Gentiles (9:1-30), Luke again showed the work of Peter in Judea, healing the lame, raising the dead, and at the same time moving geographically and ethnically closer to the edge, to the place by the sea in Joppa, where he resided with the ritually impure tanner Simon, ready to hear the call from the Gentile city of Caesarea (9:31-42). Now at last Luke is ready to show how the Church made this most fundamental and dangerous step, which would involve the greatest struggle and demand the most fundamental self-reinterpretation for the nascent messianic movement, which in fact would in principle establish its identity as a universal and not simply ethnic religion.

The space Luke devotes to this struggle is itself testimony to its importance. In a very real sense, the entire section from chapter ten through chapter fifteen is dominated by the crisis precipitated by Cornelius' and Peter's visions. After the initial detailed recital of the events in 10:1-48, they will be narrated still again in 11:1-18 and then recapitulated in 15:6-11. What is Luke trying to do in this tortuous progress?

Certainly he is in no doubt, nor has he left his reader in any doubt, concerning *God's* intentions. From the very beginning of Luke-Acts, the reader has been alerted to the promise that Jesus would be a "light of revelation to the Gentiles" (Luke 2:32); John's preaching was accompanied by the text of Isaiah that promised, "all flesh shall see the salvation of God" (Luke 3:6; Isa 40:5, LXX); at the end of the Gospel, Jesus told the apostles that forgiveness of sins would be preached "to all nations" (Luke 24:47), and in Acts 1:8 he reasserted that they would be witnesses to "the ends of the earth."

That God intended all along for the Gentiles to share in the blessings of Abraham—which Luke understands as the gift of the Holy Spirit through Jesus—could not be more clear (see also Acts 2:29; 3:25-26). In his portrayal of this momentous step, furthermore, Luke gives every possible signal that it is intended and indeed initiated by God, validated in turn by visions and the palpable outpouring of the divine Spirit.

The struggle Luke seeks to communicate to the reader is the process of *human* decision-making as the Church tries to catch up to God's initiative. And it is precisely this struggle that gives the narrative its marvellous tension. The reader is a privileged observer, knowing far more than the characters about what God wills and what God is doing. But the reader is also drawn sympathetically into the poignancy of the human confusion and conflict caused by God's action. The struggle of Peter and his fellow believers to understand what God is doing works subtly on the reader, shaping a sharper sense of the enormity and unprecedented character of the gift.

Each stage is meticulously noted: the decision to provide hospitality to these Gentiles, then to visit their home, then to preach to them, and then to confirm God's bestowal of the Spirit by the ritual act of baptism, and then finally to defend and confirm that decision. The extended descriptions of visions, hesitations, visitations, and narrations, all serve to unfold the rich significance of this new and final extension of God's people. Each retelling, we shall see, tells something more, as though the characters themselves grew to understand better what they were up to as they spoke to each other about it.

And once the acceptance of the Gentiles has become a fact, and through the work of Paul and Barnabas appears ever more to represent the future direction of growth, a still more difficult decision must be reached concerning the status of the Gentile believers: are they first-class citizens within the people or not? The story of Cornelius will be brought before the reader a final time as a key component in that greatest of Christianity's first acts of self-definition.

In this first stage, then, we see how God sets the action in motion by means of separate visions to the righteous Gentile Cornelius and the Apostle Peter. Cornelius' experience is as straightforward as his piety. Cornelius' acceptability to God is confirmed for him and for the reader by the vision, and demonstrated by his quick obedience. He does not yet know *how* his prayers and almsgiving have been "remembered" by God, but prepares himself to hear the further message from Simon.

Simon's vision, in contrast, is obscure—at least to him. The reader cannot help but sympathize with his perplexity and confusion. Luke's placing the vision at the point where Peter was hungry and waiting for a meal is a lovely narrative touch: did he imagine all this because of his hunger? No, the next intervention by the Spirit, telling him to meet his visitors, tells him that the vision was real. But what did it *mean*? Simon's vehement response, which focuses on the unlawfulness of eating common or unclean food, is not in fact so far off the point. It is indeed his symbolic world of Torah and his identity as a member of God's people that will be stretched to an unimaginable extent in the events that will follow. But for Simon's deeper grasp of the vision, we must continue to follow where

Luke leads us. Simon has been told to proceed "without debate/discrimi-
nation"; he and the reader will quickly discover the dimensions of that
directive.

For Reference and Further Study

Bovon, F. "Tradition et rédaction en Actes 10, 1-11, 18." *ThZ* 26 (1970) 22–45.
Gaventa, B. *From Darkness to Light: Aspects of Conversion in the New Testament.*
    Philadelphia: Fortress Press, 1986, 107–129.
Lake, K. "Proselytes and God-fearers." *Beginnings* 5:74-96.
Loning, K. "Die Korneliustradition." *BZ* 18 (1974) 1–19.
Plunkett, M. "Ethnocentricity and Salvation History in the Cornelius Episode."
    1985 Society of Biblical Literature Seminar Papers. Ed. K. H. Richards. Atlanta:
    Scholars Press, 1985, 465–479.
van Unnik, W. C. "The Background and Significance of Acts x, 4 and 35." *Sparsa
    Collecta: The Collected Essays of W. C. Van Unnik.* SuppNT 29. Leiden: E. J.
    Brill, 1973, 1:213-258.

20. *Gentiles Receive the Spirit* (10:23b-48)

23b. The next day he got up and went with them. Some of the brothers
from Joppa also went with him. 24. And on the following day he entered Caesarea. Cornelius was expecting him. He invited his relatives
and close friends. 25. When Peter entered, Cornelius met him. He fell
at his feet and did him homage. 26. But Peter raised him. He said, "Stand
up. I am myself also a human being." 27. And while conversing with
him, he went in and found many people gathered together. 28. He said
to them, "You do understand how it is forbidden a Jew to associate with
or to visit a person of another race. But God has shown me not to call
any person common or unclean. 29. For this reason, when I was summoned, I came without any cavil. I ask you, then, for what purpose you
have invited me." 30. Cornelius said, "Four days ago at this time I was
making my ninth hour prayer in my house. Suddenly a man with shining clothes stood before me. 31. He said, 'Cornelius, your prayer and
your almsgiving have been remembered by God. 32. Therefore send to
Joppa. Invite Simon who is called Peter. He is lodging at the house of
Simon the Tanner, near the sea.' 33. So I sent for you at once, and you
have acted graciously by coming. We are now therefore all here in God's
presence to hear everything that has been commanded you by the Lord."
34. Peter began speaking. He said, "In truth, I am grasping that God
is no respecter of appearances. 35. Rather, in every nation, the one who

fears God and acts righteously is acceptable to him. 36. He sent the message to the children of Israel. He proclaimed the good news of peace through Jesus Messiah. He is Lord of all! 37. You know the word that spread through all of Judea, beginning from Galilee after the baptism that John preached, 38. concerning Jesus from Nazareth: how God anointed him with the Holy Spirit and power. He went about doing good and he healed all those oppressed by the devil, because God was with him. 39. We are witnesses of all the things he did in the territory of the Jews and in Jerusalem. But they killed him by hanging him on a tree. 40. God raised this man on the third day and enabled him to be seen, 41. not by all the people, but by us, the witnesses appointed by God. We ate with him and we drank with him after he rose from the dead. 42. And he ordered us to preach to the people and to bear witness that he is the one designated by God to be judge of the living and the dead. 43. To this all the prophets bear witness, that everyone who believes in him receives forgiveness of sins through his name." 44. While Peter was still speaking these words, the Holy Spirit fell on all those who were listening to the speech. 45. The believers from the circumcision who had come with Peter were astonished that the gift of the Holy Spirit had been poured out even on the Gentiles, 46. for they were hearing them speaking in tongues and praising God. Then Peter answered, 47. "Can anyone refuse water for these people to be baptized, since they have received the Holy Spirit just as we did?" 48. And he directed them to be baptized in the name of Jesus Messiah. Then they asked him to remain for some days.

NOTES

23b. *brothers from Joppa:* They are identified in 10:45 as "believers (*pistoi* = faithful ones) from the circumcision (*hoi ek peritomēs*)." The fact that this event is witnessed throughout by Jewish Christians other than Peter is an important element in its validation (see 11:12).

24. *relatives and close friends:* With the *oiketai* ("household servants," 10:17), these would make up the extended family that was the Hellenistic household (*oikos*). The whole household is included in the description as "pious and God-fearing" in 10:2, and will share in the outpouring of the Spirit and baptism in 10:44-48. For "relatives" (*syngeneis*), see Luke 1:36, 58; 2:44; 14:12. As we have seen repeatedly, Luke is particularly attuned to the social mesh of friendship in the Hellenistic world (see 7:6; 11:5-6, 8; 14:10-12; 15:6, 9, 29; 23:12). The adjective *anankaios* (literally "necessary") denotes especially close ties.

25. *fell at his feet and did him homage:* We recognize "falling at the feet" as signifying submission to authority (see the note on Acts 4:35). It is accompanied by *proskynesis*, the prostration used widely in oriental courts, and sometimes translated as "worship" (see Luke 4:7, 8; 24:52, and Acts 8:27; 24:11). The Western Text elaborates the beginning of the verse considerably: "As Peter

was approaching Caesarea, one of his slaves ran on ahead and announced he had come. Cornelius got to his feet and met him."

26. *also a human being:* Peter's command to "stand up!" (*anastēthi*) echoes the healing of Aeneas (9:34) and the raising of Tabitha (9:40). His deflection of personal homage will be repeated by Paul and Barnabas in Lystra (14:15). In this and the succeeding verses, the Western Text adds a number of details which heighten the declaration.

28. *forbidden . . . to associate:* The use of the personal pronoun *hymeis* at the beginning of the statement lends it a certain formal quality. The term *athemitos* can mean simply "lawless" (see 2 Macc 10:34; 3 Macc 5:20; Josephus, *Jewish War* 4:562), but in constructions such as this it also means "unlawful" (2 Macc 6:5; 7:1; Plutarch, *Dinner of the Seven Wise Men* 5 (*Mor.* 150F). For the sense of "associate with" (*kollaomai*), see the note on Acts 5:13. The vast majority of uses of *allophylos* in the LXX translate the Hebrew for "Philistine," but can be extended to include all "foreigners" (see 1 Macc 3:41; 5:5). The degrees of "avoidance" compatible with loyalty to Torah were debated by the various parties within Judaism, and distinguished the more extreme separatists like the Essenes from the more moderate like the Pharisees, and from the least observant "people of the land" ('*am-ha-areṣ*).

    not to call any person: Literally, "any man" (*mēdena anthrōpon*). Peter's characterization represents an advance in learning; he now has made a connection between the vision and the events in which he is involved: the terms "common and unclean" apply not only to foods but also to categories of persons. God "showed him" not only through the vision but also through his interaction with these Gentiles, and hearing their story.

29. *without any cavil:* The adverb *anantirētos*, as its etymology suggests, means "without speaking against." Luke will use the adjective again in 19:36 to mean "incontrovertible fact." In the present context, it picks up the "without debate" (*mēden diakrinomenos*) of 10:20.

30. *four days ago:* The text is very difficult, especially since the combination of *apo* and *mechri* would make the literal translation, "from the fourth day up to this very hour," which would mean that Cornelius had been fasting up to the time of his declaration. But this contradicts the clear evidence of the story. Textual variations only make the situation more complicated. The best solution is to take the phrase as an awkward temporal reference to the beginning of the events related in 10:3-6.

    shining clothes: The description shows Luke's penchant for variation. The direct narrative of the event identified Cornelius' visitor as an angel of the Lord (10:3), but Cornelius is more circumspect. For the "shining clothes" as code for heavenly visitors, see Luke 24:4 and Acts 1:10.

31. *have been remembered by God:* Another example of stylistic variation from the "memorial offering" in 10:4, which places the emphasis on God's response to his deeds. In the LXX, the verb *mimnēskomai* is used for God's "remembering" of his righteous ones or his covenant with them (Gen 4:1; 9:15; Exod

2:24; 6:5; Lev 26:42; Ps 105:45; 135:23), and has this meaning also in the Gospel (Luke 1:54, 72; 23:42).

33. *all here in God's presence:* Although the Western Text has "in your presence" (*enōpion sou*), the version here translated is undoubtedly correct; the entire sequence is played out within an explicitly religious context; see also Luke 1:15, 19, 76; 12:6; 16:15; Acts 4:19; 7:46; 10:31. Notice that Cornelius assumes that Simon has been sent with a message from God.

34. *Peter began speaking:* Luke uses a periphrastic expression, "having opened his mouth, Peter said," which gives greater solemnity to his pronouncement (compare Acts 8:35, and see Exod 4:12; Num 22:28; Judg 11:36; Ezek 33:22; Dan 3:25; 10:16).

    God is no respecter of appearances: The verb *hypolambanomai* should be taken as a present progressive: Peter is just now grasping or coming to understand. The phrase *ouk estin prosōpolēmptēs ho theos* derives from the LXX's translation of *naśah panim* ("to lift the face") with *prosōpon labein*. As used in 2 Kgs 3:14, it means preference for one person over another. In Lev 19:15 it is used as a way of forbidding judgment "on the basis of appearances," that is, allowing extraneous factors, and especially bribes, to sway fair judgment. Such "impartiality" is attributed to God directly in Deut 10:17 and becomes the basis for condemning wicked human judges in LXX Ps 81:2 (see also *Psalms of Solomon* 2:18). On this rather slender basis, the early Christian writings make "God's impartiality" into a central theological axiom (Rom 2:11; Col 3:25; Eph 6:9; 1 Pet 1:17; Jas 2:1, 9; *1 Clement* 1:3; *Letter of Barnabas* 4:12; Polycarp, *Letter to the Philippians* 6:1).

35. *is acceptable to him:* The adjective *dektos* ("acceptable") is used in the LXX for the reception of sacrifices by God (Exod 28:34; Lev 1:3-4; 17:4; 19:5; Mal 2:13; Isa 56:7; 60:7; Jer 6:20; Sir 32:7), and extends it to mean generally a life pleasing to God (Prov 10:24; 11:1; 16:5; Sir 2:5). Of special interest are the statements in LXX Prov 12:22, "the one who acts faithfully is acceptable to him," and Prov 15:8, "the prayers of the righteous are acceptable to him." The notion of "working righteousness" as the basis for acceptability to the impartial God is remarkably close to Rom 2:10-11.

36. *he sent the message to the children of Israel:* The Greek text of 10:36-38 is very difficult, with awkward transitions and obscure syntactical connections; textual variants make it more confusing. Every translation must proceed by both establishing and interpreting the text, recognizing the interrelationship and the tentativeness of each task. The first decision here is to omit the relative pronoun *hon* after *logon*. Doing so means adopting the "easier reading," but it also enables us to make *some* sense of the passage. The second decision is to translate *logos* not in the "theological" sense of "Word," but in its straightforward sense of "message" (compare Luke 1:29; Acts 2:41; 4:4). This enables us to connect the previous statement about God's impartiality with the next sentence: God sends the message about his fairness to Israel through the work of the Messiah, expressed as the good news of peace.

proclaimed good news of peace: Peace as a messianic blessing is thematic in Luke-Acts (Luke 1:79; 2:14; 7:50; 8:48; 10:5-6; 19:38, 42; 24:36; Acts 7:26; 9:31), but in light of Peter's statement concerning God's *aprosōpolēmpsia* it has particular force: the Prophet Jesus called into the people all those who "feared God and did righteously," even those who were outcast because of social or ritual status (compare Eph 2:1-15).

Lord of all: The placement of the ejaculation would make it refer most naturally to Jesus (compare Rom 9:5), and the combination of ideas is similar to that in Rom 10:12: "for there is no distinction between Jew and Greek, for he is Lord of all, rich toward all who call upon him, 'for everyone who calls on the name of the Lord will be saved.' " For intimations of such inclusivity in Judaism, see 3 Macc 5:28; 6:39; Wis 6:7; 8:3; Sir 36:1. The explicit expression "Lord of all" is found in the *Testament of Moses* 4:2; *The Letter of Aristeas* 16, 18. The epithet is applied to the God Osiris in Plutarch, *Isis and Osiris* 12 [*Mor.* 355E].

37. *the word that spread:* Or, "the deed that occurred," with *to genomenon rhēma* being capable of both meanings. This translation connects the phrase to "Jesus from Nazareth" rather than to *ton logon* in v. 36.

    beginning from Galilee: The majority of *mss* have the nominative *arxamenos* but this translation accepts (with trepidation) the accusative *arxamenon*, rejected by most text-critics as the "easier" reading. It is, because it enables one to make sense of the sentence as a modification of *rhēma*. If the nominative is accepted, it still must be treated as syntactically disconnected and translated as though it were in fact accusative.

    the baptism that John preached: The movement from Galilee to Jerusalem is one of Luke's fundamental structuring devices (see Introduction to *Commentary on the Gospel of Luke*). John's baptism is taken as the starting point of Jesus' ministry in Luke 3:3; 16:16 and Acts 1:22. This mention of John's baptism anticipates the statement in 11:16.

38. *anointed him with the Holy Spirit and power:* The use of the verb *chriō*, as in Luke 4:18, shows how Luke understood Jesus' messiahship in prophetic terms. For the connection of the Holy Spirit to the divine *dynamis*, see Luke 1:17; 4:14; 24:49, and Acts 1:8. In the Gospel, the *dynamis* at work in Jesus is manifested in his healings (Luke 4:36; 5:17; 6:19; 8:46; 9:1, 11). The verb *euergeteō* ("to do good/act as benefactor") is used in the NT only here, but see Luke 22:25 and Acts 4:9. The wonderworker Apollonius is called a "benefactor" in Philostratus, *Life of Apollonius* 8:7.

    oppressed by the devil: The verb *katadynasteuō* is found in the NT only here and in Jas 2:6, where it refers to the oppression of the poor by the rich. It occurs frequently in the LXX with the same sense (Exod 1:13; 21:17; Neh 5:5; Amos 4:1; 8:4; Jer 7:6; 22:3; Ezek 18:7). That Peter attributes such oppression to the devil strengthens the image of the kingdom of God as a rule that must do battle with a counter-kingdom run by Satan and his demonic minions (see the notes on Luke 4:5 and 11:17-18).

God was with him: A Septuagintal expression for God's guidance and protection (Gen 21:20, 22; 39:2; Exod 3:12; Isa 58:11). It is particularly striking that Luke uses it to characterize Joseph in the Stephen Speech (Acts 7:9). The expression does not signify a "adoptionist Christology," but simply fits within Luke's consistent portrayal of all his leading characters in prophetic terms: God is the main actor.

39. *hanging him on a tree:* The kerygmatic statement of death and resurrection resembles those in 2:22-24; 3:13-15; 4:10. For the use of *xylon* ("tree/wood") for the cross, see the note on 5:30, where the verb *kremannymi*, with its unmistakable allusion to the curse text of Deut 21:23, "cursed be everyone who hangs upon a tree," also appears.

41. *the witnesses appointed by God:* As in Peter's speech of 1:17-25, the witnessing includes both the things done by Jesus during his ministry (10:39) and the events of his death and resurrection (10:41). The witnesses are here said to be "designated," using the same term as for Jesus' messiahship in 3:20. For the role of the apostles as witnesses, see Luke 24:48; Acts 1:8, 22; 2:32; 3:15; 5:32.

    we ate with him and we drank with him: This statement makes explicit the connection between meals and the presence of the risen Lord that was implicit in the narratives of 24:30-31, 36-43; Acts 1:3-6.

42. *designated . . . to be judge:* Luke uses the term *horizō* ("to set aside/designate") as in Luke 22:12; Acts 2:23. He will use it again with reference to Jesus as judge in Acts 17:31 (see also Rom 1:4). The conception of Jesus as judge is implicit in a number of Gospel passages (Luke 9:26; 10:13-16; 11:29-32; 12:41-48; 13:22-30; 17:25-37; 18:8; 22:69), but this future role of the Messiah is only stated explicitly in the two Acts passages. The combination "living and dead" is correlative to the attribute of being "Lord of all," and becomes a common Christian expression (Rom 14:9; 1 Thess 5:9-10; 2 Tim 4:1; 1 Pet 4:5; *Letter of Barnabas* 7:2; *2 Clement* 1:1; Polycarp, *Letter to the Philippians* 2:1; Justin, *Dialogue with Trypho* 118:1).

43. *all the prophets bear witness:* The theme of prophetic fulfillment is central to Luke-Acts; this formulation most resembles that in Luke 24:44-47. Most translations treat *touto* as though it referred to the previous sentence, and translate, "all the prophets bear witness to *him*," but this translation finds the threefold repetition of "him" excessive, and takes *touto* as neuter, and pointing forward to the clause that follows, "that everyone who believes in him." The expression *pisteuein eis auton* is found only here in Luke-Acts (or even in the NT: compare Gal 2:16; 1 John 5:10, 13). Luke prefers to use *epi* + dative, or the dative case alone (Luke 20:5; 24:25; Acts 2:44; 5:14; 8:12; 9:42; 11:17; 13:39; 16:31; 27:25).

44. *the Holy Spirit fell on all those who were listening:* This is now the fourth outpouring of the Spirit (Acts 2:1-4; 4:3; 8:17). Luke has the event "interrupt" Peter's speech, but of course he has said all that Luke wants him to. Luke will use the same technique in 17:32; 22:22; 23:7; 26:24.

46. *hearing them speaking in tongues:* Rather than describe the effects of the Spirit directly, as in Acts 2:1-5, Luke adopts the spectator's perspective, as in Acts 2:5-13. The observers deduce from the external phenomena (speaking in tongues, 2:5, and praising God, 2:11) the cause (the gift of the Holy Spirit, 2:4).

47. *can anyone refuse water:* Peter also makes an argument: the patent reception of the Spirit shows that God has accepted these Gentiles; the ritual of baptism is therefore a sign of the Church's acceptance of God's action. The key premise is expressed by the phrase "just as we did": the bond between the first believers and these new believers is the shared experience of the Spirit.

INTERPRETATION

This second stage of the Cornelius sequence itself consists of three moments: the opening exchanges between Peter and Cornelius (10:23b-33), the proclamation by Peter of the message concerning Jesus (10:34-43), and the experience of the Holy Spirit leading to baptism (10:44-48). The reader's progress through each part leads to a growing awareness of the dimensions of what God has initiated.

Luke leads us to the climactic event deliberately. Cornelius awaits Peter's arrival and gathers the members of his household; something more than a private experience will be involved. A fundamental step is taken when Peter crosses the threshold "conversing with Cornelius." He has entered into the house of a Gentile, and more: he declares how "God has shown him" not to call any person "common or unclean" (10:28). So far has his understanding of his vision reached. But a still more decisive turn is taken when Peter asks Cornelius to tell him why he was summoned (10:29). Peter is ready to have Cornelius' recital of his own experience illuminate and amplify the meaning of Peter's personal vision.

The function of Cornelius' narration, therefore, is to bring Peter to the next stage of insight: Cornelius' vision certifies him as a righteous person acceptable to God (10:31). As Peter hears his account and realizes how Cornelius' experience intersects his own, he comes to understand still more deeply the meaning of his vision. So when Cornelius invites him to speak, Peter begins with the proposition that summarizes the events to this point and opens the way to the proclamation of the good news to the Gentiles: "In truth I am grasping that God is no respecter of appearances. Rather in every nation the one who fears God and acts righteously is acceptable to him" (10:34-35). Peter is coming to see that it is not membership in a particular nation or the observance of its specific customs that makes one acceptable to God, but rather the way of responding to God that comes from "the fear of the Lord," or in more precise terms, "faith."

It is important to note that, despite the jumbled syntax of 10:36-38, the message about Jesus which Peter begins to proclaim is directly connected with that opening declaration. The "message God sent to the children of Israel," Peter now understands, already bore that implicit message of peace and reconciliation between peoples. In principle, therefore, the extension of the mission to the Gentiles is a continuation of Jesus' own words and work.

This last missionary speech of Peter is, in fact, something of a master summation of Luke's own Gospel narrative: we find the geographical movement from Galilee to Jerusalem, the starting point in John's baptism, the emphasis on healings as the overturning of the devil's counter-kingdom, the rejection by the Jerusalemites, and the appearances to the select witnesses at meals with the commission to preach forgiveness of sins (10:39-43). Of special interest however is the emphatic placement of Peter's statement that God has designated Jesus to be "judge of the living and the dead" and that "everyone who believes in him receives forgiveness of sins through his name." The expostulation that Jesus is "Lord of all" (10:36) finds its expression in Jesus' future role of judging all, and in the possibility of forgiveness for all peoples. To these realities, Peter says, "all the prophets bear witness." So quickly has the new understanding of Jesus been extended to include this new development.

Luke now has the infusion of the Spirit interrupt Peter's proclamation. It is a device he uses again later, and although in his own summary of the events Peter will say "I had just started speaking" (11:15), it is obvious that Luke has had him say everything needful. From the observer standpoint adopted by the narrator, we are allowed to follow the same logic as the Jewish companions of Peter who witness these people speaking in tongues and praising God: they conclude, as we must, that the cause of these manifestations is the Holy Spirit (10:45-46).

But are we yet ready, with Peter, to draw the practical conclusion: if God has given these Gentiles the same experience as they had at the beginning, doesn't this mean they belong as fully to the messianic community? And doesn't it follow that since they had been baptized by the Spirit by the free gift of God, the Church should ritually ratify that initiative by baptizing these Gentiles (10:47-48)? Luke does not think the reader is yet ready to move so quickly, for he makes us go through the story one more time, step by step, in Peter's defense before the Jerusalem leadership (11:1-18).

FOR REFERENCE AND FURTHER STUDY

Barthes, R. "L'analyze structurale du recit à propos d'actes x-xi." *ResScR* 58 (1970) 17-37.

Bassler, J. "Luke and Paul on Impartiality." *Bib* 66 (1985) 546–552.

Riesenfeld, H. "The Text of Acts x, 36." *Text and Interpretation*. Eds. E. Best and R. McL. Wilson. Cambridge: University Press, 1979, 191–194.

Wilckens, U. *Die Missionsreden der Apostelgeschichte*. WMANT 5. Neukirchen: Neukirchen Verlag, 1963, 46–50, 63–70.

Wilcox, M. " 'Upon the Tree'—Deut 21:22-23 in the New Testament." *JBL* 96 (1977) 85–99.

21. *Peter's Defense* (11:1-18)

1. The apostles and the brothers who were throughout Judea heard that even the Gentiles had received the word of God. 2. But when Peter went up to Jerusalem, those who were from the circumcision criticized him. 3. They said, "You went in with people who were uncircumcised and you ate with them." 4. Peter began to explain to them point by point. He said, 5. "I was praying in the city of Joppa, and in a trance I saw a vision. A certain thing like a great sheet was coming down out of heaven, being let down by four corners. It came right up to me. 6. As I was gazing at it, I looked carefully and saw the four-footed creatures of the earth, and wild beasts, and the serpents, and the birds of the sky. 7. And I also heard a voice saying to me, 'Get up, Peter, kill and eat!' 8. But I said, 'Not at all, Lord, for the common or unclean has never entered my mouth.' 9. The voice answered a second time from heaven, 'Things God has cleansed, stop making common.' 10. This happened three times, then everything was taken up again into heaven. 11. Then suddenly three men came to the house where I was. They had been sent to me from Caesarea. 12. And the Spirit told me to go with them without debating. Six of these brothers also went with me, and we went into the man's house. 13. He related to us how he had seen the angel in his house, standing and saying, 'Send to Joppa and summon Simon, the one called Peter, 14. who will speak words to you by which you and all your household will be saved.' 15. But as I was starting to speak, the Holy Spirit fell upon them just as it had upon us in the beginning. 16. And I remembered the word of the Lord, how he said, 'John baptized with water, but you will be baptized with the Holy Spirit.' 17. If therefore God gave them the same gift as to us who had believed in the Lord Jesus Messiah, was I powerful enough to prevent God?" 18. When they heard all these things, they grew quiet and glorified God. They said, "Therefore God has given repentance to life even to the Gentiles."

= 1:5 a ref to "not many days hence" (recalling Pentecost)

NOTES

1. *the apostles and the brothers:* Luke makes a deliberate distinction between these groups and those of the circumcision party he will introduce in the next verse; the distinction is significant first of all because it implies that the leaders of the Church in Jerusalem and the ordinary believers had no problem with the conversion and baptism of Cornelius, signified by their own response that they had "received the word of God." Some *mss* of the Western tradition add, "and they glorified God." For the "word of God" as thematic, see the Introduction to *A Commentary on the Gospel of Luke* and the note on Luke 1:2.

2. *when Peter went up to Jerusalem:* Codex D precedes this with a lengthy addition: "Now Peter wanted for a long time to journey to Jerusalem. He called the brothers and strengthened them. He spoke much and taught them throughout the region. He also met them and announced to them the grace of God. But the brothers from the circumcision criticized him . . . ." The motivation for this undoubtedly secondary elaboration is not clear, but may have had something to do with a desire to avoid the impression of Peter being summoned to trial.

   criticized him: Luke exploits the polyvalence of *diakrinomai* in a fascinating way. What the Spirit forbade Peter to do toward the Gentiles, namely "debate/make distinctions/doubt," (10:20), these fellow Jews are now doing toward him!

3. *you ate with them:* The fact that Peter ate with Gentiles is not stated directly by the previous narration but could be inferred from Peter's protracted stay in Cornelius' household (10:48). The sting in the charge, of course, is found in the ancient symbolism of table-fellowship: to eat with someone is to share spiritually with them as well; by implication to eat with Gentiles is to collude in idolatry (see the note on Luke 5:30, and Dan 1:8, 12-16; 2 Macc 5:27; *bT Ber.* 43b; *bT Sanh.* 104a).

4. *explain to them point by point:* The verb *ektithēmi* has the sense of "expound/set forth" (see *Letter of Aristeas* 161); Luke uses it again in 18:26 and 28:23. The adverb *kathexēs* means "in sequence," and is here translated "point by point." Its use is instructive, for it is clear that Luke understands a "recitation in order" as having a peculiarly convincing quality, and it is for that reason he uses it in the Gospel prologue (Luke 1:3).

5. *it came right up to me:* Although the opening of Peter's defense is close to the initial narrative in 10:9-11, this is a small if vivid addition, as is also the following line: "As I was gazing at it (*atenisas*), I looked carefully (*katenooun*) and saw (*eidon*)." Luke's artistic instinct is to make Peter's first-hand report more anecdotal and colorful.

11. *to the house where I was:* The *mss* are rather evenly split between reading *ēmēn* ("I was") and *ēmen* ("we were"). Either reading could be an easily understood correction, and it is difficult to decide which was original. Is there anything at stake? Only this: if the reading is "we were," then Peter has implicated his Jewish companions from the beginning (see the next verse).

12. *without debating:* Once more (as in 10:20; 11:2) the verb *diakrinō* is used, but the textual evidence is split between the active *diakrinonta* ("making no distinction"), and the middle *diakrinomenos* ("without doubting"). The translation here as in 10:20 tries to preserve the ambiguity.

six of these brothers also went with me: The phrasing is clever: "six of *these* brothers . . . and *we* went into the man's house." Since they have been identified by the narrator in 10:45 as "from the circumcision," Peter has not only made them witnesses to the events (in which capacity they are critical to his defense), but has also implicated them in his own actions; they were participants! They were with him, heard his speech, saw the result of the Spirit's outpouring, made no objection *then* to the baptism.

14. *will be saved:* Peter introduces a note that will be developed in 15:1 and 15:11 when the decision will once more be challenged and debated: the issue is not simply one of table-fellowship, but one of *salvation.* We touch on one of Luke's central themes (Luke 1:47, 69, 71, 77; 2:11; 6:9; 7:50; 8:12, 36, 48, 50; 9:24, 56; 13:23; 17:19; 18:26, 42; 19:9-10; 23:35, 37, 39; Acts 2:21, 40, 47; 4:9, 12; 5:31; 7:25). Luke has also shown a subtle progression in perception: the angel first told Cornelius only to send for Peter (10:5); the messengers report to Peter that Cornelius wanted to "hear words from you" (10:22); Cornelius next tells Peter he is ready to hear "all that has been commanded you by the Lord" (10:33); now, all of this is read back into the first message.

15. *just as it had upon us in the beginning:* The *hōsper* is emphatic: Luke is concerned to show the identity of the experience of these new believers with that of the original witnesses (*en archē*, referring back to Pentecost, 2:1-5), because this will be the basis for asserting their equality of membership in the community. A redefinition of the religion itself is in process.

16. *I remembered the word of the Lord:* This is an example of how later experience forces the *recollection* of a saying of Jesus, as well as its extension in application. Peter is referring back to the statement of the risen Lord in Acts 1:5, which in turn recast the saying that originally was attributed to John the Baptist (Luke 3:16). The disjunction between water and spirit sets up the question to follow.

17. *if therefore God gave them the same gift:* Here is the key point in Peter's argument: his action in baptizing the Gentiles was in response to God's action. Note the emphasis on the equality of the gift (*isēn dōrean*) between Jew and Gentile believers; and if it is a *gift* in both cases that establishes membership in the messianic community (rather than ethnic origin or even having been a follower of Jesus during his ministry), then neither is there room for discrimination in Church practice—which is the development to be worked out in ch. 15.

to prevent God: The construction is mixed, combining "who was I to prevent God," and "was I powerful enough to prevent God." The Western Text somewhat spoils the force of the question by adding, "from giving them the Holy Spirit since they believed in him?"

18. *they grew quiet and glorified God:* The sentence may appear confused, but "growing silent" (*hesychazō*) here means to desist from criticism (compare Luke 14:4; Acts 21:14). For "glorifying God" (*doxazō*) as a response to his activity, see Luke 2:20; 5:25-27; 7:16; 13:13; 17:15; 18:43; 23:47; Acts 4:21.

repentance to life: Or perhaps "conversion (*metanoia*) that leads to life (*zōē*)." Once more, we see a deeper understanding than was held at the beginning of the passage, where the apostles had merely recognized that the Gentiles had "received the word of God."

INTERPRETATION

The apparent redundancy of this passage is the most important clue to its interpretation. The progress through visions and narrations to the acceptance of Gentiles into the community has already been so lengthy and detailed that we must wonder what Luke is up to in Peter's defense before his critics in the Jerusalem Church. To dismiss the passage as a case of clumsy construction is to abandon interpretation. An appeal to separate sources is a sign of desperation. Our best procedure is to build on the premise that Luke has some literary and religious motivations for extending the Cornelius episode still further.

In fact, these are not difficult to find. We have already seen in the case of the Samaritan mission that Luke is concerned to show the connection to the Jerusalem Church, so he has Peter and John sent to Samaria to confirm the work of Philip (8:14-15). The same concern is at work here, but the situation is more complicated: the extension is not only across geographical boundaries but across the most radical of demographic lines. The initiative, furthermore, has been taken by Peter himself: who from the Jerusalem community can certify his work? This encounter between Peter and his Jewish critics—*not*, we notice, the other apostles—enables Luke both to defend (and interpret) Peter's action (which he will want to show is really *God's* action), and to establish the link between the Church in Jerusalem, and this first Gentile Mission; the conclusion of the passage is the glorification of God by the Jerusalem Church for the "repentance to life" now shared by the Gentiles. At the same time, this encounter enables Luke's readers to assimilate and more deeply appreciate the events being related by Peter. The readers also need to catch up with God's surprising new venture. Luke therefore constructs the sort of "trial scene" that is so frequently found in Hellenistic novels to summarize, articulate, or advance the significance of the events related by the narrative (see, for example, Achilles Tatius, *Clitophon and Leucippe* 7:7).

It is perhaps natural that "those from the circumcision" should criticize Peter (11:2); their attack, however, does not focus on the decision

to baptize the Gentiles, but returns to the level of Peter's own initial understanding: they challenge his having entered the house of the uncircumcised and eaten with them (11:3). The issue as they pose it is one of
table-fellowship. That the Gentiles have "received the word of God"—
which is explicitly acknowledged in 11:1—does not yet decide the question of their status vis-à-vis Jewish believers. Can Jewish Christians share
meals with them? Are these Gentiles members of God's people of equal
status with those who first believed?

The problem is a real one. For a Jew to eat without attending to ritual
purity or to dietary regulations meant loss of identity, for the entire ration-
ale for such regulations was the "holiness," that is the separateness, of
this people, based on the commandments of God. Such ritual separation, furthermore, was a symbolic rejection of involvement with idolatry. Therefore, the question how meals could be holy yet shared with
unclean people is not an easy one. Peter's opponents imply that by being
willing to eat with Gentiles, he has abandoned his own heritage as a Jew,
and has also jeopardized the identity of the messianic community as the
people of God.

In Peter's response to the charge, we can detect some of the elements
prescribed by ancient rhetoricians for the defense speech (see Plato,
Phaedrus 266D-E; Aristotle, *Rhetoric* 1354b). He omits the *prooemium*, and
launches instead into the *narratio* (*diēgēsis*, "narration") that dominates
his reponse. But he also includes two standard elements for the "proof"
(*probatio*), namely the attestation of witnesses (11:12), and the evidence
of "signs" (*tekmēria*, 11:15). His conclusion (*peroratio*) is extremely short,
taking the form of a rhetorical question (11:17).

The place given to narration, of course, is entirely consistent with
Luke's larger literary project. We notice that Peter is said to tell the events
kathexēs ("in order"), which this translation renders as "point by point."
It is surely no accident that this adverb is also used by Luke in the prologue of the Gospel to describe his entire two-volume work (Luke 1:3).
Luke clearly understands the recitation of events in sequence to have a
peculiarly convincing quality.

As for the elements of proof, each has its own function. The outpouring of the Spirit that Peter says interrupted his speech (11:15) is only the
culminating "sign from heaven," following the respective visions of Peter
(11:5-10) and Cornelius (11:13-14), as well as the direct order given Peter
by the Spirit itself (11:12). Out of the longer narrative Luke has selected
these elements for Peter's defense precisely because they show unequivocally that his decision was not the result of human calculation, but rather
a *response to the divine initiative,* from beginning to end. Thus, his *peroratio*
can be so compressed: "was I powerful enough to prevent God?"

The mention of the witnesses has another function. By including members of the circumcision party in his account (10:45; 11:12), Peter already implicates them in his decision: they heard the message and went with him to Caesarea; they entered with him into the Gentile man's house; they saw the Spirit being poured out. And they made no complaint. They not only can attest to the truth of Peter's recital, they would deny their own experience if they were to controvert it!

When we turn to the content of Peter's defense speech, we are struck above all by the way it reveals a growth in his own understanding. Peter is no longer fixated at the stage of table-fellowship. He has begun to think in terms of the gift of God for salvation. It is because the outpouring of the Spirit shows that *God* has given "the same gift" to Gentiles as to Jews that Peter has taken the step of baptizing them. This gift proves in fact that "God is no respecter of appearances" and accepts the righteous from every nation. The full implications of this "equality of salvation" will not be seen until the Jerusalem council.

The experience of the Spirit among Gentiles also deepens Peter's understanding of Jesus' words (11:16): it is when he sees the Gentiles speaking in tongues and praising God that he "remembers" the saying of the risen Lord about the baptism in the Spirit (Acts 1:5). What is most fascinating about this remembrance is that Jesus spoke the words to a small band of *Jewish* followers. The words of Jesus are given a new understanding because of the continuing work of the Spirit. In the Jerusalem council (Acts 15), we will see the same extension of interpretation given to the prophetic texts of Torah.

As the last two points have indicated, not even this defense speech exhausts the need to examine the implications of Peter's epochal action. Once more, the storm of controversy will arise (Acts 15) and require a final settlement. But by this repeated telling, Luke's reader is at least assured that the one guiding the community through this treacherous passage is God's Spirit.

FOR REFERENCE AND FURTHER STUDY

Haulotte, E. "Fondation d'une communauté de type universel: Actes 10, 1–11, 18. Etude critique sur la rédaction, la 'structure' et la 'tradition' du récit." *RScRel* 58 (1970) 63–100.

Johnson, L. T. *Decision Making in the Church: A Biblical Model*. Philadelphia: Fortress Press, 1983, 74–77.

Kilgallen, J. J. "Did Peter actually Fail to Get a Word in? (Acts 11, 15)." *Bib* 71 (1990) 405–410.

Kilpatrick, G. D. "The Two Texts of Acts." *Studien zum Text und zur Ethik des Neuen Testaments*. BZNW 47. Berlin: Walter de Gruyter, 1986, 188–195.

Marin, L. "Essai d'analyze structurale d'actes 10, 1–11, 18." *RScRel* 58 (1970) 39–61.

Schneider, G. "Zur Bedeutung von *kathexēs* im lukanischen Doppelwerk." *ZNW* 68 (1977) 128–131.

22. The Church at Antioch (11:19-30)

19. Those who were scattered by the affliction that occurred because of Stephen traveled across to Phoenicia and Cyprus and Antioch. They did not preach the word to anyone except Jews. 20. But some of those who went to Antioch, men from Cyprus and Cyrene, proclaimed the good news about the Lord Jesus also to the Greeks. 21. The hand of the Lord was with them, and a considerable number of believers turned to the Lord. 22. Word concerning them reached the Church in Jerusalem, and they sent Barnabas with a commission to travel to Antioch. 23. He arrived and saw the grace from God. He rejoiced. He exhorted them all to remain loyal to the Lord with their hearts' resolve, 24. because he was a good man, and he was full of the Spirit and of faith. So a considerable crowd was added to the Lord. 25. And he went to Tarsus to seek out Saul. 26. When he found him, he brought him to Antioch. Now this is how it was for them: during an entire year they met together in the church and taught a large crowd. It was indeed in Antioch that the disciples were first called Christians. 27. During that period of time, prophets came down from Jerusalem to Antioch. 28. One of them, whose name was Agabus, stood up. Through the Spirit, he predicted a great famine would come on the whole of the empire—which happened under Claudius. 29. Each of the disciples set aside what he could afford to send as relief to the brothers dwelling in Judea. 30. And this they did by sending it to the elders through the agency of Barnabas and Saul.

NOTES

19. *scattered by the affliction:* The verb *diaspeirō* ("scatter") picks up the thread dropped by 8:1-4. Luke will now use the activities of the other Hellenist missionaries to connect Paul and Barnabas. The term *thlipsis* ("affliction") is widely used in the LXX for the oppression of the people by the godless (Exod 3:9; 4:31; Deut 4:29; Judg 10:14; LXX Ps 24:22; 33:17; 36:39) and in the NT is sometimes joined with *diōgmos* ("persecution"; Matt 13:21; Mark 4:17; Rom 8:35; 2 Thess 1:4); see especially the occurrence of *diōgmos* in 8:1.

    Phoenicia and Cyprus: According to Pliny the Elder, *Natural History* 5:69, the city of Joppa would already be considered a part of Phoenicia, and Josephus considered Caesarea to be within Phoenician territory (*Antiquities* 15:333). By these definitions, the work of Philip (8:40) and Peter (9:43; 10:24) would already have made geographical inroads to Phoenicia. Its major area lay north of Caesarea, however, and included the cities of Tyre and Sidon (Pliny the Elder, *Natural History* 5:75-78; Luke 6:17; 10:13-14; Acts 21:3, 7; 27:3). Luke clearly wants us to see these missionaries pushing farther geographically than Peter and Philip had done. A connection to Cyprus was already established by reference to Barnabas' place of origin (4:36); it will (quite logically) be the place Barnabas and Saul go first on their mission (13:4), and after their split, the place to which Barnabas will return with John-Mark (15:39).

Antioch: This Syrian metropolis, located on the Orontes River (Strabo, *Geography* 16, 2, 5-7), will play a major role throughout the rest of the narrative. Josephus calls it "third among the cities of the Roman world"—after Rome and Alexandria (*Jewish War* 3:29), and indicates that it had a particularly large Jewish population (*Jewish War* 7:41-62). Luke exercises particular care in describing this foundation; it will be the sponsoring Church for the western mission (13:1-3), the place where the debate over Gentile membership will come to a head (14:26–15:2), and the place where, after an extended tenure (11:26; 15:35), Paul and Barnabas finally separate (15:36-40). Finally, Paul will make a separate visit to the Church (18:22) before beginning his final European tour.

20. *men from Cyprus and Cyrene:* At Pentecost, Jews from Libya in the area of Cyrene are said to be present in Jerusalem (Acts 2:10). "Cyrenians" are also among the Hellenists who oppose Stephen (6:9). This North African territory (Pliny, *Natural History* 5:31-33) was another important center of a Jewish population sufficiently powerful to revolt in 115-117 c.e. (Josephus, *Jewish War* 7:437-450). It is possible that Luke wants the reader to perceive "Lucian of Cyrene" in Acts 13:1 as one of these missionaries. For the tradition concerning "Simon of Cyrene" in the Gospel story, see Mark 15:21; Matt 27:32; Luke 23:26.

    also to the Greeks: Even though we meet here the same text-critical choice between *hellēnistas/hellēnas* ("Hellenists"/"Greeks") as in Acts 6:1, this case is easier to resolve in favor of the reading "Greeks" (*hellēnas*) on the basis of context. Not only does Luke clearly indicate a contrast between "only Jews" and these *hellēnai*, but those who are preaching to them are also to be understood (in the logic of his narrative) as "Hellenists," that is, Jews who speak Greek and have some Greek culture. Luke gives us a hint, in other words, of a "Gentile mission" larger than the initiative of Peter yet preceding Paul's own work.

21. *hand of the Lord was with them:* For the background and significance of this expression in the LXX (esp. 1 Sam 5:3, 6, 9; 2 Sam 3:12), see the note on Acts 4:30. As in that passage, the "hand of the Lord" signifies the presence of divine power that validates their testimony.

    considerable number of believers: Literally, "a great number that believed (sing.) turned"; the emphasis on the number of conversions is consistent with other such computations (see *arithmos* in 4:4; 6:7; 16:5). For the expression "turning to the Lord" (*epistrephein epi ton kyrion*), see already Luke 1:16-17, as well as Luke 22:32; Acts 3:19; 9:35; 14:15; 15:19; 26:18, 20; 28:27.

22. *reached the Church in Jerusalem:* The translation tidies up two awkward constructions: the first clause reads literally, "but the word was heard in the ears of the Church," and continues "that was (*tēs ousēs*) in Jerusalem." This is the only place Luke uses this participial construction familiar to us from Paul (Rom 16:1; 1 Cor 1:2; 2 Cor 1:1).

23. *grace from God:* Luke's use of *charis* elsewhere (Luke 1:30; 2:40, 52; 4:32; Acts 2:47; 4:33; 6:8) makes clear that it signifies the favor God shows to someone. It increasingly comes to mean in Luke-Acts the "gift" of that divine favor, and is so translated (see 13:43; 14:3, 26; 15:11, 40; 18:27; 20:24, 32). In this case, the community at Antioch is shown to be enjoying the same messianic blessings as the community in Jerusalem (Acts 2:47). Barnabas' response of "rejoicing" (*echarē*) not only forms an assonance (*charis/echarē*), but signals the perception of God's activity in the world (see Luke 1:14, 28; 6:23; 10:20; 13:17; 15:5, 32; 19:6, 37; Acts 5:41; 8:39).

    remain loyal to the Lord: The verb *prosmenō* means an adherence to or devotion (see Wis 3:9). The present infinitive suggests a continuing process (see also Acts 13:43; 1 Tim 5:5). Barnabas' "exhortation" (*parakaleō*) enacts his apostolic identity as *huios tēs paraklēseōs* (Acts 4:36). For other examples of such moral exhortation, see Luke 3:18; Acts 2:40; 14:22; 15:32; 16:39; 20:1-2. The phrase "heart's resolve" is literally "purpose (*prothesis*) of the heart"; the noun *prothesis* here has the sense of "moral purpose" (see Epictetus, *Discourse* 1, 21, 2; 3, 25, 1; 4, 6, 26; Rom 8:28; 9:11; Eph 1:11; 3:11; 2 Tim 1:9; 3:10).

24. *full of the Spirit and of faith:* The description resembles that of Joseph of Arimathea (Luke 23:50), except that Luke has Barnabas bear the qualities associated with the prophet (see esp. 6:5, 8). Barnabas is ideally suited to this role of confirming a new community, since he has been shown to be twice-obedient to the apostles in Jerusalem (4:36-37).

25. *to Tarsus to seek out Saul:* Saul had been sent to his home territory by the Jerusalem Church after his altercation with the Hellenists (9:30); now for the second time (see 9:27), Barnabas acts as Saul's patron. The Western Text expands vv. 25-26 considerably: "He heard that Saul was in Tarsus. He went to find him. When he found him he exhorted him to come to Antioch. When they came, for a whole year a considerable crowd was stirred up, and then for the first time the disciples were called Christians." The Western version has two interesting aspects: it gives Saul greater independence, and it makes the apostles' presence in the Church one that agitates rather than solidifies.

26. *taught a large crowd:* For the Western Text's version, see the previous note. In the Alexandrian text, we see Luke's desire to portray a community that is well-established and is being "taught" (*didaskein*) by Barnabas and Saul the way the Jerusalem Church had been by the Twelve (4:2, 18; 5:21, 25, 42). The missionary journey of these two will be based on a long-standing presence in a local community.

    disciples were first called Christians: As indicated in the note on Acts 10:22, the verb *chrēmatizo* has oracular connotations, but in the passive it also has the meaning of "being called/styled" (see e.g., Rom 7:3). The term *christianoi,* in turn, is obviously based on the title *christos/chrēstos* = Messiah. If compared to a similarly formed designation like *hērōdianoi* (Mark 3:6; 12:13), it appears to mean a follower of someone, or a member of a movement. The translation "Messianist" would also be appropriate in English. The other NT occurrences are placed in the mouths of outsiders: King Agrippa (Acts 26:28), and opponents (1 Pet 4:16). It appears to have originated, therefore, as a somewhat slighting designation given not by the "believers" themselves but by hostile observers (see also Tacitus, *Annals* 15:44). The contemporary example of the name "Moonies" given to the members of the Unification Church (based on the name of the founder, Sun Yung Moon) is instructive.

27. *prophets came down from Jerusalem:* It is a fascinating aspect of Luke-Acts that, despite describing Jesus and the apostles in terms that are unmistakably prophetic, he so rarely uses the title *prophētēs* of them. It is given directly or indirectly to Jesus only in Luke 4:24; 7:16, 39; 13:33-34; 24:19; Acts 3:22-23; 7:37), and the other "men of the spirit" in Acts are not called by this title (but see 15:32). Luke's main use of the title is for the "prophets of old" either as persons or as authors of prophecy (Luke 1:70; 3:4; 4:17, 27; 6:23; 9:8, 19; 10:24; 11:4, 47, 49, 50; 13:28; 16:16, 29, 31; 18:31; 24:25, 27, 44; Acts 2:16, 30; 3:18, 21, 24, etc.). He also applies it to John the Baptist (Luke 1:76; 7:26, 28; 20:6). Finally, he uses it for these charismatic figures in Acts (11:27; 13:1; 21:10). These are portrayed as members of local churches who travel about and make predictions. Strikingly, they lack entirely the kind of stereotypical "prophetic" coloration Luke gives to his major characters. Paul recognized such prophecy as an important charism (1 Cor 12:28-29; 14:29, 32, 37; Eph 2:20; 3:5; 4:11), and we have evidence of wandering prophets (as well as the problems they presented) in *The Didache* 11:3-12; *Shepherd of Hermas*, Mand. 11:1-21.

28. *whose name was Agabus:* He is reintroduced in much the same way again in Acts 21:10, with the difference that he is there said to be from "Judea." As in this case, his prophecy consists in a declaration concerning the future. The phrase "standing up" (*anastas*) is frequently used by Luke almost as a helping verb (Luke 1:39; 4:29; 6:8; 15:18, 20; 17:19; 23:1; Acts 5:6; 9:18, 39; 10:13). At other times, however, it has the specific sense of "standing" in an assembly, and that is the meaning here (Luke 4:16; Acts 1:15; 5:17, 34). The Western Tradition expands the verse: "There was much rejoicing. When we were gathered together, one of them whose name was Agabus spoke, indicating . . . ." The text is probably secondary, but if it were original, it would provide the first of the "we" passages (see 16:10).

through the Spirit he predicted: Literally, "he signalled/signified"; the verb *sēmainein* can have the straightforward meaning of "indicate/declare" (as in LXX Exod 18:20; Num 10:9; Acts 25:27; John 12:33; 18:32; 21:19), but it also has associations with prophetic utterances (see Plutarch, *Sayings of the Spartans*, Callicratidas 6 [*Mor.* 222F]; Epictetus, *Discourses* 1, 17, 18; Josephus, *Jewish War* 7:214; 10:241; Dan 2:23, 45; Rev 1:1). As in the anonymous prophecy of 21:4, this one takes place "through the Spirit."

famine . . . on the whole of the empire: For the translation of *oikoumenē* (literally, "inhabited world") as "empire," see the notes on Luke 2:1 and 4:5. These passages and those in Acts 17:6 and 24:5 give a thoroughly "political" nuance to the term. Compare Lucian of Samosata, *The Octogenarians* 7, and Josephus' use of *romaios oikoumenē* in *Jewish War* 3:29. The advantage of the rendering is that it not only conforms to Luke's usage elsewhere, but saves him the embarrassment of claiming a "world-wide" famine that by-passes Antioch! In fact there is good supporting evidence for extensive famine during the reign of the emperor Claudius, who ruled from 41-54 C.E.; see Suetonius, *Life of Claudius* 18; Tacitus, *Annals* 12:43. Josephus mentions a great famine in Palestine during the forties (*Antiquities* 20:101), and explicitly mentions a famine in Judea during the reign of Claudius (*Antiquities* 3:320-21).

29. *set aside what he could afford:* The Greek plural *hōrisan* "set aside" picks up the plural "of the disciples" (*tōn mathētōn*) rather than the singular *hekastos* ("each one"). The verb itself could mean either "to set aside [viz. funds]," or "to determine [viz. to send]." The construction "just as (*kathōs*) each one could afford (*euporeito*)" echoes the principle for the distribution of possessions in Acts 4:35, "just as any one had need."

    to send as relief: Literally "to send for a service" (*diakonia*); the choice of terms recalls Luke 4:39; 8:3; 10:40; 12:37; 17:8; 22:26-27; Acts 1:17, 25; 6:1, 4, as well as the language used by Paul for his collection (Rom 15:31; 2 Cor 8:4; 9:1, 12-13). The term will be picked up explicitly in Acts 12:25.

30. *sending it to the elders:* Up to this point Luke has used *presbyteroi* ("elders") only for the Jewish leaders (Luke 7:3; 9:22; 20:1; 22:52; Acts 4:5, 8, 23; 6:12). Now for the first time he uses it for leaders in the messianic community (see also 14:23; 15:2, 4, 6, 22, 23; 16:4; 20:17; 21:18). Apart from Acts, this designation for Christian leaders occurs in 1 Tim 5:1, 2, 17, 19; Titus 1:5; Jas 5:14; 1 Pet 5:1, 5; 2 John 1; 3 John 1. See also *1 Clement* 57:1; Ignatius of Antioch, *Ephesians* 2:2; 4:1; *Magnesians* 2:1; 3:1; Polycarp, *Letter to the Philippians* 6:1.

    through the agency: Literally, "through the hand." In this passage as in those that immediately follow, Luke gives first place to Barnabas (see 12:25; 13:1, 2, 7). In 13:43, he shifts the order, putting Paul in first place, and with the exception of 14:14; 15:12, 25, has Paul take first position in the team (13:46, 50; 14:20; 15:2 (twice), 22, 35). In effect, he has balanced the relationship by listing each of them in first position eight times.

INTERPRETATION

Luke has secured—at least for a time—the consent of the Jerusalem Church to the initiative taken by Peter in baptizing Gentiles (11:1-18). Now he turns at once to the mission of the Hellenists in Antioch (11:19-30). By so doing he shows that the expansion of the people to include Gentiles is not the work only of one person but is part of a larger enterprise. And by devoting special attention to the foundation of the Church at Antioch (the only new community described so fully since the Jerusalem narrative), he prepares the way for the later commissioning of Barnabas and Saul (13:1-4).

The description of the community is a model of suggestive compression. In the space of two verses (11:20-21), Luke informs the reader that the community was distinctive in that it included "Greeks" (see notes); that it was founded by messianic Diaspora Jews; that the Church was founded by the preaching of the good news about the Lord Jesus; that this preaching was accompanied by wonders (thus "the hand of the Lord" in 11:21); that the first conversions were substantial. Through the eyes of Barnabas in 11:23, he takes one verse to convey the further information that the community enjoyed the "grace of God" just as had the Jerusalem community (2:47), and was growing even larger. In a word, the community was flourishing and an authentic realization of the messianic people.

When Barnabas and Saul arrive together at the scene, still another verse provides further information: that for over a year the Church met together with these leaders, and that a large number of them received instruction from Barnabas and Saul; and that they were sufficiently visible within the city to have gained a nickname as the "Christians" (11:26). Finally, we learn that this was a community in which charismatic activity was exercised (11:27; see 13:1), that prophecy was heeded, and that a generous fellowship with possessions was practiced (11:29-30). What a full portrait of a community in so few strokes!

The role of Barnabas in this account is particularly interesting. This is now his third appearance in the narrative of Acts. In the first, he received a new name from the apostles and showed his submission to them by the donation of his property (4:36-37). In the second, he showed his main function in the story, namely to be the link between the Jerusalem Church and Saul: he championed Saul when the others in Jerusalem would have nothing to do with him, and brought him to the apostles (9:27). Now in this third appearance, we recognize why Luke noted Barnabas' birthplace in 4:36, for it turns out he is a countryman of some of those who established the Antiochean community (11:20). He is the perfect emissary from Jerusalem to this new Church (11:22).

Once more, then, we see Luke's concern to secure continuity between the restored people of God in Jerusalem, and the ever extending messianic people, now including great new areas and entire new races. When Barnabas sees the character of the new community, he "rejoices," which in Luke's shorthand means he acknowledges that this is the work of God. He then "exhorts/comforts" (*parakaleō*) the new community, fulfilling the meaning of his name. And, for the first time, he is identified by Luke as a prophetic figure, "full of the Holy Spirit and faith" (11:24). Therefore, when he recruits Saul to work with him for a year in this new foundation, the reader recognizes that this is done by one whose allegiance to Jerusalem could not be doubted.

Indeed, the communication between this new Church and Jerusalem is only confirmed further by the prophets from Jerusalem who visit the community (11:27). But the prophecy of Agabus and the collection for the Jerusalem Church taken up in Antioch once more entangle us in the issue of the historical reliability of Acts. The reason, as in other such cases, is that Luke makes statements that either concern the wider world scene (rather than the internal life of the community) or that intersect with other evidence.

The first of these problems is whether there was such a famine as Luke states "during the time of Claudius." Most discussions of this issue stumble over the part of the prediction dealing with the famine's extent, namely "the whole world." But if, as the notes suggest, the term *oikoumenē* can (and does in Luke's usage) mean pretty much the same as "empire," then Luke's statement accords extremely well with a number of statements made by our other historical sources: there were widespread famines during the reign of Claudius, and there was a particularly severe one in roughly the same period in Palestine.

The second problem is harder. It deals with the relationship between the collection described here as being delivered "through the agency of Barnabas and Saul" (11:30), and the collection "for the saints in Jerusalem" so extensively discussed in Paul's own letters (Gal 2:10; 1 Cor 16:1-4; 2 Cor 8-9; Rom 15:25-32). This is one of the classic contradictions between our sources that are discussed in the Introduction to this commentary (pp. 6-7). In the longer perspective, the sources can be said to agree on a fundamental point: at some point in his career, Paul brought a gift of money to the Church in Jerusalem. And both the letters of Paul and the Acts narrative agree as well on their overall portrayal of the network of communication maintained between these early Christian communities, involving among other things the sending of delegations and the sharing of financial resources.

But in virtually every detail concerning the timing, motivation, and significance of the collection, the sources disagree. Certainly the historian must follow Paul's account as being more reliable: the collection was taken up among Gentile Churches toward the latter part of Paul's career as a symbol of unity as well as a form of practical assistance, was taken by Paul personally to the "saints in Jerusalem," and may not have been accepted. Luke's version is historically suspect because it shows signs of hiding the true dimensions of the Pauline collection: he knew more about it than he was willing to tell the reader, perhaps out of embarrassment at the fact that the collection did not succeed in its aim of reconciling Paul with the Jerusalem Church (see the later discussion, pp. 377-379).

That may be, in fact, why Luke has shifted Paul's connection to a relief effort to this point in the narrative. He not only shows Barnabas and Paul together as the agents of the Antioch Church; he will very carefully note in 12:25 that they carried out this *diakonia* for Jerusalem, immediately before describing the start of their mission. This provides us the most important clue to *Luke's* use of the story. Paul regarded his collection not as a sign of submission but as an act of *koinōnia* (fellowship) between equals. But Luke is concerned to show how *all* missionaries maintained continuity with the authority of the Twelve in Jerusalem. Barnabas' relationship to the Jerusalem community has already been symbolized through his donation of possessions "at the feet of the apostles," but Paul's has not. Therefore Luke uses Paul's participation in the collection from Antioch, and his delivering it "to the elders in Jerusalem" as a signal of his connection to that Church and a recognition of its authority, thereby from the very beginning validating his mission.

FOR REFERENCE AND FURTHER STUDY

Benoit, P. "La deuxième visite de Saint Paul à Jerusalem." *Bib* 40 (1959) 778–792.
Cadbury, H. J. "Names for Christians in Acts." *Beginnings* 5:383-386.
Ellis, E. E. "The Role of the Christian Prophet in Acts." *Apostolic History and the Gospel*. Eds. W. W. Ward and R. P. Martin. Exeter: Paternoster Press, 1970, 129-144.
Funk, R. "The Enigma of the Famine Visit." *JBL* 75 (1956) 130-136.
Holtzmann, O. "Die Jerusalemreisen des Paulus und die Kollekte." *ZNW* 6 (1905) 102-104.

23. *Peter's Escape, Herod's Death* (12:1-25)

1. About that time King Herod set out to harm some who belonged to the Church. 2. James the brother of John he killed by the sword. 3. When he perceived that this pleased the Jews, he went on to arrest Peter. It was during the feast of unleavened bread. 4. He seized him and put him in jail, handing him over to four squads of four soldiers each to guard him. He planned to bring him out to the people after the Passover. 5. Peter therefore was being kept in the jail. But the Church kept praying fervently to God for him. 6. Now when Herod was about to bring him out, Peter was that night sleeping between two soldiers, bound with two chains, with guards before the door keeping watch over the cell. 7. Then, look, an angel of the Lord stood there! And a light shone in the building! He struck Peter's side. He raised him. He said, "Stand up quickly!"

And the chains fell off his hands. 8. The angel said to him, "Fasten your belt and put on your sandals." He did just that. He also said to him, "Throw on your cloak and follow me." 9. So as he went out he followed, but he did not know that what was happening through the angel was real. He thought that he was seeing a vision. 10. They went out through the first guard post and a second. They came to the iron gate that led out into the city. It opened for them by itself! So going out, they went down one street. And suddenly the angel withdrew from him. 11. Then Peter came to himself. He said, "Now I know for sure that the Lord sent his angel and rescued me from the power of Herod and all the expectation of the people of the Jews." 12. Realizing this, he went to the house of Mary, mother of the John called Mark. There, many were gathered together and were praying. 13. When he knocked at the door of the gate, a woman servant named Rhoda went to answer. 14. But when she recognized Peter's voice, she did not open the door because of her joy. Instead, as she ran in, she announced that Peter was standing at the gate. 15. But they said to her, "You are crazy." But she insisted that it was so. They said, "It is his angel." 16. But Peter kept knocking. When they opened, they saw him and were astonished. 17. He signalled them with his hand to keep silent. He reported to them how the Lord led him out of prison. And he said, "Tell James and the brothers these things." Going out, he went to another place. 18. When day came, there was no small commotion among the soldiers concerning what happened to Peter. 19. Herod searched for him and could not find him. He interrogated the soldiers. He ordered them to be taken away. And having gone down from Judea, he stayed in Caesarea. 20. But he was furious at the Tyrians and Sidonians. They presented themselves before him all together, and won over Blastus, the king's chamberlain. They sought peace because their country was supported by the king's country. 21. On a set day, Herod, clothed in royal garments, sat on the throne. He made a speech to them. 22. And the people cried out, "The voice of a god and not of a man!" 23. Immediately an angel of the Lord struck him, because he did not give glory to God. He was eaten up by worms and died. 24. But the word of God grew and increased. 25. Having completed their service to Jerusalem, Barnabas and Saul returned. They brought along with them John called Mark.

Notes

1. *Herod set out to harm:* Literally, "put his hand to" (compare 1 Esdr 9:20). This is now the third Herod to (briefly) enter the narrative. The first was Herod the Great (Luke 1:5). The second was Herod the Tetrarch who shadowed Jesus' ministry and death (Luke 3:1, 19; 8:3; 9:7-9; 13:31; 23:7-15; Acts 4:27). This "King Herod" is Herod Agrippa I, the grandson of Herod the Great. His checkered career as a client of Roman emperors takes up a major portion

of Books 18-19 of Josephus' *Antiquities of the Jews*. He came to exercise rule over most of Palestine by means of such patronage (*Antiquities* 18:250-256).

2. *James the brother of John:* One of the first followers of Jesus (Luke 5:10) and one of the Twelve (Luke 6:14; Acts 1:13), who enjoyed special intimacy with Jesus (Luke 8:51; 9:28, 54). His death signals the end of the short period of tranquillity enjoyed by the Jerusalem leadership after the persecution of Stephen (Acts 8:1). In his *Ecclesiastical History* 2, 9, 1-3, Eusebius of Caesarea hands on a tradition reported by Clement of Alexandria that James' jailer was converted and then executed with him.

3. *this pleased the Jews:* The reason may lie in the means of execution. The *m.Sanh.* 7:2 calls beheading the most shameful of all deaths. Who should receive such capital punishment? A murderer, which certainly would not apply to James, but also "the people of an apostate city" (*m.Sanh.* 9:1). This designation is an allusion to Deut 13:15, which calls for the extermination of the city whose inhabitants have gone over to the worship of idols. According to *m.Sanh.* 10:4, furthermore, the "inhabitants of an apostate city" have no share in the world to come. Beheading James therefore is a gesture of solidarity on Herod's part with the Jewish majority, a statement that he regarded the Messianists as apostates and idolators. In fact, Josephus makes clear that Agrippa's loyalties were with the Pharisaic version of Jewish piety (*Antiquities of the Jews* 19:292-316), which would make his desire to "please the Jews" in this fashion intelligible.

   feast of unleavened bread: See "after the Passover" (*meta to pascha*) in the next verse. Although the celebration of the feast began with the Passover meal on 14th Nisan and then the "days of unleavened bread" continued for seven days more (Exod 12:3-19), Luke collapses any distinction between them (see Luke 22:1, and also Josephus, *Antiquities* 14:21). The reader, of course, is expected to make the connection between this arrest and that of Jesus also at Passover.

4. *bring him out to the people:* The timing is puzzling. Does this reflect a pious desire not to intrude in the festival (see *m.Sanh.* 4:1)? But the summary execution of James does not suggest legal fastidiousness. Does the "bringing out" refer simply to the process of arraignment, or to the sort of ritual offering to the people suggested by the (usually rejected) text of Luke 23:17 (see Mark 15:6)? The narrative function of the delay is clear enough: it builds tension and allows the reader to see the activity of the Church working against that of the tyrant.

5. *Church kept praying fervently:* The adverb *ektenōs* denotes eagerness and earnestness. The comparative form is used for the prayer of Jesus before his arrest (Luke 22:14; see also Jdt 4:9 and Acts 26:7). The community's prayer compensates for Peter's powerlessness and prepares for his miraculous escape.

6. *sleeping between two soldiers:* The custom with such squads was to have four men on duty at a time, in four revolving watches. Here two sleep next to Peter, one is at each of the two guard posts (v. 10). The elaborate description of the security measures heightens the wonder of the escape.

7. *angel of the Lord stood there:* For the prominent role of such heavenly messengers in Luke-Acts, see the note on Acts 5:19. Together with the use of *idou* ("look/behold"), the verb *ephistēmi* gives the sense of a sudden and startling appearance; compare especially Luke 2:9 and Acts 23:11. As in the appearance to Saul, light (*phōs*) is a sign of heavenly presence (Acts 9:3; 22:6, 9-11; 26:13).

struck Peter's side: The choice of *patassō* ("strike") is odd, since it is usually used in the LXX for the "smiting" of God's enemies (Exod 2:12; Judg 1:5; Ps 3:7; 77:66), and is elsewhere used by Luke with that meaning as well (Luke 22:49-50; Acts 7:24). In fact, later in this passage, Herod will be "smited" by the angel (12:23). Perhaps this is why the Western Text changes the verb to the gentler *nuxas* ("nudged").

9. *what was happening . . . was real:* Literally, "that the thing coming to be through the angel was true." In fact, Luke manages to convey a remarkable dream-like quality to the entire sequence, including the angel's precise directions for putting on clothes! After Peter's experience on the roof-top in Joppa (10:9-16), he is certainly prepared not only to "see visions (*horama*)," but also to follow wherever they lead.

10. *opened for them by itself:* The adjective *automatos* here is used adverbially. The gate swings open "spontaneously." The fact that it is made of iron (*sideros*) only makes the event more wonderful. The dream-quality is impressive: Peter and the angel float through the obstacles unimpeded. Once through the gate, Codex D adds the beguiling detail that they went down "the seven steps."

withdrew from him: Literally, "stood away from (*aphistēmi apo*)," as in Luke 4:13; 13:27; Acts 5:38; 15:38; 19:9. The withdrawal of the heavenly companion corresponds to Peter's "coming to himself" (*en heautō genomenos*), which is similar to Luke 15:17.

11. *expectation of the people of the Jews:* As in 12:3, Luke joins the power of Herod (literally, the "hand" of Herod) to the hostile expectation (*prosdokia*) of the Jews. For the first time in the narrative of Luke-Acts, he connects the distancing designation "Jews" to the term that previously had been used in a religious sense, "people" (*laos*). The use of the term "expectation" (*prosdokia*) is somewhat ironic in light of Luke's earlier usage (see Luke 1:21; 3:15; 7:19-20; 8:40; Acts 3:5; 10:24).

12. *Mary the mother of the John called Mark:* The identification of the head of a household as a woman is striking but not unparalleled (compare Luke 10:38-42; Acts 16:14-15; 1 Tim 5:16). *Marcus* is one of the most common Latin names. Here as in the case of *Justus* added to Barsabbas in 1:23, it is added to the Jewish name *Iōannēs*. This "John-Mark" becomes an important if contentious figure in the next section of narrative. He joins Barnabas and Saul after they complete their mission to Jerusalem (12:25), and goes with them on their first missionary journey (13:5), but leaves them in Perga to return to Jerusalem (13:13). This "departure" is made the reason for the split between Barnabas and Saul in 15:37-39. Because Marcus is such a common name, we cannot be sure that all the other NT passages refer to the same person, although Col

4:10, which calls him a nephew of Barnabas, certainly does. The other passages are 2 Tim 4:11; Phlm 24; 1 Pet 5:13.

gathered together . . . praying: We now know the source of the "fervent praying" for Peter in 12:5. This portrayal of the Church is entirely consistent with Luke's understanding of the community as defined by prayer (see note on Acts 1:14). By bracketing the description of the marvelous escape by these notices of the Church's prayer, Luke suggests the origin of the power at work.

13. *woman servant named Rhoda:* The *paidiskē* ("maid-servant") recalls Peter's earlier unhappy experience with a woman servant in Luke 22:56, when Peter was confronted in the *aulē*. We are to picture here just such a courtyard before the house proper, with a wall and a "door at the gate" (*thura tou pulōnos*) on which Peter can pound. This is Rhoda's only appearance in the narrative, but it is an unforgettable one.

14. *because of her joy:* The phrase *apo tēs charas* recalls the puzzling passage in Luke 24:41, where the disciples do not believe in Jesus "from their joy." But such highly wrought and sometimes conflicting emotional responses are regularly found in Hellenistic Romances, sometimes to the degree that characters are prevented from acting appropriately (see, e.g., Longus, *Daphnis and Chloe* 2:30; Achilles Tatius, *Clitophon and Leucippe* 1:3; 2:23).

announced that Peter was standing: The use of *apangelō* ("announce") echoes the proclamation of the resurrection by the women in Luke 24:9: "They announced these things to the eleven."

15. *you are crazy:* The verb *mainomai* often bears the sense of "raving" (as in a spirit-induced frenzy; see Herodotus, *Persian Wars* 4:79; 1 Cor 14:23), but it is used by Luke in Acts 26:24-25 in the sense of "being irrational." Note how similar is this response to that of the eleven to the message of the women concerning the empty tomb (Luke 24:11): it seemed "in their view to be so much nonsense (*hōsei lēros ta rhēmata tauta*)."

it is his angel: The Western Text makes it more tentative, "Perhaps (*tychon*) it is his angel." Compare the reaction of the disciples to the visitation of Jesus after his resurrection (Luke 24:37): "They thought they were seeing a ghost (*pneuma*)." For the notion of "attendant/guardian" angels in special relationship with human persons, see, e.g., LXX Gen 48:16; Tobit 5:22; Matt 18:10; Pseudo-Philo, *Biblical Antiquities* 59:4; *Testament of Jacob* 1:10; *Shepherd of Hermas*, Mand. 6, 2, 2.

17. *tell James and the brothers:* This James, "the brother of the Lord" (see Mark 6:3; Matt 13:55 and Acts 1:14), is called by Paul one of the three "pillars" (*styloi*) of the Jerusalem Church with Cephas and John (Gal 1:19; 2:9), as well as a witness to Jesus' resurrection (1 Cor 15:7). It was "people from James" who according to Paul created the difficulties at Antioch over table-fellowship (Gal 2:12). The picture in Acts basically confirms Paul's version: James emerges as the leader of the Jerusalem Church in the present passage, and is clearly its chief spokesperson at the apostolic council (15:13) as well as at Paul's final visit to the city (21:18). It is his death under the chief priest Ananus which

is recounted briefly in Josephus, *Antiquities of the Jews* 20:200, and more elaborately by the Christian writer Hegesippus (cited in Eusebius, *Ecclesiastical History* 2, 23, 11-18). The canonical *Letter of James* is attributed to him (1:1), as well as apocryphal works such as *The Apocryphon of James*. James is the hero in the apocryphal narrative, *Kerygmata Petrou*.

went to another place: The *heteros topos* is not specified, and nothing more can be read into it about Peter's subsequent career, despite abundant speculation. Certainly Acts 1:25 cannot be taken as support for seeing this as a reference to Peter's death. Even leaving aside his role at the apostolic council (Acts 15:7-11), the tradition is unanimous in attributing to Peter a considerable period of travel: Gal 2:14 places him in Antioch; 1 Cor 1:10 and 9:5 offer circumstantial evidence for his having been in Corinth, and a body of testimony supports his ending up in Rome (1 Pet 5:13; *1 Clement* 5:4; *Acts of Peter* 7). The present passage, however, says nothing more than that he removed himself from Jerusalem.

18. *no small commotion:* The same expression (*tarachos ouk oligos*) is used in 19:23; some scribes suspected that the present passage was influenced by the later one and left it out of their *mss*. But Luke is very fond of the rhetorical trope called *litotes* (understatement), and the phrase *ouk oligos* appears also in 14:28; 15:2; 17:4, 12; 19:23, 24; see also "no mean city" in 21:39. The translation "concerning what happened to Peter" would literally be "what therefore (*ara*) Peter became"; compare Luke 1:66.

19. *interrogated the soldiers:* The verb *anakrinō* has a specific judicial sense (Luke 23:14; Acts 4:9; 24:8; 28:18). "Cross-examine" might be the best translation (see, e.g., Plato, *Symposium* 201E). When carried out by tyrants or householders, such "interrogation" could involve physical torture (see Chariton of Aphrodisias, *Chaereas and Callirhoe* 5:1-2; Pliny the Younger, *Letters* 10, 96, 8).

to be taken away: The passive of the verb *apagō* has the judicial sense of being arrested or carried off to prison (Herodotus, *Persian Wars* 2:114; 6:81; LXX Gen 42:16; Luke 22:66). It is used for the "taking away" of Jesus to his execution in Luke 23:26. Is there, then, the implication that Herod also put these soldiers to death? Certainly Codex D thought so, for it replaced this verb with *apoktanthēnai* ("to be killed"). And such summary executions for dereliction of duty were common enough (see Chariton of Aphrodisias, *Chaereas and Callirhoe* 3, 4, 18). Such behavior is comprehensible within the world of Luke's parables (Luke 12:46; 19:27), and within the range of a king who had already executed James with what we presume was less cause (12:3).

stayed in Caesarea: For the significance of Caesarea, see the note on Acts 10:1. The verb *diatribo* has the general sense of "residing/staying" (Acts 14:3, 28; 15:35; 16:12; 20:6; 25:6, 14; compare John 3:22; 11:54), which the use of the imperfect tense accentuates. Only here and in 15:15 does Luke fail to add some indication of elapsed time when using *diatribo*.

20. *furious at the Tyrians and Sidonians:* The verb *thumomacheō* can mean simply to be angry at someone, or to contend with someone; it is lacking in the LXX and elsewhere in the NT. Luke appears to be sketching a situation in which

territories adjacent to Herod's are in dispute with him, although no reason is given why there should have been such a dispute. For the cities of Tyre and Sidon, see the note on Acts 11:19, as well as the description of their importance by Strabo, *Geography* 16, 2, 22-24. In his version of Herod's death, Josephus presents a different *mise-en-scène*. He mentions no dispute between Herod and the cities. He does precede the account with a dispute between Herod and Marsan the governor of Syria (see *Antiquities of the Jews* 19:339-342).

before him all together: The Western Text tries to clarify the situation: "some from both cities presented themselves together before the king." For Luke's characteristic use of *homothymadon*, see the note on Acts 1:14.

Blastus, the king's chamberlain: This is his only appearance in the text, and he is otherwise unknown to us. The "one over the bed-chamber of the king," sometimes titled *koitōnēs*, could exercise considerable power of access to the ruler, and be a figure to reckon with, as suggested by Epictetus, *Discourses* 1, 19, 17-23; 3, 22, 15; 4, 7, 1-19.

supported by the king's country: The term "country" is supplied as the substantive understood to be modified by the adjective *basilikos* ("royal"). The establishment of treaties between Judea and Phoenicia involving food being sent to these cities is attested already in the time of Solomon (1 Kgs 5:9-12) and of Ezechiel (27:17).

21. *on a set day:* The Western Text makes this otherwise inexplicable reference ("day set [*taktē*]" for what?) somewhat easier by supplying "when he was reconciled with the Tyrians." Josephus makes the occasion "spectacles in honor of Caesar," at which were gathered "a large number of men who had office or had advanced to some rank in the kingdom" (*Antiquities of the Jews* 19:343). Luke's cryptic reference seems to assume some such setting.

clothed in royal garments: Josephus describes the clothing, and makes its splendor the occasion for the crowd's flattery (*kolakeia*), in *Antiquities of the Jews* 19:344-345; see also the reference to the clothing of kings in Luke 7:25.

throne . . . speech: The *bema* is a raised platform or rostrum; see LXX Neh 8:4; 2 Macc 13:26; also Acts 18:12, 16, 17; 25:6, 10, 17. For a king, it would properly be translated as "throne." The term *dēmēgoreō* means to make a speech in a public assembly. Luke says nothing about the content of the speech, and Josephus has the critical events take place before Agrippa could deliver one.

22. *voice of a god:* In Luke's version, the people respond to Herod's speech. In Josephus' version, they also address him as a god, but in response to the "fear and awe" generated by the vision of his splendid clothing in the sunlight (*Antiquities of the Jews* 19:345).

23. *angel of the Lord struck him:* In contrast to the use of *patassō* in 12:7, the "smiting" here has its usual connotation of divine retribution. It recalls especially the killing of the hundred and eighty-five thousand Assyrians in one night by the angel of the Lord (2 Kgs 19:35), which is recounted again in 1 Macc 7:41 and Sir 48:21. Luke's typical use of *parachrēma* ("immediately") is in contrast to Josephus, who has some time elapse between the acclamation and the onset of symptoms (*Antiquities of the Jews* 19:346).

did not give glory to God: Josephus agrees that the punishment befell Herod because "the king did not rebuke them nor did he reject their flattery as impious" (*Antiquities of the Jews* 19:346). For "giving glory to God" in Luke-Acts, see Luke 2:14, 20; 4:15; 5:25-26; 7:16; 13:13; 17:15; 18:43; 23:47; Acts 4:21; 11:18.

eaten up by worms and died: In Josephus, Herod develops severe stomach pains that last for five days before he dies (*Antiquities of the Jews* 19:346-350). Eusebius quotes Josephus' version of the event because he thinks it shows "how in this and other points Josephus confirms the truth of the divine scriptures" (*Ecclesiastical History* 2, 10, 10). The horrible manner of death described by Luke (undoubtedly rooted in the production of maggots by a gangrenous condition) finds parallels in accounts by Herodotus, *Persian Wars* 4:205; Pliny the Elder, *Natural History* 7:172; Lucian of Samosata, *Alexander the False Prophet* 59. In the biblical tradition, see Jdt 16:17 and 2 Macc 9:9 (the death of Antiochus Epiphanes). Josephus describes the death of Herod the Great in these terms (*Antiquities of the Jews* 17:169; *Jewish War* 1:656). The Western Text adds a number of details, the most vivid of which says that the king was "still alive" (*eti zōn*) when the worms ate him.

24. *word of God grew:* This is a summary statement like those of 2:47; 4:4; 6:7; 9:31; 11:24. In the present case, it is also a triumphant assertion of the movement's growth despite the attempts of a tyrant to suppress it through the harassment of its leaders.

25. *having completed their service to Jerusalem:* The verse presents a difficult textual problem. The hardest reading contains the phrase *eis Ierousalēm* ("to Jerusalem"). But if taken as the object of the verb *hypestrepsen* ("they returned"), we seem to have a flat contradiction of the movements suggested in 11:30, where Barnabas and Saul were on their way to Jerusalem with this aid package. Luke furthermore wants us to see them back in Antioch, for the next scene opens with them in the Antiochean assembly (13:1-3). Many *mss* have tried to resolve the difficulty by altering *eis* to *ex* ("out of") or *apo* ("from"), or by keeping *eis*, but having as its object *Antiochaian*. The best solution may be to keep the best attested reading of *eis Ierousalēm* but connect it to the participial phrase "having completed their service," making the main verb absolute. This keeps the best text and respects the manifest narrative intention.

INTERPRETATION

Luke's story is very shortly going to focus almost exclusively on the mission of Paul. Indeed, at the end of this passage, he reminds us that Barnabas and Saul had returned from their mission to Jerusalem, bringing with them the John-Mark who would be their companion in the first missionary venture (12:25). But before narrating the commissioning of these missionaries by the Antiochean Church (13:1-3), Luke pauses to look for a last time at events concerning the Church in Jerusalem and especially concerning the figure who until now had so dominated the story that it could fairly have been called "The Acts of Peter."

The two vignettes of Peter's escape (12:1-19) and Herod's death (12:20-25) present us once more with the puzzling character of Luke's historiography. Accounts of prison-escapes are found everywhere in Hellenistic fiction, whether their wonderful character is owed to some human virtue or relationship (see Lucian of Samosata, *Toxaris* 28-33; Achilles Tatius, *Clitophon and Leucippe* 3:9-11), or due to some divine intervention (Ovid, *Metamorphoses* 3:690-700; Artapanus, *On the Jews*, frag. three; *The Acts of Paul* 7; *The Acts of Thomas* 162-163). One of the most interesting examples of the type-scene is also one of the earliest, the escape of the devotees of Bacchus from prison by divine intervention after a tyrant had jailed them in an attempt to halt the growth of the cult (see Euripides, *Bacchae* 346-357; 434-450; 510-643).

Luke's account concerning Peter is if anything even more extravagant than the norm. Yet this tale is told as straightforwardly and unapologetically as the account of Herod's measures against James (12:1-3) and of Herod's death (12:20-25) which, while having some dramatic features, is not only supported in its essential historicity by the version found in Josephus, *Antiquities of the Jews* 19:343-352, and by Luke's subtle allusion to a source in the Herodian circle (13:1), but is in several respects less "fictional" in tone than Josephus (see notes).

Luke's primary interest in these stories is obviously not demonstrating their historical reliability but making them serve his narrative purposes. First he uses the stories to rearrange his characters. He quickly passes over "James" who is killed by Herod (12:2), so the reader can focus on the "James" who with "the brothers" is to be told of Peter's escape (12:17). Then he has Peter "go to another place," which suggests the shift in authority within the Jerusalem Church that is in fact realized by Acts 15:13-21 and 21:17-26, where James is the community's chief spokesperson. He also obliquely introduces John-Mark (12:12), who will become Barnabas' and Saul's companion (12:25) and bone of contention (15:36-41).

Luke also uses the story to make a decisive comment on the power at work in the messianic movement. He does this by arranging his materials in a pattern of reversals. Herod begins as had the Jewish Sanhedrin by seeking to harm the Church (12:1). But he ends up eaten by worms (12:23). The Church in contrast starts off having one of its leaders killed as a "member of an apostate city" (see note on 12:2), and its chief spokesperson imprisoned (12:4). But in the end its leader has escaped, the tyrant is dead, and the Church is growing and prospering (12:24).

Against the powerful resources of the king (his chamberlain, his prison, his squads of soldiers), the community has only the power of prayer, which it exercises ceaselessly (12:5, 12). But Luke makes clear that the power of prayer is mightier than that of tyrants. The angel of the Lord who strikes Peter in the side to free him of his chains and lead him from prison (12:7), also strikes Herod (who began by trying to please the Jews but ended by being seduced by pagan flattery) down from his throne, where he dies the miserable death reserved for tyrants (12:23). Once more the reader finds the narrative fulfilling the prophecy of Mary, "He has pulled down the mighty from their thrones. He has exalted the lowly" (Luke 1:52).

The charm and humor in Luke's account of Peter's escape has often and justly been remarked. It is one of the finest samples in his impressive collection of vignettes. Luke's own pleasure in the art of story-telling is obvious. The reader is quite willing to credit Peter's confusion concerning the escape ("whether what was happening through the angel was real," 12:9) because the entire sequence had in fact a dream-like quality. Who cannot identify with the bizarre obsessiveness of the angel's instructions concerning Peter's clothing, or the sense of floating through obstacles unseen while gates open ahead? The reader is also—in relief at Peter's escape—willing to chuckle over the slapstick misunderstanding of the maidservant Rhoda: an angel gets Peter out of Herod's cell, but Peter himself cannot get through the locked gate to the Christian household because he is mistaken for an angel!

But perhaps something more than a charming story is being told. Perhaps Luke wants the reader to ponder further some of the puzzling details of this account to find a deeper message concerning Peter and the power at work in his behalf. The reader is already aware that Luke establishes parallels between his prophetic characters. The portrayal of Stephen's trial and death, for example, obviously continued and mirrored the story of Jesus' passion. Alerted to this possibility, we notice first the detail that Peter, like Jesus, was imprisoned during the time of the Passover celebration (Luke 22:1; Acts 12:2), and that a "King Herod" had a role in this event (Luke 23:6-12; Acts 4:27; 12:1).

Other details of language then take on a greater significance. We notice that in the case of Peter as in the case of Jesus, there is the "laying on of hands" (Luke 9:44; 20:19; Acts 12:1), and the "arresting" (Luke 22:54; Acts 12:3), the "delivering over" (Luke 23:25; 24:7; Acts 12:4) and the "leading forth" (Luke 23:1, 26; Acts 12:4). Jesus rises from the dead and the event is announced to the women by two figures identified as "angels" (Luke 24:23). When the women deliver this message to the eleven, they are not heeded because the message seemed like nonsense (24:11). When Jesus then appears to the community as a whole, they "disbelieve for joy" (24:41). They think that Jesus is a "ghost" (24:37). After Jesus converses with them, he withdraws (24:51).

Peter obviously does not die, but he is told by the angel to "rise" (Acts

12:7) and his passage through the portals is like one who was a ghost. When he gets to the house, then, we are not surprised to find that Rhoda "did not open for joy" (12:14). We are not surprised that when she "proclaims" that "Peter is standing at the gate" (12:14), she is told, "you are crazy" (12:15) and that some think he is an "angel" (12:15). We are not surprised that after Peter "relates everything" he tells them to "announce these things to James" and then withdraws from them (12:17).

As the death of Stephen was portrayed as the extension and mirror-image of the death of Jesus in order to make the point that Stephen was a prophet who spoke with Jesus' spirit, so is the account of Peter's escape subtly fashioned by Luke to make a similar point. The escape of the prophet Peter from prison becomes a demonstration that the resurrection of Jesus continues to empower his apostles. The story of Jesus is continued in the story of his followers, and the power at work in Jesus is now even more powerfully at work in his Church.

FOR REFERENCE AND FURTHER STUDY

Cullmann, O. "Courants multiples dans la communauté primitive: à propos du martyre de Jacques fils de Zebedée." *RScR* 60 (1972) 55–68.

Dupont, J. "La mission de Paul 'à Jérusalem' (Act xii, 25)." *NovT* 1 (1956) 275–303.

_____. "Pierre deliveré de prison." *Nouvelle Etudes sur les Actes des Apôtres.* Lectio Divina 118. Paris: Editions du Cerf, 1984, 329–342.

Garrett, S. R. "Exodus from Bondage: Luke 9:31 and Acts 12:1-24." *CBQ* 52 (1990) 656–680.

Lake, K. "The Death of Herod Agrippa I." *Beginnings* 5:446-452.

Strobel, A. "Passa-Symbolik und Passa-Wunder im Act 12.3." *NTS* 4 (1958) 210–215.

Tannehill, R. *Narrative Unity* 2:151-158.

24. *Commission and Confrontation* (13:1-12)

1. In the Church at Antioch there were prophets and teachers such as Barnabas, and Simeon who was called Niger, and Lucian the Cyrenian, Manaen the childhood companion of Herod the Tetrarch, and Saul. 2. While they were worshipping the Lord and fasting, the Holy Spirit said, "Set aside for me Barnabas and Saul, so they can do the work to which I have summoned them." 3. Then, after they had fasted and prayed, and after they had placed hands on them, they sent them off. 4. Now when they had been sent out by the Holy Spirit, they went down to Seleucia. From there they sailed to Cyprus. 5. They came to Salamis.

They proclaimed the word of God in the synagogues of the Jews. And they had John along as an assistant. 6. Then they travelled through the whole island up to Paphos. They found a certain man who was a magician. He was a Jewish false prophet whose name was Bar-Jesus. 7. He was with the Proconsul Sergius Paulus, an intelligent man. He summoned Barnabas and Saul. He sought to hear the word of God. 8. But Elymas the magician—for so is his name to be translated—opposed them. He tried to turn the Proconsul away from the faith. 9. So Saul—who was also Paul—filled with the Holy Spirit, stared at him. 10. He said, "You child of the devil, full of every deception and fraud, enemy of all righteousness! Will you never stop twisting the straight paths of the Lord? 11. And look, now the hand of the Lord is upon you! You will be blind, you will not see the sun for a season!" And immediately there fell on him a dimness and darkness. He wandered about looking for someone to lead him by the hand. 12. Then the Proconsul, having seen what had happened, believed. He was astounded by the teaching about the Lord.

NOTES

1. *Church at Antioch:* For the importance of this city in the narrative of Acts, see the note on 11:19. The expression here used by Luke, *kata tēn ousan ekklēsian,* is difficult to render exactly. The participial construction is paralleled in 5:17; 11:22, and 28:17, meaning something like "local," or "in that place" (see note on 11:22). But does Luke use *kata* + the accusative in the distributive sense that it has, for example, in 2:46 ("in houses"), or in 2:47 ("day by day")? If so, then a better translation would be, "in the local churches at Antioch."

prophets and teachers: In Acts 11:27, Luke mentioned the prophets from Judea who had arrived in Antioch; for the continuing importance of the role of prophets in local churches, see the note on that verse. This is Luke's only use of the title "teacher" (*didaskalos*) in Acts, and he has prepared for it by having Barnabas and Saul "teach" (*didaskein*) in Antioch for an extended period (11:26). For teachers among the ministers of a local church, see Rom 12:7; 1 Cor 12:28-29; Eph 4:11; Jas 3:1. Luke nicely establishes the place of Barnabas and Saul within the local community by putting their names first and last, thus bracketing the others.

Simeon who was called Niger: Like Joseph Barsabbas who came to be called Justus (1:23), and like John who was called Marcus (12:12), Simeon is another Jew who bears a Latin surname. *Niger* in Latin means "black," and in fact may be a nickname suggestive of an African origin. It is tempting to identify him with "Simon of Cyrene" (Luke 23:26), but there is nothing else that might be used to support the suggestion.

Lucian the Cyrenian: Nothing more is known of this prophet/teacher, unless we can identify him in Rom 16:21 as one of Paul's companions, referred to in the same breath with Timothy. His place of origin in North Africa connects him to the group who founded this community (11:20). That the shortened form of his name (*Loukas*) might give us the author of this composition (also, of course, identified as a companion of Paul in Col 4:14; 2 Tim 4:11; Phlm 24), is a pleasant thought but one unsupported by anything more than such overlapping designations.

childhood companion of Herod: The term *syntrophos* (literally, "nurtured with"; Aristotle, *Nichomachean Ethics* 1161B) is used for someone "adopted" by a family as a childhood playmate (see Herodotus, *Persian Wars* 1:99). It can be extended to mean a court "familiar" or "companion" (Lucian of Samosata, *Nigrinus* 12; 15). This is the second reference in Luke-Acts to a special relationship with someone in Herod's household (see Luke 8:3).

2. *worshipping the Lord and fasting:* The verb *leitourgeō* had as its original setting the public activities of the Greek city-state which would include support of and participation in its religious rituals (Aristotle, *Politics* 1291A; 1335B; Julian, *Oration* 1:21D). Compare Rom 13:6; 15:16; 2 Cor 9:12; Phil 2:30. In the LXX, the verb (as well as the noun *leitourgia*) is used primarily for the "service" (Heb. *'abodah*) of the Lord in worship (Exod 28:31, 39; Num 1:50; 4:33; 18:6; Deut 17:12; 18:7; 1 Sam 2:11; Ezek 40:46; 45:5). This is its sense also in Luke 1:23; Heb 1:7; 8:2, 6; 9:21. In *The Didache* 15:1, we find it used for the work of church ministers: the bishops and deacons "also minister to you (*leitourgousi*) the ministry (*leitourgia*) of prophets and teachers." For "fasting" (*nēsteuō*), see the note on verse 3, below.

set aside for me: The particle *de* gives the command a sense of urgency (compare LXX Gen 15:5; 18:4), as it does also in Acts 15:36. The verb *aphorizō* is used in the sense of "separate/make holy" (Exod 13:12; 29:26-27; Lev 13:4; Num 12:24; 2 Sam 8:1; Isa 52:11; and especially Rom 1:1; Gal 1:15).

3. *placed hands on them:* For this gesture as the sign of transmitting power or authority, see Acts 6:6; 8:17-19; 9:17. For the combination "fasting and prayer," see also Luke 2:37; 5:33, and Acts 14:23. The combination of prayer and fasting is frequent in Jewish piety (Jer 14:12; Neh 1:4; Matt 6:5, 16; *Joseph and Asenath* 10:17-12:12; *Testament of Simeon* 2:12-3:4), and in other early Christian texts (see Polycarp, *Letter to the Philippians* 7:2; 2 Clement 16:4; *The Didache* 8:1-2). For prayer and fasting in connection with the reception of revelations, see the note on Acts 9:9 and *The Shepherd of Hermas*, Vis. 2, 2, 1; 3, 1, 2; 3, 10, 6.

4. *sent out by the Holy Spirit:* Luke emphasizes the divine character of the apostles' commission. The Holy Spirit had set them aside (13:2), and although the Church sent them off (13:3), he now repeats that they are "sent out" by the Holy Spirit. Such direct interventions by the Spirit are a characteristic recurrence in Acts (4:31; 8:29, 39; 10:44; 16:6).

4-5. *Seleucia . . . Salamis:* Seleucia is the port city of Antioch, located some 16 miles westward of the city proper which was situated on the Orontes River. Salamis is on the east coast and is the chief city on the island of Cyprus. For the presence of Jews on the island, see the note on Acts 11:19.

5. *synagogues of the Jews:* Luke makes it Paul's fixed practice to preach first in Jewish synagogues wherever he goes. For the social significance of the syna-

gogue in local Jewish life, especially in the Diaspora, see the notes on Luke 4:15 and Acts 6:9. The presence of such synagogues throughout the Diaspora is supported by archaeological as well as literary evidence (e.g., Philo, *Against Flaccus* 48-49; *Special Laws* 2:62). Among the best and earliest evidence is that provided by the narrative of Acts itself (13:14; 14:1; 16:13, 16; 17:1, 10, 17; 18:4, 19, 26; 19:8). The fact that Moses was "read every Sabbath in the synagogues" (Acts 15:21) was no small factor in preparing the moral groundwork for the Christian message (see Josephus, *Against Apion* 2:282-286).

John along as an assistant: Although Luke uses *hypēretēs* for the "ministers of the word" in Luke 1:2, and for Paul's service of "witnessing" in Acts 26:16, the term has the basic sense of being a functionary (see Luke 4:20; Acts 5:22, 26, as well as 13:26; 20:34; 24:23). Such is the sense here. Luke prepares the reader for John-Mark's departure in 13:13.

6. *travelled through . . . to Paphos:* This city was at the western end of the island of Cyprus. Perhaps to explain why no other cities are mentioned if they "travelled through" (*dielthontes*) the island, the Western Text has them travel "around" it (*perielthontōn*).

who was a magician . . . Jewish false prophet: For the title *magos*, see the note on Acts 8:9. The phrase "Jewish false prophet" (*pseudoprophētēs*) is used here as roughly synonymous with *magos*. Gentile observers sometimes connected Judaism to the practice of magic (see Strabo, *Geography* 16, 2, 39; 16, 2, 43; Pliny the Elder, *Natural History* 30, 2, 11; Apuleius, *Apologia* 90). The rough equivalence with "false prophet" is not out of line with Josephus' usage (*Jewish War* 6:285-288). Josephus, in fact, refers to "a Cyprian Jew named Atomos, who pretended to be a magician," during the time when Felix was procurator of Judea (*Antiquities* 20:142).

name was Bar-Jesus: The issue of the magician's name gets more complicated as the story proceeds, but the straightforward rendering of the Greek *bar-iēsou* (the reading of the best *mss*) is as a bilingual version of the Aramaic *Bar Jehoshua*, "son of Joshua," or, "son of Jesus." The idea of a "false prophet" who is termed "son of Jesus" and who opposes Paul is provocative enough, given Luke's prophetic coloration of his characters.

7. *Proconsul Sergius Paulus:* The magician is portrayed as a sort of court advisor to the Roman authority. The title *anthupatos* properly designates the administrator of a Senatorial province such as Cyprus had become in 22 C.E. Luke will use it also for the administrators in Corinth (18:12) and Ephesus (19:38). In contrast, the imperial provinces were administered by military prefects (*hēgemōn*) such as Pontius Pilate (Luke 2:2; 3:1); Felix (Acts 23:24, 26), and Festus (24:27). There is some epigraphic evidence supporting the existence of a Roman official named Sergius Paulus, but none that securely locates him as Proconsul of Cyprus at this time.

sought to hear the word of God: In this first encounter with a Roman authority, Luke stresses his "intelligence" (*synetos*) and his openness to the gospel message. Later officials will prove less persuadable but no less equable (18:12-17; 22:29; 23:23-30; 24:22; 25:23-27). It should not surprise us that a Roman official should have a *magos* as court advisor, for as Philo remarks, "true magic" closely resembled philosophy and was a fit subject for study even by kings (*The Special Laws* 3:100). For a lively account of such a soothsayer in a royal court, see Pseudo-Callisthenes, *Life of Alexander of Macedon* 1:1-12, and the magician Simon at the house of the Senator Marcellus in *The Acts of Peter* 8.

8. *Elymas the magician:* This verse contains a bewildering number of difficulties, all of which revolve around the identification given by Luke. The first puzzle is the reintroduction of the man identified already in v. 6 as "Bar-Jesus"; narrative logic demands that this be the same person, but it is nevertheless odd. Second, what is the name given him here? The majority of *mss* have it as *Elymas*, which is possibly (but only that) a Greek version of the Arabic *'Alim*, meaning "wise man." The Western Text, however, gives *Hetoimos*, which would be translated as "Ready." This name, in turn, has been thought by some to resemble that of the Cyprian Jewish Magician referred to by Josephus as *Atomos* (*Antiquities of the Jews* 20:142). The third puzzle is what Luke might have meant by "for so his name is translated (*methermeneuetai*)": does he mean that "Elymas" translates "Bar-Jesus?" Or does he mean that *magos* translates "Elymas"? Neither option appears to have any linguistic basis, unless we assume Luke's bilingual grasp of Arabic/Greek. If we pay closer attention to Luke's use of the Greek verb *methermēneuō*, however, we may gain some vantage point. In the case of Barnabas (4:36), "Son of Consolation" (*huios paraklēseōs*) certainly did not "translate" *bar-Nebo*. Perhaps, then, Luke uses "is translated" in a broad and non-technical sense, "was understood to mean." The difficulties are impossible to resolve. We must be content with the equation: Elymas the magician = Bar-Jesus the magician.

opposed . . . tried to turn: Luke uses the verb *anthistēmi*, which recalls the prophecy of Jesus concerning the opposition to be faced by his followers (Luke 21:25; see also Stephen in Acts 6:10). As for the verb *diastrephō* ("turn away"), it is used frequently in the LXX for distorting the truth and perverting the people, especially by false prophets or idols (see Num 15:39; 32:7; Ezek 13:18, 22; 14:5; 16:34; Prov 10:9). It is used in the charge against Jesus (Luke 23:2). Paul will use it in his speech against Elymas in 13:10.

away from the faith: Luke uses "the faith" here as in 6:7, as roughly equivalent to the Christian movement. No explicit conversion is here suggested (in contrast to v. 12, below); Codex D adds to this line, "because he was hearing them with the greatest pleasure."

9. *Saul, who was also Paul:* Luke takes this occasion to identify Saul with the name he will bear through the rest of the narrative. It is not likely that anything more than coincidence links this with the name of the Proconsul. Lucian of Samosata tells us of men who changed their names to signify a higher social status (*The Cock* 14; *Timon* 22), but in the present case it is more likely that Saul adopts the "public" name he had used all along in contexts other than Jewish.

filled with the Holy Spirit: Luke accompanies the change of name with the stereotypical identification of Paul as a prophet just as he had with Peter in the face of the challenge put by Ananias and Sapphira (Acts 5:1-11), and Simon Magus (8:20-24). For the "stare" (or "intent gaze," *atenizō*), see the "piercing look" of the soothsayer in Pseudo-Callisthenes, *Life of Alexander of Macedon* 1:4.

10. *child of the devil:* Literally, "son of the devil," which forms a neat opposition to the name "son of Jesus." The conflict between the kingdom of God and the counterkingdom of Satan, represented by the realm of magic, was noted in the stories of Ananias (5:1-11) and Simon (8:20-24).

full of every deception and fraud: The term *dolos* suggests cunning or cleverness, but as a moral quality it means fraud or treachery (see LXX Deut 27:24; Ps 23:4; Wis 5:5; and especially Sir 19:26 [*plērēs dolou*] and Sir 1:30 [*hē kardia sou plērēs dolou*]). In the NT, *dolos* appears in Rom 1:29; 1 Thess 2:3; 1 Pet 2:1; 3:10. The term *radiourgos*, in contrast, appears in Hellenistic moral teaching (see Plutarch, *On the Malice of Herodotus* 23 [*Mor.* 860D]; Philo, *On the Cherubim* 80), but is not found in the LXX or elsewhere in the NT, apart from Luke's own use of *radiourgma* in Acts 18:14.

enemy of all righteousness: Paul's language recalls the prophecy of Jesus that his followers would tread upon "all the power (*dynamis*) of the enemy (*echthrou*)," meaning the demonic opposition (Luke 10:19). For the language of "enmity" against God, see in particular Rom 8:7 and Jas 4:4.

twisting the straight paths of the Lord: Luke has Paul use the same term (*diastrephō*) that was used for Elymas' attempt to "turn aside" Sergius Paulus from the faith. In addition to the LXX passages noted for verse 6, see especially "perverting right ways" (Mic 3:9; Isa 59:8) and "he who perverts his ways" (Prov 10:9). The characterization "straight paths" recalls Hos 14:10 and especially the passage from Isa 40:3-4 cited by Luke 3:4-5, "the twisted ways will be made straight." See also the statement of Peter to Simon Magus, "Your heart is not straight before God" (8:21). The phrase wonderfully sums up a path of opposition to God's work.

11. *hand of the Lord is upon you:* The expression echoes passages such as LXX Judg 2:15 and 1 Sam 12:15, where the "hand of the Lord," which always signifies power, is taken as an active force "against" someone who opposes God's will.

blind . . . see the sun for a season: The curse is an obvious reversal of the blindness that befell Saul at his conversion in Acts 9:9. Why this form of punishment is chosen here is less clear (see Interpretation). The phrase "for a season" (*achri kairou*), in turn, recalls the ambiguous expression concluding Luke's version of the temptation of Jesus, "the devil withdrew from him for a season" (Luke 4:13).

to lead him by the hand: Another parallel to Paul's own blinding, when he needed his companions to "lead him by the hand" (*cheirogōgeō*) into Damascus (see also Acts 22:11).

12. *believed . . . astounded:* Despite the explanatory clause stating that the Proconsul was "impressed" (*ekplēssomenos*) by the "teaching about the Lord" (*didachē tou kyriou*), it is clear that in this case, as in the conflict between Philip and Simon in Samaria (8:7), it is superior thaumaturgy that wins allegiance. The

verb *ekplēssō* can mean any strong emotional response, including admiration (see Herodotus, *Persian Wars* 3:148). It may seem unlikely that a Roman Proconsul, especially one who has been called "intelligent" (*synetos*), would convert this easily, but skepticism is tempered by the recollection that he had already consorted with a magician in his court.

INTERPRETATION

In this passage Luke finally launches the final stage in his narrative argument. He has shown how God was faithful to the promises by restoring a faithful Israel in Jerusalem, and he has shown how the people were extended both geographically and demographically into the Gentile world. Now, in the figure of Paul, he will show how the gospel spread throughout the Mediterranean world, and how the Gentiles won recognition as full participants in the restored people of God. It is very much part of Luke's purpose in all of this to emphasize the ways in which Paul worked in cooperation and continuity with the other apostles.

Luke's stated goal, we remember, is to provide *asphaleia* ("security") to Gentile readers by showing how the promises first made to Israel have been extended faithfully to them as well. We do not find here, therefore, a renegade apostle who abandons Israel and delivers a suspect gospel to the Gentiles, but an apostle whose divine commission is confirmed by prophetic election and the charge of the Church, whose activities are not only filled with the prophetic spirit but also mirror those of Jesus and Peter before him, who remains in constant contact with Jerusalem, and who until the very end of the story tries to convert his fellow Jews.

The pattern is set in this first passage. By having Saul recruited by Barnabas to work in the Church at Antioch (11:25-26), Luke had signalled to the reader that Saul was acceptable to the Jerusalem leadership. Then by having him sent with Barnabas to deliver the collection to the needy Church in Jerusalem, he showed further how Saul symbolically demonstrated through the disposition of possessions his obedience to that leadership (11:27-30). Now before sending them on their first journey, Luke returns Barnabas and Saul to the local community in which they had taught for a whole year (12:25). This commission, too, must be seen as one impelled by the Holy Spirit.

The commissioning scene in 13:1-3 therefore serves to give Barnabas and Saul a two-fold validation. First, they are shown to be thoroughly enmeshed in the life of the local Antiochean community. It is there they have lived and taught for a year. It is there they exercise their gifts as prophets and teachers. It is within that community that they fast and worship God. And it is by that community that they are sent on their way as missionaries. The point, clearly, is to demonstrate the social character of the apostolic mission, and its essential continuity. Second, their mission is validated by the direct intervention of the Holy Spirit. Here the reader confronts again the strange doubleness of religious narrative, in which action taking place at the level of human freedom is encompassed by action directed by God's will. The Holy Spirit speaks in the assembly (in its own voice!), directing the setting apart of Barnabas and Saul for "the work to which I have summoned them" (13:2). And in case we miss the point, Luke repeats that they were sent out "by the Holy Spirit" (13:4).

Given Luke's penchant for parallelism, we are not surprised to find this new empowerment by the Holy Spirit followed immediately by a confrontation with demonic powers. Such was the case with Jesus after his baptism with the Spirit (Luke 4:1-13), and such was the case with Peter after the outpouring of the Spirit on the Twelve (Acts 4:23–5:11). So now Paul (with Barnabas very much in the background) confronts the "son of the devil," the Jewish false-prophet, court *Magos* with the doubled name Bar-Jesus-Elymas, and convincingly overturns his opposition to the gospel with a display of prophetic power (13:6-12).

Three literary functions of this strange story are fairly evident. The first is Luke's concern to show that Paul is a genuine prophet in continuity with Jesus and Peter. This is shown by his being "filled with the Holy Spirit," his reading the heart of his opponent, and his ability to declare a curse in the name of the Lord. The second literary function is the demonstration of the kingdom of God ("word of God") reaching new territories and overcoming the powers of Satan. As we saw Peter overcome Ananias in Jerusalem and Simon in Samaria, here we find Paul engaging in a "turf-war" with the false prophet who is a "son of the devil," and conquering him. The sign of this victory is not only the helpless condition of the *magos*, but the conversion of the Proconsul to the faith. The third function is the apologetic theme that shows Roman authorities to be fair-minded and open to persuasion. Later encounters will not prove so successful as this one; the conversion of a Proconsul in Cyprus is not yet the conversion of the empire. And as the narrative progresses, the official representatives of the empire will not always prove to be perfect models of judicial fairness. But neither are they portrayed as the fixed enemy of this new sect; they represent a structure of power that, despite its human frailties, provides at least a refuge from the active hostility of the Jewish leaders.

We cannot leave Paul's encounter with Elymas-Bar Jesus, however, without wondering whether Luke's account does not invite still further speculation. Readers cannot help but pause over the puzzling set of doublings and reversals Luke has here brought together. Are they purposeful? In the notes, some of the technical considerations are discussed. Here we can ask whether Luke has deliberately invited a second and more subtle reading of the story.

What are some of the signals he provides? There is the puzzling matter of names: Why is the false-prophet/magician named twice, and so oddly? And is there a connection between this double name and the fact that Luke chooses this moment to denominate Saul "as also Paul?" Then there are the parallels: Saul had been an opponent of "The Way" who was blinded by the light and had to be led into Damascus by the hand. Now there is a Jewish opponent who "twists the straight ways of the Lord" and who is blinded by Paul and who needs to have people guide him by the hand. Finally, there are the reversals: the one named "son of Jesus" (*bariēsou*) is called by Paul "son of the devil." Paul is identified as a prophet by being "filled with the Holy Spirit," whereas the "false prophet" is "full of deception and fraud."

It is easy enough to observe these things; making sense of them is another matter. For contemporary readers, a strong psychological reading is a temptation. Perhaps we are to see Saul, at the moment he takes on his new and proper identity as Paul the Apostle, fighting the final battle with the "Jewish false prophet" within him, blinding the hostile magician that is his former self at the moment he assumes his role as "light to the Gentiles" (see 13:47). The problem with such a reading, however, is that Luke gives it little encouragement. In fact the naming of Paul at this juncture may have as little to do with any "new sense of identity" as it does with the implied patronage of Sergius Paulus. It may simply be given now because this is the moment when Paul enters definitively into the world of Hellenistic culture. It is certainly not Luke's practice elsewhere to suggest that the psychological or spiritual progression of his characters was of great interest.

Perhaps better sense of the complex interconnections in this passage may be given by appreciating them not so much as clues to intra-psychic conflicts as to the equally ambiguous battle between spiritual forces and symbols. At this level the reader can with some confidence assert that it is Paul as "Light of the Gentiles" (as we shall soon be told he is, 13:47) who blinds the master of the dark arts Elymas; and it is the Holy Spirit that fills the prophet Paul who casts into confusion the "false prophet" Bar-Jesus.

FOR REFERENCE AND FURTHER STUDY

Best, E. "Acts 13:1-3." *JTS* 11 (1960) 344–348.
Garrett, S. *The Demise of the Devil: Magic and the Demonic in Luke's Writing.* Minneapolis: Fortress Press, 1989, 79–87.

Nock, A. D. "Paul and the Magus." *Beginnings* 5:164-188.
Tannehill, R. *Narrative Unity* 2:159-163.
Yaure, L. "Elymas-Nehelemite-Pethor." *JBL* 79 (1960) 297–314.

25. *Proclamation at Antioch of Pisidia* (13:13-41)

13. When they had set sail from Paphos, those who were with Paul came to Perga of Pamphylia. But John separated from them. He turned back to Jerusalem. 14. They themselves then continued on from Perga, arriving at Antioch of Pisidia. And going into the synagogue on the Sabbath day, they sat down. 15. After the reading of the Law and the Prophets, the rulers of the synagogue sent a message to them: "Brothers, if you have among you a word of exhortation for the people, say it." 16. So Paul stood. Making a gesture with his hand, he said, "Israelites and you who are fearing God, listen! 17. The God of this people Israel chose our fathers. He raised up the people during its sojourn in the land of Egypt. With an uplifted arm he led them out of Egypt. 18. And for a period of some forty years he took care of them in the wilderness. 19. And after destroying seven nations in the land of Canaan, he let them have their land as an inheritance 20. —for about four hundred and fifty years. After these events, he gave them judges until Samuel the prophet. 21. Then they asked for a king. God gave them Saul the son of Kish, a man from the tribe of Benjamin, for a period of forty years. 22. But having removed him, he raised up for them David to be king. To him he also bore witness. He said, 'I have found David son of Jesse to be a man after my heart. He will perform all my desires.' 23. From the seed of this man, according to promise, God brought to Israel Jesus as a savior. 24. John announced before his coming a baptism of repentance to all the people Israel. 25. And as John was finishing his race, he said, 'What do you suppose me to be? I am not he. But look, he is coming after me. I am not worthy to loosen the sandals on his feet.' 26. Brothers, children of the family of Abraham—and those among you who are fearing God— the message concerning this salvation has been sent out to us. 27. For those dwelling in Jerusalem and their leaders did not recognize this man. And by condemning him they fulfilled the sayings of the Prophets that are read every Sabbath. 28. Even though they found no charge worthy of death, they begged Pilate to have him killed. 29. And when they had fulfilled everything written concerning him, they took him down from the tree and placed him in a tomb. 30. But God raised him from the dead. 31. He appeared for many days to those who had come up with him from Galilee to Jerusalem. They are now his witnesses to the people. 32. And we are proclaiming good news to you! This promise made to

the fathers 33. God has fulfilled for us their children, by raising Jesus. So also it stands written in the second Psalm: 'You are my son. I have begotten you today.' 34. And to show that he raised him up from the dead no longer to return to corruption, he spoke this way: 'I will give to you the holy and faithful things said to David.' 35. Therefore he also says in another place, 'You will not give your holy one to see corruption.' 36. For David, having served God's will in his own generation, fell asleep. He was gathered to his fathers, and he saw corruption. 37. But the one whom God has raised has not seen corruption. 38. Let it be known to you, brothers, that through this one forgiveness of sins is being proclaimed! And from all the things which by the Law of Moses you were not able to be made righteous, 39. in this one everyone who believes is made righteous. 40. Beware, then! Don't let that which was said in the Prophets come upon you: 41. 'Look, you who are scornful! Be astonished and disappear! Because I myself am accomplishing a deed in your days, a deed which if someone should tell it to you, you will not believe.' ''

NOTES

13. *Paphos . . . Perga of Pamphylia:* The voyage goes northwest from the western end of Cyprus (see note on Acts 13:6), to the coast of present-day Turkey, known as Pamphylia. A more natural landing would have been Attalia, a port situated on the coast itself, whereas Perga was a river port some twelve miles up the river Cestus (Pliny the Elder, *Natural History* 5:96; Strabo, *Geography* 14, 4, 1-2). Luke's speaking of "those with Paul" (*hoi peri tou Paulou*) gives the impression of a larger band of travellers (including such as John-Mark), and puts the reader's attention squarely on Paul rather than on Barnabas.

    John separated . . . turned back: No reason is given, but his action becomes the bone of contention that causes Barnabas and Paul to split up at a later time (Acts 15:37-39). The two verbs used by Luke suggest something more than a simple return home: *apochōreō* can be used in the sense of "removing oneself from" someone's opinions (Epictetus, *Discourse* 4, 1, 53); the use in LXX Jer 46:5 implies a turning back in fear or cowardice, and in 3 Macc 2:33, it means something like apostasy. It is striking that Luke will use another form of the verb (*apochōrizomai*) for the later separation of Barnabas and Paul.

14. *Antioch of Pisidia:* The translation "of Pisidia" is retained because of long usage, but it reflects the Western Text's genitive *tēs Pisidias* rather than the adjectival form of the preferred text, *Antiochean tēn pisidian* ("The Pisidian Antioch"). The city was actually in the province of Phrygia, near Pisidia, from which it drew the designation. The present sequence is apparently the one referred to by the author of 2 Tim 3:11, where Paul tells his delegate to recall "what befell me at Antioch, at Iconium, and at Lystra, what persecutions I endured."

the synagogue on the Sabbath day: The setting for Paul's discourse deliberately mirrors that of Jesus' first speech in Luke 4:16-30. Luke had Jesus enter the synagogue "according to his custom" (Luke 4:16), and the same phrase is used later for Paul (Acts 17:2), whom Luke shows regularly going to synagogue on the Sabbath (13:42; 16:13; 17:2; 18:4).

15. *reading of the Law and the Prophets:* Luke will have James declare in Acts 15:21 that "Moses is read every Sabbath in the synagogue." It is difficult to reconstruct precisely the shape of synagogue worship for this period. Luke, in fact, is our fullest and one of our earliest datable sources. Some confirming evidence is given in the *Mishnah* for such elements as the recitation of the *Shema* (*m.Ber.* 1:1); the praying of the Benedictions (*m.Ber.* 1:4; 5:2), above all the *Shemone esre* ("Eighteen Benedictions," *m.Ber.* 4:3); the saying of prayers (*tefilloth, m.Ber.* 3:5; 4:1, 7); and the reading of the Law (*m.Ber.* 1:2). A discussion of various issues pertinent to the synagogal lections of Torah and Haftorah (Law and Prophets) is found in *bT Meg.* 23b-32a.

    rulers of the synagogue: For the use of *archisynagogos*, compare Luke 8:41, 49; 13:14; Acts 18:8, 17. Inscriptions confirm the title, usually in the singular. Here, as in Mark 5:23, the plural is used. Luke seems to be thinking of a collegial leadership, like that of the *presbyterion* (Luke 22:66; Acts 22:5; 1 Tim 4:14) or the *gerousia* (Philo, *Embassy to Gaius* 229; 2 Macc 1:40; 11:27).

    word of exhortation: Here as in Heb 13:22, the term *logos tēs paraklēseōs* seems to have something of a technical flavor for a sermon based on the lections. Compare the sequence in 1 Tim 4:13, "Attend to the reading, the exhortation, the teaching." Compare also 1 Pet 5:12. In *Special Laws* 2:62, Philo mentions that after the reading in the synagogue, "one of special experience rises and sets forth what is the best and sure to be profitable and will make the whole of life grow to something better."

16. *you who are fearing God:* For the problems in deciding who might be meant by the designation "God fearers" (*hoi phoboumenoi ton theon*), see the note on Acts 10:2. In the present discourse, the epithet is repeated in 13:26. In both cases, it could theoretically be in apposition to "Israelites," but the mention of "devout proselytes" in 13:43 suggests that Luke intended the reader to see the "God fearers" as a group included in the worship but not in the fullest sense of the term "Israelites."

17. *God of this people Israel:* Following the greeting, "Israelites," the name "Israel" is repeated three times in Paul's sermon (13:17, 23, 24), as it was also in Stephen's speech (7:23, 37, 42). The theme of Israel as "the people of God" is central to Luke's literary and religious purposes (Luke 1:16, 54, 68, 80; 2:25, 32, 34; 4:25-27; 7:9, 22, 30; 24:21; Acts 1:6; 2:36; 4:10, 27; 5:21, 31; 9:15; 10:36; 28:20). For the epithet, "God of Israel," see LXX Ps 40:13; 58:5; 67:8, 35; 68:6; 71:18; also Luke 1:68; Matt 15:31.

    chose our fathers: In contrast to the Stephen speech, this discourse moves rapidly over the Abraham story with this brief summary; for the "election" (*eklegomai*) of the people, see e.g., Deut 4:37; 7:7; 10:15; LXX Ps 32:12. The expression "our fathers" (more inclusively, "our ancestors"), is repeated in

13:32, 36, as it is frequently also in Stephen's speech (see Acts 7:2, 11, 12, etc.).

raised up the people: The verb *hypsoō* is used for God's saving intervention in LXX Ps 36:34, and in Ps 117:16: "the right hand of the Lord has exalted (*hypsōsen*) me." Luke uses it in the "reversal" statements of 1:52; 14:11; 18:14. In Acts, he employs it twice for the resurrection of Jesus (Acts 2:33; 5:31). For the "sojourn" (*paroikia*) of the people in Egypt, compare Acts 7:6, 29.

with an uplifted arm: The expression *brachion hypsēlos* is used as the image for God's power in LXX Exod 6:1, 6; 32:11; Deut 3:24; 4:34; 6:21; 7:8; 9:26; Ps 135:12; Isa 26:11; Jer 39:17; Ezek 20:34, as well as in Luke 1:51. After the extensive attention given to Moses in Stephen's speech, it is striking that he is passed over entirely here; this only sharpens our perception of the literary role he played in that earlier discourse.

18. *took care of them in the wilderness:* For the forty years in the wilderness, compare 7:36, which does not qualify the period with *hōs* ("about/some"). A textual variant that is almost equally well attested as the one translated (*etrophophorēsen*), reads "he put up with/bore with them" (*etropophorēsen*). Since an allusion to LXX Deut 1:31 seems intended, checking that passage would seem to settle the issue; unfortunately, the LXX *mss* have the same variation in readings. In the present context, the emphasis on the way God had been gracious to Israel seems to make more likely the version of the text translated.

19. *seven nations in the land of Canaan:* The nations are listed in Deut 7:1 (see also Gen 10:15-20). In his *Antiquities of the Jews* 5:88, Josephus uses a cognate verb (*diaireō* rather than Luke's *kathaireō*) in stating, "thus did Joshua divide six of the nations," noting that he had taken care of the seventh earlier; Pseudo-Philo's *Biblical Antiquities* 20:9 speaks of getting rid of the "thirty-nine kings." For the "inheritance" of the land, see especially Josh 14:1.

20. *for about four hundred and fifty years:* As in Stephen's speech, apparently meticulous attention is paid to periods of time (13:18, 20, 21; see 7:6, 23, 30, 36, 42), probably in order to lend the speeches historical verisimilitude. The placement of this particular temporal marker (particularly in the Alexandrian Text tradition, which is here translated) is extremely awkward, a fact indicated by the use of dashes, and makes an already uncertain chronology (compare 1 Kgs 6:1 and Josephus, *Antiquities of the Jews* 8:61) even more obscure.

judges until Samuel the prophet: The clause recalls the recital of Nathan to David, "from the time that I appointed judges over my people Israel" in 2 Sam 7:11. The charismatic leaders of the people who rallied against danger in the time before the monarchy are designated "judges" (*kritai*) in Judg 2:16, 18, 19; Ruth 1:1; 1 Chr 17:10. Samuel is designated "prophet to the Lord" in 1 Sam 3:20-21. Luke's periodization here recalls Acts 3:24: "indeed all the prophets who spoke from Samuel onwards also announced these days."

21. *Saul the son of Kish:* The story of Saul's selection is recounted in 1 Sam 10:21-24; 11:15. Luke's text reflects no negative judgment on the request for a king, although that anti-monarchical tendency is also embodied in texts such as 1 Sam 12:1-25. As we have seen in the *Commentary on the Gospel of Luke*, our

author is also comfortable with the notion of Jesus as King. How long Saul actually reigned is difficult to reconstruct from the sources: 1 Sam 13:1, which gives two years, is fragmentary and unreliable. Depending on whether one reads the Greek or Latin of Josephus, *Antiquities of the Jews* 6:378, that historian gives either forty years (thus agreeing with Luke) or twenty years (as he does also in 10:143), thus agreeing with later Jewish traditions.

22. *raised up David for them:* The rejection of Saul from the monarchy is formally stated in 1 Sam 15:23; 16:1. The choice of the verb *egeirō* ("raise up") for David's election is interesting because of its application to the resurrection of Jesus in verse 30 (as well as Luke 9:22; 24:6; Acts 3:15; 4:10; 5:30; 10:40). A typological connection is already being forged.

    I have found David: This is a mixed citation from LXX Ps 88:21 ("I have found David [*heuron Daueid*] my servant"), and 1 Sam 13:14 ("the Lord seeks a man after his heart [*kata tēn kardian autou*]"), with the "son of Jesse" added for clarity. The passages are cited in the same combination also by 1 *Clement* 18:1. In the light of the ambiguous *ta hostia daueid ta pista* in 13:34, it is perhaps significant that the passage in Ps 88:21 is preceded by: "Then you spoke on the mountain to your holy ones (*tois hosiois sou*) and you said, 'I have given timely help to the powerful, I have lifted up (*hypsōsa*) an elect one (*eklekton*) from my people. I have found David my servant, with a holy oil (*elaiǭ hagiǭ*) I have anointed him (*echrisa auton*).'" The cluster of terms provides opportunities for the kind of midrashic connections Luke will draw. The fragmentary 4QFlor from Qumran shows that just such passages concerning David were interpreted messianically (see *4QFlor* 1:10). For the use of *martureō* in contexts of God's giving witness, see 10:43 and 15:8.

    perform all my desires: Literally, "he will do all my wills (*thelemata*)." The line comes from Isa 44:28, in reference to Cyrus. In this one epithet, therefore, either Luke or the tradition before him has pulled together three Septuagintal texts.

23. *the seed of this man:* In Greek the pronoun *houtos* ("this man") is in the emphatic first position, emphasizing the connection between David and Jesus. The present translation shifts the order of the phrases in the Greek sentence. In particular, it moves *kat' epangelian* ("according to promise") closer to the phrase it is meant to modify. The reference, of course, is to the promise made to David in 2 Sam 7:12, "I will raise up (*anastēsō*) your offspring (*sperma* = seed) after you, who shall come forth from your body, and I will establish his kingdom forever" (see also 2 Sam 22:51; LXX Ps 17:50). The promise will be understood in exactly the way Luke read the promise of Deut 18:15-18 about God's "raising up a prophet," that is, as referring to the resurrection. The "raising up of your descendant" therefore means for Luke precisely the resurrection of Jesus.

    brought . . . as savior: Two textual variants affect the interpretation of this verse. Some *mss* have "raised" (*ēgeiren*) rather than "led/brought" (*ēgagen*), possibly under the influence of 2 Sam 7:12 ("I will raise up"), as well as the use of *egeirō* for the resurrection of Jesus in 13:30. The text translated here gives the best attested and harder reading. Some *mss* also have "salvation" (*sōtēria*) rather than "savior" (*sōtēr*), but in the light of Luke 2:11 and Acts 5:31, *sōtēr* is probably correct, especially since *sōtēria* can be explained as an influence from 13:26.

24. *John announced before his coming:* The intricate relationship between John and Jesus continues to be worked out (see Luke 1:17; 3:2-20; 5:33; 7:18-33; 9:7-9, 19; 11:1; 16:16; 20:4-6; Acts 1:5, 22; 10:37; 11:16), and consistent with Luke's overall presentation, John's ministry is clearly distinguished from and subordinated to that of Jesus. Note again the focus on "Israel" as the intended recipient of John's message (compare Luke 3:17, 23).

25. *finishing his race:* The term *dromos* refers first to the athletic competition and then to the place where it is held ("the course"). It easily adapts itself to being a metaphor for any effort (Epictetus, *Discourse* 3, 14, 11-14; Qoh 9:11; Wis 17:19; Jer 8:6; 2 Macc 14:45; compare Acts 20:24; 2 Tim 4:7). The sequence of clauses here once more tends to reinforce the separation of John's ministry from that of Jesus, just as in the redaction of Luke 3:18-21.

    what do you suppose me to be: Depending on how one construes the particle *ti* (or in some *mss tina*), either as the interrogative or as equivalent to a relative pronoun, John's statement could also be read as a single declarative sentence in which *ouk ego eimi* governs the present clause: "I am not whom you suppose me to be." In either case, the sense is the same. As in Acts 1:5, where a saying of John is transferred to Jesus (see Luke 3:16), we have here again a *logion* from the Baptist in a slightly altered form. The statement about loosing sandals is substantially the same, with only slightly different diction. The disclaimer, however, is far more emphatic than in Luke 3:16-17, bearing in fact some resemblance to John 1:19-27.

26. *message concerning this salvation:* Literally, "word (*logos*) of this salvation (*sōtēria*)." The use of the demonstrative "this" helps explain why some scribes wanted to read *sōtēria* rather than *sōtēr* in 13:23. As so often in Acts, the *mss* tradition is also split between reading "to us" (*hēmin*) and "to you" (*hymin*). In the present case, the reading "to you" might make more sense, in light of the deliberate contrast drawn between this audience and "those dwelling in Jerusalem." A similar sort of construction is used at the close of Acts: "This salvation from God (*sōtēria tou theou*) has been sent (*apestalē*) to the Gentiles" (Acts 28:28).

27. *did not recognize this man:* As in earlier kerygmatic statements, the sentence is long and the syntax convoluted (see 2:22-24; 3:13-17). The sentence is built on the simple statement "they fulfilled the sayings of the prophets," with two dependent circumstantial participial clauses (*agnoēsantes* and *krinantes*). In the present translation, the first of these dependent clauses is made into an independent sentence. For the theme of the non-recognition of Jesus in the time of the prophet's first visitation, see the notes on 3:17; 7:13, 25. Here as in 3:17, the leaders are included with the populace both in rejection and in ignorance.

fulfilled the sayings of the Prophets: The noun *phōnē* (literally ''voice'') has here the sense of ''saying/utterance'' (see Plutarch, *Letter to Apollonius* 9 [*Mor.* 106B]; *On the Fortune of Alexander* 9 [*Mor.* 330E]). Luke here has Paul touch on the central theme of the fulfillment of prophecy, especially in connection with the death of the prophet Jesus (Luke 24:26-27, 45-46; Acts 4:25-28). The phrase, ''read every Sabbath'' anticipates the statement by James in 15:21. The point, of course, is ironic: they had listened to the prophets' utterances every week, yet did not ''recognize'' the one of whom the prophets had spoken; thus in rejecting him they fulfilled the very texts foretelling his rejection! The Western Text is corrupt at this point, but seems to have attached the failure to understand directly to the reading of the scriptures themselves: *mē sunientes tas graphas tōn prophetōn* (''not understanding the writings of the prophets'').

28. *found no charge:* The language of ''finding'' (*heuriskō*) and ''worthy of death'' (*thanatos*) echoes precisely that used three times by Pilate in Luke's passion account, except that the Gospel uses *aition* rather than *aitia* (see Luke 23:4, 14, 22). By just such linkages does Luke join the parts of his story. Similarly, the use of *ētēsanto* (''begged/asked for''), recalls the verb *aiteomai* used in the Lukan trial scene (Luke 23:23-25) and in Acts 3:14.

29. *fulfilled everything written:* As in v. 27, an explicit emphasis on the motif of the fulfillment of prophecy. In this case the formulation is remarkably close to that put in the mouth of Jesus in Luke 22:37: *touto to gegrammenon dei telesthēnai en emoi*, compared to this passage's *etelēsan panta peri autou gegrammena*.
    they took him down from the tree: Unless we consider these third person plural verbs as equivalent to the passive (as in Luke 12:20), the same ones who asked for Jesus' death are here the ones who take him down and bury him (in contrast to Luke 23:52). For ''the tree'' (*xylon*), see the note on Acts 5:30.

31. *he appeared for many days:* The statement concerning the resurrection itself in v. 30 is extremely short, since this is the part of the kerygma that will now be expanded. Luke places the focus here on the post-resurrection appearances. As in Acts 1:3, the length of time during which appearances occurred is noted; as in 10:41, the relationship of the witnesses to the whole people is made explicit; as in 1:13-22, the shared origins of Jesus and the witnesses in Galilee is made clear.

33. *has fulfilled for us their children:* For the third time in this short section, the theme of the fulfillment of prophecy is struck (see 13:27, 29), now with specific reference to the promise (*epangelia*) made to ''the fathers'' (*hoi pateres* = ''the ancestors''; see 3:13, 25; 5:30; 7:2, 11, 12, 14, 15, 19, 32, 38, 39, 44, 45, 51, 52), the election of whom opened this discourse (13:17). In this case, the promise seems to be the one made to David, since that is the one which is now elaborated (13:23). This fulfilled promise is the content of the ''good news'' (*euangelizomai*) proclaimed by Paul. It is possible to read the pronoun *hēmin* (''to us'') as going with the next clause, ''by raising Jesus for us.''

    I have begotten you today: This is a direct citation from LXX Ps 2:7. The Psalm lacks a title, and there is some evidence that in the patristic period Psalms one and two were joined. This may account for the textual confusion in the introduction: some texts have "in the first psalm," others, "in the second psalm," and still others, "in the psalms." Luke used the first portion of this psalm already in his *pesher*-style midrash of 4:25-26. Some Western Tradition *mss* also have it in the declaration made to Jesus at the baptism (Luke 3:22). That the psalm figured elsewhere in early Christian midrash is demonstrated by Heb 1:5; 5:5.

34. *and to show that he raised him up:* The translation supplies "and to show," in order to make clear the function of the noun clause beginning with *hoti*, which appears here in Greek before the main and governing clause, "he spoke this way" (*houtos eirēken*). The argument concerning who did and who did not "see corruption," that is, die and stay dead, is similar to that in Peter's Pentecost sermon (Acts 2:31).

  the holy and faithful things said to David: The citation is from LXX Isa 55:3. The precise import of the passage is much disputed, at least in part because the LXX diverges substantially from the Hebrew's "I will make with you an everlasting covenant, my steadfast, sure love for David" (RSV). The LXX has translated the Hebrew *ḥesed* ("mercy") by "holy." This is unusual only because the LXX's *hosios* ordinarily translates *ḥasid* ("holy one"), as in Deut 33:8; Ps 4:3; 29:4; 85:2; 131:9. It is noteworthy, however, that the term *hosios* links three of the citations in this sequence. In addition to the *dōsō* ("I will give") and the *ton hosion sou* ("your holy one") in the next citation from LXX Ps 15:10, there is also the occurrence in LXX Ps 17:26 (paralleled by 2 Sam 22:26) of "with the holy (*meta hosiou*) you will show yourself holy (*hosiothēsei*)." The sense of the citation in the present argument is that what God promised David will be given to the present generation. In that light, the translation of *hosia* as "divine oracles," or as in this translation, "the holy things said" is most appropriate (compare Wis 6:10; Josephus, *Antiquities of the Jews* 8:115).

35. *your holy one to see corruption:* The citation from LXX Ps 15:10 (used also in Acts 2:27) is introduced by the strong connective *dioti:* the oracle makes clear that "not seeing corruption" is the content of what was promised David concerning "his seed" (according to Luke's reading). All that remains now is to properly identify the one to whom the oracle applies.

36. *for David . . . saw corruption:* As in Peter's speech at Pentecost (2:29), the function of this statement is to show that David could not have been the one intended by the promise, since he in fact died and saw corruption. Here the argument is more extended, with four separate statements: a) he served God in his own generation (but no other); b) he fell asleep; c) he was gathered to his fathers; d) he saw corruption. Luke's summary echoes LXX 1 Kgs 2:10.

38. *forgiveness of sins:* The phrase "let it be known" (*gnōston estō*) is used here as in Acts 2:14 and 4:10. The forgiveness of sins was the message to be spread by Jesus' followers, according to the commissioning in Luke 24:47, and was carried out in Acts 2:38; 5:31; 10:43. The *dia toutou* ("through this one"), like the *en toutǫ* ("in this one") of the next verse, refers to Jesus, "the one whom God raised up" (13:37).

39. *everyone who believes is made righteous:* Here is as close an approximation to Paul's distinctive contrast between faith-righteousness and Torah-righteousness (Rom 2:13; 3:24-26; 4:2, 5; 5:1, 9; 8:30, 33; 1 Cor 8:11; Gal 2:16; 3:11, 24) as we will find in Acts. The contrast Luke draws is between what was possible "by the Law" and what is now possible "by this one," namely the resurrected Jesus. The language of "justifying/declaring righteous" (*dikaioō*) derives from the forensic context of ancient Israel (see LXX Exod 23:7; Deut 25:1; 1 Sam 12:7; 2 Sam 15:4; Isa 5:23) and becomes a central concept for the relationship between God and humans (LXX Ps 18:9; 50:4; 81:3; 142:2; Sir 7:5; 10:29; 18:2; Isa 45:26; 50:8; 53:11). Here the concept of righteousness is directly connected to that of having one's sins forgiven. It is not certain whether the phrase "from all the things which by the Law of Moses" is intended to mean that a) the Law offered forgiveness and righteousness in some cases but not all; or, b) the Law was insufficient as a whole with regard to forgiveness and righteousness. The phrase "everyone who believes" echoes earlier passages (2:44; 10:43) and is also found in Paul (Rom 3:22; 10:4, 11).

40. *said in the Prophets:* As in the citation from Amos in Acts 7:42 ("just as it is written in the book of the prophets"), the reference here is to the collection of the twelve minor prophets, with whom Habakkuk was included. The form of Paul's warning is literally, "Beware lest there come upon," with "you" being supplied by the context (and, in fact, by some *mss* as well).

41. *look, you who are scornful:* This is a citation from the LXX of Habakkuk 1:5, with some small modifications: a) the LXX has an extra "look" (*epiblepsete*) which Luke omits, and a cognate *thaumasia* to go with the verb *thaumazete*; b) Luke has *hoti* rather than the LXX's *dioti*, and reverses the order of *ergazomai* and *egō*; c) Luke adds an extra *ergon* ("work") for emphasis. The original context of Habakkuk made this warning refer to the invasion by the Chaldeans. The operative phrase for Luke seems to be "you will not believe" (with the emphatic *ou mē*), which functions in Luke's narrative context as a self-fulfilling prophecy. The Western Text adds to the speech either the singular *esigēsen* ("he fell silent"), or the plural *esigēsan* ("they fell silent"), the last of which would conform to the pattern of Luke 9:36; 20:26.

INTERPRETATION

The first thing that draws our attention in this passage is the narrative sequence. As we have seen repeatedly, Luke in various ways shows continuity between his characters. He describes them in terms of prophetic imagery. He has the trial of Stephen echo the trial of Jesus, and Peter's escape from prison echo Jesus' resurrection. By these means Luke points to the main character in his story, the God who unseen but powerful works in similar ways through these disparate characters. For the human character who, next to Jesus, occupies the largest part of his two-volume work, we might expect an even more emphatic pattern of imitation.

When Jesus began his ministry, he was baptized and received the Holy Spirit (Luke 3:21-22). Then he went into the wilderness where he confronted the demonic powers and bested them (4:1-13). Then he preached his inaugural sermon to his countrymen in a synagogue on the Sabbath, showing how the Scripture he had read in the assembly was fulfilled in him (4:14-21). After an initial favorable response (4:22), Jesus uttered prophecies that enraged his countrymen and led them to take him out of the city and try to kill him (4:23-30).

Luke now has Paul follow, *mutatis mutandis,* the same pattern. He is commissioned by the Spirit in Antioch (13:1-3), then confronts and bests the demonic powers presented by the *magos* Bar-Jesus/Elymas (13:4-12). Then he goes into a synagogue on the Sabbath, where he reads from the Law and Prophets, then preaches a sermon showing how the Scripture has been fulfilled in the resurrection of Jesus (13:13-41). Finally, there will be the same experience of rejection by Paul's countrymen that Jesus experienced from his (13:42-52). Luke obviously intends by this sort of narrative *mimesis* to establish the continuity between the prophetic ministry of Jesus and the one who, we now learn, is the one who is to be "light to the Gentiles" (13:47; see Luke 2:32).

The narrator thereby alerts us to the proper manner in which to hear Paul's sermon. We do not expect by this time a *précis* of Pauline theology, but recognize that in his speeches Luke stretches over the discourses of several speakers a single midrashic argument concerning the messianic movement and its crucified and raised founder. Paul's speech looks in equal parts like the discourses of Peter and the speech of Stephen. In fact, we are even somewhat startled at the conclusion of the speech with its Pauline coloration, until we recognize Luke's concern for *prosōpopoiia.* The one who speaks at the end about righteousness through faith in contrast to righteousness through the Law may not be Paul, but is, after all, not a bad simulacrum.

The main point of the discourse, however, is to work once more through the history of Israel from the perspective of belief in the "prophet whom God raised up," this time with special attention to the Messiah's Davidic connection. In contrast to Stephen's speech, which lingered over Abraham, Joseph, and especially Moses (Acts 7:2-44), with only a rapid transition from the wilderness to Solomon (7:45-47), this discourse ignores the patriarchs altogether and spends only four lines getting from the Exodus to Samuel (13:17-20). When the kingship of Saul and David is reached, however, the speech lingers there, for it is precisely the way in which the promises made to David are fulfilled in Jesus that forms the point of Paul's preaching (13:21-41). This is, in fact, Paul's first and last

missionary sermon reported with any fullness, and it is all the more striking that it focuses on this most traditional, Davidic, understanding of the
Messiah.

Although in many respects this discourse resembles that made by Peter
at Pentecost (2:14-36), it gives even shared elements a distinctive turn.
First, the kerygmatic statement concerning Jesus' rejection and vindication (13:27-31) emphasizes the shared responsibility of both leaders and
"dwellers in Jerusalem." The purpose of this is to open the way to a "second chance" for these dwellers in the Diaspora. Second, the rejection
of Jesus is directly connected to the ironic fulfillment of the prophecies;
by not "recognizing this man," and by "judging" him (13:27), the Jerusalem Jews inadvertently failed to recognize their own role in the prophetic utterances. Indeed, the note of prophetic fulfillment is struck three
times in rapid succession (13:27, 29, 32-33). Both of these touches help
set up the next scene, in which the people will fail to "recognize" Jesus
in the preaching of Paul, and will in their turn ironically fulfill the prophecies of rejection (13:44-52).

Paul's sermon is like that preached at Pentecost by Peter also in the
attention it gives to a midrashic argument concerning Jesus' resurrection.
In effect this argument serves to bring together the two points noted
above: the "facts" of the kerygma (in this case, that God raised up Jesus)
and the fulfillment of prophecy. As in Peter's sermon, a key role is played
by the Davidic Psalm 15:10, "you will not give your holy one to see corruption" (13:35; compare Acts 2:25-28). At the simplest level, Paul argues that this text must apply to someone other than David, since David,
in fact, died and saw corruption (13:36-37). Underpinning this is a more
complex argument concerning the referentiality of the biblical promises.
Does Scripture itself legitimate the reader's looking to another after David
who would be the recipient of the promises?

The details of the argument are discussed in the notes, but the basic
mode of argumentation here is the practice of comparing the use of the
same words in different passages in order to discover their full or precise
meaning (later known as *gezerah shewa* in the *middoth* of rabbinic midrash).
By this logic of word-association—almost completely obscured by any English translation—the "holy and faithful things" declared to David (13:34)
and the "holy one who will not see corruption" are brought into close
and mutually interpretive connection. As a result, Paul is able to state
that the promise concerning David's "seed" is really fulfilled in the Messiah Jesus, and Scripture itself declares that this fulfillment was intended
"for you" (13:34).

The argument would obviously not be convincing for anyone who was
not already committed to its governing premise, namely that Jesus was
the resurrected one "begotten this day" (13:33), but then the speech is

not really a report of what Paul said to the Jews at Antioch, but a reflection on the first mission by the apologetic historian Luke. We will therefore not be surprised to find in the next scene Luke's stereotypical pattern of acceptance and rejection, both responses governed less by the actual content of the speech than by the demands of the narrative drama.

FOR REFERENCE AND FURTHER STUDY

Bowker, J. W. "Speeches in Acts: A Study in Proem and Yelammedenu Form." *NTS* 14 (1967-1968) 96-111.
Buss, M. F.-J. *Die Missionspredigt des Paulus im Pisidischen Antiochien.* Stuttgart: Katholisches Bibelwerk, 1980.
Dupont, J. "*TA HOSTIA DAUEID TA PISTA* (Acts 13, 34=Isaïe 55, 3)." *Etudes sur les Actes des Apôtres.* Lectio Divina 45. Paris: Editions du Cerf, 1967, 337-359.
Epp, E. J. "The 'Ignorance Motif' in Acts and Anti-Judaic Tendencies in Codex Bezae." *HTR* 55 (1962) 51-62.
Gordon, R. P. "Targumic Parallels to Acts xiii, 18 and Didache xiv, 13." *NovT* 16 (1974) 285-289.
Kilgallen, J. J. "Acts 13, 38-39: Culmination of Paul's Speech in Pisidia." *Bib* 69 (1988) 480-506.
Menoud, Ph.-H. "Justification by Faith according to the Book of Acts." *Jesus Christ and the Faith.* Trans. E. M. Paul. Pittsburgh: Pickwick Press, 1978, 202-227.
O'Toole, R. F. "Christ's Resurrection in Acts 13:13-52." *Bib* 60 (1979) 361-372.
Schmitt, A. "Ps 16, 8-11 als Zeugnis der Auferstehung in der Apg." *BZ* n.s. 17 (1973) 229-248.

26. *Acceptance and Rejection in the Diaspora* (13:42-52)

42. As they were on the way out, they were asked to speak to them on these matters on the next Sabbath. 43. And when the assembly disbanded, many of the Jews and of the devout proselytes followed Paul and Barnabas, who continued speaking to them, urging them to remain faithful to God's gift. 44. On the next Sabbath, nearly the whole city gathered to hear the word of the Lord. 45. But when the Jews saw the crowd, they were filled with jealousy. They contradicted the things being said by Paul. They uttered slanders. 46. Paul and Barnabas responded boldly. They said, "It was necessary to speak the word of God to you first. Since you are rejecting it and are deciding that you are not fit for eternal life, look, we are turning to the Gentiles! 47. For the Lord has so directed us: 'I have placed you to be a light for the nations, so you

can bring salvation to the end of the earth.' " 48. The Gentiles who were listening began to rejoice. They glorified the word of the Lord. And those destined for eternal life believed. 49. And the word of the Lord was being spread throughout the whole region. 50. But the Jews incited the pious and well-established women as well as the leading men of the city. They stirred up a persecution against Paul and Barnabas. They drove them across their borders. 51. So they shook off the dust from their feet against them! They went to Iconium. 52. And the disciples continued to be filled with joy and the Holy Spirit.

Notes

43. *Jews and of the devout proselytes:* Precisely this sort of designation in Acts creates difficulties in sorting through the historical facts concerning Proselytes and "God-Fearers" in first-century Judaism (see the note on 10:2, and above on 13:16). In this case, one of the terms usually used to describe "God fearers" (*seboumenoi*) is attached to *proselytoi* ("proselytes"), in distinction from those Luke calls, simply, "Jews." Absent total clarity about the technicalities—if they existed at all—Luke obviously wants the reader to perceive, in the environs of the synagogue, a fringe element of interested Gentiles among whom the messianic message will find its most eager listeners. The verse is considerably expanded by Codex D.

    faithful to God's gift: Literally, "to remain (*prosmenein* [see 11:23]) in the grace of God." The "grace" (*charis*) in this case must refer to the reception of Paul's message about the fulfillment of the promise through the resurrection of Jesus. For Luke's use of *charis*, compare Luke 1:30; 2:40, 52; 4:22; Acts 2:47; 4:33; 11:33.

44. *nearly the whole city:* Such mass responses to excitement are a common feature in Hellenistic Novels (see Chariton of Aphrodisias, *Chaereas and Callirhoe* 3, 4, 4-18; Heliodorus, *The Ethiopians* 4, 19, 5), as well as the apocryphal Acts of the Apostles (see *Acts of John* 31; *Acts of Peter* 3). In the present case, it is this popular response to the apostles that sets up the jealous reaction of the Jews.

45. *filled with jealousy:* The same motive is attributed to the Sanhedrin in its resistance to Peter and John (5:17). For the logic of the Hellenistic *topos* on envy, see the note on Acts 5:17 and 7:9. The theme is continued by *1 Clement* 5:4-5, which makes jealousy the source of the suffering both for Peter and Paul.

    they uttered slanders: For a discussion of the range of meanings in *blasphēmein*, see the note on Luke 12:10. In this case, the "hard words/slander" is directed against the "things being said by Paul," and is roughly synonymous with the "contradicting" by the Jewish opposition. Since Paul's words have to do with the message from God about Jesus, and are considered by Luke to be, in fact, "The word of the Lord," slander here comes very close to the properly religious sense of "blasphemy" (compare Luke 5:21; 22:65; 23:39).

It is noteworthy that in a passage which so vividly echoes Luke's portrayal of Jesus, Paul should receive the same response that Jesus had.

46. *responded boldly:* Luke uses the verb *parrēsiazomai* as he had in Acts 9:27-28. For "boldness in speech" as a characteristic of the philosopher, and as part of Luke's prophetic coloration of his characters, see the note on Acts 4:13.

necessary to speak . . . to you first: This is the only time Luke uses a construction with *anankaion* ("necessary") rather than his customary *dei*, but the meaning is the same: the necessity is one dictated by the divine plan that is being worked out in the story. The progression of proclamation must follow this plan, with the people of the promise the first recipients (see esp. Acts 3:26). The reason, in terms of Luke's literary and religious purposes, is to show that God is faithful to the promises made to the ancestors. The same pattern of "Jew first, then Gentile" is found in Rom 1:16; 2:9-10.

since you are rejecting it: The conjunction *epeidē* indicates a clear causal relationship between the two events: Paul turns to the Gentiles *because* of this Jewish rejection. Luke uses the same verb (*apōtheomai*) as in the two-fold rejection of the prophet Moses (Acts 7:27, 39). In the LXX, the verb occurs at moments of solemn rejection either from the side of God or of the people (see e.g., 1 Sam 12:22; Ps 61:5; 76:8; 77:60, 67). It is also the term used by Paul himself in Romans when he asks, "has God rejected his people?" (Rom 11:1-2).

fit for eternal life: The translation of *krinein* as "deciding" may be somewhat weak, especially in the light of its use above in 13:27. A more literal rendering would be, "since you judge yourselves unworthy of eternal life." Does Luke intend an ironic turn, in which those who "judged" Jesus to death without worthy cause are now "judging" themselves unworthy of life? The expression "eternal life," in any case, is used by Luke only in the question from the lawyer (Luke 10:25), in the passage about the rich ruler (Luke 18:18, 30), and twice in the present passage (see "destined for eternal life" in 13:48, below). For the expression, see the note on Luke 10:25.

we are turning to the Gentiles: As always, it is difficult to decide whether in a particular passage *ta ethnē* should be rendered more collectively as "the nations," or distributively as "the Gentiles." Since the focus in the present statement is on those who will be converted, "Gentiles" has been chosen. In the citation from Isaiah to follow, "nations" seems more appropriate. Paul's declaration is the first of three such "turnings" in the narrative of Acts. After this one and the second in Corinth (18:6), he nevertheless continues to work among the Jews (14:1; 19:8). The third such statement, however, closes the narrative (28:28).

47. *Lord has so directed us:* The introduction to the citation is striking on two counts: a) the use of *entellomai* echoes the command of Jesus to the Twelve before his ascension (Acts 1:2), so that *this* commandment "from the Lord" appears to be continuous with Jesus' command to be witnesses "to the end of the earth" (Acts 1:8); b) the citation gives a scriptural form to the commandment of the risen Lord to Paul which is reported in Acts 22:26 this way, "He said

to me, 'Depart, for I will send you far away to the Gentiles,' " and expressed in 26:18 in terms of opening the Gentiles' eyes, "that they may turn from darkness to light, and from the power of Satan to God."

light for the nations: On the problem of translating *ta ethnē*, see the note on 13:46 above. This citation from the Servant Song in Isaiah 49:6 is close but not exact. The LXX has "Behold, I have placed you as a covenant of the people (*genous*), as a light for the nations, for the purpose of your being salvation to the end of the earth." The full citation brings together the themes initiated by Simeon's prophecy in Luke 2:32 and continued by Jesus' programmatic prophecy in Acts 1:8: Paul is now explicitly identified as the "light for the nations" who will carry his witness *heōs eschatou tēs gēs*. Note as well that the citation brings Paul's mission into direct continuity with the "salvation" (*sōtēria*) that was the theme of his sermon (13:26). The theme of "salvation" will be elaborated throughout the following section. Finally, in its original context the Isaiah citation has before it the statement that "my servant" (*pais*) has "stood up" (*stēsai*) the tribes of Jacob and has "turned back" (*epistrepsai*) the *diaspora tou Israel* ("Diaspora of Israel"). This matches the threefold movement in Acts from a) the restoration of the tribes in Jerusalem; b) the preaching to the Diaspora; c) the turn to the Gentiles, and provides it all with scriptural backing.

48. *Gentiles . . . began to rejoice:* As earlier Luke had distinguished between leaders and ordinary people in the divided Israel, he now distinguishes between the responses of Jew and Gentile. The response of "joy" signals acceptance of God's visitation (Luke 1:14, 28; 2:10; 6:23; 8:13; 10:17, 20; 13:17; 15:5, 11, 32; 19:6, 37; 24:41, 52; Acts 5:41; 8:8, 39; 11:23), as does the response of "glorifying" (Luke 2:20; 5:25-26; 7:16; 13:13; 17:5; 18:43; 23:47; Acts 4:21; 11:18).

destined for eternal life believed: The verb *tassō* ("set/appoint") in the perfect passive participle takes on the sense of "destined/allotted." The language reminds us of that used at Qumran for those slotted for everlasting light or darkness, life or death (see CD 3:20; 1QS 3:18–4:1). The term "eternal life" (*zōē aiōnios*) picks up from 13:46, the only other time it occurs in Acts. The Jews "rejected the word of God" and judged themselves "unfit for eternal life"; in contrast, the Gentiles show that they are destined for eternal life by "glorifying" this same "word of the Lord."

49. *word of the Lord was being spread:* Literally, "was being carried (*diephereto*)." This is the typical Lukan notice of the mission's success in a region (compare Acts 2:41, 47; 6:7; 9:31; 11:24; 12:24).

50. *the Jews incited:* As shown in the reaction of the Sanhedrin to the apostles, the vice of envy (5:17) turns to murderous rage (5:33); so here the response of jealousy (13:45) turns to physical coercion and violence. There is undoubtedly a negative suggestion of the underhanded and surreptitious in this "egging on" (*parōtrynein*) of others to do mischief (compare Luke 20:20; Acts 6:11).

pious and well-established women: The inconsistency of Luke's usage prevents us from deciding whether the adjective *seboumenai* is meant to place these women among those who had converted to Judaism (see Josephus, *Jewish War* 2:560-561), or simply to indicate their active religious involvement. The adjective *euschēmenos*, in turn, can refer to physical comeliness, or decorum, or (as here), "honorable/noble" (Josephus, *Life* 32). The leading role often played by women in the Diaspora synagogue is confirmed by epigraphic evidence. For the "leading men" of a city, see Josephus, *Life* 9.

stirred up a persecution: Codex D adds "a great tribulation (*thlipsis*)" before the word "persecution." This is the second (see 8:1) and last use of the term *diōgmos* ("persecution") in Acts, and it is directed not against the new converts but against Paul and Barnabas. Like Jesus in Luke 4:29, they are taken out of the city—indeed out of the entire district (literally, "from their borders," *horiōn*).

52. *filled with joy and the Holy Spirit:* Luke is concerned to show how the word spread, but also how local communities prospered (see 14:21-23). The code words used here by Luke indicate that this foundation is an authentic realization of the Church: it is filled with joy (see note on 13:48 above), and of "the Holy Spirit" (2:4; 4:31; 8:17; 9:31; 10:44; 13:2).

INTERPRETATION

Although the necessity of breaking material into manageable portions has dictated the splitting of Paul's sermon in Antioch of Pisidia from its denouement, the present passage should in fact be read in connection with the speech that preceded it. The combination of the two shows us one of Luke's favorite literary devices, the arrangement of speech and narrative in a pattern of self-fulfilling prophecy.

We have already observed how Luke has patterned the beginning of Paul's ministry on the beginning of Jesus' ministry in Galilee, with its baptism in the Spirit, conflict with demonic forces, and initial proclamation. That narrative mimesis continues. There had initially been a positive response to Jesus' proclamation in Nazareth (Luke 4:22). But when Jesus uttered the provocative words about the rejection of the prophet in his own homeland, and compared himself to the prophets Elijah and Elisha who had extended God's visitation outside Israel (4:23-27), the townspeople were enraged and tried to kill him (4:28-29). Likewise there is an initially positive response to Paul's preaching in Antioch of Pisidia: Jews and Godfearers alike ask to hear him again, and great crowds attend the next synagogue service (Acts 13:42-44). But at the sight of this success among the larger population, the Jews are envious and attack Paul (13:44-45). They have, in fact, fulfilled the prophecy with which Paul had concluded, and turn away from the deed God is doing (see 13:41).

Rather than try to conciliate them, Paul solemnly declares a turn to the Gentiles (13:46). The extension of God's visitation that was implicit all through the Gospel (see Luke 2:32) and which was initiated by the conversion of Cornelius by Peter (Acts 10–11), is now made programmatic. The commission of the Twelve by the risen Lord to be "witnesses to the end of the earth" (Acts 1:8) is now to be carried on by Paul as "light for the nations," bringing "salvation to the end of the earth" (13:47). The statement, as we by now have grown to expect, is greeted by a "division in the people." Only now it is a division between the Gentiles, who gladly accept the message concerning this visitation, and "the Jews," who stir up a persecution and drive Paul and Barnabas out of their district (13:48-50).

The last word is the narrator's. The apostles "shake off the dust from their feet" in a gesture of rejection commanded by Jesus himself to his emissaries (Luke 10:11). Those who reject the kingdom are themselves rejected from it. In contrast, "the disciples" who remain in Antioch are described in the terms Luke uses for an authentic realization of God's people: they are filled with joy and the Holy Spirit (13:52).

The narrative of Acts has reached another turning point. Indeed, the prophecy from Isaiah 49:6, taken in context, describes the stages of the mission as it has thus far proceeded: first the restoration of the twelve tribes in Jerusalem, now the preaching to the Jews in the Diaspora, and then the "light for the nations." The story is by no means over. Paul will continue to preach to his fellow Jews. But this first statement of rejection will be followed by another (18:6) and then a definitive and book-closing one (28:28). Increasingly the narrative will focus on the mission to the Gentiles and on their "salvation" for which this Isaiah passage functions as a programmatic prophecy.

Paradoxically, as the story itself opens to this ever greater horizon, it also focuses ever more closely on the figure of Paul. He is the one who above all carries the message to the Gentiles, and it is for this reason that Luke has so diligently portrayed his first steps as an imitation of Jesus. Luke wants the reader to be in no doubt: the mission led by Paul is also in continuity with the story begun in Jesus and continued in the restored Israel of the Spirit.

For Reference and Further Study

Beydon, F. "Luc et 'les dames de la haute societé'." *ETR* 61 (1986) 331-341.
Cadbury, H. J. "Dust and Garments." *Beginnings* 5:269-276.
Cambe, M. "La *Charis* chez Saint Luc." *RB* 70 (1963) 193-207.

Gager, J. G. "Jews, Gentiles, and Synagogues in the Book of Acts." *HTR* 79 (1986) 91–99.

Tannehill, R. C. *Narrative Unity* 2:172-175.

27. The Apostles in Iconium and Lystra (14:1-18)

1. When they arrived in Iconium, they went in the same way into the synagogue of the Jews. They spoke in such fashion that a large crowd both of Jews and of Gentiles believed. 2. But the disbelieving Jews made a commotion. They turned the minds of the Gentiles against the brothers. 3. They therefore remained for a considerable period of time. They spoke boldly concerning the Lord, who was bearing witness to the message about his gift by enabling signs and wonders to be done through their hands. 4. So the population of the city was divided, with some of them for the Jews and others for the apostles. 5. But when an attempt was made by Jews and Gentiles, with their leaders, to abuse and stone them, 6. they found out. They fled to the cities of Lycaonia, Lystra and Derbe, and the surrounding territory. 7. There they continued preaching good news. 8. Now in Lystra a certain man was sitting. He could not use his feet. He was lame from his mother's womb. He had never walked. 9. This man heard Paul speaking. Paul gazed at him attentively. He saw that he had such faith as to be saved. 10. He said in a loud voice, "Stand up straight on your feet!" He jumped up and began to walk. 11. When the crowds saw what Paul had done, they shouted out in the Lycaonian dialect, "The gods have come down to us in human form!" 12. They began to call Barnabas "Zeus." They called Paul "Hermes" because he was the main speaker. 13. And the priest of "Zeus before the City" brought bulls and garlands to the gates. He wanted to offer sacrifice with the crowds. 14. But when the apostles Barnabas and Paul heard of it, they ripped their robes. They dashed into the crowd, 15. shouting, "People, why are you doing these things? We are human beings of the same nature as you! We are proclaiming good news to you so that you can turn away from these foolish things to the living God. He made the heaven and the earth and the sea and everything that is in them. 16. In past ages he allowed all the nations to follow their own paths. 17. Even so he left a witness to himself by his doing good works. He gives you rain from heaven and seasons of harvest. He fills you with food and with the gladness of your hearts." 18. And by saying these things they barely prevented the crowds from offering sacrifice to them.

NOTES

1. *arrived in Iconium:* Their departure from Antioch was noted in 13:51. The city is located in the territory sometimes designated as Phrygian (see Pliny, *Natural History* 5:145), sometimes as Lycaonian (*Natural History* 5:95; see the discussion in Strabo, *Geography* 12, 6, 3-4, and especially the problems of nomenclature in this region discussed in 12, 7, 1-5). The city was located on the *Via Sebaste* (the "Royal Road" of the *Acts of Paul and Thecla* 3, which has a fictional account of Paul's experiences at this juncture in the Acts story).

2. *disbelieving Jews made a commotion:* The verb *apeitheō* has the sense of being "disobedient" (see Epictetus, *Discourse* 3, 24, 24 for "disobedience against God"). In the LXX it frequently is used of the rebellion of the people against God (Lev 26:15; Num 11:20; Deut 1:26; 9:7, 23, 24; 32:51; Isa 30:12). Luke will use it again of the Jews in 19:9. Despite this background, it does not appear as though Luke is characterizing Jews as such, as in the phrase "perfidious Jews"; rather he is distinguishing this part of the population which rejected the good news, from that part which, with the Gentiles, accepted it (14:1). The phrase "made a commotion" translates *epēgeiran* (literally "stirred up"), which was used transitively in 13:50 but here lacks a direct object. Codex D considerably expands the verse: a) it attributes the commotion to "the chiefs of the synagogue of the Jews and the rulers of the synagogue"; and b) the "persecution against the righteous" is made explicit. Indeed, throughout the following verses, the Western Text expands in order to fill out some of the connections left obscure in the Alexandrian Text.

   turned the minds of the Gentiles: The difficult construction is literally "they made evil (*kakoō*) the souls (*psychas*) of the Gentiles against (*kata*) the brothers." The verb *kakoō* is used for the oppression of the people by Egypt (Acts 7:6, 19), and of Herod's wickedness toward the Church in Jerusalem (12:1). Luke will again use it for attacks against Paul in Corinth (18:10). In 1 Pet 3:13 also it has the sense of being done harm; see also Josephus, *Antiquities* 16:10, 205; *Jewish War* 2:261.

3. *they therefore remained:* The narrative logic is here very obscure, with the connective "therefore" appearing to be in contradiction to the circumstances. Codex D helps out by adding to the previous verse, "But the Lord soon gave peace." This emendation makes the long stay of the apostles more plausible, which is precisely why it is regarded as an addition and not as original.

   message about his gift: As always, the precise translation of densely coded expressions such as this one is difficult. The Greek literally has God bearing witness to "the word of his grace" (*logon tēs charitos autou*). This could variously be read as: a) "his gracious word"; b) "the word that was his grace/gift/favor"; c) "the word/speech/message concerning his grace/gift/favor."

   by enabling signs and wonders: Literally, "by giving" signs and wonders. The powerful deeds here as elsewhere serve to certify the message being proclaimed (2:19, 22, 43; 4:16, 22, 30; 5:12; 6:8; 7:36; 8:6, 13); compare 2 Cor 12:12. For the Lord "bearing witness" (*martyreō*) in this fashion, see Acts 13:22; 15:8; 20:23.

4. *population of the city was divided:* As so often in Luke-Acts, the precise meaning of *plēthos* ("multitude/assembly") is unclear (see Luke 1:10; 2:13; 5:6; 6:17; 8:37; 19:37; 23:1, 27; Acts 2:6; 4:32; 5:14, 16; 6:2, 5). In 14:1, it obviously refers to the entire population, but here it could also refer to a "popular assembly" (see Plato, *Apology* 31C); in that case, the better translation would be, "the civic assembly." More pertinent is the fact that the division is not between Messianist and non-Messianist but between "the Jews" and "the apostles" as rival parties. Codex D obviously takes *plēthos* as referring to the populace, and has some of them for the apostles, "clinging to them on account of the word of God."

6. *cities of Lycaonia:* Luke refers to a geographical area whose precise boundaries are unclear. In *Natural History* 5:95, for example, Pliny the Elder refers to Iconium as a Lycaonian town. The city of Lystra (see 14:8, 21; 16:1-2) is mentioned also in the personal reminiscence reported in 2 Tim 3:11, but Derbe (Acts 14:20; 16:1) is not.

7. *continued preaching good news:* The Western Text once more has significantly expanded this short notice: "The whole of the multitude was moved by the teaching. But Paul and Barnabas remained in Lystra." As elsewhere in this section, the Western Text's version is to be regarded as secondary.

8. *never walked:* The description of the man as "lame from his mother's womb" resembles that of the man healed by Peter in Acts 3:1-10. The resemblance is probably less accidental than a deliberate literary signal. Paul will do the same deeds as Peter and Jesus (compare Luke 5:17-26). The description itself is certainly redundant: a) he was sitting; b) he was powerless in his feet; c) he was lame from birth; d) he had never walked. Like the man in 3:10, he also was sitting "at the gates" of a temple!

9. *such faith as to be saved:* The connection between faith and salvation is thematic in Luke-Acts, and although the immediate reference here is to being healed, the symbolic level is also present (see Luke 7:50; 8:12, 48, 50; 17:19; 18:42; Acts 3:16). For the "attentive gaze," see Luke 4:20; 22:56; Acts 1:10; 3:4, 12; 6:15; 7:55; 10:4; 11:6; 13:9.

10. *stand up straight:* The adjective *orthos* ("straight") is used adverbially. The Western Text makes the passage resemble that in Acts 3:1-6 even more by adding at the beginning of Paul's statement, "I say to you in the name of the Lord Jesus Christ," and at the end, "and walk."

    jumped up and began to walk: The verbs *hallomai* and *peripateō* recall the healing in Acts 3:8. The Western Text once more assimilates this story to the earlier one by adding, "straightway (*parachrēma*) he at once (*eutheus*) leaped up."

11. *in the Lycaonian dialect:* This detail may be due to Luke's desire to provide "local color" to the story; we are not in the heart of the metropolis but in the hinterlands. Nevertheless, the sentiments expressed are Greek enough. In contrast to the more sophisticated response of the philosophers in Athens (17:16-34), Luke shows a spontaneous outpouring of Hellenistic religiosity (compare the response to Paul in Malta, 28:6). The use of the "foreign dia-

lect" also serves a dramatic function: Paul and Barnabas are slow to pick up on the populace's intentions.

gods . . . in human form: Literally, "the gods having taken the form of humans" (*homoiōthentes anthrōpois*); the mistaking of impressive humans for various divinities occurs with some frequency in the Hellenistic Novel (see for example Chariton of Aphrodisias, *Chaereas and Callirhoe* 1, 1, 16; 1, 14, 1; 3, 2, 15-17; Xenophon, *The Ephesians* 1, 12, 1; Heliodorus, *The Ethiopians* 1, 2, 1). These fictional accounts reflect an authentic aspect of Greco-Roman religion: the conviction that the membrane separating the realms of the human and the divine was a permeable one, with traffic possible in both directions. Not by accident is Ovid's great compendium of Greco-Roman mythology called simply *Metamorphoses* ("The Changing of Forms"; see for example 1:390-779; 2:466-495).

12. *Zeus . . . Hermes:* Zeus is the high God in the Olympian Pantheon. Hermes is the son of Zeus and Maia, and is associated especially with the role of messenger. Among the most charming tales in Ovid's *Metamorphoses* is the one about the aged couple Baucis and Philemon, who welcome to their humble cottage "in the Phrygian hills" the gods Zeus and Hermes, who had put off their divine appearance in order to seek hospitality. As a reward for the generous reception of the "gods in human form," the couple were made priests of a temple of Zeus (8:611-724). It is difficult to avoid the suspicion that Luke's account plays off such a tradition.

the main speaker: Literally, "the leader of the word" (*hēgoumenos tou logou*). According to Jamblichus (*Egyptian Mysteries* 1:1), Hermes is *theos ho logon hēgemōn*, "The God who governs speech."

13. *Zeus before the City:* The construction suggests a shrine whose name locates it outside the city walls, probably at the gates of the city; note that the attempted sacrifice takes place "at the gates." The best analogy might be churches like "St. Paul's Outside the Walls" in Rome.

bulls and garlands: The garlands (*stemmata*) are laurel-wreaths that could be worn on the head (Plato, *Republic* 617C), swathed in the temple (Lucian, *On Sacrifices* 3), or draped on the beast to be slaughtered (Herodotus, *Persian Wars* 7:197 applies this to humans about to be killed!). The bulls or oxen (*tauroi*) are widely used for sacrifice on the grand order (Lucian, *On Sacrifices* 3; 12).

14. *the apostles Barnabas and Paul:* The order of the names is interesting, since Luke has lately been putting Paul in first place; it may reflect the populace's perception of Barnabas as the higher deity. This is in fact the only time that either of the two missionaries is directly called by this title, although they are surely intended by the more general reference to "the apostles" in 14:4. So striking is this occurrence that Codex D, which ordinarily tends to expansion, omits the designation.

ripped their robes: The phrase *diarregnuein himatia* occurs frequently in the LXX as a response of extreme emotion (see Gen 37:29, 34; Num 14:6; Josh 7:6; Judg 11:35; 2 Sam 1:2, 11; 3:31; 13:31; 1 Macc 2:14; 3:47), usually as a gesture of sorrow and mourning (see also *m.Moed Kat.* 3:7). In Matt 26:65 and Mark

14:63, it is the gesture employed by the chief priest to signal the "blasphemy" of Jesus, according to the protocol of *m.Sanh.* 7:5 (see also Acts 22:23). The combination of shouting with a loud voice, tearing the clothes, and rushing into the crowd is paralleled by Jdt 14:16-17, using the same verbs. A somewhat similar gesture is recommended by Dio Chrysostom to the man who might be considered superior by others: "he should tear off his garments and leap forth naked upon the public highways, proving to the world that he is no better than any other man" (*Oration* 35:9).

15. *of the same nature as you:* Literally "of like feeling/disposition" (*homoiopatheis*); compare Plato, *The Republic* 409B. Here as in Jas 5:17, it serves to state the shared human condition, and deflect divine honor. Compare Peter's response to Cornelius' obeisance, "Stand up. I am myself a human being" (Acts 10:26; see also Rev 19:10). For a similar deflection, see the response of Alexander, "I beg off from honors equal to the gods. For I am a mortal man and I fear such ceremonies. For they bring danger to the soul" (Pseudo-Callisthenes, *Life of Alexander of Macedon* 12:22).

turn away from these foolish things: The tone of this proclamation is similar to that found in Hellenistic Jewish apologetic literature: a) the language of conversion (*epistrephein*; Luke 1:16-17; Acts 3:19; 9:35; 11:21; 15:19; 26:18); b) the characterization of idolatry in terms of "foolishness" (*mataia;* see LXX Isa 2:20; 30:7, 15, 28; 31:2; Ezek 8:10; Wis 13:1; 15:8; 3 Macc 6:11; 1 Pet 1:18); c) the turning to the "living God" (Hos 1:10; 4:15; Isa 37:4; Dan 5:23; 6:26; 2 Macc 7:33; 2 Cor 3:3; 6:16; 1 Tim 3:15; and especially 1 Thess 1:9 and Heb 6:1).

he made the heaven and the earth: The statement echoes Acts 4:24 and such Old Testament passages as Exod 20:11; Neh 9:6; Isa 37:16; LXX Ps 145:6. To say that the One God "created all that is in them" serves to eliminate any created thing's claim to ultimacy and therefore serves as a scriptural testimony against idolatry; compare Acts 7:49 and 1 Cor 8:6.

16. *to follow their own paths:* Literally, "to go in their own ways," with the term *hodos* having the sense of "custom" or "moral behavior" (see LXX Ps 1:1, 6; 2:12; 15:11; 17:21; compare Matt 10:5; Luke 1:79; 3:4; Acts 2:28; 9:2; 19:9). The contrast between the Gentiles' "former times" and the present is found also in Acts 17:27; Rom 3:25; 1 Pet 1:18.

17. *by his doing good works:* Luke uses *litotes* for emphasis: "has left himself not without witness." That the activity of God in nature is a "witness" (*martys*) to his goodness is axiomatic for monotheistic belief (see Wis 13:1; Rom 1:20). The argument anticipates the one in Acts 17:24-31. The blessings enumerated (rain, harvest, food, gladness of heart) recall passages such as LXX Ps 144:13-17; 146:8-11.

18. *barely prevented the crowds:* Despite his notice about the crowds using another dialect, a certain bilingualism pervades the encounter: the lame man hears Paul preaching (presumably in Greek, 14:9); the crowd cries out in Lycaonian (14:11), but it is when Paul and Barnabas "hear" of their bringing sacrifices (14:14) that they rush out shouting (14:15) and since their words (14:18) are what restrain the crowd, they are presumably understood in Greek. All that

this tells us is that Luke has enriched his story with "local color." Some *mss* round off the story by noting that the people return to their homes.

The implications of Paul's "turn to the Gentiles" in 13:46-47 begin to surface in this stretch of narrative. Luke shows us a sharper and more decisive turn against the apostles by the Jews, and a greater receptivity to the message among the Gentiles. The two responses are vividly etched in the events at Iconium (14:1-7) and Lystra (14:8-18).

The apostles, we recall, had gone to Iconium in the first place because of the trouble caused at Antioch by the Jews (13:50). But despite his declaration about going to the Gentiles, Paul is still shown entering the synagogue to preach (14:1). And for a second time, the same pattern emerges: success among some Jews and Greeks, but hostility aroused by the "unbelieving Jews" (14:2). Despite this opposition, the apostles stay with their mixed community for a considerable time, and Luke indicates in his usual fashion (the speaking of God's word boldly, the working of signs and wonders), that this is a genuine part of God's people. But the "turning of the minds of the Gentiles" against the apostles finally does its work, and in the face of an attempt to abuse and stone them, they flee to Lystra.

The scene is almost a replay of that in Antioch, and its literary function is much the same. Luke is at great pains to show that the turn to the Gentiles was not because God rejected the Jews, but because some Jews rejected the gospel and prevented its being spread among them. Nothing will make the point more forcibly than such repetition of patterns. We will, in fact, see it again shortly (14:19).

But Luke must also make clear the basis for the inclusion of the Gentiles in the messianic movement. And by so doing, he begins the process of redefining for the reader the character of God's People. Luke now makes even more explicit the theme that has run through his entire work, that "faith saves." From the side of God, the visitation of humans is for their salvation. From the side of humans, that visitation and salvation can only be realized by acceptance in faith. Those who accept in faith become part of the authentic Israel in the Spirit. Those who do not still remain Jews according to the previous understanding of that identity, with the hearing and observance of Torah, but they refuse the invitation to share in this realization of the people: they are "disbelieving."

The events at Lystra demonstrate the opposite tendency among the Gentiles. The sequence is of special interest because it shows the first direct contact between the apostles and a purely Gentile population. What characteristics will Luke choose to emphasize in this paradigmatic pagan population?

The reader is not by this time surprised to find the encounter initiated by a healing story, nor to find that it is a lame man who is healed (14:8-10). The usefulness of the story in securing Paul's identity as an authentic prophet in the tradition of Jesus, who healed a lame man (Luke 5:17-26), and of Peter who healed a lame man (Acts 3:1-6) is obvious. But surely by this point the reader is not in urgent need of such reassurance. We are invited to look instead at the symbolic function of the healing.

Why is this a lame man, and why is he healed? He is lame for the same reason that the characters in Jesus' and Peter's healing were lame: the incapacity to move, the powerlessness to walk, the weakness and the helplessness, all signify the condition of humans with respect to salvation. He is "saved/healed" because he "has faith" (14:9): he perceives in Paul's word the power of God's visitation and is open to its power. When Paul commands him to stand, he springs up and walks (14:10). His acceptance of God's visitation in faith—and the power of that faith to "save" him make this story, like that about Peter and the lame man at *another* "temple gate" (3:10), a literary "sign of healing" (4:22).

The paradigmatic character of the healing is made clear by Luke's portrayal of the people's response (14:11-18). It is overwhelmingly, almost embarrassingly, positive; the apostles are barely able to restrain the people from offering worship to them. As the notes suggest, Luke may well be playing off a literary motif concerning the hospitality shown to the gods Zeus and Hermes by residents of Phrygia (Ovid, *Metamorphoses*). These folk do not want to miss the chance to be the next Baucis and Philemon!

Such unsophisticated religiosity provides Luke the opportunity to have Paul and Barnabas appear both as genuine philosophers who reject such attempts at deification (14:14-15), and also as Jewish evangelists who correct misguided idolatrous impulses by means of an abbreviated but effective exhortation to conversion from such "foolishness" to belief in the one "living God" who is creator of heaven and earth (14:15-17). Yet Luke's intentions would be misread if this passage were understood only as a correction to Gentile religious convictions.

At a deeper level, Luke portrays these rustics as having precisely the conditions for genuine faith. They may misunderstand the status of the apostles, but they recognize a divine work of healing when they see one. They are open to God's visitation. They do not cavil over the possibility of "god in human form" visiting and saving humans. From the standpoint of the Christian convictions about Jesus as the raised prophet and as the Son of God, such willingness and openness must appear as part of God's providential "witness to himself" among these nations who until now had been allowed to "follow their own paths" (14:16-17). The reception of the apostles by the pagans in Lystra shows dramatically how God is "opening a door of faith for the Gentiles" (14:27).

FOR REFERENCE AND FURTHER STUDY

Bornkamm, G. "The Missionary Stance of Paul in I Corinthians 9 and in Acts." *Studies in the Acts of the Apostles.* Eds. L. Keck and J. L. Martyn. Nashville: Abingdon Press, 1966, 194–207.

Downing, F. G. "Common Ground with Paganism in Luke and Josephus." *NTS* 28 (1982) 546–559.

Gaertner, B. "Paulus und Barnabas in Lystra: zu Apg. 14, 8-15." *SEA* 27 (1962) 85–88.

Lerle, E. "Die Predigt in Lystra (Acta xiv, 15-18)." *NTS* 7 (1960–1961) 46–55.

Malten, L. "Motivgeschichtliche Untersuchungen zur Sagenforschung." *Hermes* 74 (1939) 176–206, and 75 (1940) 168–176.

Praeder, S. M. "Jesus-Paul, Peter-Paul, and Jesus-Peter Parallelism in Luke-Acts: A History of Reader Response." *SBL 1984 Seminar Papers.* Ed. K. H. Richards. Chico: Scholars Press, 1984, 23–39.

Throckmorton, B. H. "*Sōzein, sōtēria* in Luke-Acts." *Studia Evangelica.* Ed. E. A. Livingstone. Berlin: Akademie Verlag, 1973, 6:515-526.

28. Return to Antioch (14:19-28)

19. Now Jews from Antioch and Iconium came there. Having both persuaded the people and stoned Paul, they dragged him out of the city. They thought he was dead. 20. But when the disciples gathered around him, he rose up and went into the city. The next day he went with Barnabas to Derbe. 21. After proclaiming the good news in that city and making a large number of disciples, they returned to Lystra, and to Iconium, and to Antioch. 22. They strengthened the souls of the disciples. They encouraged them to remain in the faith, and said, "It is necessary for us to enter the kingdom of God through many afflictions." 23. In each church they appointed elders for them. With prayer and fasting they presented them to the Lord in whom they had come to believe. 24. Going through Pisidia, they came to Pamphylia. 25. After speaking the word in Perga, they went down to Attalia. 26. From there they set sail for Antioch, where they had been commissioned by the gift of God for the work which they completed. 27. When they had arrived and gathered the Church, they announced what God did with them, and that "He has opened a door of faith to the Gentiles!" 28. And they remained with the disciples for more than a short period of time.

NOTES

19. *Jews from Antioch and Iconium:* Luke connects these disparate incidents by the repeated harassment of Paul by the Jewish opposition from cities already

evangelized, Antioch (13:50) and Iconium (14:5). By so doing, Luke minimizes the rejection of the gospel by *local* communities; opposition appears as the vendetta of a small band of fanatics. Such movement from place to place by opponents of Paul seems to be reflected in his own letters as well (2 Cor 11:4-6; Gal 2:4-5; 5:11; 6:12).

persuaded the people and stoned: Luke provides no lapse in time between the previous scene and this one, but the narrative logic seems to demand one. The two actions (persuading and stoning) are given equal weight in balanced participial constructions; the effect is to make this not an organized action (as at Iconium, 14:5) but a mob action generated by these travelling *provocateurs*. Paul is "dragged" (*syrein*) out of the city, just as he himself had earlier "dragged" (*syrein*) Christians out of their homes (8:3). The prophecy concerning how much Paul would have to suffer for the sake of the name is being fulfilled (9:16).

thought he was dead: For the use of *nomizō* ("considered"), see Luke 2:44; 3:23; Acts 7:25; 8:20. In his lengthy catalogue of sufferings in 2 Cor 11:23-29, Paul himself states that he was "many times near death" (*en thanatois pollakis*, 11:23), and had been "by the Jews . . . stoned once" (11:25).

20. *disciples gathered around him:* Literally, "formed a circle around him" (*kykloō*), probably of protection or of support. The presence of "disciples" (*mathētai*) suggests either Paul's travelling companions (see 13:13), or converts Paul had made already in Lystra—which again would suppose some gap in time between the previous scene and this one.

rose up . . . next day he went: This rapid sequence grates on contemporary sensibilities (how could Paul act so expeditiously if he was near death?), but fits the episodic character of ancient narratives. Furthermore, the wording enables us to read the sequence in a number of ways. Is Paul a superman (or *theios anēr*) who leaps up unscathed, runs back to Lystra, then blithely proceeds on his mission? Or does Luke intend us to read this in the light of the thematic statement in 14:22 concerning the necessity of entering the kingdom through many tribulations? Then we could imagine a deeply injured Paul who only with the assistance of others is able to make his escape. Much is left to the imagination and empathy of the reader. The Western Text also felt the abruptness of the movements, and tried to provide some padding: a) the crowd of opponents leaves the scene; b) the time is evening; c) there is darkness; d) Paul got up with difficulty.

21. *in that city:* Derbe was named with Lystra in 14:6 as one of the "cities of Lycaonia" to which Paul had come to preach. That goal is now accomplished, as he "evangelizes" (*euangelizō*) and "makes many disciples." The verb *mathēteuō* is found only here in Luke-Acts, but occurs in Matt 13:52; 27:57; 28:19.

22. *strengthened the souls of the disciples:* This return through the cities already evangelized is far from a flight; it is a pastoral visitation. Given the compressed character of the narrative (the last physical harm done to Paul was only three lines previous), the image of the apostles is of truly philosophical courage as they return to the places where they had been so badly treated. For

"strengthening the souls" see especially the command of Jesus to Peter in Luke 22:32, as well as the language used by Paul himself for such pastoral behavior in Rom 1:11; 16:25; 1 Thess 3:2, 13; 2 Thess 2:17; 3:3.

encouraged them to remain in the faith: The verb *parakalō* can also be rendered as "exhort," but the context here seems to require the translation given. The task for Paul and Barnabas is the stabilization of new communities in the face of opposition. "Remain in the faith" could therefore be understood as remaining loyal to their community commitment, as well as their "belief in the gospel" (compare Acts 6:7; 13:8, and with slightly different language, Acts 11:23; 13:43).

through many afflictions: This translation puts the *hoti* clause into direct rather than indirect discourse. The language of "affliction" (*thlipsis*) is intimately connected with eschatological contexts and their attendant sufferings. Luke uses the term only here, 11:29 and 20:23, but it is frequently employed by other NT writings for situations of persecution (Matt 23:21; 24:9, 21, 29; John 16:33; Rom 2:9; 5:9; 8:35; 12:12; 2 Cor 1:4; 6:4; 7:4; Col 1:24; 1 Thess 1:6; 3:3; 2 Thess 1:4, 6).

to enter the kingdom of God: The language of this declaration is striking, if only because of the verb "to enter" (*eiselthein*), which reverses the usual spatial imagery in language about the *kingdom's* "coming" (compare Luke 10:9, 11; 11:2, 20; 17:20; 18:17; 21:31). Luke's language here is close to that he uses in Luke 18:24-25, "how difficult it is for those with possessions to enter the kingdom of God," and Luke 23:42, "when you enter your kingdom." Is Luke portraying "the kingdom" as a future condition toward which we are travelling (*per aspera ad astra*)? Is he placing Paul within a specifically apocalyptic framework, so that the present "woes" are regarded as the prelude to the eschatological moment (compare Rev 1:9)? Or is he—as appears more likely—suggesting that commitment to the "rule of God" inevitably demands (*dei*) the same sort of suffering as that experienced by Jesus, the prophetic proclaimer of that rule?

23. *appointed elders for them:* The verb *cheirotoneō* means literally to stretch out the hands, and was used for the raising of hands in an election (Plato, *Laws* 763E). It does not occur in the LXX, but in Josephus it has the sense of being "appointed" to the chief priesthood (*Antiquities* 13:45). Luke uses it synonymously with "laying on hands" (Acts 6:6; 8:17; 9:17; 13:3). The term is used by Paul himself for the "appointment" of Titus as representative of the churches (2 Cor 8:19). As with the visitation and exhortation, Luke is showing how the early communities were nurtured and stabilized (compare 11:22-24). Already in 11:30, Luke had added "elders" to the leadership in Jerusalem, and we will see them again together with "the apostles" in 15:2, 4, 6, 22, 23; 16:4. Finally, in his farewell address to the Ephesian Church, Paul will address "the elders of the Church" (20:17).

prayer and fasting: Literally, "having prayed (*proseuxamenoi*) with fastings (*nēsteiōn*); This element makes the ordination echo the appointment of Paul and Barnabas themselves as they began this mission (Acts 13:2-3). For the incidence and significance of the practice, see the notes on Acts 9:9 and 12:3.

presented them to the Lord: The verb *paratithēmi* has three uses in the LXX and in Luke-Acts: a) to present something to someone in the context of a meal (Gen 18:18; 24:33; Luke 9:16; 10:8; 11:6; Acts 16:34); b) to present a speech or commands (Exod 19:7; 21:1; Lev 6:10; Deut 4:44; Acts 17:3); c) to present to another in the sense of "entrust" (in deposit or safekeeping; Lev 6:4; Ps 30:5; Luke 12:48; 23:46; Acts 20:32). It is the last sense that applies in this case. They are being entrusted to the one in whom they have placed their trust.

25. *went down to Attalia:* On the first visit to Perga (Acts 13:13-14), no mention was made of preaching, a deficiency now remedied by the apostles' "speaking the word" there. Attalia is the seaport on the coast of Pamphylia; the Western Text adds an attempt at evangelization there as well.

26. *commissioned by the gift of God:* They were literally "handed over" (*paradidōmi*), with the "gift/grace" of God in the dative case; the context of their original commission (13:1-3) suggests that they were delivered to their task "by" the Holy Spirit (the "gift"), but the dative could also be read as "handed over *for* the gift of God" (that is, for its preaching), or alternatively, *to* the "favor of God" (this is, his keeping).

    the work which they completed: The use of *ergon* ("work") here echoes the terms of their commission in 13:2, "set apart . . . for the work to which the Lord summoned them," as well as the citation from Habakkuk in 13:41 (see also 5:38). For the "completion" (*plēroō*), compare the note on Barnabas and Paul in 12:25.

27. *announced what God did with them:* Throughout this narrative, Paul and Barnabas are portrayed as loyal and active members of the local Antiochean congregation; they had been commissioned by it, and now they report back. The relative *hosa* could also be translated "how much" God had done; it is more vivid than the translation suggests. The construction *met' autōn* ("with them") is unusual (the Western Text emends to "with their souls"), but is actually consistent with Luke's characterization of Joseph (*ēn ho theos met'autou*) in 7:9, and of Jesus (*hoti ho theos ēn met'autou*) in 10:38. For Luke, God is always the main character who acts through his prophetic representatives.

    door of faith to the Gentiles: Whether by *prosōpopoiia*, or happy chance, or historical reminiscence, Luke has hit on an expression that is distinctively Pauline. Alone in the writings of the NT, Paul uses "door" (*thyra*) in this metaphorical sense of opportunity: "A wide door for effective work has been opened to me" (1 Cor 16:9); "when I came to Troas to preach the Gospel of Christ, a door was opened for me in the Lord" (2 Cor 2:12); "pray for us, that God may open to us a door for the word" (Col 4:3). The emphasis on "faith" (*pistis*) not only picks up a major theme of the entire section (see 13:8, 12, 39, 41, 48; 14:1, 9, 22, 23), but prepares for the formal statement concerning faith as the principle of salvation in 15:9, 11.

28. *remained with the disciples:* For *diatribō*, see the note on Acts 12:19. This Lukan transition provides a space in the narrative that prepares for the next great crisis in Antioch (15:1). The "no little time" (*chronon ouk oligon*) is typical Lukan litotes (see 14:17 above, and especially Acts 12:18; 15:2; 17:4, 12; 19:2).

The growing resistance to Paul's messianic preaching by Diaspora Jews reaches a savage pitch in Lystra. Paul and Barnabas have just resisted the efforts of the eager Gentile population to offer them sacrifices (14:18) when Jews from Antioch and Iconium arrive and turn the populace against Paul (14:19). He is stoned, dragged from the city, left for dead. The narrator could offer no more dramatic display of this new division created by the prophet Paul, a division between the believing Gentiles and the disbelieving Jews.

The events immediately following this devastating attack are critical for the reader's assessment of Paul—or better, Luke's portrayal of Paul. Because of the extreme brevity of the narrative, Paul's rapid resumption of his activities may be read in an almost parodic fashion, as the triumph of the "divine man" over adversity: left for dead, he is able to return to the city and set off on a journey the following day. For some readers, it is tempting to see this as a sign of Paul's inconquerable power.

In fact, however, the portrayal is at once more somber and moving. Paul returns to the city surrounded by his followers (14:20), and his subsequent actions do not suggest irresistable power so much as indefatigable faith and loyalty. Paul does not return to the city in triumph and best his opponents in a contest of wonders; he does not outdue them in debate. He moves on to another place where he can preach freely (14:21). Only after some time does he return to the place where he experienced such danger, not in order to overwhelm his foes, but in order to attend pastorally to his communities.

Luke draws our attention here not so much to the personality or power of Paul as to the process by which early Christian communities came into being and were nurtured. The value of this text lies not so much in the accuracy of its report concerning Paul's movements, but in the feel it gives us for the pastoral practices of the early Messianists. The narrative provides a sense of the fragility inevitable for communities established in the context of resistance and persecution, and the mechanisms employed to stabilize such churches: the visitation by pastors, the exhortation to loyalty, and the securing of a leadership cadre. In this case, Luke shows us Paul and Barnabas appointing elders for each of these local churches (14:23).

The issue of what local leadership obtained in the actual Pauline communities is vigorously debated by scholars. On the one side, it is important to avoid the impression that Paul had no interest in matters of local organization, for even his undisputed letters take up such concerns repeatedly (1 Thess 5:11-13; 1 Cor 6:5; 12:28; 16:15-18; 2 Cor 8:23; Gal 6:6; Rom 12:8; Phil 1:1). On the other side, it is not clear that the sort of organizational structure supplied by 1 Timothy (with its board of elders) obtained everywhere during Paul's lifetime. Less important than the *form* of community structure is the conviction attested to both in Paul's letters, in Acts, and in other NT writings, that there is no essential incompatibility between a prophetic self-consciousness or a charismatic awareness, and ecclesiastical structure. The narrative of Acts is surely historical in this broad sense, that Christian communities needed from the very beginning to establish local leadership.

In terms of Luke's narrative purposes, this passage serves as an important bridge to the next major stage of his story, the conflict in Antioch over the Gentile mission, and the council in Jerusalem called to debate the status of Gentile believers (15:1-21). Luke has shown that the conversion of Gentiles, the "door of faith" opened to them, was not idiosyncratic or momentary. By having the apostles visit them on their return to Antioch, Luke has signalled that these are in fact authentic churches. These Gentile communities are "filled with joy and the Holy Spirit" (13:52), they have "signs and wonders" worked among them by the witnessing of God (14:3), they are truly "disciples" (14:20-21), who are testing their faith and their worthiness to enter the kingdom of God by their suffering of many tribulations (14:22; compare Luke 8:13-16). Luke has so portrayed the genuineness of the Gentiles as having "faith as to be saved" (14:9) that the burden of proof will fall on those who want to place conditions on their acceptance into God's people.

FOR REFERENCE AND FURTHER STUDY

Cosgrove, C. H. "The Divine *DEI* in Luke-Acts." *NovT* 26 (1984) 168–190.
Pervo, R. I. *Profit with Delight: The Literary Genre of the Acts of the Apostles.* Philadelphia: Fortress Press, 1987, 26.
Prast, F. *Presbyter und Evangelium in nachapostolischer Zeit: Die Abschiedsrede des Paulus in Milet (Apg 20, 17-38) in Rahmen der lukanischen Konzeption der Evangeliumsverkundigung.* Stüttgart: Verlag Katholisches Bibelwerk, 1979, 212–222.
Ross, J. M. "The Appointment of Presbyters in Acts 14:23." *ExpT* 63 (1951) 288.
Tannehill, R. C. *Narrative Unity* 2:180-182.

29. *Conflict over Gentile Conversions* (15:1-21)

1. Some people came down from Judea. They began teaching the brothers, "Unless you are circumcised according to Mosaic custom, you cannot be saved." 2. Because there was a conflict and no small debate, with Paul and Barnabas against them, it was determined that Paul and Barnabas and certain others from among them should go up to the apostles and elders in Jerusalem about this question. 3. Those who were sent off by the Church passed through Phoenicia and Samaria. They recounted the conversion of the Gentiles and gave great joy to all the brothers. 4. When they arrived in Jerusalem, they were welcomed by the Church and the apostles and the elders. They announced the things the Lord had done with them. 5. But some believers from the Pharisaic party stood up. They said, "It is necessary to circumcise them and order them to keep the Law of Moses." 6. So the apostles and elders gathered together to consider the matter. 7. After considerable debate, Peter stood up. He said to them, "Brothers, you know that from early days among you God chose the Gentiles to hear the message of the good news through my mouth and to believe. 8. And God who knows the heart bore witness. He gave to them the Holy Spirit just as he had also to us. 9. And by cleansing their hearts with faith he has made no discrimination between us and them. 10. Therefore, why are you now testing God by putting a yoke on the neck of the disciples, one which neither our ancestors nor we were strong enough to bear? 11. Instead, through the gift that is the Lord Jesus, we are believing in order to be saved, in the same way that they are." 12. The whole assembly fell silent. They listened to Barnabas and Paul as they narrated how many signs and wonders God had done through them among the Gentiles. 13. And after they fell silent, James responded. He said, "Brothers, listen to me! 14. Simeon has related how God first made visitation to take a people for his name from out of the Gentiles. 15. And the words of the Prophets agree with this, just as it stands written: 16. 'After these things I will return, and I will rebuild the tent of David that had fallen. Its ruined portions I will build again. I will restore it, 17. so that the rest of humanity might seek the Lord, and all the nations upon whom my name has been invoked, 18. says the Lord, as he makes these things known from eternity.' 19. Therefore it is my decision to stop bothering those from the Gentiles who are converting to the Lord, 20. but to write them to this effect: to avoid things polluted by idolatry, and sexual immorality, and that which is strangled, and blood. 21. For Moses from ages past has had those who proclaim him in every city, as he is read every Sabbath in the synagogue."

Amos 9:11-12

NOTES

1. *came down from Judea:* That is, to Antioch, where Paul and Barnabas have been staying "no little time" with the disciples (14:28). As in 11:1-2, "Judea" may

be a circumspect way of referring to the Jerusalem community, for the passage takes up again the issue of the legitimacy and status of the Gentile mission. Are these agitators travelling members of the "Pharisaic party" who are introduced at the council in 15:5? The Western Text identifies them as such in this verse. In his account of his conflict with Cephas in Antioch, Paul refers to "certain ones who had come from Judea" (Gal 2:24), who are possibly to be identified with "certain ones from James" in Gal 2:12 (whether or not they were his conscious agents).

circumcised according to Mosaic custom: Their statement takes the form of a conditional sentence, in which circumcision forms the condition for salvation itself. The Western Text adds the ethical dimension, "and walk" according to the custom of Moses. Circumcision was the traditional ritual of inclusion in the people from the time of Abraham (Gen 17:10-14, 23-27; 21:4; 34:15-24; Exod 12:44, 48; Lev 12:3; Josh 5:2-8). Luke nowhere expresses animus toward the custom. He has John the Baptist circumcised (Luke 1:59) as well as Jesus (2:21). The ritual is mentioned without animadversion in Stephen's speech (7:8). Indeed, Luke will have Paul circumcise Timothy, who had a Jewish mother (16:3). But Luke never connects circumcision to the issue of righteousness or salvation. It is for him a "custom of the people" (for Luke's use of *ethos*, compare Luke 1:9; 2:42; 6:14 as well as Acts 16:21; 21:21; 26:3; 28:17).

you cannot be saved: What is most striking about the declaration is its innovative character. Although circumcision was universally practiced among Jews, and its abandonment regarded as a sign of apostasy (1 Macc 1:11-15; Philo, *The Migration of Abraham* 89-92), the relationship of this ritual to "authentic Judaism" was variously understood, and it may fairly be stated that for many first-century Jews, circumcision understood as a symbol of religious commitment was more important than the literal procedure itself (Philo, *The Migration of Abraham* 92; *Special Laws* 1:8-11; 1:304-306; *1QS* 5:5; 5:28; Rom 2:12-15). Concerning the obligation even of proselytes to be circumcised, there was also debate; see *bT yeb.* 46a, and especially Josephus, *Antiquities of the Jews* 20:38-48. Not even the "Judaizers" opposed by Paul in Galatia made their desire for an additional initiation into Moses a condition for *salvation* (Gal 4:21; 5:2-4; 6:12-13). The statement is all the more shocking in the present context because of the way it controverts the theme so emphatically developed by the narrator in the previous section, that among the Gentiles "faith saves" (Acts 14:8, 22, 23, 27).

2. *conflict and no small debate:* The term *stasis* has the sense of dissent/disorder (compare Luke 23:19, 25; Acts 19:40; 23:7, 10), whereas *zētēsis* has more the meaning of "inquiry/discussion" (compare Acts 15:7; 1 Tim 6:4; 2 Tim 2:23; Titus 3:9). Luke again uses *litotes*, emphasizing the dimensions of the conflict by deliberate understatement. The Western Text expands the verse: "For Paul was saying strongly that they should remain as they had believed; but those who were from Jerusalem ordered them with Paul and Barnabas and some others to go up. . . ." The expansion obviously exalts the role of Paul as the defender of freedom against those the Western Text has identified as

"Pharisees," but also makes the Jerusalem contingent more directly control the situation.

concerning this question: The term *zētēma* is more or less synonymous with *zētēsis* in the previous verse (compare Acts 18:15; 23:29; 25:19; 26:3). For the "elders" (*presbyteroi*) sharing the leadership in Jerusalem with the apostles, see 11:30. Instead of the reading translated here, the Western Text has "that they might be judged by them," which again emphasizes the role of the Jerusalem community.

3. *recounted the conversion of the Gentiles:* Luke uses the verb *ekdiēgeomai* ("declare/relate") as in Acts 13:41 (compare LXX Ps 49:16; 117:17; Sir 34:11; Hab 1:5). Throughout the passage, the *narratio* of events plays an important role in the shaping of the community's decision (compare Chariton of Aphrodisias, *Chaereas and Callirhoe* 3, 4, 13). The Antioch legation proceeds along the path of earlier evangelization, through Phoenicia (Acts 8:40; 9:32-43) and Samaria (8:4-25). If we take Luke's semantic signals seriously, we will recognize in "all the brothers' " reception of the apostles' recitation with "great joy" (*chara*), a clear indication that the decision for the Gentile initiative will be positive (see the note on Acts 13:52).

4. *the things the Lord had done with them:* Luke takes every opportunity to communicate his own view of these events to the reader. The Antiochean delegation is "welcomed" (*paradechomai*, see 16:21; 22:18) by the Church and its leaders, and they once more "recount" (*anangelō*) how much God had done with them, from which we learn that God was the true author of the Gentile mission, not Paul and Barnabas. By the phrase *met'autou*, Luke connects this announcement with the earlier report to the Antiochean Church (14:27).

5. *believers from the Pharisaic party:* Literally, "from the party/school/sect of the Pharisees." Luke never portrays the Pharisees in positive terms (see Luke 5:17, 21, 30, 33; 6:2, 7; 7:30, 36, 37, 39; 11:37-39, 42-43, 53; 12:1; 13:31; 14:1, 3; 15:2; 16:14; 17:20; 18:10-11; 19:39). Although Paul will later identify himself as a Pharisee (23:6; 26:5), the members of that sect as such are treated no better in Acts than in the Gospel, as the passage concerning Gamaliel demonstrates (5:34-39). As in the Gospel (7:30), the Pharisees here play a role "opposing God's plan," even though they are counted among the believers—as were Ananias and Sapphira and Simon Magus! We should not automatically conclude that these are the same people as "those from the circumcision" who accompanied Peter in the Cornelius incident (10:41; 11:12).

necessary to circumcise them: Luke has the Pharisees use language the author ordinarily reserves for statements concerning the divine plan (*dei;* see notes on Luke 2:49 and Acts 1:16). They are not proposing a desirable option but a fundamental requirement, even though the language of "salvation" is not used here as it was in 15:1. The assumption of authority on their part is indicated by the double mandate: the Gentiles are to be (forcibly?) circumcised, and commanded to observe (*tērein*) the Law of Moses. Josephus, in fact, tells us of one incident in which Jews attempted such forced circumcision of inhabitants "as a condition of residence among them" (*Life* 113) and another in which a group of Gentiles willingly underwent such a group surgical procedure (*Antiquities of the Jews* 13:258; see also LXX Esth 8:17).

Law of Moses: As it pertains to one's identity as a Jew, Luke is entirely positive toward the Law of Moses (see Luke 2:22, 23, 24, 27, 39; 10:26; 16:16-17; Acts 7:53), even though its observance is not an adequate measure of righteousness or of salvation (Acts 13:39). The issue posed here therefore is whether Torah is to be an absolute norm for membership in the people, having the same authority as the principle of faith, and therefore whether initiation into the *ethnos* ("nation") of the Jews with its specific *ethos* (custom) is required to be a part of the *laos tou theou* ("people of God").

6. *apostles and elders gathered together:* The precise dynamics of the meeting as Luke portrays it are not entirely clear. The whole assembly (*ekklēsia*) appears to be present in 15:4, which makes possible the objection voiced by the Pharisaic Christians (15:5). The following discussion, however, seems only to involve the leaders (15:6-11)—although some mss add "with the congregation." Yet there is a response at the end of *pan to plēthos* ("the whole assembly") in 5:12 (compare also 5:22).

7. *Peter stood up:* The leading characters of Luke's narrative now bear witness in turn, with the response coming from the new leader of the Jerusalem Church, James. Peter's role here is not as a "prince of the apostles" but as another faithful witness whose function is to narrate his experience and draw implications from it. The Western Text gives additional prophetic character to his speech by stating, "he stood up in the [Holy] Spirit."

from early days among you: The adjective *archaios* retains something of the sense of *archē* ("beginning"); here the translation of *apo archaiōn hemerōn* must respect the context: Peter is referring to the events of Acts 10 (compare the use of *en archē* in 11:15!). The placement of the phrase "among you" (*en hymin*) argues for taking it as referring to that time when Peter continued to move among them as their leader before "going to another place" (12:17). The Western Text has *en hēmin* ("among us") which makes it refer to the group out of which Peter was chosen, the apostles.

chose the Gentiles: This translation departs, with some trepidation, from many others in making *ta ethnē* ("the Gentiles") the direct object of the verb "chose." The word order is, as so often in Luke's speeches, awkward, and this interpretation seems to accord best with the overall sense of Peter's sentence. See the construction of another sentence using *eklegomai* in Acts 1:2, and compare Acts 1:21. The choice of words, in any case, powerfully shapes the reader's perceptions. First, Luke emphasizes that what had happened was *God's* doing, and not the initiative of humans. Second, he uses the term "elected" (*eklegomai*), which is fundamental to Jewish self-understanding (Num 16:5; Deut 4:37; 7:7; 21:5; Josh 24:15; LXX Ps 32:12; 46:4; see also Luke 6:13; 9:35; Acts 1:2). The effect of the combination is oxymoronic but deliberate.

to hear . . . and to believe: Like "the people" in the Gospel narrative, these Gentiles have "glorified God" by hearing his word (Luke 5:15; 7:29; 11:28); note especially the connection between "hearing and believing" in Luke

8:11-18. The response of faith was left implicit by 10:44, although it was strongly suggested by Peter's "all who believe in him" in 10:43. The combination is also Pauline (Rom 10:14, 17; Gal 3:2, 5). The explicit emphasis here on "faith" picks up the theme Luke has been developing in the immediately preceding narrative (Acts 13:8, 12, 39, 41, 48; 14:1, 9, 22, 27). The use of the noun "gospel/good news" (*euangelion*) is unusual, being found only here and in Acts 20:24. Luke ordinarily uses the verb form *euangelizomai*.

8. *God . . . bore witness:* The epithet "knower of the heart" (*kardiognōstēs*) is used also in Acts 1:24. The function is the same in both contexts: it is because God can "see the heart" and humans cannot that God is able to "choose" appropriately to his intentions. In this case, God is able to make judgment in terms of internal dispositions rather than on external criteria. For God "bearing witness" in this fashion, see also 13:22.

gave to them the Holy Spirit: Peter now makes explicit reference to the previously narrated Cornelius story (10:44). The circumstantial participle (*dous*) can be taken as instrumental, "*by* giving them the Holy Spirit." For the equating of the gift to the Gentiles with that to the first believers, ("just as he had also to us"), see 10:47 and 11:15.

9. *cleansing their hearts with faith:* This translation reverses the order of the Greek clauses. By his use of *katharizō* ("cleanse"), Luke enables Peter to finally draw the full conclusions from his initial vision and the command, "things God has cleansed, you stop making common" (10:15). Peter has come to understand not only that the vision was about the Gentiles, but recognizes that *faith* is the principle used by God for this "cleansing of the heart." For the background of *katharizo* in ritual contexts, see the note on 10:15.

made no discrimination between us and them: The language again deliberately echoes that in the Cornelius episode: Peter had been told to join the messengers from the centurion "without debate/discrimination/hesitation" (*mēden diakrinomenos*, 10:20). In 11:12, he recounted that in fact he had done so. Now we understand why he was not to "discriminate": it was because God himself made no fundamental distinctions between peoples. The theme is attached to the theological conviction concerning God's "impartiality" (*aprosōpolēmpsia*, 10:34), and is found also in Romans 3:22; 10:12.

10. *therefore why are you now testing God:* Evaluating the role played by the Pharisaic party in this debate hinges on the weight given to this line. Three things about it deserve attention: a) the "therefore" (*oun*) should be taken at its strongest: in the light of all that God has done, why are they challenging it? b) the challenge, furthermore, is not to humans, but to God. c) the verb "test" (*peirazō*) is to be understood explicitly in terms of resistance to God's plan (see Exod 17:2; Deut 6:16, etc). Thus Satan "tested" Jesus in the wilderness (Luke 4:2); Jesus' opponents "test" him (Luke 11:16), and Ananias and Sapphira "test" the Spirit of God (Acts 5:9).

putting a yoke on the neck of the disciples: The "yoke" (*zygos*) is a restraint, whether literally, as for oxen (Deut 21:3), or figuratively, as a metaphor for political or social oppression (2 Chr 10:10; 1 Macc 8:31; LXX Ps 2:3; 1 Tim 6:1).

Gal 5:1: Τῇ ἐλευθερίᾳ ἡμᾶς Χριστὸς ἠλευθέρωσεν· στήκετε
οὖν καὶ μὴ πάλιν ζυγῷ δουλείας ἐνέχεσθε.

It was therefore already paradoxical for rabbinic Judaism to adopt the image (perhaps as early as Sir 51:26) as a symbol for the acceptance of responsibility to keep the commandments of Torah (see *Sifra* 57b; *Sifre on Deuteronomy* Re'eh 117; *m. Ber* 2:2; *Pirke Aboth* 3:5). The imagery is appropriated by Matt 11:29-30 for the "light yoke" that is the messianic instruction (see also the *Didache* 6:2), but the present passage agrees with Gal 5:1 in characterizing the yoke of Torah in terms of an unsupportable burden.

strong enough to bear: The point of view here is obviously opposed to the one which saw this yoke as the source of genuine freedom, and resembles Luke 11:46, "You pile loads on people that are hard to carry, and yourselves do not touch the burdens with one of your fingers" (compare Matt 23:4).

11. *gift that is the Lord Jesus:* Consistent with the previous cases, *charis* is here translated as "gift" rather than as the more traditional "grace," and the genitive is treated as epexegetical: the Lord Jesus is the content of the gift, rather than the one who "shows favor." A more standard rendering would be, "by the grace (favor) of/from our Lord Jesus."

we are believing in order to be saved: The construction of the Greek sentence is awkward and leads to several possible construals. The RSV has, for example, "we believe that we shall be saved by the grace of our Lord Jesus"; Cadbury has "through the grace of the Lord Jesus we believe that we shall be saved." But the infinitive *sothēnai* can function as easily as a purpose clause as it can the equivalent of a future indicative, "we shall be saved." The advantage of the present translation is that it makes explicit the connection between faith and salvation that Luke has been developing (see the note on 14:9, where the same combination of *pistis* and *sothēnai* is found). Furthermore, Luke never elsewhere explicitly connects the concept of *charis* to Jesus (even 15:40, below, has "grace of the Lord"), or to salvation.

in the same way that they are: The phrase *kath' hon tropon* (literally "according to the same way") is used by the author elsewhere (Luke 13:34; Acts 1:11; 7:28; 27:25). The most remarkable thing about the declaration is that the principle of salvation for those born Jews is *measured* by that for Gentiles, in a complete reversal of the expected order. God uses the salvation of the Gentiles to reveal to the Jewish believers the true ground of their own salvation. Peter's statement stands as a direct rebuttal to the opening attack, "if you are not circumcised, you cannot be saved" (15:1).

12. *signs and wonders God had done:* Peter's intervention silences the dispute (for *sigaō* see Luke 9:36; 18:39; 20:26; Acts 12:17, and for *plēthos*, see the note on Acts 14:4); some *mss* from the Western Tradition add, "when the elders assented to the things said by Peter." The effect of his narration and declaration is to clear the way for this narration (*exēgeomai*) by Paul and Barnabas. Once more the author's compression of the extended narrative running through all of chapters 13-14 reveals his perceptions: the *sēmeia kai terata* ("signs and wonders") always function as the signal of God's prophetic spirit at work (Acts 2:19, 22, 43; 4:16, 22, 30; 5:12; 6:8; 8:6, 13; 14:3). They serve as *tekmēria* (evidenciary signs), therefore, that the Holy Spirit was the one who accomplished the conversion of the Gentiles.

13. *James responded:* Luke unfolds the figure of James (see 1 Cor 15:7; Gal 1:19; 2:9, 12) in three stages: a) when Peter left Jerusalem, he sent word to "James and the brothers," which was our first hint of his leadership role; b) here at the council he is the spokesperson for the Jerusalem Church and indeed the one whose decision (*krinō*) influences the entire *plēthos;* c) in 21:18, he stands "with the elders" as the leader of the Jerusalem Church who confronts Paul on his last trip to the city. But in all of this there is no sign of animosity between the two leaders.

14. *Simeon has related:* The name "Simeon" (*Symeōn*) rather than "Simon" (*Simon*) or *Petros* is at first startling. The logic of the entire narrative demands that we take it as referring to Peter and not some other character (such as the Simeon Niger of Acts 13:1); otherwise the reference itself would be nonsensical. But why the alternative name? It may be due to Luke's love of archaizing (compare "Simeon Peter" in 2 Pet 1:1).

   God first made visitation: By this language, Luke makes James agree with Peter's own characterization of the events: it has been God at work in the Gentile conversion. For the significance of Luke's use of "visitation" (*epistkeptomai*) as shorthand for God's interventions in history, see the notes on Luke 1:68, 78; 7:16; 19:44; Acts 7:23.

   a people for his name: Two aspects of this expression require attention: a) the term *laos* ("people") is used by Luke almost exclusively in reference to Israel as the "people of God," that is, in its religious sense (see especially Luke 1:17, 68, 77; 2:32; 7:16, 29; 20:1; 22:66; 24:19; Acts 2:47; 3:23; 4:10; 5:12; 7:17, 34; 13:17). By having God choose "a people" from among Gentiles he suggests both an extension in the meaning of "Israel" defined in terms of faith rather than in terms of ethnic or ritual allegiance, and a claim for the continuity of the Gentile mission with biblical history; b) the term *onoma* ("name") in the LXX is virtually synonymous with God (see e.g., LXX Ps 5:11; 7:17; 21:22; 22:3; 44:17; 53:1; 78:9; 144:1; 148:1; 148:5, 13). In Acts, apart from 2:21, the primary use of the term is in reference to the "name of Jesus" (2:38; 3:6, 16; 4:7; 8:12, etc.). In the present phrase, the older biblical sense is intended, so that "for his name" means in effect "for himself." A passage that might have affected Luke is LXX Zech 2:14-15: "I will come and construct a tent (*kataskēnōsō*) in your midst, says the Lord, and in that day many nations will flee to the Lord and they will be to him as a people (*eis laon*), and they will tent among you."

15. *words of the Prophets agree with this:* Since the citation immediately following is from LXX Amos 9:11-12, the plural "the prophets" may refer here, as in 7:42 and 13:40, to the collection of the Twelve Prophets. More significant is the construction of the sentence: Luke does not have James declare that "this thing" (*touto*) agrees (*symphōnein*) with the prophets, so that the scripture text is the measure of how God can work, but the opposite: the working of God precedes the perception of the text's agreement.

16. *after these things I will return:* Although the bulk of this citation is from LXX Amos 9:11-12, it has a number of distinctive features: a) it replaces Amos'

en ekeinę hēmerą ("in that day") with *meta tauta* ("after these things"), reversing the procedure of Acts 2:17; b) it adds the words *anastrepsō* ("I will return"), possibly under the influence of Jer 12:15; c) Amos uses *anastēsō* ("will raise up") twice and *oikodomēsō* ("I will rebuild") twice, whereas Luke fails to use *anastēsō*, uses *oikodomēsō* twice, and *anorthēsō* (lacking in Amos) once; d) Amos has both *ta peptōkota* ("fallen things") and *ta kataskammena* ("ruined things"), whereas Luke has only *ta kataskammena*—both, however, have textual variants which further confuse the issue; e) Amos has *kathōs an hēmerai tou aiōnos* ("just as the days of old"), lacking in Luke; f) in Amos 9:12, Luke adds the particle *an* after *hopōs*, and also adds the words *ton kyrion* ("the Lord") as the direct object of "seek" (*ekzētēsōsin*); g) finally, the words *gnōsta ap' aiōnos* ("known from of old/eternity"), if they are to be read as part of the citation, are not from LXX Amos, and only marginally reflect the influence of LXX Isa 45:21.

tent of David: The *skēnē Daueid* occurs in the LXX only in this Amos passage and in Isa 16:5. It appears to be equivalent to the "house of David" (*oikos Daueid*) (see 1 Kgs 12:19, 26; 13:2; Ps 121:5, and especially Luke 1:27, 69; 2:4). The primary sense of the passage therefore refers to the re-establishment of the Davidic kingdom. It was taken in a messianic sense also by the Qumran sect, which cited it in *CD* 7:16 and *4QFlor* 1:12-13.

17. *rest of humanity might seek the Lord:* Precisely the divergence of the LXX from the Hebrew enables the text to be used midrashically. The MT can be translated, "that they may possess the remnant of Edom and all nations who are called by my name, says the Lord who does this." In the Hebrew the passage is a straightforward promise that Israel would possess other nations in a restored kingdom. But the LXX apparently read the Hebrew for "possess/inherit" (*yirshu*) as "they will seek" (*yidreshu*), and the Hebrew for "Edom" (*edom*) as "mankind" (*adam*), resulting in "the remnant of humanity seeks," with Luke only needing to supply what he regards as implicit, "the Lord" (*ton kyrion*). Now the restoration of David's kingdom (under the Messiah Jesus) functions as an invitation to the rest of the nations to join "the people of God."

my name has been invoked: Here the verb *epikaleō* is found in the perfect passive (compare Jas 2:7); in the active, the phrase "call on the name of the Lord" is thematic in Acts (2:21; 7:59; 9:14, 21). The use of *onoma mou* ("my name") obviously provides the midrashic link for the use of the passage by James who is discoursing on God's choice of a "people for his name."

18. *makes these things known from eternity:* This portion of the text is particularly difficult: a) is it considered to be part of the citation? It is not found in Amos, and the possible allusion to Isa 45:21 is weak; b) is it meant to be a statement by James following the citation, functioning as a transition to his concluding judgment? Certainly some *mss* took it this way, "this work is known by the Lord from all eternity." The present translation treats it as the end of the citation, which was already a loose one. But the following is also possible: "says the Lord as he does these things, which are known for a long time."

19. *my decision is to stop bothering:* The language is solemn and measured, literally, "I judge/decide" (*krinō*). Here, then, is James' "response." The "therefore" (*dio*) is strong, pointing us back to the basis for the decision, which appears to be: a) Peter's recital of God's visitation; b) the consonance of the prophecies with that event. But what is it about the text itself that justifies the decision to "stop" (negation of a present infinitive) "troubling/bothering" the Gentile converts? The choice of the verb *parenochlein* is itself revealing: it means to cause another annoyance (Aristotle, *Rhetoric* 1381B). In LXX Judg 14:17, it refers to Samson's being pestered by Delilah (see also 16:16); it is what Samuel calls his being summoned by the witch of Endor at the behest of Saul (1 Sam 28:15). In 1 Macc 10:35, it is used for the molesting of Jews during festivals. In short, James characterizes the Pharisees' demands as a form of *harassment* of the Gentiles that he wants stopped.

20. *write them to this effect:* The problems attending this so-called "Apostolic Decree" are multiple and various: a) there are three versions (15:20; 15:29; 21:25) which do not agree precisely in diction or order; b) there are substantial and significant textual variants for *each* of the versions; the Western Text, to take the most important case, omits the mention of *tou pniktou* ("of that which is strangled") in every case, and in the first two instances, replaces it with a version of the "Golden Rule": "and whatever they do not wish to happen to them, they should not do to others." c) Even if the text is stabilized, the meaning of the specific terms and of their overall intent (whether moral or ritual) is not entirely clear.

to avoid things polluted by idolatry: Or, "the contaminations of idols." The verb *apechō* when used with *apo* is used frequently for prohibitions (see LXX Job 28:28; Prov 9:18; Wis 2:16; Isa 54:14; 1 Thess 4:3; 1 Tim 4:3; 1 Pet 2:11). The noun *alisgēma*, however, occurs only here. Its meaning must be derived from the verb *alisgein*, which itself only occurs three times: in the LXX of Mal 1:7 (with reference to polluted food offered on altars), of Dan 1:8 (with reference to Daniel's excusing himself from the king's banquet), and of Sir 40:29 (with reference to "looking at the table of another," thus "contaminating one's soul"). These make it fairly certain that "the things polluted by idolatry" refers specifically to the food offered at the shrines of idols. The idea is basically the same, then, as in 15:29 and 21:25, where the term *eidōlothyton* ("meat offered to idols") is used; the prohibition therefore pertains to the issue discussed at such great length by Paul in 1 Cor 8–10.

sexual immorality: The prohibition of *porneia* is listed last in the other two versions of the decree (15:29; 21:25). Although the term *porneia* derives from *pornē* ("prostitute," see Gen 38:15-22; Josh 2:1; 6:16; Judg 11:1; Ezek 16:30), and has its first association with prostitution (Hos 1:2; 2:2-4; 4:12) it takes on the broad sense of any form of sexual immorality (Tob 4:12; 8:7; Sir 23:23). Because sexual imagery was used by the prophets as the metaphor for covenantal fidelity, the association of *porneia* with idolatry was inevitable, particularly since ritual prostitution seemed in fact to have played some role in the native Canaanite cults. Just as marriage is associated with covenantal fidelity, sexual immorality symbolizes idolatry (Hos 5:4; 6:11; Ezek 16:15-46; 23:7-35; Jer 3:6-8).

The relationship is stated in causal terms by Wis 14:12: "the idea of making idols was the beginning of fornication (*porneia*)." All forms of *porneia* are condemned by the NT (1 Cor 6:18; 7:2; 2 Cor 12:21; Gal 5:19; Eph 5:3; Col 3:5; 1 Thess 4:3; Heb 13:4), and it is even considered cause for divorce by Matt 5:32; 19:9. Note particularly the explicit connection between such sexual immorality and idolatry in 1 Cor 10:8 and Rev 2:14, 20.

from that which is strangled and from blood: The textual status of "that which is strangled" (*tou pniktou*) is uncertain, since the Western Text, which regularly expands, here omits it entirely. If with a majority of texts it is to be read, its precise meaning remains unclear. It is a substantive formed from the verb *pnigein*, which means to strangle or choke (compare Mark 5:13; Matt 13:7; 18:28, and Luke's *apopnigō* in Luke 8:7, 33). But to what does the term refer? The LXX uses *pnigein* straightforwardly for choking someone (1 Sam 16:14-15; Sir 51:4), but never uses the term in a ritual context. This brings us to the related problem of *haima* ("blood"). An obvious meaning would be the prohibition of murder (see Deut 21:7-8; 2 Sam 1:16; 2 Kgs 9:7; Ps 5:6; 9:12; 25:9). But a more frequent connection in Torah is to animal sacrifices. Since the "life of every creature is in the blood" (Lev 17:14), the Israelites were forbidden to drink the blood of any creature (Lev 17:10-13). The blood (symbolizing life) is to be offered to the Lord, before any creature is eaten. This enables us to connect the terms *haima* and *pniktou* into a single ritual prohibition: to abstain from "strangled things" and "from blood" is equivalent, since when something is strangled and then eaten, the blood remains within it. Note that this is the "sin" attributed to the people in 1 Sam 14:33.

21. *Moses from ages past:* Luke has James give this as his reason (*gar*) for the elements of the decree. The statement is witness to the long-standing ("from ages past") and widespread ("in every city") and regular ("every Sabbath") practice of reading and studying Torah throughout the Diaspora. For supporting evidence, see the note on Acts 13:14, as well as Philo, *On the Creation* 128; Josephus, *Antiquities of the Jews* 16:43). Josephus, in fact, attributes the custom to the command of Moses himself (*Against Apion* 2:175). But how does this fact lend support to James' decision? Undoubtedly because Luke regards these conditions as rooted in Torah, and that Torah's own norms for proselytes and sojourners (Lev 17:8, 10, 13, 15) would be known already to Gentiles close to the synagogue such as had converted. Such norms fell far short of circumcision or the implication that "salvation" hinged on their observance.

INTERPRETATION

No reader can miss the obvious importance Luke attaches to this Jerusalem Council. Preparation for it began already in Acts 10–11, with Peter's conversion of Cornelius and his household. The first mission of Paul and Barnabas among the Gentiles continued that preparation through Luke's repeated emphasis on faith as the basis for salvation.

Luke's capacity for composing a sustained narrative is nowhere more impressively displayed than in the way he weaves these earlier thematic strands together in this scene.

The reader of Hellenistic Novels recognizes the use of a standard narrative device: the assembly (*plēthos/ekklēsia*) of the people for debate allows an author the opportunity to recapitulate the story, reveal its implications, and strengthen its premises by means of public discussion and dialectic (compare e.g., Chariton of Aphrodisias, *Chaereas and Callirhoe* 3, 4, 4-18; 8, 7, 1-16). As so often, Luke's appropriation of such hackneyed devices is impressively fresh, in part at least due to his ability to compress narratives to their essence and so provide the reader with a new perspective on them. Peter's third and final retelling of the Cornelius episode, for example, is more than a mechanical repetition; by reducing the complex story to its constitutive components, Luke provides the reader with a far deeper understanding of that event.

The importance of the meeting is signalled as well by the proposing (15:20) and issuing (15:29) of a formal decree, the only such official directive in the entire narrative. Luke gathers his main characters together for the first time only for the fashioning of this decision, and then disbands them. The only time two of the participants meet again, the subject of the decree will also surface: when James meets Paul on his last visit to Jerusalem, he reminds Paul of the terms of this conciliar decision (21:18-25).

We are justified, therefore, in regarding the Apostolic Council as a watershed in the narrative of Acts. Before this point, Luke has followed the movements (at least ostensibly) of all the apostles; after this, it is Paul alone who dominates the story. Before this point, the mission to the Jews was the first priority; after this, attention is given unequivocally to the establishment of Gentile communities. But how does the narrative effect this literary (and perspectival) transition?

First, the meeting allows Luke to legitimate in formal fashion the Gentile mission: the human Church now catches up with the divine initiative, and formally declares itself on the side of God's plan to save all humanity. Second, the debate enables Luke to define more precisely the basis for this legitimacy, by establishing *faith* as the basis of salvation (and of inclusion within God's people) for all, both Gentiles and Jews. Third, the discussion provides the opportunity to emphasize the essential *continuity* between these stages in the divine plan: the inclusion of the Gentiles does not mean the replacement of "Israel" but its expansion; the elimination of Mosaic *ethos* (custom) for the Gentiles does not mean the elimination of Torah, but rather the fulfillment of its prophetic intention, "made known from long ago" (15:18), as well as the continuation of those aspects of Torah that have always applied to the proselyte and sojourner.

Having secured these points, Luke can confidently lead the reader into the final part of his story, showing through the ministry of Paul how the good news reaches "the end of the earth" (Acts 1:8).

Precisely the impressive and central staging of this event we have come to call the "Jerusalem Council," however, has raised questions concerning its historical character. Once more, the reader faces the problem posed by multiple sources and their disagreement. In this case, Acts tells a story that in some respects agrees with and in other respects comes into conflict with the version found in Paul's letters. The most important overlap and divergence is found in Gal 2:1-14, which describes both a conflict in Antioch and a meeting in Jerusalem, but in terms quite different than Luke's. A second, less direct, conflict is suggested by the lengthy discussion in 1 Cor 8–10 concerning the propriety of eating food that had been sacrificed to idols, a discussion in a letter surely written after this putative council, by a major participant in it, dealing with the same subject, yet which never in any way alludes to the "apostolic decree" supposedly issued by that council.

The problem in assessing the historical character of these events is rendered more difficult by the fact that neither Paul nor Luke are disinterested observers; each has a purpose to telling the tale the way he does. If the version in Acts cannot be taken as reliable in every respect, neither can that in Galatians. The discrepancies are many and the questions they pose real. Was there only one meeting, concerning which the sources disagree, or were there several? Do the sources refer to the same or different meetings? When Paul went up (after fourteen years) to Jerusalem with Barnabas (Gal 2:1), did he go as part of an Antiochean delegation (Acts) or in response to a "revelation" (Gal), or both? Did he bring Titus along (Gal 2:3), and was Titus among the anonymous "certain others" (Acts 15:2)?

More critically, did this meeting *follow* a harsh encounter involving Paul and Barnabas in Antioch (Acts) or *precede* such an encounter (according to the usual way of reading Gal 2:11)? Was that encounter, in either case, between Paul and Barnabas (on one side) against anonymous members of the Pharisaic party, as Acts 15:1 would have it, or was it a conflict primarily between Paul and Cephas (with Barnabas siding with Cephas) stimulated by the arrival in Antioch of "certain men from James" (as in Gal 2:11-13)? Was this encounter the real reason for the split between Barnabas and Paul, rather than the personal dispute over John-Mark reported by Luke (Acts 15:36-40)? Was James, in fact, a figure of reconciliation (as in Acts) or a provocateur (as possibly in Galatians)? Of historical importance for the understanding of Paul's later career is the issue whether the meeting *closed* an issue in amicable fashion (Acts), or whether it only *opened* the issue and further disagreement (Gal).

The disagreements touch also on other critical aspects of Paul's career.

Did the meeting issue in decrees concerning the basic requirements of Gentile converts (Acts)? If so, why did Paul not refer to them in his discussion of the issue in 1 Corinthians? Is it because those decrees had application only to the areas cited in the apostolic letter (Antioch, Syria, Cilicia [Acts 15:23]), and not in Achaia? Is it because Paul disagreed with the council's decision and ignored it in his own churches? Or is it because there never were any such decrees? Was the outcome of the meeting the conditions for table fellowship among Jewish and Gentile Christians at all (Acts) or perhaps an agreement concerning the division of the mission between Peter and Paul (Gal 2:7-8) and a commitment from Paul to raise a collection for the Jerusalem Church (Gal 2:10)?

The disagreements are real, and the historical questions they raise are of legitimate interest. Sane historiography, however, is not paralyzed but empowered by such conflicts, for the divergence of sources on so many important details makes their agreement on other points the more impressive. This underlying agreement enables us to state with considerable confidence that in the first decades of the Christian movement an important meeting was held concerning the legitimacy and basis of the Gentile mission; that participants included the leaders Paul and Peter and James and Barnabas; that certain agreements were reached which, in one way or another, secured the basic freedom of the Gentile initiative. The most striking agreement between the sources, in fact, comes at the religious level. With only very slight variation, both Luke and Paul agree that the basis of the mission to the Gentiles was a matter of God's gift (Acts 15:11; Gal 2:9), and that God was equally at work in the Apostle Paul as he was in the Apostle Peter (Acts 15:7-8, 12; Gal 2:8).

The critical historian need reject absolutely neither the account in Acts nor in Galatians. Both sources are partial and tendentious. Both can be used with care to make a firm if finite statement about early Christianity. That said, the historian must yield to the literary critic and the theologian, for the value of Luke's narrative is hardly limited to its historical accuracy. We have by this point learned enough about the character of Hellenistic historiography and apologetics to approach this story confidently in terms of its literary fashioning. We know that, as at every other point in the story, our author is concerned less with "what happened" than with "what should have happened," is indeed constructing a narrative which (no less than the idyllic summaries of the early Church or the speeches of Peter and Paul) is meant to have a paradigmatic character for his readers.

Recognizing the fundamentally edifying quality of the story, therefore, we are able to engage the author's narrative perspective and thereby engage a quality of narrative "truth" which is not confined to referential accuracy. The structure of the story calls our attention, for example, to the dynamics of decision-making in the Church. This formal gathering of the Church (*ekklēsia*) is called in order to respond to a crisis that not only threatens the peace of the community but raises fundamental questions concerning the community's identity and the grounds for its fellowship. The attention Luke gives to *how* the Church makes the decision required of it is an intrinsic part of his narrative message.

In brief, Luke enables the reader to see the early Church reaching decision by means of an articulation of its faith, as a process of *discernment* of God's activity. Priority is given to the narratives of faith, for it is such narratives which enable private religious experience to reach the level of public discernment. Here Peter does not appear as the judge but as another witness, whose story of how God himself "bore witness" to the Gentiles by giving them the Holy Spirit "just as he had to us" led him to the deepest and final insight of his long journey from the tanner's rooftop: that the basis of salvation for both Jews and Gentiles was faith (15:7-11). Here Paul and Barnabas do not appear as advocates pleading a case but as simple witnesses of "the signs and wonders God had done with them" among the Gentiles (15:12).

Such narratives open up the possibility of perceiving God working in unexpected ways. They also open up the possibility of new understandings of Torah. The second component of decision-making as an articulation of faith is the reinterpretation of the Scripture. What is striking about James' citation of Amos 9:11-12 is not simply the dependence on the LXX version (see notes) or the way in which that version enables James to perceive a mission to the Gentiles after the "restoration" of David's tent, but the way in which James puts the case. He says that "the prophets agree with *this*" rather than that "this agrees with *the prophets*" (15:15). In other words, it is the experience of God revealed through narrative which is given priority in this hermeneutical process: the text of Scripture does not dictate how God should act. Rather, God's action dictates how we should understand the text of Scripture.

The third component in ecclesial decision-making may be the most surprising, but Luke clearly sees conflict and debate as legitimate and perhaps even necessary elements in the process of discernment. Both in the Antiochean community (15:2) and in the Jerusalem assembly (15:7) there is considerable dissension and debate. Luke is unembarrassed by it, for such disagreement serves to reveal the true bases for fellowship, and elicit the fundamental principles of community identity. In this case, the Pharisaic challenge to the Gentile mission, precisely because of its unequivocal and massive character, forced the community to deal with the issue of membership and status in a far more substantial way than if the challenge had not been raised.

We must, of course, distinguish Luke's approbation of debate and dis-

→ pp.
15-16,
279

agreement as legitimate components in the process of decision-making, from his equally emphatic *disapproval* of the Pharisees who raised the objection as well as of their position! As indicated in the notes, Luke never shows the least favor toward the Pharisees, and this incident is no exception. The fact that they are "disciples" is irrelevant, for so were other characters who served as negative narrative foils (Judas, Ananias and Sapphira, Simon Magus). Everything in Luke's shaping of the narrative from chapter 10 forces us to see the Pharisees personifying the same opposition to "the plan of God" as they did in the Gospel (see especially 7:29-30).

Four pieces of evidence make Luke's intentions unmistakable. First, their statement that the Gentiles *cannot be saved* without circumcision flies in the face of Luke's whole previous narrative, which made the emphatic point that Gentiles could and did receive salvation through the principle of *faith* (see notes). Second, Peter's characterization of their position as "testing God" places their opposition in the same category as the challenge of Ananias and Sapphira, a refusal to recognize the work of the Spirit. Third, James' expression "stop bothering" (*mē parenochlein*) makes clear that the Pharisees have engaged in a form of harassment of those whom James himself regards as having "turned to God" (15:19) and forming "a people for his name" (15:14). Fourth, the careful reader cannot but notice the contrast between this "assembly" of the disciples with that of the Sanhedrin in 5:28-40. In that assembly, the Pharisee Gamaliel was the chief advisor. His apparently banal but essentially faithless interpretation of history led to the beating of the disciples, signifying the rejection of the Spirit's work. In this assembly, another attempt by the Pharisees to control the movement is rejected, and the Church's leaders fulfill the statement made by Peter in that earlier encounter: "we are witnesses of these things, as well as the Holy Spirit whom God has given to those who obey him" (Acts 5:32).

We will take up the final component in decision-making, the consent of the community, in the next section. But we must observe now that the decision by James emphatically agrees with the perception of Peter, Paul, and Barnabas, that God was at work in the Gentile mission and that the Church must respond obediently to God's initiative. The Pharisaic position is emphatically rejected. The equal status of the Gentiles in the messianic community is confirmed by the head of the Jerusalem community. What, then, are we to make of the "apostolic decree" James wants sent to these Gentiles?

The complexity of the issues these prohibitions raise for the text of Acts and for the historical analysis of early Christianity, have been touched on earlier in this discussion and more extensively in the notes. But how does Luke want us to understand them? To assess this, we must take into account the character of the prohibitions themselves, the characterization of them by James as something other than "harassment," and their basis in the fact that "Moses is read" throughout the Diaspora.

According to Luke's presentation, therefore, the prohibitions are neither new to these Gentile converts nor a burden to them. This implies that they would have learned of the prohibitions through their association with the synagogue, and would have already been observing them. Looked at in this light, the prohibitions themselves clearly seem to fit within the sort of requirements for "proselytes and sojourners" already spelled out in Leviticus 17–18, and elaborated in the rabbinic discussions of the so called "Noachian precepts." These were the commandments given to the sons of Noah for observance, and include (among others) the prohibitions listed here by Luke (see *bT Sanh.* 56b).

The logic of James' position is either a) that these primordial commands would be known to all nations, or b) that those frequenting the synagogues would already know them. In either case, no burden would be put on the Gentiles by demanding their observance.

But why insist even on these? The point would seem to be to provide the basis for table-fellowship and full communion between Jew and Gentile Messianists. The commandments in Leviticus in particular give as their motivation the avoidance of "defiling the land" and "defiling the people," and the consequences of breaking these commandments is "being cut off from the people" (Lev 17:7, 9, 10, 14; 18:21, 24-25, 28-30). But according to the protocol of table-fellowship in the ancient world, one would eat only with someone who shared the same values. Table-fellowship symbolized spiritual fellowship (see 1 Cor 10:14-22). How could *Jews* eat with those whose practices fundamentally defiled themselves and the land and the people? These requirements of the Gentiles therefore enabled Jews to remain in communion with them, since the Gentiles would not be engaging in practices in radical disharmony with the Jewish *ethos*, and the Gentiles would be "keeping the Torah" as it was spelled out for "proselytes and sojourners in the land."

For Reference and Further Study

Dahl, N. " 'A People for His Name' (Acts 15:14)." *NTS* 4 (1957–1958) 319–27.

Dibelius, M. "The Apostolic Council." *Studies in the Acts of the Apostles.* Trans. M. Ling. London: SCM Press, 1956, 93–101.

Dupont, J. "*LAOS EX ETHNON.*" *Etudes sur les Actes des Apôtres.* Lectio Divina 45. Paris: Editions du Cerf, 1967, 361–365.

_____. "Un peuple d'entre les nations (Actes 15:14)." *NTS* 31 (1985) 321–335.

Haenchen, E. "Quellenanalyze und Kompositionanalyze in Acts 15." *Judentum, Urchristentum, Kirche.* Ed. W. Altester. Berlin: A. Töpelmann, 1960, 153–164.

Lake, K. "The Apostolic Council." *The Beginnings of Christianity* Part One: *The Acts of the Apostles*. Eds. F. J. Foakes-Jackson and K. Lake. Vol. 5: *Additional Notes to the Commentary*. Eds. K. Lake and H. J. Cadbury. London: MacMillan and Co., 1933, 195–212.

Richard, E. "The Creative Use of Amos by the Author of Acts." *NovT* 24 (1982) 37–53.

Schwartz, D. R. "The Futility of Reading Moses (Acts 15:21)." *Bib* 67 (1986) 276–281.

Weiser, A. "Das Apostelkonzil (Apg 15, 1-35): Ereignis, Uberlieferung, lukanishe Deutung." *BZ* n.s. 28 (1984) 145–167.

Wilson, S. G. *The Gentiles and the Gentile Mission in Luke-Acts*. Cambridge: University Press, 1973, 171–195.

30. *The Church Decides for Gentile Freedom* (15:22-35)

22. The apostles and elders, together with the whole Church, then decided to choose men from among them who were leaders among the brothers—Judas called Barsabbas, and Silas—to send to Antioch with Paul and Barnabas. 23. Through them they wrote: "The brothers who are apostles and elders send greetings to the brothers from among the Gentiles in Antioch and Syria and Cilicia. 24. Since we have heard that certain people coming from us have disturbed you, upsetting your minds with words we did not authorize, 25. we decided after gathering together to choose men to send to you with our beloved Barnabas and Paul, 26. who have dedicated their lives to the name of our Lord Jesus Messiah. 27. We have therefore sent Judas and Silas, and they will announce the same things orally. 28. The Holy Spirit and we have decided to place no further burden on you apart from these necessary things: 29. to keep away from food offered to idols, and from blood, and from things strangled, and from sexual immorality. You will do well by keeping yourselves from these things. Stay well!" 30. They were therefore sent off. They went down to Antioch. When they had gathered the assembly, they delivered the letter. 31. Upon reading it, they rejoiced at the consolation. 32. Judas as well as Silas were themselves prophets. They comforted the brothers with many words and strengthened them. 33. After spending some time, they were sent back by the brothers in peace to those who had sent them. 35. But Paul and Barnabas remained in Antioch. With many others as well, they continued to teach and preach the word of the Lord.

Handwritten margin notes:
OED 1. full of mng (of persons:) full of intelligence
or wisdom
2. of the nature of a sentence or aphoristic saying
3. (of discourse) abounding in pointed maxims, aphoristic
in recent NOTES use sts in a bad sense, affectedly
or pompously formal

22. *then decided:* Literally, "it seemed good to the apostles." Luke uses *dokeō* + the dative in the same way as in Luke 1:3. The expression will occur three times in the passage (15:25, 28, [34]). Its slightly sententious tone derives from its use in formal declarations (see Herodotus, *Persian Wars* 1:3, and compare Josephus, *Antiquities of the Jews* 6:321 and especially 16:163).

to choose men from among them: The aorist participle of *eklegomai* in some *mss* agrees with its governing subject and is therefore in the dative; the majority of *mss*, however, have it agreeing with the object in the accusative. The circumstantial participle can be used to express purpose, but here it properly modifies the act of sending; literally, "having chosen, to send." For the resonances of the verb *eklegomai* ("choose/elect"), see Luke 6:13; 9:35; Acts 1:2, 24; 6:5; 13:17; 15:7.

Judas called Barsabbas, and Silas: The surname means "Son of Sabbath." Although the construction is precisely the same, Luke draws no connection between this character and the "Joseph called Barsabbas" who was a candidate for the apostolic circle in Acts 1:23. Judas is characterized as a "prophet" (15:32), but does not appear again outside this account (15:27, 32). Silas, in contrast, will play an important role as Paul's new partner after the split between Paul and Barnabas (15:41; 16:19, 25, 29; 17:4, 10, 14-15; 18:5). He is undoubtedly to be identified with the Silvanus who is Paul's coworker in 2 Cor 1:19; 1 Thess 1:1; 2 Thess 1:1 (see also 1 Pet 5:12). For the expression "leaders among the brothers" (*hēgoumenoi en tois adelphois*), compare Luke 22:26; Acts 7:10; 14:12; Heb 13:7, 17, 24.

23. *through them they wrote:* Literally "writing through their hand"; the *dia* ("through") in this case suggests that they were the deliverers of the letter. Compare *dia . . . Silouanos egrapsa* in 1 Pet 5:12. Some *mss* of the Western Tradition considered this too cryptic and variously expanded it.

brothers who are apostles and elders send greetings: Some *mss* add a *kai* ("and") before *adelphoi*, so that this reads, "the apostles and elders and brothers," making it agree with the inclusion of "the whole Church" in v. 23. The infinitive *chairein* ("to rejoice") is a standard greeting in Hellenistic letters (see 1 Macc 10:18, 25, 26; 11:30, 32; 13:36; 2 Macc 1:1, 10; 11:16; 3 Macc 1:8; Jas 1:1, and below, Acts 23:26).

Antioch and Syria and Cilicia: Luke uses the preposition *kata* + the accusative to demarcate a geographical area, as in Luke 9:6; 13:22; 21:11; Acts 2:10; 8:1; 11:1. The inclusion of the city of Antioch is obvious, since that is where the commotion began and from which the delegation was sent (15:1-2). Syria-Cilicia is the double province of which Antioch is the capital city. Luke has not yet explicitly related any activity by Paul in that area, but in 15:41 Paul and Silas go through the region "strengthening" those churches. Paul himself refers to his early work "in Syria and Cilicia" in Gal 1:21 (compare Acts 9:30). In James' reminder concerning this letter in 21:25, there is no geographical restriction: the letter was intended for "the Gentiles who have believed."

24. *since we have heard:* The *epeidē* has a formal sense ("inasmuch"), like the *epeid-ēper* in the prologue to the Gospel (Luke 1:1), and the use of *dokeō* in v. 25. Luke chooses language appropriate to such solemn declarations by assemblies. See the precise parallel (*epeidē . . . edoxe tē boulē kai tō dēmō*) in Diogenes Laertius, *Lives of the Philosophers* 2:142.

    certain people coming from us: Although any responsibility for their actions is immediately denied ("with words we did not authorize"), this expression is as close as Luke comes to agreeing with Paul's version in Gal 2:12 that the trouble in Antioch originated with "certain men come from James" (*elthein tinas apo Iakobou*). Some *mss* drop the participle *exelthontes*, which makes that point of origination even more explicit.

    disturbed you, upsetting your minds: For Luke's use of *tarassō* ("disturb"), see Luke 1:12; 24:38; Acts 17:8, 13; the language used by Paul in Gal 1:7 is once more intriguing: *ei mē tines eisin hoi tarassontes hymas* ("unless there are some who are disturbing you"). The verb *anaskeuazō* (translated as "upsetting") occurs only here in the NT and is not found in the LXX. It has a range of negative connotations, from "distracting" to "destroying." Some *mss* expand the verse by adding the words that were supposed to have upset them: "saying that it is necessary to be circumcised and keep the Law." The older and best *mss* have the shorter reading.

25. *to choose men:* The same options with regard to textual variants and grammar apply in this use of *eklexamenois/ous* as in 15:22. In this case, the textual evidence for the dative case is stronger. For the sending of four men on a legation, see Chariton of Aphrodisias, *Chaereas and Callirhoe* 3, 4, 17: "two from the people, and two from the council" (*duo men apo tou dēmou, duo de apo tēs boulēs*).

    beloved Barnabas and Paul: Notice that although James is made to call Peter by the name "Simeon" (15:14), the assembly does not use "Saul" but Paul. The adjective *agapētos* ("beloved") occurs only here in Acts. In the Gospel it is used only with reference to Jesus (3:22; 20:13), once in a textual variant to the adjective "chosen" (*eklelegmenos*, 9:35). It is used very widely in the NT epistolary literature (Rom 1:7; 12:19; 16:5, 8, 9, 12; 1 Cor 4:14, 17; 10:14; 15:58; 2 Cor 7:1; 12:19; Eph 5:1; 6:21; Phil 2:12; 4:1; Col 1:7; 4:7, 9, 14; 1 Thess 2:8; 1 Tim 6:2; 2 Tim 1:2; Phlm 1, 16; Heb 6:9; Jas 1:16, 19; 2:5; 1 Pet 2:11; 4:12; 2 Pet 1:17; 3:1, 8, 14, 15, 17; 1 John 2:7; 3:2, 21; 4:1, 7, 11; 3 John 1, 2, 5, 11; Jude 3, 17, 20).

26. *who have dedicated their lives:* The Greek makes clearer than the translation is able that this characterization applies specifically to Paul and Barnabas. The perfect participle of *paradidōmi* ("hand over") is here translated as "devoted," rather than as the RSV's "risked their lives," which is overly dramatic. Note particularly the use of the same verb in Acts 14:26 with reference to these same people, "where they had been commissioned for the gift of God" (see also 15:40, below). The Western Text, however, seems to agree with the RSV translation, since it adds *eis panta peirasmon* ("they handed over their lives to every trial").

27. *announce the same things orally:* Literally, "through speech" (*dia logou*). The emissaries are to confirm with personal testimony the contents of the letter; compare the role of the letter-bearer in Eph 6:21-22; Col 4:7-8; 1 Macc 12:23. The participle is used to denote purpose and could be rendered, "in order that they might report the same things orally."

28. *The Holy Spirit and we have decided:* Literally, "it seemed good to the Holy Spirit and to us," with *dokeō* used in the same way as in 15:22. Compare Chariton of Aphrodisias, *Chaereas and Callirhoe* 3, 4, 18, and especially Josephus, *Antiquities of the Jews* 16:163: in a letter from Caesar to the Jews in Asia, we find *edoxe moi kai tọ emọ symbouliọ meta orkōmosias,* "it has been decided by me and my council under oath." The invocation of the Holy Spirit as a partner to the decision has an odd sound to contemporary ears, but it nicely captures the dynamics of the process as portrayed by Luke. For similar language establishing an interplay between the activity of humans and of the Holy Spirit, see Acts 13:1-3.

    apart from these necessary things: The spirit of this statement is exactly the same as in James' earlier declaration, with the expression "no further burden" standing in place of "stop bothering" (15:19). The term "necessary" (the adverb *epanankēs* used as a substantive) obviously has nothing to do with "necessary for salvation" as in the Pharisees' position (15:1, 5), but means rather "the minimal requirements for communion between Jew and Gentile believers." For *baros* as an oppressive weight, see 2 Macc 9:10; Matt 20:12; 2 Cor 4:17; Gal 6:2; Rev 2:24.

29. *food offered to idols:* For a detailed discussion of the separate terms of the decree, see the notes on 5:20. The major textual consideration is Codex D's dropping of "things strangled" and adding of the Golden Rule, as in 15:20. The term *eidōlothyton* (literally "something sacrificed to an idol") replaces "things polluted by idolatry." It occurs in 4 Macc 5:2, as well as in 1 Cor 8:1, 4, 7, 10; 10:19; Rev 2:14, 20. The item "sexual immorality" occurs here in last place, rather than in second place.

    by keeping yourselves: The circumstantial participle *diatērountes* here functions virtually as the prodosis of a conditional sentence = "if you keep yourselves." The verb appears in the LXX in contexts of fidelity to the covenant and commandments (see Gen 17:10; 37:11; Num 18:7; Deut 7:8; 33:9; Sir 1:25).

    you will do well: The expression *eu praxete* or its near equivalent appears at the end of letters in 2 Macc 9:19 (where it is synonymous with "be healthy"); 11:26, and in the letters of Ignatius of Antioch, *Eph* 4:2; *Smyr* 11:3. See also the *kalōs poieis* in Jas 2:19. The expression can be read as signifying both moral rectitude and fittingness.

    stay well: The perfect passive imperative of the verb *rhōnnumai* ("be strong") literally means to "fare well." It is a frequent conclusion to Hellenistic letters (2 Macc 9:20; 11:21, 33; 3 Macc 3:12; 7:1, 9); see also Acts 23:20 (in some *mss*). The Western Text adds *pheromenoi en tọ hagiọ pneumati* ("being borne along in the Holy Spirit"), although it could as easily be read with the beginning of the next verse, "they were sent off," by assimilation from Acts 13:4. Similar pious additions are made to *errōsthe* in the letters of Ignatius of Antioch (*Eph* 21:2; *Magn* 15:1; *Rom* 10:3; *Phil* 11:2; *Smyr* 13:2).

31. *rejoiced at the consolation:* For Luke's thematic use of "rejoicing" (*chairein*) as a positive response to God's visitation, see the note on Acts 13:48. The term *paraklēsis* could also be translated as "exhortation," but consolation seems to fit the context better.

32. *were themselves prophets:* Luke restricts this term in Acts to those who function as spokespersons within communities (see notes on 11:27 and 13:1). In the present case, however, the fact that Silas will become Paul's new partner in 15:40 gives this designation a sharper connotation. Codex D adds, "filled with the Holy Spirit," which is consistent with one of that manuscript's thematic tendencies. The verb *sterizō* ("strengthen") is used by Luke for the act of building up or establishing a group (Luke 22:32; Acts 15:41; 18:23). For the combination of "comforting and strengthening," see Acts 14:22.

33. *to those who had sent them:* They have been sent back "in peace" (see Luke 7:50; 8:48; 10:5-6; 24:36), which in the present context has more than a formulaic significance; the legation achieved its mission of reconciliation, and relations between the communities are good. Many later *mss* have "back to the apostles," with an obvious interest in exalting their role. The present translation follows the best *mss*. These also lack v. 34, which in the later *mss* on which most English translations were based read "Silas decided to remain there" (again using *dokeō*). The purpose of the addition seems obvious: since Silas joins Paul in 15:40, he should be in Antioch rather than in Jerusalem. Still other *mss* make the situation even clearer by adding "Judas alone went."

35. *continued to teach and preach:* Luke again gives the reader the sense that Paul and Barnabas are rooted in the life of this local community, as they continue their ministry of teaching and preaching (*euangelizomai*). Compare the earlier notices in 11:26; 13:1; 14:26-28.

INTERPRETATION

This segment of the text obviously continues the account of the Jerusalem Council (15:1-21) and is considered separately only for reasons of convenience. Luke draws the meeting of apostles, elders, and people to a close with a decision in favor of Gentile freedom and the resolve to send a legation with a letter to that effect to the churches first troubled (15:22-29), and rounds off his account with the happy conclusion of that reconciling effort (15:30-35).

In our analysis of the council, we saw how Luke portrayed as a theological process the resolution of the crisis posed by God's activity among the Gentiles and the challenge to their inclusion among God's people. The members of the community affected bore witness to God's activity among them by the narrative of their experience, and how they had come to understand it (15:7-12). These narratives in turn provided the key for the interpretation of the tradition, both that coming from Jesus himself (11:15), and the words of Torah (15:15-17). Within this process, disagreement and dissent played an important role in forcing the discernment of the essential from the accidental, the genuine from the false (15:1, 5, 7).

Now Luke shows the final component in that process, the consensus of the entire Church. James makes judgment (*krinō*, 15:19), but does not decide alone. The apostles and elders must agree *with the whole Church* for that decision to be carried (15:22). In fact, it is not enough for the Mother Church to decide the issue unanimously; the local churches who are addressed must also "rejoice at the consolation" and send the emissaries back "in peace" for the decision truly to have been reached (15:31, 33). Not only the communication of a decision from on high, but the steady presence in the affected community of prophets who can console and strengthen, teach and preach the word of God, finish off this process of decision-making in Luke's idealized rendition (15:32, 35).

Luke's version is indeed idealized, which is precisely why it has had such a powerfully evocative force through the history of the Church. It is too seldom noticed how subtly Luke interweaves the elements of divine intervention and human discernment, so that the decision of the Church appears finally neither as an abject submission to the divine impetus it cannot understand, nor as a willful manipulation of religious symbols by politically motivated leaders, but as a dialectical synergism of God's intrusions and human faith. Precisely this synergism is suggested by the language of the community: "The Holy Spirit and we have decided." It is not as though they were equal partners; rather the Church's decision is one that has finally caught up with and therefore confirmed a decision made already by God.

By so structuring this story, Luke has provided his readers with a further glimpse of a developing messianic *politeia*. Just as in Acts 2 and 4 he provided a "foundation story" which expressed the ideals of life together, so here he provides a model for making decisions within this people constituted by faith. Here now is a community capable of resolving difficult issues concerning membership and status: it calls a council (*plēthos*), hears testimony, interprets its sacred texts, declares its convictions in propositions of faith, sends out legations with letters, establishes peace between local communities.

The influence of this portrayal is unmistakable in the account of Eusebius of Caesarea concerning the second century debate over the observance of Easter (the so-called "Quartodecimam Controversy"). Without ever explicitly quoting Luke's version, his own narrative resonates the same convictions and bears independent testimony to the same ideals: the use of narratives of faith in council, the discernment of tradition, the valuing of *koinōnia* ("fellowship") over theoretical correctness, the tolerance of diversity of practice within a framework of shared belief (Eusebius, *Ecclesiastical History* 5:23-25). Luke's sense of "how things should have happened" played no small role in shaping the way things subsequently did happen, at least in moments when the Church partially realized its own best self.

Equal credit must be given Luke's narrative for its effectiveness in summarizing in a single emblematic sequence what must surely have been, historically, a messier and more complex development. The way he shaped the rhetoric of the Jerusalem meeting is far more important than the historicity, applicability, or reception of the "apostolic decree." That decree could have been, in any case, of only temporary significance. It is in the enunciation of the basic issues and their resolution that Luke's narrative shows its true power.

Subtly but surely he uses the apostles' statements to shape a new definition of "the people of God" as one based on messianic faith rather than on ethnic origin or ritual observance. He establishes as a fundamental principle that the Church's responsibility is not to dictate God's action but discern it, not to close the Scriptures to further interpretation but to open them. He asserts unequivocally that the authentic people of God is one in which all nations can share as equals, and that since God has shown himself to be without discrimination, so must the Church itself.

In some fashion, of course, all of these propositions can be located somewhere in Paul's letters. But the point is that they must be found, elicited, and analyzed. Alone in the New Testament writings Luke has given fundamental and programmatic expression to the nature of Christianity as a people of faith and as potentially inclusive of all humans; he has done so, moreover, in a narrative of paradigmatic force, so that despite every other dispute and division Christianity subsequently experienced, this issue never again required resolution.

Nor does it in Luke's own story. Acts 15 is a watershed within the narrative because it frees Luke finally to concentrate almost entirely on the mission of Paul, and the effective opening of "the door of faith for the Gentiles" (14:27). In this light, the most significant clue to the literary function of the account we have just read may be the sending back of the Jerusalem delegation "in peace" (15:33): attacks may still come from the outside, but Luke wants the reader to see the Church—as it expands to include ever more of the Gentiles—internally unified, with its first and most serious division reconciled.

For Reference and Further Study

Blomberg, C. "The Law in Luke-Acts." *JSNT* 22 (1984) 53–80.
Bruce, F. F. "The Apostolic Decree of Acts 15." *Studien zum Text und zur Ethik*

des Neuen Testaments. Ed. W. Schrage. BZNW 47. Berlin: Walter de Gruyter, 1986, 115–124.

Jervell, J. *Luke and the People of God*. Minneapolis: Augsburg Press, 1972, 185–207.

Johnson, L. T. *Decision-Making in the Church: A Biblical Model*. Philadelphia: Fortress Press, 1983, 46–58, 67–87.

Perrot, C. "Les decisions de l'assemblée de Jérusalem." *RScR* 69 (1981) 195–208.

Sahlin, H. "Die Drei Kardinalsundin (Götzendienst, Blutvergiessen, Unsucht) und das N.T." *ST* 24 (1970) 93–112.

Sieben, H. J. "Zur Entwicklung der Konzilidee." *TPhil* 50 (1975) 481–503.

Turner, C. H. "Jewish Christianity: The Apostolic Decree of Acts XV and the Apostolic Church Orders—I." *Theology* 20 (1930) 4–14.

Wilson, S. G. *Luke and the Law*. SNTSMS 50. Cambridge: University Press, 1983.

III. THE APOSTLE TO THE GENTILES

31. *The Mission to Europe* (15:36–16:10)

36. After some days Paul said to Barnabas, "Let us go back and visit the brothers in each city where we proclaimed the word of the Lord, to see how they are doing." 37. Now Barnabas wanted to also take along John who is called Mark. 38. But Paul thought it better not to take along with them this one who had abandoned them in Pamphylia and had not gone on with them. 39. And there was such sharp disagreement that they separated from each other. Barnabas took along Mark and sailed to Cyprus. 40. But Paul chose Silas, and after being dedicated to the gift of the Lord by the brothers, he departed. 41. He went through Syria and Cilicia, strengthening the churches. 16:1. He also went down to Derbe and Lystra. A certain disciple there was named Timothy. He was the son of a Jewish woman who was a believer. But his father was a Greek. 2. The brothers in Lystra and Iconium testified to him. 3. Paul wanted this man to accompany him. He took him and circumcised him because of the Jews who were in those areas; for they all knew that his father was a Greek. 4. Now as they went through the cities, they delivered to them for their observance the decrees that had been decided by the apostles and elders in Jerusalem. 5. The churches therefore were strengthened in faith and every day increased in number. 6. They then went through the Phrygian and Galatian region, since they had been prevented by the Holy Spirit from speaking the word in Asia. 7. And when they came opposite Mysia, they tried to go into Bithynia. But the Spirit of Jesus did not allow them. 8. So passing by Mysia, they went

down to Troas. 9. A vision appeared to Paul during the night. A certain Macedonian man was standing and exhorting him. He was saying, "Come over to Macedonia! Help us!" 10. When he saw the vision, we sought at once to go to Macedonia, since we were convinced that God had called us to proclaim the good news to them.

NOTES

36. *visit the brothers:* Here the term *episkeptomai* ("to visit") has the sense of "over-see/inspect" (Num 14:34; Ps 26:4; Zech 11:16; 2 Macc 11:36; Acts 6:3), rather than the more religiously freighted sense of Luke 1:68, 78; 7:16; Acts 7:23; 15:14. This is made clear by the final clause "[to see] how they are doing" (literally "having," *echousin*). Compare the pastoral circuit reported in 14:22-23.

37. *now Barnabas wanted to also take along:* The next four verses are something of a rough chiasm: a) Barnabas' desire; b) Paul's perception; c) the split; a') Barnabas' action; b') Paul's action. The Greek conjunctions are repetitive and bland (*de/te*), so this English translation tries to supply some of the intended narrative movement. John-Mark had accompanied Paul and Barnabas in the first leg of their previous journey (13:5-12). The verb *symparalambanō* ("to take along with," see 3 Macc 1:1), is the same as used for John-Mark's initial recruitment in 12:25. Paul uses it himself for his taking Titus with him to Jerusalem (Gal 2:1).

38. *Paul thought it better:* The verb *axioō* (literally, "consider worthy") here has the sense of a prudential judgment rather than a moral one; it has the sense "he was resolved" (compare 2 Macc 4:19; 4 Macc 5:17; Acts 28:22).

    this one who had abandoned them: Luke obviously shares Paul's hard judgment on the nature of the original departure, since *touton* ("this one") holds a place of emphasis at the end of the Greek sentence. The verb *aphistēmi*, furthermore, has the clear sense of "apostasy" in the present context (compare Acts 5:37-38). Codex D expands the sentence and puts Paul's sentiments in indirect discourse. Its addition of "work for which they had been sent" probably derives from 14:26, but represents a good sense of the basis for Paul's position: the mission was not a matter of human whim but of divine commission; commitment to it was therefore not a matter of personal taste (see 1 Cor 9:16-18).

39. *such sharp disagreement that they separated:* The translation "sharp disagreement" tries to capture the combination of *paroxusmos* (see LXX Deut 29:28; Jer 32:37) and the result clause (*hōste*). The noun *paroxusmos* is related to the verb *paroxunein* which in the LXX has the sense of "provoke/irritate/enrage" (see Num 14:11; 15:30; Deut 1:34; 9:19; Ps 9:34). Their conflict, then, has a strong emotional quality. The verb used for "separate" (*apochōrizomai*), in turn, is cognate with the one used originally (*apochoreō*) to designate the departure of John-Mark from the mission (Acts 13:13; compare 3 Macc 2:33)!

    Barnabas . . . sailed to Cyprus: The whole sequence of events takes on a new meaning if the report in Col 4:10 is trustworthy, that John-Mark was Barnabas' nephew. If such were the case, we then have a story about the conflict between the demands of the apostolic commission and family loyalties. By having Barnabas return to his own place of origin (see Acts 4:36) with Mark, Luke places an implicit but no less real judgment against him. He no longer appears in the story. Were it not for Col 4:10 and 1 Cor 9:6 (compare Gal 2:13), which suggest some sort of working relationship with Paul, we would think the rupture here had been permanent.

40. *dedicated to the gift of the Lord:* There is nothing particularly solemn about Paul's choice (*epilegomai*) of Silas (for his role in the narrative, see the note on 15:22), but the formal dedication (*paradidōmai*, see the note on 15:26) resembles the formula used in 14:26. For the options in translating *chariti* ("to/for" the "grace/gift/favor"), see also the note on 14:26. Some *mss* have "of God" (*tou theou*) rather than "of the Lord" (*tou kyriou*), possibly by attraction from 14:26.

41. *strengthening the churches:* This makes explicit the purpose for the mission expressed in 15:36. For "strengthening" (*epistērizein*), see the note on 15:32. Codex D adds that "they delivered to them the commandments (*entolas*) from the elders," but this undoubtedly is a scribal anticipation of 16:4. In effect, this "missionary journey" began as a continuation of the work assigned to Silas and Judas. For the question of when the areas of Syria and Cilicia were evangelized, see the note on 15:23.

16:1. *also went down to Derbe and Lystra:* Since Paul is going in the opposite direction, these cities are listed in the reverse order of 14:6. The initial mission to these places is recounted in 14:6-21. The Western Text provides an easier transition between 15:41 and this verse by supplying "and when he had come through these nations, he came . . . ." Notice that despite the fact that Paul and Silas are supposed to be a team, the verbs here are singular.

a certain disciple . . . Timothy: Here we meet one of the most important figures in the Pauline mission. He is mentioned explicitly in Acts 17:14-15; 18:5; 19:22; 20:4, but is also acknowledged by Paul as a "fellow worker" (Rom 16:21) and special delegate (1 Cor 4:17; 16:10; Phil 2:19; 1 Thess 3:2, 6). He is listed as one of the co-sponsors (cowriters?) of several of Paul's letters (2 Cor 1:1; Phil 1:1; Col 1:1; 1 Thess 1:1; 2 Thess 1:1; Phlm). He is the intended reader of 1 Timothy and 2 Timothy, which reveal something of the filial relationship between Paul and his helper.

Jewish woman who was a believer: The adjective *pistē* could be translated simply as "faithful," but the usage matches that in Acts 10:45 and 1 Tim 5:16; see also below, 16:15. She is, therefore, herself already a Christian, as is her son (*mathētēs*/"disciple"). In 2 Tim 1:5, Paul makes mention of the sincere faith of Timothy's mother Lois and his grandmother Eunice, and in 2 Tim 3:15, notes that Timothy learned the Scriptures "from childhood."

his father was a Greek: Their marriage was therefore a mixed one, which since the time of the restoration had been problematic for the maintenance of Jewish identity (see Neh 13:23-27; Ezra 9:1–10:44; Mal 1:10-16; *The Book of Jubilees* 30:7-17). The fact that both mother and son were members of the messianic movement yet the son had remained uncircumcised until now is susceptible of several explanations: a) the mother's commitment to this new cult was stronger than had been her commitment to Judaism; b) according to custom at the time, as a son of a Gentile father, Timothy would not be considered Jewish and therefore have no need of circumcision; c) the Greek father (who had sway in such matters) had prevented her from having Timothy circumcised. The last explanation seems supported by verse 3, below. The principle that Jewish descent was traced matrilineally cannot be dated with certainty before the period of the Mishnah (see *m.Qidd.* 3:12; *m.Yeb.* 7:5), but this passage's implicit assumptions seem to support the fact that Luke considered this to be the case.

2. *testified to him:* Literally, "he was witnessed to by the brothers," with the translation changing the voice to active. For this use of *martureō* in the passive to mean accreditation or reputation, compare Luke 4:22; Acts 6:3; 10:22; 22:12.

3. *circumcised him because of the Jews:* To see Paul circumcise someone after the events so painstakingly laid out in chapters 14–15 is certainly startling. If we assume Luke had control over his narrative and characterization, we must conclude that he saw no conflict in Paul's action. The reader is therefore expected to take Paul's action as motivated by prudential considerations. If Timothy were Gentile, then his circumcision is not carried out for his salvation (15:1-2). If Timothy were Jewish (which is what Luke seems to want us to think), then his circumcision is not a condition for discipleship (he is already called that) but rather a means of assuring acceptability among the Jews with whom (together with Paul) he will work.

for they all knew that his father was a Greek: The sentence structure makes this clause introduced with *gar* ("for") the reason for Paul's action. But why would the Jews' knowledge that Timothy's father was Gentile motivate Paul to circumcise him? Certainly if Luke thought this fact made Timothy a Gentile himself, Paul's fellow Jews would also know this, and his circumcising Timothy would be seen not only as opportunistic but also futile. On the other hand, if Timothy was regarded as Jewish, then the act of circumcision signifies loyalty to the ancestral traditions (the *ethos* of the Jewish *ethnos*). Why would the Jews of the area then take it seriously? Because they knew the Gentile father (who had authority in such matters) had prevented the circumcision before this.

4. *the decrees that had been decided:* The delivery of these beyond Cilicia had not been part of their original charge; inserting the notice here also helps clarify Luke's intention in the previous verse. It goes beyond comprehension (if Timothy were supposed to be Gentile) that Paul should in the space of two verses both circumcise a Gentile and deliver the decrees which required no such thing. The term *dogma* derives from the verb *dokeō* (see 15:22, 28), and is widely used for official declarations and laws (see Plato, *Laws* 926D). The perfect passive participle *kekrimena* in turn echoes the use of *krinō* ("judge") in Acts 15:19. The verb *paradidōmi* ("hand over") has been used extensively in this section (14:26; 15:26, 40), but here has the sense of the handing over of traditions (compare 1 Cor 11:2, 23; 15:3). The Western Text adds the ele-

ments that they preached boldly and handed over the "commandments (*entolas*) of the apostles."

5. *increased in number:* This is another in the series of statements concerning the growth (internal and numerical) of the community (Acts 2:41, 47; 4:4; 5:14; 6:1, 7; 8:25, 40; 9:31; 11:24-25; 12:24; 14:21-23).

6. *the Phrygian and Galatian region:* The join between the sentences here is unclear, with the English translation no better than the Greek; the implied subject of this sentence is, however, "Paul and his companions." The textual variants for the present verse testify to the confusion concerning the precise geographico-political relationships designated by the terms "Phrygia" and "Galatia." Since these were themselves changeable, the confusion cannot totally be eliminated (see the notes on 13:51; 4:1, 6, 20, as well as the extensive discussion of the confusion concerning this region in Strabo, *Geography* 12, 7, 1-5).

    prevented by the Holy Spirit: The circumstantial participle of *koloō* (see Luke 9:49-50; 11:52; 23:2; Acts 8:36; 10:47; 11:17) is to be understood as the reason for their taking the path they did. "Asia" could refer to the coastal territory (including cities such as Ephesus which Paul does not reach until 18:19, and spends no time in until 19:1-10), or to the Roman Province of Asia which (since 166 B.C.E.) included such geographical designations as "Phrygia." Although endless scholarly discussion has been devoted to determining the precise route Paul took—at stake in the minds of some being whether Paul in fact carried out a mission in so called "North Galatia"—it is in fact unsolvable, and does not answer the question asked; for by no means does the verb *dierchomai* yield any information whether a preaching endeavor was made. That question, furthermore, has no relevance for Luke's narrative point, which is that the Holy Spirit once again directly and dramatically directs the movement of the mission (see 4:31; 8:29, 39; 10:44; 13:2, 4).

7. *tried to go into Bithynia:* As the apostles proceed northwestwardly (having been prevented from heading due west into Asia proper), they arrive at a point "opposite" (*kata*) Mysia, the territory which abuts the Aegean to the west, the Hellespont to the north, Bithynia to the east, and Lydia to the south (Strabo, *Geography* 12, 4, 5). They try to turn eastward to Bithynia, a territory which in 65-63 B.C.E. was organized by Pompey into a single Roman province. The presence of Christians there at an early date is attested by 1 Pet 1:1, as well as by Pliny the Younger, *Letter* 10:96.

    the Spirit of Jesus did not allow them: This is the only time the expression "Spirit of Jesus" (*pneuma Iēsou*) occurs in Acts. Some *mss* correct it to the more frequent "Holy Spirit" or "Spirit of the Lord." The reading translated, however, is probably the correct one; we have seen before that Jesus continues to take an active role in the story (7:56; 9:5).

8. *passing by Mysia:* The Western text alters *parelthontes* ("passing by") to *dielthontes* ("passing through"), which provides an easier reading: they had to go through some portion of Mysia, after all, to reach Troas on the coast (see the confusion expressed by Strabo, *Geography* 12, 4, 5). Despite the un-

certainty and clumsiness of these geographical indicators (clumsy perhaps only to us because of our uncertainties), the narrative point is clear enough: the Spirit blocked every direction sought by human initiative, and left only an opening to Europe.

9. *a vision appeared to Paul:* Just as in the call of Paul (9:10) and in the conversion of Cornelius (10:3, 10; 11:5), the vision plays a key role in advancing the plot; for literary parallels, see the note on 10:3, and especially the dream experienced by Apollonius of Tyana: a woman appears to him and asks to see him before he leaves for Rome, a dream he interprets as meaning he should visit Crete (Philostratus, *Life of Apollonius of Tyana* 4:34); similarly, Alexander has a dream-vision that warns him not to destroy Tyre, in Pseudo-Callisthenes' *Life of Alexander of Macedon* 1:35.

   a certain Macedonian man: The *anēr* ("man") is explicit in the Greek. Since the narrative immediately and inexplicably shifts to the first person plural ("we"), it is pleasant to connect this vision personage with a member of Paul's entourage, perhaps even the author, Luke. Any such hypothesis must deal with the problem that the person included in the "we" appears to be not a new addition but an existing member of the group. Macedonia, of course, is the territory north of Achaia, facing to the west the Adriatic Sea, and to the east, the Aegean Sea, whose major cities are clustered on the eastern coast.

   help us: The use of the verb *boēthein* ("help/assist") is deeply evocative of biblical prayer, which uses this language for the help from God that is salvation (see Gen 19:25; Exod 18:4; Deut 33:26; Pss 9:35; 17:2; 36:40; 39:13; 40:3; 43:26; 45:5; 53:4; 61:8; 78:9; 85:17; 93:17; 108:26; Isa 41:10, 14; 49:8; 50:9).

10. *we were convinced:* Thus Luke casually begins an extended "We" passage; the critical problems concerning such passages are discussed in the interpretation of the next section, pp. 296–297. For the range of meanings of *symbibazō*, see the note on Acts 9:22. In contrast to that passage, the translation here takes it in the sense of "reaching the conclusion." The textual variation between "Lord" and "God" are probably due to the recognition by scribes that Luke is alluding (by the use of *proskaleomai*) to the thematic statement in 2:39 (which itself echoes Joel 3:5), "the promise is for you and for your children and all those far off, whomever the Lord our God summons."

INTERPRETATION

Luke's narrative takes a decisive turn after the apostolic council. Paul and his mission dominate the story. Nothing more is heard of the other apostles. Jerusalem, now under the leadership of James, will reappear only briefly, and entirely within the framework of its response to Paul. Between the council in ch. 15 and Paul's arrest and imprisonment in ch. 21, Luke compresses a vivid account of Paul's missionary work in Europe and Asia, his continuing struggles with Jewish opposition, and his ever more decisive turn to the Gentiles. The present passage is a transition between these stages of the story. Paul and Barnabas separate (15:36-39). Paul recruits new helpers (15:40–16:3). He is called by God to a new field of missionary work (16:4-10).

The smoothness with which Luke accomplishes this transition does not entirely conceal its ambiguity. In particular for Paul's split with Barnabas, and his circumcision of Timothy, our possession of other contemporary information demands consideration of the complexity presented by the divergence between historical sources, not in order to resolve the historical problem itself, but in order to sharpen our perception of Luke's narrative purposes.

The case of Barnabas actually continues the set of problems dealt with in the account of the Jerusalem council. As we have seen, Barnabas occupied a central role in Luke's story up to this point: he intervened for Paul with the other apostles (9:27), he recruited Paul for work in the Antiochean Church (11:25-26), he was Paul's companion on the mission (13:1-14:28), he spoke with Paul in defense of that mission at the council (15:12). But after this separation scene, he is never mentioned in Acts again. Indeed, he is mentioned in only three other places in the NT. In Col 4:10, Mark is called the nephew of Barnabas; in 1 Cor 9:6, Paul includes Barnabas in a question concerning his own rights as an apostle: "Is it only Barnabas and I who have no right to refrain from working for a living?" There is no hint in these passages either of a particularly close working relationship between Paul and Barnabas, or an estrangement.

In contrast, Paul's account of the events following his meeting with the Jerusalem leaders in Gal 2:11 appears to implicate Barnabas more deeply in the Antiochean conflict between Paul, Cephas, and the "men from James." He does not accuse Barnabas of malice but of weakness: "Even Barnabas was carried away by hypocrisy," since he apparently joined Cephas in stopping table-fellowship with Gentiles once that was put under attack by the Jewish Christians. Neither does Paul explicitly state that this event placed his and Barnabas' relationship under a strain. Indeed, if we had as additional sources only 1 Cor 9:6 and Col 4:10, the most obvious construal would be that Paul and Barnabas were loosely associated in the mission from beginning to end, never either particularly closely connected nor deeply alienated.

Are we then to conclude that Luke's version of a personal division between Paul and Barnabas whitewashes a more fundamental ideological conflict involving the Gentile mission? On the basis of the sources we have available to us, that position is difficult to sustain, precisely because Paul's own references to Barnabas are oblique and lacking specificity. As in so many other cases, Luke's account seems to be required even for its own rebuttal! If it is his version that leads us to think that Paul and Barnabas had ever been closely associated in the first place, and it is only his version that speaks of their estrangement in such definitive terms, then it appears that his version must also be given some credit for the factors at work in both.

But it is also a misreading of Luke's own account to take it as a matter of personal preference or pique. His language is too strong for that, and suggests that beneath the *paroxysmos* there was a matter of principle. By characterizing John-Mark's departure from the field as an *apostasy*, Luke suggests that it represented a failure in obedience to the mission. They had been commissioned, after all, by the Church and sent out by the Holy Spirit. Luke's view of the matter seems strongly shaped by the sayings of Jesus on discipleship in Luke 9:57-62, especially the last: "No one who has once grasped the plow yet keeps looking backward is fit for the kingdom of God" (Luke 9:62). And when Barnabas, in the face of Paul's objection, then chooses to return to Cyprus *with* Mark rather than continue on the mission with Paul, the reader must see this also as a kind of apostasy. Even if the information in Col 4:10, that Barnabas was Mark's uncle, is not accurate, we must as readers assume that a personal loyalty has here superseded a commitment to the work of the mission. This is particularly clear since Luke makes no mention of the two continuing any sort of evangelization, and since Cyprus is Barnabas' place of origin. In Luke's story, he has, simply, taken his relative/friend, and gone home.

Paul then replaces Barnabas with Silas. Like Barnabas, he had previously been commissioned by the Jerusalem Church (15:27); like Barnabas and Paul, he has also been certified by Luke as a prophet (15:32). But Paul's next task is to replace Mark as the "assistant" (*hypēretēs*, 13:5). He chooses a disciple in the city of Lystra named Timothy (16:1-3). His action of circumcising Timothy "because of the Jews who were in those areas," however, appears as problematic on several counts.

For those who credit Paul not only with consistency concerning the circumcision of Gentiles (see the case of Titus in Gal 2:3), but also elevate his position on circumcision to a principled rejection of it for all Messianists, this account must be dismissed as a fictional construct by Luke, part of his systematic reconstruction of the whole series of events surrounding the conflict between early Christian leaders. But for those who are more hostile toward Paul, who think there is some basis in the suggestion that Paul tailored his principles to expediency (see 1 Cor 9:19-23; 2 Cor 1:17), Luke's version is taken as historical evidence to the discredit of Paul, an indication that Paul's question in Gal 5:11, "But if I, brothers, still preach circumcision, why am I still persecuted," was not without basis and not so easily answered.

Our reading cannot hope to settle the historical issue of Paul's views or moral consistency, but can only address the question of Luke's perception. Here, everything depends on two factors: a) whether Luke wants the reader to perceive Timothy as a Jew, and b) whether Luke regards circumcision as a legitimate expression of national *ethos* for Jews. The answer to the first question must be in the affirmative. It is certainly true, as the notes indicate, that we have no firm evidence for the first century that the matrilineal principle for determining Jewish identity was either legally formalized or universally applied. But it is equally true that Luke's language suggests precisely that *he* so viewed matters. There would have been no reason for him to bring up the mixed heritage of Timothy at all if the point were not that he was in fact Jewish.

This is made especially clear by Luke's explanatory clause concerning the Jews of the area: "for they all knew that his father was a Greek." If this meant they considered Timothy to be a Gentile, then Paul's circumcision of him would scarcely win approval among Jews already suspicious of the messianic movement; it would be expediency without point. But if their knowledge of Timothy's paternal ancestry serves (as the notes suggest) to excuse Timothy's delay in being circumcised, then the action would signify a belated but genuine commitment to the Jewish heritage by one previously prevented from it, and would in fact serve Paul's purposes in gaining a hearing for himself and his entourage in the synagogues.

The question then arises whether this was pure expediency on Paul's part? We obviously cannot answer for the historical Paul, but the narrative does give us important clues to *Luke's* perceptions. And this brings us to the second critical consideration: did Luke think circumcision appropriate for Jewish Christians? Once more, the answer is, emphatically, yes. The decision concerning the freedom of the Gentiles by the council did not affect the traditions of the Jewish people. Luke throughout his work considers the normativeness of Torah for the messianic community to consist primarily in its prophetic function. It is not the norm for righteousness or salvation. But as the *ethos* of the Jewish people, it is a legitimate expression of identity and their ancestral commitment to God.

However faithful Luke might be to *Paul's* perceptions, then, this account is consistent with Luke's own previous presentation. In fact, the circumcision of Timothy at this juncture serves three important narrative functions. First, it clarifies exactly what was and what was not decided by the council. By opening a door of freedom to Gentile Christians, the Church did not close the door to Jewish Christians; everything appropriate to that tradition could still be practiced, so long as it was understood to have cultural rather than soteriological significance. Second, Luke is concerned to show that Paul's "mission to the Gentiles" is not in any way an abandonment of his commitment to Judaism. At the very beginning of his turn to Europe, he asserts that commitment through this action, and he will continue to the end trying to bring "the hope of Israel" to his own people. Third, Luke provides an early answer to the objection that James will later voice, that "you teach all the Jews who are among the Gentiles to forsake Moses, telling them not to circumcise their children or observe the customs (*ethē*)" (21:21). The reader knows this to be a canard, for Paul has from the very start himself shown a commitment to the Jewish *ethos* by circumcising his coworker.

Finally, Luke shows us how, having transcended ethnic limits, the Messianist movement crossed still another geographical boundary. We can by now recognize Luke's familiar narrative devices and how they work to reveal his religious perceptions. On one side there is the role of human calculation: Paul, Silas and Timothy try turning to more familiar paths, first directly westward to Asia, then eastward to Bithynia. On the other side, there is the divine intervention and guidance, now more direct and urgent than ever. They are "prevented" by the Spirit from pursuing their own projects. Finally, just as Peter was drawn to the edge of Palestine before being shown that he was to preach to Gentiles, so is Paul given a vision of a "certain Macedonian man" who implores him for help. On the basis of that vision, Paul and his companion decide that God is "summoning them" to preach the gospel also in Europe. The adventures of that mission we will turn to next.

For Reference and Further Study

Bowers, W. P. "Paul's Route through Mysia: A Note on Acts 16:8." *JTS* n.s. 30 (1979) 507–511.

Bryan, C. "A Further Look at Acts 16:1-3." *JBL* 107 (1988) 292–294.

Cadbury, H. J. " 'We' and 'I' Passages in Luke/Acts." *NTS* 3 (1957) 128–132.

Cohen, S. J. D. "Was Timothy Jewish (Acts 16:1-3)? Patristic Exegesis, Rabbinic Law and Matrilineal Descent." *JBL* 105 (1986) 251–268.

Delebecque, E. "De Lystre à Philippes (Ac 16) avec le *Codex Bezae*." *Bib* 63 (1982) 395–405.

Kaye, B. N. "Acts' Portrait of Silas." *NovT* 21 (1979) 13–26.

Lake, K. "Paul's Route in Asia Minor." *Beginnings* 5:224-240.

Praeder, S. M. "The Problem of First-Person Narration in Acts." *NovT* 29 (1987) 193–218.

32. *Events at Philippi* (16:11-24)

11. When we had set sail from Troas, we made a straight run to Samothrace, and the next day to Neapolis, 12. and from there to Philippi, which is a colony, a chief city of the district of Macedonia. We remained in this city for some days. 13. On the Sabbath day we went out from the gates to go along the river. We thought a house of prayer would be there. When we had sat down, we began speaking to the women who had gathered. 14. There was a certain woman listening whose name was Lydia. She was a purple-goods merchant from the city of Thyatira. She was a woman who feared God. The Lord opened her heart to accept the things being spoken by Paul. 15. When she and her household had been baptized, she made a request. She said, "If you have decided that I am a woman faithful to the Lord, come and stay in my house." And she was insistent toward us. 16. But as we were proceeding to the house of prayer, a certain slave girl encountered us. She had a Pythian spirit. By making prophecies, she brought considerable profit to her owners. 17. She began following after Paul. She cried out concerning us. She was saying, "These people are the servants of the highest God! They are announcing to you a way to salvation!" 18. Now she was doing this over a period of several days. And when Paul had grown weary of it, he turned around. He said to the spirit, "I command you in the name of Jesus Messiah! Come out of her!" And that same hour it came out. 19. But when her owners perceived that the hope for their profit had gone out, they seized Paul and Silas. They dragged them into the city-center and before the authorities. 20. And when they had brought them before the magistrates, they said, "These people are Jews! They are overturning our city! 21. They are proclaiming customs which we as Romans are not allowed to accept or practice!" 22. The crowd joined in against them. The magistrates ripped their clothes from them. They ordered them to be beaten. 23. And after hitting them with many blows, they threw them into jail. They ordered the jailer to hold them secure. 24. He accepted the order. He threw them into the inside cell, and he fastened their feet to the stocks.

NOTES

11. *We made a straight run to Samothrace:* The first person plural is used through verse 15, as the "we-narrative" begins in earnest. Samothrace is a mountainous island in the Aegean off the coast of Macedonia (Strabo, *Geography* 2, 5, 21; frag. 7:47). As for Neapolis, it was the port for Philippi, in the same way that Attalia was for Perga in Pamphylia (Acts 13:13; 14:25). Philippi itself was about ten miles inland, along the *Via Egnatia* that ran from the eastern to western coasts of Macedonia.

12. *a colony, a chief city of the district of Macedonia:* Luke goes into unusual detail in describing Philippi (see Strabo, *Geography* frag. 7:34, 41), which as we know

from Paul's own letters was an important center for his European mission. It was a community that had "a partnership in the gospel from the first day" (Phil 1:5), and which supported Paul financially (Phil 4:15-18; 2 Cor 11:9). Paul regarded this community with great affection (Phil 4:1-7). Roman colonies were originally garrisons of soldiers, and always retained special privileges connected to their direct relationship with the Roman *imperium*. Other cities visited by Paul, such as Antioch of Pisidia, were also Roman colonies. The particular attention paid to the fact here may be related to the legal entanglements in 16:19-40. The textual variants in this line have two causes: a) the use of *prōtē* ("first/chief") for Philippi is difficult, because Thessalonica was actually the capital city of Macedonia; b) the term *meris* ("portion/share") was not recognized as a term used for "district." Some *mss* therefore have corrected to "a city of the first portion of Macedonia."

13. *thought a house of prayer would be there:* The *mss* tradition reflects confusion over what *proseuchē* might mean. The present translation is based on *enomizomen proseuchēn einai*, which is found only in a few *mss*, but which seems to be presumed as the basis for many of the other readings. In light of the company's further progress "toward *tēn proseuchēn*" in 16:16, the translation as "house of prayer" is undoubtedly correct. In Hellenistic Jewish literature, the term is virtually synonymous with *synagōgē* (see e.g., 3 Macc 7:20; Philo, *Against Flaccus* 45, 47, 49; Josephus, *Against Apion* 2:10; *Life* 277, 280, 293; in *Antiquities of the Jews* 14:258, Josephus refers to the building of "houses of prayer" by the sea as an ancestral custom). Scribes may have been influenced by Luke's use of *nomizō*, which in every other case introduces a false supposition (Luke 2:44; 3:23; Acts 7:25; 8:20; 14:19; 16:27; 17:29; 21:29). In fact, Luke's usage may be consistent, for the women Paul speaks to on the riverside may not yet be the *proseuchē* he is seeking (see 16:16).
    speaking to the women who had gathered: Much of the confusion concerning this passage stems from Luke's failure to make clear whether or not this encounter with a group of women on the riverbank is a synagogue service. The text does not really force us to decide, therefore, whether this could be a "true" synagogue (since women were taking part) or whether this passage provided evidence to the contrary, that women took an active role in Diaspora synagogue meetings. The most obvious reading of the story would be to see this as a separate encounter *on the way* to the synagogue (see 16:16), in which Paul takes advantage of a crowd of women on the beach (*synelthousais gynaikais*), to preach.

14. *purple-goods merchant:* Lydia is one of the ancient kingdoms subsumed by the Roman Province of Asia (Pliny the Elder, *Natural History* 5:10), and among its industries was the production of textiles and dyes. This woman's name could in fact be a nickname ("the Lydian woman"), but it is also attested elsewhere. The Church at Thyatira receives one of the harsher letters from the seer in the Book of Revelation 2:18-29. Purple clothes were for the wealthy (Luke 16:19) and the royal (1 Macc 10:62; Dio Chrysostom, *Oration* 4:71). Her trade, therefore, as well as her ownership of a household (*oikos*, 16:15) of ade-

quate resources to provide hospitality to the missionaries, suggests that she is a woman of substantial means.

woman who feared God: The noun "woman" is supplied by the translation for the feminine form of the participle *sebomenē ton theon*. Luke's usage is sufficiently flexible to make it impossible to know for certain whether the designation in this case means that she was a Gentile attracted to the synagogue's teachings, or whether she was in fact a pious Jew; Josephus tells us that in the time of Antiochus IV, some two thousand Jewish families were transported from Mesopotamia to Lydia and Phrygia (*Antiquities of the Jews* 12:147-153). It is not necessary to take the imperfect "she was listening" (*ēkouen*) to mean a series of meetings with Paul, any more than it is to take the imperfect *elaloumen* that way. In fact, this entire scene moves with great rapidity.

Lord opened her heart: Although the "biblical" sound of this is undeniable, the actual expression occurs only in 2 Macc 1:4, "May he open your heart to his law." Luke does use *dianoigō* for the opening of the disciples' eyes after the resurrection (Luke 24:33) as well as the opening of the Scriptures (24:32) and of the disciples' minds (24:45) by the resurrected Jesus.

to accept the things being spoken: The verb *prosechō* ("accept") has the sense of "being attracted/devoted/committed" to someone or something; compare the close parallel in Acts 8:6, 10, 11, as well as 1 Tim 4:13; Heb 2:1; 2 Pet 1:19. Notice also that she attends to *Paul's* speech, even though the earlier subject was "we" (*elaloumen*).

15. *she and her household had been baptized:* The phrasing recalls Acts 7:2, 10, and 10:2. For that reason, some *mss* add the adjective *pas* ("all") before *oikos* ("household"). The baptism takes place abruptly, but no more so than in other instances (compare 2:41; 8:12, 38; 9:18; 10:48).

    she was insistent: The term (*parabiazomai*) is used in the Gospel (Luke 24:29) for the urging of the disciples that Jesus stay the evening with them, and has the same sense here (see also LXX Gen 19:3, 9; 2 Kgs 2:17).

16. *proceeding to the house of prayer:* The entire episode with Lydia and the women can be seen as a narrative interlude, since this transition picks up the missionaries' original intention (in 16:13) to seek out a "house of prayer" (*proseuchē*). Alternatively, the next episode can be read as a narrative flashback, which picks up the first encounter between Paul and the Pythian Servant Girl, when he was initially on the way to the synagogue, the continuation of which encounter is now related.

    had a Pythian spirit: The *python* was the mythical serpent/dragon slain by Apollo (Ovid, *Metamorphoses* 1:438-447), from which the prophetesses at the shrine at Delphi took one of their names (Plutarch, *On the Obsolescence of Oracles* 9 [*Mor* 414E]; see also 40-41 [*Mor* 432C-433C], and *The Oracles at Delphi* 21 [*Mor* 404B-405A]; Lucian of Samosata, *Phalaris* 2:12). The authority of the Delphic Oracle in the Hellenistic world was great (see e.g., Herodotus, *Persian Wars* 1:51, 66, 67; 5:42-43), as was mantic prophecy in general (see Plato, *Phaedrus* 244A, *Timaeus* 71E-72B; Plutarch, *The E at Delphi* 6 [*Mor* 386D-387D]), a fact that was taken advantage of by wandering charlatans (see the note below).

by making prophecies: Luke uses the term *manteuomai*, which is the technical term for ecstatic prophecy in the Hellenistic world (e.g., Herodotus, *Persian Wars* 1:46; LXX Deut 18:10; 2 Kgs 17:17; Mic 3:11 [also for money]; Ezek 22:28 ["foolish lies"]; Josephus, *Antiquities of the Jews* 6:330).

considerable profit to her owners: The psychic powers of the slave-girl (*paidiskē*) are exploited by her owners/masters (*kyrioi*); for savage satirization of such charlatanism, see e.g., Lucian of Samosata, *Alexander the False Prophet*, and Apuleius, *The Golden Ass* 8:26-30. The mention of profit-taking places these religious merchandizers with others in Luke's narrative whose wickedness is connected to avarice (Luke 12:21; 16:1-9, 16, 19-26; Acts 1:16-21; 5:1-11; 8:18-24).

17. *cried out concerning us:* Codex D omits *tō Paulō kai*, apparently thinking that it was redundant with *hēmin* ("us"): "followed Paul and us." But in the present translation, the dative *hēmin* is taken with *ekraxen* ("cried out") rather than with "followed," and is read as the dative of reference ("concerning us") rather than as indirect object ("cried out *to* us").

servants of the highest God: The designation *douloi* ("slaves/servants") has here a specifically religious sense (compare LXX Judg 2:8; 1 Sam 3:10; Ps 77:70; 115:7; Isa 49:3; Luke 2:49; Acts 2:18; 4:29), but forms an interesting parallel to the relationship between the *paidiskē* and her *kyrioi*. The title "Most High God" (*hypsistos theos*) is used with some frequency in the narrative (Luke 1:32, 35, 76; 2:14; 6:35; 8:28; 19:38; Acts 7:48), but in this context has a more polemical edge: the God the missionaries serve is "higher" than the one she serves, and the pythian spirit within her, like the demonic spirits in the Gospel (e.g., Luke 4:34; 8:28), recognizes that fact.

a way to salvation: For the use of *hodos* ("way") in its ethical/religious sense, see the note on 9:2, and for *sōtēria* ("salvation") as a Lukan theme, see Luke 1:69, 71, 77; 19:9; Acts 4:12; 7:25; 13:26, 47. Some mss have *hēmin* ("to us") rather than *hymin* ("to you").

18. *grown weary of it:* Luke uses the same verb (*diaponeō*) as in Acts 4:2, where it refers to the response of the Sanhedrin to the efforts of the apostles. The verb means basically "to work/labor," and in the passive has the sense of the contemporary usage, "worked over."

he said to the spirit: It is possible also to read "in the Spirit he said," or "turning in the spirit," but since the confrontation is between the Christian prophet and the Pythian prophetess, it is better to take *tō pneumati* as characterizing the object of Paul's speech (see Acts 4:8; 11:28; 13:9).

come out of her: Paul uses the exorcism formula *exelthein ap'autēs*, just as Jesus did in the Gospel (Luke 4:35; 8:29); the notice of the Spirit's departure is also formulaic (see Luke 4:36, 41; 8:33; 11:14; Acts 8:7). The difference here is that Paul's exorcism is "in the name of Jesus Messiah," with *to onoma* ("the name") having the same sort of power as in Acts 3:6, 16; 4:10, 30).

that same hour it came out: Codex D adds the adverb *eutheōs* ("immediately"). What is most significant about this language is that it communicates Luke's perception that the Pythian spirit is demonic and therefore to be treated as such; for "the same hour," compare Luke 2:38; 7:21; 10:21; 12:12; 13:31; 20:19.

19. *hope for their profit had gone out:* The translation tries to catch the parallelism between the two phrases: the profits went out (*exerchomai*) with the demon! It is also characteristic of Luke to link the fate of persons and their possessions (compare Luke 11:21-22; 12:20-21; Acts 8:20). At the same time he has managed to attribute to this wandering divination show avaricious motives rather than genuine religious sensibility, a motif that he develops more fully in Acts 19:23-40.

    city square . . . authorities: The precise translation of *agora* depends on its context, since the central public space of the *polis* had a variety of functions, including public assembly and judgment (see Epictetus, *Discourses* 3, 24, 80; 4, 9, 13). Luke uses the general term *archontes* for "authorities" in this line (see Luke 12:58; 18:18; 24:20; Acts 4:5, 26; 7:27, 35; and compare Rom 13:3).

20. *before the magistrates:* The term *stratēgos* is widely attested for the legal authorities in Greek cities (see Herodotus, *Persian Wars* 5:38; Epictetus, *Discourses* 2, 1, 26), and is equivalent to the Latin *praetor* (see Cicero, *On the Agrarian Law* 2, 34, 93). It specifies the more generalized title of *archōn* used in the previous line. The plural refers to the *duoviri* who held the position at any time.

    Jews . . . overturning our city: The translation reverses the order of the clauses in order to suggest the causal rather concessive character of the circumstantial participle, *Ioudaioi hyparchontes*. Literally, the line goes, "These men are overturning our city, being Jews." But the charge is scarcely an afterthought; it is an appeal to the xenophobia of a Roman Colony. The verb *ektarassō* is an intensive form of *tarassō*, and combines the sense of civic disorder and mental confusion (see Josephus, *Jewish War* 7:41 [the context is a city excited by false charges made against Jews], and *Antiquities of the Jews* 17:253). This first part of the complaint resembles that made against Jesus (Luke 23:2) and later against Paul (Acts 17:6-7).

21. *proclaiming customs:* There is no specific content to this charge, only the generalized fear of the alien that was so frequently the source of antisemitism in the Hellenistic world. We see here the conflict between the customs (*ethē*) that the apostles are charged with purveying as "Jews" (*Ioudaioi*), set against those which the *romaioi* were not allowed (*exestin*) to receive or practice. The xenophobic mood cut both ways: this reminds us both of Peter's statement in 10:28, that it was *athemitos* for a Jew to asssociate with Gentiles, and the charge against Stephen in 6:14, that he was trying to "change the customs (*ethē*) that Moses handed down to us." This passage is important for helping us grasp Luke's notion of what is involved in a people's *ethos*.

22. *crowd joined in against them:* The rabble-rousing character of the slave-owner's complaint is obvious from the crowd's response. They have raised the sort of charges that would guarantee local resentment against a population that resided within a *polis* (or in this case a *kolōnia*) without fully participating in its civic life. Philo and Josephus provide some vivid descriptions of what Philo calls the "unstable rabble" in the city of Alexandria, always quick to react

hostilely to Jews (see *Embassy to Gaius* 18, 19, 20, 25, 26; *Against Flaccus* 5; also Josephus, *Against Apion* 1:11; 2:3). Luke's text suggests that the situation obtained elsewhere as well.

ordered them to be beaten: Literally, "ordered a beating" (*ekeleuon rhabdizein*). The act would in all likelihood be carried out by the *rhabdouchoi* (see 16:15), who carried the *rhabdoi* (wooden rods/*fasces*). For the public beatings as a possible fate for the true philosopher, see Epictetus, *Discourses* 3, 22, 54. In 2 Cor 11:25, Paul says that he was "three times beaten with rods," and in 1 Thess 2:2 recalls to his readers that he had been "shamefully treated at Philippi."

24. *fastened their feet to the stocks:* The security measures resemble those in the imprisonment of Peter (Acts 12:4). The authorities wanted the men locked up "securely" (*asphalōs*), and so they are: placed in an inner cell, with feet fastened (*asphalizomai*) to, literally, "the wood" (*to xylon;* see Herodotus, *Persian Wars* 9:37).

INTERPRETATION

The most striking shift in Luke's story at this point is the narrator's adoption of the first person plural ("we"). No explanation is provided, so the interpretation of it is left to the reader. Are we to assume the presence of an eyewitness at the events so reported, perhaps even the participation of Luke himself? In that case, perhaps Luke is providing examples of how he himself had "examined everything carefully" (Luke 1:3). Or is Luke making use of a written source, perhaps a diary or itinerary, that was written in that fashion by a participant in the action? In that case, Luke is providing material from "eyewitnesses who also became ministers of the word" (Luke 1:2); the use of such diaries was an accepted practice in historiography (see Lucian of Samosata, *How to Write History* 16).

The determination is impossible to make, for these sections are stylistically uniform with the sections surrounding them; as always, if Luke has used sources, he has, like a good Hellenistic historian, rewritten them. Indeed, Luke may once again be following one of the conventions of ancient historiography. Particularly in accounts of journeys and sea voyages, such first person narration was frequently employed, even if the narrator patently was not party to the events (see for example the parody of such accounts in Lucian of Samosata, *A True Story* 5-9). But for that matter, biblical histories also provided Luke with examples of such shifts from third to first person narration (see Ezra 8:23-31; 8:35–9:15).

The "We-Narratives" in Acts are rich in detail, and most of the geographical data corresponds to the facts, insofar as we are able to determine them. Lucian insists on this sort of fidelity to detailed accuracy in the historian (*How to Write History* 24), but it can be found as well in narratives which are clearly "fictional" in character (see Xenophon of Ephesus, *The Ephesians* 11-12). In fact, the presence of these first person passages seems to have little impact on the development or meaning of the story, and this commentary will not take up the issue again until we examine Paul's sea voyage in ch. 27.

We turn, then, to the content of Luke's story at this important juncture. Paul has come to Macedonia, and begins his European mission in the Roman Colony of Philippi. He makes converts, confronts an alien spirit, and is imprisoned. These first steps remind us of earlier beginnings in Jerusalem, in Samaria, and in Cyprus. Luke is fond of such repetitive patterns, but within each cycle, he has lively specific details that camouflage his limited repertoire of structural devices.

In this case, we have the charming scene by the riverside that leads to the beginning of the Messianist community in Philippi (16:13-15). Not a formal proclamation in a synagogue, but a casual conversation between Paul with his company and a group of women, leads to the conversion of a wealthy woman and her household, and a new base of operations for Paul's entourage (see 16:40). Lydia may or may not herself be a Jew. Luke calls her *sebomenē* ("devout"), which could mean either that she was formally a Jew or one of those "God-fearers" among whom the gospel found its readiest audience. But she is certainly portrayed as wealthy: she is a purple-goods merchant, and the mistress of a household. Luke is typically interested in noting those converts whose wealth or social status was above the ordinary, as part of his apologetic agenda: such nobler adherents of the gospel helped accredit it in the eyes of status-conscious Hellenistic readers (compare 13:12; 17:4; 28:7). In her openhearted generosity, however, Lydia also demonstrates her enthusiastic reception of the good news (16:14-15); as always, Luke connects spiritual dispositions to the disposition of possessions.

The careful reader might by now be prepared for the next scene, the encounter between Paul and the Pythian Prophetess (16:16-18). As in Peter's confrontation with Ananias and Sapphira (5:1-11), or with Simon Magus (8:17-24), and Paul's encounter with Bar-Jesus/Elymas (13:6-11), we find the Prophet doing battle with demonic forces and besting them, establishing in still another turf-war a further territorial gain for the "kingdom of God" being proclaimed by the apostles, and enacted by their power to heal and exorcize. The details of this story are, as always, distinctive: the agent of the demons is here an oppressed slave-girl whose mantic powers are being exploited by religious charlatans. As with the story of Simon Magus and the magician Bar-Jesus/Elymas, we are informed about still another side to popular Hellenistic religion: now not the mighty wonder worker who sets a provincial territory aflame (Simon), nor a court magician who has access to regional political power (Bar-

Jesus/Elymas), but the equivalent of an urban dog-and-pony show, a Sybil and her keepers, prophesying for pay through the Macedonian cities.

As in the case of Simon Magus, this prophetess acknowledges the superiority of the divinity being proclaimed by the apostles: they are proclaiming "the highest God," and are offering "to us" a path of salvation (16:17). In fact, it is only the language used for Paul's response that enables us to recognize in her proclamation the work of demons, for Paul uses the formula of exorcism to command the spirit's removal (16:18).

There is also, typically, the role of possessions: as with Judas, Ananias and Sapphira, and Simon Magus, the profit motive figures in the tale. In the Jerusalem section, it will be remembered, Luke juxtaposed Barnabas and Ananias as positive and negative examples of obedience to the prophetic Spirit at work in the apostles: Barnabas' submission was symbolized by his placing of possessions at their feet; Ananias' (and Sapphira's) conspiracy against the Holy Spirit was symbolized by their holding back of possessions (4:36–5:11). In just the same way, Lydia and the owners of the slave-girl provide the same set of examples: the wealthy but devout Lydia expresses her openness to the message by opening her house; the avaricious owners symbolize their rejection of the apostles by dragging them to court because of losing "their hope for a profit" (16:19).

Finally, Luke recounts the tumultuous scene in the *agora*, where the angry owners drag Paul and Silas before the city magistrates (16:19-24). The sketch is thumbnail in size but full of the authentic feel of Mediterranean urban life. Most of all, Luke manages to communicate the peculiar position occupied by Paul and Silas in their society. To the pagan purveyors of prophecy, they appear to be Jews, and the dormant antisemitic tendencies of the urban rabble are quickly incited by the xenophobic charges brought against the apostles by the complainants (16:20-22). Yet the missionaries have already, and will again, suffer equal indignities from Jews who regard them as apostates (13:50; 14:5, 19; 17:5-8). Small wonder in such a squeeze that Paul should invoke his rights as a Roman citizen (see the next section, on 16:37-38).

As for the local magistrates, they do not perform well. They succumb at once to the antisemitic tirade of the slave-owners and the incipient threat of violence from the crowd. With no judicial deliberation at all, they have the missionaries stripped and flogged, then sent to the securest part of the local jail, with their feet fastened to the stocks (16:22-24). The magistrates thereby become foils for Luke's presentation of Paul in the next section.

FOR REFERENCE AND FURTHER STUDY

Finn, T. M. "The God-Fearers Reconsidered." *CBQ* 47 (1985) 75–84.

Harnack, A. *Luke the Physician: The Author of the Third Gospel and the Acts of the Apostles.* Crown Theological Library 19. London: Williams and Norgate, 1907, 8–11.

Schwartz, D. R. "The Accusation and Accusers at Philippi (Acts 16, 20-21). *Biblica* 65 (1984) 357–363.

Smallwood, E. M. *The Jews Under Roman Rule From Pompey to Diocletian.* Studies in Judaism in Late Antiquity 20. Leiden: E. J. Brill, 1976, 120–143.

van Unnik, W. C. "Die Anklage gegen die Apostel in Philippi (Apostelgeschichte 16, 20f)." *Sparsa Collecta: The Collected Essays of W. C. Van Unnik.* NovTSupp 29-30. Leiden: E. J. Brill, 1973–1980, 1:374-385.

Wehnert, J. *Die Wir-Passagen der Apostelgeschichte: Ein lukanisches Stilmittel aus jüdischen Tradition.* Göttingen: Vandenhoeck & Ruprecht, 1989.

Wilcox, M. "The 'God-Fearers' in Acts—A Reconsideration." *JSNT* 13 (1981) 102–122.

33. *Imprisonment and Release* (16:25-40)

25. In the middle of the night Paul and Silas were praying by singing hymns to God. The prisoners were listening to them. 26. Suddenly there was an earthquake so severe that the foundations of the prison were shaken. Immediately all the doors were thrown open and everyone's chains were loosened. 27. The jailer woke up. He saw the prison doors open. He drew out his sword. He was ready to kill himself, because he thought that the prisoners had escaped. 28. But Paul shouted out loudly, "Don't do yourself any harm, because we are all here!" 29. He asked for lights. He rushed in. Trembling, he fell down before Paul and Silas. 30. He then led them out. He said, "Masters, what must I do to be saved?" 31. They said, "Believe in the Lord Jesus, and both you and your household will be saved." 32. They spoke the word of the Lord to him and to all those in his house. 33. And at that hour of the night he took them and washed their wounds. He himself was at once baptized and so was all his family. 34. He then led them up into his house. He provided a meal. With his entire household he rejoiced because he had come to believe in God. 35. When it was day, the magistrates sent the police to say, "release these people." 36. The jailer reported these words to Paul, "The magistrates have sent to have you released. Therefore come out now. Go in peace!" 37. But Paul said about them, "They beat us in public without a trial, even though we are Roman citizens, they threw us into prison, and now they are dismissing us in secret? No! Instead let them come themselves to lead us out!" 38. The police

reported these words to the magistrates. They grew fearful when they heard that they were Roman citizens. 39. So they went to implore them. And when they had led them out, they asked them to leave the city. 40. But when they left the prison they went to Lydia's. They saw and comforted the brothers, and they left.

NOTES

25. *in the middle of the night:* More precisely, "towards (*kata*) midnight (*mesonyktion*)"; see also Luke 11:5; Acts 20:7 and 27:27. All these dramatic events happen between midnight and daybreak.

    praying by singing hymns: Luke typically shows the disciples turning to prayer at a time of crisis, in imitation of Jesus (see Luke 3:22; 6:12; 9:18, 28-29; 10:21-22; 11:1; 18:1-8; 22:31, 41-46; 23:46; Acts 1:14; 2:42, 47; 4:23-31; 6:4; 7:60; 9:11; 10:2, 9; 12:12; 13:2-3). For the singing of hymns (*hymneō*), see 1 Chr 16:9; 2 Chr 23:13; 29:30; Tobit 12:22; Pss 21:22; 70:8; 136:3; Sir 39:35; 47:8; Dan 3:24; Eph 5:19; Col 3:16. The prison experience is one that tests one's philosophical mettle. Epictetus says, "Then we shall be emulating Socrates, when we are able to write paeans in prison" (*Discourses* 2, 6, 26-27), and in the *Testament of Joseph* 8:5, the patriarch "sang praise in the house of darkness."

26. *suddenly there was an earthquake:* For the motif of miraculous prison escapes in Hellenistic literature, see the notes on Acts 5:19-20 and 12:6-10. For the earthquake (*seismos*) as a sign of theophany in Hellenistic religion, see Ovid, *Metamorphoses* 9:782-83; 15:669-78, and Lucian of Samosata, *The Lover of Lies* 22, and for the "shaking" (*saleuein*) in the biblical tradition, see LXX Pss 17:7; 47:5; 81:5; 96:4; 98:1. The divine intervention here is less direct and personal than in the escapes of Peter but no less decisive.

27. *he was ready to kill himself:* A prominent theme in Hellenistic Novels, and in the Apocryphal Acts which so much resemble them, is the threat or deed of suicide in the face of disappointment, loss, and especially shame or dishonor (see e.g., Chariton of Aphrodisias, *Chaereas and Callirhoe* 3, 1, 1; 1, 5, 2; 5, 9, 9-10; Xenophon of Ephesus, *The Ephesians* 2, 4, 6; Apuleius, *The Golden Ass* 6:12, 17; *Acts of John* 20; 24; *Acts of Andrew*, Narr. 36).

29. *trembling he fell before Paul and Silas:* Although the needed transition is lacking, the jailer is clearly the subject of this new sentence. His reactions appear extreme, but fit the fashion of the Hellenistic Novel, where strong emotions are always being extravagantly displayed (see e.g., Longus, *Daphnis and Chloe* 2:30; Achilles Tatius, *Clitophon and Leucippe* 1:4; 2:23; 5:19; Heliodorus, *The Ethiopians* 2, 1, 2; 2, 2, 2). For "trembling" (*entromos*), compare LXX Ps 17:7; Wis 17:10; 1 Macc 13:2 and Acts 7:32. For falling before someone (the Western Text understandably adds *pros tous podas* ["at the feet"]), see Luke 5:8; 8:28, 41, 47; 17:16; Acts 5:10; 10:25.

30. *Masters, what must I do:* As with Lydia in the previous episode, the jailer emerges as a personality in his own right. The Western Text extends his role even further by adding that before he led them out, "he secured the other prisoners." In his question to Paul and Silas, the term *kyrioi* could mean "sirs"/"Lords." If the jailer attributes the earthquake to the songs spoken by the apostles, the title "Lords" might be better, since he would be greeting them as magicians or divine men. In that case, Paul's response would be a deflection of glory. The phrase "to be saved" (*hina sōthō*) picks up the theme established programmatically in 13:47 by the citation of Isaiah 49:6, and last encountered in the announcement by the Pythian spirit (16:17).

31. *believe in the Lord Jesus:* The formula resembles that in 5:14; 9:42; 11:17. For the connection of faith to salvation throughout this section of Acts, see 14:9 and 15:11. The inclusion of "your household (*oikos*)" echoes the story of Lydia (16:15) and of Cornelius (11:14).

34. *rejoiced because he had come to believe in God:* The verb *agalliaō* ("rejoice") is used by Luke for specifically religious responses to God's visitation (Luke 1:47; 10:21; Acts 2:26; compare LXX Pss 2:11; 5:11; 9:2; 15:9; 30:7; 118:162). The circumstantial perfect participle of *pisteuō* provides the reason for the rejoicing. Notice, however, that this conversion is expressed in terms of believing in *God* rather than in the Lord Jesus.

35. *when it was day:* Throughout the next five verses, the mss of the Western Tradition expand the story. In the present verse it adds, "when it was day, the magistrates came together into the city-center (*agora*). And because they remembered the earthquake that had occurred, they grew frightened . . . ." The function of the expansion seems obvious: it provides a motive for the magistrates' otherwise unexplained decision to release the apostles.

    sent the police: The *rhabdouchoi* (carriers of the *rhabdoi* = wooden rods) could be several kinds of functionaries. In the present case, they are the officials below the magistrates (*stratēgoi*) and above the jailer (*desmophylax*), so the translation "police" is appropriate.

37. *beat us in public without a trial:* Literally "without having been condemned" (*akatakritos*). There is a contrast here between the public (*dēmosia*) beating, and the secret (*lathra*) dismissal. The first gave shame to Paul, the second is to save the magistrates from shame. Note how Paul himself in 1 Thess 2:2 refers to the suffering experienced by himself, Silas, and Timothy (see 1 Thess 1:1) in Philippi as *hybristhentes* ("treated shamefully/insultingly").

    even though we are Roman citizens: Two things are revealed by this concessive participial construction: a) the charge made by the slave-owners ("these men are Jews") is revealed as antisemitic, yet the magistrates were all too willing to accept it at face value, *and* treat those so charged shamefully, with no fear of reprisal; b) Paul lays claim, not for the last time (see 22:25-29) to the rights guaranteed the *rōmaioi*, sharers in the citizenship rights of the city of Rome, which during this period had been widely extended. It is impossible, given the state of our evidence, to state whether in fact Paul *was* a citizen, but the fact is critical to Luke's narrative. Magistrates in a Roman Colony in particular would need to be careful not to infringe those rights, which included freedom from such arbitrary treatment (see Livy, *History of Rome* 10, 9, 3-6; Cicero, *Against Verres* 2, 5, 66: "To bind a Roman citizen is a crime, to flog him an abomination, to slay him almost an act of parricide").

38. *they grew fearful:* As with the terror of the jailer at the prospect of a prison-break, so in the magistrates' reaction we see the kind of fear of severe retribution that enabled Rome to rule over its vast empire (see also the fear of the Tribune in 22:29). The whole burden of Cicero's orations *Against Verres* was that such ancestral rights had been flagrantly violated (see esp. 2, 5, 53-54), for which Verres had to pay the penalty.

39. *went to implore them:* The Western Text expands this verse considerably: a) it adds the presence of the magistrates' "friends" (*philoi*); b) it has the magistrates recognize that the apostles are "righteous/innocent" (*dikaioi*); c) most oddly, they add to their plea that the apostles leave this motivation: "lest they again gather against us, crying out against you." This exonerates the magistrates and fits them to the mold of Pilate, as having been swayed to their injustice by the anger of a mob.

40. *saw and comforted the brothers:* The return to Lydia's household (see 16:14-15) is a gesture of independence by Paul, and nicely pulls these three Philippian vignettes into a neat unit. For the "exhortation/comfort" (*parakalein*) of the brothers in a new community, compare 11:23; 14:22; 15:31-32. The Western Text has again expanded the verse: "they narrated (*diēgēsato*) the things the Lord had done for them" (compare 14:27; 15:12).

INTERPRETATION

In Luke's narrative, the interplay between the divine plan and human circumstance is subtle. It is possible to read this section of his story as a snippet of the social history of the early empire. In the chance meeting with an Asian tradeswoman by the riverside, and the progression to the Jewish synagogue; in the encounter with the Pythian Prophetess and her owners; in the near-riot caused by the apostles being identified as Jews in the *agora*; in their imprisonment without trial and then elaborate, face-saving release, we see the multiform, pluralistic, and intensely vibrant life of the Mediterranean world of the first century.

We can identify the social usages of that world. We see how women such as Lydia, with no reference made to a spouse, could exercise significant means and power, not only in trade, but also as the patron of a cult (16:15, 40). We see how Judaism, despite its privileged status in the Diaspora under the emperors, remained at the local level terribly susceptible to sudden surges of antisemitic fury, so that local magistrates (even in a Colony) could be swayed by the mob (16:20-24).

Above all, we see some of the social-psychological factors that acted as powerful motivators of behavior. The jailer is a case in point. He is quick to attempt suicide when he thinks his prisoners have escaped (16:27). Why? Because he is fearful of retribution, surely, but also because of shame at having failed his responsibility. He is quick to call Silas and Paul "Masters" (*kyrioi*), and seek salvation from them (16:30). Why? Because they have become his benefactors. They saved him from shame by not escaping themselves and restraining the other prisoners from escaping. The jailer cannot contain himself in his gratitude. From having his "skin" saved, he is opened to another form of salvation in this God whom such powerful benefactors are propagating (16:31-34).

The importance of honor and shame in that world are displayed as well in the encounter between the apostles and the magistrates. Luke does not explain why the magistrates decided to release them, although the Western Text is quick to connect their decision to the earthquake, no doubt interpreted as a divine warning (see notes). Perhaps, in fact, they simply had placed them in protective custody to save them from a worse fate at the hands of the mob (another possibility suggested by the longer Western Text Tradition). Or perhaps Luke has not thought about it, but considered their action from the beginning an arbitrary and short-termed bit of injudicial justice.

In any case, their behavior provides the occasion for a shame-honor showdown between Paul and them (16:37-39). Paul regards their public (*dēmosia*) beating without a trial to have been a dishonoring, which the magistrates are now trying to rectify "in secret" (*lathra*). But Paul will not be content with freedom if his honor as a citizen still stands publically impugned. He faces down the magistrates. They come to beg him to leave the prison and the colony. Only when his honor has thus been vindicated does Paul consent to leave the prison, and even then he does not leave the city at once, but first visits and comforts the nascent community at Lydia's house; he is indeed acting like a *rōmaios*, a citizen of the city of Rome!

But beneath all this interaction which is perfectly explicable on the basis of the social-psychology of the ancient Mediterranean world, Luke weaves another narrative line concerning God's visitation of the nations for salvation. Paul's failure to find the house of prayer led to a conversation with a congregation of women by the river. And his meeting with Lydia leads in turn to her baptism and that of her household, and also to the founding of a messianic community in Philippi. Paul's encounter with the Pythian spirit leads to the (unwitting) proclamation through the streets of Philippi of "the Highest God" and "the path of salvation" offered by the apostles. The imprisonment enables the other prisoners to perceive the philosophical calm of the apostles as they pray with the singing of hymns. The earthquake and its sequel leads to the baptism of the jailer and his entire household. Each of these occasions for proclamation and witness was unplanned, spontaneous, even accidental, unless one perceives, as Luke surely did, that God's visitation is enabled by just such human experiences.

FOR REFERENCE AND FURTHER STUDY

Cadbury, H. J. *The Book of Acts in History.* New York: Harper and Brothers, 1955, 73–82.
Mommsen, T. "Die Rechtsverhaltnisse des Apostels Paulus." *ZNW* 2 (1901) 81–96.
Sherwin-White, A. N. *Roman Society and Roman Law in the New Testament.* London: Oxford University Press, 1963, 71–98.
Tajra, H. W. *The Trial of St. Paul.* WUZNT 2: 35. Tübingen: JCB Mohr (Paul Siebeck), 1989, 3–29.
Tannehill, R. *Narrative Unity* 2:198-205.

34. *Troubles in Thessalonica* (17:1-15)

1. They travelled through Amphipolis and Apollonia. They came to Thessalonica, where there was a synagogue of the Jews. 2. According to his custom, Paul went in among them. For three Sabbaths he held discussions with them on the basis of the scriptures. 3. He opened their meaning. He set out how the Messiah had to suffer and to rise from the dead. And he said, "This one is the Messiah, the Jesus whom I am proclaiming to you." 4. Some of them were convinced and were committed to Paul and Silas. So was a large crowd of devout Greeks as well as more than a few of the important women. 5. But the Jews became jealous. They recruited some wicked fellows from the rabble, and gathering together a crowd, they put the city in tumult. They came to Jason's house. They were seeking to bring them before the assembly. 6. But since they could not find them, they proceeded to drag Jason and certain brothers before the city leaders. They shouted, "These people have been subverting the empire, and now they are here! 7. Jason has welcomed them! And these people are all acting contrary to Caesar's decrees by saying there is another king, Jesus." 8. They stirred up the crowd as well as the city leaders, when they heard these things. 9. These took bail from Jason and the rest, and released them. 10. But the brothers immediately sent off Paul and Silas to Beroea by night. When they arrived, they went to the synagogue of the Jews. 11. These people were more refined than those in Thessalonica. They received the message with complete eagerness. Every day they examined the scriptures to see whether these things

were so. 12. And many of them came to believe, as well as some well-placed Greek women and more than a few men. 13. But when the Jews from Thessalonica heard that the word of God had been proclaimed by Paul also in Beroea, they came there in order to stir up and disturb the crowds. 14. Then the brothers immediately sent off Paul to travel to the sea, while Silas and Timothy remained there. 15. And those who were conducting Paul led him to Athens. Taking along an order for Silas and Timothy to come to him as soon as possible, they departed.

NOTES

1. *through Amphipolis and Apollonia:* Luke earlier used *diodeuō* ("making a way") in the Gospel for Jesus' travels through Galilee (Luke 8:1). These towns were on the *Via Egnatia*, upon which Paul appears to be travelling; they are named in Pliny the Elder, *Natural History* 4:38. The Western Text implies that he stopped at these places rather than simply travelled through them.

    came to Thessalonica: This was the capital city of the province, called by Pliny the Elder a "free city" (*Natural History* 4:36); the circumstances of the founding of the church there are also recounted in 1 Thess 1:5–2:16. In Acts 20:4, Aristarchus and Secundus are identified as companions of Paul from the Thessalonian community, and Aristarchus is mentioned still again in 27:2.

2. *according to his custom:* The same expression is used for Jesus' trip to the synagogue in Nazareth (Luke 4:16). In fact, this has been Paul's regular practice (13:14, 44; 14:1; 16:13, 16), and will continue to be so in Corinth (18:4) and Ephesus (19:8). Luke does not want the reader to lose sight—after the recent encounters with Gentiles—of Paul's fundamental commitment to spreading the good news among his own people.

    held discussions with them: The verb *dialegomai* here has the sense of a philosophical discussion (compare Plato, *The Republic* 454A; 511C) on the basis of the texts of Torah (*apo tōn graphōn*). Such activities of study and discussion were a common feature of the synagogue in its realization as *Beth ha Midrash* ("house of study"); see *m.Shab* 16:1; *bT Meg.* 26b-27a.

3. *he opened their meaning:* The use of *dainoigō* ("open") here does not refer simply to the opening of the scrolls but to the act of interpretation; the translation therefore supplies the implied "their meaning." Compare Luke 24:31, 32, 45; Acts 16:14.

    he set out: The verb *paratithēmi* ("to set out"), which Luke uses elsewhere in its sense of "spreading a table" (Luke 9:16; 10:18; 11:6; 12:48; Acts 16:34), or "presenting" (Luke 23:46; Acts 14:23; 20:32), has here the rhetorical meaning of adducing evidence or examples by way of proof (Lucian of Samosata, *A Professor of Public Speaking* 9; Josephus, *Life* 6; Dio Chrysostom, *Oration* 17:10). In the present case, Luke undoubtedly means those passages of Torah that demonstrate his thesis that "the Messiah must suffer" (compare Luke 9:22; 17:25; 24:26, 46; Acts 3:18).

this one is the Messiah, the Jesus whom I am proclaiming: Luke uses an abbreviated form of syllogism called the *enthymeme,* one of whose terms is left implicit (see Aristotle, *Rhetoric* 1356A-1358A). Here the middle term left unspoken is: "Thus Jesus has suffered." The odd presence of two definite articles (*ho christos ho Iēsous*) led some *mss* to omit either one or the other, or (as Codex D) both articles.

4. *committed to Paul and Silas:* For "being convinced" (*peithō*), see Luke 16:31; 20:6; Acts 5:36-37; 13:43; 18:4. The verb *prosklēroomai* ("committed to") is rare, occurring neither in the LXX nor elsewhere in the NT. The root *klēros* ("lot") and the use of the "divine passive" suggest that "God assigned them" to Paul and Silas.

so . . . as well: The translation tries to catch the sense of the balanced clauses connected by the particles *te. . . te.* For the "God fearing (or devout) Greeks," see the note on 10:2. Three observations on "more than a few of the important women": a) the Greek has "not a few" (*ouk oligai*), another example of Luke's *litotes:* he means "many"; b) the adjective *prōtai* ("important") is literally "first/leading"; c) another possible translation of the Greek as it stands is "wives of important/leading men." Codex D makes this reading explicit by writing *kai gynaikes tōn prōtōn.* In light of 17:12, below, however, the majority reading and the present translation are correct.

5. *Jews became jealous:* The translation takes the aorist as inceptive, as "the Jews turned jealous." For earlier examples of this theme of jealousy (envy) see the notes on 5:17; 7:9; 13:45. Codex D supplies the characterization, "the disbelieving Jews."

wicked fellows from the rabble: While the adjective *ponēros* has a definite moral connotation (see Luke 3:19; 7:21), the phrase "from the rabble" has more of a class-conscious perspective: *agoraios* is used to refer to people who hang about in the public square (*agora*), and could rightly be translated as "low-lifes" (see Aristotle, *Politics* 1291A; Herodotus, *Persian Wars* 2:141). They are the sort of folk who as day-laborers were often at loose-ends and therefore ready for mischief (see Plato, *Protagoras* 347C). Note the social consciousness in Luke's distinction between those who convert and those who do not!

put the city in tumult: The term for "gathering a crowd" (*ochlopoieō*) is literally "making a crowd" and is unattested earlier than Luke. The verb *thorubein* has the primary sense of making lots of noise by shouting, and from there takes on the sense of frightening (Plato, *Phaedrus* 245B; LXX Nah 2:3; Dan 8:17; Sir 40:6; Wis 18:19). Luke will use it again in 20:10, and *thorubos* in 20:1; 21:34; 24:18.

Jason's house: As in the case of Lydia's, we are to picture a house-church already in existence, even though Paul has been at work in Thessalonica only a matter of weeks (17:2). The Greek name Jason is attested among Jews both in Palestine (see Josephus, *Antiquities* 12:415; 14:146) and in the Diaspora (2 Macc 2:23), but we cannot be certain that this Jason was himself Jewish. Paul in Rom 16:21 mentions a Jason with "Luke and Sosipatros" as being among his "fellow workers," but once more, any connection with the person whose presence in Acts in confined to this story, is entirely speculative.

bring them before the assembly: The implied subject of "they" throughout these sentences is the mob, or its Jewish instigators. The implied referents of "them" in this sentence are Paul and Silas. The term *dēmos* (literally "the people") is used in its sense of "popular assembly" (compare Plato, *The Republic* 565B).

6. *before the city leaders:* Luke is concerned to assign the proper political offices to the various urban magistracies faced by Paul. In the Roman Colony of Philippi, they were the *stratēgoi;* here they are the *politarchai*, a term whose appropriateness for the Macedonian territory at this period is well supported by inscriptional evidence.

subverting the empire: For the translation of *oikoumenē* as "empire," see the note on Acts 11:28; the political connotation here is unmistakable, and any other translation would miss the point of the charge. The verb *anastatoō* (literally "upset," as in Gal 5:12), is translated as "subvert" to suit the charge of political disruption. It is used in LXX Dan 7:23 and again in Acts 21:38.

now they are here: The translation adds "now" to capture the stress placed by *kai enthade pareisin*. The tone is one of patriotic panic, as in "The Russians are coming!"

7. *another king, Jesus:* The translation of *basileus* is difficult: from one point of view, it should be rendered as "emperor," for such was Caesar's title in the East (although see Luke 23:2; Acts 25:8), and such is the burden of this charge; from another point of view, the translation "king" enables the reader to recognize the theme of Jesus' kingship that runs through Luke's two-volume work (Luke 1:33; 19:11, 12, 15, 38; 22:29-30; 23:2-3, 37). As in the trial of Jesus (Luke 23:2) the confession of Jesus as "Messiah" is put in the most politically inflammatory form. Such activity is generally subversive, and for an empire chronically suspicious of any unapproved social gatherings (see Pliny the Younger, *Letters* 10:34), surely to be regarded as against the *dogmata* ("decrees"; compare Luke 2:1) of Caesar.

9. *took bail from Jason:* The expression *lambanein to hikanon* ("to take that which is sufficient/necessary") means here to accept bail money or security (compare a similar though not identical usage in Diogenes Laertius, *Lives of the Philosophers* 4:50). These magistrates do not give in to the demands of the mob, as did those at Philippi (16:23-24), but follow legal procedure.

10. *to Beroea by night:* As in earlier occasions in Damascus (9:23-25), Jerusalem (9:30), Antioch of Pisidia (13:50-51), and Lystra (14:20), Paul is forced to make a rapid and less than glorious exit because of the trouble he has generated. A remarkable amount of the action in Acts takes place *dia nyktos* ("at night"); see 5:19; 9:25; 12:6; 16:33. The city of Beroea is some 60 miles south of Thessalonica (see Pliny the Elder, *Natural History* 4:33).

11. *more refined than those in Thessalonica:* Luke emphasized the rabble-character of the opposition in Thessalonica (*ponēroi/agoraioi*). The term *eugenēs* means literally "well born" (see Luke 19:12; 1 Cor 1:26), and is used primarily to

designate the social status of nobility; from there it can mean to act in a noble or gracious fashion (see e.g., 4 Macc 6:5; 9:13; 10:3). Here the emphasis is entirely on behavior, demonstrated by their "complete eagerness" (*prothymia*).

every day they examined the scriptures: As at Thessalonica (17:3), Luke places emphasis on the reading and (here) the critical examination of Torah. For *anakrinō*, compare Luke 23:14; Acts 4:9. The Beroeans "complete eagerness" is shown by the fact that they engage in this activity "every day" (*kath'hēmeran*) rather than simply on the Sabbath.

12. *well-placed Greek women:* The term *euschēmōn* properly means "decent" or "proper." It is used by Luke in the sense of social standing, once more in explicit contrast to the "rabble" at Thessalonica. Codex D has a split response, "Some of them believed and some did not believe," and also changes the present clause so that the role of the women is less prominent: "a large number of men and women from among the Greeks and the well-placed came to believe."

13. *word of God:* Despite the thoroughly Hellenistic coloration that Luke's narrative has taken on in this section, the presentation of the apostles as prophets from God is not fundamentally altered, as this way of characterizing their message indicates (compare Luke 5:1; 8:11, 21; 11:28; Acts 4:29-31; 6:2, 7; 8:14, 25; 11:1; 12:24; 13:5, 44, 46, 48-49; 15:35; 16:32).

stir up and disturb the crowds: The participles *saleuontes* ("stir up/shake"), and *tarassontes* ("disturb") are translated as expressing purpose. Luke pictures this in precisely the same way as the pursuit of Paul to Lystra by the Jews of Antioch and Iconium (14:19).

15. *led him to Athens:* Although the verb *kathistēmi* is otherwise used by Luke in the sense of "establish/appoint" (Luke 12:14, 42, 44; Acts 6:3; 7:10, 27, 35), the meaning of "conducting/leading down" is also well-attested (see, e.g., Herodotus, *Persian Wars* 1:64). Codex D adds these words: "He passed by Thessaly, for he was prevented from preaching the word to them," which explains the lack of missionary work between Beroea and Athens.

taking along an order: Literally "a commandment" (*entolē*); precisely such commands concerning the movement of delegates are contained or alluded to in the Pauline letters (see Titus 3:12-13; 2 Tim 4:21; 1 Tim 1:3; Col 4:10; Phil 2:19; 1 Cor 16:10-11). The sequence of events described in this part of the narrative corresponds exceptionally well with the information contained in 1 Thess 3:1-2.

INTERPRETATION

In this section of Acts we find the highest degree of correspondence between Luke's narrative and the information given by Paul's letters. More than at any other place in Paul's career, we are able with confidence and some precision to trace his movements. In 1 Thessalonians, Paul recounts for his readers his earliest experiences with them, as well as his present circumstances. These agree in outline with the presentation in Luke's narrative: a) the humiliation that Paul had suffered in Philippi before coming to Thessalonica (1 Thess 2:2); b) the opposition faced his preaching in Thessalonica (2:2), especially from the Jews with respect to preaching to Gentiles (2:16), so that the Thessalonian Church received the word "with much affliction (1:6); c) Paul's staying in Athens after leaving Thessalonica (3:1); d) his sending Timothy to them "to establish you in the faith and to exhort you" (3:2).

There are things in each source lacking in the other. Acts includes the Beroean episode, and the participation of Silas in the legation with Timothy. Paul includes "Silvanus" in the greeting of his letter (1 Thess 1:1), but says nothing more about Silas. And rather than recount his experiences after his leaving Thessalonica, he concentrates on his concerns for that community (1 Thess 3:6-8). Perhaps most puzzling, Acts concentrates on Paul's work (and partial success) among the Jewish community in Thessalonica (17:4) and in Beroea (17:11). But Paul's language in 1 Thess 1:9; 2:14 and 4:13 suggests he is writing to a community that is almost entirely if not exclusively made up of Gentiles. These disparities make it unlikely that Luke was using the Thessalonian correspondence as one of his sources, and helps the historian's confidence that in this section of Paul's story the basic events are confirmed by two independent sources.

Luke's own shaping of the narrative, of course, is influenced by the overriding concerns that motivate his story. We notice first how Luke has returned the reader to a perception of Paul that may slightly have been eroded in the Philippian section, where Paul interacted so vigorously with the Gentile world: in Thessalonica and again in Beroea, Paul reverts to his custom of going to the synagogue and debating with his fellow Jews. Despite his first great "turn to the Gentiles" in 13:46, Paul is still presented as the "Teacher of Israel," seeking to convince his compatriots of the message he bears. Luke presents Paul as the philosopher who calls his hearers to an "examination" of the text (17:11), and enters into "debate" with them (17:2), is able to marshal his arguments, "setting out" to them the evidence and "opening its meaning" to them by means of syllogism: "This one is the Messiah, the Jesus whom I am proclaiming to you" (17:3-4). But he is also very much the Jewish philosopher, whose texts are not those of Plato but of Moses, whose examples come not from mythology but from Torah (17:3).

Despite Paul's commitment to this mission of convincing his fellow-Jews, however, he continues to receive at best a mixed response. Even while Luke acknowledges some success among the Jews ("some of them were convinced," 17:4; "many of them came to believe," 17:12), he notes a much greater receptivity among the Gentiles, ("a large crowd of devout Greeks," 17:4, and "some well-placed Greek women and more than a few men,'' 17:12). The Jews who refuse to accept this proclamation, furthermore, are presented in negative terms. Like the leaders in Jerusalem, they grow envious of the apostles' success (17:5), and like the Jews of Pisidian Antioch and Iconium, those of Thessalonica follow Paul to Beroea to create trouble for him there as well (17:13). In the riot they create in Thessalonica, the Jews bring against Paul the same sort of charges of disrupting the social order and challenging the rule of Caesar that the Jerusalem leadership had brought against Jesus (17:6-7). The delicacy of the Messianists' position is obvious: in Philippi they could be thrown in jail because of the antisemitic charge that as Jews they were purveying foreign customs; in Thessalonica the Jews themselves could charge them with subversion against the political order. In terms of Luke's narrative, whatever small success Paul does have among the Jews is obliterated by such vigorous counterattack.

We observe in this passage as well Luke's apologetic interest in showing the success of the messianic movement among the ''better classes'' of society. It does not take a great deal of reflection to perceive that any social one-upmanship would be at least in implicit tension with Jesus' teaching in the beatitudes, and the entire theme of the good news to the poor which is so characteristic of Luke's Gospel. What, then, are we to make of Luke's gleeful note that ''important'' and ''well-placed'' Greek women were converting to the messianic movement?

At one level, we can see these comments as a sort of naive glee at the social success of the movement: because those who are powerful take it seriously, it seems more important. At another level, there is also a slighting of the Jews who form the opposition. The jealous Jews in Thessalonica must find their allies among the riff-raff of the streets (17:5) and not among the better people who have accepted the gospel. And the Jews who are ''eager'' to hear Paul in Beroea are thereby shown to be ''more refined'' (literally ''more noble'') than the Jews who rejected Paul in Thessalonica.

However understandable such social claims may be for a marginal and persecuted movement which was—even at the time of Luke's writing— scarcely a social or political success in any meaningful sense of those terms, they are less easy for us to read after centuries of Christian antisemitism that fed off such relatively innocent characterizations and made of them truly hostile stereotypes. Nevertheless, historical perspective is important for appreciating still another aspect of these authorial touches. The reader must remember that Luke's story is one that must argue for the legitimacy of the Gentile mission within a context dominated by the symbols of Torah and the people that can lay first claim to those symbols. In this light, the conversion of Greek women of social standing can also be read as a statement about the good news to the outcast.

FOR REFERENCE AND FURTHER STUDY

Beydon, F. "Luc et 'ces dames de la haute société'." *ETR* 61 (1986) 331–341.
Cassidy, R. J. *Society and Politics in the Acts of the Apostles.* New York: Orbis Press, 1987, 83–95.
Judge, E. A. "The Decrees of Caesar at Thessalonica." *Reformed Theological Review* 30 (1971) 1–7.
Kurz, W. S. "Hellenistic Rhetoric in the Christological Proof of Luke-Acts." *CBQ* 42 (1980) 171–195.
Slingerland, D. " 'The Jews' in the Pauline Portion of Acts." *JAAR* 54 (1986) 305–321.
Tajra, H. W. *The Trial of St. Paul.* WUNT 2:35. Tübingen: JCB Mohr (Paul Siebeck), 1989, 30–44.

35. *Paul in Athens* (17:16-34)

16. While Paul was in Athens waiting for them, his spirit was irritated within him, because he saw that the city was filled with idols. 17. He was therefore debating in the synagogue with the Jews and with those who feared God, as well as every day in the city-square with those who happened to be there. 18. And some philosophers of the Epicurean and Stoic schools entered into discussion with him. Some of them were saying, "What is the meaning of this busybody's speech?" And since he was announcing good news about Jesus and the resurrection, others said, "He seems to be the proclaimer of foreign deities." 19. So they took him and led him to the Areopagus. They said, "May we know what this new teaching is that you are speaking? 20. For you are bringing certain strange things to our attention. We therefore wish to learn what these things mean." 21. Now all the Athenians and the foreigners who lived there liked nothing better than speaking or hearing something novel. 22. Paul stood in the middle of the Areopagus. He said, "Athenians! I perceive that you are in every respect exceptionally religious, 23. for as I was passing through and gazing at your shrines I saw also an altar on which was inscribed, 'To an Unknown God.' Therefore the one whom you unknowingly worship I am proclaiming to you. 24. This God is the one who made the world and everything in it. Since he is Lord of heaven and earth he does not dwell in temples made by hands. 25. Neither is he served by human hands as though he needed anything, since he himself gives life and breath and everything to everyone. 26. And from one human being he has made every nation of humans to dwell over the entire face of the earth. He has set apart designated seasons and the territories for their habitation, 27. so they might seek God,

perhaps even sense and find him. Indeed he is not far from each one of us, 28. 'For by him we live and move and are,' as even some of the poets among you have said, 'for we are also of his family.' 29. Therefore since we are of God's family we ought not to think of the divine as similar to gold or silver or stone, shaped by human craft and conception. 30. God has accordingly overlooked the times of ignorance, but now is commanding all people everywhere to repent, 31. because he has established a day in which he is going to judge the world with justice, by a man whom he has appointed. He has provided proof to all by having raised him from the dead." 32. When they heard "resurrection of the dead," some of them began to mock. But others said, "We will listen to you another time concerning this matter." 33. So Paul went out from among them. 34. But some men joined him and believed. Among them was Dionysius of the Areopagus, and a woman named Damaris, and others with them.

Notes

16. *waiting for them:* Namely, Silas and Timothy (see 17:15); the effect of this transition statement is not only to link this story with the previous one, but also to provide the clear impression that Paul's subsequent experiences in Athens were the result of accident rather than a set missionary plan.

    his spirit was irritated within him: There are no *mss* that omit "his" (*autou*), so the *pneuma* that is irritated is Paul's own and not the prophetic "Holy Spirit" (compare 16:18). For the psychology presumed, compare 1 Thess 5:23 (*pneuma, psychē, soma*). The term for "irritation" (*paroxynomai*), which we recognize from the dispute between Paul and Barnabas (15:39) could perhaps be translated "angry" or even "outraged."

    city was filled with idols: The construction *kateidōlon* occurs only here, and clearly reflects a Jewish perspective on Greek piety! The many statues to be found in Athens are mentioned in such sources as Livy, *History of Rome* 45:27; Pausanius, *Description of Greece* 1, 14, 1-1, 15, 7.

17. *he was therefore debating:* Although the connective *men oun* is very frequent in Acts as a simply narrative transition that does not really require translation (Acts 1:18; 2:41; 5:41; 8:4, 25; 9:31; 11:19; 12:5; 13:4; 14:3-4; 15:3, 30; 16:5; 17:12), it is translated here because it describes an action consequent on Paul's previous perception. The term "debate" (*dialegomai*) as in 17:2 recalls the philosophical style associated with Socrates (Plato, *Apology* 19D), an association that is made more emphatic in the verses to follow.

    as well as every day in the city-square: Here is the point of innovation in Paul's procedure: for the first time he deliberately takes up the position of the Cynic philosopher, who would confront folk in the *agora* (for the range of meanings of this term, see the note on 16:19). It is a step sufficiently important to have been prepared for by the psychological comment in v. 16. For the "open-air" style of preaching of the Cynic, see Epictetus, *Discourses* 3, 22, 26-30; Dio Chrysostom, *Oration* 32:9.

18. *Epicurean and Stoic schools:* The translation supplies the word "schools" (literally, "and some both of the Epicurean and Stoic philosophers"). The Epicureans were founded ca. 300 B.C.E. by Epicurus, and the Stoics at about the same time by Zeno. A sketch of their lives, teachings, and followers can be found in Diogenes Laertius, *Lives of Eminent Philosophers*, Books 7 (Zeno and the Stoics) and 10 (Epicurus). Together with the Platonists and Peripatetics, these schools continued to have subsidized "chairs" in Athens (see Lucian, *The Eunuch* 3). The Stoic school was by far the more obviously "pious" with its views concerning providence and divine immanence, and in thinkers such as Marcus Aurelius and Epictetus reached a genuine religious spirit (see, e.g., Marcus Aurelius, *Meditations* 1:17; 2:3; 2:11-12; 4:23; 5:7, 8, and Epictetus, *Discourses* 1, 16, 15-21; 3, 5, 8-11; 3, 22, 2-8; 4, 1, 89). In contrast, the Epicureans were as ostentatiously "impious" with regard to traditional belief, saving their piety for their founder (see Plutarch, *Reply to Colotes* 17 [*Mor* 1117 B-C]). Their commitment to a Democritean explanation of reality in terms of atomic particles was connected to a resolute rejection of religion (see Lucretius, *On the Nature of Things* 2:581-725; 5:81-90; 5:146-194). Lucian of Samosata pictures the Epicureans as the consistent deflators of religious charlatans (see *Alexander the False Prophet* 25; 43-44).

the meaning of this busybody's speech: Luke uses the phrase *ti thelei* (literally "what does he wish") in the optative with *legein* with the sense "what does it mean/intend" (see Luke 1:62; Acts 2:12; 17:20). The term *spermologos* ("busybody") derives from the image of a bird picking up and dropping a seed (*sperma*), hence a "gossip" (Philo, *Embassy to Gaius* 203) or the peddler of second-rate religious opinions (see Philostratus, *Life of Apollonius of Tyana* 5:20), which seems to be the sense here. In his treatise *On Being a Busybody* 2 (*Mor* 516C), Plutarch appears to have this in mind when he refers to Aristippus picking up only "seeds and samples" of Socrates' words (*tōn logōn autou spermata kai deigmata*).

good news about Jesus and the resurrection: This translation reverses the order of the Greek clauses to give a better sense of the first clause's explanatory function. The explanatory clause is in fact omitted by some *mss* (including Codex D) of the Western Tradition. The author's perspective on Paul's activity is indicated by the use of *euangelizomai!*

proclaimer of foreign deities: Although the NT writings generally understand *daimonia* as "demons," the term here has the sense of "deities" (see Herodotus, *Persian Wars* 5:87; Euripides, *Bacchae* 894). Acts uses the verb *katangello* ("proclaim") frequently (3:24; 4:2; 13:5, 38; 15:36; 16:17, 21; 17:3, 23), this is the only use in the NT of the noun *katangeleus*. The charge of introducing "foreign deities" not only resembles the charge of changing customs brought at Philippi (16:21), but more particularly echoes the charge made against Socrates (Xenophon, *Memorabilia* 1, 1, 1; Plato, *Apology* 24B). The defense made by Socrates against the attacks made by his fellow Athenians became in Hellenistic Philosophy the model for philosophical integrity (see e.g., Lucian of Samosata, *Demonax* 11). The odd phrasing of the previous clause, "Jesus and the resurrection" (we would have expected "the resurrection of Jesus"), may have given rise to the misapprehension about multiple deities.

19. *led him to the Areopagus:* The interpretation of the following scene depends on: a) how we understand the participle of *epilambanō;* does it mean simply a "taking along" (as in Acts 9:27; 23:19), or does it mean "arrest" (as in 16:19; 18:17)? b) how we construe the *areios pagos* (literally "Mars' Hill/Ares' Hill"); does it mean simply the location, or does it refer to the formal Athenian Council (*boulē*) which met at that location (Aristotle, *Politics* 1273B-1274A; Pausanias, *Description of Greece* 1, 28, 5)? At issue is how Luke wants us to regard the scene: is it a friendly inquiry, or is it a trial? The tone of the proceedings makes us think rather of a discussion than a formal hearing or trial. For a wonderful parody of a trial at the Areopagus, see Lucian of Samosata, *The Double Indictment* 4-12. Diogenes Laertius tells us that the philosopher Cleanthes was haled before the Areopagus, so that the court could determine how he made his living (*Lives of the Philosophers* 7:168-169).

    may we know: Literally "are we able (*dynametha*) to know." These two verses show an elaborate politeness, and place an emphasis on the desire to learn (*gnōnai* is used twice), rather than on the desire to investigate or cross-examine. For the expression *kainē didachē* ("new teaching") compare Mark 1:27. The note of "newness" will be picked up explicitly in v. 21.

20. *certain strange things:* The *xenizonta tina* are equivalent to the *kaina* ("new things"); we see again the similarity to the charges made against Socrates (Plato, *Euthyphro* 3B; *Apology* 24 B-C). In the present case the attitude of the council (or of gathered philosophers) is one open to instruction.

21. *speaking or hearing something novel:* The comparative *ti kainoteron* ("something newer") is used in the sense of "the latest thing/novelty." The Athenians' reputation in this respect is wonderfully captured by Chariton of Aphrodisias' *Chaereas and Callirhoe* 1, 11, 6-7.

22. *in every respect exceptionally religious:* The adjective *deisidaimonisteros* is in the comparative with the superlative sense intended, as is made clear by the use of *pantachou* ("in every respect"). The quality of being *deisidaimōn* was ambiguous, and the precise meaning depends on the attitude of the writer. Positively, it means "religious/devout" (see Dio Chrysostom, *Oration* 61:9); negatively, it means "superstitious" (see Strabo, *Geography* 16, 2, 37), a quality that Plutarch, at least, regards as worse than atheism (*A Pleasant Life Impossible* 21 [*Mor.* 1101 C-D]). Since Paul's statement is clearly intended to be a *captatio* (he builds on rather than condemns their piety), the translation "religious" is here appropriate. Luke does use the term in the sense of "superstition" in Acts 25:19. For the reputation of the Athenians for religiosity, see Josephus, *Against Apion* 2:130; Pausanias, *Description of Greece* 1, 17, 1.

23. *gazing at your shrines:* The noun *sebasma* means that which is an object of reverence or worship; in Wis 14:20 and 15:17 it is used for the worship of idols; see also Josephus, *Antiquities of the Jews* 18:344.

To an Unknown God: There is no independent evidence for such an inscription to a single god, but a fairly impressive collection of literary references to a practice in Athens of erecting altars to unknown deities (see especially Diogenes Laertius, *Lives of Eminent Philosophers* 1:110; Philostratus, *Life of Apollonius of Tyana* 6:3).

whom you unknowingly worship: There is a rhetorical play on the "unknown god" who is "unknowingly worshipped." The participle *agnoountes* also anticipates the "times of ignorance" in v. 30. The verb *eusebeō* ("worship/reverence") finds its only NT usage here and in 1 Tim 5:4; but see *eusebēs* in Acts 10:2, 7 and *eusebeia* in Acts 3:12. The verb is cognate with *sebasmata* in v. 23. Paul's "I am proclaiming" (*katangellō*), in turn, picks up the designation of him as a *katangeleus* in v. 18.

24. *this God is the one:* The present translation shifts the emphatic demonstrative pronoun *houtos*, which in Greek introduces the next clause, to the beginning of the entire sentence, which enables a better sense of the emphasis to be put on the circumstantial participle *hyparchōn*. For the background of this *topos* on creation, see the note on Acts 14:15.

    does not dwell in temples made by hands: The participle *hyparchōn* is explanatory: it is because God is Lord of all things that he cannot be circumscribed by any of them. This statement is obviously similar to that in Stephen's Speech (7:48-50). For the background to the theme in Judaism, see the note on 7:48; see also such Greco-Roman texts as Lucian of Samosata, *On Sacrifices* 11; Pseudo-Heraclitus, *Letter* 4:2.

25. *as though he needed anything:* The verb *therapeuō* is used elsewhere for "healing" (Luke 4:23; 6:7; 7:21; Acts 4:14; 5:16), but the meaning of "giving service" to a deity is widely attested (see e.g., Herodotus, *Persian Wars* 2:37; LXX Isa 54:17). The verb *prosdeomai* can mean either simply "to be in need" (LXX Prov 12:9; Sir 4:3), or actively "to request" (LXX Sir 18:32; 4 Macc 9:26). For the theme of God not needing human service, see 2 Macc 14:35; Josephus, *Antiquities of the Jews* 8:111.

26. *from one human being:* The Western Text supplies the word *haimatos* to *ex henos* (here translated as "one human being") to form the phrase "from one blood." Luke is clearly alluding to the Genesis story (Gen 1:27-28; 2:7), just as Paul does in Rom 5:12.

    designated seasons . . . territories: Despite the temptation to place these phrases within the context of Greek philosophy or Jewish apocalypticism, they are more likely to be a standard statement of God's creative power, which has as one of its essential elements the "separating" (*horizō*) of space and time in orderly fashion (see Gen 1:24; Deut 32:8; LXX Ps 74:17; Wis 7:17-19, and compare Acts 14:17).

27. *so they might seek God:* The translation gives particular emphasis to *zētein* as expressing purpose: God has done all this for humans precisely so that they might seek him. The idea of "seeking God" is axiomatic for the biblical tradition (see e.g., LXX Pss 26:8; 104:4; Prov 16:15; 28:5; Wis 13:6; Sir 2:15; Jer

27:4; Isa 31:1; 55:6). Some *mss* substitute "Lord" for "God," probably because "Seek the Lord" is such a well-established biblical phrase and scribes
could easily slip into it. An argument longer but essentially similar to the one
here is developed by Philo, *Special Laws* 1:32-40. The famous Olympic Discourse of Dio Chrysostom, of course, takes the argument the other direction,
but builds from the same premise that all people seek God (*Oration* 12:60-61).

perhaps even sense and find: The indirect question (*ei ara ge*) with the optative
mood (*psēlaphēsaian, heuroiein*) expresses a possibility which the translation
might make too definite. The Greek verb translated "sense" (*psēlaphaō*) has
a definite physical connotation of "groping, touching" (see LXX Gen 27:12;
Isa 59:10).

not far from each one of us: If the construction of the previous clause emphasized mere possibility, this one expresses stronger confidence. Since God not
only "makes" things, but sustains them in existence at every moment, God
is always near to every creature (see Deut 30:11; Josephus, *Antiquities of the
Jews* 8:108); the classic statement of this is Augustine, *Confessions* 1:1.

28. *live and move and are:* The traditional translation of *esmen* as "have our being"
is difficult to avoid, but gives too much the impression of an ontologically
loaded statement. The same is true of the translation of *en autǭ* as "in him,"
making it appear as a kind of participation in the divine rather than a *dependence* on it, as the translation "by him" suggests. Codex D adds the puzzling
words "day by day" (*to kath'hēmeran*). It is possible that Luke is alluding to
a poem attributed to the Cretan poet Epimenides, one of the seven sages of
Greece (Diogenes Laertius, *Lives of the Philosophers* 1:109-115), possibly the
same poem cited by Paul in Titus 1:12. It is not certain that Luke intended
this to be a direct quotation, and the precise form of the line in Epimenides
(if such it was) is not known.

as even some of the poets among you: The phrase *kath'hymas* ("among you") is
equivalent to "your." The phrasing and placement is sufficiently ambiguous that it might be taken with the foregoing or following statements, or both.
More important is the fact that Luke has Paul citing pagan *auctoritates* in virtually the same way that he cites Torah for his Jewish listeners.

we are also of his family: It was recognized already by Clement of Alexandria
(*Stromateis* 1, 19, 91) that this citation came from the *Phaenomena* of the Greek
poet Aratus (born ca. 310 B.C.E.). As in his midrashic arguments, Paul immediately picks up the key word, *genos* ("family/offspring") for his conclusion. It is probable that Luke understood this kinship along the lines of being
created in God's image (Gen 1:26), for that is the direction the argument takes.
A Hellenistic Jew like Aristobulus was also comfortable citing this poem of
Aratus in support of his thesis that "it is necessary to hold holy opinions
concerning God" (Aristobulus, frag. 4).

shaped by human craft and conception: Literally "engraved of craft and
thought/plan of man." We recognize a standard Jewish charge against idolatry (see Deut 4:28; LXX Pss 113:12; 134:25; Isa 40:18; 44:9-20; Wis 13:5, 10;
15:3-17; Rom 1:23), but it is also a motif in Hellenistic Philosophy (Dio

Chrysostom, *Oration* 12:80-83). The implicit appeal is to think of "the divine" (*to theion* used only here in the NT) in terms appropriate to rational creatures.

30. *overlooked the times of ignorance:* This theme was applied earlier to the ignorance of the Jews who rejected the Prophet Jesus (Acts 3:17; 13:27). Now it is applied to the erroneous conceptions of the divine rampant in the Gentile world (note the use of *agnōstos* and *agnoeō* in 17:23). For the "overlooking," compare Rom 3:25-26, and notice that *chronoi* is used here rather than *kairoi*, cautioning us from overloading the significance of *kairoi* in 17:26.

   commanding all people everywhere to repent: Some mss have "is announcing" (*apangellei*), but *parangellein* is a favorite Lukan word and fits the context (Luke 5:14; 8:29, 56; 9:21; Acts 1:4; 4:18; 5:28, 40; 10:42; 15:5; 16:18, 23). The theme of universal repentance (*metanoia*) is sounded in Luke 24:47, but this is its most explicit expression. It is also a vivid rebuttal of the position that a "natural revelation" is itself without need of correction and supplement.

31. *established a day:* The belief in a "day of judgment" is everywhere in the NT (Rom 2:5, 16; 1 Cor 1:8; Phil 1:6, 10; 1 Thess 5:2, 4; 2 Thess 1:10; 2:2; 2 Tim 1:18; 2 Pet 3:10), and based on such prophetic passages as Amos 5:18; Isa 2:12. See especially Luke 10:12; 12:46; 17:24, 30; Acts 2:20.

   judge the world with justice: The phrase derives directly from the LXX *krinei tēn oikoumenēn en dikaiosynē*, which is repeated verbatim in Pss 9:8; 66:4; 95:13; 97:9. The translation of *oikoumenē* as "world" is obviously justified in this case.

   by a man whom he has appointed: The use of *anēr* demands the translation by "man." The use of *horizō* ("appoint") reminds us not only of the separation of the seasons and territories by God (17:26), but especially of the conclusion of Peter's speech in 10:42: "He is the one designated (*horismenos*) by God to be judge (*kritēs*) of the living and the dead." Some Western mss add the name "Jesus" after "man."

   provided proof: The phrase *parechō pistin* can mean here either a) to provide a pledge or assurance (see Herodotus, *Persian Wars* 3:74), or b) to provide a proof or demonstration (Aristotle, *Nichomachean Ethics* 1173A; Josephus, *Antiquities of the Jews* 15:69).

32. *began to mock:* Luke pictures the same sort of response as at Pentecost: some hearers are dismissive (we would imagine the Epicureans), and some more receptive (compare 2:12-13); indeed, the verb *chleuazō* ("mock") is cognate with that used in the earlier passage (*diachleuazō*). Compare the mocking response to the speeches of the pretender Cynic in Lucian of Samosata, *The Passing of Peregrinus* 7-8, 34.

33. *went out from among them:* It may be possible in this to hear an echo of Luke 4:30, where Jesus passes through his would-be murderers after the speech in Nazareth, but it is a faint one at best. The conclusion is somewhat anticlimactic, and the lack of clear resolution argues in favor of a casual inquiry rather than a formal trial.

34. *joined him and believed:* Luke typically notes the success that leads to the foundation of a community. In this case, the success is obviously modest. Luke con-

tinues a recent preoccupation by a) noting the social rank of the male convert Dionysius; the designation *areopagitēs* suggests he is a member of the Athenian council and therefore of high social rank (Aristotle, *Politics* 1273B-1274A); b) noting the conversion of a woman, Damaris (see 16:15; 17:4, 12).

INTERPRETATION

Luke uses the space made available by Paul's short stay in Athens to craft one of his most impressive scenes. No ancient reader could miss the piquancy of a wandering Jewish preacher confronting the cultured sages of Athens. Although scarcely in her prime, Athens was still the city that most represented the greatness of Greek culture (Cicero, *De Officiis* 1:1), whose every locality evoked great teachers of the past (Cicero, *De Finibus* 5:1-8), whose reputation was so great that even obsessive describers of places needed to say no more than, "Athens is a free city, and requires no advertisement here, as her celebrity is more than ample" (Pliny the Elder, *Natural History* 4:24). Luke's sources (and our own, see 1 Thess 3:1-2) confirmed that Paul had spent time in Athens, but it was Luke's literary skill that created a scene that has continued to fascinate artists and theologians ever since. He made what historically could only have been the meagerest and most casual of contacts into a moment frozen in time, the exemplary meeting between Jerusalem and Athens, and the anticipation of the Christianized Hellenistic culture for which it provided the symbol.

No more than in the speeches of Peter at Pentecost or Stephen at his stoning or Paul at Pisidian Antioch are we to look here for a straightforward report of Paul's words. The speech for all its portentousness is as succinct as any other in Luke-Acts, and like all the others, is entirely the creation of Luke. So, for that matter, is the setting of the scene and its denouement. As in other such set-pieces, we discover here not what happened but Luke's idealized version of what ought to have happened, so marvelously wrought that for its readers it provided the emblem of what possibly could happen.

What impresses every reader with even the slightest knowledge of Hellenistic culture is how cunningly Luke has got everything right. There is no mistaking this scene in Athens for any other scene in Acts. The presence of statues and shrines everywhere, including those to "anonymous gods," which in fact gave the Athenians precisely the reputation for "piety/superstition" that Paul ascribes to them; the ubiquitous presence of the Philosophers always ready for a debate, especially one picked with a religious "proclaimer" who frequented the *agora* and confronted passers-by there, some of these philosophers notoriously skeptical of religious claims (the Epicureans), some of them more cautiously open (the Stoics); the traditions associated with Socrates—the charge of inculcating "foreign gods," and the hearing before the Areopagus—Luke gets all of this as vibrantly as any sketch in Lucian of Samosata (compare *Zeus Rants, The Double Indictment,* and above all, *The Eunuch*).

There is little doubt that Luke consciously set about to create the impressions he has. The difficulty for the interpreter is to avoid overloading an after all slender scene with more significance than it can bear, and to respect the proportion the author has himself assigned to this scene within his larger narrative. It is not the end of the book, not its singular climax, but another in a series of symbolic encounters between the word of the gospel and the many aspects of the world it was destined to transform.

In the same way, we should not ask of Luke a more profound engagement with Greek Philosophy than he could manage in these few lines placed in the mouth of Paul. His compressed sentences represent something of a sample of the far more sustained efforts at negotiating the religious and philosophical perceptions of the Greek world and those of Torah that could be found, for example, in the writings of Hellenistic Jews like Philo Judaeus (see *Special Laws* 1:32-44) and Aristobulus (frag. 4). We can detect echoes as well of the Hellenistic attempts to seek beneath the plurality of religious forms and representations a more fundamental conception of the divine (see Dio Chrysostom, *Oration* 12).

Yet neither should we miss the significance of what Luke has managed in this scene. If he does not creatively reshape Greek philosophy, he does something more important: he recognizes it as a legitimate conversation partner in the approach to God. He does not find it necessary to condemn "the poets among you" in order to assert the truth of the gospel. The "groping after" the God whom all humans seek—whether expressed in statuary or shrine or poetry or philosophy—can provide the foundation for hearing about "The Lord of heaven and earth." Luke does not construct or canonize a "natural theology"; he simply shows Paul picking up the inchoate longings of this "exceptionally religious" people and directing them to their proper object.

Certainly Luke shows Paul also calling them to "repentance" just as the Jews were called. Their groping search is not itself the finding. They need to be told of the appointment of Jesus as judge of the living and the dead and the surety represented by his resurrection. But it is of fundamental significance that they are called *from where they began,* just as were the Jews. Their "times of ignorance" are not treated any differently than the "ignorance" that excused the first rejection of Jesus the Prophet by the Jewish people. Indeed, it might be argued that just as the Greeks are called from the "ignorance" that sees an adequate representation of the divine in physical forms, so are the Jews called from the "ignorance" that requires of its Messiah the credentials of physical rule rather than the gift of the Holy Spirit. As the gospel calls all humans (especially the outcast) without discrimination, so does it demand of all humans a "repentance."

No more impressive confirmation could have been provided for the decision of the Jerusalem Council "to place no greater burden" on the Gentiles than Luke's willingness to show Paul establishing a *rapprochement* with the distinctive forms of Gentile thought and piety. Here truly is a fundamental step, an affirmation of human culture not as sufficient in itself, but as a worthy vehicle for the truth of the gospel toward which, unwittingly, it was striving. The answer to the question of the Areopagus, "Are we able to know this new teaching?" is a resounding "Yes!"

But the possibility does not always become an actuality. Nor is understanding yet faith. Luke's story concludes on an ambiguous note. In contrast to the openhearted accceptance of the backwater provincials of Lystra to whom Paul gave a very similar discourse, though one stripped of literary allusions (14:8-18), Luke here shows that the gospel was no more universally received by the educated of the Gentile world than it was by the learned of the Jewish world. Paul receives from these philosophers and councillors at best a mixed response. Luke uses language to echo the response to the Pentecost experience. Some "mock" his preaching of the resurrection! And others simply defer a decision, "we will listen to you another time." Only a few join themselves to Paul and believe. God's impartiality which extends the message of salvation to all humans cannot all at once or altogether overcome the fact of human partiality, especially among those who always "know better."

FOR REFERENCE AND FURTHER STUDY

Balch, D. L. "The Areopagus Speech: An Appeal to the Stoic Historian Posidonius against Later Stoics and the Epicureans." *Greeks, Romans, and Christians.* Ed. D. Balch et al. Minneapolis: Fortress Press, 1990, 52–79.

Calloud, J. "Paul devant l'Aréopage d'Athens (Act 17, 16:34)." *RScR* 69 (1981) 209-248.

Conzelmann, H. "The Address of Paul on the Areopagus." *Studies in Luke-Acts.* Eds. L. E. Keck and J. L. Martyn. Nashville: Abingdon, 1966, 217-230.

Downing, F. G. "Common Ground with Paganism in Luke and Josephus." *NTS* 28 (1982) 546-559.

Dupont, J. "The Salvation of the Gentiles and the Theological Significance of Acts." *The Salvation of the Gentiles: Studies in the Acts of the Apostles.* Trans. J. Keating. New York: Paulist Press, 1979, 11-33.

Gaertner, B. *The Areopagus Speech and Natural Revelation* (Acta Seminarii Neotesteamentici Upsaliensis 21. Lund: Gleerup, 1955.

Lake, K. "The Unknown God" and "Your own Poets." *Beginnings of Christianity:* Part One: *The Acts of the Apostles.* Eds. F. J. Foakes-Jackson and K. Lake; Vol. 5: *Additional Notes to the Commentary.* Eds. K. Lake and H. J. Cadbury. London: Macmillan and Co., 1933, 240–246, and 246–251.

Neyrey, J. "Acts 17, Epicureans, and Theodicy." *Greeks, Romans, and Christians.* Ed. D. Balch et al. Minneapolis: Fortress Press, 1990, 118–134.

Schubert, P. "The Place of the Areopagus Speech in the Composition of Acts." *Transitions in Biblical Scholarship.* Ed. J. C. Rylaarsdam. Chicago: University of Chicago Press, 1968, 235–261.

[handwritten:] οὐ παντὸς ἀνδρὸς ἐς Κόρινθον ἐσθ' ὁ πλοῦς (LCL 194; 363 x.d) Greek proverb referring to the great expense of a self-indulgent life in Corinth.

[handwritten:] non cuivis homini contingit adire Corinthum (Horace, Ep. 1.17.36 LCL 194: 362)

36. Founding the Church at Corinth (18:1-11)

1. After these events he left Athens. He went to Corinth. 2. He found a certain Jew whose name was Aquila, a native of Pontus, who with his wife Priscilla had recently arrived from Italy because Claudius had ordered all the Jews to leave Rome. He went in to visit them, 3. and since he shared the same craft, he stayed with them and set about working. For their craft was tentmaking. 4. But every Sabbath in the synagogue he engaged in debate. He was persuading both Jews and Greeks. 5. And when Silas and Timothy came down from Macedonia, Paul began to devote himself to the word. He bore witness to the Jews that the Messiah was Jesus. 6. But when they opposed him and spoke harshly against him, he shook out his garments. He said to them, "Your blood be on your head. I am innocent of it. From now on I will go to the Gentiles." 7. He left there and went into the house of a certain man named Titius Justus, one who feared God. His house was next door to the synagogue. 8. And the ruler of the synagogue, Crispus, believed in the Lord together with his entire household. And many of the Corinthians when they heard believed and were baptized. 9. And the Lord said to Paul in the night by means of a vision, "Fear no longer. Rather, keep speaking out and do not be silent, 10. because I am with you, and no one will attack so as to harm you. For there is a great people for me in this city." 11. So he settled down for a year and six months, teaching the word of God among them.

Notes

1. *he came to Corinth:* The older city on the Isthmus of Corinth had been destroyed by the Romans in 146 B.C.E., but had been restored by Julius Caesar as a colony (Pausanias, *Description of Greece* 2, 1, 2), and in 27 B.C.E. became the capital city of Achaia (see the residence of the proconsul in v. 12). We have unusu-

ally rich literary and archaeological evidence concerning Corinth, which enables us to flesh out the portrait of that community supplied by Acts and Paul's Corinthian correspondence. As a port city, it was a bustling center of trade and commerce, with a large transient population, a reputation for sexual immorality, and a variety of religious cults, including (as archaeology has uncovered) a "Synagogue of the Hebrews," a temple to Apollo, and an Isis Shrine, as well as the famous temple to Aphrodite (the goddess of love) on the Acrocorinth (see Strabo, *Geography* 8, 6, 20-23, and especially Pausanias, *Description of Greece* 2, 2, 3-2, 4, 7).

2. *Aquila . . . Priscilla:* The two are always mentioned together (Acts 18:18, 26), and play an active role in Paul's ministry. In 1 Cor 16:19, Paul (writing from Ephesus) sends greetings from them (and from the church that met in their house) to the Corinthians. In 2 Tim 4:19 and Rom 16:3, Paul sends them greetings, calling them in the Romans passage his "fellow workers" (*synergoi*). Since neither 1 Cor nor Acts makes mention of their conversion, we can suppose that they were already Christian before their expulsion from Rome. The present translation ("who with his wife . . . .") inadvertently comes closer to the Greek of Codex D, which tends generally to slight the role of women. The majority text reads literally: "Aquila . . . arrived, and Priscilla his wife . . . ."

Claudius had ordered: The edict is referred to in Suetonius, *Life of Claudius* 25:4, and attributed to a commotion caused *impulsore Chresto*, a possible reference to the preaching about Jesus in Rome (see the previous note). The date of the edict is usually put at 49 C.E., and is considered one of the key dates for establishing the possibility of an absolute chronology for Paul's career.

3. *set about working:* The imperfect *ergazeto* is translated as inchoative. Codex D provides a fuller narrative transition, stating that Aquila and Priscilla left Rome "and settled in Achaia. And Paul became known to Aquila, since they had the same craft." The amplification was probably elicited by the obvious abruptness of the majority text.

their craft was tentmaking: Literally "by craft they were tentmakers." Associations and guilds formed on the basis of shared crafts were a common feature of the Hellenistic world; the partnership of Aquila, Priscilla, and Paul appears as an informal example. Luke identifies them as *skēnopoioi*, which means literally "tentmaking," but could apparently include a range of leatherworking. Paul himself makes a considerable point of his "working with his hands" (1 Thess 2:9; 2 Thess 3:6-8; 1 Cor 4:12; 9:6), in this following one ideal for teachers of wisdom, found among at least some of the Rabbis (see *Pirke Aboth* 2:2; 4:7; *Aboth de Rabbi Nathan* 11), as well as among certain Cynic Philosophers (see Diogenes Laertius, *Lives of Eminent Philosophers* 7:168 (Cleanthes); Epictetus, *Discourses* 3, 26, 23; Musonius Rufus, frag. 11).

4. *engaged in debate:* As in 17:2 and 17:17, the verb *dialegomai* is used for this scholastic disputation within the synagogue, here serving clearly as *beth ha midrash* ("house of study"). Codex D has a remarkable addition to the text, saying that Paul "was inserting the name of the Lord Jesus" (*entitheis to onoma*

tou kyriou Iēsou). The most obvious way he could do this would be by "reading" the name Jesus into those places of Torah where the title *Kyrios* is used, on analogy with the way in which *adonai* is read by pious Jews to avoid the pronouncing of the tetragrammaton (*YHWH*). This could indeed be considered provocative, and one wonders whether it reflects some actual practice.

5. *began to devote himself to the word:* The verb *synechō* has the sense here of "involving oneself," and since it marks a transition from a split occupation to a single one, the imperfect tense is correctly read as inchoative. As in other places, "the word" is shorthand for the task of preaching (see 4:29, 31; 6:2, 4; 8:4). For the movements of Silas and Timothy (note their ranking), see the notes on Acts 17:15 and 17:16.

6. *they opposed him and spoke harshly:* The Western Text provides once more a smoother transition here by adding, "after much speech and interpretation of scripture . . . ." This is Luke's only use of *antitassomai* ("oppose"), which has the connotation of an organized front of resistance (see Herodotus, *Persian Wars* 4:134). For "spoke harshly," and its possible translation as "blasphemed," see the note on Acts 13:45.

   shook out his garments: The gesture is one of rejection toward those who have rejected him. Compare the instructions of Jesus in Luke 10:11, and Paul's behavior in 13:51. Paul's declaration ("Your blood . . . .") makes them responsible for the division rather than him (compare Matt 27:25 and Acts 5:28). The formula derives from 2 Sam 1:16; 1 Kgs 2:33; 3:1. Note the variation of this in Paul's farewell discourse at Ephesus (Acts 20:26).

   I will go to the Gentiles: This is now the second of Paul's solemn declarations of his intention, but no more than the first (13:46) does it prevent him from continuing his work among the Jews (see 18:19; 19:8). Luke's narrative has the double function of legitimating the Gentile mission but also asserting God's fidelity to his people; thus this narrative tension which remains unresolved till the end.

7. *the house of a certain man named Titius Justus:* The Western Text adds "from Aquila," apparently because a scribe thought that Paul was changing his place of lodging rather than the center for his teaching. The pattern here is like that in 19:9. Some *mss* supply the name *Titus* in place of Titius, apparently in an attempt to find in him the delegate of that name known from the letters but not otherwise attested in Acts (see 2 Cor 2:13; 7:6, 13, 14; 8:6, 16, 23; 12:18; Gal 2:1, 3; 2 Tim 4:10; Titus 1:4). The connection is in fact possible, but there is no other evidence to support it. More pertinent is the fact that, as in the case of Lydia (16:15), a center for the new community is found in the household of one who was a God-fearer (*sebomenos ton theon*).

8. *ruler of the synagogue, Crispus:* Luke uses the term *archisynagōgos* in the singular, whereas in Acts 13:15 he used the plural. Notice, however, that in v. 17, we meet another person with the same title, so Luke still may have been thinking in terms of a collegial leadership. The name Crispus occurs again in 1 Cor 1:14, where Paul asserts "I did not baptize any of you except Crispus and Gaius." Luke does not, however, make any mention of Stephen, whom

Paul in 1 Cor 1:16 and 16:15 calls his first convert in Corinth. For the phrase "with his entire household," compare Acts 10:2; 11:14; 16:15, 31.

when they heard: The participle *akouontes* does not make clear whether the reason for conversion was the "hearing of Paul" (as the RSV translation supplies), or the "hearing about the conversion of Crispus."

9. *by means of a vision:* For Luke's frequent use of this plot mechanism, and for the parallels to it in Hellenistic literature, see the notes on Acts 9:10; 10:2; 16:9. The "Lord" who appears in the vision must be understood to be the risen Jesus (as in 9:5).

fear no longer: The use of the Greek tenses is deliberate, and the translation attempts to catch the nuance of each. We are not told why Paul should have been frightened in the first place (in anticipation of the events to follow?), although the fact itself seems confirmed by 1 Cor 2:3, "I came to you in weakness and fear and much trembling." The expression, "I am with you," echoes the reassurance made to the prophets (see Isa 41:10; 43:5; Jer 1:8, 19).

10. *attack so as to harm you:* It is striking that this reassurance comes immediately before Paul is in fact attacked! Trusting that the author knows what he is about, it is better to translate *tou kakōsai se* as a result clause rather than a purpose clause, since the attack on Paul in 18:12-17 does not bring Paul any personal harm.

a great people: The translation may be slightly misleading, if "great" here is read as *megas;* in fact it translates *polus,* "considerable/many." It is important, nevertheless, to retain the word "people," since Luke uses *laos,* his consistent reference to Israel as "people of God" (see the notes on Luke 1:10 and Acts 2:47). This announcement is particularly significant in light of 15:14 that God was visiting the Gentiles to take from among them "a people (*laos*) for his name."

11. *teaching the word of God:* Luke's attention to Paul's travels and founding of communities should not blind the reader to the long periods of time (longer by far than those spent in travel) that Luke has Paul working within specific communities and (later) in captivity (see 11:26; 14:28; 15:35; 19:10; 24:27; 28:30).

INTERPRETATION

This part of Luke's story continues to dovetail with the facts about Paul's movements derived from his letters. Once more, the points of agreement tend to confirm the basic reliability of the Acts account, while the points of omission or disagreement tend to suggest Acts did not use 1 Corinthians as one of its sources. The most impressive points of agreement beyond the obvious ones that Paul founded this Church (Acts 18:4, 8; 1 Cor 1:17; 4:15) and worked among both Jews and Gentiles in the city (Acts 18:4; 1 Cor 1:22-25; 9:19-23), are: a) Paul's involvement with

Priscilla and Aquila (Acts 18:2; 1 Cor 16:19); b) his earning a living by the practice of a trade (Acts 18:3; 1 Cor 9:12, 15-18); c) his conversion and baptism of Crispus (Acts 18:8; 1 Cor 1:14); d) his association with Sosthenes (Acts 18:17; 1 Cor 1:1); e) his experience of "fear and trembling" (Acts 18:9; 1 Cor 2:3); f) the participation of Timothy in this part of Paul's ministry (Acts 18:5; 1 Cor 4:17; 16:10-11).

But the attempt to connect the God-fearer Titius Justus in whose house Paul began to teach after leaving the synagogue (Acts 18:7) with the Titus who was Paul's special delegate to the Corinthians (see 2 Cor, *passim*), reflected already in the textual variants, has nothing more than sheer possibility to recommend it. Acts fails to mention, furthermore, the names of others whom Paul considered especially important in the founding of the community, such as Gaius (1 Cor 1:14) and Stephanus (1 Cor 1:16; 16:15). And although Silas is mentioned as working with Paul in Corinth together with Timothy (Acts 18:5), and this fact is confirmed by 2 Cor 1:19, Paul makes no mention of Silas in 1 Corinthians. It is doubtful that anyone using 1 Corinthians as a source would fail to include these facts. The impression given by a comparison of the two sources is that they are in agreement rather than that one is dependent on the other.

A more likely source of information would appear to be Priscilla and Aquila themselves, who uniquely would be in a position to supply information about their place of origin, their trade (never specified by Paul in his letters), and the beginnings of their association with Paul (18:1-3), not to mention experiences they had apart from Paul (Acts 18:24-28). It is through Priscilla and Aquila, in fact, that Luke is able to establish another connection to a broader historical context. By referring to the expulsion of the Jews from Rome under Claudius (usually dated around 49 C.E.), Luke mentions an event known to us from an independent source (Suetonius, *Life of Claudius* 25:4), and (as he does also with the story about Gallio in 18:12-17) thereby provides considerable assistance to the critical historian who wishes to construct an absolute chronology for Paul's career. Luke does not mention what Suetonius does, that the Jews had been expelled *impulsore Chresto*, a comment that may represent in a somewhat garbled fashion our earliest evidence for the presence of the messianic movement in Rome already by the middle of the first century, and may tell us even more about Aquila and Priscilla than either Paul or Luke does: that they were independent and original missionaries among their fellow Jews before ever encountering Paul.

There is, therefore, the stuff of genuine history within Luke's account. But his narrative is not itself a critical history. It is an *apologia* for God's action in history, and Luke provides the sort of literary touches required to shape the story in that direction. Themes that are elsewhere of fundamental importance for Luke find their way into this account as well.

First, there is the theme of rejection of the good news by Paul's fellow Jews and his turning to the Gentiles (18:5-6). The formal and artificial character of these "declarations of turning" by now should be obvious to the reader. They serve to give structure to Luke's story, by making what must have been an extremely complex and never completely resolved tension, into one with a narrative logic and resolution. Why does Luke include such a declaration in this place? The most obvious reason would be the story that follows, in which the issue of messianic claims and Jewish identity are brought before a disinterested Roman judge, with little effect except the narrative demonstration of the increased hostility between Messianists and non-Messianist Jews.

Second, we find the theme of the divine guidance of the mission. As at other key points in the story, there is a dream/vision that serves to direct and reassure the apostle (9:12; 10:10-15; 16:9-10). The "Lord" of this vision is undoubtedly the risen Jesus who also appeared to Paul on the road to Damascus (9:5) and in the Jerusalem temple (22:17-21). The prophet whom God raised up is alive and active in the story, not only through the sharing of his Spirit, but directly through the enlightenment of minds and the strengthening of hearts.

Third, Luke continues the theme of God's people. The story he tells is not simply one of action-filled adventures by philosophers or prophets. It is the story of how God enters human experience to shape a "people for his name" (15:14). In the present case, it is startling to realize that despite the formal "turning" to the Gentiles and the leaving of the synagogue, Luke clearly communicates that Paul enjoyed unusual success among the Jews of this city. It was no small accomplishment to convert the ruler of the synagogue and have him baptized (18:8)! Whether they were Jewish or Gentile, whether it was because they "heard the Word" of the gospel or simply of Crispus' conversion, "many Corinthians" believed and were baptized. And in the vision, the Lord explicitly identifies these converts as the *laos*, the people that belongs to him.

FOR REFERENCE AND FURTHER STUDY

Bruce, F. F. *Jesus and Christian Origins Outside the New Testament*. Grand Rapids: Eerdmans, 1974, 2–21.

Deissmann, A. *Light from the Ancient East*. Trans. L. R. M. Strachan. Grand Rapids: Baker, 1978 (1922), 15–17.

Fitzmyer, J. A. "The Pauline Letters and the Lukan Account of Paul's Missionary Journeys (Acts 18:24–19:7)." *SBL 1988 Seminar Papers*. Ed. D. Lull. Atlanta: Scholars Press, 1988, 82–88.

Hock, R. *The Social Context of Paul's Ministry: Tentmaking and Apostleship*. Philadelphia: Fortress, 1980, 20–49.

Smallwood, E. M. *The Jews under Roman Rule From Pompey to Diocletian.* Leiden: E. J. Brill, 1976, 211–216.
Tannehill, R. *Narrative Unity* 2:221-229.

37. Troubles and a New Recruit (18:12-28)

12. When Gallio was proconsul of Achaia, the Jews got together against Paul and led him to the court. 13. They said, "This fellow incites people to go against the Law in reverencing God." 14. But as Paul was about to open his mouth, Gallio said to the Jews, "If it had been some crime or wicked fraud, O Jews, I would have accepted it as a matter of course. 15. But since these are disputes over speech and names and your own Law, you see to it yourselves. I do not wish to be a judge of these matters." 16. And he dismissed them from the court. 17. But they all seized Sosthenes the ruler of the synagogue. They began beating him in front of the court. And none of this bothered Gallio. 18. Now when Paul had spent a considerable number of days, he said farewell to the brothers. He sailed for Syria, and with him were Priscilla and Aquila. In Cenchrae, he cut his hair, since he had a vow. 19. They came to Ephesus, and he departed from them there. He himself went into the synagogue. He debated with the Jews. 20. Although they asked him to stay for a longer time, he did not agree, 21. but said farewell to them. He declared, "If God is willing, I will return to you again." He set sail from Ephesus and 22. went down to Caesarea. And having gone up to greet the Church, he went down to Antioch. 23. And having spent a certain period of time, he left. He went through in succession the Galatian region and Phrygia. He strengthened all the disciples. 24. Now a certain Jew named Apollos, an Alexandrian by birth, came to Ephesus. He was an eloquent man, powerful in the scriptures. 25. He had been instructed in the way of the Lord, and ardent in the spirit, he was teaching accurately the things concerning Jesus, even though he knew only the baptism of John. 26. He began to speak boldly in the synagogue. When Priscilla and Aquila heard him, they took him aside. They explained the way of God to him more accurately. 27. And when he wanted to cross over to Achaia, the brothers encouraged him. They wrote to the disciples that they should welcome him. When he arrived, he contributed much to those who through gift had come to believe, 28. for in public he was vigorously refuting the Jews by demonstrating through the scriptures that the Messiah was Jesus.

NOTES

12. *Gallio was proconsul of Achaia:* This is another example of Lukan synchronicity (see Luke 1:5; 2:1-2; 3:1-2; 13:1-2; Acts 12:1, 20; 18:2). An inscription found at Delphi (issued by the emperor Claudius between the end of 51 and August of 52 C.E.) locates Gallio as proconsul (*anthupatos*, compare Sergius Paulus in Acts 13:7) in 51 C.E. Corinth was the chief city of Achaia, and therefore the place of the administrator's residence. He was the brother of the court philosopher Seneca, who refers to the sickness Gallio experienced while he was proconsul in Achaia (*Moral Epistles* 104:1). Together with the edict of Claudius (discussed in the note to 18:2), this reference to Gallio is of first importance for establishing a Pauline chronology.

    led him to the court: The *bēma* is an elevated platform (Latin: *tribunal*) from which public declarations could be given or (as here) justice could be decided. The English translation "bench" (Cadbury) captures the sense of function as well as form. Archaeologists have uncovered a large specimen of such a *bēma* in Corinth, possibly the one mentioned in this account. The Western Text expands the story: "having talked together among themselves against Paul, and laying hands on him, they led him to the proconsul, crying out and saying . . . ."

13. *against the Law in reverencing God:* In contrast to the charges in 16:20-21 and 17:7, this one is both mild and couched in terms specific to the tradition (notice "the Law" and the singular *ho theos*), rather than in terms of a social or political threat. The verb *anapeithō* ("incite") means to persuade, but with the nuance of "seduce/mislead" (Herodotus, *Persian Wars* 3:148).

14. *some crime or wicked fraud:* The term *adikēma* carries the sense of a wrongdoing deliberately carried out (Aristotle, *Nichomachean Ethics* 1135A; Acts 24:20). In something of a contrast, *radiourgia* has the nuance of thoughtless wrongdoing; it can bear the sense of "fraud" (as in Plutarch, *On Exile* 7 [*Mor.* 602A]); see the combination of *dolos kai radiourgia* applied to Bar Jesus/Elymas by Paul in Acts 13:10.

    O Jews: Gallio's interjection, together with Luke's designation of it being addressed "to the Jews," serves not only to set the context for Gallio's rebuke, but also serves (contrary to their apparent wishes) to place Paul within the context of an intra-Jewish conversation.

    accepted it as a matter of course: The construction of the conditional sentence suggests that the supposition is contrary to fact. The phrase *kata logon* can mean simply "reasonably," (see Plato, *Laws* 689D) but in this context could also have the sense of "according to rule/law." The same is true of the verb *anechomai*; although it often means "to put up with" in the moral sense (Luke 9:41; 1 Cor 4:12; Eph 4:2), here it bears the more forensic sense of "accepting a case."

15. *since these are disputes:* The two conditional sentences are balanced by *men . . . de*, with the second, simple, conditional here being translated inferentially ("since"). In context *zētēmata* is better translated as "disputes" than as "in-

quiries/questions" (compare Acts 15:2; 23:29; 26:3). The parallel in Acts 25:19 is particularly close: "disputes about their own superstition."

speech and names and your own Law: It is probably unwise to attempt making this dismissive characterization more precise; the term *onomata*, for example, could mean "titles" as well as "names," but the fundamental distinction Gallio is making is between "actions" subject to judicial inquiry and this "dispute over speech." There is also the implied distinction in the command "you see to it," between the matters that fall within his purview as magistrate, and those which can be settled by the Jews' own court (*gerousia*), since they ordinarily enjoyed the privileges of being a *politeuma* (see Josephus, *Against Apion* 2:35-47).

16. *dismissed them from the court:* The translation may err on the side of gentleness: the verb *apelaunō* is sometimes used in the sense of a physical expulsion (see LXX Ezek 34:12), and in the light of the violence that follows, the translation could equally read, "he drove them away from the bench (*bēma*)." In either version, he brusquely dismisses their case!

17. *they all seized Sosthenes:* Sosthenes is identified here as "the ruler of the synagogue." Was he then the replacement of Crispus who had converted (18:8)? Or was he part of a collegial leadership of the synagogue (Acts 13:15)? More important, was Sosthenes a member of the messianic community as well? In 1 Cor 1:1, Paul lists a Sosthenes as a co-sponsor of the letter. But Luke gives us no indication that Sosthenes either now or later became a Messianist. Nor does he tell us why "they" should have attacked him. Indeed, it is not at all clear who "they" are! Some *mss* add the words "the Jews." This would make some dramatic sense, if we understood those frustrated in their suit turning in anger on their leader who had failed to carry it through. But why would Gallio not care about such a flagrant flouting of his authority before his *bēma*? This would be actionable indeed! The Western Text supplies "the Greeks," and in this case may have made an inspired guess. In this reading, Gallio would have the same casual anti-semitism as reflected in the Philippi scene (16:20-22): he does not interfere with the violence taken against Jews by Gentiles, even before his bench. But the scene remains obscure except in one respect: Paul, in accordance with his vision (18:10) comes to no harm.

18. *in Cenchrae:* The seaport is actually something of a suburb of Corinth, about seven miles east and facing the Aegean Sea. Pausanias reports a shrine of the goddess Isis there (*Description of Greece* 2, 2, 3) and Apuleius locates Lucius' vision of Isis on the beach at Cenchrae (*The Golden Ass* 10:35). According to Rom 16:1, there was a church there whose deacon was Paul's financial patron, Phoebe.

cut his hair: The singular verb demands that we see Paul as the one cutting his own hair and having the vow. Some *mss* make Aquila or Aquila and Priscilla together the subjects.

since he had a vow: The term *euchē* here seems clearly to refer to the "Nazarite" vow that is described in Num 6:1-21. A Jew could dedicate himself or herself to God in a special way by abstaining from strong drink and uncleanness, and the symbol of this was letting the hair grow during the period of the vow (Num 6:5). According to *m.Nazir* which discusses the subject extensively, such vows could be taken for life, or for varying periods of time, but in any case, the shaving of the hair would come at the *end* of the vow rather than at the beginning, and was to take place in the Temple (Num 6:18). Luke is obviously aware of this last regulation, since he has James suggest to Paul in Acts 21:24 that he accompany some men "under a vow" who were going to the Temple to have their heads shaved. But what does Luke mean by having Paul cut his hair in Cenchrae? Is he confused or in error? Apparently not, since he knows the procedure at the other end. Practice, furthermore, does not always correspond to legislation, especially that compiled much after the fact. The *Mishnah* has two regulations which could be apropos: a life-long Nazarite was obliged to cut his hair every thirty days—at least according to one opinion (*m.Naz.* 1:4); likewise, if one vowed two such vows, a hair-cutting could come between them (*m.Naz.* 3:2). Perhaps the best resolution involves: a) noting that Luke uses "cut" (*keirō*) here rather than the "shave" (*xureō*) of 21:24 (for the distinction, see 1 Cor 11:6); b) a long period of time is to pass before Paul reaches Jerusalem—at least two years; c) perhaps therefore Paul is cutting his hair *before* beginning the Nazarite period. In this case the translation of the imperfect as "he was making a vow" would probably be better.

19. *departed from them there:* Luke uses the infrequent *autou* as the adverb "there" rather than *ekei* (see Matt 26:36; Luke 9:27; Acts 21:4). The separation is amicable, and enables Luke to include the incident with Apollo for which Paul was not present (18:24-28). The city of Ephesus was the capital city of Asia, and a great commercial and religious center. In the next chapter, Luke will provide some vivid snapshots of its first-century life. For the rights of Jews in Ephesus, see Josephus, *Antiquities of the Jews* 14:225-227; 262-264; 16:167-168; 172-173; *Against Apion* 2:38-39.

21. *if God is willing:* The genitive absolute *theou thelontos* expresses a pious conditional found already in Plato (see *Phaedo* 80D) and used as well by other NT writings (Jas 4:15; 1 Cor 4:19). At the beginning of Paul's statement, the Western Text adds, "It is necessary for me by all means to make the approaching feast in Jerusalem," which probably anticipates Acts 20:16.

22. *gone up to greet the Church:* The language of "going up" and "going down" suggests that this is a visit to the *Jerusalem* Church (*anabainō* in Luke 2:4, 42; 18:31; 19:28; Acts 11:2; 15:2; *katabainō* in Luke 2:51; 10:30; 8:15, 26; 24:1; 25:6). For the early Christian practice of maintaining contact by "greeting" (*aspazomai*), see Rom 16:3-23; 1 Cor 16:9-20; Phil 4:22; Col 4:10-15; 1 Thess 5:26; Titus 3:15; Phlm 23; Heb 13:24; 1 Pet 5:13; 2 John 13; 3 John 15. Luke once more demonstrates Paul's loyalty to and unity with the Jerusalem community (see Acts 9:26; 11:30; 12:25; 15:2, 25-26).

23. *a certain period of time:* Despite the special side-trip to greet the Jerusalem Church, it is obvious that Antioch, which had sponsored him as an apostle

in the first place, remains Paul's "home community," and it is there he consistently spends the most time (11:26-30; 13:1-3; 14:26-28; 15:30-35).

strengthened all the disciples: The use of "in succession" (*kathexēs*) here suggests a picture of Paul systematically moving through all the communities that had been established by the earlier mission (14:6), carrying out a pastoral visitation similar to those described in 14:21-22 and 15:41. The determination of the precise territories encompassed by this *Galaktikēn chōran kai Phrygian* has the same problems as those discussed in the note on 16:6.

24. *Jew named Apollos:* For the first time since 15:36, the narrative takes up an account that does not involve Paul. Codex D supplies the full version of Apollos' name, Apollonios; still other *mss* have Apelles. This character appears only here in Acts, but his movements match those presupposed by the frequent mention of him in 1 Cor 1:12; 3:4-6, 22; 4:6; 16:12. Despite the impression given that some Corinthians preferred Apollos and tried to make rivals of the apostles (1:12), Paul considers him a collaborator and coworker. The reference to an Apollos in Titus 3:13 is much harder to place.

Alexandrian by birth: The phrase *tǭ genei* for a person's place of origin is used also in Acts 4:36 and 18:2 (see also Mark 7:26). The Egyptian city of Alexandria was founded by Alexander the Great himself in 323 B.C.E. and quickly became a great metropolis (Pliny the Elder, *Natural History* 5:62-63). For a lively account of the building of the city with its five sections, see Pseudo-Callisthenes, *Life of Alexander of Macedon* 1:31-33. With its Museum and Library, it was universally regarded as a center of learning. It was also the center for Hellenistic Jewish literature, beginning with the translation of the Septuagint (*Letter of Aristeas* 301-321), whose most important extant representative is Philo Judaeus. A sketch of the privileges and problems experienced by the Jews in Alexandria is provided by Philo's *Against Flaccus*.

an eloquent man: The adjective *logios* can mean "learned" (Aristotle, *Politics* 1267B), or "eloquent" (Lucian of Samosata, *The Cock* 2); since in this account Apollos shows signs of both, deciding between the two is difficult. Since ancient rhetoric demanded learning of the eloquent, however, it seems best to use the more inclusive adjective. It is impossible to know whether Paul's somewhat defensive allusions to "speech and wisdom" in 1 Cor 1:17 and 2:1-4, as well as to his own "weakness in speech" in 2 Cor 10:10 may be based on a contrast made between him and Apollos.

powerful in the scriptures: Such command of sacred texts would make Apollos *logios* in the sense of "learned." His ability is later demonstrated by his refutation of the Jews *dia tōn graphōn* (18:28). Precisely this quality leads some to think it possible that Apollos was the author of the anonymous treatise/ homily called *To the Hebrews*, for the intricate and rhetorically polished argument of that letter relies heavily on the interpretation of Scripture along the lines associated with Hellenistic Judaism (see esp. Heb 7:1-14; 9:1–10:10).

25. *instructed in the way of the Lord:* The verb *katecheō* is the same used in the prologue of the Gospel for Luke's intended reader Theophilus (Luke 1:4). Some *mss* change *hodos* ("way") to *logos* ("word"), which would make it resemble

Luke 1:4 even more (as well as Gal 6:6); for that reason it is less likely to be original. For Luke's use of *hodos* for the messianic movement, see the note on 9:12. The Western Text also adds the words "in his homeland," which would make explicit the suggestion that Apollos became a follower of Jesus (though still not baptized) already in Alexandria; the foundation of Christianity in that important center is otherwise unknown.

ardent in the spirit: The verb *zeō* means literally "to boil" but can be used metaphorically for passion. It is not certain whether *tō pneumati* should be taken as a psychological statement: "he had a passionate spirit," or as a religious statement: "he was fervent in the [Holy] Spirit." In either case it is striking that Luke here avoids his stereotypical prophetic characterization: Apollos is *not* said to be "full of the Holy Spirit."

teaching accurately the things concerning Jesus: Some *mss* correct "Jesus" to "Lord," in order to conform this statement to the previous sentence, but "Jesus" is the best-attested reading. The adverb *akribōs* ("accurately") once more echoes the Gospel prologue (Luke 1:3). Although Apollos is not himself baptized into Jesus, he is teaching about him; the phrase *ta peri Iēsou* resembles *ta peri tēs basileias* ("things concerning the kingdom") in Acts 1:3, and could include both sayings and stories concerning Jesus; see Paul teaching *ta peri tou kyriou Iēsou Christou* in Acts 28:31.

knew only the baptism of John: Luke consistently portrays John's baptism as a preparation for the baptism in the Holy Spirit connected with Jesus (Luke 3:16; Acts 1:5; 11:16). The connection will be stated thematically in the next passage (19:3-5).

26. *Priscilla and Aquila:* The Western Text tends to downplay the role of women, and characteristically reverses the order of the names here, placing Aquila first (compare Acts 18:3, 18, 21).

    the way of God: In this case, the Western Text is the shorter, having only "the way" (*tēn hodon*), which would fit the context better. It is, after all, the "messianic way" that Priscilla and Aquila are explaining, not merely "the way of God" in general. Still other *mss* have "word of the Lord." Note that Priscilla and Aquila improve Apollos' knowledge by making it "more accurate," picking up again the *akribōs* of v. 25.

27. *cross over to Achaia:* The Western Text expands this verse by providing the motivation for his intention: "In Ephesus certain Corinthians were residing. They heard him speaking. They begged him to come with them to their homeland. When he consented, the Ephesians wrote . . . ." Paul's entire discussion in 1 Cor 1-4 presupposes that Apollos came to Corinth after he did.

    wrote to the disciples: This is the sort of letter between churches that Paul himself refers to (2 Cor 3:1), sometimes writes (Rom 16; 2 Cor 8), and in Acts 15:22-29 is shown carrying. The word translated "encouraged" (*protreptomai*) means to urge on someone to an action or task (see Plato, *Laws* 711B), and forms the basis for the sort of discourse called *protreptikos* (see Pseudo-Isocrates, *To Demonicus* 3-4).

28. *in public he was vigorously refuting:* The verb *diakatēlenchetō* is a *hapax*, but it suggests the total rout of the opposition. In this case it is carried out "in public" (*dēmosia*) and powerfully (*eutonōs*; compare Luke 23:10), which would be particularly shameful (see Acts 16:37). Recall the characterization of Apollos as "powerful (*dynatos*) in the scriptures" (18:24).

demonstrating through the scriptures: The verb *epideiknymi* can mean to "display" (see Luke 17:14; Acts 9:39), but also "to prove" (Plato, *The Republic* 391E; 4 Macc 1:1, 7). Apollos' use of the Scripture here is identical to that attributed to Paul in 17:2-3; see also the language used in 9:22.

INTERPRETATION

The more deeply we move into that part of Luke's narrative concerning Paul's mission, the less confident we grow in our literary assertions. Unlike the early chapters of Acts, whose events had no supporting evidence and whose literary and religious motivations seemed clear, the historical character of the Pauline section must be taken more seriously, precisely because we have available to us much more by way of supporting evidence, and because the reasons why some materials are included (apart from the possibility that "they happened") is not always clear. This is far from suggesting that Luke is simply putting down the facts. He continues to shape the story as best he can for his apologetic purposes. But it is to suggest that for us as readers such motivations are at times less obvious, and the weight of historical verisimilitude heavier.

The first incident reported in this section is a fine example. The Jewish attempt to have Paul convicted by the proconsul Gallio breathes the air of plausibility. The extant skein of literary and archaeological evidence supports all the scene's elements: the title of the proconsul, his name, the time of his tenure, his *bēma*, his apparently casual anti-semitism; the privileges of the Jews to decide matters of their own *ethos* as a *politeuma*; the sudden turn of violence by the anti-semitic population. Everything seems just right. Yet we can go no further towards asserting that the event did in fact happen. Paul makes no reference to it in his letters to the Corinthians, and the identity of Sosthenes (here a ruler of the synagogue, in 1 Cor 1:1 a co-sponsor of Paul's letter) is uncertain. It may be that Luke has again constructed a scene out of historical props in order to make his apologetic point, or it may be that a real event is being shaped by him in order to make that point.

The literary and religious functions served by the Gallio story, in fact, seem rather clear. The first concerns the relationship of the messianic movement vis-à-vis the Roman Empire. Gallio's refusal to hear the case against Paul on the grounds that it was an intramural dispute that Jews could "see to themselves" establishes a precedent: Roman authorities should not treat Christianity as a subversive cult but as a disputed option within one of the approved religions (*religio licita*) of the empire.

But it is unlikely that a Roman ruler would read Luke's account. What message, then, did this incident bear for his Christian readers? Is he suggesting that the Roman rule is uniformly enlightened and reliable? The riot in front of Gallio's *bēma* does not seem to make that point: if Gallio has dismissed the suit as a Jewish matter and then allowed an anti-semitic riot to break out without interfering, his "judicial restraint" does nothing to positively protect the Christians. It is more likely that the point Luke wants to make is that the prophecy delivered to Paul in his dream (18:10) has in fact been fulfilled within the story: Paul was attacked but came to no harm. Luke's *apologia* is ultimately not for Paul or for the Christian movement or for the Roman Empire, but for the power of God at work in human lives. Jews and Gentiles alike are prone to violence; in God alone is salvation truly to be found.

The second episode in this sequence concerns Paul's rapid trip eastward that seems to have no real effect except to bring him back to the same place he had left Priscilla and Aquila (19:1). Once more, the surface impression given by the text is one of a straightforward itinerary. Paul moves from one point to another in sequence. Luke provides no dramatic stories, no overt commentary. It is in fact in principle possible that he was using some travel source. Yet the reader must still ask why Luke includes the details he does. Selection is itself interpretation. In the present case, two such details draw our attention. The first is Paul's stopping in Cenchrae to cut his hair "for he had a vow" (18:18). The second is the fact that before stopping in Antioch for a longer stay preceding his visitation of the churches in the Galatian/Phrygian region, Paul "went up to greet the Church" (18:22).

The detailed difficulties attendant on these two remarks are discussed in the notes. But the reason why Luke has chosen to include them is clear. They serve to assert Paul's continuing allegiance to Judaism, and specifically to the Jewish-Christian Church in Jerusalem. We can speculate concerning the specific point made by Paul's Nazarite vow: its timing, purpose, even its factualness. But of all the events that surely occurred on this long expedition, Luke has chosen to tell the reader about this one for a single purpose: following an incident which serves to *separate* Paul from the Jews in Corinth who have brought him to court, the cutting of hair because of a Nazarite vow asserts that Paul indeed remains committed to the *ethos* of Judaism. Likewise for the greeting of the Jerusalem Church: Paul's obvious destination was Antioch, the Church which had sponsored his mission and which was truly his homebase. Why does

Luke, even so hurriedly, have Paul "go up" to greet the Church? For one reason only: to assert his continuing fidelity to the original apostolic community.

Within the narrative of Luke-Acts as a whole, these details serve the larger program of demonstrating how the Gentile mission emerged in continuity with the Jewish Church in Jerusalem, and always remained in contact with its authority. For the reader, it also serves to reinforce the portrait of Paul in particular as one who remains from first to last faithful to Judaism, so that the charge made against Paul when he finally arrives for his final visit to Jerusalem, that he was teaching the abandonment of the Jewish *ethos* (21:20-24), is known by the reader to be false.

The third incident, which recounts the recruitment of Apollos by Priscilla and Aquila (18:24-28) is in some ways the most intriguing to the historian. Not only does the information it provides coincide nicely (though not *too* precisely) with the picture provided of Apollos by Paul in First Corinthians (see notes), it also appears to derive from another source than Paul himself, since it deals with matters happening in his absence. Is it simply because Priscilla and Aquila (say) made the story available to him that Luke used it? Or does this special attention given to Apollos testify to an importance that went beyond his association with Paul?

Whatever lies behind the story, we can make some guesses as to the impression Luke wanted to convey from the way he handled the information at his disposal. The first thing that strikes us is that although Apollos is described in highly favorable terms, Luke refrains from portraying him in the stereotypically prophetic terms that he has used for all his major protagonists. Apollos is "ardent in the spirit" and "eloquent" but he is not "full of the Holy Spirit" nor does he speak "God's word," or perform "signs and wonders." He is, the reader learns, not of the same rank as those called to be prophets by Jesus and the Spirit. We notice also that Apollos is in need of a further initiation (the baptism of Jesus rather than simply that of John—more on that in the next story) as well as a "more accurate" instruction in the way of God. And these are to be provided by Paul's companions.

This shaping of the story may have had different causes, but the effect of it is to make Apollos a helpful but secondary participant in the messianic movement, not a prophet commissioned by the Spirit of God, but a teacher instructed by the Pauline school and commissioned by the churches. But Apollos is also, we should note finally, another part of Paul's team—like Priscilla and Aquila themselves—whose origins are in Judaism. For Apollos to go to Corinth and engage in open disputation with Jews in the synagogue on the basis of Scriptures is to make the point once more that the Pauline mission was not one exclusively and definitely

directed to the Gentiles, but remained engaged in the effort to win a
"people for his name" among the Jews as well.

FOR REFERENCE AND FURTHER STUDY

Barrett, C. K. "Apollos and the Twelve Disciples of Ephesus." *The New Testa-
ment Age.* Ed. W. C. Weinrich. Mercer, Ga.: Mercer University Press, 1984,
1:29-39.
Hemer, C. J. "Observations on Pauline Chronology." *Pauline Studies: Essays
Presented to F. F. Bruce.* Eds. D. A. Hagner and M. J. Harris. Exeter: Pater-
noster Press, 1980, 3-18.
Käsemann, E. "The Disciples of John in Ephesus." *Essays on New Testament Themes.*
London: SCM Press, 1964, 136-148.
Lake, K. "The Proconsulship of Gallio." *Beginnings* 5:460-464.
Schweizer, E. "Die Bekehrung des Apollos, Apg. 18, 24-26." *Evangelische The-
ologie* 15 (1955) 247-254.
Tajra, H. W. *The Trial of St. Paul.* WUNT 2:53, Tübingen: JCB Mohr (Paul Sie-
beck), 1989, 30-44.
Wolter, M. "Apollos und die ephesinischen Johannesjünger (Act 18:24-19:7)."
ZNW 78 (1987) 49-73.

38. *The Mission in Ephesus* (19:1-20)

1. While Apollos was in Corinth, Paul—having passed through the upper
regions—came down to Ephesus. He found certain disciples 2. and said
to them, "Since you are believers, have you received the Holy Spirit?"
They told him, "But we have not even heard that there was a Holy
Spirit!" 3. He said, "Then into what were you baptized?" They said,
"Into John's baptism." 4. But Paul said, "John baptized a baptism of
repentance for the people. He said they should believe in the one who
was coming after him, that is, in Jesus." 5. When they heard this, they
were baptized in the name of the Lord Jesus. 6. And when Paul placed
hands on them, the Holy Spirit came upon them. They spoke in tongues
and prophesied. 7. And there were in all about twelve men. 8. He went
into the synagogue. He was speaking boldly for about three months,
arguing and persuading concerning the kingdom of God. 9. But when
some of them grew hardened and disbelieved, speaking harshly against
the way before the assembly, he withdrew from them. He separated his
disciples, holding debates daily in the lecture hall of Tyrannus. 10. This
took place over a two-year period, so that all those dwelling in Asia heard
the Word of the Lord, both Jews and Greeks. 11. God did extraordinary

wonders through the hands of Paul, 12. so that handkerchiefs and aprons were being carried from his skin to the sick, and their illnesses were taken away, and the evil spirits were departing. 13. But some of the wandering Jewish exorcists attempted to pronounce the name of the Lord Jesus over those who had the evil spirits. They said, "I charge you by the Jesus whom Paul is proclaiming." 14. Now those who were doing this were the seven sons of a certain Scaeva, a Jewish chief priest. 15. The evil spirit answered. It said to them, "I know Jesus and I recognize Paul. But who are you?" 16. And the man who had the evil spirit leaped upon them. He overwhelmed them all. He overpowered them so that they fled that house naked and wounded. 17. This event became known to all the Jews and Greeks who were dwelling in Ephesus. Fear fell on all of them. The name of the Lord Jesus was extolled. 18. And many of those who had begun to believe came to confess and announce their practices. 19. A considerable number of those who practiced magical arts brought with them their books. They burned them before all. They added up their price and found it to be fifty thousand pieces of silver. 20. Thus powerfully did the word of the Lord grow and prevail.

NOTES

1. *while Apollos was in Corinth:* The construction is periphrastic, with *ginomai* controlling infinitival and participial phrases; the translation simplifies. The Western Text again provides an elaboration: "When Paul wanted to go, according to his own plan, to Jerusalem, the Spirit told him to return to Asia . . . ." The expansion fits the tendency of this text tradition to emphasize the role of the Holy Spirit and to provide motivation for actions. In this case the expansion appears to correlate with the Western expansion in 18:21.

2. *since you are believers:* The translation turns an indirect question (*ei*) into a direct question, and takes the aorist participle *pisteusantes* as the question's motivation. It could be phrased more neutrally as, "When you became believers, did you receive the Holy Spirit?" If they are in fact *mathētai*, the natural assumption would be that they had been baptized into Jesus and had received the Spirit; the question therefore has the literary function of enabling a final distinction between John and Jesus.

   not even heard that there was a Holy Spirit: The Western Text alters this to, "that some are receiving the Holy Spirit," perhaps because the scribes found it incredible that an absolute ignorance of the Holy Spirit would be possible for those who had been followers of John! But the question, even as it stands, can mean only that they did not know there was a Holy Spirit in connection with baptism.

3. *into John's baptism:* For the idea of "being baptized *into*" someone or something, see Rom 6:3; 1 Cor 1:13, 15; 10:2; 12:13; Gal 3:27. As in the case of Apollos (18:25), these "disciples" and "believers" are portrayed as yet unfinished and in need of the messianic baptism in the Spirit.

the one who was coming after him, that is, in Jesus: For John's baptism as one of repentance for "the people" (*ho laos*), see Luke 3:3-15; for the statement that "a stronger one is coming after me," see Luke 3:16. This is now the fifth time in Acts that John's role as a precursor to Jesus has been clarified (Acts 1:5; 11:16; 13:25; 18:25). The need to repeatedly take up the issue, plus the fact that John apparently has disciples twenty years after his death in places as far from the Jordan as Alexandria (Apollos) and Ephesus, supports the portrait of John as an important religious figure in his own right (see especially Josephus, *Antiquities of the Jews* 18:116-119, as well as John 3:23-30). In Luke's Gospel, of course, John does *not* say that people should "believe" in the one coming after him, or that this one is Jesus (see Luke 7:19). These are the conclusions derived from the perspective of messianic faith.

5. *name of the Lord Jesus:* It is striking that "Lord Jesus" occurs three times in this passage (see 19:13, 17). For the use of "the name" with reference to baptism, see Acts 2:38; 8:16; 10:48. The Western Text expands by adding the words, "unto the forgiveness of sins." This misses the point, since Paul has already stated that this was the purpose of John's baptism as well (v. 4).

6. *Holy Spirit came upon them:* As in the Samaritan mission, the bestowal of the Spirit accompanies the laying on of hands rather than the baptism itself (8:17). As in that story as well, the fact that it is the apostle Paul who is the medium for this bestowal has a legitimating function: these erstwhile Johannine disciples are brought within the apostolic community and authority.

   spoke in tongues and prophesied: For the meaning of *glōssais lalein* and its connections to prophecy in the ancient world, see the note on Acts 2:5. As in the case of Cornelius' household, the ecstatic utterances give physical evidence of the presence of a transforming spiritual energy (see 10:46). Less obviously, it helps place Paul in the prophetic succession with Peter: the laying on of his hands brings the prophetic spirit. After "speaking in tongues," the Western Text adds "other tongues, and they themselves knew them, which they also interpreted for themselves, and certain ones also prophesied"; the addition seems to reflect awareness of the discussion in 1 Cor 14.

7. *in all about twelve men:* Literally, "all the men were about twelve." Luke regularly uses "about" (*hōs/hōsei*) with numbers (2:4; 4:4; 5:7, 36; 10:3; 13:18, 20; 19:34), and he clearly intends this one to symbolically represent a realization of "Israel" (compare Acts 1:15-2:13).

8. *speaking boldly:* Despite the solemn announcement of a turn to the Gentiles in 18:6, we once more find Paul in the synagogue. The characterization of speech as "bold" (*parrēsia/parrēsiazomai*) is part of Luke's prophetic/philosophical presentation of the apostles (Acts 2:29; 4:13, 29, 31; 9:27-28; 13:46; 14:3; 18:26). The Western Text adds (redundantly) "with great power."

   concerning the kingdom of God: The language is similar to that used earlier for the synagogal contacts: for *dialegomai* ("argue/debate") see 17:2, 17; 18:4, 19; for *peithō* ("persuade") see 17:4; 18:4. The theme of the kingdom of God runs throughout Luke-Acts; note in particular that Paul's proclamation is shown to be in continuity with that of Jesus (Luke 4:43) and in obedience to his command (Luke 9:2).

9. *grew hardened and disbelieved:* It is consistent with Luke's two-stage understanding of God's visitation through the prophets that "hardness of heart" is *not* attributed to the Jews during the time of Jesus' ministry (contrast Matt 19:8; Mark 10:5), whereas it is applied to the leaders by Stephen (Acts 7:51), and now to these Diaspora Jews by the narrator. The language of "hardening," of course, recalls the biblical characterization of Pharaoh (LXX Exod 4:21; 7:3; 8:19; 13:15), and of the people Israel in its turning from the Lord (Deut 2:30; 10:16; Ps 94:8; Isa 63:17; Jer 7:26; 17:23; 19:15). It signifies a stubborn resistance in the face of God's visitation (compare Rom 2:5; 9:18; Heb 3:8, 13; 4:7). For "disbelieved" (*apeitheō*), see the note on Acts 14:2.

speaking harshly: Paul not only fails to convert them all, but there is active conflict: "some of them" (*tines*) engage in a public reviling (for *kakologeō*, see Herodotus, *Persian Wars* 7:237). This corresponds to the "blaspheming" (*blasphemein*) Paul experienced in 18:6. The public character of this slander (before the *plēthos*) forces Paul to remove himself and his disciples, since he can no longer find in the synagogue the atmosphere of civil discourse (*scholē* in its meaning of leisurely study).

separated his disciples: The language evokes the sort of *hairesis* that creates separate philosophical schools. The term *aphistēmi* is sometimes used for the "avoidance" of evil (Num 16:27; Tob 1:15; Ps 6:8; Wis 10:3; compare 2 Tim 2:19; Acts 5:38; 15:38). The verb *aphorizō* ("set apart") reminds us in this instance of Luke 6:22, "when they exclude (*aphorizō*) and revile you," but also other formal "separations" between people (see Exod 13:12; 19:23; Lev 13:4; Num 8:11; Deut 4:41; Isa 52:11; 56:3; Ezek 45:1; compare Matt 13:49; 25:32; 2 Cor 6:17; Acts 13:2).

daily in the lecture hall of Tyrannus: The term *scholē* means in the first place "leisure" and by extension is applied to the things associated in the Hellenistic world with leisure, above all discussions; it therefore came to mean also a "school," either in the sense of a gathering or of a place for gathering (see e.g., Aristotle, *Politics* 1313B; Epictetus, *Discourses* 3, 21, 11). Dio Chrysostom (*Oration* 32:10) speaks of Philosophers who do not declaim in public, but "exercise their voices in what we call lecture-halls (*akroatēriois*)." Of Tyrannus, we know nothing further. The Western Text supplies further detail by adding to "daily" these words: "from the fifth hour to the tenth." The case for thinking that this represents a reliable tradition is about the same as that for the "seven steps" in Acts 12:10.

10. *all those dwelling in Asia:* The statement is manifestly hyperbolic, but has the function of asserting the success of Paul's work among *both* Jews and Greeks, despite his separation from the synagogue. We begin to see the emergence of Christianity as a separate movement. For the "word" as shorthand for the mission, see Acts 4:4, 31; 6:2, 7; 8:4, 14, 25; 11:1; 12:24; 13:5, 49; 15:7, 36; 16:32; 18:11.

11. *extraordinary wonders:* Literally, "not ordinary (*ou tychousas*) powerful deeds (*dynameis*)." This is part of Luke's prophetic characterization (see Acts 2:22; 4:33; 6:8; 8:13; 10:38), and certifies that Paul's mission in Ephesus is also a "visitation by God."

12. *being carried from his skin to the sick:* We are to picture small bits of cloth, pressed to Paul's skin, and then applied to the sick. This portrayal of healing through the physical transmission of power reminds us of 5:15-16. As in that case also, the expulsion of spirits accompanies the healing of illness. The theurgic associations are obvious. Luke himself, it should be noted, betrays no embarrassment about combining the "word of God" with such "popular religiosity"; for the Hellenistic parallels, see the notes on Luke 8:44 and Acts 5:15-16.

13. *some of the wandering Jewish exorcists:* The term *exorkistēs* ("exorcist") occurs only here in the NT. It is cognate with *orkizō* ("I charge/adjure") used in the next sentence. By his language, Luke suggests that there were a number of such exorcists besides these, who "wandered" (*perierchomenoi*) through the cities of Asia. For the reputation of the Jews for magic, see the note on Acts 13:6; for their particular skill in exorcisms, see especially Josephus, *Antiquities of the Jews* 8:42-49, who traces the knowledge back to Solomon, and tells of the practice of a contemporary named Eleazar; Josephus also attributes exorcistic power to certain plants in *Jewish War* 7:185. Outsider perspectives are given by Lucian of Samosata, *The Lover of Lies* 16, and Justin Martyr, *Dialogue with Trypho* 80:9-10.

    the Jesus whom Paul is preaching: The verb *orkizō* ("charge/bind/adjure") takes the accusative of the one being invoked as authority (compare Mark 5:7). As in the story of Simon Magus (8:19), the attempt to use the apostolic power functions as an implicit compliment to its superiority (see also the testimony of the Pythian spirit in Philippi, 16:17).

14. *seven sons of a certain Scaeva:* The Western Text tries to correct the apparent disconnectedness of this verse: "among them also were the [seven] sons . . . ." The textual evidence for "seven" is uncertain, possibly because of the inconsistency that Luke introduces with the use of *amphoteros* ("both") in v. 16. We know nothing about any Scaeva, and it is difficult to assess the characterization of him as a "chief priest." There are two historical possibilities: a) Scaeva was part of a priestly family—he certainly was not one of the Jerusalem priests we know about from other sources; b) he advertised himself as such, the way Mark Twain's charlatan in *Huckleberry Finn* advertised himself as the "Lost Dauphin." But it is also possible that: a) the Latin name Scaeva could bear some of its etymological weight of "untrustworthy," and that b) Luke had no historical information to deal with here at all.

15. *know . . . recognize:* Luke uses two different verbs, *ginōsko* and *epistamai*, but probably only for the sake of variety, since he otherwise uses the terms with roughly the same range of significance; compare Acts 10:28 and 15:7 (*epistamai*) with Acts 2:36 and 9:24 (*ginōskō*). The more essential point in that the demon refuses to yield to their invocation, suggesting: a) that faith in the "name

of the Lord Jesus" is not simply a theurgic technique to be used by anyone; b) the extraordinary power over demons is connected to the apostles.

16. *leaped upon them:* Although this is the only time that Luke uses the verb *aphallomai* ("leap upon"), it is used three times in the LXX for the leaping of the *Spirit of the Lord* (1 Sam 10:6; 11:6; 16:13). The irony involved in the choice of verbs should be obvious.

    overwhelmed . . . overpowered: The translation renders the participial phrase *katakyrieusas amphoteron* as an independent sentence. There is an obvious tension between the "seven sons" in v. 14 and the "both" who are overwhelmed here, unless we take *amphoteroi* in the broad Hellenistic sense of "all." There is also the unexpected appearance of "that house" which had not previously been mentioned. In general, this is not the most carefully crafted of Luke's vignettes. As for *ischuō*, Luke ordinarily uses it to mean "be able," but with the preposition *kata*, it takes on the transitive sense (compare LXX Judg 6:2; Esth 4:17; Ps 12:4; 1 Macc 10:49).

17. *became known to all the Jews and Greeks:* The notice is similar to those in 1:19; 4:16 and 9:42, and helps prepare the way for Paul's emphatic statement in 26:26, "this was not done in a corner." For the response of fear, compare especially Acts 5:5, 11.

    name of the Lord Jesus was extolled: Literally, "made great/magnified" (*megalunō*), the same verb as used in Luke 1:46, 58; Acts 5:13; 10:46. Luke has brought together all the typical responses to a miracle story: a) the spread of the news (see Luke 4:37; 7:17; 8:39); b) the response of awe or fear (see Luke 5:26; 7:16; 8:35); c) the glorification/praise of God (see Luke 5:26; 7:16; 8:39; 9:43; 13:17; 17:15; 18:43).

18. *confess and announce their practices:* For *exomologeomai* as the confession of sins, see Jas 5:14; *Didache* 4:14; *Letter of Barnabas* 19:12. The term "practice" (*praxis*) means generally "business/deed," but appears in Magical Papyri as "spell." In the light of the following verse, it is possible that it has that meaning here, but not likely, since the *doing* of magic is being confessed rather than the *forms* of its practice.

19. *who practiced magical arts:* The term *perierga* can mean simply "curious things," but is used as well for the doing of magic (see Plutarch, *Life of Alexander* 2). This is now the third encounter between the gospel and the practice of magic. As in the case of Simon Magus (8:4-25) and Bar Jesus/Elymas (13:4-12), the gospel triumphs in explicit and dramatic fashion.

    brought with them their books: Such books contained the magic spells and formulae; see the *Great Magical Papyrus* for examples, and Lucian of Samosata's reference to "Egyptian Books" in *The Lover of Lies* 31. In Plutarch's *Table Talk* 7:5, reference is made to the *ephesia grammata* ("ephesian letters") as a magical formula against demons (*Mor.* 706E).

    burned them before all: The practice of burning books as a way of controlling the spread of unacceptable ideas was fairly well attested in antiquity. Some examples: a) books of philosophy and prophecy (Livy, *History of Rome* 39:16;

40:29); b) more than two thousand prophetic books other than the approved Sybilline Oracles (Suetonius, *Life of Augustus* 31:1); c) the writings of Protagoras by the Athenians in the *agora* (Diogenes Laertius, *Lives of Eminent Philosophers* 9:52); Epicurus' *Sovereign Maxims* by the charlatan Alexander (Lucian of Samosata, *Alexander the False Prophet* 47). Instances are found also in the biblical tradition (see Jer 36:20-27; 1 Macc 1:56). In contrast to the usual pattern, the volumes are here voluntarily offered.

fifty thousand pieces of silver: Luke does not specify the kind of silver coin, though the *denarion* (Roman) and *drachma* (Greek) silver coins were roughly equivalent in value. Whatever the rate of exchange, fifty thousand of such coins obviously represents a fortune (compare Matt 26:15). Luke would not have included the number had he not thought it particularly impressive.

20. *word of the Lord grow and prevail:* The verb "prevail" (*ischuō*) is the same one used for the "overpowering" of the exorcists by the demonic spirit! For similar statements concerning the growth of the community, see 2:47; 6:7; 9:31; 12:24; 16:5.

INTERPRETATION

The Ephesian narrative provides us with another fascinating glimpse of Luke's narrative techniques. He tells us three anecdotes in quick succession: the encounter between Paul and the disciples of John, leading to their baptism (19:1-6), the separation of Paul from the synagogue and his continued success among both Jews and Greeks (19:8-10), and the overwhelming of the Jewish exorcists, leading to the conquest over magic in the city (19:11-20). As in other parts of the story the impression of fullness and vivid realism is achieved by a combination of stock scenes and special effects.

When we look at the section carefully, we quickly realize that Luke had very little real historical information with which to work. The "disciples of John," for example, are not only a convenient symbolic twelve in number but lack both specific identity (names, origin) and future role in the story. Like Apollos, they share a connection to John the Baptist, but unlike Apollos, they are undetectable in any other historical source. At best, these converts from a Johannine version of "discipleship" bear testimony to the independent importance of the baptist movement associated with John (see notes).

The lack of verifiability is even more evident in the conflict with the Jews in the synagogue, and the account of the Jewish exorcists. Luke tells us that Paul shifted his teaching from the synagogue to the lecture hall of Tyrannus; a lively detail, but one we are utterly unable to confirm. And in the case of the "chief priest" Scaeva and his "seven sons," supporting evidence is even less likely.

It is of course possible that there is some nugget of tradition with which Luke is working, at least in broad terms. The fact that we can't verify facts does not thereby make them untrue. Tyrannus may have been as real as Tarsus, Scaeva as historical as Scaevola. And there is no mistaking Luke's skill in depicting local color. In the burning of the magic books and (in 19:21-41) in the riot of the silversmiths, Luke captures the particular attributes of ancient Ephesus as well as he did those Athens. But even if we grant all of this, the character of the scenes themselves suggests that they owe most of their construction to Luke.

The main reason for asserting this is that the "events" reported here by Luke can by now be recognized by the reader as typical rather than as unique. The encounter with the Johannine disciples has its special touches, but it is essentially a standard "foundation account" in which Luke shows the effective birth of Christianity in a new locale by means of conversion, baptism, the apostolic laying on of hands, the outpouring of the Holy Spirit and its manifestation in tongues and prophecy (compare Acts 2:1-4; 8:15-17; 10:44-48). The conflict within the synagogue can also be recognized as part of a consistent literary pattern that Luke has used throughout Paul's mission (see 13:44-52; 17:1-5, 13-14; 18:5-7). We can observe in the "Sons of Scaeva" scene another in a series of "turf-battles" between the powers to heal and exorcise that Luke associates with the apostolic preaching through the Holy Spirit, and the powers of magic which Luke attributes to demonic forces (see 8:9-24; 13:4-12; 16:16-18). The description of the "extraordinary wonders" being worked by Paul, in fact, is another standard Lukan filler (see 2:43; 4:33; 5:12-16; 6:8; 8:6-7), as is the closing comment on the growth of "the word of the Lord" (see Notes).

Luke has therefore filled in the space between Paul's journeys the way he has filled other narrative lacunae: by a series of set-scenes connected by summaries. Perhaps the truest compliment readers pay to Luke can be found in the realization that despite the remarkably repetitive, indeed predictable character of his narrative, it retains its capacity to entertain and instruct. But the more we are aware that this part of his story owes almost everything to Luke himself, the freer we are to ask what he was seeking to accomplish by the effects he has created.

What is most striking about the arrangement of typical materials here is that this is the first time they have been applied so systematically to Paul himself. None of Paul's other "foundings" have received this sort of attention; this is by far the most extended treatment of Paul's "prophetic" powers to bestow the Spirit, heal and cast out demons. The question therefore arises why they are applied to him in this place. We can get at that question by taking "place" both geographically and textually.

As important as Ephesus was in the early history of Christianity, Acts suggests that it may not in fact have been a Church founded by an apostle. These stories about Priscilla and Aquila, Apollos, and the Twelve Disciples of John skirt the implication that Paul himself did not actually establish Christianity in this city. He only stopped in the synagogue for a short time on his way to Jerusalem (18:19-21). While Paul was gone, there were already "brethren" able to communicate with the Corinthians and commission Apollos (18:27). It is more than a little possible that Paul's encounter with the Johannine disciples with its spectacular, Pentecost-like, outpouring of the Spirit, has the effect of giving apostolic legitimacy to the Ephesian founding. For Luke, Paul is the center of the mission, and although in this and other places he gives us unwitting evidence that the first Christian expansion was far wider than the Pauline effort, he himself tries to bring the cities he knows of as "Pauline" firmly within the authority of that apostle.

This leads us in turn to the reason why such attention is given to Paul's prophetic powers at this *narrative* "place." Luke not only focuses on the powers that emanate from Paul himself, but also on the way these lead to the triumph of "the name of the Lord Jesus" (repeated three times, 19:5, 13, 17), and to the spread of the "word of the Lord" among the population of Asia, "both Jews and Greeks" (19:10, 17). The reason seems fairly obvious when we see what happens next: Paul begins plans for his fateful trip to Jerusalem and eventual arrival at Rome (19:21), and after the riot in Ephesus over "the way" (19:23) Luke's narrative concentrates on Paul's progression toward his end.

The present passage therefore compresses into three vivid scenes the essence of Paul's prophetic ministry as an apostle and serves to "legitimate" him firmly in the reader's eyes as having fulfilled precisely what was predicted of him, before his own series of calamities and defenses begin. The Ephesian Church, established by an apostle, triumphant over the demonic powers of magic, independent of the synagogue yet drawing into itself both Jews and Gentiles, is the final evidence within Luke's text for the success and integrity of Paul's mission. That he so intends us to see it is shown further by the fact that it is to this Church that Paul directs his final testimony (20:17-35).

FOR REFERENCE AND FURTHER STUDY

Garrett, S. R. *The Demise of the Devil: Magic and the Demonic in Luke's Writings.* Minneapolis: Fortress Press, 1989, 89-99.
Käsemann, E. "The Disciples of John the Baptist in Ephesus." *Essays in New Testament Themes.* Trans. J. Montague. London: SCM Press, 1964, 136-148.
Mastin, B. A. "Scaeva the Chief Priest." *JTS* 27 (1976) 405-412.

Pease, A. S. "Notes on Book Burning." *Munera Studiosa*. Eds. M. H. Shepherd and S. E. Johnson. Cambridge: Episcopal Theological School, 1946, 145–160.

Strange, W. A. "The Sons of Scaeva and the Text of Acts 19:14." *JTS* n.s. 38 (1987) 97–106.

Wolter, M. "Apollos und die ephesinischen Johannesjünger (Act 18:24–19:7)." *ZNW* 78 (1987) 49–73.

39. *Riot in Ephesus* (19:21-40)

21. When these matters were completed, Paul decided to travel through Macedonia and Achaia in order to go to Jerusalem. He said, "After I am there, I must also see Rome." 22. And he dispatched to Macedonia two of those who were ministering with him, Timothy and Erastus. He himself stayed for a time in Asia. 23. Now during that period of time there was no small disturbance concerning the way. 24. A certain man named Demetrius was a silversmith. By making silver temples of Artemis he earned for his craftsmen no meager business. 25. He gathered them and the workers in related crafts together. He said, "Men, you recognize that we get our prosperity from this business. 26. And you see and hear that this Paul has converted a considerable crowd not only in Ephesus but in nearly all of Asia, persuading them that the things made by hands are not gods. 27. There is danger not only that our share in this is coming to be discredited, but that even the temple of the Great Goddess Artemis will be reckoned as nothing. Indeed, she may even be brought down from her greatness, she whom all of Asia and the inhabited world reverences." 28. When they heard this they were filled with fury. They began to cry out, "Great is Artemis of the Ephesians!" 29. The city was filled with confusion. They rushed together to the theater. They took along with them Gaius and Aristarchus, who were Macedonians, fellow travellers with Paul. 30. Even though Paul wanted to go into the assembly, the disciples did not allow him. 31. Even some of the Asiarchs, who were Paul's friends, sent to him the request that he not present himself in the theater. 32. Now some were shouting one thing, others something else, for the assembly was in confusion and most of the people did not know why they had come together. 33. Some from the crowd pressed together against Alexander after the Jews had put him forward. And Alexander signalled with his hand. He wanted to address the assembly. 34. But when they recognized that he was a Jew, a single cry came from them all. For up to two hours they kept shouting, "Great is Artemis of the Ephesians!" 35. The city-clerk calmed the crowd. He said, "Men of Ephesus, who among people, after all, does not know that the city of the Ephesians is the keeper of the temple of

the Great Artemis and of the sacred stone from the sky? 36. Since these things are undeniable, it is necessary for us to remain calm and do nothing rashly. 37. For you have brought these people neither as temple-robbers nor as blasphemers of our goddess. 38. If therefore Demetrius and the craftsmen with him have a case against someone, there are court-days and there are proconsuls. Let them bring cases against each other. 39. But if you seek something further, it will be solved in the legal assembly. 40. In fact we are in danger of being charged with rioting because of today, since there is no cause we will be able to give to account for this disturbance." After he said these things, he dismissed the assembly.

NOTES

21. *Paul decided:* Literally "proposed in the spirit" (*etheto en tǫ pneumati*); as in other places (16:18; 17:1; 18:25), the absence of *hagion* from "spirit" makes it uncertain whether Luke intends us to read this simply as Paul "decided within himself" or "proposed under the guidance of the Holy Spirit."

    in order to go to Jerusalem: Luke provides the first signal for the turning point to be taken by the narrative: after the riot, Paul will begin making his way to Jerusalem (20:1), and arrive there in 21:17. Eventually he will end up in Rome (28:16). Luke fails to provide the motivation for Paul's trip to Jerusalem. According to Paul himself, he was delivering a collection of money taken up from his Gentile churches (1 Cor 16:1-4; 2 Cor 8–9; Rom 15:25-32). Paul's expressed desire to "see Rome" corresponds exactly to the sentiment he expresses in Rom 15:24, 32.

22. *ministering with him:* Or possibly "ministering (*diakoneō*) to him" (compare Luke 8:3; 10:40; Acts 6:2, 4). Luke uses the term *diakonia* for the collection taken up by the Antiochean Church for the Church in Jerusalem (11:29; 12:25). Paul also characterizes his collection for the saints as a *diakonia* (Rom 15:31; 2 Cor 8:4; 9:1). For the work of the collection in Macedonia, see 2 Cor 8:1-2; 9:2-4; Rom 15:26. The Macedonian community at Philippi had a longstanding participation in Paul's financial support (Phil 4:10-20). The language Luke uses, in short, suggests they were participating in Paul's collection effort.

    Timothy and Erastus: For the role of Timothy as Paul's delegate, see the note on Acts 16:1; he is reported as having worked primarily in Macedonia (18:5; Phil 2:19-24) as well as in Corinth (1 Cor 4:17; 16:10). Paul names an Erastus as "treasurer (*oikonomos*) of the city" (that is, Corinth) in Rom 16:23. 2 Tim 4:10 also places an Erastus in Corinth. This is his only appearance in Acts.

23. *no small disturbance:* This transition sentence nicely splices the travel notice and the long account which follows. As so often, Luke uses *litotes* (compare v. 24, "no meager business"). The "disturbance" (*tarachos*) was in fact large; Luke uses precisely the same construction in 12:18 (compare also 17:8). For "the way" (*hē hodos*) as a designation for the messianic movement, see 9:2; 16:17; 18:25-26; 19:9.

24. *silver temples of Artemis:* The cult of Artemis at Ephesus is well-documented both in literature (see e.g., Strabo, *Geography* 14, 1, 22-23; Herodotus, *Persian Wars* 1:26, 92; Achilles Tatius, *Clitophon and Leucippe* 7:13-8:14; Xenophon, *The Ephesians* 1, 2, 2-7; 1, 11, 5), and in archaeological evidence. In the Olympian Pantheon, Artemis (Latin: Diana) was identified as a huntress-goddess (see Ovid, *Metamorphoses* 3:154-252), but the worship of her in Ephesus had as many associations with the mother-goddess cults of the East. There are a number of extant examples of terra-cotta replicas of her temple, coins with representations of the temple, and silver reproductions of the goddess herself, but no "silver shrines" such as Luke seems to intend. A first-century inscription from Ephesus identifies a certain Demetrius as a *neopoios*, but this seems to be the title for a temple official rather than a maker of images. It is possible, of course, to imagine various ways in which this evidence might be combined. More significant for the reader of Luke-Acts is the way it shows the author's firm grasp on the specifics of "local color."

    no meager business: In this and the next verse, the term *ergasia* is used. It can mean both "business" and "gain from business = profit" (compare Luke 12:58; Acts 16:16, 19). It is tempting in this case to translate the term as "profit," since Luke regularly connects acquisitiveness to the resistance of God's visitation (see Luke 16:1-14; Acts 1:17-20; 5:1-11; 8:20-22; 16:16-18).

25. *workers in related crafts:* The characterization is vague (literally, "those workers concerning such things"), as is that of the town-clerk in v. 38, "Demetrius and the craftsmen with him." We are to picture the members of an artisans' guild (*collegium*) who have been called together to respond to a threat to their livelihood. There remains abundant evidence for the wide proliferation of such guilds during the period of the empire, including at least one papyrus from Egypt concerning a silversmiths' guild (see also the note on 18:3).

    our prosperity: The term *euporia* includes wealth but suggests "the good way of life" as well (Aristotle, *Politics* 1279B). For *epistamai* as "recognize," see the note on 19:15, above.

26. *converted a considerable crowd:* The phrase "this Paul" (*houtos Paulos*) is wonderfully dismissive, but the substance of Demetrius' complaint, although couched in negative terms (*methistēmi* tends to mean "changing things" in social or political terms [Herodotus, *Persian Wars* 1:65; Aristotle, *Politics* 1301B]; compare Col 1:13; Luke 16:4; Acts 13:22), confirms what the narrator had stated in positive terms, Paul's great success "through all of Asia" (19:10)!

    things made by hand are not gods: In backhanded fashion once more Demetrius is made a spokesperson for the position that Paul himself (and Luke) vigorously espouses (see Acts 7:48-50; 14:15-17; 17:23-31).

27. *our share . . . discredited:* The sentence is difficult to translate because the adjective *apelegmos* is a *hapax*, and because *meros* is used in an unusual way. The verb *apelenchō* means to "discredit/disprove/refute," so the rendering "discredited" seems right in the context. As for *meros*, Luke uses it elsewhere for one's participation in something, or financial stake (Luke 12:46; 15:12; Acts 5:2).

Great Goddess Artemis: The attribute "great" (*megalē*) anticipates the phrase "brought down from her greatness" (*megaleiotēs*) later in the sentence, as well as the repeated acclamation in vv. 28 and 34, "Great (*megalē*) is Artemis of the Ephesians!" The designation is not uncommon for gods (see Ps 46:2; 75:1; 94:3; Dan 9:4; [especially *Bel and the Dragon* 18]; Titus 2:3; Acts 8:10). The specific acclamation for Artemis can be found in Xenophon, *The Ephesians* 1, 11, 5.

Asia and the inhabited world: In the case of such hyperbole, "inhabited world" seems the appropriate translation of *oikoumenē*, rather than the "empire" that has been preferred generally in the present translation (compare Luke 2:1; 4:5; Acts 11:28; 17:6). For the widespread worship of the Ephesian Artemis, see Pausanias, *Description of Greece* 2, 2, 5; 4, 31, 8.

brought down from her greatness: For the verb *kathairein* ("pull down"), see Luke 1:52; Acts 13:19; for the threat of Christianity to the system of sacrifices to the gods, see the first-hand testimony given in the early second century by Pliny the Younger, *Letters* 10:96.

28. *filled with fury:* Compare the response of the townspeople in Nazareth (Luke 4:28). It is characteristic of Hellenistic Romances to have such violent emotional responses, but it is also a feature of Hellenistic Historiography, as can be seen in similar situations reported by Philo, *Embassy to Gaius* 243; Josephus, *Jewish War* 2:402; 5:420; 7:42, 57. The Western Text adds the detail that they "ran out into the street," which provides a helpful narrative transition from this smaller group to the larger assembly in the next verse.

29. *rushed together to the theater:* Archaeologists have uncovered a theater of very considerable proportions (seating some 25,000) in Ephesus; such spontaneous meetings of the "popular assembly" (*dēmos*, v. 30; *ekklēsia*, v. 32) are a feature of Hellenistic novels (see only Heliodorus, *The Ethiopians* 4, 19, 5; Chariton of Aphrodisias, *Chaereas and Callirhoe* 1, 5, 3; 3, 4, 4-18; for a riot in Ephesus, see Tatius Achilles, *Clitiphon and Leucippe* 7:9). It should be noted as well, however, that Luke's account also strikingly resembles Josephus' chilling story concerning the riot against the Jews in Antioch (*Jewish War* 7:46-62).

Gaius and Aristarchus: The name Gaius is very common (see 3 John 1), but the information here corresponds roughly with Paul's reference to the Gaius he baptized in Corinth (1 Cor 1:14), and who was also a "host" (*xenos*) to him and to the Church (Rom 16:23). He is here identified as a "Macedonian" but his place of origin was not terribly significant in this peripatetic messianic movement: like Paul he is *ekdēmos*, a traveller away from his homeland. He will reappear in the list of Paul's delegates in Acts 20:4. The name Aristarchus is also connected elsewhere to the Pauline mission (Col 4:10; Phlm 24), and reappears as a companion of Paul in 20:4 and 27:2.

30. *disciples did not allow him:* No explanation is given for Paul's companions' being hauled off to the theater. Even odder is Paul's systematic removal from the center of the story. Is the background to this story formed by Paul's own allusions to having "fought with the beasts in Ephesus" (1 Cor 15:32), and to the "afflictions we experienced in Asia" (2 Cor 1:8)? It is difficult to see

why, if Paul had been directly involved or even had his life threatened (2 Cor 1:8-9), Luke should have so camouflaged it.

31. *the Asiarchs:* Although there remains some uncertainty concerning their precise political and religious functions, the existence of this prestigious office in Asia is well-attested (see e.g., Strabo, *Geography* 14:649-665; *The Martyrdom of Polycarp* 12). As in similar situations, Luke shows an excellent grasp of local political and social arrangements (16:20; 17:6, 22; 18:12). That such socially elevated folk became "friends" (*philoi*) of Paul and showed concern for his welfare is consistent with Luke's recent efforts to show the success of the mission among the better classes (17:4, 12, 34), as well as his consistent attention to the niceties of obligation demanded by *philoi* in the Hellenistic world (see the notes on Luke 7:6; 11:5-8; 14:10-12; 23:12).

33. *pressed together against Alexander:* The translation given here is unusual, and its tentative quality should be recognized. The entire sequence involving Alexander is obscure. We know nothing about him otherwise (there being no good reason to connect him to the Alexander of 1 Tim 1:20 or 2 Tim 4:14). The passage is nearly as confused as the crowd's state of mind! The precise translation of *synebibēsan* is particularly difficult, for the verb *symbibazō* (compare Acts 9:22; 16:10) never appears in this sort of context. If we translated it as "instructed Alexander," the meaning is only more obscure. Notice the corrections in the Western Text, which recognize the difficulty. Like the present translation, they take *ek tou ochlou* as the subject, and read the verb as *katabibazō* ("pull down"). In order to give some meaning to Alexander's subsequent need to "silence the crowd," the present translation reduces *symbibazō* to its root sense of "press together" in the physical sense. The passage is only made harder by Luke's neglecting to provide a reason why the Jews should have "put him forward" in the first place.

    address the assembly: Luke uses the verb *apologeomai*, which is employed elsewhere for the "defenses/apologies" made by Christians (Luke 12:11; 21:14; Acts 22:1; 24:10; 25:8, 16; 26:1). The terms *dēmos* and *ekklēsia* are used interchangeably throughout this passage.

34. *recognized that he was a Jew:* As in the stories of conflict in Philippi (16:16-24) and in Corinth (18:12-17), Luke suggests that to the casual Gentile observer, Messianist and non-Messianist Jews were indistinguishable, and therefore Messianists experienced some of the casual anti-semitism that was directed against Jews at the local, popular level in the Hellenistic Diaspora (see Josephus, *Against Apion*; Philo, *Embassy to Gaius*; *Against Flaccus*). A more difficult question is whether Luke himself shared some of that attitude by having Alexander "put forward" by the Jews and then having him shouted down.

35. *city-clerk calmed the crowd:* The noun *grammateus* is used by Luke everywhere else for the "scribes" who were the associates of the Pharisees (Luke 5:21, 30; 6:7), and participated in the Sanhedrin (Acts 4:5; 6:12; 23:9). In the Hellenistic city, the *grammateus* was a part of the bureaucracy, functioning as keeper of records, registrar, and so forth, as we learn from inscriptions; for Ephesus in particular, see also Apollonius of Tyana, *Letters* 32. For

Josephus' claim that such record-keeping among the Jews was assigned to "priests and prophets" see *Against Apion* 1:29. For the translation of *katastellō* as "calm," see 2 Macc 4:31; Josephus, *Antiquities of the Jews* 20:175.

keeper of the temple: The term *neokoros* probably derived from the humble task of "keeping" a shrine in the sense of cleaning and tending (Philo, *Special Laws* 1:156; Josephus, *Jewish War* 1:153), but came to be a title for cities that housed important temples or shrines. For Ephesus, the title appears on coins of the period.

sacred stone from the sky: The substantive *to Diopetes* means literally "that which fell from Zeus." It may have referred to a meteorite, or to the image of the goddess, or both. The implication, in either case, is that this cult, too, "came from heaven," and thus had special legitimacy. For a similar legend concerning images of Athene that fell from heaven for the Athenians, see Pausanias, *Description of Greece* 1, 26, 7.

36. *do nothing rashly:* There is a balance to the clerk's discourse: here, for example, *propetes* ("rashly") matches *diopetes*, just as *katastelmenous* ("remain calm") picks up the *katasteilas* which introduced his speech. Note the similar sort of advice given by the *stratēgos* to a like assembly in the novel by Heliodorus, *The Ethiopians* 4, 20, 1-3.

37. *temple-robbers nor as blasphemers:* The term *hierosylos* can mean a literal robber of temple treasures, or one who is in any way sacrilegious (see Plato, *Republic* 344B; 2 Macc 4:42; Josephus, *Jewish War* 1:654; Rom 2:22); the seriousness of the crime—shrines were supported by the gifts of their patrons and devotees—is indicated in Lucian of Samosata, *Phalaris* 1:6; 2:12-13. The Ephesians had special reason to be sensitive to such attacks, for in their history was the tradition of an attempt to burn down the temple of Artemis (see Lucian of Samosata, *The Passing of Peregrinus* 22). For the meaning of "blasphemers" see the discussion on Acts 6:11; 13:45; 18:6.

38. *court-days . . . proconsuls:* The sentence is laden with legal terminology: "have a case against someone" (*logon echein pros tina*; see Aristotle, *Rhetoric* 1402A); "bring cases" (*enkaleō*; Plato, *Apology* 26C); "court days" (*agoraioi*; see Josephus, *Antiquities* 14:245); "proconsuls" (Acts 13:7; 18:12). These are all means and occasions for the proper settlement of disputes rather than this mob-action.

39. *seek something further:* Some mss have here *peri heterōn* ("concerning other things"), but the comparative adverb *peraiterō* is probably the correct reading. Notice again the emphasis on the "legal assembly" (*ennomō ekklēsia*) in contrast to this illegal one.

40. *charged with rioting:* The term *stasis* retains some of its original sense of forming a party for the sake of revolt or sedition (see Herodotus, *Persian Wars* 1:59; Dio Chrysostom, *Oration* 38:14; Luke 23:19, 25).

to account for this disturbance: For "give an account" (*apodounai logon*), compare Luke 16:2. The term "disturbance" (*sustrophē*) can have the sense of a seditious gathering (Josephus, *Jewish War* 4:601; 1 Macc 14:44; 3 Macc 5:41;

Acts 23:12), which would clearly make it even more dangerous in an empire chronically suspicious of any unregulated assembly (see Pliny the Younger, *Letters* 10:34).

INTERPRETATION

Luke's final lines devoted to Paul's Ephesian sojourn continue to combine revealing detail with puzzling reticence. The announcement of Paul's plan to travel to Jerusalem and from there to Rome plays an important role in the overall narrative, analogous to Jesus' formal decision to proceed toward Jerusalem in Luke 9:51. Paul has been (recently with great emphasis) certified as a prophet in the line of Jesus and the other apostles (18:24-19:20). Now his resemblance to Jesus is marked even more decisively by the carefully plotted and portentous journey to the city which "kills the prophets" (Luke 13:34). The actual journey will not begin until 20:1-5, but Paul's announcement of his intention begins the process and functions as a programmatic prophecy for the narrative to follow.

Within Luke's overall narrative, Paul's journey to Jerusalem works perfectly well within his geographical structure (which centers the entire story on Jerusalem) and his prophetic structure (which has all his heroes follow the pattern of the rejected prophet). But the reader who knows something of Paul's movements at this point from his letters as well must be puzzled at what Luke does *not* tell us about this journey. As we will see as the plot unfolds, Luke's reticence on this point grows ever more puzzling. If Luke knew so much about the movements of Paul and his delegates, why did he choose not to tell us of Paul's own reasons for going to Jerusalem, namely to deliver a collection of money for the Church in Jerusalem from his Gentile communities (see note on vv. 21-22)? His language about Paul's assistants ("those ministering with him") only teases us, for Luke uses the same term (*diakonein*) that Paul himself does for the collection, yet he never tells us that Paul was engaged in such a collection! Was he camouflaging a fact that proved in the end to be an embarrassment to his hero? Or was he simply transforming the event to fit his overall literary pattern?

A similar puzzlement attends the reading of the "Riot in Ephesus" (19:23-40). The story itself justly deserves its reputation as the liveliest of all Luke's vivid vignettes. As the notes indicate, Luke once more gets the local color precisely right: what he has to say about the cult of Ephesian Artemis, the fame of the city of Ephesus as its "keeper," the presence and prestige of the "Asiarchs," is all abundantly confirmed by other literary and archaeological evidence. In a remarkably few strokes, he also compresses all the features associated with the unruly mobs and popular assemblies of the Hellenistic cities, known to us both from histories and romances of the period: the violent emotions, the throngs in the street, the convergence on the theater, the noise and confusion, the efforts of the local leaders to quell the disturbance in the name of good order and out of fear of reprisal. Luke also effectively conveys the way in which Jews could be caught up in such disturbances and made their victims.

As a literary set-piece, the account is flawless. The puzzlement begins with any attempt to read it as historical evidence, particularly with regard to Paul. Three things in the story itself are difficult to understand: the first is the reason why Paul's delegates were swept up by the mob and carried to the theater; the second is why Paul himself is so marginal to the entire account, especially when he has otherwise dominated virtually every scene; the third is what Alexander and the Jews were up to and why they were shouted down. It is possible to make sense of it: the silversmiths identified Gaius and Aristarchus as Paul's fellow workers and decided to bring them to account with a sort of rough mob-justice; Paul's tremendous success has won him the allegiance of important figures who do not want him harmed; Alexander is put forward by the Jews to stir the crowd against Paul, but is mistakenly identified by the crowd instead as one of the Messianists and only makes matters worse. Read this way, the account would resemble that in Corinth (18:12-16). But it must be said that Luke does not himself make these connections.

A more serious problem for the historian is trying to align Luke's evidence with that found in Paul's own letters. In 1 Cor 15:32 and 2 Cor 1:8-9, Paul refers to serious, even life-threatening "afflictions" he had experienced in "Asia/Ephesus." In fact, Luke's own subsequent account of Paul's travels down the coast of Asia Minor, in which he by-passes Ephesus "so he would not spend time in Asia" (20:16), even though he summons the elders from Ephesus to meet him in Miletus (20:17), seems to suggest a real danger to Paul in Ephesus—so great he could not return there—that Luke prefers not to mention.

It is possible that things happened this way, and Paul characterized them the way he did for his own reasons. It is possible that things happened roughly this way, but involved Paul much more directly and threateningly than Luke suggests. It is possible that Luke replaces a far more dangerous event with this highly colored but ultimately stock account, simply because his information was not better, or because his own literary and religious goals motivated him to slant the account this way. The historian, alas, is not able to gain any further certainty on the matter.

We are able to observe, however, that certain consistent Lukan preoccupations are also present in this story: the desire to show the social level of Christianity's new converts and "friends," the interest in applauding the regular procedures of law rather than the vagaries of mob assembly.

But of special importance here is the way Luke continues one of his major subthemes: the way in which responses to God's visitation are symbolized by attitudes toward material possessions. As we have seen repeatedly both in the Gospel and in Acts, the acceptance of God's call is accompanied by the sharing of possessions (see only Luke 8:1-3; Acts 4:32-37). With equal regularity, we have seen how opposition to the Gospel is expressed by the love of money.

The silversmiths' concern for their loss of revenue, and their violent rejection of a message that denies the reality of "gods made with hands," is a characteristic quality of idolatry, according to the prophetic and wisdom traditions of Israel (see e.g., Wis 13:10; 15:11-13); for Luke, such self-protectiveness and acquisitiveness is a sign of rejecting God's call (Luke 6:24; 16:10-31; Acts 1:17-20; 5:1-11; 8:18-24; 16:16-19). The triumph over the exorcists in Ephesus led to the symbolic dispossession of their wealth by those who came to believe in the good news (19:19-20). The continuing resistance to the gospel by the ancient and deeply entrenched patterns of idolatrous worship is expressed in the same way that the resistance of the Jewish leadership to the prophet was: in murderous fury fed by the desire for gain.

FOR REFERENCE AND FURTHER STUDY

Duncan, G. S. "Paul's Ministry in Asia." *NTS* 3 (1957) 211–218.

Lyonnet, S. " 'La Voie' dans les Actes des Apôtres." *RScR* 69 (1981) 149–164.

Pervo, L. *Profit with Delight: The Literary Genre of the Acts of the Apostles.* Philadelphia: Fortress, 1987, 9–10, 37–39.

Plümacher, E. *Lukas als hellenistischer Schriftsteller.* Göttingen: Vandenhoeck & Ruprecht, 1972, 98–100.

Stoops, R. F. "Riot and Assembly: The Social Context of Acts 19:23-41." *JBL* 108 (1989) 73–91.

Taylor, L. R. "Artemis of Ephesus" and "The Asiarchs." *Beginnings* 5:251-256 and 256-262.

40. *Heading Toward Jerusalem* (20:1-16)

1. After the disturbance quieted down, Paul summoned the disciples and exhorted them. Bidding them farewell, he left to go to Macedonia. 2. He passed through those regions and after exhorting them with many speeches, he came to Greece. 3. He stayed there three months. When a plot was made against him by the Jews just as he was about to set sail for Syria, he determined to return through Macedonia. 4. Accompanying him were Sopater from Beroea (the son of Pyrrhus); and from the Thessalonians, Aristarchus and Secundus; Gaius from Derbe and Timothy; and the Asians Tychichus and Trophimus. 5. These went on ahead. They waited for us in Troas. 6. But after the days of unleavened bread, we set out from Philippi. We came to them in Troas in five days. We stayed there seven days. 7. On the first day of the week, we gathered together to break bread. Paul spoke to them. Since he was about to depart the next day, he extended his discourse until midnight. 8. There were many lamps in the upper room where we were gathered. 9. A certain youth named Eutyches was sitting in the window. He was being carried off by deep sleep as Paul continued speaking at length. Overcome with sleep, he fell down from the third story. He was picked up dead. 10. Paul went down. He leaned over him and lifted him up. He said, "Don't stay upset, for his life is within him." 11. He went up and broke bread and ate, continuing to discourse extensively until daybreak. Thus he departed. 12. They took away the boy alive, and they were comforted greatly. 13. We had gone ahead into the boat. We set sail for Assos. From there we were going to pick up Paul, for so he had arranged it, since he was going to go over land. 14. And when he met us in Assos, we picked him up and we came to Mytilene. 15. And from there on the next day we arrived opposite Chios, and on the second day we sailed past Samos, and on the next we came to Miletus, 16. for Paul had decided to sail past Ephesus so that he would not spend time in Asia. For he was hurrying to be in Jerusalem, if possible, for the day of Pentecost.

Notes

1. *the disturbance quieted down:* The transition sentence rounds off the previous story and reconnects the reader to the travel plans Paul had expressed in 19:21-22, to go through Macedonia and Achaia to Jerusalem, and from there to Rome.

2. *exhorting them with many speeches:* The verb *parakaleō* here and in the next sentence could also be translated as "comfort" (compare Acts 11:23; 14:22; 15:32; 16:40). Paul is shown engaging in the same sort of pastoral visitation of churches that he had previously founded, as in 14:21-22; 15:36; 16:4-5; 18:23. The phrase "many speeches" translates the sense of *pollō logō*.

3. *plot was made against him by the Jews:* An *epiboulē* is an organized conspiracy (see Herodotus, *Persian Wars* 1:12; 2 Macc 5:7; 3 Macc 1:2, 6). The term recurs with reference to Paul in 9:24; 20:19; 23:30. Such repetition certainly reinforces the perception of Paul's Jewish opponents as dishonorable.

he determined to return: Literally, "he was of the opinion" (*gnōmēs egeneto*); Codex D makes two changes: a) the initial intention to go to Syria is occasioned by a plot of the Jews; b) the change of direction is determined by the Holy Spirit: "the Holy Spirit told him to return through Macedonia." It is one of the characteristic features of Codex D to emphasize the role of the Holy Spirit in directing the mission.

4. *accompanying him:* In the following list, Codex D makes three significant alterations: a) the first group is said to accompany Paul "as far as Asia (*mechri tēs Asias*); b) Gaius is said to be *Derberios* ("of Derberios") rather than *Derbaios,* ("of Derbe"); c) rather than Tychichus and Trophimus, there appear "the Ephesians Eutyches and Trophimus." The emendations apparently seek to clarify the respective movements of the delegates, eliminate intratextual conflicts (Acts 19:29 identifies Gaius as a Macedonian rather than from Derbe, and Derberios is a town in Macedonia), and anticipate the following narrative (see the appearance of Eutyches in 20:9).

Sopater . . . Trophimus: For the textual variations in this list, see the previous note. Although we were told of Paul's work in Beroea (17:10-12), this is our first glimpse of Sopater, and our last (unless he is to be identified with the Sosipater of Rom 16:21). Aristarchus was identified as a Macedonian in 19:29, but this is the first appearance of Secundus. Timothy is well known to us (16:1-3). Gaius is a common name, and there is probably no need for the correction attempted by the Western Text (see above). This is Tychichus' only appearance in Acts, although he is known to us from Pauline letters (Eph 6:21; Col 4:7; 2 Tim 4:12; Titus 3:12). Trophimus will reappear in Acts 21:29, and is also mentioned in 2 Tim 4:20. The most obvious feature of the list is its inclusion of representatives from the diverse geographical areas in which Paul worked. The passage testifies to the complexity of the Pauline mission. But it is once more strangely reticent concerning the function of the delegates, which we suspect—from Paul's own testimony—to have been connected to the collection for the saints in Jerusalem.

5. *waited for us in Troas:* This is the place from which Paul had initiated his European mission (16:8, 11). The fact that the delegation travels together ahead of Paul and then makes rendezvous with him again suggests its real role as one of arranging the delivery of the collection to the Jerusalem Church (Rom 15:25-27).

6. *days of unleavened bread:* For Luke's treating "Passover" and the "days of unleavened bread" as identical, see the note on Luke 22:1. All the other travel notices seem to have no other purpose than reporting the facts, with no special meaning attached to "five days" or "seven days." But the mention of Passover and of Paul's desire to be in Jerusalem for the feast of Pentecost serve to demonstrate again the apostle's dedication to the *ethos* of Judaism.

7. *first day of the week:* In this case, the deliberate designation of the day, together with the activity of "breaking bread," seems to suggest a definite day of Christian worship as a celebration of the resurrection (see Luke 24:1; 22:19; 24:30; 24:35; Acts 2:42, 46; 1 Cor 16:2; Rev 1:10; *The Didache* 14:1).

8. *where we had gathered:* The "we-narrative" had resumed in 20:5, and it continues through this sequence. This charming story is filled with incidental detail: the many lamps in the upper room, the time of the night, the length of the discourse, the number of stories of the house, the name of the youth, his position in the window, the gradual increase in sleepiness. Such detail could derive equally from an eyewitness or from a good fictional imagination. We know nothing more about Eutyches, whose name ("good fortune/ lucky") is perhaps not coincidental. The Western Text tries to make him a delegate of Paul's in 20:4, but the way Luke designates him as *neanias/pais* ("youth") argues against that.

10. *leaned over him:* The gesture faintly resembles the actions of the prophets Elijah (1 Kgs 17:17-24) and Elisha (2 Kgs 4:33-36) in their resuscitations, although there are no actual verbal echoes, and Paul's action is less elaborate.
    life is within him: It matters little to the symbolic point of the story whether the child was clinically dead or only "as good as dead," whether Paul's statement was simply declarative or performative; compare the discussion of the *thauma* of the resuscitation of the young bride in Philostratus, *Life of Apollonius of Tyana* 4:45.

12. *took away the boy alive:* Codex D reads, "as they were bidding farewell, he brought the boy alive." In either version, the separation of this notice from Paul's statement that he was alive remains awkward. For "comforted" (*parakaleō*), see the note on 20:2. Luke engages in *litotes* again by using the expression *ou metriōs* (literally, "not moderately," that is, "greatly").

13. *going to go over land:* From Troas to Assos, the delegates are in a boat, making their way down the coastline of Asia. The verb *pezeuein* means literally to go on foot as opposed to riding on a horse; in this context it means to go by land rather than by sea. No motivation is given for Paul's preference.

14-15. *Mytilene . . . Miletus:* As was customary for sea-voyaging at that time, the boat makes its way by short stages from one coastal port to another in short, one-day journeys. Mytilene is a town on the island of Lesbos, Chios is another Aegean island further south, and so is Samos. The sailers are therefore going from island to mainland and back on this trip. After "Samos," some *mss* add "and after staying in Trogylla" (a promontory opposite Samos). Miletus itself is on the mainland some thirty miles south of Ephesus.

16. *had decided to sail past Ephesus:* The pluperfect tense (*kekrikei*) suggests a fixed decision rather than a spur-of-the-moment impulse. Luke would want us to think that stopping at Ephesus would be too involving, but does not make clear why stopping at Miletus and waiting for a delegation would not be. We must wonder, therefore, whether it was actually the danger to Paul in Ephesus which might have been the real determining factor. For the signifi-

cance of Paul's desire to make the great pilgrimage feast of Pentecost in terms of his allegiance to the *ethos* of Judaism, compare the note on v. 6. And for Luke's use of *speudō* ("hurry"), see Luke 2:16; 19:5-6; Acts 22:18.

INTERPRETATION

After having Paul declare his intention to go to Jerusalem and prepare for it by sending his delegates ahead of him (19:21-22), Luke now shows the first steps on that journey. More significant by far than any single stage of the journey is the way in which Luke has so obviously structured it to mirror the great journey of the prophet Jesus to his death and triumph in Jerusalem (Luke 9:51-19:44). Paul announces his intention, sends out delegates ahead of him, and then proceeds to move steadily toward a destiny that is ever more clearly enunciated as he approaches the city of Jerusalem. Luke shows through this journey not only that Paul shared the prophetic spirit of Jesus that was demonstrated through the proclamation of the word in boldness, and in the doing of signs and wonders, but also and above all that he replicated the pattern of the prophet who was rejected in Jerusalem.

The literary and religious purposes that motivate Luke at this point may shed more light on elements that are otherwise somewhat puzzling. Why, for example, does Luke pay such attention to the gathering of Paul's delegates at the start of this journey? He does not tell us. From reading Paul's letters, we suspect that Paul's motivation for making the journey to Jerusalem was to deliver the collection from the Gentile churches to the Jerusalem community (see notes). In this light, the gathering of delegates (in pairs) from all the various areas of Paul's work makes perfectly good sense: they had gathered the money, and were going with Paul *en masse* as representatives of the Gentile communities. We would have a glimpse, in other words, of the way a "Pauline school" functioned during Paul's life.

The only problem with this plausible reconstruction is that Luke himself gives us not the slightest hint (here) that Paul was taking up such a collection or that this was the reason he was going to Jerusalem. And this despite the fact that he later drops clear hints to the effect that Paul was in fact delivering such "alms to his nation" (24:17). We can only speculate on the reasons for Luke's silence. Possibly the failure of the Jerusalem Church to rally to Paul's aid when he was arrested was an embarrassment and a sign that Paul's intended gesture of reconciliation had failed. We will return to the point later. But for now, we can notice that the failure to provide a motivation for the journey to Jerusalem only has the effect of heightening the resemblance to Jesus' own journey. The gathering of these "disciples" (named in pairs), and the "sending of them on ahead" provide a mirror image of Jesus' gathering and sending on of his emissaries ahead of him on the way to Jerusalem (Luke 9:1-6; 10:1-12).

Within this literary framework, the story of Eutyches (20:7-12) takes on a similar symbolic dimension. Why has Luke chosen to tell this particular story in this place? It is preceded by prosaic travel notices, and followed by more of the same. And the story itself is a strange blend of incidental detail and inconclusiveness. Luke's dramatic sense seems to have abandoned him completely. He tells us about the many lamps in the room, and the length of Paul's preaching, and the gradually increasing sleepiness (a nice touch), but the dramatic moment of falling and dying and being restored are handled almost casually, and with very little detail. It is possible, of course, that this combination of bare structure and incidental (and relatively disconnected detail) is itself a signal to the reader as to how Luke intends the account to be read.

If we suggest that this is an account that shows how the power of resurrection is at work in Paul, then Luke's *choice* of details begins to appear somewhat less arbitrary. Is it by accident that the story takes place on the first day of the week (Luke 24:1), or that it occurs in an "upper room" (Luke 22:12; Acts 1:13), or that the disciples are gathered to "break bread" (Luke 24:30-35)? All of these are clear verbal pointers back to the resurrection of Jesus and the experience of his risen presence by the first disciples. We are rightly hesitant to go further in seeking to find a mystical sense to the "many lamps" in the upper room or the "three stories" that the young man fell, as though the entire narrative were entirely an allegory. The small details already noted clearly indicate the message Luke wants the reader to derive from the tale: the power of the raised prophet Jesus is at work in the Apostle Paul precisely at the moment he sets off on his own journey to "chains and afflictions" in Jerusalem (20:23).

FOR REFERENCE AND FURTHER STUDY

Delebecque, E. "Les deux versions du voyage de saint Paul de Corinthe à Troas (Ac 20, 3-6)." *Bib* 64 (1983) 556–564.

Menoud, Ph.-H. "The Acts of the Apostles and the Eucharist." *Jesus Christ and the Faith: A Collection of Studies.* PTMS 18. Pittsburgh: Pickwick Press, 1978, 84–106.

Plümacher, E. "Wirklichkeitserfahrung und Geschichtsschreibung bei Lukas: Erwagungen zu den Wir-Stucken der Apostelgeschichte." *ZNW* 68 (1977) 2–22.

Praeder, S. M. "The Problem of First Person Narrative in Acts." *NovT* 29 (1978) 193–218.

Tremel, B. "A propos d'Actes 20, 7-12: Puissance du thaumaturge ou de témoin?" *RTP* 112 (1980) 359-369.

41. *Paul's Farewell Discourse* (20:17-38)

17. Sending into Ephesus from Miletus, he summoned the elders of the Church. 18. When they came to him, he said to them: "You know the way I have been with you the entire time since the first day I set foot in Asia. 19. I have been serving the Lord with all lowly-mindedness, with tears, and with testings that have come upon me from the plots of the Jews. 20. I have held back nothing that was helpful, proclaiming to you and teaching you in public and from house to house, 21. as I have given witness both to the Jews and Gentiles concerning repentance to God and faith in our Lord Jesus. 22. And now, look, since I am bound by the Spirit, I am going to Jerusalem. I don't know what will meet me there, 23. but the Holy Spirit is testifying to me city by city. It is telling me that chains and afflictions await me. 24. But I make of no account the value of my life to myself, so long as I can complete my course and the ministry that I received from the Lord Jesus, to bear witness to the good news of the gift of God. 25. And now, look! I know that you will no longer see my face, all of you among whom I have passed preaching the kingdom. 26. Therefore I declare to you this day that I am innocent of the blood of all persons, 27. for I did not hold back from announcing to you all the will of God. 28. Look to yourselves and to all the flock in which the Holy Spirit has placed you as overseers to shepherd the Church of God, which he acquired with his own blood. 29. I know that after I leave fierce wolves will come in among you. They will not spare the flock. 30. And from among them will arise men who will speak deceptive things in order to draw the disciples after them. 31. Be on the watch, therefore! Remember that for three years, night and day, I did not cease admonishing each one of you with tears. 32. And now I am entrusting you to God and to the word that is his gift, to the one who is able to build and to bestow an inheritance among all those who have been made holy. 33. I have desired no one's silver or gold or garment. 34. You yourselves know that these hands have attended to my needs as well as those who are with me. 35. I have given an example of these things to you, because by so laboring it is necessary to help those who are weak, as you remember the words of the Lord Jesus. Because he himself said, 'It is more blessed to give than to receive.' " 36. After saying all these things, he fell to his knees. He prayed with all of them. 37. Everyone wept greatly. They embraced Paul and kissed him. 38. They were anguished most of all because of the word he had spoken, that they would no longer see his face. But they sent him off on the boat.

NOTES

17. *summoned the elders of the Church:* The solemn character of the discourse is anticipated by the "summoning" (*metakaleomai*): compare Acts 7:14; 10:32. The presbyteral structure of the local church from the beginning is assumed by Luke (11:30; 14:23; 15:2, 4, 6, 22, 23; 16:4). See also the evidence offered also by 1 Tim 5:1, 2, 17, 19 (Ephesus!); Titus 1:5; Jas 5:14; 1 Pet 5:1; 2 John 1; 3 John 1.

18. *the way I have been with you:* Literally, "how (*pōs*) I have been with you": the adverb indicates the *manner* of Paul's life. A series of clauses over the next three verses all depend on this opening declaration which appeals to their knowledge of his behavior. After the word "Asia," Codex D adds the words "for about three years or even more," deriving that information either from 19:10, or v. 31 below.

19. *serving the Lord with all lowlymindedness:* The translation makes the circumstantial participle *douleuontes* into an independent verb. The use of *doulos/douleuein* for describing Christian existence taps into the biblical tradition of the "servant of God" (LXX Ps 18:11; 33:22; 77:71; 85:2; Isa 49:3, 5), but is also typical of Paul (Rom 1:1; 2 Cor 4:5; Gal 1:10; Phil 1:1; 2:22; Titus 1:1). Equally Pauline is the corresponding attitude of "slave-mindedness" (*tapeinophrosynē*), as in Rom 12:16; 2 Cor 7:6; 10:1; 11:7; 12:21; Phil 2:3, 8; 3:21; 4:12; Col 3:12.

    with tears and with testings: The mention of "tears" (*dakryōn*) here and in v. 31 again echoes Paul's own language, as in 2 Cor 2:4 and 2 Tim 1:4. Although the construction of the Greek sentence demands that "lowlymindedness, tears, and testings" be controlled by *meta* ("with"), it is obvious that there is a difference between the first two terms (which refer to Paul's subjective attitudes) and the *peirasmoi* ("testings") that come on him from the "plots" (*epiboulai*, see 20:3) of the Jews. For Paul's own uses of "testing" in reference to his ministry, see 1 Thess 3:5 and Gal 4:14.

20. *held back nothing that was helpful:* The construction *hypostellō tou mē anangeilai* is difficult to render idiomatically in connection with the next phrase, *kai didaxai.* The translation aims at the sense, which seems clear enough. Luke is stating in negative terms the *parrēsia* ("open speech/boldness/frankness") that he elsewhere attributes to Paul and which was a quality of the genuine philosopher/prophet; see the note on Acts 4:13, as well as 9:27-28; 13:46; 19:8. Plato uses the same idiom, "to restrain from speaking," in Socrates' self-defense (*Apology* 24A). The use of *sympherō* is particularly interesting here since in Luke's other use of the verb (Acts 19:19) it does not bear this same sense of "helpful/useful" that is so characteristic of Paul himself (see 1 Cor 6:12; 7:35; 10:23, 33; 12:7; 2 Cor 8:10; 12:1).

    in public and from house to house: The narrative ascribes both activities of "proclaiming" (*anangellein*; Acts 14:27; 15:4) and "teaching" (*didaskein*; 11:26; 15:35; 18:11) to Paul. The terms "in public" (*dēmosia*) and "house to house" (*kat'oikon*) means "public and private." His mode of life was consistent in every circumstance, unlike the false philosophers, whose private activities contradicted their public proclamations (see, e.g., Lucian of Samosata, *Timon* 54).

21. *both to the Jews and Gentiles:* Another encapsulation of a Lukan narrative emphasis, particularly in recent chapters (13:44-48; 14:27; 17:4, 11, 17; 18:5-6, 19; 19:8-10, 17). It is also an emphasis of Paul's ministry according to his letters as well (Rom 1:16; 3:9; 10:12; 1 Cor 1:24; 10:32; 12:13; Gal 3:28).

    repentance to God: The two responses are balanced: repentance (*metanoia*) is "unto" (*eis*) God, and faith (*pistis*) is "unto" (*eis*) the Lord Jesus. For the theme of repentance in Luke-Acts, see the note on 5:31. This summary of his proclamation most resembles that by Paul in 1 Thess 1:9-10.

22. *since I am bound by the Spirit:* As in 19:21, the construction allows us to understand this either in psychological terms ("I am determined"), or in religious terms ("I am obliged by the Holy Spirit"). In the present case, the religious meaning is most likely, for two reasons: a) the Holy Spirit is immediately mentioned in v. 23; b) the participle "being bound" initiates a theme that is an ironic reversal of Paul's initial trip to Damascus to deliver back to Jerusalem "bound" disciples; Paul also will be "bound" (see 21:11, 13, 33; 22:5, 29; 24:27). In this light, the participle is translated as explanatory, "since I am bound." It is somewhat surprising that the Western Text, which otherwise tends to emphasize the role of the Holy Spirit (see, e.g., 19:1), made no improvement in this verse.

    I am going to Jerusalem: Paul's statement resembles Jesus' passion predictions, even though he explicitly eschews having "knowledge" of what will happen to him. As in the Gospel's "journey narrative," the name Jerusalem recurs with great frequency in this part of the story (19:1, 21; 20:16, 22; 21:4, 15, 17).

23. *Holy Spirit is testifying to me:* Luke makes every effort to assure the reader that what awaits Paul is part of God's plan, in conformity with the pattern of the rejected prophet Jesus. For the active role of the Holy Spirit in Paul's ministry, see 9:17; 13:2, 4, 9; 16:6-7, 18, as well as the further revelations given in 21:4, 11. The prophetic resonances are patent.

    chains and afflictions: The more specific meaning of "being bound" is defined by the term "chains" (*desma*), which stands for being imprisoned; reference will be made to them again in 23:29; 26:29, 31. Paul had earlier told his churches that "it is necessary for us to enter the kingdom of God through many afflictions (*thlipseis* 14:22)." For Paul's own references to his "chains," see Phil 1:7, 13-14, 17; Col 4:18; 2 Tim 2:9; Phlm 10, 13; and for his "afflictions," see 2 Cor 1:4, 8; 2:4; 4:17; 6:4; 7:4; Eph 3:13; Phil 1:17; 4:14; Col 1:24; 1 Thess 3:7.

24. *complete my course:* The comparison of moral effort to athletic activity is common in Hellenistic moral teaching (see only Epictetus, *Discourses* 1, 2, 25-29; 1, 4, 13; 3, 15, 1-13), and Luke uses the image of the "race" (*dromos*) earlier with reference to John the Baptist (Acts 13:25); Paul himself uses the same image in 1 Cor 9:24 and Phil 3:14. The phrasing here is particularly close to that in 2 Tim 4:7, *ton dromon teteleka.*

the ministry that I received: The phrasing is very close to Paul's own in 2 Cor 5:18, where it is the "ministry of reconciliation" (*diakonia tēs katallagēs*). The term *diakonia* in this case could allude again to the collection (see the note on Acts 19:22), or refer to Paul's entire task of "bearing witness to the good news." It is also possible to combine the two notions, as Paul himself does in 2 Cor 9:13, where participation in the work of the collection is called obedience to "the gospel of Christ," and 2 Cor 8:9, which interprets the collection in terms of "the gift (*charis*) of our Lord Jesus Christ."

25. *you will no longer see my face:* Such formal statements of departure (see also later v. 29) are a staple of the "farewell discourse" or "final testament," which this discourse so much resembles (see Gen 48:21; *Testament of Reuben* 1:4-5; *Testament of Dan* 2:1; *Testament of Naphtali* 1:3; *Testament of Job* 1:4; 2 Tim 4:6; 2 Pet 1:13, and Luke 22:15-16).

    preaching the kingdom: Some mss from the Western Tradition add the words "of Jesus," or "of the Lord Jesus," while still other witnesses have "of God"; but Luke is capable of having "kingdom" without modifier (as in Acts 1:6). He clearly intends *basileia* to be in continuity with the theme that runs throughout Luke-Acts (see the notes on Acts 1:3; 14:22).

26. *innocent of the blood:* This picks up Paul's declaration to the Jews in Acts 18:6; for other examples of the expression, see the note on that verse. In the present case, Paul's innocence is based in his having declared to them openly all they needed to know; the decision is in their hands. For a similar use of the disclaimer, see *Testament of Simeon* 6:1; *Testament of Levi* 10:1.

27. *all the will of God:* For "not holding back," compare v. 20. The phrase *pasan tēn boulēn tou theou* could also be translated "the entire plan of God." For Luke's distinctive use of *boulē*, see Luke 7:30; Acts 2:23; 4:28; 5:38; 13:36; it is close to that of Paul's *thelēma tou theou* in 1 Cor 1:1; Gal 1:4; Eph 1:9, 11; Col 1:9.

28. *look to yourselves and to all the flock:* The wording of the warning "look to yourselves" recalls LXX Gen 24:6; Exod 10:28; Deut 4:9; Wis 13:8; Hos 5:1, and Jesus' words in Luke 12:1; 17:3; 20:46; 21:34. For similar exhortations, see *Testament of Judah* 13:1; *Testament of Asher* 6:1. For the "flock/herd" (*poimnion*) as an image for the people of God, see e.g., LXX Ps 77:52, 70; Mic 5:4; Isa 40:11; Jer 13:17; Ezek 34:12; there is a very extended use of the image in *1 Enoch* 89:13–90:39. The language here most resembles that in 1 Pet 5:2-3.

    Holy Spirit has placed you as overseers: This is the only time Luke uses the term *episkopos* ("overseer/guardian/inspector"), although his use of *episkopē* in 1:20 is suggestive in context. In the Hellenistic world, the term is used for a variety of social and political offices, including that of educator (Plato, *Laws* 795D). The office of the *mebaqqer* at Qumran seemed to have similar functions (*1QS* 6:12; 6:20; *CD* 9:18-19; 13:6). Paul mentions such officials (in the plural) together with the *diakonoi* in Phil 1:1. In 1 Tim 3:2 and Titus 1:7, the office of the *episkopos* is, as here, not sharply differentiated from that of the *presbyteros*. Certainly there is no hint here of the hierarchical ordering reflected in Ignatius of Antioch, *Ephesians* 4:1-2; 6:1; *Trallians* 3:1. The NT passage closest to the present one is 1 Pet 2:25: "Turn now to the shepherd (*poimēn*) and guardian (*episkopos*) of your souls." Attaching the office to the appointment of the Holy Spirit obviously has a strongly legitimating effect.

to shepherd the Church of God: The verb *poimainein* carries forward the image of the flock and the shepherd, and points to Luke's understanding of the presbyterate/episcopate as an administrative position. The textual evidence is evenly split between two readings: "the Church of God" (*ekklēsia tou theou*), and "the Church of the Lord" (*ekklēsia tou kyriou*). The first is the reading translated here, for two reasons: a) the expression "Church of the Lord" never occurs elsewhere in the NT (although see Paul's "churches of Christ" in Rom 16:23), whereas "the Church of God" occurs frequently in Paul (1 Cor 1:2; 10:32; 11:16, 22; 15:9; 2 Cor 1:1; Gal 1:13; 1 Thess 2:14; 2 Thess 1:4; 1 Tim 3:5, 15), and Luke's usage throughout this discourse is remarkably faithful to Paul's own; b) the shift to "Church of the Lord" is more explicable because of the awkwardness of the following phrase, "acquired with his own blood," which is obviously difficult to read with "God." The harder reading is here preferred.

acquired with his own blood: The verb *peripoieō* ("acquire") has associations with Israel as the elect people (see LXX 2 Sam 12:3; Isa 43:21; Mal 3:17, and [with *ktaomai*] Ps 73:2); compare also Gal 1:14; 1 Pet 2:9. The phrase "by his own blood" is notoriously difficult to combine with "God," accounting for the textual variant, "Church of the Lord." It is just possible to read *tou haimatos tou idiou* here as "the blood of his own [son]," if *idios* is understood as equivalent to *yaḥid/agapētos*.

29. *fierce wolves will come in among you:* The prediction of evil following upon the death of the hero is a common element in the "Farewell Discourse" (see *Testament of Levi* 4:1; 10:2-5; 14:1-3; *Testament of Judah* 18:1-3; *Testament of Issachar* 6:1-4; *Testament of Napthali* 4:1-5; 2 Tim 3:1-5; 4:3-4; 2 Pet 2:1-3; 3:3-4). The term *aphixis* ("departure") is not found elsewhere in the NT, but seems clearly to refer not only to Paul's "leaving the Ephesians," but his death. The image of "fierce wolves" is particularly appropriate to the portrayal of the Church as a flock of sheep (see Ezek 22:27; Matt 7:15; 10:16; John 10:12); compare its use for a philosopher in Philostratus, *Life of Apollonius of Tyana* 8:22. In the Gospel, Jesus had told his missionaries that they would be "like sheep among wolves" (Luke 10:3). The image becomes stereotyped in early Christian literature (see *The Didache* 16:3; Ignatius of Antioch, *Philadelphians* 2:2; *2 Clement* 5:2-4).

not spare the flock: The verb *pheidomai* in such a context means to withhold from ill-treatment (Plato, *Apology* 31A), to be forebearing (Rom 11:21; 1 Cor 7:28; 2 Cor 1:23; 13:2; 2 Pet 2:4, 5), or possibly, have compassion (LXX Ps 18:13; 71:13; Joel 2:17).

30. *speak deceptive things:* Or "perverted things"; this resembles the charge made against Jesus (Luke 23:2), and made by him against unbelievers (Luke 9:41). Paul also accuses Bar Jesus/Elymas of "perverting the ways of the Lord" (Acts 13:10); see also Matt 17:17 and Phil 2:15.

draw the disciples: Although Luke uses the middle voice of *apospaō* in the sense of "withdraw" (Luke 22:41; Acts 21:1), the active voice matches the metaphor of the sheep and wolves, for the verb has the sense of violently "tearing away" someone or something (Herodotus, *Persian Wars* 3:1).

31. *Be on the watch, therefore:* The command *grēgoreite* is a more vigorous version of the earlier exhortation to "look to yourselves and to the flock" (v. 28), and the "therefore" (*oun*) shows it to be an inference from the danger to the flock/disciples. For the exhortation to watchfulness, see Luke 12:37-39, but even more so, Matt 24:42-43; 25:13; 26:38, 41; Mark 13:35, 37; 14:34, 38; 1 Cor 16:13; Col 4:2; 1 Thess 5:6; 1 Pet 5:8; Rev 3:2-3; 16:15.

    remember that for three years: The remembrance (*mnēmoneuō*) of a model is a regular element in Hellenistic paraenetic instruction, and therefore also of the "farewell discourse" which is in reality a species of that larger genre (see Pseudo-Isocrates, *Demonicus* 9, 11; Lucian of Samosata, *Demonax* 1-2; *Nigrinus* 6-7; Plutarch, *The Education of Children* 13 [*Mor.* 9F]; *Progress in Virtue* 15 [*Mor.* 85A]). See also 2 Tim 1:3-6; 2:8; 2 Pet 1:9, 12-13. In Luke 17:32, the disciples are told to "remember Lot's wife" as a negative example. The phrase "night and day" echoes Paul's own language in 1 Thess 2:9; 3:10; 2 Thess 3:8; 1 Tim 5:5; 2 Tim 1:3, as does also the use of *noutheteō* ("admonish"), which is found only here in Luke-Acts, but with some frequency in Paul (Rom 15:14; 1 Cor 4:14; Col 1:28; 3:16; 1 Thess 5:12, 14; 2 Thess 3:15).

32. *I am entrusting you:* The verb *paratithēmi* is here used in the sense of "committing what is one's own into the care of another" (see Luke 12:48; 23:46); the usage is close to that in 1 Tim 1:18; 2 Tim 2:2; 1 Pet 4:19. Translating the phrase *tǭ logǭ tēs charitos autou* presents the same problems as the other constructions with *charis:* "the word that comes from him by gift/favor," "the message concerning his gift/favor," "the message/word that is his gift/favor."

    able to build: Luke uses "build up" (*oikodomeō*) very much in the Pauline sense both here and in 9:31, to refer to establishing and nurturing a community identity and stability (see Rom 14:19; 15:2; 1 Cor 3:9; 8:1; 10:23; 14:3-5, 12, 17, 26; 2 Cor 10:8; 12:19; 13:10; 1 Thess 5:11; Eph 4:12, 16, 29).

    bestow the inheritance: The rich and allusive image of "inheritance" (*klēronomia*) appears in Luke's parable of the vineyard (Luke 20:14, 32; for the biblical background, see the note on Luke 10:25). It is a symbol vigorously employed by Paul himself (1 Cor 6:9-10; 15:50; Gal 3:18, 29; 4:30; 5:21; Eph 1:14, 18; 5:5; Col 3:24; Titus 3:7).

    those who have been made holy: The perfect passive participle of *hagiazō* is used here as a substantive, as it is in another statement put in Paul's mouth (Acts 26:18), *tou labein autous . . . klēron en tois hēgiasmenois.* This construction also is familiar from Paul's letters (Rom 15:16; 1 Cor 1:2; 6:11; 7:14).

33. *silver or gold or garment:* The use of *epithymeō* is particularly striking not only because it recalls the commandment, "Do not covet" (*ouk epithymēseis*, LXX Exod 20:17), but also because it is the commandment of God singled out by Paul himself for special consideration in Rom 7:7; 1 Cor 10:6; Gal 5:17. For his own protestations against defrauding his communities in matters of

money, see 1 Cor 9:12; 2 Cor 7:2; 11:7-11, and for the prototypical expression of such a disclaimer, see the farewell discourse of Samuel to "all Israel" in 1 Sam 12:3-5. Disavowing the vice of *philargyria* ("love of money") was also a standard element in the *apologia* of the authentic philosopher (see Philostratus, *Life of Apollonius of Tyana* 1:34; Dio Chrysostom, *Oration* 32:9, 11; 1 Thess 2:5).

34. *these hands have attended to my needs:* In 18:3, Luke showed Paul working as a craftsman with Priscilla and Aquila. The statement here corresponds with Paul's own protestations concerning his self-support (1 Cor 4:12; 9:15-18; 1 Thess 4:11). The statement in 2 Thess 3:6-10 is remarkably close in spirit to the present passage. Nowhere does Paul himself suggest, however, that he supported others as well.

35. *I have given an example of these things:* The verb *hypodeiknymi* can mean simply "tell" (see Tob 1:19; 4:2; Luke 12:5; Acts 9:16), but at times it can take on the sense of "drawing a pattern" (see Luke 3:7; 6:47), and therefore of "providing an example"; compare the use of *deiknymi* in LXX Exod 25:40 and in 1 Cor 12:31.

necessary to help those who are weak: Luke's use of *kopiaō* ("labor") here is distinctive (compare Luke 5:5; 12:27), but is thoroughly Pauline in tone (see 1 Cor 4:12; 16:16; Gal 4:11; 2 Tim 2:6; above all, see Eph 4:28). The verb *antilambanomai* in the meaning of "help/assist" is found in the NT here, in Luke 1:54, and in 1 Tim 6:2. As for the designation "the weak," Luke otherwise applies it to those who are physically *ill* (Luke 4:40; 9:2; Acts 9:37), whereas the present use comes closer to Paul's application to those within the community who are "not strong" (Rom 14:1-2, 21; 1 Cor 1:27; 4:10; 8:11-12; 9:22; 12:22).

remember the words of the Lord Jesus: Although Luke uses "Lord Jesus" from the beginning of Acts (1:21; 4:33; 8:16; 11:17, 20; 15:11, 26; 16:31), the title has appeared with particular frequency in the Ephesian section, being used three times in this discourse (19:5, 13, 17; 20:21, 24, 35). For the use of "memory" in paraenesis, see the note on 20:31. The citation of Jesus' words here is similar to Peter's in 11:16, "I remembered the word of the Lord." In that case, Peter "remembered" a saying not found in the gospel as attributed to Jesus, but found instead in the mouth of the risen Jesus in Acts 1:5.

more blessed to give than to receive: For Luke's use of *makarios* ("blessed/happy"), see the note on Luke 1:45. This saying of Jesus does not occur in the present gospel tradition, although a variant of it appears in *1 Clement* 2:1. The sentiment has fairly wide distribution both in Jewish wisdom (Sir 4:31) and in Greek (see Plutarch, *Sayings of Kings and Commanders* (Ataxerxes 1) [*Mor.* 173D]; *Sayings of Kings* (Ptolemy Son of Lagus) [*Mor.* 181F]); Thucydides, *Peloponnesian War* 2, 97, 4). The gist of the statement is found in passages such as Luke 6:35-36, 38. See also *The Didache* 1:5; *Shepherd of Hermas* Mand. 2:4-6.

36. *fell to his knees:* Given the way Luke has portrayed Paul's trip to Jerusalem according to the pattern of Jesus, this gesture can be regarded as an imita-

tion of what Jesus did after *his* farewell discourse: *theis ta gonata proseucheto* (Luke 22:41).

38. *no longer see his face:* Luke conveys an unusual amount of emotional outpouring in response to Paul's words: tears, embraces, kisses, and the feeling of anguish (*odynōmenoi*; see Luke 2:48: 16:24-25). Since these are all made to focus on the statement of Paul's departure (thus highlighting it again for the reader), there can be no doubt that Luke is writing from a perspective given by a time after Paul's death. For such outbursts of emotion, even in sober historical accounts, see Philo, *Embassy to Gaius* 243; Josephus, *Jewish War* 2:402.

INTERPRETATION

Before setting Paul on the final leg of his journey to Jerusalem, Luke has him deliver a last discourse to the elders of the Church at Ephesus. We have noted often how deftly Luke employs the literary conventions of his age. At Jesus' last meal with his disciples, for example, we could see how Luke combined the conventions of the Hellenistic *symposium* with those of the "Farewell Discourse" or "Testament" that was found not only among philosophers (as in Diogenes Laertius, *Life of Epicurus* 10:16-22), but especially in Jewish literature running from Gen 49:1-28 to the *Testaments of the Twelve Patriarchs*.

Luke makes use of the same literary conventions here. By so doing, he accomplishes two things: a) the form enables him to deliver the final "insider" interpretation of Paul before his long series of trials and defense speeches, so that the reader is able to grasp "how Paul was" for his churches—in effect supplying the sort of intimate portrait that the frantic pace of travels and tribulations had not till now allowed; b) the discourse reminds the reader once more of the prophet Jesus, whose own passion Luke wants the reader to perceive as the template for Paul's own—like Jesus before *his* death, Paul reminds his readers of his own pattern of life which is to be a model for their imitation, and warns them of things to come.

The elements of the "Farewell Discourse" are present in a highly compressed form: the sketch of Paul's life and activity (20:18-21); the prediction of his own destiny (20:22-23, 25); the prediction of what will befall the Church after his departure (20:28-30); the exhortation of how they should behave in his absence (20:28, 31). Within these bare bones, Luke has packed a number of behavioral norms as well: Paul's openness in proclamation (20:20) that has led to the disclosure of "all God's will" (20:27); his constant admonishment over a three-year period (20:31); his lack of covetousness and his working to support himself and others (20:33-34). And Luke has added as well an impressive collection of spiritual dispositions to accompany this behavior: lowlymindedness (20:19) and tears (20:19, 31), devotion to the ministry even in the face of chains and afflictions (20:24).

These components remind us that the "Farewell Discourse" is in reality a kind of paraenetic discourse, in which the main point is the instruction of the listener in certain moral values. As always in such discourses, there is the presentation of a model that they are to remember and to imitate, with the specific maxims making the example more explicit. In the present case, all of Paul's actions and dispositions are intended to communicate an example that the elders after him (and the readers of Luke-Acts) can imitate (20:31, 35). The final thing they are all to "remember," we notice, are "the words of the Lord Jesus," which connect Paul's behavior and that of the elders after him to the story of Jesus, summarized in this otherwise unattested saying, "It is more blessed to give than to receive." The ultimate model for imitation is the one who was "in your midst as the one who serves at table" (Luke 22:27).

But when all these formal conventions have been computed, it is undeniable that Luke's *prosōpopoiia*, or ability to deliver a speech in character, here is shown in convincing fashion. This is surely not Stephen or Peter delivering the speech. It is unmistakably Paul, and a Paul who presents himself to this community in terms remarkably like the ones we recognize in the letters we know Paul himself wrote to his communities. There is no need to repeat here all the textual evidence displayed verse by verse in the notes. But it is important to recognize that Luke accurately represents not only a number of distinctively Pauline themes, but does so in language which is specifically and verifiably Paul's. As so often in this intriguing work, just when Luke seems totally definable in terms of literary convention, he surprises us with a grace note that escapes such reduction.

FOR REFERENCE AND FURTHER STUDY

Barrett, C. K. "Paul's Address to the Ephesian Elders." *God's Christ and His People.* Eds. J. Jervell and W. A. Meeks. Oslo: Universitetsforlaget, 1977, 107–121.

Dupont, J. *Le discours de Milet. Testament pastoral de Paul Actes 20, 18-36.* Paris: Editions du Cerf, 1962.

Lambrecht, J. "Paul's farewell-Address at Miletus (Acts 20:17-38)." *Les Actes des Apôtres: traditions, rédaction, théologie.* Ed. J. Kremer. Gembloux: Leuven University Press, 1979, 307–337.

Michel, H.-J. *Die Abschiedsrede des Paulus an die Kirche Apg 20, 17-38: Motivgeschichte und Theologische Bedeutung.* SANT 35. Munich: Kösel-Verlag, 1973.

Munck, J. "Discours d'adieu dans le Nouveau Testament et dans la littérature biblique." *Aux Sources de la Tradition Chrétienne.* Bibliotheque Theologique; Melange Maurice Goguel. Neuchatel: Delachaux et Niestle, 1950, 155–170.

Prast, F. *Presbyter und Evangelium im nachapostolischer Zeit: Die Abschiedsrede des Paulus in Milet (Apg 20, 17-38)*. Forschung zur Bible 29. Stüttgart: Verlag Katholisches Bibelwerk, 1979.

42. *Prophecy of Paul's Fate* (21:1-14)

1. Having set sail, we withdrew from them. We made a straight run and came to Cos, and on the next day to Rhodes and from there to Patara. 2. When we found a boat that was crossing to Phoenicia, we went on board and set sail. 3. We sighted Cyprus and as we went past it we turned left, sailing to Syria and going down to Tyre, for there the boat had its cargo unloaded. 4. When we located the disciples we remained there for seven days. Through the Holy Spirit, they warned Paul not to go up to Jerusalem. 5. But when we had completed the days, we left. We went outside the city, with all of them, including women and children, seeing us off. Falling to our knees on the beach, we prayed. 6. We said farewell to each other. We went up onto the boat, and they returned to their own homes. 7. When we finished the voyage from Tyre, we reached Ptolemais, and greeting the brothers we remained one day with them. 8. The next day we departed. We came to Caesarea. We went into the house of Philip, the proclaimer of the good news, who was one of the seven. We remained with him. 9. He had four virgin daughters who practiced prophecy. 10. While we were staying there for many days, a certain prophet named Agabus came down from Jerusalem. 11. He came toward us. He picked up Paul's belt. He bound his own hands and feet. He said, "Thus says the Holy Spirit! So will the Jews in Jerusalem bind the man whose belt this is, and they will hand him over to the power of the Gentiles!" 12. Hearing this, we and the local people began to entreat him not to go up to Jerusalem. 13. Then Paul responded, "What are you doing, weeping and breaking my heart? For I am prepared not only to be bound but even to die in Jerusalem for the name of the Lord Jesus." 14. Since he was not persuaded, we grew quiet, saying, "May the will of the Lord be done."

NOTES

1. *Cos . . . Patara:* The first person plural ("we") narration picks up again from 20:15. Luke names three stops along the coastline of Asia, with Cos and Rhodes being islands (Pliny the Elder, *Natural History* 5:132-134), and Patara a seaport on the coast of Lycia. Codex D adds the words "and Myra" after Patara, referring to a town further east of Patara and an important port for

the Egyptian sea-trade (see Acts 27:5). A similar itinerary is traced for the lovers Habrocomes and Anthia in Xenophon's novel, *The Ephesians:* they start in Ephesus (1, 10, 4), stop in stages in Cos and Rhodes (1, 11, 6), are waylaid by Phoenician pirates (1, 13, 1) who take them eventually to Tyre (1, 15, 2).

3. *we sighted Cyprus:* The participle *anaphanantes* is here transitive and active (compare the use of *anaphaino* in Luke 19:11). The boat approaches Cyprus from the northwest, and as it moves past its eastern coast, turns to the left (port) and heads for Syria and then Tyre in Phoenicia.

4. *located the disciples:* The verb *aneuriskō* means to "discover/find out," but is used here in the same sense as in Luke 2:16 (compare also 4 Macc 3:14). The Gospel had portrayed people from Tyre coming to hear the preaching of Jesus (Luke 6:17), and in Acts 11:19 missionaries were said to have passed through Phoenicia. According to Acts 15:3, Paul and the Antiochean delegation were able to greet the Christians in Phoenicia on the way to the great council. Paul is not therefore "discovering" Christians as though their presence was a surprise, but "locating" them.

through the Holy Spirit they warned Paul: Literally, "they said to Paul," but the context allows the stronger translation, "warned." The narrative now provides the "city by city" testimony from the Holy Spirit that Paul had referred to in his discourse to the Ephesian elders (20:23). We will shortly (v. 23) see an even more dramatic example.

5. *on the beach we prayed:* Here as in 20:36, the group prayer enhances the solemn religious character of Paul's journey to Jerusalem; for the theme of prayer in Luke-Acts, see Luke 1:10; 3:21; 6:12; 9:18, 28-29; 10:21-22; 11:1-4; 18:1-8; 22:31, 39-46; 23:46; 24:53; Acts 1:14, 24; 2:47; 4:23; 6:6; 8:15; 9:11; 10:2, 9; 12:5, 12; 13:3; 16:25.

6. *returned to their own homes:* The phrase *ta idia* means literally "one's own things/interests/property" especially as opposed to public ones; see the contrast between *idion* and *koinon* in Acts 4:32. The usage here resembles that in Luke 18:28 as well as John 1:11 and 19:27.

8. *the house of Philip:* For a sketch of the city of Ptolemais, see Strabo, *Geography* 16, 2, 25. The narrative had brought Philip to Caesarea at the end of his missionary work in 8:40. Here Luke identifies him again for the reader as "one of the seven," referring back to his appointment with six others by the apostles in 6:3 almost as if it were a title. Philip is also identified as *ho euangelistēs* ("evangelist/proclaimer of the good news"), a title that appears only here in Luke-Acts (compare Eph 4:11; 2 Tim 4:5), although it defines Philip's characteristic activity (*euangelizomai ton logon*) within the story (8:4, 12, 35, 40).

9. *daughters who practiced prophecy:* There may be no special point attached to the reference to Philip's daughters as "virgins" (*parthenoi*), although prophetesses in Hellenistic religion such as those who were the mouthpieces of Apollo at Delphi were often *parthenoi* (see Plutarch, *The Oracles at Delphi* 22 [*Mor.* 405C]); Pausanias, *Description of Greece* 10, 12, 6). In later apocryphal Acts of the Apostles, we begin to see the formation of distinct groups of Christian

"virgins" (see *Acts of Paul and Thecla* 7). The anarthrous present participle *prophēteuousai* should be taken as referring to their customary practice and as a means of identifying them rather than to something they did on this occasion. For the prophetic portrayal of their father Philip, see the interpretation of Acts 8:4-25.

10. *prophet named Agabus:* Another character from earlier in the story reappears. In contrast to the careful cross-referencing given to Philip, however, Luke introduces Agabus in much the same way as he had in 11:27, with no indication that the reader should remember him.

11. *picked up Paul's belt:* Like some of the prophets of old (Jer 19:1-13; Ezek 4:1-17), Agabus seems to have specialized in prophecies that involved symbolic gestures. Thus in 11:28 he "signed" (*esēmanen*) the coming famine, and here he uses Paul's belt/girdle (*zōnē*) to physically enact the import of his words.
    thus says the Holy Spirit: The introduction *tade legei* ("thus says," from the demonstrative pronoun *hode*), is familiar from legal decrees of the ancient world (Josephus, *Antiquities of the Jews* 11:26) and above all from the LXX version of the prophets, many of whom began their oracles with "Thus says the Lord" (see Amos 3:11; 5:16; Nah 1:2; Haggai 1:6; Zech 1:16; Isa 3:16; Jer 2:31; Ezek 4:13). The only other instance in the NT is found in the "Spirit Letters" of the Book of Revelation, which probably derive at least in part from the oracles of Christian prophets (see Rev 2:1, 8, 12, 18; 3:1, 7, 14). The use of "the Holy Spirit" with the formula is, so far as I can tell, unparalleled.
    bind the man: The symbolic act of binding (*deō*) and the oracle concerning binding (*deō*) together pick up Paul's own statement that the Spirit was telling him "in every city" that "chains" (*desma*) awaited him in Jerusalem (20:23), and in fact creates of 20:22 a pun: Paul says, "bound (*deō*) by the Spirit I am going to Jerusalem." The fulfillment of this part of the prophecy is found in 21:33, though it is not actually "the Jews" who are responsible for the binding.
    hand him over to the power of the Gentiles: The use of the verb *paradidōmi* and the phrase "to the power of" (literally "the hands of") the Gentiles (*ethnōn*) makes this prophecy echo the passion predictions of Jesus himself in Luke 9:44; 18:32.

13. *weeping and breaking my heart:* The emotional level in this scene is very high, as it was also in the farewell at Miletus (Acts 20:36-38). The verb *synthruptō* means literally "to break/crush" (see the literal use in Josephus, *Antiquities* 10:207). In the last several scenes, Luke has portrayed Paul as a deeply sympathetic human being who generated warmth and affection among his followers. For the motif of turning away pleas of followers to avoid one's death, see Socrates in Plato, *Phaedo* 116E-117A.
    I am prepared . . . to die in Jerusalem: Paul's statement echoes the one Luke has him make in his farewell discourse (20:24), as well as the fears Paul himself expressed concerning his acceptance in Jerusalem (Rom 15:31-32). The prospect of "death in Jerusalem" also inevitably recalls the motif of Jerusalem as the murderer of the prophets (Luke 11:49-51; 13:33-34).

for the name of the Lord Jesus: The willingness to suffer "in behalf of the name" (*hyper tou onomatos*) places Paul in line with the first apostles (Acts 5:41), and in fulfillment of Jesus' own prophecies concerning the destiny of his followers (Luke 6:22; 21:12, 17). The Jerusalem council had earlier certified Paul and Barnabas as having "dedicated their lives for the name of our Lord" (15:26); see also the statement to Ananias in 9:16.

14. *will of the Lord be done:* This petition is lacking from the best *mss* for the Lukan version of the Lord's Prayer in Luke 11:2 (compare Matt 6:10), but does appear as Jesus' prayer before his passion (Luke 22:42; compare Matt 26:42). See also Paul's use of "God willing" in Acts 18:21.

INTERPRETATION

In Paul's "Farewell-Discourse" to the elders of Ephesus (20:17-35), Luke provided the readers a summation of Paul's ministry and character, as well as a programmatic prophecy of what awaited him at the end of his journey to Jerusalem. As the narrative of that journey once more resumes (21:1), the reader continues to be prepared—in the space provided by "reading time"—for the shocking events to come.

At one level, the journey continues to have the character of a bald itinerary that we observed in 20:13-16. The first-person plural narration continues. The stages of the journey are noted dispassionately and, so far as we can tell, accurately. The island and mainland harborages for the typical coast-hugging Mediterranean sea voyage correspond, for example, with those described in Xenophon's novel, *The Ephesians* (see notes), except that the novel's narration is not in the first person plural. The need to wait for a ship sailing in the proper direction (21:2), and the determination of destination by the ship's place of unloading cargo (21:3) fit the realities of sea-travel in that world.

At another level, Luke infuses the passage over sea and land with a weight of prophetic significance. When the travellers touch down in Caesarea, they meet characters from earlier in the story, who remain where Luke had left them: Philip the proclaimer of the Gospel had reached Caesarea at the end of his mission through Samaria and the coastal towns (8:40). Now he has four grown daughters who are also prophets (21:8-9)! The Jerusalem prophet Agabus had "come down from Jerusalem" to Antioch with a prophetic sign much earlier in the story (11:27-28); now he "comes down from Jerusalem" again with a grimmer sign and oracle (21:11). By enmeshing Paul with these characters, Luke reminds the reader that Paul and the narrative are completing a full circle. The trip to Jerusalem is not simply a trip to a geographical location, but a return to a narrative "place" that is, for Paul, filled with the memories and possibilities of conflict.

The Holy Spirit, as Paul had declared in his discourse (20:23) continues to "witness in every city" to him concerning what awaits him (see 21:4, 11). The prophetic act and oracle of Agabus simply give the most explicit expression to the mood of foreboding. Things will not turn out, in fact, exactly as the prophet says: the "Jews" will not be the ones who bind Paul, although they surely create the occasion for it. But the language of the oracle once more conforms Paul to the image of the prophet Jesus on *his* journey to Jerusalem: Agabus declares that Paul, too, will be "handed over" and "into the power of the Gentiles," which makes his prophecy remarkably close to the passion predictions of Jesus (9:44; 18:32). And like Jesus, Paul declares his willingness to die in Jerusalem for the name of his Lord (21:13).

The response of those who witness these things is to provide dramatic commentary and emphasis. The chorus expresses in place of the reader the anguish and dismay that must be felt in face of these hard realities (21:12-13), but also gives the reader an example of the appropriate response of obedient faith, to declare, finally, "May the will of the Lord be done."

For Reference and Further Study

Corssen, P. "Die Töchter des Philippus." *ZNW* 2 (1901) 289-299.

Ellis, E. E. "The Role of the Christian Prophet in Acts." *Apostolic History and the Gospel*. Eds. W. Gasque and R. P. Martin. Exeter: Paternoster Press, 1970, 55-67.

Mattill, A. J. "The Jesus-Paul Parallels and the Purpose of Luke-Acts: H. H. Evans Reconsidered." *NovT* 17 (1975) 15-46.

Talbert, C. H. *Literary Patterns, Theological Themes, and the Genre of Luke-Acts*. SBLMS 20. Missoula: Scholars Press, 1974, 15-18.

Tannehill, R. *Narrative Unity* 2:262-267.

43. *Paul and the Jerusalem Leadership (21:15-26)*

15. After these days we prepared ourselves and went up to Jerusalem. 16. Some disciples from Caesarea also went with us. They brought us to Mnason, a certain Cypriote, an early disciple, so we could lodge with him. 17. And when we arrived in Jerusalem, the brothers welcomed us gladly. 18. On the next day, Paul went in with us to James. And all the elders were present. 19. After he greeted them, he related to them one by one the things God had done among the Gentiles through his ministry. 20. When they heard, they gave glory to God. But they said to him, "You see, brother, how many thousands among the Jews have come to belief. They are all zealous for the Law. 21. But they have been informed concerning you that you are teaching apostasy from Moses to all the Jews among the Gentiles, that you say they are not to circumcise their children nor to follow their customs. 22. What then should be done? They will surely hear that you have come. 23. Do this thing, therefore, that we are telling you: there are four men with us who have taken a vow upon themselves. 24. Take them with you and be purified with them. And supply the funds for them to have their heads shaven. Then everyone will realize that the things they have been told about you have nothing to them. Instead, you live by and keep the Law. 25. Now concerning the Gentiles who have come to belief, we have sent the decision that they should keep themselves from food offered to idols, and blood, and that which is strangled, and sexual immorality." 26. Then Paul took along the men. On the following day he was purified with them. He was going into the Temple in order to announce the completion of the days of purification until the offering was made for each one of them.

NOTES

16. *Mnason, a certain Cypriote:* His hospitality was considerable, for by the narrative sequence, Paul was accompanied still by the delegates he had gathered in 20:4! This is the only mention of Mnason in the NT. The adjective *archaios* is similar to Luke's use of *archē* (see Luke 1:2; Acts 11:15, 25; 15:7). Perhaps Luke wants the reader to recognize him as one of those missionaries "from Cyrene and Cyprus" who early on had preached the gospel in Phoenicia (11:20).

so we could lodge with him: As in several other places, Luke gives us a glimpse of the network of hospitality established from the first because of the demands of itinerant missions (Acts 9:43; 10:6; 16:15, 40; 21:4, 8). The Western Text adds, "and when we arrived at a certain village, we stayed . . . ." which makes the stopover at Mnason's occur before the arrival in Jerusalem.

17. *brothers welcomed us gladly:* Luke makes every effort to show that Paul was not, in fact, rejected by the Jerusalem community (see Paul's own fears as

expressed in Rom 15:31). This is the only use of *asmenōs* ("gladly") in the NT, but see 3 Macc 3:15; 5:21, and especially Josephus, *Antiquities of the Jews* 4:131. For *apodechomai* as a gesture of hospitality, see Luke 8:40; 9:11; Acts 18:27; 28:30.

18. *all the elders were present:* James is clearly the leader and spokesperson, just as in 15:13—note that he is mentioned first and then the elders—but as in that earlier passage as well, the supporting presence of the board of elders is explicit (15:4, 6, 22-23).

19. *God had done . . . through his ministry:* The language echoes that used by Luke for Paul and Barnabas in their report to the Jerusalem council in 15:12: the use of *exēgeomai* ("relate"), and "what God had done among the Gentiles" is found in both passages. The main difference here is "through his ministry" (*diakonia*), which picks up the language of Paul's farewell discourse (20:24) not to mention the ambiguity of that term itself: is there an allusion here to the collection? The phrase "one by one" (*kath'hen hekaston*) is roughly equivalent to the *kathexes* of Peter's narration to the Jerusalem leadership in 11:4.

20. *gave glory to God:* As so often in Luke-Acts, this response (*doxazein ton theon*) signals a recognition of God's visitation in human experience (Luke 2:20; 5:25-26; 7:16; 13:13; 17:15; 18:43; 23:47; Acts 4:21). Note especially that this was also the response of the Jerusalem leadership to Peter's narration concerning the first Gentile converts (11:18).

they said to him: In contrast to James' individual judgment at the Jerusalem council (15:19), the whole board of elders is made to speak here (*eipon*); the only significant textual variant is the equally plural participle *eipontes*. Compare the joint statement of the Jerusalem council in 15:23-29.

thousands among the Jews: The invitation to "see" can be taken quite literally, since Luke has in fact shown in his Jerusalem narrative how "thousands" of Jews responded to the apostolic preaching: three thousand (Acts 2:41), five thousand (4:4), and more (6:7). Such substantial success among the historic Israel is, as this entire commentary has tried to demonstrate, a critical stage in Luke's apologetic argument, or historical theodicy, that intends to show how God remained faithful to his promise.

zealous for the Law: The adjective *zēlōtēs* is applied in the LXX mainly to God (Exod 20:5; 34:14; Deut 4:24; 5:9; 6:15; Nah 1:2), but in 2 Macc 4:2 is used for those who were "zealous for the Law" (see also the use of *zēloō* in 1 Macc 2:26-27, 50, 54, 58). Paul refers to himself in Gal 1:14 as being *zēlōtēs* for the traditions of his ancestors. The term suggests not only "zeal" for observance, but also "jealousy" for honor to be paid to Torah, and therefore hostility toward any perceived derogation of that honor. In Luke's list of the Twelve, Simon is identified as "the one called *zēlōtēs*" (6:15; see Acts 1:13). The origins, complexion, and associations of the Jewish resistance party called the zealots, the "fourth philosophy" described by Josephus (*Antiquities of the Jews* 18:3-15; *Jewish War* 2:118) are difficult to define precisely, but no such technical reference seems intended here.

21. *teaching apostasy from Moses:* Paul is not himself accused of breaking Torah. The charges rather have a strong resemblance to those brought against Stephen in 6:13-14, with "Moses" standing as equivalent to "the Law" (see also Luke 16:29; 24:27; Acts 6:11; 15:1, 21). For "apostasy" (*apostasia*) in this context, compare 1 Macc 2:15.

    Jews among the Gentiles: It is possible that *ethnē* should be translated here as "nations," since the reference seems clearly to be to the Diaspora, with the complaint reflecting the expectable worry in the national cult center about the observance of those far afield. The concern in general seems not to have been entirely without basis, as we can see from the remarks concerning non-observance among Alexandrian Jews in Philo, *Migration of Abraham* 89-92.

    circumcise their children or follow their customs: The use of *mē* with the present infinitives could also be translated, "teach them to *stop* circumcising/following." The reader knows, of course, that Paul has taught no such thing, and his own practice shows that the charges are a canard: he has circumcised his own associate Timothy (16:3), has taken a Nazarite vow (18:18), has observed the feasts (20:5, 17). On the other hand, Luke is here consistent in characterizing such things as the "customs" (*ethē*) of the Jewish people, which are appropriate to their cultural identity but have no direct pertinence to the life of faith (see 6:14; 15:1; 16:21; 26:3; 28:17). In Paul's own letters, there is no suggestion that he ever advocated *Jewish* believers forsaking circumcision or their customs; his debates concerning circumcision revolved completely around the *necessity* of Gentiles undergoing the process for full inclusion in the community.

22. *what then should be done:* The question reads literally, "what therefore is it (*ti oun estin*)," a form of rhetorical question which, with several variations, is found widely attested in diatribal literature (see Epictetus, *Discourses* 1, 6, 12; 1, 7, 7; 2, 4, 8), and in Paul's letters (see 1 Cor 14:15, 26). The question is intended to set up its own immediate response.

    will surely hear: The Western Text interjects the phrase "there must be (*dei*) gathered an assembly (*plēthos*)," but this seems to miss the point of the subsequent statement, which makes perfectly clear that these zealots for the Law among the Jewish Christians must be appeased by Paul's demonstration of piety.

23. *taken a vow upon themselves:* The mention of the shaving of the head in the next line indicates that this is again a case of the Nazarite vow (Num 6:1-21). For the complexities of the legislation concerning that vow in Numbers and in the rabbinic tradition, see the Mishnah tractates *Nedarim* and especially *Nazir;* and the notes on Acts 18:18.

24. *be purified with them:* The ritual of purification (*hagnizō*) is frequently found in connection with the cult (Num 8:21; 19:12; 31:19; 1 Chr 15:12, 14; 2 Chr 29:16), but is not in fact mentioned in connection with the Nazarite vow in Num 6:1-21. The legislation of *m.Naz.* 6:5–8:2, however, envisages a number of cases in which someone who had taken a vow, which forbade "uncleanness, cutting off the hair, and aught that comes from the vine" (*m.Naz.* 6:5),

could contract ritual uncleanness and require purification before being able to shave the head in completion of the vow (*m.Naz.* 6:6). Paul could also have been considered, by a strict construal of the Law by those "zealous" for it according to Pharisaic interpretation, to have been rendered unclean by his journey among the Gentiles, and in particular by his contact with a "corpse" (see the story of Eutyches, 20:7-12). It is not clear to us, in short, what is going on.

supply the funds: The legislation in Num 6:21 speaks of the Nazarite making an offering "according to his vow, apart from what else he can afford" (using the language of "gift," *dōron*). See the discussion of the "hair-offering" in *m.Naz.* 2:5-6. Josephus provides the example of Herod Agrippa I as someone who (according to the most likely reading of the passage) assumed the expenses for the hair-offering of a large number of Nazarites (*Antiquities* 19:294). This is the first clear indication given by Luke that Paul came to Jerusalem with substantial funds (see also 24:17, 26).

live by and keep the Law: The verb *stoicheō* means literally "to be in line with," and from that means to "live in accord with" (see Paul's usage in Rom 4:12; Gal 5:25; 6:16; Phil 3:18). For "keeping" (*phylassō*) the Law in the sense of observance, see Acts 7:53; Rom 2:26; Gal 6:13. The implicit logic here is that Paul would not preach something contrary to his own practice, therefore his observance of this act of piety would refute that charge concerning his "teaching." In his letters, Paul seems not to have enjoyed the same assumption among his opponents (see Gal 5:11).

25. *we have sent the decision:* Literally, "we have sent [a letter/delegation] deciding," with the same use of *krinō* as in 15:19. The actual letter sent by the Jerusalem council to the Gentile churches is in 15:23-29. The real oddity is why they should need to inform Paul about this letter, if he had taken part in the original deliberations (15:12) and had been one of the deliverers of the letter (15:25). It is possible that Luke is, in one direction or another, altering the historical reality, or, more likely, exercising his accustomed authorial right to remind the reader of important points. Codex D has a fascinating addition to the text: after "concerning the Gentiles who have come to belief," it inserts, "they have nothing to say against you, for" and then continues, "we have sent the decision . . . ." The emendation makes clear that the charge against Paul does not concern either the validity of the Gentile mission *or* what he has taught them, but strictly what concerns Jewish believers.

from food offered to idols: For the complex textual issues surrounding the three versions of the "apostolic decree" (15:20, 29; 21:25), see the notes on 15:20. The present version is noteworthy most of all for: a) changing the order of the prohibitions; b) the Western Text's *not* having a version of "the golden rule."

26. *going into the Temple:* Num 6:13 calls for the vow to be completed at the "tent of meeting" which was taken to mean the Temple. The imperfect of *eiseimi* ("to go in") suggests a repeated action by Paul, although the situation as a whole remains somewhat obscure. Why did Paul need to "announce" any-

thing? Was he simply accompanying the men, or was he also undergoing the completion of his own vow (18:18)? The likeliest possibility is that he was required to "announce," in the sense of "check off" with some priest each day of purification as it passed.

completion of the days of purification: The legislation in Num 6:9 calls for the Nazarite who has been defiled by someone dying suddenly beside him to purify himself for seven days, before shaving his head on the seventh day and making the offering on the eighth day (see also *m.Naz.* 6:6). Compare the reference in 1 Macc 3:49, "they stirred up the Nazarites who had completed the days" (*hoi eplērōsan tas hēmeras*).

INTERPRETATION

With Paul's arrival in Jerusalem, the reader also comes to one of the most difficult and painful parts of Luke's narrative. Some of the difficulty and pain are connected to the conflicts Paul will experience in the city. But some is attached to the reader's sense that there may be some distance between the story as Luke tells it and the historical realities as they are suggested by Paul's letters. Luke's account is not utterly transparent, and its obscurities may owe something to an attempt to make his story come out better than the evidence suggests it did.

The scene between Paul and the Jerusalem leaders (especially James) is even on its own terms somewhat odd. But when we read it against the backdrop of the information provided in Paul's letters concerning his planned trip to Jerusalem, puzzlement deepens. Was Paul accepted by the Jerusalem community or not? Was his eventual arrest and imprisonment something entirely outside the community's control and concerning which it was powerless to intervene? Or was Paul abandoned by the Jerusalem community? Was he, possibly, even set up?

We can begin to sort through the problem by reminding ourselves of what we know otherwise about Paul's last trip to Jerusalem. As we have seen, he had taken up an elaborate collection from the Gentile churches as a symbol of reconciliation between these communities and the Jewish believers in Jerusalem (Gal 2:10; 1 Cor 16:1-4; 2 Cor 8-9). He saw the collection as a way of completing his Eastern mission before beginning a new venture in the West, for which Rome was to be his new base of operations (Rom 15:22-29). We know as well that Paul was fearful that he faced danger in Jerusalem. He asked the Roman Church to pray that "my service (*diakonia*) for Jerusalem may be acceptable to the saints," and also that he "may be delivered from the unbelievers in Judea" (Rom 15:31). As Luke himself shows us, and as Paul's captivity letters confirm, he did not escape from the "unbelievers in Judea": he was arrested, and eventually brought to Rome as a prisoner.

The more difficult question is whether Paul's "service for Jerusalem" was rejected by "the saints" as well. On this point, Luke's narrative is at best unclear. Certainly he attributes Paul's troubles to the "Jews from Asia" rather than members of the messianic community (21:27). But it is striking that apart from the (very private and personal) help given by Paul's nephew (23:16-22) and the single mention in 24:23 of "Paul's associates" being allowed to attend to him while in prison at Caesarea, Luke says nothing about Paul being supported. And even these aids were offered by a family member and Paul's own co-workers. Nothing is said about any role played by the Jerusalem community itself during the whole period of Paul's troubles, either in Jerusalem or in Caesarea. This passivity is even stranger if we take seriously the emphatic point made by his earlier narrative concerning this community's size and influence among the people (see especially Acts 4-6).

Luke's silence about community support for Paul is rendered even more startling when we observe his almost total silence concerning the collection. As noted earlier, Luke knew of Paul's movements and those of his delegates, and has them all coming to Jerusalem as a solemn delegation. Paul's "report" to the elders concerning all that God had done among the Gentiles through his ministry actually uses the same term (*diakonia*) that Paul himself had used for his collection (Rom 15:31). Later, we will see that he has Paul himself make reference to the "alms for his nation" that he was carrying on this trip (24:17), which clearly indicates that Luke knew at least that Paul came for the purpose of delivering a large sum of money. This is confirmed also by Luke's recognition that Felix was expecting to receive a bribe from Paul (24:26).

In light of all this, Luke's portrayal of the meeting between Paul and the Jerusalem leadership is deeply ambiguous. Not only does James and the board of elders assume an authority over Paul that appears at odds with Paul's own statements concerning his relations with the Jerusalem leaders (Gal 2:5-10); not only do they recommend that he perform a "gesture of reconciliation" (taking part in a ritual of purification) for the sake of appeasing his opponents that Paul himself would, on the evidence, regard as a craven capitulation (see Gal 2:3); but—most shockingly—their recommendation completely ignores his own gift of money which he interpreted as an act of *koinōnia* ("fellowship"), and according to Paul's own testimony was in fact part of his agreement with the Jerusalem leadership (Gal 2:10).

More than at any other place in his long narrative, the historian is made to wonder whether Luke's specific religious preoccupations—above all his concern to show a peaceful relationship between the apostles, and the fundamental continuity between the Jewish and Gentile missions—have here led to a distortion of the historical facts that even the author seems to have known. Possibly not, but the evidence not only from Paul but even from his own text seems to support that conclusion.

The purpose of this commentary, however, has not been historical reconstruction, even if some things along those lines are required if we are to have a sufficiently sharp perception of Luke's literary and religious aims. And in this case the apparently difficult character of the "facts" helps us understand both the author's desire to reshape the events and his difficulty in doing so. How then does Luke portray the encounter?

First, he obviously seeks to make this meeting mirror that of the Jerusalem council in Acts 15. As Paul and his party move through a series of local stops before reaching Jerusalem, they are welcomed just as the Antiochean delegation had been (15:3). Like that earlier delegation, this one is "welcomed gladly by the brothers" (15:4). Like the earlier delegation as well, this one "relates what God had done" (15:4, 12). And like the Jerusalem leadership's response to Peter's defense of his Gentile initiative, we find the brothers "giving glory to God," (11:18), which is Luke's signal for a recognition of God's visitation. In every way available to him, Luke signals that Paul's arrival is one welcomed by the Jerusalem leadership; they and Paul are in fundamental agreement, as is shown further by James' otherwise odd repetition of the "apostolic decree" in 21:25. The issue, as Luke puts it, does not have to do with the Gentile mission or the terms in which Paul is carrying it out. Luke does not picture James and the Jerusalem leadership renewing the earlier debate (15:5-7); that, Luke is saying, is finished.

Instead, the issue is Paul's own fidelity to his Jewish heritage, and whether he has in fact "taught apostasy from Moses," not to *Gentiles*, but to "Jews among the Gentiles," by telling them to stop circumcising their children and abandon the practice of the Mosaic customs. We recognize a new version of the attack raised in 15:1, 5 by the "party of the Pharisees" among the Jerusalem Church who are now further characterized as "zealous for the Law" (21:20). Any reader of Acts up to this point will recognize the canard for what it is; Luke has gone out of his way to portray Paul as a Jew and as a particularly observant one (see notes).

But by posing this "challenge from within," Luke can account for the odd request from the leadership (it is under pressure for its zealous majority) and for Paul's presence in the Temple, as well as why once he is arrested, Paul is not helped by the community as such: it was divided from within concerning Paul's loyalty to Judaism. Everything in Luke's subsequent narrative (particularly in Paul's defense speeches) will continue to show why this was an unjust suspicion. But by expressing it so sharply, Luke makes convincing to the readers why Paul must undergo a test of his fidelity on the terms of his critics. He also thereby shifts the blame for Paul's subsequent troubles entirely onto the outsiders who attack him in the Temple.

For Reference and Further Study

Achtemeier, P. J. *The Quest for Unity in the New Testament Church.* Philadelphia: Fortress, 1987.

Berger, K. "Almosen für Israel: zum historischen Kontext der paulinischen Kollekte." *NTS* 23 (1977) 180–204.

Bruce, F. F. "The Church in Jerusalem in the Acts of the Apostles." *BJRL* 67 (1984–85) 641–661.

von Campenhausen, H. "Die Nachfolge des Jakobus: zum Frage eines urchristlichen 'Kälifats'." *ZKG* 63 (1950–51) 133–144.

Diehl, H. "Das sogenannte Aposteldekret." *ZNW* 10 (1909) 277–296.

Jervell, J. "James: The Defender of Paul." *Luke and the People of God.* Minneapolis: Augsburg Press, 1972, 185–207.

Kittel, G. "Die Stellung des Jakobus zu Judentum und Heidenchristentum." *ZNW* 30 (1931) 145–157.

44. Riot in Jerusalem (21:27-40)

27. When the seven days were about to be completed, the Jews from Asia saw him in the Temple. They agitated the whole crowd and laid hands on him. 28. They cried out, "Israelites, help! This is the man who is teaching everyone everywhere against the people and against the Law and against this place! More than that, he has even led Greeks into the Temple and has profaned this holy place!" 29. For they had earlier seen Trophimus the Ephesian in the city with him. They thought that Paul had taken him into the Temple. 30. The whole city was disturbed, and people came running together. Seizing Paul, they dragged him out of the Temple, and immediately the gates were closed. 31. While they were trying to kill him, a report reached the tribune of the cohort that all of Jerusalem was in turmoil. 32. He immediately gathered soldiers and centurions and rushed down on them. When they saw the tribune and the soldiers, they stopped beating Paul. 33. The tribune approached and apprehended him and ordered him to be bound with two chains. He asked who he was and what he had done. 34. Different people in the crowd shouted out different things. Since he could not gain firm knowledge because of the tumult, he ordered him to be led into the barracks. 35. When they reached the steps, it came to him being carried by the soldiers because of the violence of the crowd, 36. for the mass of the people

was following. They were crying out, "Away with him!" 37. As he was about to be taken into the barracks, Paul said to the tribune, "Is it allowed for me to say something to you?" He responded, "Do you know Greek? 38. Then you are not the Egyptian who some time ago stirred up and led into the desert the four thousand men who were assassins?" 39. Paul said, "I am a Jew from Tarsus of Cilicia. I am a citizen of no mean city. I beg you, allow me to speak to the people." 40. When he gave permission, Paul stood on the steps. He made a gesture to the people with his hand. When there was substantial silence, he addressed them in the Hebrew dialect.

NOTES

27. *the Jews from Asia:* For the seven-day period of purification, see the note on v. 26, above. Luke had earlier noted the hostility of the Asian (Ephesian) Jews towards Paul (19:9; 20:19). As in 2:5, we are not surprised to find Diaspora Jews in Jerusalem for the great pilgrimage feasts such as Pentecost (20:16); see Josephus, *Antiquities of the Jews* 14:337; 17:254; *Jewish War* 1:253; 2:42.

    agitated the whole crowd: The volatility of the great crowds at the pilgrimage feasts, where a perceived slight against the ancestral customs could quickly generate a riot that required suppression by the military authorities, is well attested by Josephus, *Jewish War* 1:88-89; 2:8-13; 2:42-48; 2:169-174; 2:223-227; 2:229-231; 2:315-320; 2:406-407; 2:449-456.

28. *against the people:* The first part of their charge picks up what was reported about Paul to the church elders (21:21), and Luke thus invites us to see these Asian Jews as the source of such "informing" (*katecheō*, 21:21, 24). The last part of their charge ("against this place") recalls the specific complaint made against Stephen in Acts 6:13-14.

    profaned this holy place: Literally, "he has made common" (*kekoinōken*, compare 10:15; 11:9). This is a far more serious charge since it involves action rather than simply "teaching." Gentiles were allowed into the outer court of the Temple, but were forbidden under penalty of death from entering into the inner court, or "holy place" (see Josephus, *Antiquities of the Jews* 15:417; *Jewish War* 5:193-194; 6:124-126; Philo, *Embassy to Gaius* 212). There is extant a version of the inscription which declares that any one "of another race" (*allogenēs*) who enters is liable to death (*aitios estai . . . thanaton*).

29. *Trophimus the Ephesian:* Luke makes clear that the charge is in fact false. Yes, they did see Paul "in the city" with a man whom as Asians themselves they could recognize as a Greek compatriot (see 20:4), but they were wrong about Paul's bringing him into the Temple.

30. *people came running together:* For other such urban excitations of the populace, see Acts 2:6; 8:1; 13:44, 50; 16:22; 17:5, and for the literary parallels in Hellenistic novels, see especially the note on 19:29. That in Jerusalem such scenes

were more than a fictional motif, however, see again the references from Josephus, *Jewish War*, cited in the note on 21:27.

the gates were closed: The action makes good sense on the literal level: the keepers of the Temple close the gates once the polluter has been expelled from it in order to keep the riot outside the sacred precincts. But does Luke also intend a symbolic "shutting of the gates" that marks Paul as an outsider to the cultic life of Judaism, and at the same time the final response of the non-Christian Jerusalem Jews to the apostle?

31. *the tribune of the Cohort:* We learn in 23:2 that his name is Claudius Lysias. The *chiliarchos* ("leader of a thousand") is the head of a "Cohort" (*speira*) which ideally consisted of a thousand soldiers, though the numbers in reality could vary. Since this unit could muster two centuries and some four hundred and seventy soldiers as an escort for Paul's journey to Caesarea (23:23), it must have been at full strength. That the action taken here corresponds with the realities of life in Jerusalem during those tumultuous years, see Josephus, *Jewish War* 2:315-320. From this point on in the narrative, Paul will have almost constant contact with the Roman military.

33. *bound with two chains:* Probably thus bound to a soldier on each side; in approximate fashion, the prophecy of Agabus is coming true: Paul is "bound" and is handed over to the power of the Gentiles (21:11). For the use of "two chains" compare the imprisonment of Peter in 12:6.

34. *could not gain firm knowledge:* The shouting of different things from the crowd reminds us of the scene in the theater at Ephesus (19:32). The phrase *gnōnai to asphales* is literally "know something certain," in the sense of "getting the facts" as opposed to all these shouted opinions. The expression will recur at Acts 22:30 and 25:26.

because of the tumult: The term *thorubos* (see Acts 17:5; 20:1) is frequently used for such riotous events (see Philo, *Against Flaccus* 120; 3 Macc 5:48; Josephus, *Jewish War* 1:201; 2:611). In his *apologia*, Paul will deny that he had himself created any *thorubos* in the Temple (Acts 24:18).

led into the barracks: The *parembolē* is literally an enclosure, and specifically a military camp. Here as in the remainder of the narrative (22:24; 23:10, 16, 32; 28:16), it will refer to the barracks where soldiers were kept and where prisoners could be kept. In this case the Fortress Antonia is meant. It was built by Herod the Great on the basis of an earlier Hasmonean fortification (Josephus, *Antiquities of the Jews* 18:91-92) to the northwest of the Temple and connected to the Temple precincts by steps. A full description of this great building, "from its possession of all conveniences it seemed a town, from its magnificence a palace," is found in Josephus, *Jewish War* 5:238-247.

36. *mass of the people:* The translation is made difficult because Luke once more uses *plēthos tou laou*, which could hypothetically mean "assembly of the people" (see Luke 8:37; 19:37; 23:27; Acts 6:2; 14:4; 15:12), an identification which would gain special piquancy from their cry of "away with him" (*aire auton*). The cry means in context, "kill him," and echoes the cry of "the crowd" against Jesus in the hearing before Pilate, "away with this one" (*aire*

touton) in Luke 23:18 (see also John 19:15). But since in this case Luke makes *plēthos* roughly equivalent to *ochlos*, the less precise meaning of the term is to be preferred.

38. *then you are not the Egyptian:* However fallaciously, the tribune concludes (*ara*) from Paul's ability to speak Greek that he is not an Egyptian revolutionary. Josephus informs us of an Egyptian charlatan (*goēs*) who claimed to be a prophet during this period (the prefecture of Felix, ca. 54 C.E.; see 23:24). He led some 30,000 men to the Mount of Olives on the promise that his command would bring the city walls down. The Romans killed and captured hundreds of his followers, though he himself escaped. The tribune's assumption that he could be around and fomenting an uprising (*anastatoō*, see 17:6) in the Temple was not therefore unreasonable (see Josephus, *Jewish War* 2:261-263; *Antiquities of the Jews* 20:168-172).

led into the desert the four thousand men: Luke's account differs from that of Josephus in two important respects: a) he has four thousand men, rather than Josephus' thirty thousand; b) he has the Egyptian lead them *into* the desert, whereas Josephus had him lead the men either from Jerusalem or from the desert to the Mount of Olives.

who were assassins: The designation *sikarios* ("assassin") comes from the Latin name for a short dagger (*sica*), and thus, *sicarius* = "dagger-man." Josephus once more tells us about such violent revolutionaries in *Jewish War* 2:254-257 and *Antiquities of the Jews* 20:186-188. Josephus attributes to them many of the misfortunes that fell on the Jews during the revolt against Rome and its aftermath (see *Jewish War* 7:252-263; 7:409-419). It is difficult to disentangle with precision the different resistance groups in Palestine during this turbulent period, particularly since not only Luke but also Josephus himself tends to cluster them together: note, for example, the sequence of incidents involving gatherings in the desert, the first with Sicarii, the second with the Egyptian charlatan (Josephus, *Jewish War* 2:259-263).

39. *I am a Jew:* Literally, "I am a Jewish man"; Paul's response is noteworthy not only because it distinguishes him from "the Egyptian," but because it forms the point of his series of defense speeches that follow. He may speak Greek, but he also speaks Aramaic; he may be from a Diaspora city, but his upbringing is in Jerusalem; he may work among the Gentiles, but his zeal for God is the same as his compatriots.

a citizen of no mean city: Tarsus (9:30; 11:25) was in fact an important center of Hellenistic culture (Strabo, *Geography* 14, 5, 13-15), and in particular of Stoic philosophy (Dio Chrysostom, *Oration* 33:48; 44:3; Lucian, *Octogenarians* 21). Paul has earlier (16:37) and will again (21:25) claim Roman citizenship, but that privilege was not in itself incompatible with being a citizen (*politēs*) in another city. The more serious issue raised by his statement is the general likelihood of Jews having full citizenship in Hellenistic cities, as opposed to the rights granted by means of membership in a *politeuma*. A passage in Philostratus, *Life of Apollonius* 6:34 concerning the citizens of Tarsus seems to suggest that Jews were in fact to be considered part of that group; see also

Josephus, *Against Apion* 2:38-39. The *litotes* of "no mean city" (*ouk asēmos polis*) is, of course, a form of boasting, and is paralleled in Achilles Tatius, *Clitophon and Leucippe* 8, 3, 1: "I am a free man and from no mean city (*eleutheros te ōn kai poleōs ouk asēmou*)."

40. *addressed them in the Hebrew dialect:* However unlikely it may appear that a commander in such a situation would allow his prisoner to address the mob—although Paul's Hellenistic credentials might have slightly overawed the tribune momentarily—this first defense (*apologia*) begins a series of such speeches by Paul that will dominate the rest of the narrative. The gesture of waving the hand appears also at Acts 13:16; 19:33; 26:1; that the gesture was part of rhetorical style is suggested by *The Golden Ass* 2:21. The phrase "substantial silence" translates *pollēs sigēs*, for the crowd does not quiet "completely" until 22:2. As for the "Hebrew dialect," meaning Aramaic, see Acts 1:19; 22:2; 26:14, as well as John 5:2.

INTERPRETATION

In the previous passage, Luke's shaping of the account seemed to struggle against the historical facts and even his own earlier narrative. But now he delivers Paul from the claustrophobic and ambiguous last meeting with the elders of the church, into the wider world whose colors he can make so vividly real. The specific details of the present passage correspond precisely with what we know from other sources. Luke seems to grasp better than we do, for example, the intricacies of fulfilling the Nazarite vow; at least, what he says fits within the discussion of those vows in the Mishnah with remarkable plausibility. As for the setting, he does not burden the reader with the extended descriptions of the Temple or of the Fortress Antonia that we find in Josephus or *The Letter of Aristeas*, but we can tell from those fuller descriptions that Luke puts things in their proper place.

He knows why Paul's supposed transgression of the Temple limits with a Gentile was a grievous offense, and why the mob could assume to get away with murdering him for it. He knows the way the Temple is connected to the fortress area by stairs, and how rapidly a military contingent could get from one place to the other. He knows the sorts of officers and soldiers involved in the Jerusalem garrison. He is aware of the revolutionary movements that stirred the mobs in the Temple precincts at the time of the great pilgrimage feasts. And like our other major source for the events of this period, he is not altogether clear on the distinctions between the various revolutionary forces. To any reader of Josephus' *Jewish War* for this period, this riot scene in the Temple rings absolutely true.

There is nothing, in other words, intrinsically unlikely about a figure like Paul creating just such a scene as Luke describes. The "zeal for the

Law'' of Jerusalem Jews during that time often expressed itself in terms of a "jealousy for the holy place." Neither is the appearance of the tribune with his soldiers implausible, for such was standard operating procedure (see notes). Perhaps the only unlikely element in the account is the part Luke is leading to, namely Paul's *apologia* delivered on the steps leading to the barracks. It is barely possible that a Roman officer would be impressed enough by Paul's show of sophistication to allow him a word, but it is far less likely that a crowd so wrought up would have silenced itself for the speech that Luke has Paul deliver.

These less verifiable parts of the account, however, are essential to Luke's literary purposes. The Temple scene is a necessity for him, and necessary to describe at such length, precisely because it will be the main charge brought against Paul, and therefore the point that he must repeatedly address as a prisoner in his self-defenses. The first thing that Luke has established, therefore, is the grounds for the charge (a misunderstanding combined with hostility toward Paul) and its fundamental injustice (he did not profane the Temple).

At the same time, as in the Philippi incident (16:35-39), he shows us an image of Paul that will be even further developed as the story continues. Paul is fully conscious of his rights and is willing to take advantage of them; he is by no means shy about his heritage or the privileges that accompany it—both from the Greek and from the Jewish side. Paul is also a philosopher who will stand up with courage to the wrath of a mob and speak in his own behalf. Here is the sharpest difference between the philosopher/prophet Jesus, who went to his death without self-defense, and his philosopher/prophet successor. Luke's Paul is much more a character of late antiquity, at home in the *paideia* of Hellenism and the *politeia* of the Roman world.

The most impressive literary accomplishment in this scene is Luke's use of "misapprehensions" to set up Paul's own *apologia*. The Jews of the city misunderstand his attitude toward the Law, and accuse him of profaning the Temple. The Roman tribune confuses Paul with a revolutionary who is fomenting a rebellion within the Temple precincts. These erroneous identifications enable Paul to define himself in the series of speeches that dominate the next section of Luke's story. How *are* we to understand Paul's relationship with his people and ancestral heritage?

FOR REFERENCE AND FURTHER STUDY

Bickermann, E. J. "The Warning Inscriptions of Herod's Temple." *JQR* 37 (1947) 387–405.

Guillet, J. "Theme de la marche au desert dans l'Ancien et le Nouveau Testament." *RScR* 36 (1949) 161–181.

Horsley, R. A. and J. S. Hanson. *Bandits, Prophets, and Messiahs.* New York: Harper and Row, 1985, 135-243.

Tcherikover, V. *Hellenistic Civilization and the Jews.* Trans. S. Appelbaum. New York: Athenaeum, 1970, 309-332.

Trites, A. A. "The Importance of Legal Scenes and Language in the Book of Acts." *NovT* 16 (1974) 278-284.

45. Paul's Speech in the City (22:1-29)

1. "Brothers and fathers! Listen to my defense now before you!" 2. When they heard that he was addressing them in the Hebrew dialect, they grew quieter. He said, 3. "I am a Jew. I was born in Tarsus of Cilicia. I was raised in this city. I was educated at the feet of Gamaliel according to the strictness of our ancestral Law. I was zealous for God just as all of you are today. 4. I persecuted this Way to the death, binding and handing over to prison both men and women. 5. So even the chief priest and all the council of elders testify to me. Having received letters from them to the brothers, I was journeying to Damascus to bring those who were there bound to Jerusalem so that they would be punished. 6. And it happened to me that as I was travelling and getting near to Damascus, around midday, a great light from heaven flashed around me. 7. I fell to the ground, and I heard a voice saying to me, 'Saul, Saul, why are you persecuting me?' 8. I answered, 'Who are you Lord?' And he said to me, 'I am Jesus the Nazorean, whom you are persecuting.' 9. Those who were with me saw the light but they did not hear the one speaking to me. 10. But I said, 'What shall I do, Lord?' And the Lord said to me, 'Get up. Go to Damascus. There you will be told all the things that have been prescribed for you to do.' 11. And since I could not see because of the glory of that light, I came to Damascus guided by my companions. 12. But a certain Ananias, a pious man according to the Law, testified to by all the Jews who lived there, 13. came to me and stood by me. He said to me, 'Brother Saul, regain your sight!' And at that hour, I looked up at him and regained my sight. 14. He said, 'The God of our fathers has chosen you to know his will and to see the righteous one and to hear a voice from his mouth, 15. because you will be a witness for him before all people of the things you have seen and heard. 16. And now, why are you waiting? Get up! Be baptized and cleansed of your sins by calling on his name.' 17. But it happened to me that when I returned to Jerusalem and was praying in the Temple, I experienced a vision. 18. I saw him as he was speaking to me: 'Hurry, and leave quickly from Jerusalem, because they are not accepting your witness concerning me.' 19. And I said, 'Lord, they themselves know that I was imprisoning and binding those who believed in you, synagogue by synagogue,

20. and when the blood of your witness Stephen was poured out, I was myself standing by and giving approval and holding the clothes of those who killed him.' 21. And he said to me, 'Go, for I will send you far away to the Gentiles.' " 22. They listened to him up to this statement, and they lifted up their voices. They said, "Away from the earth with such as this! He does not deserve to live!" 23. As they were shouting and tearing their garments and throwing dust into the air, 24. the tribune ordered him to be led into the barracks. He commanded him to be examined by flogging, so that he might discover the reason why they had thus cried out against him. 25. But as they were stretching him out for the flogging, Paul said to the centurion who was standing there, "Are you allowed to flog a person who is a Roman citizen and who has not been convicted?" 26. When the centurion heard this, he went to the tribune. He said, "What are you going to do? For this fellow is a Roman citizen." 27. The tribune came and said to him, "Tell me, are you a Roman citizen?" And he said, "Yes." 28. The tribune responded, "I purchased this citizenship at a considerable cost." And Paul said, "I on the other hand was born to it." 29. Those who were about to flog him immediately stood back from him, and the tribune became fearful, since he realized that he was a Roman citizen and he had bound him.

NOTES

1. *listen to my defense:* Luke uses the term *apologia*, which had the technical sense of a defense speech (see Plato, *Apology* 28A; *Phaedrus* 267A; Wis 6:10; Josephus, *Against Apion* 2:147); see also Acts 25:16; 1 Cor 9:3; 2 Cor 7:11; Phil 1:7, 16; 2 Tim 4:16; 1 Pet 3:15. In all of Paul's speeches that follow, we will observe the elements of such *apologiae* as rhetoricians described them (see e.g., Quintilian, *Institutes* 3, 9, 1; Cicero, *De Inventione* 1, 14, 19).

2. *they grew quieter:* Paul's waving of his hand had already silenced them "substantially" (21:40), but now hearing him speak in Aramaic (the "Hebrew dialect," see the note on 21:40), they grew even more quiet. By choosing Aramaic rather than Greek, Luke's Paul shows a fine sense of what is demanded in the *exordium* of a defense speech: winning the attention and sympathy of the audience.

3. *born . . . raised . . . educated:* Luke uses the standard tripartite biographical formula: birth (*gegennēmenos*), upbringing (*anatethrammenos*), and education (*pepaideumenos*), as he did also in the case of Moses (7:20-22). See also Plato, *Crito* 50E, 51C; Philo, *Life of Moses* 2:1; *Against Flaccus* 158. For Tarsus (Cilicia) as Paul's home, see 9:30; 11:25; 21:39; 23:34.

   raised in this city: Knowing that Luke uses a standard formula enables us to make the appropriate punctuation: "at the feet of Gamaliel" should go with *pepaideumenos,* so that Paul is raised and not only educated in Jerusalem. Luke's having called Paul a *neanias* ("youth") at the stoning of Stephen (7:58), and having Paul's nephew living in the city (23:16) enhance this picture. Is this claim incompatible with Paul's statement in Gal 1:22, "I was unknown by face to the churches of Christ in Judea?" Possibly, but not necessarily.

educated at the feet of Gamaliel: In Luke-Acts, the phrase "at the feet" always symbolizes submission (Luke 7:38; 8:35, 41; 10:39; 17:16; 20:43; Acts 2:35; 4:35, 37; 5:2, 10; 7:58; 10:25). The Gamaliel mentioned here is to be identified with the Pharisaic leader in 5:34, called Gamaliel I ("the Elder"). For more information on him, see the references in the note on 5:34.

strictness of our ancestral Law: The term *akribeia* can be translated as "exactness" and refers to the punctilious performance of the *mitṣwôth* by the Pharisaic school; Josephus says they "have the reputation of being distinguished from others by the strictness (*akribeia*) concerning the ancestral laws (*patria nomima*)," *Life* 191; see also *Jewish War* 2:162. In Acts 26:5, Paul will call it the "strictest sect" (*akribestatēn hairesin*).

zealous for God: In light of the characterization of the Jewish Christians in 21:20 as *zēlōtai tou nomou* ("zealous for the Law"), and in light of Paul's self-characterization in Gal 1:14 as *zēlōtēs hyarchōn tōn patrikōn mou paradōseōn* ("being zealous for the traditions of my fathers"), it is not at all surprising that some Western Tradition *mss* alter the harder reading "zealous for God" (*zēlōtēs tou theou*) to "zealous for the Law." The basic agreement with Gal 1:14 is striking in any case, even if we retain here the harder reading; note also Paul's tribute to his fellow Jews in Rom 10:2, "they have zeal (*zēlos*) for God."

4. *I persecuted this Way:* For the designation "Way" (*hē hodos*) for the messianic movement, see 9:2; 19:9, 23. Paul's self-presentation now picks up the thread of the Lukan narrative in 8:3. The language here resembles that used by Paul himself in 1 Cor 15:9 ("I persecuted the Church of God"), in Gal 1:13 ("I excessively persecuted the Church of God"), and Phil 3:6 ("according to zeal I persecuted the Church"). The phrase "to the death" (*achri thanatou*) could mean "to the end," since despite the mention in 9:1 that Paul was "breathing threat and murder," there is no indication that he succeeded in putting anyone (except Stephen) to death.

5. *the chief priest and all the council of elders:* This forensic version presents some variations from the direct narrative: a) in 9:2 only the chief priest was involved, whereas here the *presbyterion* (see Luke 22:66) is also made the source of authority for his actions; b) in 9:2, Paul brought letters "to the synagogues," whereas here it is "to the brothers" (rhetorically another *captatio benevolentiae*); c) this version makes explicit that they were to "be punished" (*timōreō*, see 26:11). The main point is that these leaders stand as "witnesses" (*martureō*) for Paul's deeds and motivations; the citation of such witnesses was a key component in ancient defense speeches.

6. *around midday:* In Paul's recitation of the conversion event, we find the addition of incidental detail and the emergence of points of discrepancy. There is no mention in 9:2 of the time of day, for example (but see 26:13), and the light from heaven is not called "great" (*hikanon*) as it is here, although the verb for "flashing" (*periastraptō*) is the same as in 9:3. These additional de-

tails could be attributed to Luke's skill in representing the story from the participant's perspective.

7. *heard a voice:* Influenced by the version in 26:14, which makes the voice speak "in the Hebrew dialect," some *mss* add those words here. Still others also add the words "it is hard for you to kick against the goad" from that later version.

8. *Jesus the Nazorean:* Only in this version is the title *ho Nazōraios* added to the simple name, Jesus. For the background of the designation, and the warning not to automatically equate it with "from Nazareth," see the note on Luke 18:37 and Acts 2:22; see also the use in 24:5.

9. *saw the light:* This exactly contradicts the first version of the story, which had Paul's companions hear the voice but not see the light (9:7). In 26:13, Luke simply has the light fall on Paul and the companions together. The Western Text adds "and grew afraid."

10. *what shall I do:* This question, as well as the directions given in response to it, are lacking in the direct narrative of 9:8. The version in 26:16, in contrast, elaborates the message at this point even further, making it into a commissioning. The phrase "things that have been prescribed" (*tetaktai*) could also be translated as "ordered" or "appointed" (see the use of *tassō* in Luke 7:8; Acts 13:48; 15:2; 18:2; see also Rom 13:1).

11. *because of the glory of that light:* The literal translation of *doxa* as "glory" rather than as "brightness" is preferable here because of the thematic associations throughout the work between light and the "glory of God" by which Luke means God's effective presence in the world (see esp. Luke 2:9, 14, 32; 9:31-32). Once more, the language here is strikingly like that used by Paul himself in a passage that is best understood as a reference to the experience of his calling: "the God who said, let light (*phōs*) shine out of darkness, has shined in our hearts the light of the knowledge of the glory (*doxa*) of God in the face (*prosōpon*) of Jesus Christ" (2 Cor 4:6).

12. *pious man according to the Law:* In 9:10, Ananias was described simply as "a disciple." Luke's present description of him is obviously appropriate to the context in which Paul seeks to establish connections to his audience that is "zealous for the Law." It should not for that reason be taken simply as a ploy, for it also echoes earlier descriptions of Lukan characters: In the Gospel, Zechariah and Elizabeth (Luke 2:6), Anna (2:37), the centurion with a sick slave (7:5), and Joseph of Arimathea (23:50); in Acts, Tabitha (9:36), and Cornelius (10:2). For the use of "testified to" with the meaning of enjoying a good reputation, see Acts 6:3; 10:22; 16:2.

13. *looked up at him and regained my sight:* In contrast to the expansionist tendency otherwise exhibited in this speech, Ananias' message to Paul is shorter than that in 9:7, as is the account of Paul's regaining of sight. So cryptic is Luke in this version, in fact, that his *aneblepsa eis auton* must be spelled out in two separate phrases to capture both meanings of the term *anablepsō*: "to look up"/"to regain sight." Some *mss* understandably seek to remove the ambi-

guity by removing the phrase *eis auton,* which then yields simply "I regained my sight."

14. *God of our fathers has chosen you:* For the traditional-sounding "God of our fathers," see Acts 3:13; 5:30; 7:32; 13:23. For "chosen" (*procheirizomai*), see 3:20. Ananias' language has the archaizing or "biblical" tone of the early speeches in Acts. Notice that he is made to characterize Jesus as "the righteous one" (*ho dikaios*), as in Luke 23:47; Acts 3:14; 7:52.

15. *you will be a witness for him:* This declaration places Paul in succession to the other apostles who were defined primarily in terms of this function of bearing witness to the resurrection (Acts 1:8, 22; 2:32; 3:15; 5:32; 10:39; 13:31), which for Paul comes by way of what he has "seen and heard" in this experience. The title will be applied to Paul once more in 26:16.

16. *why are you waiting:* The verb *mellō* is used by Luke frequently as a helping verb in its sense of "to be about to"/"coming" (Luke 3:7; 7:2; 9:31, 44; Acts 3:3; 5:35; 12:6, and later in this same passage, 22:26), but the verb can also be used absolutely to mean "delay" and that is the sense here.

    calling on his name: This version again expands Ananias' speech in order to explicate the meaning of the bald statement that Paul was baptized in 9:18. This is the only time that Luke uses the verb *louo* ("cleanse") with reference to baptism, but it is found also in Paul's statement about baptism in 1 Cor 6:11. The phrase "calling on (*epikaleō*) the name of the Lord" picks up the language of conversion in Acts 2:21 that is used also for the followers of the Way in 9:14, 21.

17. *praying in the Temple:* This statement is startling not only because it introduces an incident totally lacking from the earlier direct narrative, but because it also follows a complete omission of any mention why Paul had to leave Damascus, namely his conflict with the Jews there (9:23-25). Luke accomplishes four things with this addition: a) Paul's visit to the Temple signifies, as an implicit rebuttal of the charge against him, his long-standing devotion to the *ethos* of Judaism and in particular to the Temple; b) the fact that he *prayed* there also proves his piety, and his recognition of the Temple as a place of prayer; c) for the messianic reader, Paul's *ekstasis* while in prayer connects him to the experiences of Peter (10:11; 11:5); and d)—perhaps most threateningly to his hearers—Paul appears as a prophet like Isaiah who has a vision of the Lord in the Temple and receives a commission to be "sent" (see Isa 6:1-10).

18. *leave quickly from Jerusalem:* Once more, the defense speech presents a different perspective from that in the direct narrative. In 9:30, Paul's departure was orchestrated by the disciples. The accounts do agree substantially that Paul's message was not accepted in Jerusalem, although Acts 9:29 specifies his opponents as "Hellenist" Jews.

19. *they themselves know:* Having Paul voice this objection is rhetorically very effective. It invites his listeners to bear witness to his former sincerity as a persecutor of the Christians. If they do so, they should also be willing to grant the sincerity of his new experience and perspective.

20. *blood of your witness Stephen:* Paul gives Stephen the title (*martys*) by which he will always be known. The verb used (*ekchynnomai*) suggests the "pouring out" of sacrificial blood (Exod 24:6; Num 35:33). Using it for Stephen places him in continuity with all the prophets (Luke 11:50), and in particular with the prophet Jesus (Luke 22:20). The same verb is used for the "pouring out" of the Spirit in Acts 2:17 and 10:45. Luke shows us an ironic reversal: Paul had originally stood with and approved the "witnesses" to the death of this man who had a vision of the risen Jesus (7:58-60). Because he has now also had such a vision, Paul himself becomes a "witness" and is able to designate Stephen also as "your witness."

21. *go, for I will send you far away to the Gentiles:* This prophetic commissioning resembles most of all that of Isaiah in the Temple (Isa 6:10). The reader now knows the source of Paul's self-referential citation of Isa 49:6 concerning the "light to the Gentiles" (Acts 13:47), and is also better able to grasp the full import of the prophecy of Simeon (Luke 2:35). Luke places in a vision to Paul substantially the same message that in 9:15 he assigned to Ananias' vision of the Lord.

22. *away from the earth with such as this:* Luke makes it appear as though the reaction interrupts the speech, but of course he has had Paul make all the points required (see the similar "interruptions" in 23:7 and 26:24). The crowd responds to this intimation of universalism in the way that Jesus' townspeople had responded to the suggestion that God's visitation extended beyond Israel: by seeking to kill the prophet (Luke 4:24-29). The Greek for "he does not deserve to live" (*ou kathēken auton zēn*) might also be rendered, "It is not fitting for him to go on living." For a similar response by an excited crowd, see Philo, *Against Flaccus* 144.

23. *throwing dust into the air:* The crowd goes through the whole repertoire of apotropaic gestures exhibited elsewhere in the narrative: shouting (Acts 7:57; 14:14), tearing the garments (14:14; 18:6), throwing dust (13:51). They are repelling the wickedness of Paul's words.

24. *examined by flogging:* The verb *anetazō* means to make a legal inquiry. The use of torture to obtain information was by no means unusual (see, e.g., Chariton of Aphrodisias, *Chaereas and Callirhoe* 1, 5, 2; Pliny the Younger, *Letters* 10:96). Information gained by such means, as a matter of fact, could have considerable evidenciary value (see Quintilian, *Institutes* 5, 4, 1). The tribune seeks the "cause" (*aitia*) not simply of the shouting but of the entire commotion caused by Paul.

25. *stretching him out for the flogging:* The verb *proteinō* means to "extend/stretch out," especially of the hands (2 Macc 3:20; 7:10; 14:33). The translation decision here is whether to take the dative plural of *himas* ("thong") as instrumental ("stretching him out with thongs"), or as purpose, ("stretching him out for the thongs").

Roman citizen and who has not been convicted: The entire situation reminds us of the incident at Philippi (Acts 16:19-39). Paul again appeals to his status as a citizen of the city of Rome (*Rōmaios*) and the fact that he has not been convicted in a hearing (*anakritos*), just as in Acts 16:37, but on the present occasion, his timing is better! For the illegality of beating a Roman citizen, see the note on Acts 16:37. Evidence for the widespread extension of Roman citizenship rights, apparently even among Jews, is offered by Josephus, *Against Apion* 2:40-41.

28. *purchased . . . at a considerable cost:* The term *kephalaion* ("of the head/principal"), can be used financially of "capital" (see Plato, *Laws* 742C), or generally of a large sum of money (see *Letter of Aristeas* 24; Josephus, *Antiquities of the Jews* 12:30). The practice of purchasing citizenship in the first century is attested by Dio Cassius, *Roman History* 60, 17, 4-9. Since it was customary to take the name of the emperor in whose reign this citizenship was acquired, the tribune's name (Claudius Lysias, 23:6) might suggest the time of his purchase during the reign of Claudius (41-54 C.E.). Dio confirms that under Claudius, citizenship rights were purchased for "great amounts" (*megalōn . . . chrēmatōn*, 60, 17, 6). For the reaction of fear by the tribune and the torturers, see the note on 16:38.

Interpretation

Paul has been mistaken for a polluter of the Temple and for an Egyptian revolutionary. Now as Luke places him on the steps leading up to the Fortress Antonia to address the crowd that seeks his death, Paul has the opportunity to interpret his identity for himself. The process of Paul's defense has begun. But it has only begun. The remainder of the Acts narrative will in one way or another deal with the charges against Paul, the legal process of hearing and appeal, and above all the speeches that Luke places in the mouth of his hero.

Throughout this commentary on Luke's two volumes, we have noted how thoroughly and comfortably Luke employs the appropriate conventions of Hellenistic literature. We should not be surprised, then, to discover an embattled character like Paul, whose career was at best ambiguous, engaging in the sort of *apologia* that occurs so frequently in the literature of a culture fundamentally shaped by forensics, whether in histories (see e.g., Thucydides, *The Peloponnesian War* 3, 10, 52-60; Josephus, *Antiquities of the Jews* 16:105-120) or in fiction (see, e.g., Chariton of Aphrodisias, *Chaereas and Callirhoe* 5, 6, 1-10).

Neither are we by this point surprised to find in Paul's several defenses scattered through the next chapters the basic components of the ancient Greek defense speech as found in rhetorical sources: the *exordium* or *proemium* in which Paul recommends himself to his listeners and establishes his credibility (Quintilian, *Institutes* 4, 1, 1-79); the *narratio*, which provides his version of the events pertinent to the charge (Quintilian, *Institutes* 4, 2, 1-132; Cicero, *De Inventione* 1, 19, 27); the *probatio*, or proof, in which he invokes such elements as human witnesses and divine omens in testimony (Cicero, *De Inventione* 1, 23, 34; Quintilian, *Institutes* 5, 2-12); and the *refutatio*, wherein he answers various charges (Cicero, *De Inventione* 1, 41, 77; Quintilian, *Institutes* 5, 13).

These elements are unevenly distributed over the discourses in 22:1-21; 24:10-21; 26:2-18. Since Luke, for his own dramatic purposes, usually has Paul interrupted in mid-speech, the element of *peroratio*, or conclusion, is less in evidence (see Plato, *Phaedrus* 266D-267E; Aristotle, *Rhetoric* 1354B; Cicero, *De Inventione* 1, 52, 98). As always, Luke uses the conventions without being bound by them; taken individually, Paul's speeches retain a freshness and spontaneity together with a brevity that in the Hellenistic world was always admired (Cicero, *De Inventione* 1, 20, 28).

This first speech also provides us with the second of the three versions of Paul's conversion experience. The ways in which these retellings differ from the direct narration in Acts 9 are analyzed in the notes. More important for understanding Luke's overall narrative is to observe the simple fact that he does tell this story *three* times. By now we have learned that the lessons Luke wants learned well he repeats: so with the passion of Jesus, and so with the conversion of Cornelius. In Luke's resurrection stories, the passion prophecies of Jesus were interpreted in the light of his "entering into glory." In each of Peter's retellings of the first Gentile conversion, new dimensions of its meaning were unfolded.

The same is the case in the two retellings of Paul's conversion. The fact *that* he retells them tells the reader how important this experience of Paul is: for Luke and for the reader, Paul is a prime "witness of the resurrection," on whose credibility a great deal rests. The *way* he retells them shows us the lesson we are to derive from the experience. Luke isolates and elaborates those parts of the story that he wants the reader to see again more closely.

When Paul emphasizes in this first *apologia* his Jewish roots, therefore, we are to recognize not only the obvious way in which this functions as a *captatio benevolentiae* for his Jewish audience, but also a genuine aspect of Paul's identity that should be of importance for the Gentile reader of Luke's narrative, for in his own life, Paul enacts the movement of the good news from the historic Israel to the restored people of God made up of Jews and Gentiles.

The information Luke provides about Paul's early life corresponds with what we learn from Paul's own letters, particularly that he had been a Pharisee and "zealous for God" according to the norms of Torah as understood by the strict construction of the Pharisaic tradition, and that he had persecuted the messianic community "to the death." In this speech, Luke has Paul appeal to the Jewish authorities and even to his hearers: they can bear witness to the sincerity of this part of his life. And if they do attest that he speaks the truth about these matters, his credibility in the matters more offensive to them is increased.

It is in Paul's retelling the story of his conversion, however, that Luke makes the most alterations from his first narrative version. Some differences, again, can be attributed to this specific setting: the emphasis on Ananias' Jewish piety and reputation, and the elimination of any mention of opposition to Paul from Jews in Damascus. This is not the time to stress Paul's past conflicts with his people! But more striking is the amplification of the role played by the Risen Lord, above all in the (previously unnarrated) vision in the Temple. As the notes suggest, this incident ought to provide Paul with a number of important credentials, not only with respect to his fidelity to the *ethos* of his nation, but above all as a prophet whose own "Temple vision" issues in a commission like that of the great Isaiah.

But it is precisely this part of the story, naturally, which generates the violent response among those listening. The commission to go far away to the Gentiles is bad enough. Worse is Paul's implication that this hated Jesus is in fact alive and appearing in visions within the Temple precincts! We are not surprised that this crowd of Paul's "countrymen" respond just as had Jesus' "townspeople" in Nazareth (Luke 4:24-29), by seeking once more to kill him.

The next scene, in which the tribune takes Paul into custody for his own protection, sets up the entire narrative sequence to follow. Paul's appeal to his Roman citizenship saves him from a flogging and places him under the protection of the empire, but also makes him captive to its judicial process, whose various stages the reader will now follow.

FOR REFERENCE AND FURTHER STUDY

Budesheim, T. L. "Paul's *Abschiedsrede* in the Acts of the Apostles." HTR 69 (1976) 9–30.

Cassidy, R. J. *Society and Politics in the Acts of the Apostles.* New York: Orbis Press, 1987, 96–144.

Hubbard, B. J. "The Role of Commissioning Accounts in Acts," *Perspectives on Luke-Acts.* Ed. C. H. Talbert. Danville, Va.: Association of Baptist Professors of Religion, 1978, 187–198.

Long, W. R. "The *Paulusbild* in the Trial of Paul in Acts." *SBL 1983 Seminar Papers.* Ed. K. H. Richards. Chico: Scholars Press, 1983, 87–105.

Neyrey, J. "The Forensic Defense Speech and Paul's Trial Speeches in Acts 22-26: Form and Function." *Luke-Acts: New Perspectives from the Society of Biblical Literature Seminar.* Ed. C. H. Talbert. New York: Crossroad, 1984, 210–224.

Retif, A. "Témoignage et Prédication Missionaire dans les Actes des Apôtres." NRT 73 (1951) 152–165.

van Unnik, W. C. *Tarsus or Jerusalem: The City of Paul's Youth.* London: Epworth, 1962.

Veltman, F. "The Defense Speeches of Paul in Acts," *Perspectives on Luke-Acts.* Ed. C. H. Talbert. Danville, Va.: Association of Baptist Professors of Religion, 1978, 243–256.

IV. THE IMPRISONED APOSTLE

46. *Paul's Defense before the Sanhedrin* (22:30–23:11)

22:30. The next day he wanted to find out for certain what he was being charged with by the Jews. He untied him and ordered the chief priests and the whole Sanhedrin to meet. He brought Paul down and stood him among them. 23:1. Paul gazed at the Sanhedrin. He said, "Brothers, up until this day I have continued to conduct myself toward God with a completely good conscience." 2. But the chief priest Ananias ordered those in attendance on him to strike his mouth. 3. Then Paul said to him, "God is going to strike you, you whitewashed wall! And are you sitting to judge me according to the Law, while against the Law you are ordering me to be struck?" 4. Those in attendance said, "Are you reviling the chief priest of the people?" 5. Paul said, "I did not know, brothers, that he was a chief priest. For it stands written that 'You shall not speak wickedly against a leader of the people.' " 6. But since Paul knew that one group was made up of Sadducees and the other was made up of Pharisees, he shouted out in the Sanhedrin, "Brothers! I am a Pharisee, a son of Pharisees. I am being judged concerning the hope that is the resurrection of the dead." 7. When he said this there was a conflict between the Pharisees and the Sadducees, and the assembly was divided. 8. For the Sadducees say that there is no resurrection, nor angel, nor spirit. But the Pharisees confess all of them. 9. There was a great roar. Some of the scribes of the party of the Pharisees took up the battle. They said, "We don't find anything wicked about this fellow. Perhaps a spirit spoke to him or an angel." 10. As the conflict grew greater, the tribune feared that Paul would be torn apart by them. He ordered the troops to go down and take him away from the midst of them, and lead him into the barracks. 11. The next night the Lord stood by him. He said, "Have courage! For as you have given witness concerning me in Jerusalem, so must you give witness also in Rome."

NOTES

22:30. *what he was being charged with:* Neither the shouting of the crowd in the Temple precincts nor Paul's spontaneous address have made clear to the tribune what was happening, and he has been prevented from extracting that information by flogging, so he must seek another way of "finding out for certain" (*gnōnai to asphales,* as in 21:34). For "being charged," Luke uses *katēgoreō,* as in Luke 6:7; 11:54; 23:2, 10, 14; the verb will naturally recur in the subsequent chapters (24:2, 8, 13, 19; 25:11, 16; 28:19).

ordered . . . the whole Sanhedrin to meet: Luke uses the term *synedrion* only once in the Gospel (Luke 22:66) for the hearing of Jesus before the "college of elders of the people" (*presbyterion tou laou,* see also Acts 22:5), whose make-up is discussed in the note on Luke 22:66. Jesus' prophetic successors are shown to suffer before this court just as he did: the apostles in Jerusalem (Acts 4:15; 5:21), Stephen (6:12, 15), and now Paul. All of this is in fulfillment of Jesus' own prophecy concerning his followers (Luke 21:13). Luke appears to assume that the Sanhedrin would be responsive to the demands of the Roman military authority; Josephus mentions at least one other incident in which the procurator claims the sole right to convene the Sanhedrin (*Antiquities of the Jews* 20:202).

23:1. *conduct myself toward God:* The verb *politeuomai* has the sense of "living as a citizen," and therefore of "conducting one's life" (see 2 Macc 6:1; Philo, *Special Laws* 4:226; and especially Josephus, *Life* 12); also Paul's instruction in Phil 1:27, "conduct yourselves (*politeuesthe*) worthy of the goodness of Christ."

a completely good conscience: Apart from its use here and again in 24:16, the term *syneidesis* ("conscience") is, within the NT, thoroughly Pauline (Rom 2:15; 9:1; 13:5; 1 Cor 8:7, 10, 12; 10:25, 27, 28, 29; 2 Cor 1:12; 4:2; 5:11). For a "pure" (*katharos*) or "good" (*agathos*) conscience, see 1 Tim 1:5, 19; 3:9; 2 Tim 1:3. His present statement does not contradict his earlier confession of persecuting the Church, for in fact he nowhere suggests (notwithstanding 1 Tim 1:13-15) that his behavior on either side of his conversion was ever motivated by anything other than "zeal for God."

2. *chief priest Ananias:* We learn something about this chief priest (47-59 C.E.) from Josephus, *Jewish War* 2:243, 426-29; *Antiquities* 20:103. His great wealth is especially noted by Josephus (*Antiquities* 20:213-214) as well as his violent death at the hands of brigands (*Jewish War* 2:441-442). His luxurious way of life is also suggested by the (exaggerated) reference in *bT Pes.* 57a. By "those who stood by him (*paristēmi autǭ*)," Luke has in mind his entourage, as in Luke 19:24. The order to strike Paul reminds us vividly of the scene involving Jesus in John 18:22-23, but the motivation in either case is obscure, and its unexpectedness (or irregularity) may account for Paul's response.

3. *God is going to strike you:* In Deut 28:22, the curse levied against those who disobey the commandments includes "the Lord will smite you . . . ." and this is taken to be an appropriate form of cursing by *m.Sheb.* 4:13. The LXX,

however, uses the verb *pataxai* rather than the *typtein* used here. The accusation of being a "whitewashed wall" (*toiche kekoniamene*) recalls the "whitewashed tombs" applied to the scribes and Pharisees in Matt 23:27 because of their hypocrisy. Compare the allusion to Ezek 13:10, "the builders of the wall and those who daub it with plaster," applied to the Jewish leadership in *CD* 8:12.

sitting to judge me: For the judge "sitting," compare Matt 23:2; 25:31; Luke 22:30; Acts 12:21; 25:6, 17. Note the singular "you": until the destruction of the Temple, the chief priest functioned as president of the Sanhedrin; in addition to the evidence of the gospels (e.g., Mark 15:33) and Acts (5:17; 7:1), see Josephus, *Antiquities* 14:167; 20:200; *m.Sanh.* 2:1.

according to the Law . . . against the Law: The verb *paranomeō* is stronger than "act illegally"; it has the sense of "flouting" the law (see Aristotle, *Politics* 1307B; Plutarch, *Superstition* 3 [*Mor.* 166B]). Herein is the chief priest's hypocrisy: he has treated Paul as a malefactor before having heard the witnesses such as are demanded by the proper procedure (*m.Sanh.* 3:6-8). Paul's charge is similar to that made by Stephen against the Sanhedrin: "You are the ones who received the Law as commandments from angels, yet you did not keep it" (Acts 7:53).

5. *speak wickedly against a leader of the people:* Paul quotes Exod 22:27, except that the LXX has the plural *archontes* instead of Luke's singular *archonta*. The citation of the commandment is obviously intended to show Paul's continuing devotion to Torah, and his desire to live *kata ton nomon* ("according to the Law"), even if the chief priest does not! This is also the best way to explain Paul's otherwise disingenuous statement, "I did not know that he was a chief priest"—the chief priest's behavior was not in accord with his status and function. Far from an "apology" for a mistake, Paul's statement is another prophetic criticism of the chief priest, whose behavior makes him "unrecognizable."

6. *Sadducees . . . Pharisees:* In the Gospel, Luke mentions the Sadducees only once (Luke 20:27), with reference to their disbelief in the resurrection of the dead. For their membership in the Sanhedrin and their special links to the priesthood, see Acts 4:1; 5:17. He pays much more attention to the Pharisees (Luke 5:17, 21, 30, 33; 6:2, 7; 7:30, 36, 37, 39; 11:37, 38, 39, 42-43; 12:1; 13:31; 14:1, 3; 15:2; 16:14; 17:20; 18:10-11; 19:39). Their presence in the Sanhedrin is shown by Acts 5:34.

a Pharisee, a son of Pharisees: Although Paul had identified himself in 22:3 as one who followed the Law strictly, this is the first time he explicitly identifies himself as a member of the Pharisaic sect, a self-description that recurs in 26:5, and which agrees with Paul's own testimony in Phil 3:5, where he declares that he was *kata nomon pharisaios*, "according to the Law, a Pharisee." No more than in the case of Roman citizenship is it possible entirely to prove this assertion for Paul himself, much less so for his own father. If the evidence is reliable, it serves to show the spread of Pharisaism in the first century into the Greek Diaspora.

the hope that is the resurrection of the dead: The Greek reads literally, "hope and resurrection of [the] dead" (*peri elpidos kai anastaseōs nekrōn*). It should be understood as a *hendiadys*, two phrases joining in a single concept. Paul is now made to state the issue that defines not only what truly stands between him and his opponents—whether in Jesus the resurrection of the dead has genuinely occurred—but also between Messianist and non-Messianist Jews generally. The issue is not only the resurrection as a general belief (Acts 24:15, 21), but whether in fact *Jesus* has been raised (26:23). Once more, Luke has identified a theme central also to Paul himself; see Rom 1:4; 6:5; Phil 3:10; but especially 1 Cor 15. For the connection of "hope" (*elpis*) to resurrection, see 2 Macc 7:14, 20; 1 Cor 15:19; Col 1:5; 1 Thess 4:13; Titus 1:2; 3:7; Heb 6:18; 7:19; 1 Pet 1:3.

7. *the assembly was divided:* The noun *plēthos* here clearly has the sense of being an organized assembly, a usage that throws light on more difficult passages such as the remarkably similar one in Acts 14:4. Luke portrays this division as the result of Paul's deliberate ploy. But Paul's statement concerning the resurrection also serves to demonstrate the continuity of Paul's convictions from his former to his present life.

8. *no resurrection, nor angel, nor spirit:* Their denial of the resurrection is extensively displayed by Luke 20:27-38. Luke's perception is in agreement with that of Josephus, *Jewish War* 2:164-165, where their denial of a future life is made explicit, and *Antiquities of the Jews* 18:16: "The Sadducees hold that the soul perishes along with the body." Josephus makes no mention of their views on "spirit and angel," but the rejection of these would be consistent with their conservative attitude toward tradition, keeping "no observance apart from the laws" (Josephus, *Antiquities of the Jews* 8:16).

   Pharisees confess all of them: The phrase *ta amphotera* means literally "both of them" (see Luke 1:6-7; 5:7; 6:39; Acts 8:38), but can expand to include more than two items (see also Acts 19:16). For the language of "confession" (*homologein*), compare Luke 12:8; Acts 24:14, and especially Rom 10:9; 1 John 1:9; 2:23; 4:2. The Pharisaic belief in the resurrection builds on traditions developed in the Maccabean period (see Daniel 12:2-3; 2 Macc 7:9, 11, 14), and is attested by Josephus, *Jewish War* 2:163; *Antiquities of the Jews* 18:14, as well as by countless references in the Rabbinic materials (see e.g., *bT Sanh.* 91b; *bT RoshHaShan* 16b-17a). So firmly was this established that the Mishnah decrees, "he that says there is no resurrection of the dead prescribed in the Law" has no share in the life to come (*m.Sanh.* 10:1).

9. *took up the battle:* The imperfect tense of *diamachomai* is translated as inchoative; for the verb's meaning of "contending," see Sir 8:1; Josephus, *Jewish War* 2:55; *Antiquities of the Jews* 14:475). Luke's designation of them as "scribes from the party of the Pharisees" resembles most closely Mark 2:16, "the scribes of the Pharisees." Although Luke sometimes calls them "lawyers" (Luke 7:30; 10:25; 11:45, 46, 52, 53; 14:3) or "teachers of the Law" (Luke 5:15; Acts 5:34), he regularly associates this group of "scribes" (*grammateis*) with the Pharisees (Luke 5:21, 30; 6:7; 11:53; 15:2), although they are also associated with the

chief priest and Sanhedrin (Luke 19:47; 20:1, 19, 39, 46; Acts 4:5; 6:12). The Mishnah provided for "two scribes" [or three] for the taking down of testimony, but also for "three rows of disciples of the sages," who sound more like the people intended here (see *m. Sanh.* 4:3-4). The scriptural expertise of the scribes made them the natural allies of those who favored the development of an "oral Torah" developed by the process of midrash.

perhaps a spirit spoke to him: The Greek construction here is actually that of a protasis of a conditional sentence (*ei de*), but it lacks an apodosis; thus the translation as a hypothetical, "perhaps." The *mss* of the Byzantine text tradition fill in the gap by supplying as an apodosis, "let us not fight against God," which makes their position resemble the one recommended in 5:39. The Pharisaic willingness to recognize *some* sort of transcendental experience (that they can fit within their categories and at the same time use against the Sadducees) works to Paul's purpose, but also falls far short of recognizing the key point, which is the reality of the resurrection in Paul's experience of Jesus as Lord.

10. *lead him into the barracks:* The necessity of rescuing Paul from the highest court in Judaism for fear that they would "tear him apart" (*diaspaō*; see Judg 14:6; 16:12; Hos 13:8), implies that the Sanhedrin is no more orderly or "according to the Law" than the mob in the courtyard from whom the tribune earlier was required to rescue the apostle (Acts 22:24).

11. *give witness also in Rome:* Paul has had a series of visions which have directed his ministry (9:4; 16:9; 22:17); this one, precisely like that in 18:9-10, has the effect of showing the reader that Paul's "witnessing" has the Lord's approval (see the use of *dei* for marking the "necessity" of the divine plan throughout the narrative: Luke 4:43; 9:22; 24:7; Acts 1:21; 5:29; 9:6; 14:22). It also functions as a programmatic prophecy which shows the direction the plot will continue to take (compare 19:21). Finally, it indicates that the form of Paul's witness in Rome will be as it is here, in captivity. For the use of visions to advance and interpret the narrative in Hellenistic novels, see the references in the note on Acts 10:3. An even more impressive parallel to the present vision is found in Josephus' *Life* 208-209, where the general is told through a *thaumasion oneiron* by someone "standing by" him that he "must fight also against the Romans" (*kai Rōmaiois dei se polemēsai*).

INTERPRETATION

With Paul's being taken into "protective custody" by the Roman tribune, the final section of Luke-Acts begins. The next six chapters cover a period of some four years in Paul's life (Acts 24:27; 28:30) during which he remains a prisoner. Yet in diverse ways Luke will show how Paul continues to bear witness to the Lord, undaunted by his condition or circumstances; in this narrative, the brave declaration made by Paul in one of the captivity letters attributed to him is enacted: "the word of God is not fettered" (2 Tim 2:9). As Paul moves from one stage to another through the slow progression of legal appeals, (which the vision that concludes this section assures us by programmatic prophecy will end up in Rome), Luke is able to demonstrate through his defense speeches not only Paul's innocence of the charges brought against him by the Jews, but the reality for which Paul truly stands in witness: that in the resurrection of Jesus the authentic "hope of Israel" was realized (28:20).

We have noted how Luke has portrayed Paul's passage to the city in terms strongly reminiscent of Jesus' final journey to Jerusalem and death. We should not be surprised, then, to find after Paul's "arrest" that he too, in imitation of Jesus, is made to face the Sanhedrin (see Luke 22:66-71). Whatever the historical plausibility of the event—and there is no reason to dismiss it out of hand as "impossible"—it is certainly unverifiable, and its literary usefulness is obvious: Paul's *imitatio Christi* serves to show how the prophetic Spirit continues to work in Jesus' witnesses, and also thereby certifies Paul as a trustworthy bearer of that witness. Like the account in the Gospel, Paul does not really experience a trial so much as a "hearing." But unlike the passivity and taciturnity of Jesus in the Gospel, Paul seizes the initiative and disrupts the assembly by his incisive behavior and speech. Not for the first time, Luke shows that the prophetic Spirit at work in Jesus' followers reveals itself in a more obvious philosophical boldness (*parrēsia*) than was evident in Jesus himself (see Acts 4:13; 5:29).

When we examine Paul's words before the Sanhedrin, we can see points of continuity with his previous defense speech in the city. Three points are made emphatically: first, that Paul has continuously had a "good conscience" in the way he has conducted himself toward God, "up to this day"; the claim here is that his sincerity was equally real in the days before and after his conversion experience (23:1). Second, when disciplined by the chief priest (for pronouncing the divine name? for speaking out of turn? for claiming a sincere conscience?), he responds first with a good Jewish curse, and then with an appeal to Torah; this shows that whether they accept it or not, Paul defines himself within the symbolic framework of Torah accepted by all his fellow Jews (23:5).

It is the third apologetic motif that is most significant. Paul lays claim to the title of Pharisee, and specifically of the Pharisaic confession of the resurrection of the dead (23:6). At one level, Luke portrays this as a clever rhetorical ploy; Paul sees a way of dividing the assembly and thus extricating himself. But it is also a way of exposing to the reader for the first time the most fundamental issue dividing Paul from his opponents, and Messianists from all non-Messianist Jews: the resurrection of Jesus as the realization of the hope of Israel. This requires further attention.

By appealing to the belief in the resurrection, Paul is by no means deviating from his own witness to Jesus, or seeking a softer position vis-à-vis the Sanhedrin. The contrary is true: he appeals to a shared belief in the *possibility* of the resurrection in order to confront the Pharisees with the claim that in Jesus this resurrection has *happened*. Forget the chief priest—his behavior marks him as unworthy even of his office. Forget the Sadducees—at the time of Luke's writing they have disappeared as fully as the Temple and its priesthood. It is Pharisaism as it becomes "normative Judaism" after the fall of the Temple that is Luke's target.

Luke shows first that the Messianist claim to the resurrection in Jesus is consistent with the convictions shared by that part of Judaism which in his time claims normative status. The Messianists operate within the same symbolic framework. But he shows also that by not being willing to acknowledge Jesus' resurrection, the dominant form of Judaism is in fact unfaithful to its own best convictions. For Luke, it is Paul who represents the authentic "Pharisaic" position.

Luke indicates their "bad faith" by having them acknowledge only the peripheral possibilities: "Perhaps a spirit spoke to him or an angel." By acknowledging even so much, they have positioned themselves over against the Sadducees, yes, but they have also shown that their refusal to entertain another possibility—that Jesus truly was raised—is self-condemned. If a "spirit or angel" could have spoken to Paul, if he is not a fraud but had what might have been an authentic religious experience, then they also implicitly testify that there is no intrinsic reason why it could not have been "the spirit of Jesus" or "Jesus' angel" that appeared to him!

In this incident, we once more discern the specific complaint that Luke has against the Pharisees throughout Luke-Acts. As we saw in the Commentary on the Gospel of Luke, readers sometimes confuse Jesus' frequent interactions with the Pharisees with a positive attitude toward them. In fact, although their theology tends to be the right one, their attitude toward the prophet is always the wrong one. They are consistently closed to "the plan of God" (Luke 7:29-30) and "God's visitation" (Luke 19:39-44). The fact is that their openness to a continued revelation through the "oral torah" only makes their failure to recognize this visitation in the prophet Jesus all the worse: "they do not enter themselves and they hinder those who are entering" (Luke 11:52).

The case of the Pharisees in the Acts narrative is precisely the same. We have now seen the Pharisees in action three times. In Gamaliel's advice to the Sanhedrin, we saw that he had the right theology, but the wrong response: his "wait and see" attitude was actually a form of disobedience to God's call (Acts 5:32-40). In the conflict over the status of Gentile believers, the Christians from the Pharisaic party align themselves with "those from Judea" who made circumcision a condition of salvation (Acts 15:1, 5), and therefore showed themselves closed to the fundamentally new thing God was doing among the nations. Now, we see that although the Pharisaic party is closer to the Messianists in its abstract belief concerning the resurrection, it is all the more to blame for not following through on that conviction and acknowledging at least the possibility of its realization in Jesus. In sum, Luke's view of the Pharisees is not positive: like the chief priest whose behavior makes his status as a leader of the people unrecognizable, so does their closure to the message of Jesus close them from their own deepest "hope of the resurrection," and therefore of the claim to be the authentic realization of the people.

FOR REFERENCE AND FURTHER STUDY

Cosgrove, C. H. "The Divine *Dei* in Luke-Acts." *NovT* 26 (1984) 168–190.
Jervell, J. "Paul the Teacher of Israel: The Apologetic Speeches of Paul in Acts."
     Luke and the People of God. Minneapolis: Augsburg, 1972, 153–183.
Schubert, P. "The Final Cycle of Speeches in the Book of Acts." *JBL* 87 (1968) 1–16.
Strousma, G. "Le couple de l'ange et de l'esprit: traditions juives et chrétiennes."
     RB 88 (1981) 42–61.
Tannehill, R. *Narrative Unity* 2:285–292.

47. *Escape to Caesarea* (23:12-35)

12. When day came, the Jews formed a conspiracy. They bound themselves by an oath. They said they would not eat or drink until they had killed Paul. 13. More than forty of them made this plot. 14. They went to the chief priests and the elders. They said, "We have taken upon ourselves an oath not to eat until we kill Paul. 15. Now therefore you, together with the Sanhedrin, give notice to the tribune that he should lead him down to you, as though you were going to discern matters concerning him more closely. And we are prepared to kill him before he arrives." 16. But the son of Paul's sister heard of the ambush. He came to the barracks and went in. He told Paul. 17. Paul then summoned one of the centurions. He said, "Take this young man to the tribune, for he has something to tell him." 18. So he took him along and brought him to the tribune. He said, "The prisoner Paul summoned me and asked that I bring this young man with something to say to you." 19. The tribune took his hand and withdrew with him alone. He asked, "What is it that you have to tell me?" 20. He said, "The Jews have agreed to ask you to bring Paul down tomorrow to the Sanhedrin as if they were going

to make some more rigorous inquiry concerning him. 21. Don't believe them, for more than forty men of them are laying an ambush for him. They have taken an oath upon themselves to neither eat nor drink until they have killed him. And now they are ready, awaiting the word from you." 22. The tribune therefore dismissed the young man. He commanded him, "Tell no one that you told these things to me." 23. And he summoned two of the centurions. He said, "Prepare two hundred soldiers, and seventy horsemen, and two hundred swordsmen, to go to Caesarea from the third hour of the night; 24. prepare also animals that they can put Paul on to deliver him safely through to Felix the governor." 25. He wrote a letter with this character: 26. "Claudius Lysias to the most excellent governor Felix, greetings! 27. This man was seized by the Jews, and was about to be killed by them, when I came up with the troops and extricated him. Having learned that he was a Roman citizen, 28. I wanted to discover the reason they had a complaint against him. I brought him to their Sanhedrin, 29. which I discovered to be making complaints concerning questions about their Law, but no accusation worthy of death or imprisonment. 30. Since it was revealed to me that there was a plot against this man, I immediately sent him to you. I also ordered those accusing him to declare the matters against him before you." 31. The soldiers therefore brought Paul according to their order. They led him by night to Antipatris. 32. The next day, they turned back to the barracks, allowing the horsemen to depart with him. 33. These entered Caesarea. They handed over the letter to the governor. They also presented Paul to him. 34. When he read it, he asked from what province he was, and when he learned that he was from Cilicia, 35. he said, "I will hear your case when your accusers also arrive." He ordered him to be kept in the praetorium of Herod.

NOTES

12. *Jews formed a conspiracy:* Some *mss* soften this to "some (*tines*) Jews." Luke uses three roughly synonymous terms for their plan. In this verse, it is a *systrophē*, which has the sense of "gathering," especially for seditious purposes (Herodotus, *Persian Wars* 7:9; Polybius, *History* 4, 34, 6; see also LXX Ps 63:2; Amos 7:10; 1 Macc 14:44). In v. 13, he calls it a *synōmosia*, which has the political nuance of a "league bound by oath" (Plato, *Apology* 36B). And in the tribune's letter it is referred to as an *epiboulē*, (compare Josephus, *Antiquities of the Jews* 10:166) which focuses explicitly on the plan of action, which picks up earlier such attempts made against Paul (Acts 9:24: 20:3, 19).

    bound themselves by an oath: With slight variations, Luke also repeats this three times: here and in v. 21, the form is *anathematizein heauton* ("to put oneself under the ban"); in v. 14, the cognate dative is used, *anathemati anathematizein heauton*. The swearing of such vows is found in the LXX (Num 21:2, 3), but the verb *anamethematizein* is used unreflexively for "placing something under the ban (*ḥerem*)," that is, utterly destroying it (Deut 13:15; 20:17; Josh 6:21; Judg 1:17; 21:11; 1 Sam 15:3). The making of such a solemn oath is attested in *1 Enoch* 6:4-5, and there are prescriptions for the making of oaths, some at least of which involve not eating or drinking, in *m.Sheb.* 3:1-5. Jesus' resolve in the Gospel not to drink of the wine until he drank it new in the kingdom (Luke 22:18) has some resemblance, although taking an oath to kill someone or else starve to death is an extreme form. Given what we are told by Josephus about the fratricidal character of Palestine in the first century, however, this endeavor is not in the least implausible; see *Life* 201-203; *Jewish War* 2:418-422; 4:129-134, 326-333.

15. *give notice to the tribune:* Luke uses *emphanizō* here and in v. 22 in its sense of "report/reveal/represent" (compare Josephus, *Antiquities of the Jews* 4:43), whereas in 24:1; 25:2, 15, he uses it in the sense of "bring a charge against/accuse" (compare Josephus, *Antiquities* 10:166). In the present instance, the subsequent result clause (*hopos*) suggests a better translation might be, "make a representation to the tribune such as . . . ." The Western text expands this verse at the beginning and at the end, where it adds after the words "before he comes," this avowal, "even though we must die also."

    discern matters concerning him: The verb *diaginōskō* is used in 24:22 in its more judicial sense of "determining" a case; here it seems to have more the sense "analyzing/deliberating" the issue.

16. *son of Paul's sister:* Like the connection of Barnabas to John Mark and his household in Jerusalem (12:12), this mention of Paul's relatives provides suggestive but unverifiable information about Paul's earlier presence in Jerusalem. As for the role of the young man, Hellenistic Romances frequently use family members or slaves to communicate messages between central characters (see e.g., Xenophon, *The Ephesians* 2, 3, 2-8; Chariton of Aphrodisias, *Chaereas and Callirhoe* 3, 1, 1-3). Access to prisoners by family or associates (see 24:23; 28:17, 30) was not uncommon; compare 2 Tim 1:16-17; Phil 2:25, and the frequent visitation of the imprisoned in later Christian writings: see *The Acts of Andrew* 14; *Acts of Paul and Thecla* 18-19; *The Passion of Saints Perpetua and Felicity* 3. For further confirmation, see the wonderful depiction in Lucian of Samosata, *Passing of Peregrinus* 12-13.

17. *take this young man:* Paul's status has gradually been elevated as the story has progressed. He "summons" the centurion and sends him on an errand! The following verses have the combination of repetition with minor variations that Luke obviously enjoys using.

21. *don't believe them:* Or, "Don't be persuaded by them." The young man proceeds with the third of four retellings of the plot: he had heard of the "ambush" (*enedra*, in the LXX, Josh 8:7-9), and now speaks of them "laying an ambush" (*enedreuein*, LXX Josh 8:4; Judg 9:32).

    awaiting the word from you: The term *epangelia* usually refers to a "promise" in Luke-Acts (see Luke 24:49; Acts 1:4; 2:33, 39; 7:17; 13:23, 32; 26:6), but here it refers simply to a message (or "the promise he was coming").

23. *two hundred soldiers:* The total number of 470 soldiers seems large, and we may be witnessing the inflation of numbers (which functions to inflate importance) typical of ancient historians; on the other hand, the numbers fit within the complement of a full cohort, and such numerical superiority to the forty conspirators (ten to one) in a desert context would not be entirely unreasonable if the point were the prevention of a killing. The real issue, of course, is whether even the fact of Paul's citizenship would win such attention. The translation is made difficult by the fact that *dexiolaboi* is unattested before this time. It obviously has something to do with "taking by the right hand," but could mean anything from "guard," to "spearman," to "swordsman."

24. *animals that they can put Paul on:* The aorist participle *epibibasantes* is active ("set on a mount") as in Luke 10:34; 19:35, so that a more literal rendering would be, "prepare animals so that setting Paul on them, they might lead him safely." This would, however, be misleading, since the subject of *diasōzō* ("lead through safely"; see lxx Deut 20:4; Judg 3:26; 1 Sam 19:18; Acts 27:43-44; 28:1, 4) is the soldiers rather than the mounts. The Western Text has a number of elaborations in vv. 23-24, the most notable being to supply a motivation for the tribune's action: "he was afraid the Jews would seize him and kill him [that is, Paul], and he himself would afterwards be blamed for having taken money."

    Felix the governor: As in the case of Pilate, Luke uses *hēgemōn* for the procurator (compare *hēgemoneuō* in Luke 3:1). According to the account in Tacitus, *Annals* 12:54, Antonius Felix had already had something to do with the ruling of Palestine together with Cumanus (procurator from 48-52). Josephus does not mention this earlier presence, but refers only to Claudius having "sent" Felix as governor of Judea in 52 (*Antiquities of the Jews* 20:137; *Jewish War* 2:247). This uncertainty concerning an earlier role may have something to do with Paul's otherwise puzzling comment in Acts 24:27 that Felix had "for many years" been a benefactor to the nation. In any case, Felix remained as governor until the year 60, when he was replaced by Festus (Acts 24:27; Josephus, *Jewish War* 2:271).

25. *a letter with this character:* The term "character" translates *typos*, which here has the sense of "pattern." The usage is found in 3 Macc 3:30 and *The Letter of Aristeas* 34. The letter itself is similar to the matter-of-fact messages between leaders such as we find in 1 Macc 11:30-37; 12:19-23; 2 Macc 11:16-21. See also the letter from the Jerusalem council in Acts 15:23-29. Some *mss* contain the usual farewell in v. 30, (*errōso/errōsthe*), but others lack it.

27. *having learned that he was a Roman citizen:* The Greek sentence is usually punctuated so that the aorist participle *mathōn* goes with the previous sentence, but the present translation actually corresponds better with the intended sense, since their discovery of Paul's citizenship is not prior to the rescue but subsequent to it. The tribune's letter is a model of concision, which enables him to pass over the embarrassing fact that he had been about to flog Paul before "discovering" his real identity!

29. *questions about their law:* This opinion coincides with that of the Roman governor of Achaia in Acts 18:15: Gallio also refers to *zētēmata* about words and names and the Law. Luke is building a set of legal precedents for regarding the Messianists not as revolutionaries threatening to Rome, but as a legitimate variation within Judaism. Ideally, the issue should be settled within the *politeuma* of Judaism rather than by the Roman judicial system; see also the judgment in 25:19, "certain questions about their superstition," as well as 26:3. Unfortunately, the entrenched hatred of the Jewish leadership towards Paul will make this sort of solution impossible. The Western Text for this verse adds after "their law," the words "of Moses and a certain Jesus."

30. *a plot against this man:* The mixed construction of the sentence (the genitive absolute slides into an indirect statement), together with the use of the rare future infinitive (*esesthai*), has generated a number of textual variants, none of which affect the basic sense of the verse.

31. *by night to Antipatris:* Josephus says that this city was founded by Herod the Great in honor of his father Antipater in a plain that was well watered and fertile (*Antiquities of the Jews* 13:390; *Jewish War* 1:99). It was on the road running from Jerusalem to Caesarea, about ten miles northeast of Joppa and 35 miles southwest of Caesarea.

32. *allowing the horsemen to depart:* The reasons for this are obvious: a) the farther the party is from Jerusalem, the less grave the threat from the conspiracy and therefore the less need of manpower; b) Paul on his mounts and the cavalry could make the longer leg of the journey faster and more safely than could the foot soldiers.

34. *from what province he was:* The Western Text changes this exchange from indirect to direct discourse. The question concerns legal jurisdiction, similar to Pilate's decision to refer Jesus to Herod upon discovering that he was from Herod's territory of Galilee (Luke 23:6-7). In the present case, it seems that Felix's decision to proceed with the case despite Paul's origin in Cilicia must have something to do with distance: Paul could not face his accusers if he were extradited so far away.

35. *kept in the praetorium of Herod:* A *praitōrion* took its name from the *praetor*, or military governor, of a territory. It was both strong-place and residence. We do not know of this particular building from literary sources, but we do know that Herod was the great builder of Caesarea Maritima (see Josephus, *Antiquities of the Jews* 15:331-341).

INTERPRETATION

This part of the story forms a transition. Paul is transferred from the grasp of his Jewish opponents to the protective custody of the Roman legal system. The Jewish opposition to Paul is now shown to be more than a (perhaps understandable) emotional response to the putative transgression of a holy place; it is identified as a fixed and fanatic intention to kill Paul. The gathering resistance to Paul's mission among Diaspora Jews (Acts 13:45; 14:2-5; 14:19; 17:5-9; 18:12-16; 19:9; 20:3) which reached a riot pitch at the instigation of Asian Jews in the Temple precincts (21:28-36; 22:22) is now hardened into a deadly resolve to ambush and assassinate Paul; and as in the resistance to Jesus (Luke 22:52, 66-71), as well as in Paul's former persecution of the Church (9:1), the chief priests and members of the Sanhedrin are actively involved (23:12; see 4:1-5; 5:17-18; 6:15).

The string has not run out entirely. There will be more debate and defense in the presence of the Jewish leaders. In Rome, Paul will even find some partial acceptance by the local leaders (Acts 28:24). But the official Jewish leadership, represented by the chief priest and council, shows itself to be what it had been from the beginning: closed to the message of the prophet whom God had raised up, envious of the success found by this message among the populace, and moved to murderous rage against its most prominent preachers.

The contrast between the Jewish leadership and the Roman military tribune is instructive. The Sanhedrin has committed itself to Paul's death by its cooperation with these assassins, and will continue that commitment by its pursual of Paul by legal harassment (24:1-9). The tribune seeks to save Paul's life simply on the basis of Paul's Roman citizenship and the young man's report, and commits himself and his resources to securing Paul safely within the Roman legal system.

The message is clear. If the Christians are to argue what they regard as their legitimate claims to represent the authentic Israel, it will not be possible within the context of direct confrontation with the Jewish leadership, which has shown itself not only unwilling to hear those claims but unwilling to let those making them continue to live. Any debate or defense can take place only within the protection offered by the Roman order. The tragic dimensions of this are clear if we observe that the identity Paul claims only as an expedient (his Roman citizenship) secures him a safety and a hearing based on a recognition of that right, whereas the identity Paul claims to be his own with all sincerity for his entire life (his Jewish heritage) is utterly rejected, and he is given no fair hearing by the leaders of his own people.

Regarded simply as a story, this section has the intrinsic charm of a boy's adventure: Paul's nephew just happens to hear of the plot, and he is not only allowed to visit Paul in the barracks, but the entire machinery of the army post bends itself to Paul's request, with the young man being allowed to deliver the message to the mighty military presence. There is the excitement of a fanatic plot foiled by an even bolder counterplan, the gathering of forces, the escape by night, the safe arrival.

And each stage is connected by the fourfold repetition concerning the conspiracy.

The details of the story, however, also serve to embellish the basic point concerning the two divergent responses to Paul. From the side of the Roman authority, the nephew is allowed to deliver the message to Paul, and is brought to the tribune, and is taken by the arm to a spot apart for the delivery of the message to the tribune's ears alone. The tribune does take extraordinary precautions to protect Paul; he does send a letter that is scrupulously fair in the statement of the situation, while adding his own opinion that "nothing worthy of death or imprisonment" had been done by Paul. The soldiers do carry out their mission and deliver Paul safely. The governor does receive the prisoner, and follows the appropriate legal steps: finding out Paul's place of origin to check on jurisdiction, postponing any decision until Paul can face his accusers and answer them, and, above all, providing the safety that otherwise was no longer available to Paul. In short, the behavior of the empire is better in every respect than that of the Jewish leadership.

Luke's readers are not likely to miss Luke's point by concluding either that all Jews are closed to the good news (much of his narrative has been constructed to show the exact opposite), or that the Roman state is an unequivocally just and benign force. Luke will show us the inconsistency and moral inadequacy of Roman leaders (24:25-26), and the continuing openness of some Jewish leaders to dialogue (28:17-22). Rather, Luke is showing how God was making it possible for Paul, in fulfillment of his vision, to "bear witness as well in Rome" (23:11), by extricating Paul from his Jewish enemies and placing him within the frame of a Roman system that will in the end also reject him, but will before that enable him to bear witness as the Lord desired.

For Reference and Further Study

Cadbury, H. J. "Roman Law and the Trial of Paul." *Beginnings* 5:297-306.

Legasse, S. "L'Apologetique à l'égard de Rome dan le procès de Paul (Acts 21, 27-26, 32)." *RScR* 69 (1981) 249–256.

Sanders, J. T. "The Salvation of the Jews in Luke-Acts." *Luke-Acts: New Perspectives from the Society of Biblical Literature Seminar.* Ed. C. H. Talbert. New York: Crossroad, 1984, 104–128.

Sherwin-White, A. N. *Roman Society and Roman Law in the New Testament.* Oxford: University Press, 1963, 48–70.

48. *Paul's Defense before Felix* (24:1-23)

1. After five days the chief priest Ananias went down with certain elders and Tertullus, a certain advocate. These made a representation to the governor against Paul. 2. When he was called upon, Tertullus began to make an accusation. He said, "The great peace we have experienced through you and the reforms accomplished for this nation through your foresight, 3. we welcome, O Excellent Felix, in every respect and in every place with all thanksgiving. 4. So that I do not take too much of your time, I ask that in your graciousness you listen to our brief presentation. 5. For we have found this fellow to be a pest. And he stirs up a disturbance among all the Jews living throughout the empire as a leader of the sect of the Nazoreans. 6. He was even trying to profane the Temple, and we arrested him. 8. You yourself will be able to find out from him by examination all these things of which we are accusing him." 9. And the Jews also joined the attack by stating that these things were so. 10. When the governor gave him the nod, Paul responded. He said, "Since I know that you have been a judge in this nation for many years, I make my defense cheerfully. 11. You are able to discover that it is no more than twelve days since I went up to worship in Jerusalem. 12. Furthermore, they did not find me disrupting anyone or collecting a crowd, either in the Temple or in the synagogues or throughout the city. 13. Neither are they capable of offering evidence to you concerning the things of which they are now accusing me. 14. But I do confess this to you, that it is according to the way they call a heresy I worship the ancestral God. I believe all the things written throughout the Law and in the Prophets. 15. I have a hope in God which these people themselves accept, a coming resurrection of the just and the unjust. 16. Because of this I myself strive to have an unwavering conscience toward God and toward humans. 17. After many years I came to give alms to my nation and offerings. 18. As I was doing these, they found me purified in the Temple. Not with a crowd! Not with a disturbance! 19. But some Jews from Asia ought to present themselves before you and make accusation if they have something against me. 20. Or let these people themselves say what crime they found when I was standing before the Sanhedrin, 21. or concerning the one declaration I cried out while standing among them, that 'I am being judged by you today concerning the resurrection of the dead.'" 22. Felix put them off, since he had accurate knowledge concerning the way. He said, "When Lysias the tribune comes down, I will make a decision on your case." 23. He ordered the centurion to hold him leniently, and not to forbid his associates from ministering to him.

NOTES

1. *Tertullus, a certain advocate:* The term *rhētor* can mean any sort of public speaker (see Lucian of Samosata, *A Professor of Public Speaking* 1), but here has the

sense of a legal advocate (see Josephus, *Antiquities of the Jews* 17:226; Dio Chrysostom, *Oration* 76:4). It is not clear whether he himself is Jewish: he uses the first person plural (24:3, 5, 6, 8), but this is not decisive. In v. 9, Luke says "the Jews also contributed," as though they were separate from Tertullus. At the very least he identifies himself with the perspective of his clients.

made a representation . . . against Paul: In the present context, the verb *emphanizō* (see the note on 23:15) has its specific legal nuance of making a charge. They report "information" which constitutes a brief against Paul (see the use of *katagoreō* in the next verse).

2. *when he was called upon:* The obvious subject of the genitive absolute construction *klēthentos autou* is Tertullus; note the corresponding "nod" given to Paul when it is his turn to speak, also in the same sort of construction (*neusantos autou tou hēgemonos*, 24:10).

   the great peace: The rhetorician begins with an obviously fulsome *captatio benevolentiae*, which when applied to Felix is particularly inflated, since he was a notoriously bad administrator, and under his administration, Jewish unrest and violence reached new heights (Tacitus, *Annals* 12:54; Josephus, *Jewish War* 2:253-270).

3. *we welcome . . . with all thanksgiving:* The Greek sentence does not have a proper direct object for *apodechometha* ("we welcome"), but instead two genitive absolute constructions that provide the explanation for the gratitude ("because of the great peace . . ." etc.). For *apodechomai*, see Luke 8:40; 9:11; Acts 2:41; 18:27; 21:17; 28:30. The title "Excellent Felix" (*kratiste Phēlix*) was used also in the tribune's letter (23:26), and will be used again later by Paul (26:25). It reminds us also of Luke's designation of his patron Theophilus in Luke 1:3.

4. *take up too much of your time:* The verb *enkoptō* means generally "to hinder" (Rom 15:22; Gal 5:7; 1 Pet 3:7; 1 Thess 2:18), but when applied to time, means "delay." Judicial discourses were timed by the use of a water clock (see Lucian of Samosata, *The Double Indictment* 15, 19), and the advocate was required to keep his speeches short (*syntomōs*). Brevity, in fact, was generally an ideal of ancient rhetoric (*The Double Indictment* 20-21; Quintilian, *Institutes* 8, 3, 82; Longinus, *On the Sublime* 9:14; 42:1-2; Heb 13:22; 1 Pet 5:12), even though it was an ideal more often praised than practiced.

   in your graciousness: The quality of *epieikeia* ("graciousness") is one which allows someone to go beyond the strict bounds of legality because of reasonableness, patience, or mercy (see LXX Ps 85:5; 2 Macc 9:27; Philo, *Life of Moses* 1:198); in the NT, see 2 Cor 10:1; Phil 4:5; 1 Tim 3:3; Titus 3:2; Jas 3:17; 1 Pet 2:18.

5. *to be a pest:* The term *loimos* can mean "pestilence" as a noun or "pestilential" as an adjective. The problem with the translation as "pest" is that in contemporary English usage that term is trivialized to mean a bothersome irritation. In LXX 1 Sam 30:22, the *anēr loimos* is equivalent to an *anēr ponēros* ("evil man").

stirs up a disturbance: In 19:40, the term *stasis* has its strong sense of "riot," but since the context here is "among the Jews," the milder translation is warranted. His sponsorship of the "sect of the Nazoreans" is here said to have the same divisive effect among all Jews as that demonstrated locally by 15:2; 23:7, 10. For the translation of *kata tēn oikoumenēn* as "throughout the empire," see the note on 11:28. The charge of sedition resembles those made in 17:6-7; 18:12 against Paul, and that made in Luke 23:2 against Jesus.

leader of the sect of the Nazoreans: The *protostatēs* is the "one who stands in the first place," and appears only here in the NT. The Jewish leaders assign to Paul the same importance as standard bearer of the messianic movement that Luke himself does. The term *hairesis* applied here and in 28:22 to the Messianists can mean either "sect" or "party"; the same word is used for the divisions between Sadducees and Pharisees (Acts 5:17; 15:5; 26:5), and is used for philosophical parties in Hellenism (see the references in the note on Acts 5:17). When used by outsiders, of course, the term can take on the negative connotation of "heresy," which is the implication of Paul's appropriation of the word in 24:14. This is the only time that the plural form of *nazōraios* has been used. We noted earlier that it derives from a title for Jesus which now remains somewhat obscure (perhaps from the Hebrew *nazir*, from which "Nazarite" derives); see the note on Luke 18:37; Acts 2:22. In the present context, the designation has the same force as *christianoi* in 11:26: "those who follow the Nazorean" = "those who follow the messiah."

6. *profane the Temple:* The verb *bebēloō* means to "make profane" (*bebēlos*) that which was supposed to be sacred. In Judaism, the profanation of the Sabbath (Neh 13:17; Ezek 20:13; 1 Macc 1:43) and of the Temple (Ps 73:7; Ezek 28:18; 2 Macc 8:2; 1QpHab 12:9) were regarded as particularly heinous. In Exod 31:14, in fact, those who profane the Sabbath are declared worthy of death. Paul's compatriots show they have the same view with regard to the profanation of the Temple (21:28-31).

we arrested him: The use of *krateō* ("arrest") lends a specious air of legality to what Luke had described as a lynch mob (21:31; 22:22-23). It also implies that Paul's case should be within the disposition of the Sanhedrin. The Western Text makes this more explicit: "and we wanted to judge him according to our law," then continuing in v. 7, "but Lysias the tribune came and took him away from us with great violence, ordering those accusing him to come before you." The entirety of v. 7 is absent from the best *mss*, and is also excluded from the present text, although some scholars argue that it is original. Certainly, it has psychological plausibility in its favor, and allows Tertullus to suggest in still another way that the Jews resent this "violent" intrusion into their right to manage the affairs of their national shrine.

8. *find out from him by examination:* If v. 7 from the Western tradition were to stand, then the *par' autou* ("from him") would refer not to Paul but to Lysias the tribune. But in Luke's usage, *anakrinō* applies mainly to the examination of prisoners (see Luke 23:14; Acts 4:9, with 12:19 being a very special case!). Paul will refer back to his "examination" in 28:18.

9. *Jews also joined the attack:* The verb *synepitithēmi* means literally to "put in together," and is used for "helping" in an attack (see Aristotle, *Politics* 1311B;
LXX Deut 32:27; Ps 3:6; Zech 1:15; Josephus, *Antiquities of the Jews* 10:116).
The reader is reminded of those insistent voices from the crowd in the trial
of Jesus before Pilate (Luke 23:10, 18, 21, 23).

10. *you have been a judge . . . for many years:* Paul begins his defense with a shorter
and simpler *captatio* than that of Tertullus. His reference to "many years"
may simply be formal (compare the use of *pollēs, pantē, pantachou, pasēs* in
vv. 2-3), or it may reflect the knowledge (reported at least in Tacitus, *Annals*
12:54) that Felix had served as an administrator in Palestine together with
Cumanus before succeeding him as governor.

    make my defense cheerfully: A very similar statement is made by Paul to Agrippa
    in 26:2, again using the verb *apologeomai*. Why should Felix's putative long-
    standing as a judge provide Paul with "cheer/encouragement" (*euthumōs*)?
    Is it because the procurator had good reason to know firsthand the sort of
    internecine disputes that pervaded Jewish life in that territory during the
    middle years of the first century (see the note on v. 3, above)? Is it because,
    having a Jewish wife (24:24), he would already be aware of the boundaries
    of Jewish confession, and even of the messianic claims (24:22)?

11. *twelve days since I went up to worship:* Neither the mode of calculation nor the
point is entirely clear. If we follow the markings of the text itself (21:27; 22:30;
23:11, 12, 31), then twelve days elapsed since Paul's arrival in Jerusalem and
his night-flight to Caesarea, but 24:1 indicates the passage of another five
days before this hearing. And what is Paul's point? Is it that there was too
short a time to carry out the things of which he was accused? More important perhaps to his defense is the way he has crafted his motivation for the
trip to Jerusalem. It was to "worship" (*proskynesōn*, a future participle expressing purpose). This obviously contradicts the charge of deliberate profanation, and places Paul within the most traditional form of pilgrimage piety
(see LXX Ps 5:7; 85:9; 131:7; 137:2; Acts 7:43; 8:27).

12. *Temple . . . synagogues . . . city:* The three terms are joined by *oute,* and extend Paul's defense beyond the Temple to other Jerusalem venues. Once more,
we have indirect evidence for the multiplicity of synagogues within the city
itself at this period (compare Acts 6:9).

13. *offering evidence:* The phrase *parastēnai peri hōn* means literally, "to make presentation concerning the things." The verb *paristēmi* can carry the legal sense
of providing sufficient evidence for proof (see Epictetus, *Discourses* 2, 26, 4;
Josephus, *Life* 27), and is used with much the same sense in Acts 1:3; 4:10.

14. *I do confess this:* In forensic terms, this is a breathtaking turn: after a series
of emphatic denials, the accused is about to make a confession (*homologeō*)!
The "this" (*touto*) is emphatic: Paul himself defines what the real issue is
in the dispute. For the language of confession as profession, see Luke 12:8;
Acts 23:8.

    the way they call a heresy: If *hairesis* is the outsider designation for the Mes-
    sianists, "the way" (*hodos*) is the insider designation (see 9:2; 16:17; 18:25-26;

19:9, 23; 22:4). The critical difference here is the messianic claim to represent a legitimate (indeed, *the* authentic) form of Judaism.

I worship the ancestral God: The phrase *tǭ patrǭǭ theǭ* could equally be translated "the God of the ancestors." Paul justifies himself (and his fellow Messianists) *within* Judaism. Compare the "ancestral law" in Acts 22:3, and "ancestral customs" in 28:17, as well as the use in 2 Macc 4:15; 6:1, 6; 7:2; 3 Macc 1:23. The exact expression, "ancestral God," appears also in 4 Macc 12:18 and Josephus, *Antiquities of the Jews* 9:256.

I believe in all the things written: The English translation makes an independent statement out of the participle *pisteuōn* ("believing"). Paul's profession of faith in "the Law and the Prophets" is familiar (Luke 16:19, 31; 24:27, 44; Acts 13:15; 28:23). The phrase *kata nomon* is here translated as "throughout" rather than "according to," since the point seems to be the inclusiveness of his attachment to Scripture.

15. *a hope in God:* The translation again changes a participial construction (*echōn*) into an independent sentence. Three separate observations about this statement: a) As in his Sanhedrin hearing (23:6), Paul defines his defense to be of the resurrection, which he calls a "hope" (*elpis*), see 24:20; b) he claims that this conviction is one shared by his accusers, even though the Sanhedrin hearing made clear that some of them did not (23:7-8); c) resurrection, as in Judaism, is a future reality (*mellein esesthai*), and—more strikingly— involves both the just and the unjust, a depiction in basic agreement with Dan 12:2; John 5:28-29; Rev 20:12-13, but less so with 1 Cor 15:12-57; Luke 14:14; 20:35. According to Josephus, the Pharisaic expectation was only for the resurrection of the just (*Jewish War* 2:163); although the evidence in *Antiquities of the Jews* 18:14 is less clear.

16. *strive to have an unwavering conscience:* The term *askeō* suggests active exertion, as in physical exercise, for which it comes to mean moral striving (see Lucian of Samosata, *Demonax* 4; *Toxaris* 27; Epictetus, *Discourses* 3, 12, 10; *Letter of Aristeas* 168). For Paul's statement of conscience, see also 23:1. The adjective *aproskopos* could also mean "without stumbling/giving offense" (compare 3 Macc 3:8; *Letter of Aristeas* 210; Phil 1:10; 1 Cor 10:13).

17. *to give alms to my nation and offerings:* A completely satisfactory translation is difficult. It is uncertain whether to read *eis to ethnos mou* ("to my nation") as the object of the arrival of Paul, or (as in this translation) as the object of his almsgiving. Knowing what we do from Paul's letters, we are tempted to read this simply as a reference to his collection for "the saints in Jerusalem" (Gal 2:10; 1 Cor 16:1-4; 2 Cor 8-9; Rom 15:25-32). But since Luke has not otherwise told us of this collection, how are we to evaluate it simply within his own narrative? a) Does the designation "alms for my nation" camouflage the gift to the Church as a donation to the Jews as a whole, and therefore further portray Paul as loyal to the people? b) Why include "offerings" (*prosphoras*) as part of Paul's original intention, when in fact it was suggested to him by James and the elders as a gesture of reconciliation (21:23-26)? c) Why has Luke left it until now to reveal—even to the reader!—the purpose

of Paul's visit, after such a long reticence? For the locution "my nation" (*ethnos mou*), compare Luke 7:5; 23:2; Acts 10:22; 24:2, 10. For "alms" (*eleēmosynē*), see Luke 11:41; 12:33; Acts 3:2-3, 10; 10:2, 4, 31.

18. *found me purified in the Temple:* Far from profaning the holy place, Paul claims— and the narrative supports him (21:27)—to have been in a state of ritual purity (*hēgiasmenon*). And he was peacefully going about his business; the two denials are translated as separate exclamations to give them their proper emphasis.

19. *Jews from Asia:* The sentence is anacolouthic, but the point is clear enough. Paul addresses the credentials of the witnesses against him: the Sanhedrin members were not witnesses to the Temple disturbance, and they can offer nothing but hearsay. The only ones who could legitimately bring a charge were those who witnessed the events (and could also be rebutted), namely the Jews from Asia (21:27).

20. *what crime they found:* The credibility of the witnesses who *are* present (*autoi houtoi*, "these people here"), is challenged from another direction. All that they can bear witness to is the council meeting (23:1-10). But they can scarcely claim that any crime was detected there, only that a dispute broke out when Paul declared he was on trial for the resurrection (23:6). And if they acknowledge that they are in no position to testify concerning disturbance or profanation, then the case should be thrown out. And if they insist on taking part, then they must agree that the issue is the resurrection!

22. *accurate knowledge concerning the way:* The verb *anaballō* has the legal sense of "delaying/putting off" a case (see Josephus, *Antiquities of the Jews* 14:177). But the precise relationship between Felix's calling for a delay and his "accurate knowledge of the way" is not clear; the translation treats it as explanatory: he leans toward Paul because of his knowledge of the messianic movement, but wants to await the personal testimony of the tribune Lysias. Why would he have this awareness? Because of his having served for a long time as judge with Cumanus (23:24)? Because his wife Drusilla was a Jew (24:24)? Note the similar knowledge concerning Judaism attributed to Petronius by Philo, *Embassy to Gaius* 245.

    make a decision on your case: In contrast to Acts 23:15, the verb *diaginōskō* in the present setting clearly means to "determine/decide" a case rather than simply to "investigate" it (compare Josephus, *Antiquities* 4:121; Philo, *On Husbandry* 116). The fact that Felix subsequently fails to follow through on this promise does not affect the meaning.

23. *to hold him leniently:* Literally, "to hold him in custody, but with relaxation," with *anesis* having the sense of leniency or relief (see the exact parallel in Josephus, *Antiquities of the Jews* 18:235). For the ability of associates (*hoi idioi*, see 4:23) to visit those being held in captivity, see the note on 23:16. It is just such circumstances that support the possibility of Caesarea as one of the places from which Paul could have written such letters as Colossians, Ephesians, Philemon, Philippians and Second Timothy.

Before looking at the specifics of this passage, it is useful to pause to consider once more what Luke is up to in Paul's lengthy trial. Something more than the desire for historical or biographical plenitude is at work. Luke, after all, has shown himself elsewhere to be perfectly capable of passing over years of busy activity with a one-line summary (18:11; 19:10). He could easily have passed over the embarrassment of Paul's captivity with an equally brief allusion, and moved on to the excitement of the sea voyage to Rome. Why does he linger here? It is not due to a wealth of source material, for he was no more likely to have had accurate records of the exchanges between Paul and his accusers than he was of Stephen's speech before the Sanhedrin. What Luke chooses to tell us, we have learned, serves his literary and religious purposes.

In this instance, the drawn-out legal process, with all its false starts and delays, serves the literary function of unfolding (slowly and in segments) Paul's true identity and integrity, not for the characters in the narrative, but for Luke's readers themselves. Even more than the conversion of the Gentiles initiated by Peter (Acts 10–15), the conversion of Paul and his Gentile mission require slow digestion. The reader, too, wants to understand how Paul fits into Luke's story of the prophet and the people. In what sense does he continue the work of Jesus and the apostles? What are the grounds of opposition to Paul? These are critical questions precisely for Gentile readers, for their answers help define the "security" (*asphaleia*) of the Gentile Christians' sense of inheriting an authentic realization of the blessing to Abraham.

Luke uses these hearings to eliminate once and for all any false apprehensions concerning Paul: he is not a charlatan but sincere, not a renegade from Judaism, but one faithful to the ancestral customs and beliefs, not a fomenter of unrest, but a prophetic witness to the resurrection, not a cowardly opportunist, but a loyal and obedient disciple whose path of suffering replicates that of Jesus himself. By the rebuttal of the attacks on Paul's person, Luke also focuses the reader on the real issue: the hope of Israel that is the resurrection of the dead.

What makes Paul (and the Messianists) genuine members of Israel is the conviction they share with the Pharisees concerning the resurrection of the dead. This says more than it appears to, for that conviction involves (or should involve, from the Messianist standpoint) a number of subsidiary points: a) that God's revelation extends beyond the written text of Torah into new experiences and interpretations; b) that the authentic Israel is not defined in terms of such localized symbols as kingship, land, or temple, but in terms of faith in the one and living God; c) that the definitive establishment of God's rule comes about not by human accomplishment but by God's action. What separates Paul (and the Messianists) from the Pharisees and other Jews is their (experience and) conviction that the "pledge" (*pistis*, see 17:31) of this resurrection has occurred already in Jesus, the prophet whom God "raised up."

In the present passage, we find the only real "trial" in the sequence, held before the Roman governor, with all parties present and able to speak their piece. The odds appear at first to be grotesquely skewed: the chief priest and his elders come down from Jerusalem with a professional advocate to speak for them, whereas Paul, already held as a captive, must speak for himself. When the advocate Tertullus begins his address for the prosecution, furthermore, fear strikes the reader's heart: what an oleaginous *captatio* he delivers (24:2-4), and what a twisted version of the events! Will Felix fall for this obvious flattery, and will he be swayed by the rhetoric into accepting not only the local charge that Paul has profaned the Temple (24:6), but the universal charge against Paul as disturber of Jews throughout the empire (24:5)? Or will the governor recognize beneath these charges the barely hidden resentment of the Jews against the Roman order which surfaces only briefly in the statement "*we* arrested him," but which underlies the implicit claim that Paul is someone who should fall under *their* jurisdiction as a court over the Jewish *ethnos/politeuma*?

Paul, of course, turns out to be perfectly capable of defending himself. Once more, we are reminded of the way in which Luke's portrayal of Jesus' prophetic successors fits more comfortably within the conventions of the Hellenistic philosopher, who is ready to speak his own *apologia* before the court (like Socrates) with straightforward simplicity and confidence (*parrēsia*). His introduction is neither flattering nor arrogant: he places his hopes in Felix's long acquaintance with the circumstances he is now called upon to judge, an invitation to the governor to read between the lines: he should know by now the character of intramural Jewish conflicts (24:10).

Paul takes up the charge of causing a disturbance in the Temple (24:12), but quickly shifts to a more comprehensive self-defense, which touches on a) his clear conscience before both God and humans (24:16); b) his commitment to the ancestral beliefs and customs which he "professes" according to "the way they call a heresy" (24:14); c) his particular commitment to the coming resurrection of the dead, stated twice for emphasis (24:15, 21); d) his actions which demonstrate his loyalty to the people (bringing them alms) and the Temple (making offerings in a state of ritual purification, 24:17-18). In the notes and in previous discussions, the knotty historical problem posed by this reference to the purpose of Paul's trip to Jerusalem with a large sum of money has been taken up. What is clear in the present context is that Luke has made every effort to establish the basic *continuity* between Paul (with the messianic movement), and the sort of Judaism represented by the Pharisaic party.

But Luke does not have Paul neglect his own legal status. He goes on the counterattack against the specific charges in the way that a good contemporary defense lawyer would: by challenging the credibility and standing of his accusers. In a few deft lines, Paul isolates those who now stand before him. They were not present for any events "throughout the empire" or even in the Temple. Their evidence for that is only hearsay. Only the Asian Jews who started all this could bear witness against Paul directly on that charge, and they are not present. The charges ought therefore to be dropped! But if the Jews wish to continue the case, then they must do so on the grounds of what they *can* bear witness to, which is Paul's defense of the resurrection of the dead, for that is the only substance of their personal involvement with Paul (23:1-9).

Now for the first time, the reader has reason to grow uneasy about the protection offered by the Roman legal system. In sharp contrast to the tribune Lysias who had done everything according to the numbers, the governor Felix begins to reveal himself as vacillating and indecisive. Despite the "accurate knowledge of the way" (24:22), which would indicate the substantial truth of Paul's assertions, and despite Paul's brilliant discrediting of the Sanhedrin as legitimate witnesses to the charges as brought, Felix stalls for time. Despite knowing already Lysias' firm judgment on the matter, that Paul had done nothing worthy of death or even imprisonment (23:29), Felix refuses to make the appropriate judgment until "Lysias the tribune comes down" (24:22). No matter that Paul's captivity is a lenient one, with the opportunity to see his associates (24:23); the reader begins to perceive that Paul's progress to Rome will be neither swift nor smooth.

FOR REFERENCE AND FURTHER STUDY

Bowen, C. R. "Paul's Collection and the Book of Acts." *JBL* 42 (1923) 49–58.

Losch, S. "Die Dankesreden des Tertullus: Apg. 24, 1-4." *ThQ* 112 (1931) 295–319.

Neyrey, J. "The Forensic Defense Speech and Paul's Trial Speeches in Acts 22-26: Form and Function." *Luke-Acts: New Perspectives from the Society of Biblical Literature Seminar.* Ed. C. H. Talbert. New York: Crossroad, 1984, 210–224.

Nickle, K. *The Collection: A Study in Paul's Strategy.* SBT 48. Naperville: Allenson, 1966.

49. *Paul and Festus* (24:24–25:12)

24. After some days Felix came with his wife Drusilla, who was Jewish. He sent for Paul. He listened to him concerning faith in Messiah Jesus. 25. As he was discoursing about righteousness and self-control and the coming judgment, Felix grew alarmed. He responded, "Go for now. When I get the opportunity I will call you." 26. He was hoping at the same time that he would be given money by Paul. Therefore he summoned him even more frequently to converse with him. 27. But when two years had passed, Felix received his successor, Porcius Festus. And since Felix wanted to do a favor to the Jews, he left him in captivity. 25:1. When Festus had come into the province, he went up after three days from Caesarea to Jerusalem. 2. The chief priests and leaders among the Jews made a representation to him against Paul, and they made an appeal to him, 3. asking as a favor that he transfer him to Jerusalem, while they lay an ambush to kill him along the road. 4. Festus thereupon responded that Paul was being kept in Caesarea, but that he himself would be departing shortly. 5. "Therefore," he said, "let those who are powerful people among you come down together. If there is any wrong in the man, let them make an accusation." 6. After staying among them no more than eight or ten days, he went down to Caesarea. The next day he took his seat on the judicial bench and ordered Paul to be brought. 7. When he arrived, the Jews who had come down from Jerusalem surrounded him. They levelled against him many and weighty charges which they could not prove, 8. with Paul stating by way of defense that he had committed no offense either against the Law of the Jews or against the Temple or against Caesar. 9. But Festus wanted to do a favor for the Jews. He responded to Paul, "Do you wish to go up to Jerusalem and there be judged by me concerning these things?" 10. Paul said, "I am standing before Caesar's bench, where I must be judged. I have done no harm to the Jews as you also well know. 11. If therefore I am a wrongdoer and am worthy of death, I do not seek to be excused from dying. But if there is nothing in these things of which these people accuse me, no one is able to deliver me to them as a favor. I appeal to Caesar!" 12. Then, after Festus conferred with his council, he responded, "You have appealed to Caesar. To Caesar shall you go."

Notes

24. *Drusilla, who was Jewish:* She was the daughter of Herod Agrippa I (Josephus, *Antiquities of the Jews* 19:354; see Acts 12:1). According to the gossip reported by Josephus, she was originally married to the king of Emesa as part of her brother's dynastic arrangements. But Felix was struck by her beauty when he saw her and arranged for a *magos* to persuade her to leave her husband and marry him. So, says Josephus, she "transgressed the ancestral laws" and married Felix (*Antiquities of the Jews* 20:141–143). She provides another

reason why Felix might have had accurate knowledge of "the way" (24:22). The Western Text expands her narrative role by adding: "she asked to see Paul and hear the word (*logos*). Desiring to please her, he sent for Paul." The expansion helps to account for the remarkable fact that Paul was allowed to proclaim "faith in Messiah Jesus" to them!

25. *righteousness . . . self-control . . . judgment:* It is possible to interpret this in two ways. First, it can be understood as a sort of ethical translation of "messianic faith" for Gentile ears, in which "righteousness" (*dikaiosynē*) is defined in terms of a virtue (compare 1 Tim 6:11; 2 Tim 2:22; 3:16), which in turn is enacted by "self-control" (*enkrateia*, see 1 Cor 9:25; Gal 5:23; 2 Pet 1:6), with an eye toward God's future judgment (Rom 2:5-10; 14:10-12). Paul's discourse would focus on a subject dear to other Hellenistic moralists (see e.g., Epictetus, *Discourses* 4, 1, 10; frag. 10:6; *Letter of Aristeas* 278; 4 Macc 5:34-35). Second, it can be understood as having a more direct narrative function of rebuking the sexual irregularities of the royal couple. In this case, *enkrateia* would be understood in the narrower sense of *sexual* self-control (see *Testament of Naphtali* 8:8; *Acts of Paul and Thecla* 4-6). The difficulty of this interpretation is that it presupposes in the readers a knowledge of these characters that the narrative itself does not supply. On the other hand, it would account for the "alarm" experienced by Felix and the dismissal of Paul.

26. *hoping . . . that he would be given money:* Following upon Paul's reference to "alms for my nation" in 24:17, Luke provides a second indication that he knew of Paul's being in possession of considerable funds. Some *mss* seek to spell things out, by adding, "that he might release him." For the general willingness of a procurator to entertain such a consideration, see Josephus' report on Albinus, who was willing to make money in a variety of extra-legal ways, so that "the only ones left in prison as evildoers were those who did not pay the price" (*Jewish War* 2:272-274). The reader begins to suspect that Felix's devotion to justice is not absolute: he keeps Paul on a string in the hopes of getting a bribe, and fails to call Lysias down to confirm Paul's story.

27. *received his successor, Porcius Festus:* Josephus gives a brief notice to the governorship of Festus, which probably began in 59-60; his reign was short, but in contrast to that of *his* successor Albinus, a just one. In light of Luke's portrayal of him as one who wanted, if he could, to do a favor to the Jews, it should be noted that the one thing Josephus does specify in his account is that Festus captured and put to death a large number of the brigands, and in Josephus' interpretation, this would have made him at one with the ruling priestly class (*Antiquities* 20:182-188; *Jewish War* 2:271-272).

left Paul in captivity: Felix's lack of a steady moral compass is indicated by his willingness to leave Paul "in bonds" (*dedemenon*) in order to "do a favor" (*katathesthai charita*) for the Jews (the same idiom occurs with *charin* in 25:9; see Philo, *On Joseph* 231). Given the fact that Felix was, immediately after his replacement, charged by a delegation of Jews to the Emperor with various "injustices to the Jews" (Josephus, *Antiquities* 20:182), such a gesture may have been a final if futile attempt to forestall his own downfall. Consistent with Drusilla's expanded role in 24:24, however, the Western Text omits the mention of Felix's desire to please the Jews, replacing it with "but Paul was kept in prison on account of Drusilla."

25:1. *come into the province:* Or, "took up his office"; the phrase *epibas tȩ eparcheia* can be read either way (see Josephus, *Jewish War* 5:520, and Acts 23:24), with the meaning much the same. In the present case, the geographical context seems to favor the translation provided here.

2. *leaders among the Jews:* For only the second time, Luke uses the designation *hoi prōtoi* ("the first men"); see also Luke 19:47. In the Gospel, they were "the leaders of the people" (*laos*); here, a more distancing "leaders of the Jews." The translation "making a representation" is consistent with the use of *emphanizō* in 23:15, 22; 24:1; 25:15. Since this takes place only three days after the governor takes up office, the Jews are shown to be getting their oar in very quickly. According to Josephus, the chief priest would now be the Ishmael appointed by King Agrippa (*Antiquities of the Jews* 20:179).

3. *asking as a favor:* The construction is unusual: *aitoumenoi charin kat' autou* ("asking a favor against him"); the phrase apparently picks up the "granting a favor" of 24:27 and 25:9. If the precarious position of the governor (because of the charges being made against Felix by the Jewish leaders in Rome) is as Josephus reports it, then the Jewish leaders probably feel in a position to ask such a favor. Festus can demonstrate a stronger position against rabble-rousers and bandits than his predecessor had done.

while they lay an ambush: One should not be misled by the translation into thinking that Festus was party to this plot. For "laying an ambush" (*enedran poiountes*), see 23:16. The council's strategy is precisely the same as that of the forty oath-swearers in 23:14-15, with the difference that the leadership is now actively generating the plan. After two years, feelings against Paul still run high in Jerusalem! Luke indicates by this intention, of course, how far the Sanhedrin has come from any semblance of commitment to fair process for Paul. For the reader this helps explain Paul's complete unwillingness even to risk a trip to Jerusalem (25:10).

5. *powerful people among them:* There is a shift in this verse from indirect discourse to direct. The adjective *dynatos* is used as a substantive for powerful and influential people (Herodotus, *Persian Wars* 1:53; 1 Sam 2:9; 9:1; 2 Sam 20:7; 1 Cor 1:26). Here it is roughly equivalent to the earlier *hoi prōtoi* ("the leading men," 25:2).

anything wrong in the man: The term *atopos* (literally "out of place") can be used for anything amiss, from the strange to the wicked. Here it obviously bears the sense of "wrongdoing" (see LXX Job 27:6; 34:12; Prov 24:55; 2 Macc 14:23; 2 Thess 3:2, and especially Luke 23:41). What is most striking in Festus' sentence is the conditional construction; it is as if he were reopening the case entirely.

6. *took his seat on the judicial bench:* There is no good English equivalent for *bēma* (see Acts 12:21; 18:12, 16-17), the elevated platform or rostrum from which a magistrate would hear cases and deliver judgment (see Epictetus, *Discourses* 4, 10, 21; *Jewish War* 2:172).

7. *many and weighty charges:* The note that the Jews "surrounded" (*periistēmi*) Paul is ominous (see Herodotus, *Persian Wars* 1:43; 2 Macc 14:9), but although their charges are many and serious (*barus*), the Jews still have no proof to bring (*apodeiknymi* = demonstration, as in 4 Macc 1:8).

8. *or against Caesar:* Paul's denial of wrongdoing against Law and Temple pick up the earlier charges from 21:28 and 24:5-6, but the mention of Caesar in this context is new. We remember that Paul's accusers in 17:7 had claimed he was advocating practices against the "decrees of Caesar," but up to this point, Paul's Jewish accusers had focused only on the internal disturbance Paul had caused the Jews. Have the Jews shifted field, and picked up on Lysias' misapprehension in order to portray Paul as a brigand/revolutionary fighting against Rome? In any case, this mention of the emperor prepares for the appeal to Caesar which will follow shortly (25:10). The verb *hamartanō* here obviously has its general sense of "committing an offense" against custom or law, rather than the specific religious sense of "committing sin" (see Plato, *Phaedrus* 242E).

9. *wanted to do a favor for the Jews:* The same idiom is used here as in 24:27; Festus' suggestion can be seen as a response to the Jews' request of a "favor against Paul" in 25:3. But even though Festus declares that Paul would be heard by Festus himself rather than the Sanhedrin (*ep' emou*), Paul no longer sees any safety in Jerusalem, especially since his imprisonment to this point has been the result of another "favor" to the Jews by Felix (24:27).

11. *seek to be excused from dying:* The verb *paraiteomai* ("to request") can be used to mean "excuse" (see Luke 14:18-19), and here has the sense of "refusing/declining" (there is a precise parallel in Josephus, *Life* 141). Luke wants the reader to perceive Paul's legal maneuvering not as cowardice, but as a way of fulfilling the commission of the Lord to witness in Rome (23:11); like Socrates, he is not afraid of death if it should come to that (Plato, *Apology* 29A; 35A-B).

    deliver me to them as a favor: The verb *charizomai* means simply to "grant/give," but in the present context, where the bestowal of favors has played such a key role, the translation seeks to provide that extra nuance which Luke's word choice clearly intended (see 24:27; 25:3, 9).

    I appeal to Caesar: The emperor in question was by this point Nero, who had succeeded Claudius, and reigned from 54-68 C.E. (see Suetonius, *Life of Nero* 8). The right of a citizen to appeal was an ancient one in Roman law, and could take the form of redress from a previous decision, or a direct appeal at an earlier stage of proceedings. It was, of course, restricted to those who had citizenship rights in the city of Rome (see Pliny the Younger, *Letters* 10:96), although those who created political unrest threatening to the Roman state as such could be remanded directly to Rome for their trial even when they were not citizens—which, of course, is a form of extradition (see Josephus, *Jewish War* 2:243; 2:253). Luke's account obviously presumes that Paul's claim to be a Roman citizen (16:37-38; 22:25, 26, 27, 29) was true, and had been communicated from Felix to Festus (see Lysias' letter, 23:27). The punishments for falsely claiming citizenship were severe (Epictetus, *Discourses* 3, 24, 41), at times amounting to execution (Suetonius, *Life of Claudius* 25:3). Contemporary readers are in no position to verify Paul's claim, but the logic of Luke's narrative rests on the governor's believing it; for supporting evidence on the widespread extension of citizenship see Josephus, *Against Apion* 2:41-42.

12. *conferred with his council:* The *symboulion* functioned as a group of advisors for a magistrate (see 4 Macc 17:17; compare Philo, *Embassy to Gaius* 254; Josephus, *Antiquities of the Jews* 16:163). Since the authority of a procurator in matters *extra ordinem* (outside the code of law) was broad, and Festus could probably have ignored Paul's appeal with no one the wiser, his consultation apparently led him to believe that allowing Paul's appeal would help remove him from an awkward situation.

INTERPRETATION

With what mastery Luke has focused our attention on Paul's fate! Bit by bit, Luke has left behind all the other Christian characters. We have not heard from James and the Jerusalem Church since the fateful meeting in 21:17-25. From the time of Paul's arrest in the Temple precincts, the story has seemed to abandon every other interest except Paul. We have seen that Luke uses Paul's defense speeches to clarify the relationship of the Messianist movement to "the hope of Israel" and to Roman law. But these apologetic concerns are addressed within the compelling drama of Paul's personal destiny.

We are now led through another critical moment in Paul's progression to Rome. Paul seems more than ever to be the passive pawn of characters and events outside his control. The governor Felix had promised to send for Lysias to have Paul's story confirmed (24:22) but fails to do so. Instead, he keeps Paul in captivity for two years, partly for his entertainment value and partly as a possible source of revenue through a bribe (24:24-26). But it is when Festus enters into office that Paul's real peril begins. The Jewish leaders at once agitate for Paul's extradition to Jerusalem, hoping again to be able to kill him before his case comes to trial (25:1-3). Festus resists this first overture, but the precedent of "doing a favor for the Jews" has been set, and Paul's situation is genuinely precarious. In this light, his appeal to Caesar, which sets his course once for all toward Rome (25:10-11), is to be seen less as a deliberate plan than as a desperate maneuver.

The political maneuvering reveals more about each of the characters. Concerning the Jewish leadership we learn only that their hostility to Paul has not waned in the least despite a two-year period of imprisonment. At the first opportunity, they seek from the new governor a reversal of venue, to get Paul back in their own control. More than that, they have abandoned any pretense of legal process: they actively seek to kill Paul by way of ambush (25:3). Yet, when they are brought to Caesarea and "surround" Paul, their "many and weighty charges" come to nothing, for they bring no proof for any of them (25:7).

The Roman authorities fare little better. Festus we can blame but little, for he came into a very ticklish situation (how ticklish, we shall see below). He observes the proper procedures, but it is obvious that if there is any way he can bend them to "do a favor to the Jews," he will do so. The character who emerges least favorably from the sequence is the governor Felix. Despite his promise to bring the case to a close, he fails to summon Lysias to testify; he keeps Paul in prison for two years; he invites Paul to give a lecture on the Messiah, but when the message strikes too close to his own tangled life, he grows alarmed and refuses to listen further (24:25). But he keeps seeking conversations with the prisoner in the hope that Paul will give him a bribe (24:26). Finally, in an arbitrary attempt at winning Jewish favor, he leaves Paul in prison for his successor to deal with (24:27); an altogether shameless performance. Against this backdrop of hostility, corruption, and time-serving, Paul's character emerges as truly philosophical. Paul knows his legal rights, and makes use of them. He fearlessly proclaims before the governor and his wife the demands of righteousness and self-control. He is not afraid to die.

All these things we learn simply from Luke's narrative, and assuming nothing beyond the narrative world he has constructed. But if we expand our horizon to take in what we know of the characters from other sources, Luke's account not only gains in plausibility but also in richness. Paul is now moving in the realm of official Roman society. Governors and kings, and their tangled family relations, are the very stuff of ancient histories. From authors such as Josephus, Suetonius, and Tacitus, we are able to construct a fuller context for Luke's narrative. Knowing, for example, that the marriage of Felix and Drusilla was, in fact, rooted in adultery and betrayal (see notes) gives a special force to Paul's discourse on self-control and God's judgment.

But even more important for understanding the motivation for the political maneuvering of the two Roman governors is the knowledge that Felix's term of office was notorious not only for its corruption, but also for its failure to deal with the social unrest caused by the brigands and revolutionaries (see notes). Now in this setting, if we are to believe Josephus, the Jewish priesthood and Sanhedrin wanted a strong Roman hand, since they themselves were against the brigands. In fact, so angry were the Jewish leaders at Felix's failure in this respect, that after his removal, they went to Rome with formal complaints against him (see notes). In contrast, Festus is given generally good marks for his handling of the brigandage issue.

Now, if Paul could be regarded as a revolutionary—Lysias at first saw him that way, and the Jewish charges concerning "the entire empire" also point in that direction—then Felix's desire to keep him in jail "as a favor to the Jews" makes perfectly good sense. Having failed to control the serious revolutionaries, he could at least demonstrate with Paul a certain attention to the matter. In the same way, the new governor Festus would also want immediately to do everything possible to assuage the anger of the Jewish leadership on this question of brigandage. So he was at least open to the possibility of "doing the Jews a favor" as well, by holding hearings in Jerusalem.

Once more, the better our knowledge of the social and historical context, the more plausible Luke's account becomes. Knowing these things is not essential for grasping Luke's portrayal of Paul, but it does enrich our appreciation for the historical character of Luke's narrative at this point. For Luke, Paul is the center of the story, and its most important character. But Luke shows his readers that this view is not shared by the other characters, for whom Paul is a convenient pawn for the advancement of their own projects. But at another level entirely—even when Paul seems most passive and his message most powerless—Luke's narrative suggests that God is at work to bring his historical purposes to completion.

FOR REFERENCE AND FURTHER STUDY

Cadbury, H. J. "Roman Law and the Trial of Paul." *Beginnings* 5:312-319.
Mommsen, T. "Die Rechtsverhältnisse des Apostels Paulus." *ZNW* 2 (1901) 81-96.
Sherwin-White, A. N. *Roman Society and Roman Law in the New Testament.* Oxford: University Press, 1963, 57-70.

50. *Before Governor and King* (25:13-27)

13. After some days went by, Agrippa the king and Bernice came to Caesarea to greet Festus. 14. Since they were staying there several days, Festus put Paul's case to the king. He said, "There is a certain man left behind as a prisoner by Felix. 15. When I was in Jerusalem, the chief priests and elders of the Jews made a representation concerning him. They asked for a judgment against him. 16. I answered them that it was not a Roman custom to turn over anyone before the accused has his accusers face-to-face and is given a chance to make a defense concerning the charge. 17. When they gathered together here, therefore, I made no delay. The next day I took my seat on the judicial bench. I ordered the

man to be brought. 18. His accusers stood around him. They brought none of the charges of evil deeds that I had supposed, 19. but certain disputes they had with him concerning their own superstition and concerning a certain dead man, Jesus, whom Paul declared to be alive. 20. Since I was at a loss how to investigate such matters, I asked if he wished to go to Jerusalem and there be judged concerning these matters. 21. But since Paul made appeal to be held for the decision of Augustus, I ordered him to be kept until I could send him up to Caesar." 22. Agrippa said to Festus, "I myself would also like to hear this fellow." He said, "Tomorrow you shall hear him." 23. The next day therefore, when Agrippa and Bernice had arrived in full state, and they had entered the audience hall together with the tribunes and the leading men of the city, Festus ordered Paul to be brought. 24. Festus said, "King Agrippa and all the men who have joined us, you see this fellow concerning whom the whole assembly of the Jews approached me in Jerusalem and here, shouting that he should no longer go on living. 25. But I have understood him to have done nothing worthy of death. And since this man has himself appealed to Augustus, I have decided to send him. 26. I don't have anything definite to write to the Lord concerning him. Therefore I have brought him before you—and especially you, King Agrippa—so that after an inquiry has been made, I might have something to write. 27. For it seems unreasonable to me to send on a prisoner without signifying the charges laid against him."

NOTES

Agrippa the king and Bernice: Herod Agrippa II was the son of Herod Agrippa I, whose death was recounted in Acts 12:23. This Agrippa was granted his father's kingdom by Claudius (see Josephus, *Jewish War* 2:223; *Antiquities of the Jews* 19:360), and several other principalities in Palestine by Nero (*Antiquities* 20:138), and as a client of the Romans (see *Antiquities* 20:135) was loyal to them throughout the period of the Jewish War; see his passionate speech dissuading from war in *Jewish War* 2:345-401. Bernice was his sister, also the daughter of Agrippa I (*Jewish War* 2:220). After the death of her husband, she lived with her brother, Agrippa II (*Jewish War* 2:427), which caused scandalous gossip in Roman circles (Juvenal, *Satires* 6:156-160). Although she was apparently herself devout—to the extent of herself performing a Nazarite vow—and petitioned the governor Florus on behalf of Jews (Josephus, *Jewish War* 2:310-314), she was also part of the Roman circle, in fact becoming for a time the companion of the conqueror Titus (Suetonius, *Life of Titus* 7:1). Paul could scarcely appear before figures more "well placed" in society.

to greet Festus: Despite being in the aorist tense, the participle *aspasamenoi* can only be read as expressing purpose; this thoroughly pro-Roman family comes to pay its respects to the new governor in a state visit.

14. *put Paul's case to the king:* The verb *anatithēmi* here has the sense of "report/refer" (compare 2 Macc 3:9; Gal 2:2). Festus seeks the king's advice on, literally, "the things having to do with Paul" (*ta kata ton Paulon*).

16. *not a Roman custom:* Pride in the Roman order by one of its administrators is evident in the statement. For Luke's characteristic use of *ethos* ("custom"), see Luke 1:9; 2:42; 23:39; Acts 6:14; 15:1; 16:22; 21:21. The principle cited here is clearly stated in Appian, *The Civil Wars* 3, 8, 54, and Josephus, *Antiquities of the Jews* 16:258. Christian apologists would later make appeal to this process (see Justin, *Apology* 1:3). The phrase "given a chance to make a defense" is literally "receive a place (*topos*) for an apology (*apologia*)."

18. *his accusers stood around him:* Although the phrase *peri hou* could be taken with *aitia* to read "the charge concerning him," this is not only awkward, it also fails to recognize that Festus is recapitulating the previous narrative, which clearly stated that the Jews "surrounded" (*periistēmi*) Paul (25:7).

19. *disputes . . . concerning their own superstition:* Once more through a neutral observer, Luke declares Paul innocent of any "evil deeds" (*ta ponēra*). He is only caught up in the disputes (*zētēmata*) dividing parties of Jews (compare the declarations in 18:14-15; 23:29). The translation of *deisidaimonia* is difficult; for the options, see the note on Acts 17:22. The translation here chooses the negative meaning "superstition" rather than "religion," primarily because Festus is obviously treating Agrippa as if he were as much an outsider to these disputes as himself (note "their own" superstition).

    Jesus, whom Paul declared to be alive: Festus gives a masterful "outsider" characterization of the central Christian claim: that one who was dead (*tethnēkotos*) is now declared to be living (*zēn*). The reader notices that by so stating the governor also concurs with Paul that the real dispute between him and the other Jews has to do with the resurrection (see 23:6; 24:15, 21).

20. *how to investigate such matters:* For *aporeō/diaporeō* as mental confusion or indecision, see Luke 9:7; 24:4; Acts 2:12; 5:24; 10:17. The content of his confusion could be translated two ways, depending on the construal of *zētēsis*: a) "I was at a loss in a dispute (*zētēsis*) on these things; b) I was at a loss how to investigate (*zētēsis*) such matters." Because of the offer immediately made to Paul, the latter translation is preferable. It is obvious that for a Roman administrator to confess incompetence to judge is itself a declaration that matters internal to religious disputes rather than criminal law are involved.

21. *the decision of Augustus:* The Greek is *ho sebastos*, a substantive meaning "revered/worthy of reverence." In Luke 2:1, the Latin equivalent, *Augustus*, is used. As the conclusion of the verse indicates, the honorific of the first emperor (Josephus, *Antiquities of the Jews* 16:173) had become a title for his successors as well.

23. *arrived in full state:* As the term suggests, *phantasia* can mean "appearance" in a variety of contexts, ranging from "imaginings" to "pomp/pageantry," as here in the case of a royal retinue. One can hardly avoid the impression that Paul is intended to supply the entertainment for this splendid assem-

blage, as they enter the "audience hall" (*akroatērion*). The entourage includes "tribunes" (in the plural!) and "leading men of the city" (*hoi kat' exochēn tēs poleōs*) which here would mean Caesarea. Compare "the first men of the city" in 13:50.

24. *whole assembly of the Jews:* In this as in other cases (Luke 8:37; 23:1; Acts 4:32; 6:2, 5; 14:1; 15:12, 30), the term *plēthos* stands for the legal assembly rather than "the multitude." The point may seem minor, but at issue is Luke's portrayal of the Jewish people. He has consistently attached the resistance to the prophets to the *leadership*, not the population as such. This translation, furthermore, respects the narrative context, since it was in fact only the council that had approached Festus in Jerusalem and in Caesarea (25:2, 7). We are to read this, therefore, not as an exaggerating distortion of the events, but— at least on this point—an accurate representation of them. Some *mss* of the Western Traditon expand the text, recapitulating the scene of 25:2-12 more fully.

25. *nothing worthy of death:* This is now the second declaration by a Roman authority that Paul has done nothing deserving death (see the letter of Lysias in 23:29). There will be another in 26:31, so that Paul (like Jesus) will three times be exonerated by Roman justice (compare Luke 23:4, 15, 22).

26. *certain to write to the Lord:* Although according to Suetonius, *Life of Augustus* 53:1, the first emperor eschewed the title "Lord" (*kyrios*), inscriptionary evidence shows that by the time of Nero, the title was used ever more frequently of the emperor. This passage in Acts, however, is the first literary evidence for its absolute use ("the Lord"). The phrase *ti asphales* as in 21:34 and 22:30 has the sense of "definite facts." Although Festus' rationalization for Paul's address is the most transparent sort of literary ploy, it has the twofold effect of a) stating once more that up to this point there *were* no "facts" on which to try Paul, and b) enabling other royal witnesses—and Jewish ones at that—to confirm the previous judgments by the Roman officials "after an inquiry (*anakrisis*) has been made" (see 26:30-32).

INTERPRETATION

The introduction to Paul's final defense statement is unusually elaborate. The occasion of a state visit from the local royalty to the Roman governor enables Paul to fulfill the prophecy of Jesus concerning his disciples, that "they will lead you away to kings and governors on account of my name" (Luke 21:12).

The pretense that Festus needs still another hearing so that he could have something definite to write in a letter accompanying Paul to Rome is transparent (25:26). He surely had enough of the "facts" (such as they were) by this time. But we are to understand in his deference and referral to Agrippa a very clever political maneuver. Agrippa II and his sister

Bernice were, after all, the perfect powers to consult and coopt. On one side they represented the Jews. On the other side, they were ardent clients of the Roman state, and familiar with Caesar's family (see notes).

It was clear by this point that the Jewish Sanhedrin would never let go its desire to get Paul and have him killed. But Paul's appeal to Caesar had made any possible "favor" to the Jewish council hazardous. The Herodian family, in contrast, would be viewed by Festus' masters as perfectly sound spokespersons for the Jews who mattered, namely those who were thoroughly Hellenized and Romanized. If they could be brought into agreement with Festus' own view of the case, then—Festus could well reason—he had slipped between two unpleasant dangers and enabled everyone to save face. The Jewish council could grumble, but would recognize that matters had been taken out of Festus' hands by Paul's appeal. And the Emperor would respect the judgment of a "Jewish king" that Paul's troubles stemmed from disputes over a superstition and that it was only his stubborn appeal that forced his delivery to the higher court (26:32).

The panoply surrounding the hearing may at first seem excessive and a sign of fictional coloring: Paul is to be heard by a governor, by a king and his influential wife, by the military officials, and the leading citizens of Caesarea (25:23). But the procedure Luke describes does not in any way conflict with what we know of Palestinian politics in the first century. Josephus, for example, relates at least two such incidents which in their basic structure and in many of their details resemble the Lukan account. The first involved Herod the Great, who had invited the Roman governor Varus to consult on the matter of Antipater. After a preliminary interview, Josephus says, "On the following day Varus and the king held a council, to which were invited the friends of both sides and the relatives of the king, including his sister Salome . . . ." (*Antiquities of the Jews* 17:93; compare *Jewish War* 1:620). Another similar incident involved Marcus Agrippa, before whom the Jews of Ionia made an appeal. Josephus describes the opening of the hearing: "And when Agrippa had taken as councillors the Roman officials and those kings and princes who were present, Nicolas arose and spoke in behalf of the Jews" (*Antiquities* 16:30). Luke's portrayal of the scene, as so often in his narrative, conforms impressively to the customs of the place.

Paul is therefore placed before a first century "show trial" that is part entertainment for the guests, part a subtle political maneuver. Indeed, Agrippa and Bernice are made to play for Festus exactly the role taken by Herod in the trial of Jesus (Luke 23:6-12). For the Jewish king, there is the reward of political flattery and deference: the Romans recognize his importance! For the procurator, there is a sharing of responsibility: that's what friends are for (see Luke 23:12)! The trials of Paul therefore match in still another respect those of Jesus, *his* Lord. Paul, however, will be allowed to fulfill the other prophecy of Jesus concerning those who are brought before governors and kings: "it will turn out to be a chance for you to bear witness" (Luke 21:13).

Paul's defense speech is prepared for by the reports of Festus to Agrippa, the first private (25:14-21), the second public (25:24-25). They take the form of a recapitulation of the events up to that point. As in the letter of Lysias to Felix (23:26-30), controlling the data flow enables the official to put the best possible construal on his own actions. Festus most of all emphasizes his own steadfastness and correctness: in this version, the Jews who met him in Jerusalem wanted a "judgment" against Paul and not simply a new hearing; he gives the impression that he was under great pressure, especially since the Jews followed up by sending "the whole assembly" to Caesarea, and "surrounding" the prisoner, and making "many and weighty charges" and shouting that he should no longer live (25:15, 18, 24)! In contrast, Festus omits any desire to "do a favor for the Jews" such as he had actually contemplated (25:9). Instead, he "remembers" his impressive invocation of the Roman legal precedent (25:16). Luke shows neither shock nor surprise at such creative shaping of the story. Politicians do such things.

Most important for Luke's purposes, of course, is the way Festus also sets the stage for Paul's final defense. He reasserts Paul's fundamental innocence of any criminal charge: when the dust settled from the Jews' "many and weighty charges," Festus discovered no evil actions (25:18), and certainly nothing that was deserving of death (25:25). Instead, Festus decided that the issue between Paul and the Jewish leaders concerned "their own superstition," was in fact just another party dispute like that between the Pharisees and Sadducees, unworthy of Roman attention. More than that, Festus agrees with Paul (albeit with quite a different sort of language) concerning the nature of that dispute, concerning "a certain dead man, Jesus, whom Paul declared to be alive" (25:19). Festus has been made to say everything Luke could want him to say: the Messianist movement is not a crime and should be of no interest to the Roman order; it is a legitimate claimant to Jewish status and represents a variety of belief within that strange superstition, no worse than any other; it defines itself in terms of belief in the resurrection of Jesus. The way could not have been more pleasantly prepared for Paul's final defense.

FOR REFERENCE AND FURTHER STUDY

Cassidy, R. J. *Society and Politics in the Acts of the Apostles.* Maryknoll, New York: Orbis Books, 1987, 96–144.

Dupont, J. "Aequitas Romana: Notes sûr Actes 25, 10." *RScR* 49 (1961) 354–385.

Tajra, H. W. *The Trial of St. Paul.* WUNT 2:35. Tübingen: JCB Mohr (Paul Siebeck), 1989, 76–89.

Tannehill, R. *Narrative Unity* 2:309-329.

51. *Paul's Defense before Agrippa* (26:1-32)

1. Agrippa said to Paul, "You are allowed to speak for yourself." Then Paul stretched out his hand. He began his defense. 2. "King Agrippa! I consider myself happy to make a defense before you today concerning everything I am accused by the Jews, 3. most of all because you are expert in all the customs and controversies of the Jews. Therefore I beg you to listen to me patiently. 4. Now all the Jews know that from youth my way of life from the beginning was carried out within my nation and in Jerusalem. 5. They know me from the first. If they wanted they could testify that I lived as a Pharisee according to the strictest sect of our religion. 6. And now I stand being judged for a hope in the promise that was made by God to our fathers. 7. Our twelve tribes hope to attain it by worshipping intently night and day. For this hope I am being accused by the Jews, O King! 8. Why is it considered incredible by any of you if God raises the dead? 9. Now I myself thought it necessary to do many things against the name of Jesus the Nazorean, 10. and I did so in Jerusalem. I shut up in prison many from among the saints, since I had received authority from the chief priests. While they were being killed, I gave my approval. 11. Many times in all the synagogues I would force them to blaspheme by punishing them. Furious at them beyond measure, I was pursuing them even to the outlying cities. 12. While engaged in these things, I was proceeding to Damascus with the authority and commission of the chief priests. 13. Along the road at midday, O King, I saw a light from heaven brighter than the sun, shining on me and those travelling with me. 14. When all of us had fallen to the ground, I heard a voice speaking to me in the Hebrew dialect, 'Saul, Saul, why are you persecuting me? It is hard for you to kick against the goads.' 15. But I said, 'Who are you Lord?' And the Lord said, 'I am Jesus whom you are persecuting. 16. But get up and stand on your feet! I have appeared to you for this reason, to appoint you as a minister and witness of how you have seen me and how I will appear to you. 17. I am rescuing you from the people and from the nations to whom I am sending you 18. to open their eyes, so they can turn from darkness to light, and from the power of Satan to God, that they might receive forgiveness of sins and a share among those who have been made holy by faith in me.' 19. Because of this, King Agrippa, I was not disobedient to the heavenly

vision, 20. but I declared first to those in Damascus and in Jerusalem, then in all the territory of Judea and to the nations that they should repent and turn to God by performing deeds appropriate to conversion. 21. On account of these things the Jews seized me while I was in the Temple and attempted to kill me. 22. With God's help up to this day, I stand bearing witness to small and great. I say nothing other than the things the prophets as well as Moses said were going to happen, 23. whether the Messiah would suffer, whether as first from the resurrection of the dead he would proclaim light both to the people and to the Gentiles." 24. As Paul was making a defense on these matters, Festus said in a loud voice, "You are raving, Paul! Your great learning has turned you to madness." 25. But Paul said, "I am not mad, Most Excellent Festus, but I am declaiming words of truth and sanity. 26. For the king understands these things. To him I speak with boldness. For I am convinced that none of these things has escaped his attention. For this has not taken place in a corner. 27. Do you believe, King Agrippa, in the prophets? I know that you do believe." 28. But Agrippa said to Paul, "You are persuading me to play the Christian a little!" 29. And Paul said, "I would pray to God that both in little and in much, not only you but also all those hearing me today would become so, even as I am, with the exception of these chains." 30. The king and the governor and Bernice and those seated with them arose. 31. They withdrew and began talking to each other. They said, "This fellow has done nothing worthy of death or imprisonment." 32. And Agrippa said to Festus, "This fellow could be released if he had not appealed to Caesar."

NOTES

1. *began his defense:* The imperfect tense of the verb *apologeomai* (see 19:33; 24:10; 25:8) is here treated as inchoative. For the gesture of waving or extending the hand when beginning an oration, see Apuleius, *The Golden Ass* 2:21; Acts 13:16; 19:33; 21:40. The Western Text heightens the solemnity and prophetic character of Paul's discourse by adding, "confident and having received the encouragement of the Holy Spirit . . . ."

2. *I consider myself happy:* Paul begins with a short and simple *captatio benevolentiae* (see 24:2-4, 10). The vocative *basileu Agrippa* ("King Agrippa"), is moved to the beginning of the sentence for effect. The exclamation is repeated in vv. 7, 13, 27. The perfect tense of *hēgeomai* ("reckon/consider") is here equivalent to the present, and is the only time Luke uses the verb with this meaning (compare 2 Cor 9:5; Phil 2:3, 6). Although Luke ordinarily uses the word *makarios* in the "biblical" sense of "blessed" (Luke 1:45; 6:20, 21, 22; 7:23; 10:23; 11:27-28; 12:37, 38, 43; 14:14-15; 23:29; Acts 20:35), it here has the strictly secular sense of "fortunate." The entire discourse, in fact, has an elegance of phrasing appropriate to this high company, another fine example of Luke's use of *prosōpopoiia.*

3. *expert in all the customs and controversies:* The participial phrase *gnōstēn se onta* is in the accusative case and does not fit within the syntax of the sentence; it functions, however, much like a genitive absolute construction. The noun *gnōstēs* designates someone with particular knowledge: in LXX 1 Sam 18:3, 9; 2 Kgs 21:6 and Isa 19:3, for example, it refers to wizards. Josephus tells us more about Bernice's involvement in Jewish practice than about Agrippa's (*Jewish War* 2:310-314), but in any case, the king would be more "expert" than the Roman governor. Note the similar flattery paid to Felix in 24:10.

listen to me patiently: The adverb *makrothymōs* is used only here in the NT, but the cognate terms describe attitudes appropriate to a judge, especially that of "long-suffering/tolerance" (see Matt 18:26; 1 Pet 3:20; 2 Pet 3:9, 15; Rom 2:4; 9:22; 1 Tim 1:16; and especially Luke 18:7).

4. *from youth my way of life:* The transition to the defense proper is marked by *men oun* (here translated as "now"), which connective Luke uses frequently in Acts for a variety of fairly loose transitions (1:6, 18; 2:41; 5:41; 11:19; 15:3; 23:18). For *biōsis* as "way of life," see LXX Sir prol. 12. The translation of the verse is made awkward by Luke's use of three temporal qualifiers in succession: *ek neotētos* ("from youth"), *ap'archēs* ("from the beginning"), and *anōthen* ("from the start"). Paul's entire life has been lived openly as a Jew, and they know it!

within my nation and in Jerusalem: Luke uses *ethnos* here to mean "my own people" (compare Luke 7:5; 23:2; Acts 10:22; 24:2, 10, 17). For Luke's presence in Jerusalem during the period of his education, see Acts 22:3.

5. *if they wanted, they could testify;* The compressed Greek of *ean thelōsin martyrein* demands the sort of expansion given by the translation. The precise relationship of the clauses in this sentence is difficult. The circumstantial participle *proginōskontes me anōthen* could be translated as an explanatory clause, "since they knew me from the start," but this translation makes it an independent statement. For the ability of Paul's fellow Jews to witness to his earlier behavior, compare 22:5.

I lived as a Pharisee: For the significance of this claim, see the note on Acts 23:6, and for the characterization of "strictest sect," see the note on Acts 22:3. Paul here uses the term *thrēskeia* ("religion") rather than the more ambiguous *deisidaimonia* ("religion/superstition") used by Festus (25:19); see Jas 1:26-27, as well as 4 Macc 5:7; Josephus, *Antiquities of the Jews* 12:253.

6. *being judged for a hope in the promise:* The importance of this statement for evaluating Luke's purposes is hard to exaggerate. Paul once more claims to be on trial for "the hope that is the resurrection" (23:6; 24:15; 25:19). But now he makes explicit what was implied by his statement that he believed nothing else than "all that was written" (24:14): the resurrection of Jesus with the sending of the Spirit is the fulfillment of "the promise (*epangelia*) that was made by God to our fathers." Here is the clear statement of the theme of prophecy/fulfillment, but also the most express connection between belief in Jesus' resurrection and the claim to represent the authentic realization of the people Israel as the children of the promise made to Abraham (see the

notes on Luke 1:55, 73; 3:8; 13:28, and above all on Acts 3:24-26; 7:1-8; 13:32-33).

7. *our twelve tribes hope to attain it:* Both the substantive and the personal pronoun are significant here. The adjective *dōdekaphylos* is used absolutely as a noun, and obviously evokes the image of Israel as a whole people (compare *Sybilline Oracles* 3:248; Jas 1:1). In Luke-Acts, as we have seen, the symbolism of the Twelve is directly related to the restoration of the people Israel (Luke 6:13; 8:1, 42-43; 9:1, 12, 17; 22:30; Acts 1:15-26; 7:8). The possessive "our" (*hēmōn*) is also significant, for it expresses Paul the Messianist's solidarity with the hopes of the people.

by worshipping intently night and day: The Christians are in continuity with Israel understood as a religious people, rather than as a set of national boundaries or ethnic customs. Thus, the act of "worshipping" (*latreuō*) is constitutive of "the people of God." Luke has provided a model of this Israel in the prophetess Anna who "with fasting and prayers worshipped night and day" (Luke 2:37). Paul identified himself with Israel thus understood when he said that he "worshipped the ancestral God" (24:4; also 27:23). Most of all, this statement reminds us of the opening of the Gospel, when in his canticle Zechariah declared that the effect of God's visitation of the people in fulfillment of the oath made to Abraham was that they might "worship him fearlessly in holiness and righteousness before him all our lives" (Luke 1:74-75).

8. *incredible by any of you if God raises the dead:* The adjective *apistos* is used this way in *The Letter of Aristeas* 296, and Josephus, *Antiquities of the Jews* 6:198; in the NT otherwise it bears the sense of "unbelieving" (as also in Luke 9:41; 12:46). The Greek here makes a shift from the singular to the plural, which the translation tries to capture by "any of you." But who is the implied audience? Is the question meant to follow on the previous statement and be regarded as a rebuke to the Jews who do not follow through on their own convictions? Or is it a rhetorical question aimed at the hypothetically Gentile audience which would be skeptical about any talk of the future life (compare Acts 17:32)? The second possibility fits the narrative scenario, the first fits Luke's argument better.

9. *do many things against the name:* For the translation of *men oun* as "now," see the note on verse 4; in the present case, the transition seems to build on the implicit acknowledgement that it was Paul's previously finding it "incredible" that God should have raised Jesus that accounted for his rage and hostility against the Messianists who claimed he had. This recollection of Paul's former life (vv. 9-12) recalls 22:4-5. Two aspects of the present statement deserve particular notice: a) Paul pictures his former activities as motivated by a certain sense of obligation (*dein*); b) he uses "the name" as representing the Christian movement (compare 2:38; 3:16; 4:7, 12, 17-18; 9:14-16).

10. *I did so in Jerusalem:* The entire sequence from verse 9 to verse 12 is one long Greek sentence that any English translation must break up into smaller and simpler units. Something of the elegance of the Greek is thereby lost, but clarity is gained. The Greek sentence builds on the first verb (*epoiēsa*, "I did"),

with four specifications: "I shut up" (*katekleisa*), "I gave approval" (*katēnenka*), "I was forcing" (*ēnankazon*), "I was pursuing" (*ediōkon*).

shut up in prison: Luke has Paul himself confirm what was stated in the narrative (8:3) and by Ananias (9:13). Once more (see 22:5), Paul claims to have had the authority from the chief priests (plural!), as the narrative also had stated (9:2) and Ananias reported (9:14). The difference now is that Paul has adopted the perspective of Ananias by referring to those he persecuted as "the saints" (*hoi hagioi*, 9:13).

I gave my approval: The most obviously new thing here is the impression that more than one Messianist was killed (*anairō*, see Luke 22:2; 23:2; Acts 2:23; 5:33; 9:23), even though the narrative recounted only the death of Stephen (7:60). The phrase Paul uses here is literally, "I cast my pebble against." The idiom derives from the use of a pebble (*psēphos*) in voting; see Philo, *The Unchangeableness of God* 75; Josephus, *Antiquities of the Jews* 2:163; 10:60). The most obvious translation therefore would be "I cast my vote against them." But there are problems: a) the present participle of *anairō* seems to suggest simultaneous action rather than a prior judicial proceeding; b) even though Luke struggles to make the Sanhedrin responsible for Stephen's death (Acts 6:15–7:1), his account bears none of the marks of a judicial process with votes taken on the fate of the defendant; c) Paul's own role is nowhere else described in terms of membership in the Sanhedrin or as voting, but rather he is pictured as colluding and approving of the death (perhaps with the implication that he was an *agent provocateur* (Acts 7:58; 8:1; 22:20). On the other hand, a literal translation would serve Paul's purpose of having the Sanhedrin formally responsible for all these deaths, abetting his picture of Paul not as a maverick but as an agent authorized by the council. For the reader today, there is an excellent pun to be found in the idiom if Paul describes his participation in the stoning of Stephen as "I also cast my pebble."

11. *force them to blaspheme by punishing them:* This puts a slightly new twist on the version in 22:5, which said Paul travelled to Damascus to bring Christians back to Jerusalem "so they could be punished" (*timōreō*). Here the "punishment" (*timōreō*) takes place in Jerusalem. Acts 8:3 spoke of Paul going from house to house and dragging people out, but not of his doing this in the synagogues. The use of *blasphēmein* once more shows Paul's adoption of the Messianist point of view.

    furious at them beyond measure: The description of rage is exceptionally vivid (compare Josephus, *Antiquities of the Jews* 17:174-175), and picks up the description of him "breathing threat and murder" in 9:1. The word-choice here is particularly interesting. Paul's "raging" (*emmainomai*) against the Christians is after his conversion changed to "truth and sanity" (26:25), but that is now regarded by the outsider Festus as "raving" (*mainomai*) and "madness" (*mania;* 26:24).

12. *while engaged in these things:* The phrase *en hois* could be taken as temporal (see Luke 12:1), or as circumstantial (see Acts 24:18); for the sake of a more intelligible transition, this translation spells out what the phrase implies. Note again that Paul insists that he had the "authority" (*exousia*) given by the chief

priests (9:2, 14; 22:5; 26:10), but now strengthens that even further by referring to their "commission" (*epitropē*; compare Josephus, *Antiquities of the Jews*
8:162).

13. *along the road at midday:* The time of day was missing in the first narrative
account (9:3), but was included in Paul's first defense speech (22:6). Visions
had in daytime might be thought to be more credible than those at night,
and in this case, the light is compared to that of the sun when it was at its
brightest.

    a light from heaven brighter than the sun: That the light was "from heaven"
is found also in the earlier recountings (9:3; 22:6), but this version elevates
the "great" (*hikanon*) force of the light (22:6) to "beyond the splendor (*lam-
protēs*) of the sun." And whereas the earlier versions used the verb *peristraptō*
("flash around"), this one uses *perilamptō* ("shine around"); see Philo, *On
Dreams* 1:900. Such small stylistic variations are characteristic of Luke.

14. *all of us had fallen to the ground:* The earlier versions spoke only of Paul falling to the ground (9:4; 22:7). Here the companions both see the light and
fall to the ground. The Western Text marks the transition from this communal
to Paul's private experience by adding, "On account of fear only I could
hear . . . ."

    speaking to me in the Hebrew dialect: This qualification of the voice is lacking
in the earlier accounts. By "Hebrew dialect," Paul seems to mean Aramaic
(see 21:40). Does Luke insert this to account for the voice's using "Saul" when
his listeners know him as "Paul"? The repetition of the name is, in any case,
a feature of theophanies (Gen 22:11; 46:2; 1 Sam 3:4; 4 *Ezra* 14:1; 2 *Baruch*
22:2) and also favored by Luke (Luke 8:24; 10:41; 22:31).

    hard for you to kick against the goads: This statement also is missing from the
two earlier accounts except by scribal assimilation in some *mss.* The *kentron*
(here in the plural) is a sharp pointed stick used to move cattle in the desired
direction (Prov 26:3); a more contemporary equivalent would be "cattle prod."
The last part of the statement, "kicking against the goad," is widespread in
Greek literature. It is found in Euripides *Bacchae* 795, and in Julian the Apostate *Oration* 8:246B, it is found as a "proverb" (*paroimia*). The idea of God
(or a companion spirit) using a "goad" to direct behavior is found in *Psalms
of Solomon* 16:4 and Philo, *On the Decalogue* 87, but not in the proverbial form.
The idea here is that God has been pushing Paul to become a Messianist and
he has resisted. The phrase *sklēron soi* should not be read in the sense of "difficult," however, but as pointing to Paul's stubbornness in resisting the goad,
echoing the theme of "hardness" (*sklēros*) in Torah (see Exod 6:9; Deut 15:18;
31:27; 1 Sam 25:3).

15. *I am Jesus:* This central portion of the vision remains the most constant in all
three versions. The Western Text, however, adds here, "the Nazorean,"
under the influence of 22:8.

16. *I have appeared to you for this reason:* The phrase *eis touto* ("for this") introduces
the most significant expansion in this version of Paul's experience: in contrast to the brief directive in 9:6 and the somewhat more formal commission

in 22:10, this account from the start provides the answer to the most intriguing question of all about Paul's encounter: "why?"

appoint you as a minister and witness: For the significance of "appointing" (*procheirizomai*), see the note on Acts 3:20. In contrast to Paul's vision in the temple (22:14), which declared that he had "been appointed to know God's will and see the righteous one," the appointment this time concerns Paul's function; the idea, of course, is substantially the same. The correlation of "minister" (*hypēretēs*) and "witness" (*martys*) is intriguing because of the similar combination in the Gospel prologue, which stated that the "things fulfilled among us" were handed on by "eyewitnesses who became ministers (*hypēretai*) of the word" (Luke 1:2). The designation of Paul as a "witness" here once more establishes his essential continuity with his prophetic predecessors, Stephen (22:15, 20) and the Twelve (1:22; 2:32; 10:39, 41).

how you have seen me: This is a very difficult text, mainly because of the presence of the direct object *me* in the first clause which disrupts the otherwise acceptable syntax. We are presented with a classic problem in text criticism. The *mss* evidence for including *me* is about equal to that for omitting it. To omit it, of course, would give the shorter reading, which is usually to be preferred because scribes tend to expand rather than contract texts. But which is the "harder" reading? This is not clear. On the one hand, the passage clearly echoes 22:15 which says simply *hōn heōrakas kai ēkousas* ("the things you have seen and heard"). The "easier" reading would therefore omit the *me* and translate "of the things you have seen." But that does not take into account the *ophthēsomai* ("I will appear to you") in the second clause. There is no reason to amend it to *ophthēsontai/ophthēsetai* to provide a more intelligible sense. It is possible, of course, that Luke simply constructed an anacolouthic sentence (he has done so elsewhere!), beginning with "things you have seen and heard" (in agreement with 22:15), but then shifting to *ophthēsomai* without realizing he was messing up the sentence. This could have led scribes to "improve" the first clause by adding *me*, even though it left the sentence hopelessly tangled. The textual problem, however, should not obscure the most important new element in the declaration, the promise of new revelations to Paul, which in fact we have seen carried out in the narrative (16:7; 18:9; 22:7; 23:11).

17. *I am rescuing you:* The present participle of *exaireō* is in the middle voice, which Luke customarily uses in the sense of "extricating/delivering" (see Acts 7:10, 34; 12:11; 23:27), consistent with the biblical precedents (LXX Exod 3:8; 18:4; Deut 32:29; Ps 36:40; 58:1). The meaning of "selecting" is also possible, but since that has already been stated by *procheirizomai*, it would be redundant here. Furthermore, Paul was not "selected from the people and the nations" alike, whereas he *was* rescued from them both, as the narrative has demonstrated (16:35-40; 18:2-16; 19:23-41; 20:3). This is one of the few times that Luke uses *ho laos* ("the people") in a context of opposition to the prophetic visitation (compare Luke 23:27; Acts 4:25).

to whom I am sending you: The Greek phrase *eis hous* makes clear that this refers to the nations/gentiles (*ta ethnē*). The commission corresponds to 9:15; 13:47; 22:21, and will be elaborated in the following verse.

18. *to open their eyes:* The "opening of the eyes" echoes the servant song of LXX Isa 42:7, "I the Lord have called you in righteousness and I will grasp your hand and I will strengthen you, and I have made you a covenant of the people, to be a light for the nations, to open the eyes of the blind, to lead the captives from their chains, and from the house of imprisonment those who sit in darkness." The same Isaiah passage continues later, "I will make for them the darkness into light" (Isa 42:16). The language of transference from darkness to light fits the context of religious conversion (see *Poimandres* 28; *Joseph and Aseneth* 8:10; 15:12; 1 Thess 5:4-7; Col 1:12-13; Eph 5:8; and above all 1 Pet 2:9).

power of Satan to God: Or, "from the authority (*exousia*) of Satan," which echoes a major theme of both the Gospel and Acts, that the proclamation of the kingdom of God involves a battle with and a victory over the counter-kingdom under the *exousia* of Satan (see the notes on Luke 4:6; 11:14-23). In Acts, the demonic power has been identified above all with the practice of magic (8:11, 20-23; 13:10; 19:13-19). For the turn "to God," see the conversion summaries of 1 Thess 1:9-10; Heb 6:1; 1 Pet 2:10.

forgiveness of sins: Another important theme in Luke-Acts: that the "liberation" (*aphesis*) brought by the prophetic Messiah consists in the forgiveness of sins (Luke 1:77; 3:3; 4:18; 5:20-21, 24; 7:47-49; 11:4; 17:3-4; 24:47; Acts 2:38; 5:31; 10:43; 13:38).

made holy by faith in me: The use of *klēros* ("share") and the perfect passive participle *hēgiasmenoi* echoes Paul's statement to the Ephesian elders (20:32), as well as several passages in Pauline letters (Rom 15:6; 1 Cor 1:2; Col 1:12). For the symbolism of *klēros/klēronomia*, see Acts 1:17, 26; 7:5; 8:21. The emphatic "faith that is in me" (*pistē tē eis eme*) follows on the two earlier statements of Paul that likewise define the object of faith: *eis ton kyrion hēmōn Iēsoun* (20:21), and *eis Christon Iēsoun* (24:24).

19. *not disobedient to the heavenly vision:* Another example of Lukan *litotes*, which in this case is not so far from Paul's own (see Rom 1:16). Indeed, the boast of having been obedient to the apostolic call is thoroughly in character (1 Cor 15:10; 2 Cor 11:23-28).

20. *in all the territory of Judea:* The text is difficult because this phrase (in the accusative case) does not fit with the others (in the dative). The scribal corrections do not help and the scholarly emendations have no basis. The idea in any case is quite clear: just as Paul had pursued the Messianists in Jerusalem and beyond, he now sketches the progress of his mission in their behalf in Damascus (see 9:20-25) and in Jerusalem (see 9:26-30), then on to the Gentiles. The problematic phrase here being discussed, which describes a mission throughout Judea, is *not* described in the earlier narrative (unless reference is being made to 15:3-4). For similar summaries from Paul himself, see Gal 1:17-18 and Rom 15:19.

deeds appropriate to conversion: Paul uses here both *metanoeō* ("changing the mind," Luke 3:3; 5:32; 10:13; 11:32; 13:3-5; 15:7, 10; 16:30; 17:3-4; 24:47; Acts

2:38; 5:31; 8:22; 11:18; 13:24; 19:4; 20:21), and *epistrephō* ("turning," Luke 1:16-17; 17:4; 22:32; Acts 9:35; 11:21; 14:15; 15:19). The combination occurs earlier in Acts 3:19. For the demand for "deeds appropriate to conversion" (literally "worthy of repentance,") see the preaching of John the Baptist in Luke 3:8.

21. *on account of these things:* In the present speech this is the only reference to the ostensible charges against Paul that started the entire legal process (21:28). Luke considers those charges already well laid to rest (24:5-6, 11-12, 18), and focuses now on what he regards as the real issue.

22. *with God's help to this day:* The term *epikouria* ("aid/assistance") is absent from the LXX but is found in Philo, *Special Laws* 1:298; Josephus, *Antiquities of the Jews* 1:281. The idiom is found in *Antiquities* 2:94. The inclusive "small and great" (*mikrō kai megalō*) anticipates the later play *en oligō kai en megalō* (26:29).
    the prophets as well as Moses: The discourse now moves back to the central argument of Luke-Acts as a whole: that "everything brought to fulfillment" is in fact also a fulfillment of God's promises in Torah (see Luke 16:29-31; 24:25, 27, 44; Acts 2:16; 3:18, 24; 10:43; 13:15, 27, 40; 15:15; 24:14). It is this part of Paul's argument that will form the basis of the exchange between Paul and Agrippa in vv. 27-28.

23. *whether the Messiah would suffer:* The Greek here is more subtle and resistant to reader expectations than the translation can adequately convey. This is not simply another repetition of the conviction "the Messiah had (*dei*) to suffer" (Luke 24:26; Acts 17:3). First, the verbal adjective *pathētos* actually means "to be capable of suffering" (in opposition to *apathos*). Second, the form of the clause (introduced by *ei*) resists being reduced simply to a "content" clause. These features suggest that Paul is proposing a topic or proposition that can be debated on the basis of Moses and the Prophets concerning the future Messiah. A strikingly similar point is made by Justin, *Dialogue with Trypho* 89.
    whether as first from the resurrection of the dead: Once more, the translation tries to retain the "propositional" character of this clause which is also introduced by *ei* ("whether"). Luke (through Paul) obviously thinks that the specific Christian claims *can* be located and argued on the basis of the prophetic texts, since a great deal of his narrative has been taken up precisely with that chore. For the Messiah as the "first-born/first fruits" of the general resurrection, compare 1 Cor 15:20-21.
    proclaim light both to the people and to the Gentiles: The term "people" (*ho laos*) refers here as most often in Luke-Acts to the Jews considered as "the people of God." We can recognize in Paul's statement an echo of Simeon's "programmatic prophecy" in Luke 2:32, as well as the application of Isaiah 49:6 to the preaching of Paul in Acts 13:47. For Paul's own sense of the good news moving "first to Jews then to Gentiles," see Rom 1:16.

24. *you are raving:* The Roman governor "interrupts" Paul's defense (note the present tense of the genitive absolute construction), but not before Luke has had him say all that he wanted. The verb *mainomai* means literally to be in a rage, but it comes to mean "be beside oneself" in a variety of ways, whether

through divine inspiration (see Herodotus, *Persian Wars* 4:79) or infatuation (Lucian of Samosata, *The Ignorant Book Collector* 22). From there it can mean simply "to be crazy" (Dio Chrysostom, *Oration* 12:8). Luke uses the verb earlier for the response of those hearing Mary's report concerning Peter (Acts 12:15).

great learning has turned you to madness: Festus is befuddled by the *arcana* of Jewish messianism and replies as the bluff Roman administrator. The phrase "knowing letters (*ta grammata*)" usually means simple literacy, but can also point to higher levels of learning (see *Letter of Aristeas* 121; Plato, *Apology* 26D). The expression "turn to madness" is found in Lucian of Samosata, *Disowned* 30.

25. *words of truth and sanity:* This could be read as a *hendiadys*, "words of sober truth." Paul shows he is not crazy by being in control of his faculties, as shown by his solemn declamation (*apophthengomai*, Acts 2:4, 14). Luke used *sōphroneō* in describing the state of mind of the former demoniac after his exorcism (Luke 8:35). The contrast between *sōphrosynē* and *mania* is found in Xenophon, *Memorabilia* 1, 1, 16. It would be difficult to find a term more descriptive of the Greek philosophical ideal (see e.g., Plato, *Republic* 430E-431B; *Symposium* 196C; Diogenes Laertius, *Lives of the Philosophers* 3:91; 4 Macc 1:3, 31; 3:17; 5:23).

26. *for the king understands these things:* Paul turns from the obtuse Roman to the supposedly "expert" (*gnōstēs*) Agrippa, hoping that his "understanding" will win his approval. He therefore speaks with boldness (*parrēsiazomai*), showing himself in this respect once again thoroughly the philosopher/prophet, who even before hostility and skepticism proclaims his convictions (see Acts 2:29; 4:13, 29, 31; 9:27-28; 13:46; 14:3; 18:26; 19:8).

none of these things has escaped his attention: The sentence is an elaborate exercise in *litotes*, literally, "I am not persuaded that none of these things is hidden from him (*lanthanein auton*). The expression "not in a corner" is still another *litotes*, meaning "well-known/public." The expression *en gōnią* is proverbial for what is private or secret (see e.g., Plato, *Gorgias* 485D; Plutarch, *On Being a Busybody* 2 (*Mor* 516C); Epictetus, *Discourses* 2, 12, 17. Throughout his narrative, Luke has emphasized the *public* character of the prophetic visitation through Jesus and the apostles. The apologetic intent, of course, is to demonstrate that Christianity is neither secret nor subversive.

27. *do you believe . . . in the prophets:* The central part of the argument is now brought out in dialogue: the Christian convictions about the suffering and resurrection of the Messiah are rooted in the Scriptures. For Luke, "the prophets" include the first and greatest of them, Moses, whose career is taken as paradigmatic for the sending and rejection of the prophets (Acts 7:17-44). The question, as Agrippa is quick to recognize, is tricky. It suggests not only a commitment to the prophetic texts as Scripture, but also to the prophetic principle, that God can speak in every age in new and powerful ways.

28. *to play the Christian a little:* The proper understanding of Agrippa's reply is made difficult by several factors: a) *en oligǫ* often functions idiomatically as a temporal reference "in a short while"; on the other hand, Paul's immediate riposte uses *oligos* and *megalos* in what appears to be a non-temporal sense;

b) the verb *peithō* means, straightforwardly, "persuade," and the verb *poieō* means, straightforwardly, "to make/do," but how can Agrippa actually be saying to Paul that he is persuading him to become a Christian? Some commentators therefore make *peithein* conative, "you are trying to persuade." A better resolution is to take *en oligō* in a non-temporal sense, and to read *poieō* as "play the role" as in LXX 1 Kgs 21:7 (*poieis basilea epi Israel*). This enables us to make good sense both of Agrippa's statement (he sees that "in for a dime is in for a dollar," that an agreement to the prophets already brings him into partial agreement with Paul's position, and he does not want to be led down that logical path), and of Paul's punning response.

29. *I would pray to God:* The optative of *euchomai* ("pray") is a graceful way of expressing a desire dear to Paul but distasteful to his listener. Paul would indeed like them to "play the Christian," not only a little but a lot; he wants them *toioutous hopoios kai egō eimi* ("precisely as I am") excepting his status as a prisoner.

31. *withdrew and began talking to each other:* The consultation is similar to that held in the Sanhedrin concerning the apostles (5:33-39), except that in the earlier case the apostles were removed from the chamber, whereas here the notables withdraw.

    nothing worthy of death or imprisonment: The assembled worthies agree with the conclusion previously reached by the tribune Lysias (23:29), and by the governor Festus (25:25). Like Jesus, who was declared innocent three times by the Roman authority Pontius Pilate (Luke 23:4, 14, 22) with the agreement of the Tetrarch Herod (23:5), so is Paul three times declared innocent of the charges against him by Roman authorities with the agreement of a representative of the Herodian family.

INTERPRETATION

Paul's speech before Festus, Agrippa, and Bernice (26:2-23) is his last major discourse. After this, we will overhear only short exchanges with his fellow-travellers (27:10, 21-25, 33), and a final sad encounter with the Jews of Rome (28:17-28). This is also Paul's longest *apologia*, and Luke has prepared for it elaborately in 25:13-27, by assembling the Roman governor, the Jewish king, their entourage, and the nobility of the city of Caesarea, to hear the strange man who apparently claims that "a certain dead man, Jesus, was alive" (25:19). Such authorial placement and preparation invite us to pay particular attention to the speech itself.

Paul's final defense can be read also as Christianity's first real *apologia* before the sophisticated Greek world. The speech is both lengthy and the most elegantly constructed of Paul's discourses, with exactly the sort of elevated diction, subtle syntax, and paranomasia that delighted Hellenistic rhetoricians. Luke's skill in *prosōpoiia* has not failed him in this final challenge. Paul's speech has just the qualities desired for an aristocratic audience, down to the final verbal fencing with governor and king (26:24-29). It is all the more striking, therefore, that the speech does not transmute the messianic movement into a philosophy, but instead reasserts all the more vigorously the two features that would remain most problematic to the educated Greek world: its scandalous affirmation of a crucified and raised Messiah, and its insistence on identifying itself as a legitimate claimant to the Jewish heritage.

The specific emphasis Luke wanted to impress on Paul's audience (that is, his readers) is made clearer by showing how this speech retains, drops, or develops the motifs of Paul's earlier defenses. We notice at once, for example, that Paul's insistence on a good conscience, that was stated so emphatically in the earlier speeches (22:3; 23:1; 24:16) is virtually absent, unless in the altered form of his specific obedience to "the heavenly vision" (26:19). Even more startling is the realization that this speech spends no time at all on the legal charges against Paul. After the point-by-point refutation of these charges earlier (24:11-13, 19-20; 25:8, 11, 18, 25), Luke feels no need to rehash them again. In fact, Paul is allowed to claim that it was "for this reason"—namely his preaching of repentance to Jews and Gentiles—that the Jews seized him in the Temple and tried to kill him (26:21)!

Some elements found in his earlier defenses are carried over to this one. Paul briefly sketches his former life as a Pharisee (26:4-5; see 22:3; 24:14-16). But here he builds on his former perceptions as a possible motivation for his rabid persecution of the Messianists, now described in the fullest and most frightening detail (26:9-12; see 22:5). The confession of his rage and violence toward "the saints" makes all the more dramatic his second retelling of his experience of the risen Lord on the road to Damascus (26:12-18), bringing to three the number of versions to which the reader has been exposed (see 9:1-9; 22:6-11). More significant than the incidental details distinguishing this version from the others (the time of day, the brightness of the light and who saw it, who fell to the ground, the language spoken by the voice) is the evidence in this retelling of Paul's growing awareness of the meaning of the event.

Now, he remembers the voice as telling him that it was stubborn of him to "kick against the goads" (26:14), an image that suggests that Paul had been at once being pulled toward the Messianists even as he stubbornly refused to heed them. Now also he remembers his entire commissioning as taking place, not through the mediation of Ananias or through another vision while in the Temple (9:15-16; 22:14-21), but entirely and fully through the voice of the risen Lord. The experience of the risen Lord bore implicitly within itself all the mandate and significance for Paul's life.

In fact, one entirely new element that Luke has Paul introduce in this speech is a brief recital of his missionary activities following his conversion (26:19-20). In terms of his legal defense, this summation serves to define his activities not in terms of hostility toward humans but in terms of obedience to God, not in terms of social upheaval or impiety, but in terms of traditional Jewish convictions: he has preached repentance and turning to God and doing the deeds appropriate to conversion. Luke has this summary lead into Paul's emphatic declaration that he proclaims nothing apart from what was found in Moses and the Prophets (26:22). And it is here that we find the real point of Paul's final defense speech: the combined assertion concerning the resurrection hope and the fulfillment of the Scripture.

These are the themes that Luke has carried over from the earlier speeches. Before the crowd in the temple precincts, Paul declared that he had been chosen to "see the righteous one," and had been appointed as a witness of what he had heard and seen (22:14-15). Before the Sanhedrin, Paul stated that he was on trial "for the hope that is the resurrection of the dead" (23:6). Before Felix, Paul connected this conviction that there would be a resurrection of the just and unjust, to belief in the Law and the Prophets shared by his fellow Jews (24:14-15), and concluded his *apologia* before the governor by repeating that he was being judged concerning "the resurrection of the dead" (24:21). This had made sufficient impression on Festus that he reported the dispute between Paul and his Jewish accusers as revolving around Paul's claim that a dead man was alive (25:19). Now once more, with even greater emphasis, the reality of the resurrection is stated both specifically with regard to Jesus (26:16), and more generally to the fulfillment of the promise made to the fathers (26:6-8). In the most emphatic fashion, Luke identifies the blessings for which all the "twelve tribes" of Israel hope with the resurrection of Jesus. He makes even more explicit, furthermore, that the suffering and resurrection of the Messiah realized in Jesus are the "fulfillment" of what "the Prophets and Moses said were going to happen" (26:22-23).

Luke has therefore enabled Paul to pull together the threads of his narrative argument. The Messiah who was rejected and died was raised from the dead to proclaim "light both to the people and to the Gentiles" (26:23; see Luke 2:32), and this was all stated plainly in Torah (26:22; see Luke 24:44-49), so that acceptance of the resurrection of Jesus and the gift of his Spirit was to realize the hope of Israel itself (26:6-7; see Acts 3:24-26). Paul's defense provides a retrospective interpretation of the narrative of Luke-Acts.

That these are precisely the points that Luke wants to establish is shown by the dialogue following the speech. Festus challenges the sanity of anyone proclaiming the resurrection. But Paul insists that he is speaking "truth and sanity" (26:24-25). Indeed, he issued the challenge earlier in the speech, "Why is it considered incredible by any of you if God raises the dead?" (26:8). It is Agrippa's role to elicit the second emphasis, that belief in the resurrection is rooted in the prophetic character of Scripture. This time Paul's challenge is direct: if Agrippa believes in the Prophets, he ought to perceive the validity of Paul's claims. Agrippa is sufficiently perceptive to see that if he agrees concerning the Prophets, he is already—for Paul's purposes—already "playing the Christian a little," so he sidesteps the challenge by humorously identifying Paul's ploy (26:26-28).

Paul's *apologia* is at one level successful. The notables withdraw and consider his fate. They see no cause for death or imprisonment. Only Paul's own appeal requires his continued custody. So Luke has him declared innocent of his charges for a third time, establishing still another resemblance between Jesus and his prophetic successor (see notes). And Paul will fulfill his destiny of bearing witness also in Rome, "the end of the earth" (23:11; see 1:8).

But at another level, Paul's *apologia* is not successful. He is not, after all, simply seeking his own survival. He is under a mandate from the Lord to proclaim Jesus to both Jews and Gentiles. He is not simply "playing the rhetorician," nor is he interested simply in Agrippa's "playing the Christian." Paul really does want all those hearing him, "small and great," to become as he is (26:29). To the Roman administrator, however, this is now not only superstition (25:19) but even madness (26:24). And to the "Jewish King" who is "expert in all the customs and controversies of the Jews" (26:3), who "understands concerning these things" (26:26), Paul's challenge concerning the implications of prophetic belief is worth only dismissive humor. Even when stated in more elegant language, the good news of a crucified and raised Messiah is a stumbling block to Greeks who seek for wisdom and Jews who look for signs (1 Cor 1:21-25).

For Reference and Further Study

Harle, P. "Un 'private-joke' de Paul dans le livre des Actes (xxvi, 28-29)." *NTS* 24 (1977-1978) 527-533.

Hickling, C. J. A. "The Portrait of Paul in Acts 26." *Les Actes des Apôtres: Traditions, rédaction, théologie.* Ed. J. Kremer. BETL 48. Gembloux: J. Duculot & Leuven: Leuven University Press, 1979, 499-503.

Malherbe, A. J. " 'Not in a Corner': Early Christian Apologetic in Acts 26:26." *Paul and the Popular Philosophers.* Minneapolis: Fortress Press, 1989, 147-163.

O'Toole, R. F. *Acts 26: The Christological Climax of Paul's Defense (Ac 22:1-26:32).* AB 78. Rome: Pontifical Biblical Institute, 1978.

Stegemann, W. "War der Apostel Paulus ein römischen Burger?" ZNW 78 (1987) 200-229.

52. Perils at Sea (27:1-26)

1. When it was decided that we should sail for Italy, they handed over Paul and some other prisoners to a centurion named Julius, of the Augustan Cohort. 2. We embarked on a ship of Adramyttium. It was about to sail to places along the coast of Asia. We put to sea. With us was Aristarchus, a Macedonian from Thessalonika. 3. The next day we arrived in Sidon. Julius acted humanely toward Paul. He allowed him to go to his friends to have his needs attended. 4. Setting out from there we skirted Cyprus because the winds were against us. 5. But we made across the open sea opposite Cilicia and Pamphylia. We went down to Myra in Lycia. 6. There the centurion found an Alexandrian ship bound for Italy. He put us on it. 7. Sailing slowly for several days, we barely arrived off Cnidus. Because the wind did not allow us to go forward, we skirted Crete off Salmone. 8. Barely hugging its shore, we arrived at a place called Fair Havens, near the city of Lasea. 9. Since much time had gone by and the voyage was perilous because the fast had already passed, Paul began to offer advice. 10. He said to them, "Men, I see that the voyage is going to mean damage and great loss, not only to the cargo and the ship, but also to our lives." 11. But the centurion listened to the captain and the owner of the vessel more than to the things being said by Paul. 12. Since the harbor was not suitable for spending the winter, the greater number of them made a plan to leave there, reaching if possible Phoenix, a port of Crete that looks northwest and southwest, to spend the winter. 13. When the south wind blew gently, they thought their plan was working. They raised anchor and skirted close to Crete. 14. But soon a great wind called a Northeaster swept down from land. 15. The ship was caught up. It could not face into the wind. We gave up and were carried away. 16. But we ran under a certain small island called Cauda. We were barely able to secure the lifeboat. 17. They raised it and took means to lash down the ship. Since they feared they would crash on the Syrtis, they lowered the mainsail, and thus we were carried off. 18. As we were being violently buffeted, the next day they began to throw the cargo overboard. 19. And on the third day they threw over the ship's gear with their own hands. 20. Neither sun nor stars appeared for many days. We were under a severe storm. All hope of our being saved was disappearing. 21. When we had been without food for a long time, Paul stood among them and said, "Men, you should have listened to me and not left Crete only to gain this injury and loss! 22.

And now I advise you to take courage. There will be no loss of life among you, only the loss of the ship. 23. For there appeared to me this night an angel of the God to whom I belong and whom I worship. 24. He said, 'Fear no longer, Paul! You must stand before Caesar! And Look, God has granted you all those sailing with you.' 25. Therefore, men, take heart. For I believe in God, that it will turn out in just the way he has spoken to me. 26. But we must crash on some island.''

NOTES

1. *sail for Italy:* The "we-narrative" that had left off in 21:18 is now resumed—although with some fluctuations (notice the shift to the third person narrative in 27:13, 17, 19, 28, 29, 38, 39-44)—and continues up to 28:16. For "Italy" (*Italia*), see Acts 10:1; 18:2; 27:6; Heb 13:24. The Western Text has a more elaborate transition here, making clear that "the governor decided to send him to Caesar."

   Julius, of the Augustan Cohort: There is inscriptional evidence for an Augustan Cohort stationed in Syria during the first century, although the title could also be given as an honorific to auxiliary troops. Another possibility is that the *sebastē* refers to the cohorts called by Josephus the *sebastēnoi*, which were under Agrippa I's command (Josephus, *Antiquities* 19:365-366; *Jewish War* 2:52) and whose name derived from the city Sebaste in Samaria. The identification of the cohort is of interest for historical reconstruction but of little significance for the meaning of the narrative.

2. *ship of Adramyttium:* The place name refers to a town on the coast of Asia Minor. The planned itinerary gives the picture of a ship that moved in daily legs from one coastal port to another (compare Acts 20:13-16; 21:1-3). There is a certain catch-as-catch-can quality to the travel connections!

   with us was Aristarchus: This associate of Paul was identified as a Macedonian in Acts 19:29, and as a Thessalonian in 20:4. In Col 4:10, he is referred to as a "fellow prisoner" and in Phlm 24 as among Paul's "fellow workers." Under the influence of Acts 20:4, the Western Text adds here the name of "Secundus."

3. *acted humanely:* The adverb *philanthrōpōs* is cognate with *philanthrōpia* (see Acts 28:2; Titus 3:4), a term that occurs rarely in the NT, but is widely employed in Hellenistic moral literature to describe high qualities of ethical and "civilized" behavior (see e.g., 2 Macc 4:11; 6:22; 9:27; 14:9; 3 Macc 3:15, 20; Esth 8:13; Philo, *The Special Laws* 2:141; Josephus, *Antiquities* 12:46; *Against Apion* 1:153; Plutarch, *Oracles at Delphi* 16 (*Mor.* 402A).

   have his needs attended: for the idiom *epimeleias tynchanein*, see Philo, *Special Laws* 3:106. That a captive frequently had access to friends and associates is shown in the note on Acts 24:23; see also 28:30; 2 Tim 1:16-17. Luke has not specifically mentioned a Christian community in Sidon, but it could be included among the churches of Phoenicia referred to in 11:19 and 15:3.

4. *we skirted Cyprus:* The verb *hypopleō* means literally "to sail under," and in nautical parlance means to "sail under the lee," meaning to have the protection from severe wind offered by a land-mass. The less technical rendering "skirt" is used here and in verse 7. In fact, they were hugging the shore rather than risking the open sea. Unable to head directly west toward Italy, they are moving north (on the east side of Cyprus) toward the coast of present-day Turkey.

5. *opposite Cilicia and Pamphylia:* Coming north of Cyprus, they turn directly westward across the "open sea" (*to pelagos*) passing in front of the coasts of the provinces of Cilicia and Pamphylia. Some *mss* of the Western Text add the words "for fifteen days" to describe the length of this leg of the voyage; compare the "fourteen days" in 27:27.

    Myra in Lycia: The choice of the verb *katerchomai* ("go down") perhaps reflects how the boat hugged the coast, for the land-mass of Lycia lies southwestward of Pamphylia. The city of Myra is close to Patara (Pliny the Elder, *Natural History* 5:100), where Paul had touched down on his earlier voyage to Jerusalem (Acts 21:1); in fact, some *mss* had added "Myra" to that earlier passage.

6. *an Alexandrian ship bound for Italy:* Egypt had for a long time been the granary of the empire, and the securing of regular shipments from Alexandria to the city was a constant concern for the emperors faced with a large and often restive urban population and periodic shortages of food. Claudius, for example, guaranteed insurance coverage for the loss of ships and a special bounty for shipments that came across in the dangerous winter months (see e.g., Suetonius, *Life of Claudius* 18:2). For the distinctiveness of the "Alexandrian ships," see Seneca, *Moral Epistles* 77:1-2. And for an account of the voyage of one such grain-ship from Sidon onward that provides a remarkable parallel to the one here recounted by Luke, see Lucian of Samosata, *The Ship* 1-9.

7. *arrived off Cnidus:* This is a seaport mentioned already by Thucydides as frequented by merchant ships from Alexandria (*Peloponnesian War* 8, 24, 35). It is on a peninsula at the southwest extreme of the province of Asia Minor.

    skirted Crete off Salmone: For the translation of *hypopleō* as "skirt," see the note on v. 4. Once more, the adverse winds make a straight run impossible, so the ship moves southward to sail "under the lee" of Crete. The city of Salmone would appear to be on the northwest tip of the island (Pliny the Elder, *Natural History* 4:58; Strabo, *Geography* 10, 4, 2). For a parallel account in which temporary safety from a storm is found in Crete, see Heliodorus, *The Ethiopians* 5, 22, 7.

8. *barely hugging its shore:* The verb *paralegomai* has the sense of "coasting," and the adverb *molis* ("barely"), as in vv. 7 and 16, gives the impression of proceeding with great difficulty (compare Luke 9:39; Acts 14:18; Rom 5:7; 1 Pet 4:18). Once more we gain the impression of first-century Mediterranean travel as subject to a variety of adverse conditions and often reduced to a series of short and difficult efforts. The towns mentioned here, "Fair Havens" and "Lasea"

are not among those mentioned by Pliny the Elder, but although he speaks of "the hundred cities" of Crete that made it famous, he mentions only forty, and concludes with, "and about sixty other towns of which only the memory exists" (*Natural History* 4:69).

9. *perilous because the fast had already passed:* The "Fast" (*nēsteia*) when used absolutely as here, refers to the Day of Atonement on 10th Tishri (Sept/Oct). See Josephus, *Antiquities of the Jews* 14:66; 18:94; Philo, *Embassy to Gaius* 306; *m.Men.* 11:9. The Mediterranean was considered "closed" during the winter months (variously computed, but certainly running from November to March), because of the severe weather; thus the bonuses offered for delivering grain in these dangerous conditions (Suetonius, *Life of Claudius* 18:1). For similar notices about sailing in winter, compare Josephus, *Jewish War* 1:279; Chariton of Aphrodisias, *Chaereas and Callirhoe* 3, 5, 1.

10. *the voyage is going to mean damage:* Given the circumstances described in the previous note, Paul's "prophecy" here appears as simple common sense and prudence. For "damage" (*hybris*) in this sense, compare 3 Macc 3:25 and Josephus, *Antiquities of the Jews* 1:60; and for "loss" (*zēmia*), see *Antiquities of the Jews* 4:211; Epictetus, *Discourses* 2, 10, 14-15.

11. *to the captain and the owner:* The "owner" (*nauklēros*) would be the chief authority over the disposition of the ship and its cargo, with the "captain" (*kybernētēs*) next in line (see Plutarch, *Precepts of Statecraft* 13 [*Mor.* 807B]); the usage seems to have been flexible, however, so that the "captain" could refer to the chief in command, with the *nauklēroi* referring to pilots (see Plutarch, *Dinner of the Seven Wise Men* 18 [*Mor.* 162A]; Josephus, *Antiquities of the Jews* 9:209; and compare as well Petronius, *Satyricon* 101). In this case, of course, Luke makes the centurion the final authority, and—most surprisingly—has the prisoner Paul given a voice in the deliberations. In the end, it is the "majority" (*hoi pleiones*) making the decision (v. 12).

12. *Phoenix, a port of Crete:* The city is located in Crete by the geographer Strabo (*Geography* 10, 4, 3), but its location is uncertain; so are the terms here translated as "northwest" (*kata liba*) and "southwest" (*kata chōron*). Not a great deal hinges on the identification of the place, since the ship never even reaches it anyway!

14. *great wind called a Northeaster:* The phrase *anemos typhōnikos* might almost be translated, "a wind of the typhoon class." The specific name of the wind is otherwise unattested, and appears to be a hybrid form made up of the Latin *aquilo* ("north wind") and the Greek *euros* ("southeast wind"), thus *eurakylon*. The designations of various winds was not, in any case, entirely agreed upon by experts (see Strabo, *Geography* 1, 2, 21). The expression "swept down from land" is literally "down from it" (*kat'autēs*), with the pronoun referring back to Crete.

15. *gave up and were carried away:* The participle *epidontes* is somewhat indeterminate ("giving over"), and is taken here to mean that they stopped fighting the wind, and let themselves be carried. The Western Text amends slightly

to yield "giving way to the wind and having furled the sails." In any case, they are now out of control and at the mercy of the winds. This is, for obvious reasons, one of the most common motifs of sea-voyage narratives: see *Odyssey* 9:82-84; Heliodorus, *The Ethiopians* 5, 27, 2; Achilles Tatius, *Clitophon and Leucippe* 3, 1-2; Petronius, *Satyricon* 114; Lucian of Samosata, *Toxaris* 19; *A True Story* 1:6; 2:46; *The Ship* 7.

16. *ran under a certain small island:* The verb *hypotrechō* ("run under") has the same sense as *hypopleō* in vv. 4 and 7. They are able to drift under the shelter offered by the island—though not to land—and carry out emergency measures to prepare for their re-emergence into the full force of the winds. Cauda appears to be southwest of Crete, as the ship continues to push into the open Mediterranean.

secure the lifeboat: The adjective *perikratēs* means to have control over something (see Ps.-Callisthenes, *Life of Alexander of Macedon* 2, 4, 3). The small lifeboat (*skaphē*) was ordinarily towed behind the ship (Heliodorus, *The Ethiopians* 5, 27, 6). But in a great storm, it might be cut loose and lost. So it was lashed to the ship itself.

17. *took means to lash down the ship:* The precise action here is obscure, although the general idea is clear: they "undergird" (*hypozynnumi*) the ship. But what are the "aids/helps/means" (*boētheia*), and how are they used? Perhaps the term refers to cables that were used to wrap the ship planks either end-to-end or side-to-side, either internally or externally, in order literally to hold the ship together against the force of the waves.

crash on the Syrtis: The term refers to a zone of shallows and quicksands off the coast of Cyrenaica (the Gulf of Sidra), which was well-known as a terrible hazard to mariners (see Dio Chrysostom, *Oration* 5:8-11; Pliny, *Natural History* 5:26). Josephus said "its very name strikes terror" (*Jewish War* 2:381). Less clear is the action now taken by the sailors to avoid that hazard. What is the *skeuos* ("vessel") that they lower? A good guess is one of the sails, perhaps the mainsail (compare the use of *skeuos* in Peter's vision, Acts 10:11). Thus, they would not be driven so rapidly toward the hazardous coast of North Africa.

19. *threw over the ship's gear:* On two successive days of being buffeted by the fierce wind (*cheimazomai*), the crew progressively lightens the ship by getting rid first of the cargo (*ekbolē*), and then the "gear" (*skeuē*, plural of the term *skeuos*, above) of the ship itself. For cutting down the mast as a response to extreme danger, see the satirical treatment of Juvenal, *Satires* 12:52-60. As for the throwing over of cargo, Aristotle notes that it is not something a sane person would do in ordinary circumstances, but it will be done in order to save one's life (Aristotle, *Nichomachean Ethics* 1110A); the practice is widely attested: see LXX Jonah 1:5; Josephus, *Jewish War* 1:280; Achilles Tatius, *Clitophon and Leucippe* 3, 2; Heliodorus, *The Ethiopians* 5, 27, 7; Juvenal, *Satires* 12:29-50.

20. *hope of our being saved was disappearing:* The imperfect *periēreito* suggests a steadily deteriorating situation. Although the emotion is certainly intelligible in

the circumstances, it is also one with literary parallels (see *Odyssey* 5:297-304; 12:277-279; Aelius Aristides, *Sacred Tales* 2:12; Achilles Tatius, *Clitophon and Leucippe* 3, 2, 4; Lucian of Samosata, *Toxaris* 20; Thucydides, *Peloponnesian War* 1, 2, 65).

21. *only to gain this injury and loss:* Paul's words (*hybris kai zēmia*) deliberately echo those of his "prophecy/advice" in v. 12, and sound ironically in combination with the verb *kerdainō* ("gain"); compare Luke 9:25.

22. *advise you to take courage:* The verb *parainō* ("advise") is used in the NT only in v. 6 and here. The first case seems more appropriate than this one, since Paul is not really offering "advice" this time around, but encouragement. It is typical of Luke, however, to use the same term repeatedly in a small patch of narrative, and never employ it again. For *euthymeō* ("be of good spirit"), see below in v. 25 and 36 as well as Acts 24:10.

23. *an angel of the God:* From beginning to end, Luke-Acts employs these emissaries from God to deliver messages and comfort to characters in the story, as well as acts of deliverance (Luke 1:11; 26; 2:9, 13; 22:43; Acts 5:19; 7:26; 10:3; 12:7, 23).

    to whom I belong and whom I worship: The Greek is oddly arranged but nevertheless impressive (*tou theou hou eimi egō hō kai latreuō angelos*) as an expression of intense and personal piety. For Paul's *latreia* of God, compare Acts 24:14, and especially Rom 1:9; 2 Tim 1:3. In this case, Paul identifies *his* "tutelary spirit" to whom he turns for help in contrast to others (see Aelius Aristides, *Sacred Tales* 2:12; Plutarch, *The Bravery of Women* 8-9 [*Mor.* 247E-248A]; Petronius, *Satyricon* 105; Jonah 1:5, 7-12).

24. *fear no longer:* The content of this vision is similar to that of Paul's vision of the Lord in Jerusalem (Acts 23:11): there he was told that he must bear witness in Rome, here it is specified as "standing before Caesar." The main difference, of course, is the assurance given concerning his companions: God has "granted" (*kecharistai*) all of them "to" or "for" Paul (*soi*). The motif of rescue at sea by means of divine intervention is a common one in the parallel literature (see, e.g., LXX Ps 106:28-29; Plutarch, *Dinner of the Seven Wise Men* 18 [*Mor.* 161F]; Lucian, *The Ship* 9; *Salaried Posts* 1; Achilles Tatius, *Clitophon and Leucippe* 3:5; *Testament of Naphtali* 6:8-9).

25. *turn out in just the way he has spoken to me:* Paul is thus shown to have the sort of faith that is praised by Elizabeth in Luke 1:45. For the motif of "things turning out just as was said," compare Luke 2:20; 22:13. For a similar expression of piety, that everything happening in a shipwreck was guided by a divine agency, compare Aelius Aristides, *Sacred Tales* 2:12-13, and for one's fate at sea as the fulfillment of a prophecy, see *Odyssey* 5:300-302.

26. *crash on some island:* Paul saves the bad news for last. The verb *ekpiptō* is the same used in v. 17. In reference to sea-voyaging, it can mean to "run adrift" or to be "cast ashore" in a shipwreck (see Herodotus, *Persian Wars* 3:138). The prophecy is shown to have come true in 28:1. Ships coming to grief on rocky shores is again a favorite shipwreck motif (see Dio Chrysostom, *Ora-*

tion 7:2; Lucian of Samosata, *Salaried Posts* 2; *A True Story* 1:6; Achilles Tatius, *Clitophon and Leucippe* 3:4).

INTERPRETATION

Luke's account of Paul's voyage to Rome is one of the most puzzling parts of his narrative. The voyage can be seen as a literary *tour de force:* the language is elevated, the adventure high, the classical motifs associated with sea-voyage, sea-storm, and shipwreck all wonderfully displayed. But precisely the obvious literary quality of the account raises questions concerning Luke's purposes. Why does he spend so much time and care on what was after all only a voyage?

Although the narrative should be read straight through, it is helpful to divide the discussion of it. In this section I will focus on the interpretive questions raised by the account: its literary connections and how these affect judgments concerning its historical or fictional character. In the next section, I will discuss more fully Luke's use of the account and how it serves his overall purposes.

Perhaps no feature of Luke's narrative more clearly suggests his Hellenistic culture than this sea-voyage. The ancient Israelites, it appears, were land-bound as much by preference as by circumstance; although the author of Proverbs marvels at "the way of a ship on the high seas" (Prov 30:19), we sense that the observation was made at a distance. The psalmist speaks wonderingly of "some who went down to the sea in ships" and describes in vivid detail the disastrous character of that endeavor (Ps 107:23-30). The terrible things that could happen to Jews on sea voyages are reflected as well in the accounts of sea storms in Jonah 1:4–2:10, the *Testament of Naphtali* 6:2-10, and such Rabbinic tales as that of the little boy who calmed the sea in *jT Ber.* 9:1. The sparsity of the accounts, however, suggests the fundamental abhorrence of the sea as a place too deeply identified with the powers of chaos (Gen 1:2; Ps 104:6; Ezek 26:19-20).

In sharp contrast, Greek and Roman prosperity, culture, and empire alike were rooted in the ability to transverse the waters of the Mediterranean. Yet despite the positive benefits of sea-travel, these people knew even better the harsh reality that when setting out on the deep four things can happen, and three of them are bad. The good thing was safe arrival, but even that was sometimes achieved at the cost of pirates, storms, or shipwrecks, the "terrors of the sea" (Apuleius, *The Golden Ass* 7:6). The epic literature in which Greco-Roman cultural ideals found their first and finest expression are filled with sea adventures, including terrible storms and wrecks (*Odyssey* 5:291-332; 9:62-81; 12:201-303; *Aeneid* 1:44-153).

Not surprisingly, the same themes find their way into the popular romances of the Hellenistic period, so much so that a sea-voyage complete with storm and shipwreck is a regular element of the genre. As the notes to this section illustrate, the novels of Chariton of Aphrodisias, Achilles Tatius, Petronius, Heliodorus, Xenophon of Ephesus and Longus, all have at least one of these adventures as a feature of their plot. And the plot mechanism continues into the apocryphal acts that continue the tradition of the popular romance (see e.g., Pseudo-Clementine *Homilies* 12, 9, 3-10, 4).

So predictable were the voyage, storm and shipwreck that satirists poked fun at the conventions (Juvenal, *Satires* 12:17-82; Lucian of Samosata, *On Salaried Posts in Great Houses* 1-2), or parodied them (Lucian of Samosata, *A True Story* 1:6). The setting of storm and shipwreck could also, however, be used for the teaching of moral lessons, such as the placidity (or lack thereof) shown by a philosopher in crisis (e.g., Diogenes Laertius, *Lives of Eminent Philosophers* (Aristippus) 2:71; Lucian of Samosata, *Passing of Peregrinus* 43-44) or the beauty of loyalty and friendship (Lucian of Samosata, *Toxaris* 19-20), or the efficacy of prayer made to the true God (*jT Ber.* 9:1).

No reader in the least familiar with these literary antecedents could fail to notice their presence in Luke's account. Indeed, as so often in his appropriation of such conventions, Luke's version is a highly compressed compendium of the motifs. When read against the comparative backdrop, the narrative does not appear excessive or exaggerated just at this point or that; rather, it appears to be totally defined by the conventions of the genre. The question of Luke's historical reliability is once more raised with peculiar sharpness. Has he simply inserted into his narrative a tale of high adventure for the entertainment and perhaps edification of his readers? Are we to understand this voyage of Paul to Rome as the best evidence for the unhistorical and perhaps even fictional character of Acts?

Such a conclusion would be precipitous. As this commentary has tried to show repeatedly, there is no hard and fast line between the narrative conventions of ancient history and fiction. All ancient historians used what contemporaries would regard as "fictional" techniques; indeed, contemporary historians too, insofar as they try to construct a "narrative of events," also use them! The fact that Luke demonstrably follows the conventions of ancient sea-voyage writing does not by itself determine the basic historicity of his account.

Only a short reflection is required, furthermore, to remember that the literary conventions became so stereotyped because in the Hellenistic world sea-voyages were common, and storms were frequent, and shipwrecks did take place. It is not only in epics and romances that we read of these matters but also in historical writings (see e.g., Thucydides,

Peloponnesian War 2, 6, 26; 6, 20, 104; 8, 24, 31; 8, 24, 34; Herodotus, *Persian Wars* 3:138; 7:188) and in biographical accounts (Josephus, *Life* 15; Diogenes, *Lives of Eminent Philosophers* 7:3; Aelius Aristides, *Sacred Tales* 2:11-17, 65-67; 4:35-37). Luke's version is not notably more colorful or exaggerated than other such accounts. Apart from the interventions made by Paul—to be discussed later—this voyage narrative resembles the rest of Luke's story in its generally accurate portrayal of places, times, and procedures. The ports of call, directions of wind, places of danger (such as the Syrtis) and of safety (such as the southern coast of Crete) are all where they should be. The periods of time (for sailing generally, for being driven by a storm) are within the range of other ancient accounts (see Thucydides, *Peloponnesian War* 8, 24, 34; Aelius Aristides, *Sacred Tales* 2:68). Most of all, the essential plausibility of the event is given further support by the evidence provided by Paul himself that by mid-career he had already experienced "a day and a night adrift at sea" as well as "shipwreck three times" (2 Cor 11:25).

A sound interpretation of this section of Acts, therefore, should avoid the extreme either/or of fiction vs. history. To cling ferociously to the factual character of every detail is not only to ignore the obvious literary motifs, but also to avoid the question most pressing for answer: why does Luke devote so much attention to this voyage? Yes, the recurrence of "we" throughout the account may suggest the presence of an eyewitness companion (although the use of the plural was frequently used in voyage accounts as a convention). But other "we" sections lack anything like this amount of detail. On the other hand, to move directly from the presence of literary motifs to the claim that Luke was simply fabricating the entire incident is, as I have suggested, reckless. There is nothing implausible about the basic series of events as they are described, if we leave aside the disproportionate role ascribed to Paul. A sound position recognizes the possibility that the narrative is as a whole essentially historical, but also acknowledges its literary (or even "fictional") shaping.

Having sorted through some of the fundamental questions facing any interpretation of the sea-voyage, we are left with the question of its literary and religious function within Luke's narrative as a whole. And this consideration is best left for the next section of the commentary.

FOR REFERENCE AND FURTHER STUDY

Broughton, T. R. S. "The Roman Army." *Beginnings* 5:427-445.
Haenchen, E. "Acta 27." *Zeit und Geschichte: Dankesgabe an R. Bultmann.* Ed. E. Dinkler. Tübingen: J. C. B. Mohr, 1964, 235-254.

Hemer, C. J. *The Book of Acts in the Setting of Hellenistic Historiography.* Ed. C. H. Gempf. WUZNT 49. Tübingen: J. C. B. Mohr (Paul Siebeck), 1989, 132–158.

Pervo, R. I. *Profit with Delight: The Literary Genre of the Acts of the Apostles.* Philadelphia: Fortress, 1987, 50–54, 155–157.

Praeder, S. M. "Acts 27:1–28:16: Sea Voyages in Ancient Literature and the Theology of Luke-Acts." *CBQ* 46 (1984) 683–706.

Robbins, V. K. "By Land and by Sea: The We-Passages and Ancient Sea Voyages." *Perspectives in Luke-Acts.* Ed. C. H. Talbert. Danville, Va.: Association of Baptist Professors of Religion, 1978, 215–242.

Ronge, J. "Acts 27:1–10." *Vigiliae Christianae* 14 (1960) 193ff.

53. *Shipwreck and Safety (27:27-44)*

27. As the fourteenth night arrived, we were drifting in the sea of Adria. About the middle of the night, the sailors perceived that some land was approaching them. 28. And when they made a sounding, they found the depth to be twenty fathoms. After a short interval, they made a sounding and found the depth to be fifteen fathoms. 29. Fearing that they would crash somewhere against rocky places, they dropped four anchors from the stern. They began to pray for the day to come. 30. But the sailors were looking to flee the ship. They lowered the lifeboat into the sea, pretending as if they were going to drop anchors from the bow. 31. Paul said to the centurion and soldiers, "If those fellows don't stay on ship, you will not be able to be saved." 32. The soldiers then cut the lifeboat's ropes and allowed it to be cast off. 33. At the point when day was about to come, Paul began to exhort everyone to take food. He said, "Today is the fourteenth day you have completed in suspense without food. You have taken nothing. 34. Therefore I exhort you to take food. It is for your welfare. For from none of your heads shall a hair be lost!" 35. He said these things, and he took bread. He gave thanks to God in front of them all. He broke the bread and began to eat. 36. Everybody grew encouraged. They also began to take food. 37. In all there were two hundred and seventy six of us in the ship. 38. When they had eaten enough food, they began to lighten the ship by throwing the grain into the sea. 39. But when day came, they did not recognize the land. They did however perceive a certain bay that had a beach. They planned if possible to run the ship aground on it. 40. So releasing the anchors, they let them fall into the sea. At the same time they loosened the rudder cables. Raising the foresail to the wind, they headed toward the beach. 41. They came across a sandbar and ran the ship aground. The bow stayed fixed and immovable, but the stern was breaking up under the force of the waves. 42. Then a plan was made by the soldiers to kill the

prisoners, so they could not escape by swimming away. 43. But the centurion wanted to save Paul. He prevented them from achieving their purpose. He ordered those who were able to swim to go overboard first to reach land, 44. and the rest went on planks and on pieces from the ship. And thus all came safely to the land.

NOTES

27. *drifting in the sea of Adria:* This appears to refer to the section of the Mediterranean between Crete and Malta, with Sicily and the foot of Italy to the northwest. What is now called the "Adriatic Sea" was then referred to as the "Gulf of Adria." The location mentioned here is also where Josephus says he experienced shipwreck (*Life* 15). The verb *diaphero* picks up the note of "drifting/being carried" from 27:15, 17.

    some land was approaching them: The construction *prosagein tina autous chōran* is distinctive, as though the perspective were that of the sailors themselves ("the land is coming toward us!"). The oddness of the construction perhaps accounts for the variants for *prosagein* supplied by some *mss.*

28. *made a sounding:* The verb *bolizō* is rare but seems to mean simply the throwing of a line weighted with a lead weight (*bolis*) overboard in order to measure the depth of water. Luke's account here is dramatic, as the successive soundings follow at short intervals with the depth growing rapidly shallower. Not surprising that they were praying for day: the prospect of running aground with no visibility is indeed a frightening one. For the expression "after a short interval" (*brachu de distēsantes*), compare Luke 22:59.

30. *looking to flee the ship:* The sailors (*nautai*) have been the subject of all the action since verse 27. They above all perceive the danger to the ship and seek to save themselves. Their "pretense" (*prophasei*, see Luke 20:47) consisted in lowering the boat as though they were going to lower the bow anchors as they had those from the stern; once in the boat, they could cut themselves free and get clear of the inevitable wreck. For the untrustworthiness of sailors, see Plutarch, *Dinner of the Seven Wise Men* 18 [*Mor.* 161C], and for their incompetence in a crisis, see Aelius Aristides, *Sacred Tales* 2:12, 65-67. The motif of sailors' abandoning ship by means of the lifeboat is found also in Achilles Tatius, *Clitophon and Leucippe* 3:3; Petronius, *Satyricon* 102.

31. *you will not be able to be saved:* Paul once more enters the action, as earlier in 27:10, 21-26. This time the centurion listens to him! The lifeboat is cut away and set adrift before the sailors can carry out their plan of escape. This also of course keeps the boat from being used by anyone else; but in the circumstances, it would not in any case have been capacious enough to carry the entire complement of the ship. For the cutting off of the lifeboat in a storm, see Heliodorus, *The Ethiopians* 5, 27, 6.

33. *day was about to come:* Luke marks the sequence of time carefully: they near land at midnight (v. 27), then after making soundings pray for day to come

(v. 29), now day is about to arrive (v. 33), and finally day comes in v. 39. This is Paul's fourth intervention, and he is now obeyed by everyone! The storm at sea or shipwreck or encounter with pirates provides a fine setting for testing the philosopher's mettle for good or for bad; see *Odyssey* 12:270-300; Lucian of Samosata, *Toxaris* 20; Epictetus, *Discourses* 4, 1, 92; 4, 1, 174; Diogenes Laertius, *Lives of Eminent Philosophers* 2:71, 77 (Aristippus); 2:130 (Menedemus); 4:50 (Bion); 6:74 (Diogenes); 7:2 (Zeno); 9:68 (Pyrrho).

34. *it is for your welfare:* Literally "toward (*pros*) your salvation (*sōtēria*)," but the term here has clear reference to physical safety rather than something spiritual. As in 27:10, Paul is portrayed as giving straightforward, practical advice. Having gone so long without food, they will be too weak to make the necessary exertions to reach shore, unless they take nourishment. In his autobiographical *Sacred Tales*, Aelius Aristides tells of being adrift for fourteen days, with no one on board being able to eat during that time (2:68).

hair be lost: Paul's reassurance echoes that spoken by Jesus in the Gospel (Luke 21:18); see also Luke 12:7, and the background for the expression in LXX 1 Sam 14:45; 2 Sam 14:11; 1 Kgs 1:52.

35. *broke the bread and began to eat:* The fourfold action of taking (*labōn*), giving thanks (*eucharistēsen*), breaking (*klasas*) and beginning to eat (*ērxato esthiein*) need not refer to the Eucharist, since all Jewish meals involved the saying of blessings (see e.g., *bT Ber.* 16a, 17a, 20b, 21b, 34b; 1 Tim 4:4); but the sequence is sufficiently allusive to point the reader back to earlier passages where the Eucharistic gestures seem deliberately to be invoked (see Luke 6:4; 9:16; 22:19; 24:30). The addition of "having given also to us" in the Western Text makes the allusion even stronger. The real point of the gesture, however, is found in the phrase *enōpion pantōn* ("in front of them all"): Paul is presenting an example for them, one which in fact they imitate (v. 36, see also Luke 24:43).

37. *two hundred and seventy six:* Notice the shift to the "we" again in this verse—which may also help to account for the Western addition in v. 36—the first since v. 27. Concerning the size of the company, some *mss* give variant numbers (mostly smaller). But this larger number is possible; compare the six hundred whom Josephus claims were with him when he was shipwrecked (*Life* 15). The dimensions of the Alexandrian grain ships could be considerable, as we find in the dimensions provided for the ship "Isis" in Lucian of Samosata's *The Ship* 5-6.

38. *lighten the ship:* There had already been a jettisoning of the cargo (*ekbolē*) in v. 19; the literary parallels are given in the note to that verse. Here the *sitos* ("grain") may in fact be the ship's provisions in contrast to its cargo (compare *sitometrion* in Luke 12:42). Now that they had eaten and planned to make a run for the shore, they needed no more provisions but maximum buoyancy so as to ride as high as possible up on the shore—or such seemed to have been the plan.

40. *headed toward the beach:* The verse describes an obviously tricky maneuver, involving three coordinated actions: First, they released the anchors on both

sides (of the stern, since those at the bow had not been lowered; *periaireō tas ankyras*). Apparently they left them (or let them fall) in the sea. Second, at the same time (*hama*), they freed the rudder from the cables that had secured it (see v. 17); or, they cut the cables attaching the ship to the rudder. The first would allow them to steer, and seems to be the point. Third, they raised a sail (*artemōn*), probably a foresail. These steps enabled them to catch the wind and head toward the beach. For the expression *katechein eis ton aigialon*, see Herodotus, *Persian Wars* 7:188.

41. *ran the ship aground:* The Greek *topos dithalassas* is very difficult. Literally, it means "place of two seas," and it suggests something like a ridge of sand dividing the water, perhaps as a natural breaker: the translations of sandbar, spit, or shoals would all seem to be appropriate. What is clear is that the ship is not resting safely on the actual shore of the island, but has hit an obstacle offshore. The bow is jammed solid, but the stern still beaten by the waves and starting to break apart (*elueto*). This is now properly "shipwreck," and the problem remains of how to cross the remaining water to genuine safety on shore.

42. *escape by swimming away:* The danger seems remote, given the conditions of a sea sufficiently strong to break apart the ship. But the realistic fear of penalties for soldiers who let prisoners escape has already been well-established by the narrative (Acts 12:19; 16:27). For Luke's purposes, the line serves to set up the centurion's resolve to save Paul.

43. *prevented them from achieving their purpose:* Luke makes the centurion's concern focus solely on Paul, and in this way the prophecy in the vision is fulfilled, that God "granted all those sailing with him" to Paul (27:24); v. 44 makes it clear that "all" made it to shore safely.

44. *on planks and on pieces from the ship:* The use of planks to make it to shore from a shipwreck is found also in *Testament of Naphthali* 6:6 and Xenophon, *The Ephesians* 2, 11, 10. The concluding line, "thus we came safely to the land," is reminiscent of Aelius Aristides, *Sacred Tales* 2:12.

INTERPRETATION

In the discussion of the previous section of the sea-voyage account, the literary antecedents and basic options of interpretation were exposed. Now, having followed the voyage to its completion on the shore of Malta, we can try to assess its meaning within Luke's overall narrative.

Most readers find the claim that Luke is engaged in simple historical reportage to be unsatisfactory. While the hypothesis of an eyewitness companion can help explain the highly detailed character of the narrative, it does not tell us why Luke chose to include it all, when other portions of the story possibly reported by a companion were treated so telegraphically: the sea-journey of Paul to Jerusalem in 21:1-7 (also a "we" narrative!) is the obvious example. Nor does such historical positivism enable us to appreciate which moments out of a very long and frightening journey are selected for narration: was nothing of moment said or done by any of the characters during the fourteen days of drifting?

Even less satisfactory, however, is the leap to the other extreme, in the attempt of some interpreters to derive a "symbolic" significance to the sea-voyage and shipwreck. Several threads are pulled together to sew this theory: the general parallel between the paths of Paul and Jesus toward their respective fates; the associations of sea and water with cosmic and religious motifs of chaos/creation, death and resurrection; the use in the account of terms such as "being saved" (27:31). In this approach, the sea-voyage and shipwreck appear as a broadly symbolic or allegorical parallel of the death and resurrection of Jesus.

The problems with this approach are fairly obvious: apart from its desperate need to find parallels where the text offers no suggestion of one, it is so highly schematic that it can be removed from the particulars of the text completely. If the author's point was so patently allegorical, we have even less understanding of why the pedestrian elements of the story were retained. Why did Luke distract us with so much detail, if the detail was supposed to be ignored in favor of the overall pattern? Most of all, treating the account as an elaborate allegory ignores Luke's consistent practice elsewhere in his long narrative; nowhere else does the author invite the reader to make such a leap, certainly not for such a distance.

A third approach to the voyage and shipwreck is to regard it as fictional, providing Luke the opportunity (like the authors of Greek and Roman Romances) to provide some edification while entertaining his readers. The value of this approach is that it recognizes the clear presence of Hellenistic literary motifs within Luke's narrative and tries to account for them: Luke chooses to highlight certain moments in the voyage because they are the conventional moments within such tales to describe, and he shapes them to serve certain purposes.

The category "fictional" can, however, be misleading if it is taken to mean that the events were created entirely out of the author's imagination (or the stuff of literary convention) without any basis in fact. Indeed, the amount of space and detail (so much of it utterly pedestrian) given to the voyage in an out-and-out fiction also appears problematic.

It is by far the best approach to deal with this narrative as we have the rest of Luke-Acts. This means avoiding a hasty leap to allegory, and avoiding as well a treatment of ancient history and fiction as though they were utterly disparate categories. It means recognizing that ancient historians used "fictional" techniques even when they were relating events that had every claim to be considered historical, since narrative of any sort requires both strong selection and shaping if it is to yield any meaning at all. And Luke, like all ancient historians, was not interested simply in the chronicling of facts, but in the communication of meaning: history bore a moral message, a set of *exempla* for instruction and imitation. Finally, it means paying close attention to *how* Luke has made his selections and done his shaping, so we can detect what meaning of the events he wished to communicate to his ancient readers.

We can, in fact, observe several overall narrative interests that Luke advances by means of the sea-voyage of Paul to Rome. The most immediate and obvious reason for extending the account in this place is to provide narrative space, so that the reader has time to assimilate what has happened to Paul and what will happen to him. In the details of the voyage the reader's imagination is allowed a time of freedom that enables it to adjust to the finality of Paul's condition and the inexorability of his future. And in the dramatic account of his perils at sea, the reader is reminded of how close to death Paul really is. Even as he steps onto the shore of Malta "saved" from shipwreck, he is still a prisoner heading (as Luke's reader surely knows) toward his martyrdom.

But Luke's narrative as a whole is an *apologia* for God's work in history, and that theme is certainly present in this account. It is striking that Luke has none of the dramatic reversals of fortune at sea that could be attributed to a direct intervention by the deity. Once their bad judgment had committed them to a certain course of action, nature is allowed to take its course: Paul does not pray to have the winds silenced or the winds stilled. He is *not* portrayed as a *theios aner* ("divine man") whose will can bend the forces of nature to his own.

Instead, God's control over history appears in subtler ways: God speaks prophecies through Paul and they are fulfilled (27:10, 21, 24-25, 34, 44). God appears in a vision to Paul and offers assurance (27:23-25). Paul shares that assurance with the others and strengthens them (27:24-37). And throughout this series of events, God's overall plan to have Paul reach Rome in order to bear witness there is in process of fulfillment (27:24). An extraordinarily important set of messages is being communicated to the readers: God's mastery of history is available not to empirical test but to the eyes of faith; even more important, the work of God in history does not have to do with tinkering with natural and human processes by arbitrary interventions, but in the direction of the human heart to the perception of these processes as revealing the purposes and call of God.

Paul's reiteration of Jesus' words, "from none of your heads shall a hair be lost" is meant by Luke to trigger in the reader a recollection of how that statement is continued by these words of Jesus: "You will gain possession of your lives by your endurance" (Luke 21:19). Like Paul,

Luke's readers are caught in depths beyond their control: they too are always close to death in the risky adventure of living, they too are caught as prisoners of complex social entanglements. Their faith in God must not be focused so much on the elimination of these circumstances (that would be fatuous) or even on their amelioration (that might be foolhardy), but on God's power that enables them to "endure" and so "gain possession of their lives."

The portrayal of Paul throughout the voyage also fits Luke's characteristic narrative shaping. From one perspective, Paul can be seen as a philosopher: he is prudent and perspicacious in his advice (27:10, 33), he is calm in the face of danger and able to rally others to courage (27:22, 36). The relationship between Paul and the centurion Julius is particularly intriguing. From the first, the centurion treats Paul "humanely" (27:3); but when it came to making a decision concerning the ship, the centurion heeded the experts rather than Paul (27:11). Paul's predictions, however, came true (27:21), and he takes an ever more active role in maintaining morale. When the sailors formed their plan to abandon ship, Paul's advice to the centurion is quickly and decisively followed (27:31). And by the end of the trip, Luke makes it appear that the centurion's reason for preventing the soldiers from killing all the prisoners is solely his wish to "save Paul" (27:43).

From another perspective, Paul is portrayed, as he has been throughout the narrative, as a prophet. He not only predicts the future and sees his prophecies reach completion, he is also a spokesperson for God among his fellows: he advises, exhorts, comforts, strengthens, challenges. And he does this entirely with reference not to a Cynic *parrēsia* or Stoic *apatheia*, but in "service" (*latreia*) to the God "to whom he belongs" (27:23). In the most dangerous moment of all, Paul pauses to break bread and give thanks to God "in front of them all" (27:35) as a witness to whose power and whose unseen presence was truly at work. At the end, Paul's path is one marked not by thaumaturgy but by faith. In circumstances as naked and humanly hopeless as those of the young girl Mary at the beginning of Luke's story, he places his trust in the word spoken by God: "I believe in God, that it will turn out in just the way he has spoken to me" (27:25; compare Luke 1:45).

FOR REFERENCE AND FURTHER STUDY

Barrett, C. K. "Paul Shipwrecked." *Scripture: Meaning and Method. Essays Presented to A. T. Hanson.* Ed. B. P. Thompson. Hull: Hull University Press, 1987, 51–64.

Ladouceur, D. "Hellenistic Preconceptions of Shipwreck and Pollution as a Concept for Acts 27-28." *HTR* 73 (1980) 435–449.

Menoud, Ph.-H. "The Acts of the Apostles and the Eucharist." *Jesus Christ and the Faith*. Trans. E. M. Paul. Pittsburgh: Pickwick Press, 1978, 84–106.

Miles, G. B. and G. Trompf, "Luke and Antiphon: The Theology of Acts 27-28 in the Light of Beliefs about Divine Retribution, Pollution, and Shipwreck." *HTR* 69 (1976) 259–267.

Pokorný, P. "Die Römfahrt des Paulus und der antike Roman." *ZNW* 64 (1973) 233–244.

Praeder, S. M. "Acts 27:1–28:16: Sea Voyages in Ancient Literature and the Theology of Luke-Acts." *CBQ* 46 (1984) 683–706.

54. *From Melita to Rome* (28:1-16)

1. And once we had come to safety, we recognized that the island was called Melita. 2. The natives showed us unusually humane treatment, for having lighted a fire because of the rain that had started and the cold, they welcomed all of us. 3. Now Paul had gathered together a certain amount of dry wood and had put it on the fire. A viper came out from the heat. It fastened itself on his hand. 4. When the natives saw the creature hanging from his hand, they began saying to each other, "This fellow is surely a murderer! Although he has escaped from the sea, Lady Justice will not let him live!" 5. But when he had shaken the beast off into the fire, he suffered no harm. 6. They were expecting him to begin to swell up or to suddenly fall over dead. But as they waited and watched him for some time with nothing evil happening to him, they changed their minds. They began saying that he was a god. 7. In the area around that location was an estate that belonged to the leading man of the island whose name was Publius. Welcoming us in a friendly fashion, he showed us hospitality for three days. 8. And it happened that Publius' father was lying ill, overtaken by fever and dysentery. Paul went in to him. And after praying, he placed hands on him. He healed him. 9. After this happened, the rest of those on the island who had illnesses also started to approach, and they were being healed. 10. They also paid us many honors, and as we were departing, they gave us the things we needed. 11. After three months, we left on an Alexandrian ship with the sign of the Dioscuri. It had wintered on the island. 12. When we reached land at Syracuse, we remained there three days. 13. Setting off, we reached Rhegium, and after one day when a south wind arose, we came on the second day to Puteoli. 14. There we found brothers. We were requested by them to remain for seven days. And in this way we came to Rome: 15. The brothers from there heard about us. They

came to meet us at the Forum of Appius and the Three Taverns. When Paul saw them, he gave thanks to God and took courage. 16. And when we came into Rome, Paul was allowed to remain by himself with the soldier guarding him.

NOTES

1. *island called Melita:* Other mss read *melitēnē*, but those supporting *melitē* are to be preferred; the location is in all likelihood the Mediterranean island south of Sicily known as Malta.

2. *the natives:* The Greek has "the barbarians" (*hoi barbaroi*), which marks the distinctively Hellenistic outlook of the author: the *barbaroi* were those who did not speak the Greek language (Herodotus, *Persian Wars* 2:57), or Greek cultural customs (Chariton of Aphrodisias, *Chareas and Callirhoe* 6, 3, 7). It is a designation with many uses, including simple alien status (1 Cor 14:11), or cultural inferiority (Aristotle, *Politics* 1252B). Here and in v. 4 it is used in a neutral sense (see also Rom 1:14; Col 3:11), and apparently correctly, for Malta was in fact of Phoenician/Punic language and culture (Strabo, *Geography* 17, 3, 15-16), as inscriptional evidence also demonstrates.

   showed us unusually humane treatment: For the *litotes* "not ordinary" (*ou tēn tychousan*), compare Acts 19:11. We saw the same "love of humanity" (*philanthrōpia/philathrōpōs*) shown toward Paul by the centurion Julius in 27:3. See the note on that verse for the peculiarly Hellenistic valuation of that quality. Here it is attributed to "barbarians." This should not surprise us, for although the theory had it that Greek culture was superior, in fact Greeks were fascinated and often impressed by aliens, and were willing to grant in them virtues they perceived as deficient in themselves (see e.g., Philostratus, *Life of Apollonius of Tyana* 2:26; 2:30; 3:24-25).

   they welcomed all of us: The verb *proslambanomai* has been used by Luke in several of its meanings (compare Acts 17:5; 18:26; 27:33, 36); here it can mean either "they gathered all of us" (that is, around the fire), or "they welcomed all of us" (compare 2 Macc 10:15; Rom 14:1, 3; 15:7; Phlm 17). Throughout Luke-Acts, the theme of hospitality has been an important symbol of receptivity to God's visitation (e.g., Luke 5:29; 7:36-50; 9:4-5; 10:1-16, 38-42; 19:1-10; Acts 10:24; 16:11-15). The motif of sailors finding refuge among kindly barbarians is fairly standard in shipwreck accounts (see Dio Chrysostom, *Oration* 7:5; Xenophon, *The Ephesians* 2, 2, 4; Petronius, *Satyricon* 114; Lucian of Samosata, *True Story* 1:28-29; 2:46).

3. *gathered together . . . dry wood:* The picture of Paul is consistent with that in Acts and in his letters as one who is willing to work with his own hands in order to serve the needs of others (Acts 18:3; 20:34; 1 Cor 4:12; 1 Thess 2:9; 2 Thess 3:7-8), in the image of Jesus who also modeled the true character of authority as service (Luke 22:24-27). Throughout the journey narrative, Paul's actions and advice have been of the most practical and helpful sort (27:10, 22, 31, 34).

viper . . . fastened itself on his hand: The Greek *echidna* refers generally to snakes or vipers (see Lucian of Samosata, *Alexander the False Prophet* 10). It is used metaphorically for wicked folk in Luke 3:7 (compare Matt 3:7; 12:34; 23:33). The Greek does not describe a "strike" so much as a "gripping" (*kathēpsen;* for the verb *kathaptō* see Epictetus, *Discourses* 3, 20, 10). It is useless to pursue herptological questions (what sort of snake/viper was it, for example) for which we have no real means of finding answers. The perceptions reported are in any case not of a scientific character. For some of the common beliefs about snakes held even by the educated (that they are all poisonous, that they seek vengeance on the killer of their spouses), see Pliny the Elder, *Natural History* 8:85-86.

4. *surely a murderer:* The adverb *pantōs* has the same strength here as in Luke 4:23 (see also Acts 18:21; 21:22). The conclusion that Paul is a murderer (*phoneus*) immediately follows from the expected retribution of being killed. The punishment fits the crime.

   Lady Justice will not let him live: The translation of *hē dikē* as "Lady Justice" is necessary because the term here refers not to "justice" in the philosophical sense, but to "justice" (*dikē*) as a personification of retribution or vengeance (see Hesiod, *Theogony* 901; Arrian, *Anabasis* 4, 9, 7; Wis 1:8; 4 Macc 18:22; Josephus, *Jewish War* 1:84). A parallel account of a shipwrecked sailor who is saved from the sea only to be killed by a viper is found in the *Greek Anthology* 7:290: "The shipwrecked mariner had escaped the whirlwind and the fury of the deadly sea, and as he was lying on the Libyan sand, not far from the beach, deep in his last sleep, naked and exhausted by the unhappy wreck, a baleful viper (*echnis*) slew him. Why did he struggle with the waves in vain, escaping then the fate that was his on the land?" An even more striking example is found in *Greek Anthology* 9:269. For the "eye of justice" (*opthalmos tēs Dikēs*) watching over all that happens at sea, compare Plutarch, *Dinner of the Seven Wise Men* 18 [*Mor.* 161F].

6. *began saying that he was a god:* Once more the logic is sound enough once the premise is granted: if someone can withstand deadly serpents, then some divine *dynamis* must be at work in him (compare Mark 16:18). Notice, however, that there may also be here a subtle allusion to Luke 10:18-19: the fall of Satan is connected to "authority to walk over snakes and scorpions (*opseōn kai skorpiōn*), over every power of the enemy." The reaction of the natives here is similar to that of the Lycaonians in Acts 14:8-13; for the motif in Hellenistic novels, see notes on 14:11-12. It is found as well in the apocryphal acts, such as *Acts of Thomas* 106; *Acts of Peter* 29.

7. *leading man of the island:* It is characteristic of Luke to associate Paul with the leading figures of a locality (see 13:7; 16:22; 17:19; 18:12; 19:31). As so often, Luke also has the nomenclature for the specific locality (*ho prōtos tēs nēsou*) correct, at least so far as epigraphical evidence can confirm. It is not clear whether Publius has a Roman magistracy, or is the patron/benefactor of the region. The possession of an estate and its accessibility to the sick of the territory seems to suggest the latter.

showed us hospitality for three days: For the theme of hospitality as symbolizing receptivity to the good news, see the note on 28:2. The phrase, "friendly fashion" tries to capture the adverb *philophronōs*, a term frequently associated with hospitality (see 2 Macc 3:9; *Letter of Aristeas* 183; Josephus, *Antiquities* 11:340).

8. *overtaken by fever and dysentery:* The expression "overtaken by fever" is the same as in the story of Peter's mother-in-law (Luke 4:38), except that here the noun is in the plural (*synechomenon pyretois*). This is the only mention of dysentery in the NT or LXX. There is reportedly a "Malta Fever" that is particularly associated with this island.

   after praying he placed hands: For the laying on of hands for healing, see Luke 4:40; 10:30; 13:13; Acts 16:23; for prayer accompanying the laying on of hands, see Acts 6:6 and 13:3. The ministry of healing has throughout Luke-Acts been closely associated with the proclamation of the kingdom of God (Luke 4:38-44; 6:17-20; 7:20-23; 9:1-11; Acts 3:12-16).

9. *started to approach and they were being healed:* Compare the account at the beginning of Jesus' ministry, when the healing of Peter's mother-in-law of a fever turns into a general press of the populace to be healed of a variety of illnesses (Luke 4:38-44). The first of these two imperfects (*prosērchonto*) is taken as inchoative, and second (*etherapeuonto*) as indicating an ongoing process.

10. *paid us many honors:* The translation of *pollais timais etimēsan* is uncertain, since *time* can refer either to honor (Herodotus, *Persian Wars* 1:168; 2 Macc 9:21; John 4:44; Rom 13:7; 1 Cor 12:24; 1 Tim 1:17) or to payment/price (see Josephus, *Life* 153; 1 Cor 6:20; 1 Tim 5:7). Luke tends to use the term in the monetary sense (Acts 4:34; 5:2-3; 7:16; 19:19). Despite that, the translation chooses "honors" since the next phrase spells out the gift of possessions.

    gave us the things we needed: The general meaning is clear, but the precise translation is uncertain: *epitithēmi* could be taken in the physical sense: "as we were sailing away (*anagomenois*), they put on board the things we needed (*ta pros tas chreias*, see 20:34)," or could be taken in the broader sense, they "bestowed." As always in Luke-Acts, the sharing of physical possessions is a symbol of sharing in the good news (Luke 6:32-36; 8:3; 12:32-34; 14:13-14; 18:22; 21:1-4; Acts 2:42-47; 4:32-37).

11. *Alexandrian ship with the sign of the Dioscuri:* Like the ship caught at Myra (27:5), this one is apparently part of the fleet dedicated to the grain trade between Egypt and Rome. The *parasēmon* is a "mark/ensign" that is placed at the prow of a ship and therefore effectively becomes its name (Plutarch, *Dinner of the Seven Wise Men* 18 [*Mor.* 162B]; *The Bravery of Women* 9 [*Mor.* 248A]; Lucian of Samosata, *The Ship* 5). The *Dioscuri* are the twin sons of Zeus, Castor and Pollux. They were particularly associated with protection at sea (Epictetus, *Discourses* 2, 18, 29; Lucian of Samosata, *The Ship* 9; Aelius Aristides, *Sacred Tales* 4:35-37).

12. *reached land at Syracuse:* This is the main city of Sicily and an important port as well as a center for Greek culture (Cicero, *Against Verres* 2, 4, 117-119). Located northeast of Malta, it would be the logical stopping place for a voyage from the island, if the destination was Rome via the straits of Messina.

13. *setting off we reached Rhegium:* The telegraphic style of earlier journey narratives is resumed (compare Acts 18:18-23; 20:3-6, 13-16; 21:1-8). The city of Rhegium was a Greek colony at the toe of Italy, strategically located for passage through the straits of Messina (Strabo, *Geography* 6, 1, 6). The phrase here translated as "setting off" is difficult. Some *mss* contain the participle *perielontes,* which is found with a direct object in 27:40, and seemed to mean there something like "weigh/cut away anchors." But here it has no direct object, which makes its meaning obscure. Some *mss* furthermore, have another participle, *perielthontes,* which means, roughly, "going around/in a circuit." Is this meant to describe a nautical maneuver required to reach Rhegium? No great issue is involved, so the translation chooses a meaning sufficiently broad to contain both others.

    came on the second day to Puteoli: This port city is on the Bay of Naples, near the cities of Naples, Pompeii, and Herculaneum. It was the most important port in Italy (Strabo, *Geography* 5, 4, 6), where both cargo and passengers disembarked, until the new harbor of Portus was built at Ostia on the Tiber by Claudius (Suetonius, *Life of Claudius* 20:1); after that, the cargo went to Ostia, but passengers continued to disembark at Puteoli. Seneca describes the crowds that watched the "Alexandrian ships" come in (*Moral Epistles* 77:1-2). See also Suetonius, *Life of Titus* 5:3; Josephus, *Life* 16.

14. *there we found brothers:* Luke means other members of the messianic movement (Acts 1:16; 6:3; 9:17, 30; 10:23; 11:1; 12:17; 15:1, 32; 16:40), although the term can encompass fellow Jews as well (2:29; 13:26). For the phrase, compare Acts 19:1. There is no confirming evidence for the presence of Christians at Puteoli, but there is for the existence of a Jewish community (Josephus, *Jewish War* 2:104; *Antiquities of the Jews* 17:328).

    we were requested by them: Some *mss* replace the infinitive *epimeinai* with the participle *epimenontes,* perhaps in an effort to correct the impression that Paul the prisoner had the freedom to make such decisions. With the participle, the sentence would read: "staying with them seven days, we were comforted."

    and in this way we came to Rome: The structure of this short sentence is clear but its function is not. Is the adverb *houtōs* ("thus") to be taken resumptively (as in Acts 12:8; 13:8; 19:20; 20:11; 27:17, 44)? If so, then it is misplaced, since Paul has not yet arrived in the city itself. But it is possible for Luke to use *houtōs* in an anticipatory way: "Here is the way we arrived in Rome" (compare Acts 1:11; 13:34, 47; 27:25). In either case, the statement marks the fulfillment of the prophecy made in 23:11.

15. *the brothers from there:* As in the case of Puteoli, we find that missionaries have established communities in Italy before Paul's arrival there, a fact certainly in agreement with Paul's Letter to the Romans (1:8, 15; 16:3-16)! That Luke has not found it necessary to say anything about the establishment of these important communities shows how deliberately his attention is fixed on Paul.

    the Forum of Appius and the Three Taverns: These are locations on the Appian Way heading toward the city of Rome. The Forum of Appius was forty-three miles from the city. The satirist Horace refers to it as "full of sailors and wicked tavern-keepers" (*Satires* 1, 5, 3-4). The Three Taverns was closer, some thirty-three miles from the city. It is mentioned several times by Cicero in his *Letters to Atticus* (1, 13, 1; 2, 12, 2; 2, 13, 1), as a place where letters were exchanged, and in one of his short notes to Atticus, it is identified as the place of composition (2, 10).

gave thanks to God and took courage: The line wonderfully compresses both the intensely religious character of Paul and his humanity. He had poured out his own courage for those sailing with him (27:21-25) and in those terrifying circumstances had also given thanks to God (27:35). Now in safety, he gives thanks again and takes courage (*tharsos*) from the presence of welcoming brethren, who have come out from the city to meet him.

16. *allowed to remain by himself:* The first part of this sentence ("when we came into Rome") concludes the "we" narrative. This is natural enough in any case, since Paul is separated from his companions. But its literary effect is to focus attention even more exclusively on Paul. The Western Text expands the verse. At the beginning, it adds, "the centurion handed over the prisoners to the stratopedarch, but Paul. . . ." and after "by himself," it adds, "outside the barracks."

with the soldier guarding him: We are to envisage a sort of house arrest (see v. 30), in which Paul is accompanied by (and indeed attached by a chain to [v. 20]) a single soldier for a period of two whole years (v. 30). Paul has truly come to rest at last.

INTERPRETATION

This quiet interlude between the terrifying shipwreck and the tragic last encounter between Paul and the Jewish leaders of Rome is filled with charming touches but also serves a definite narrative function within Luke's apologetic. In the Malta scenes, Luke once more shows himself master of Hellenistic literary motifs. He needs only six verses to weave three staples of popular Greek imagination into a single memorable incident: first, he evokes the theme of the kindly barbarians who show a natural *philanthrōpia* to those washed up on their shore (28:2); second, in the response of the natives to the viper's attack, he voices popular religious perceptions concerning the inexorability of retribution for crimes (28:4); finally, in the reversal of the natives' opinion concerning Paul, Luke once more shows how the presence of *dynamis* led quickly to the conclusion that the divine was thereby present (28:6; see 14:8-13).

Luke uses these scenes to establish for the last time two themes that are of first importance for his overall literary and religious argument. The first is the image of Paul. Luke portrays Paul as a prophetic figure, one specially marked by God's protection and power. The incident of the viper/snake does not prove that Paul is innocent of murder (that was never in question for the reader), nor does it make him divine (that is only a popular perception). The popular acclamation can, however, be read by the discerning reader as offering confirmation that Paul was innocent of "any charge worthy of death" (23:29; 25:25; 26:31). But most of all, it marks him as one who is a proclaimer of God's kingdom who conquers the forces of evil wherever he goes, in accordance with the promise of Jesus: "Look, I have given you authority to walk over snakes and scorpions, over every power of the enemy. He will in no way get back at you" (Luke 10:19). This incident therefore resembles earlier scenes which show the power of the Gospel conquering a new territory by means of exorcism and healing (8:14-24; 13:4-12; 16:16-18; 19:11-20).

Paul's immunity from the power of snakebite shows that the prophetic power of the resurrected one is at work in him (see Mark 16:18). Paul can therefore, like Jesus, perform healings as signs of God's kingdom breaking into this new territory. In a scene probably deliberately reminiscent of Jesus' first healing (of Peter's mother-in-law from fever, Luke 4:38-39), Paul heals Publius' father of fever and dysentery (Acts 28:8); and, as Jesus' powerful deed had turned into a general demand for healing from the populace of Capernaum (4:40-41), so does Paul's powerful deed turn into a general ministry of healing for the populace of Malta (28:9). The divine *dynamis* at work in Paul, therefore, is not his own, but continues the presence of the resurrected Lord. In imitation of Jesus, it is manifested in service to others; by no means is the homely picture of Paul gathering wood for the fire accidental.

Finally, Luke shows us a Paul in communion with other Christians. The terrible isolation of Paul during his years of imprisonment and trial—and especially the deeply ambiguous significance of the events of his reception in Jerusalem by the leaders of that Church—might have made the reader forget how deeply Paul had been enmeshed in the wider fellowship of the messianic movement. When Paul arrives in Puteoli, therefore, and not only finds fellow Christians, but is invited to stay with them for seven days; when the brethren from Rome, on hearing of his arrival, go out to meet him forty and thirty miles from the city, not only Paul has reason to thank God and take courage (28:11-15), but the reader does as well. The Paul who comes as prisoner to Rome comes in the power of the prophetic Messiah and is accepted as such by the members of the Church in that city.

Equally important for Luke, however, is to establish for a final time the openness of the Gentiles to the good news. The Maltese barbarians serve the role admirably. No more than Paul is described as preaching the Word of God, are the Maltese said to have received the gospel. But in Luke's narrative, that is no longer necessary; as Jesus had declared of his prophetic representatives, "The one who listens to you listens to me. The one who rejects you rejects me. The one who rejects me rejects the one who sent me" (Luke 10:16). Conversely, we have come to recognize, those who *accept* his emissaries also accept Jesus and the message of the kingdom of God. And in every way, Luke shows these barbarians receptive to the power of God at work in Paul. Indeed, those now familiar with Luke's lexicon of symbols can recognize in the *hospitality* shown by the natives (28:2) and by Publius (28:7), and in the *sharing of possessions* by the populace (28:10) the infallible indicators of their openness to the visitation of God.

Luke has therefore brought Paul to Rome with these perceptions in place: Paul is innocent of any charge worthy of death; he comes in the power of God and is an acknowledged representative of the messianic movement. The reader therefore is able to read Paul's final encounter with the Jewish leaders of Rome from that perspective: their acceptance or rejection of Paul is not that of a criminal or a renegade, but rather of a prophet of God. Finally, the reader is able from the events at Malta to know the truth of Paul's final declaration, "This salvation of God has been sent to the Gentiles. *They* will listen" (28:28)!

FOR REFERENCE AND FURTHER STUDY

Cadbury, H. J. "Lexical Notes on Luke-Acts III: Luke's Interest in Lodging." *JBL* 45 (1926) 305–322.

Hemer, C. J. *The Book of Acts in the Setting of Hellenistic Historiography.* Ed. C. H. Gempf. WUNT 49. Tübingen: JCB Mohr (Paul Siebeck), 1989, 152–158.

Ladouceur, D. "Hellenistic Preconceptions of Shipwreck and Pollution as a Concept for Acts 27-28." *HTR* 73 (1980) 435–449.

Miles G. B. and G. Trompf, "Luke and Antiphon: The Theology of Acts 27-28 in the Light of Pagan Beliefs about Divine Retribution, Pollution, and Shipwreck." *HTR* 69 (1976) 259–267.

Praeder, S. M. "Acts 27:1-28:16: Sea Voyages in Ancient Literature and the Theology of Luke-Acts." *CBQ* 46 (1984) 683–706.

Warnecke, H. *Die tatsächliche Römfahrt des Apostels Paulus.* Stuttgart: Katholisches Bibelwerk, 1987.

55. *The Hope of Israel, the Salvation of Gentiles* (28:17-31)

17. After three days he called together those who were leaders of the Jews. When they had gathered, he told them, "Brothers, without having done anything against the people or our ancestral customs, I was handed over as a prisoner from Jerusalem to the power of the Romans. 18. After examining me they wanted to release me, because there was no reason to put me to death. 19. But when the Jews spoke in opposition, I was obliged to appeal to Caesar—not as though I had any charge to bring against my nation. 20. For this reason therefore I asked to see and talk to you, because it is for the hope of Israel that I wear this chain." 21. But they said to him, "We have not received any letters concerning you from Judea. Nor have any of the brothers arrived to report or declare anything evil concerning you. 22. We consider it right to hear what you think, for we know about this sect that it is opposed everywhere." 23. When they had set a day for him, many of them came to him at his lodging. He began his argument by bearing witness to the kingdom of God. From morning until evening he tried to persuade them concerning Jesus from the Law of Moses and the Prophets. 24. Some of them were persuaded by the things he was saying. But others were disbelieving. 25. Still disagreeing with each other, they departed, with Paul making one statement: "The Holy Spirit rightly spoke through the prophet Isaiah to your fathers 26. when he said, 'Go to this people and say, "You will hear and you will not understand. You will look and you will not see. 27. The heart of this people has become obtuse. They have listened reluctantly with their ears. They have shut their eyes, so that they might not see with their eyes and hear with their ears and understand with their heart, and turn to me, and I shall heal them." ' 28. Therefore let it be known to you that this salvation from God has been sent to the Gentiles. And they will listen!" 30. And he remained for two entire years at his own expense. He welcomed all those who came to him. 31. He preached the kingdom of God and he taught the things about the Lord Jesus Messiah with complete boldness and without interference.

Notes

17. *leaders of the Jews:* Literally, "the first men (*hoi prōtoi*) of the Jews," a designation Luke uses also for the Jerusalem leaders in Luke 19:47 and Acts 25:2. It is striking that this last encounter involves Jewish *leaders* who have throughout the story been portrayed as fundamentally hostile to Jesus and to the movement proclaiming him as Messiah. The Jewish community in Rome may go back to the mid-second century B.C.E., and by Paul's time the community seems to have been a large one (see 1 Macc 14:16-18; 15:15-24; Josephus, *Life* 13; *Jewish War* 2:80-92; *Antiquities of the Jews* 17:300; 18:81-83; Philo, *Embassy to Gaius* 155-158; Dio Cassius, *Roman History* 60, 6, 6). The vicissitudes of the Roman community included periodic expulsions, as under Tiberius (Josephus,

Antiquities of the Jews 18:83) and Claudius (Suetonius, *Life of Claudius* 25:4; Acts 18:2).

the people of our ancestral customs: As he had consistently in his defense speeches, Paul once more declares his fidelity to the Jewish people and its traditions (22:3; 23:6; 24:14-16; 26:4-8). Luke does not have him use *ethnos* ("nation") here as he does in 24:10, 17; 26:4, and in the following verse (28:19). Instead, he uses *ho laos*, which throughout Luke-Acts has designated Israel as "God's people" (see e.g., Luke 1:68; 2:32; 7:29; 18:43; 20:1; Acts 2:47; 3:23; 4:10). The translation supplies the possessive pronoun "our," and it could be assumed to cover both nouns. For the use of "ancestral" (*patrōos*), compare 22:3; 24:14.

18. *after examining me:* The reference is to the series of hearings Paul had to endure (23:1-10; 24:2-21; 25:6-12; 26:2-29). The Western Text expands this to read, "examined me concerning many things." The purpose for mentioning the examination is to show that the desire to release Paul "for lack of cause" was not a casual one (26:31-32).

    no reason to put me to death: The language is actually more legal sounding: "because there was no cause (*aitia*) for death (*thanatou*)," a phrasing which compresses the point of 22:24; 23:28; 25:18, 27.

19. *Jews spoke in opposition:* Luke uses the genitive absolute construction with *antilegō*. He has not used the term since 13:45, but will use it again quickly in 28:22. It is entirely characteristic of Luke to thus cluster and vary his diction. Notice that in the previous verse, he has used *aitia* in the sense of a legal charge, but in v. 20 he will use it again in a different sense. For the Jewish opposition at Paul's hearings, see 24:2-9; 25: 2, 7, 15, 18, 24; 25:2. The Western Text expands the verse with, "and they cried out, 'Take away our enemy.'" We have noticed how this version of the text tends to be more hostile to the Jews.

    charge to bring against my nation: Paul makes clear that he comes to Rome as a defendant and not as a plaintiff. The difficulty between himself and Judaism is not his doing, but that of the Jewish leaders towards him. The use of "my nation" (*ethnos mou*) identifies Paul with his Jewish heritage (compare 26:4). Some *mss* of the Western Tradition find this construction truncated, so they fill it out with a further explanation, "but so that I might deliver my life (*psychē*) from death."

20. *the hope of Israel:* The phrase echoes Paul's defense, which made clear that Paul understands Israel's authentic hope (*elpis*) to be in the resurrection of the dead (23:6), which he regards as the fulfillment of the promise made to the ancestors, now realized in Jesus (24:15; 26:6-7). Once more, Luke attributes Paul's status as a prisoner directly to his identification with values that are essentially Jewish in character.

    I wear this chain: The expression is not purely metaphorical; Paul has apparently been chained through much of his long ordeal (21:33; 22:5, 29; 23:29; 24:27; 26:29, 31). He may in fact have been lightly bound by a single chain (*alusis*) to the soldier assigned to guard him (28:16). In his captivity letters,

Paul shows himself constantly aware of his condition of being "in chains" (Phil 1:7, 13; Col 4:18; Eph 6:20; 2 Tim 1:16; 2:9; Phlm 10, 13).

21. *any letters concerning you:* We cannot tease the response of these leaders to yield more than it says: we cannot deduce that the Jerusalem leaders had given up their prosecution, or that they had failed to contact the Roman Jewish community, or that the mails were running slower than Paul's ships! The function of the two-part statement is to provide a picture of a Jewish audience that is biased against the messianic sect, but not against Paul personally. The statement does give indirect evidence for the common practice of maintaining communication between communities by means of letters, which is confirmed not only by the narrative of Acts (9:2; 15:22-31) but also by the entire NT epistolary literature.

    nor have any of the brothers arrived: This seems to point to the sort of "embassy" or "legation" (*presbeia*) that would be sent to represent the Jewish community in a legal dispute (see, e.g., 2 Macc 4:11; Philo, *Embassy to Gaius* 239; Josephus, *Antiquities of the Jews* 17:299-314).

22. *it is opposed everywhere:* Literally, "spoken against," picking up the *antilegō* from v. 19. For the designation of "sect" (*hairesis*), see the notes on Acts 5:17; 15:5; 24:5, 14; 26:5. Once more, Luke's choice of language places the messianic movement within the controversies of first-century Judaism concerning the authentic realization of "Israel" as the "people of God," in which the Christian voice was only one among many.

23. *many of them came to him in his lodging:* The "setting of a day" gives the encounter an official tone, as does the larger number (*pleiones*) of leaders who appear for this second session. The term *xenia* most often refers to "hospitality," but in its two NT uses, it appears to mean also a place where hospitality can be offered, or lodging (see Phlm 22). This might be the sense also in Philo, *Life of Moses* 2:33; Josephus, *Antiquities* 1:200; 5:147.

    began his argument: Or, "began to explain/expound," using *ektithēmi* as in 11:4; 18:26. The imperfect is inceptive, for the argument will continue from morning until evening, a long session indeed! For the sense of the passage, compare Acts 17:1-4; 18:4, 28; 19:8-9.

    by bearing witness to the kingdom of God: The circumstantial participle is treated as instrumental, indicating the means by which he carried forward his case. From the beginning of Luke-Acts (Luke 4:43) to the very end (Acts 28:31), the "kingdom/rule of God" has been the constant content of preaching both with Jesus (Luke 6:20; 7:28; 8:1; 9:11; 11:20; 12:31-32; 16:16; 17:20-21; 18:29; 19:11; 21:31; 22:30; 23:42; Acts 1:3), and with his prophetic representatives (Luke 9:2; 10:9-11; Acts 8:12; 14:22; 19:8; 20:25).

    tried to persuade them concerning Jesus: The participle *peithōn* is here translated as conative: he was trying to persuade, not necessarily successfully (compare Acts 13:43; 14:19; 17:4; 18:4; 19:8, 26; 21:14; 26:28). For the basis of the argument in Torah, see especially Luke 24:27, 44; Acts 13:27; 26:22.

24. *persuaded . . . disbelieving:* For the divided response to the preaching about
Jesus in Acts, see 2:12-13; 4:1-4; 5:12-17; 6:8-14; 9:21-25; 13:42-45; 14:1-2; 17:1-5;
18:4, 12-17; 19:8-10.

25. *still disagreeing with each other:* It is not clear whether the division among the
Jewish leaders is one of faith versus unbelief or, as is perhaps more likely,
an internal conflict generated by Paul's claims, such as was created by his
proclamation of the resurrection in 23:6-9. In any case, their failure to respond
positively motivates the "one statement" (*rhēma hen*) of Paul, which concludes
the long struggle of Paul and the Jews on such a bleak note. The sentence
structure almost allows us to hear Paul addressing these words to the backs
of the departing Jews.

    to your fathers: Although some *mss* have "our fathers," the scribal confusion
between *hymōn* and *hēmōn* is notorious, and as in the conclusion to Stephen's
Speech (7:51-52), the distancing character of Paul's statement makes the reading "your fathers" far more likely. For the Holy Spirit speaking through the
Torah as through a prophet, see Acts 1:16; 4:25.

26. *go to this people:* The citation is from the LXX of Isa 6:9-10. The original context
for the passage is the call of the prophet Isaiah in the Temple (Isa 6:1-13).
It is widely used in early Christian apologetic as a proof-text for the Jewish
rejection of the gospel. It is paraphrased by Paul in Rom 11:8, and alluded
to in Mark 4:12 and John 12:40. A full citation appears in Matt 13:14-15. It
is characteristic of Luke that he should have only a brief allusion to it in the
Gospel story which concerned only the first rejection of the prophet (Luke
8:10), and save its full citation until the end of Acts, when every effort had
been made to "visit the people" again through the proclamation of the risen
prophet Jesus.

    and say: The citation is verbatim from the LXX except that Luke has "go to
the people and say," whereas the LXX (in agreement with the Hebrew) has
"go and say to this people." The LXX in turn has some small but important
differences from the Hebrew: a) The Hebrew has "make the heart of this
people fat/heavy (*šamen*)" in the imperative, whereas the LXX has the aorist
indicative, "was made/has become fat/heavy (*epachynthē*)"; b) the Hebrew
concludes with the third person "and I heal him," whereas the LXX has "I
will heal him" (*iasomai*), which is odd as well because it is in the indicative
rather than the subjunctive mode demanded by the *mēpote* construction. Not
surprisingly, some NT *mss* do supply the subjunctive form.

    hear . . . look: The translation eliminates the cognate constructions which serve
to intensify the Hebrew/Greek versions. The sentence reads literally, "with
hearing (*akoē*) you will hear (*akousate*) and will not understand (*synēte*); looking (*blepontes*) you will look (*blepsete*) and you will certainly not see (*ou mē
idēte*). A freer translation would capture the sense this way: "although you
listen and listen you still will not hear; even though you gaze attentively you
certainly will not see."

27. *heart of this people has become obtuse:* The Hebrew "make fat" has in this context the meaning of "arrogant/unresponsive/dull," which is the metaphori-

cal sense also of the Greek *pachynō* which literally means "make/become fat," as we see, e.g., in Plutarch, *The Eating of Flesh* 1:6 [*Mor.* 995D]: ". . . eating of flesh . . . makes us spiritually coarse and gross"; see also Philostratus, *Life of Apollonius* 1:8: ". . . flesh diet . . . made the mind gross." The "heart" in this saying refers to the internal disposition of freedom (compare 7:39 and especially 7:51, "uncircumcised in hearts and ears!").

listened reluctantly: The adverb *bareōs* (from *barys*, "heavy") could be translated as "with difficulty," but the context seems to demand a recognition of the willfulness of their behavior: they are "slow to hear/unwilling to hear." For the way a word can be "heavy" compare LXX Num 11:14.

shut their eyes: The LXX again makes this a deliberate action on the part of the people. The verb *kammyō* means literally to close the eyes, but can be used figuratively for a deliberate mental blindness (see Philo, *On Dreams* 1:164). For the image elsewhere in Isaiah, see 29:10 and especially 33:15.

so that they might not: The conjunction *mēpote* with the subjunctive is often translated as "lest," but that usage is now so rare in English that a fuller translation is given. In the Hebrew, the inability to hear, see, and understand is the direct result of the prophet's speech itself. In the LXX and here, it follows as a result from their deliberate choice to listen reluctantly and to close their eyes.

and I shall heal them: For the theme of the people "being healed" by God in the prophets, see LXX Hos 7:1; 11:3; 14:5; Jer 3:22; 17:14, and especially Isa 7:4; 19:22 (for Egypt); 30:26; 53:5; 57:19; 61:1. In Luke-Acts, healing is correlated to the proclamation of God's rule and the restoration of the people (Luke 5:17; 6:18-19; 9:2, 11; 14:4; Acts 3:1-10; 9:34; 10:38).

28. *this salvation from God has been sent to the Gentiles:* Compare "the way of salvation" in 16:17 and "this word of salvation" in 13:26. The truth of Paul's statement has been established throughout the narrative since Acts 10 and most recently by the events in Malta (28:1-10). The use of *sōtērion* here echoes earlier statements concerning God's desire for the salvation of all peoples (Luke 2:30; 3:6); see also Luke 1:69, 71, 77; 19:9; Acts 4:12; 7:25; 13:47.

and they will listen: This is the third and final "turn to the Gentiles" in the narrative of Acts (see 13:46-47; 18:6). It is also the final prophecy spoken in Luke-Acts, one which Luke knows the reader will recognize as having reached fulfillment. The use of the intensive pronoun *autoi* marks a sharp contrast to the disbelieving Jews: *they* will believe! The Western Text has another verse here, which is not included in the best critical editions, being recognized as an addition: "When he had said these things, the Jews departed, engaging in considerable debate among themselves." The line is not sufficiently well-attested to be considered original, and seems to have been written in an attempt to round off what was regarded as an overly abrupt ending to Paul's colloquy with the Jewish leaders.

30. *at his own expense:* The term *misthōma* ordinarily means "rent" (see Philo, *Special Laws* 1:280), and its precise sense here is debated, particularly since the

adjective *idios* ("his own") makes it emphatic. Another rendering might be "in his own rented place," especially if *xenia* in v. 23 is translated as "lodging."

two entire years: It is impossible to determine whether Luke was making any particular point by this period of time or not (compare 24:27). References to a "two year period" in parallel accounts (Philo, *Against Flaccus* 128; Pliny the Younger, *Letters* 10:56) or even longer periods (Josephus, *Life* 13) do not support the suggestion that Luke was referring to a period of time that would elapse and—absent an appearance by the Jewish plaintiffs—result in Paul's release.

welcomed all those who came to him: The Western text adds "both Jews and Greeks." As at Caesarea, the conditions of Paul's Roman captivity are sufficiently lenient to allow visitors (see the note on 24:23). Such accessibility makes the practical directives issued by Paul's captivity letters appear more plausible (see Phil 2:19-30; 4:18; Col 4:7-17; 2 Tim 1:16-17; 4:9-13).

31. *preaching . . . teaching:* After "teaching" the Western Text adds, "that this is Christ Jesus, son of God, through whom the whole world will begin to be judged." The secondary character of the addition seems clear. In this final scene, Luke portrays Paul as continuing the characteristic work of Jesus and the other apostles. For the preaching of the kingdom of God, see the note on 28:23, above. For "teaching" (*didaskein*), see Acts 4:2, 18; 5:21; 11:26; 18:11; 20:20. The phrase "the things about Jesus" (*ta tou Iēsou*) is intriguing; see especially the instruction of Apollos by Priscilla and Aquila (18:25). The phrase seems to imply a fuller instruction in the relation of the earthly Jesus to the kingdom of God, such as Luke has undertaken in his own two-volume work (see Acts 1:1).

with entire boldness and without interference: For the "boldness" (*parrēsia*) of the apostles as prophets/philosophers, see Acts 2:29; 4:13, 29, 31; 9:27-28; 13:46; 14:3; 18:26; 19:8; 22:26. Corresponding to Paul's "free speech" is the lack of external hindrance expressed by the adverb *akolytōs*, which in Josephus is used to describe the freedom to practice the ancestral religion (*Antiquities of the Jews* 16:41) as well as for carrying out tasks "without interruption" (*Antiquities of the Jews* 12:104). Luke therefore ends his work with a positive affirmation, much like that stated by Paul himself from his captivity, "I am suffering and wearing fetters like a criminal. But the word of God is not fettered" (2 Tim 2:9).

INTERPRETATION

With Paul's last encounter with the Jewish leaders of Rome in his own rented lodgings, Luke draws his long narrative argument to a close. In his apology for God's faithfulness to his promises, he has shown how the prophet Jesus was sent to Israel a first time, yet was rejected. But having raised him up and having poured out his prophetic spirit on his disciples, God offered the gift of repentance once more to the people of the promise. Those leaders of the people who had been responsible for the death of Jesus continued to spurn this second visitation of the prophet. But within the Jerusalem messianic community, there was a realization of a restored and authentic Israel, living out the true blessings of Abraham which were brought to realization by the gift of the Holy Spirit. Having fulfilled the promises to Israel, therefore, God could carry out his plan of extending his salvation to all people. The Apostle Paul has been the chosen instrument for this mission. Yet Paul himself never ceased his attempts to turn his own people to this "word of salvation" from God. Even in captivity, Paul continued to insist that the messianic faith was in reality for the "hope of Israel" that was the substance of the promises (26:6).

If the endings of books, like beginnings, deserve special attention from those seeking clues to an author's intentions, then Luke's ought in some sense provide a satisfying closure to his narrative argument. And in fact it does. But before considering that, some consideration must be given to whether this, in fact, represents Luke's intended ending. Some readers find the conclusion all too abrupt and inconclusive. Why doesn't Luke continue the story further? After giving such careful attention to Paul's trials, why leave the reader in doubt as to the outcome? Was Paul freed, to continue his mission for a time before a second and fatal arrest? Or was this his last imprisonment?

As early as the *Muratorian Canon* (late second century), an explanation for Luke's incompleteness at this part of the story seemed called for, and the compiler of that canonical list explained that Luke did not tell of the martyrdom of Peter or Paul's subsequent journey to the West, because he wanted to relate only those things that had occurred in his presence! Other "explanations" of greater or lesser probability have not been lacking: that Luke finished this volume before Paul's case came to its conclusion—and necessarily, if it was intended to present his case! Alternatively, that Luke died before he could finish this volume, or before he could undertake still a third volume that he contemplated. This last theory has recently taken on new life in the proposal that the Pastoral Letters are written by Luke as the third volume of Luke-Acts.

Such theories are demanded only if Luke is regarded as the sort of historian whose main purpose is factual completeness and accuracy. In fact, however, we have seen that everywhere Luke's account is selected and shaped to suit his apologetic interests, not in defiance of but in conformity to ancient standards of historiography. The questions are generated as well by the presumption that it is Paul's fate which most concerns Luke, and a failure to clearly indicate his end demands an explanation. But in fact, we have seen that Luke's argument involves far more than Paul's personal destiny. As important as Paul is to Luke and as dominant as he has been in the second half of Acts, he remains for Luke ulti-mately only another in a series of prophetic figures through whom God's message of salvation is brought to the people.

It is through attention to Luke's overall narrative interests that we are best able to appreciate this ending not as the result of historical happen-stance or editorial ineptitude, but as a deliberately and effectively crafted conclusion to a substantial apologetic argument. Even concerning Paul's fate, Luke has left us with no mystery. By this time, the reader must ap-preciate that all prophecies spoken in the narrative will reach fulfillment—even if their fulfillment is not recounted in the narrative itself! Thus, the reader knows on the basis of authoritative prophecy that Paul made his defense before Caesar (27:24), and knows further that Paul died as a wit-ness to "the good news of the gift of God" (20:24) because of the prophe-cies the narrative itself contains to that effect (20:22-23, 29, 38; 21:10-14). But the fact that Luke does not find it necessary to tell us these events is a most important clue as to how we should read the conclusion of his work: the point is not the fate of Paul, but the fidelity of God.

So when Paul arrives in Rome his first step is to invite the Jewish leaders to his presence. In his initial meeting with them, Paul makes clear not only his innocence of any charges worthy of death, but more impor-tantly, his complete lack of animus against Judaism. He has not come as one bearing "a charge against my nation" (28:19). Indeed, his desire to speak at length with them has nothing to do with his own fate but with his message, which concerns "the hope of Israel" (28:20). Even after his repeated rejections by his fellow Jews which caused him to turn to the Gentiles (13:46-47; 18:6), even after their seeking to kill him in Jerusa-lem by treachery (23:12-15), and cooptation of the Roman system (25:1-5), Paul still seeks out his own people. The reason is not his personal hero-ism but God's fidelity to the promises. They have still another chance to respond.

The initial reaction of the Jewish leaders is carefully neutral. They have heard bad things about "this sect" but have had no instructions concern-ing Paul himself. They are therefore willing to hold a second and more formal meeting. The effort Paul expends in that second conference is extra-ordinary: from morning to evening he argues the case for Jesus. As we would expect, he bases his appeal on "the Law and the Prophets" (28:23). The response is mixed. Some of the Jewish leaders are positively inclined, some are disbelieving (28:24). It is difficult to assess accurately what Luke intends the reader to understand by this: do we have another instance of the "divided people of God," so that even among these Jewish leaders of Rome there is a realization of the restored people? Perhaps, but the fact that they *all* leave while "disagreeing with each other" (28:25) holds out only minimal hope.

The final word spoken to the Jewish leaders is therefore one of rejection, but it is a rejection that they have taken upon themselves. Luke now has Paul stand truly as a prophet, speaking *against* the people of Israel as the prophets of old had done. Luke had not made full use of the Isaiah 6:9-10 passage in his Gospel, for that was the time of the first visitation of the prophet, and the rejection of that prophet was mitigated by the "ignorance" of the people. It has been the argument of the narrative of Acts that God did not stop making the offer of salvation to Israel through the proclamation of the raised Prophet Jesus. Only now, after so many attempts at persuading this people, is it time to employ this most chilling prophecy, spoken first of the ancient people but now "fulfilled" in the events of Luke's story. Paul *has* "gone to this people" and spoken the Word. And they have neither heard, nor seen, nor understood. But as the LXX version of the text makes clear, the blame is not God's nor is it the prophet's. The message itself does not deafen, or blind, or stun. It is because the people have grown obtuse that they do not perceive in the message about Jesus the realization of their own most authentic "hope."

For the final time, therefore, Paul announces a turn to the Gentiles with a ringing affirmation: the salvation from God *has* been sent to them, and *they* will listen! Luke's readers recognize this as the prophecy that has indeed taken place "among us" (Luke 1:1), and which has generated the question that made the writing of this narrative necessary in the first place: how did the good news reach the Gentiles, and did the rejection of it by the Jews mean that God failed in his fidelity to them? Luke's answer is contained in the entire narrative up to this point. In every way, God has proven faithful; not his prophetic word and power, but the blindness of the people has led to their self-willed exclusion from the messianic blessings.

The final sight Luke gives us of Paul is, in this reading, entirely satisfactory. Absolutely nothing hinges on the success or failure of Paul's defense before Caesar, for Luke's apologetic has not been concerned primarily with Paul's safety or even the legitimacy of the Christian religion within the empire. What Luke was defending he has successfully concluded: God's fidelity to his people and to his own word. And that point concluded, the ending of Acts is truly an opening to the continuing life of the messianic people, as it continues to preach the kingdom and teach the things concerning Jesus both boldly and without hindrance, knowing now that although increasingly Gentile in its growth, its roots are deep within the story of people to whom God's prophets have unfailingly been sent.

For Reference and Further Study

Bovon, F. " 'Schön hat der heilige Geist durch den Propheten Jesaja zu euren Vätern gesprochenen' (Acts 28:25)." *ZNW* 75 (1984) 226-232.

Brown, R. E., and J. P. Meier. *Antioch and Rome: New Testament Cradles of Catholic Christianity.* New York: Paulist Press, 1982, 89-127.

Davies, P. "The Ending of Acts." *ExpT* 94 (1983) 334-335.

Delling, G. "Das letzte Wort der Apostelgeschichte." *NovT* 15 (1973) 193-204.

Dupont, J. "La conclusion des Actes et son rapport a l'ensemble de l'ouvrage de Luc." *Les Actes des Apôtres: traditions, rédaction, théologie.* Ed. J. Kremer. Gembloux: J. Duculot, 1979, 359-404.

Mealand, D. L. "The Close of Acts and Its Hellenistic Greek Vocabulary." *NTS* 36 (1990) 583-597.

Moessner, D. P. "Paul in Acts: Preacher of Eschatological Repentance to Israel." *NTS* 34 (1988) 96-104.

Puskas, C. B. *The Conclusion of Luke-Acts: An Investigation of the Literary Function and Theological Significance of Acts 28:16-31.* St. Louis University PhD Dissertation, 1980.

Trompf, G. "On Why Luke Declined to Recount the Death of Paul: Acts 27-28 and Beyond." *Luke-Acts: New Perspectives from the Society of Biblical Literature Seminar.* Ed. C. H. Talbert. New York: Crossroad, 1984, 225-239.

Volkel, M. "Zum Deutung des 'Reiches Gottes' bei Lukas." *ZNW* 65 (1974) 57-70.

INDEXES

SCRIPTURAL INDEX

1:13	166	2:20-21	165
1:16	432	2:22	50, 419
1:17	463	2:23	259
1:18	364	3:1-5	363
1:19	396	3:10	204
1:20	349	3:11	229, 247
3:2	362	3:15	283
3:3	410	3:16	419
3:5	363	4:1	193
3:9	396	4:3-4	363
3:11	36	4:5	369
3:15	249, 363	4:6	362
4:3	266	4:7	233, 361
4:4	455	4:9	473
4:13	230, 293	4:10	323, 346
4:14	230	4:11	213, 221
4:15	84	4:12	355
5:1	206, 360	4:14	349
5:2	206, 360	4:17	171, 387
5:3	106, 178	4:19	322
5:4	315	4:20	355
5:5	204, 364	4:21	308
5:7	463		
5:10	106		
5:16	212, 283	*Titus*	
5:17	206, 360	1:1	360
5:19	206, 360	1:2	398
6:1	262	1:4	323
6:2	276, 365	1:5	44, 206, 360
6:4	259	1:7	362
6:9	149	1:12	316
6:11	419	2:3	348
		3:2	410
2 Timothy		3:4	445
1:2	276	3:7	364, 398
1:3	364, 396, 449	3:9	259
1:4	360	3:12	13, 308, 355
1:5	283	3:13	331
1:9	204	3:14	177
1:16	404, 445, 470, 473	3:15	330
1:18	317		
2:1	171	*Philemon*	
2:2	364	1	276, 283
2:6	365	10	361, 470
2:8	364	13	361, 470
2:9	361, 400, 470, 473	17	461
2:19	339	22	470

INDEX OF ANCIENT WRITINGS

2. Greco-Roman Writings

ACHILLES TATIUS

INDEX OF AUTHORS

2014.12.05 B   49.95 (35.88)